TM

GUILD WARS 2®

TABLE OF CONTENTS

Please visit **www.bradygames.com/GW2updates** for a downloadable list of crafting recipes and other updates as they become available.

A NEW DAWN FOR TYRIA

Tyria hasn't seen many easy times, and some of its darkest days are yet upon it. Those who have followed the saga of *Guild Wars* know of the Searing, the heroics of Destiny's Edge, and of their downfall and separation, as well. The rise of the Elder Dragons and their tyranny over the world has begun, but it stands to grow much worse if the free races of the land cannot come together to oppose this vile threat.

The humans, norn, asura, charr, and sylvari are the greatest hopes for Tyria to remain free and stand defiant against the dragons. They need all of the soldiers, adventurers, and scholars they can find. Are you willing to join their ranks? Will you fight against the spirits of the past? Can you stand against corrupted and twisted monsters? Would you brave the risen Continent of Orr, where only the undead stir?

Well, good! Then let us aid you. Tyria is a massive place to explore, and we give you every possible advantage while you learn your way around it. We have maps of the regions, explanations for hundreds of events around the world, and tips describing how to beat them. If you wish to master your chosen profession, we'll tell you about its skills and attributes, and how to play them against monsters or in player-vs.-player battles.

Craftsmen of all types: do not despair! We have introductions to your skills, and we explain how to level them without wasting time or materials. Whether you plan to craft for yourself or for a guild, or trade with others, these tips can get you up to speed in no time.

If you're new to *Guild Wars* and want to find out about the history of the world and its people, we've compiled the lore and legends that were introduced in the first game and developed in the novels afterward. You can start *Guild Wars 2* as if you'd been there all along, watching as the events unfolded.

There's something for everyone in this book. We want to show you how awesome this world has become. Join us in exploring it!

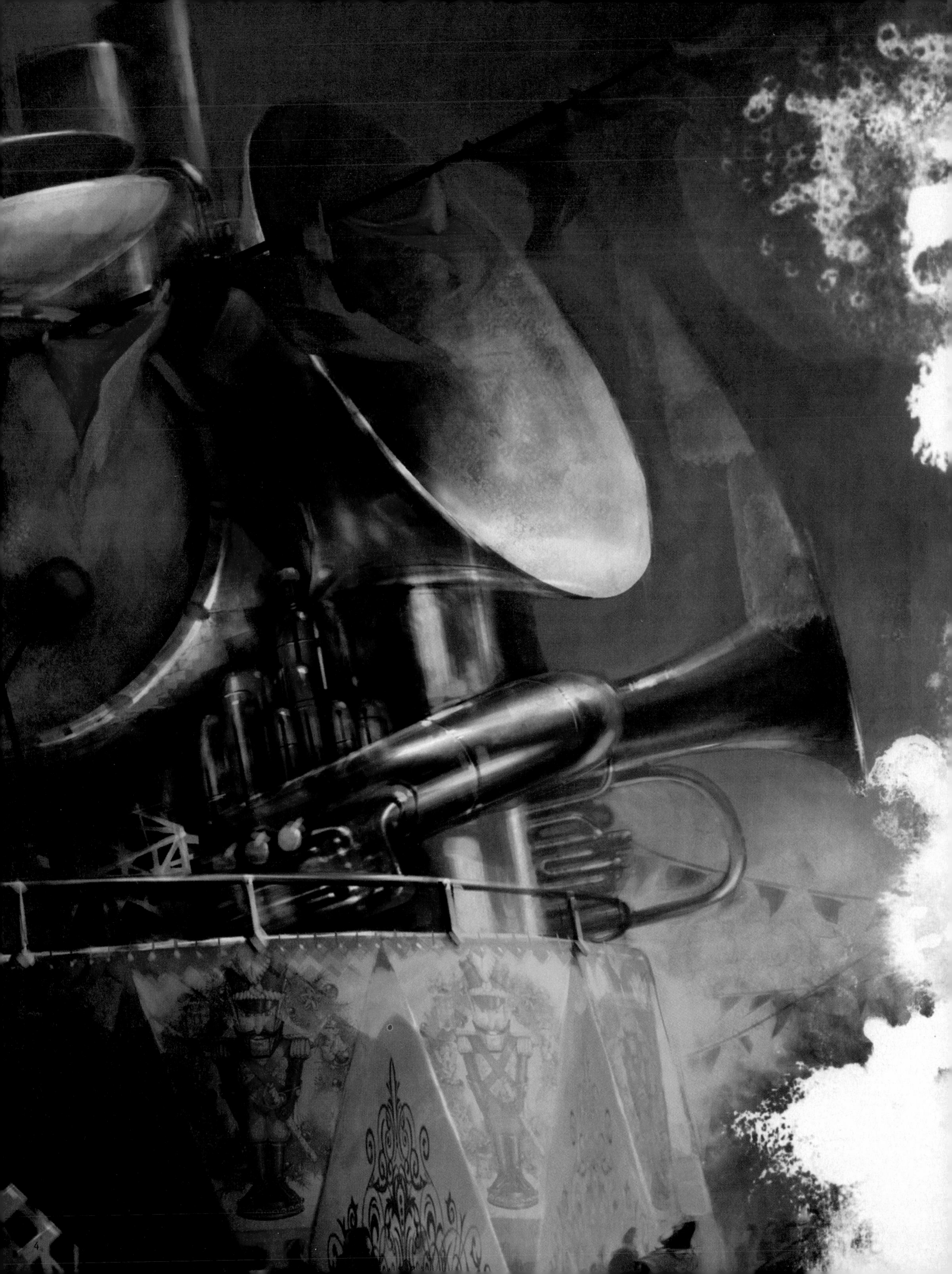

HOW TO USE THIS GUIDE

This book is large enough that you might get lost when you first page through it. Before we start, let's describe the various chapters so you can see where to go when you want to find something specific.

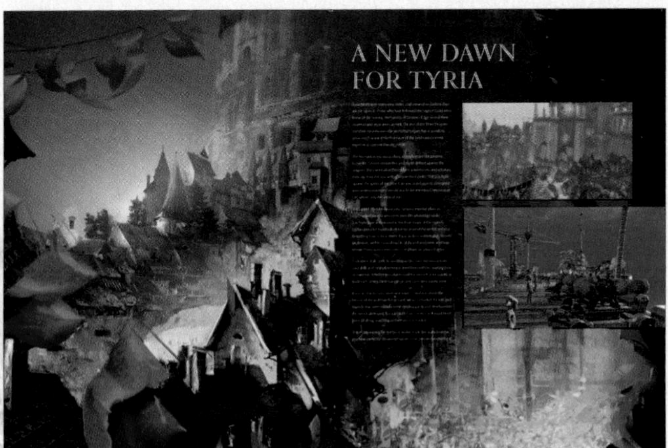

1. Introductory Chapter

Page 2

Our first chapter is mostly for those new to *Guild Wars* and to massive online games in general. After this introduction, we talk about general terminology for this game, the world and its playable races, and then the history of *Guild Wars*. At the end of the chapter, we discuss common online features and gaming etiquette. If online gaming is unfamiliar to you, this is a very important section of the guide. If you've played through several online games before, you might want to skip to the history section, read that, and then move on to the next chapter.

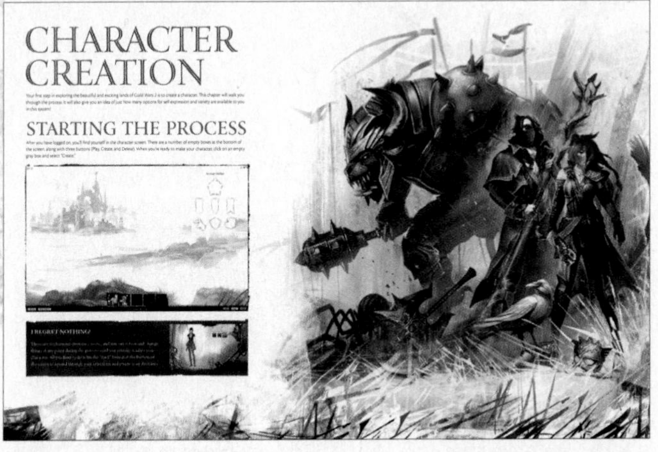

2. Character Creation

Page 50

The next chapter goes over the character-creation process. This section tells you more about race-specific skills and starting locations. We also explain the ramifications of the choices you select during character creation—and how they influence your personal story for the rest of your leveling experience.

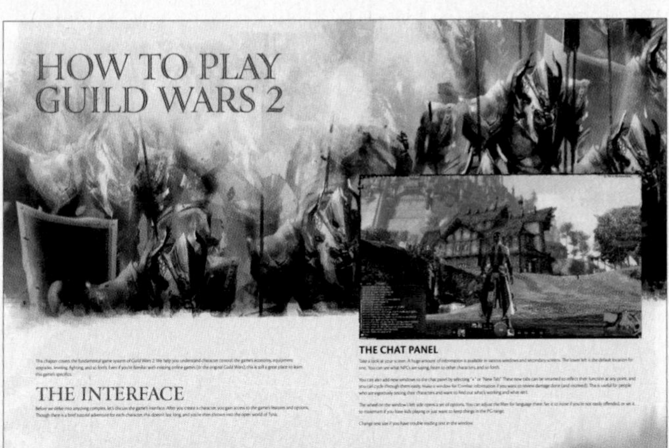

3. The Mechanics of *Guild Wars 2*

Page 60

In the third chapter we start to discuss specifics about the game's internal systems. Learn how to move, dodge, fight, gain levels, explore, and trade with others. This is a very intricate chapter, and anyone who is new to the game should read it thoroughly. It's a primer for how to play *Guild Wars 2*!

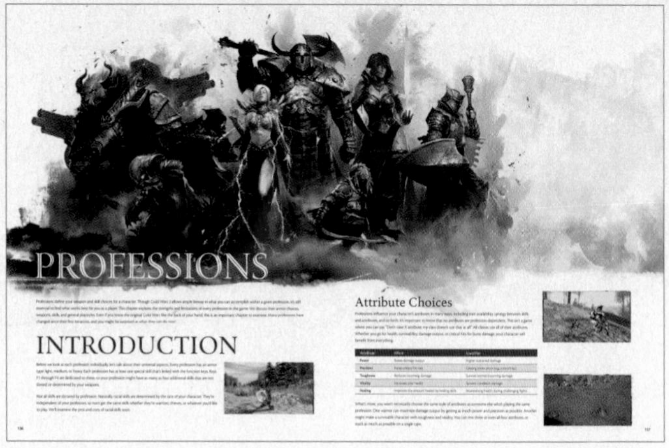

4. First Experiences

Page 122

Each race has a tutorial area that lets you get into the game without putting you in any real danger. It's a way to introduce the world without throwing everything at you at once. We take you through all five of the starting areas to give context to the events that you experience in each.

5. Professions

Page 136

There are eight classes of characters in *Guild Wars 2*. These are called professions, and they determine your character's allowable weapons and armor, his or her skills, and much about how you'll play your hero. This chapter explores every weapon and slot skill for every profession, their attributes, and how to play your character against monsters or other players. Look up the professions that interest you, or read through all of them if you have the time.

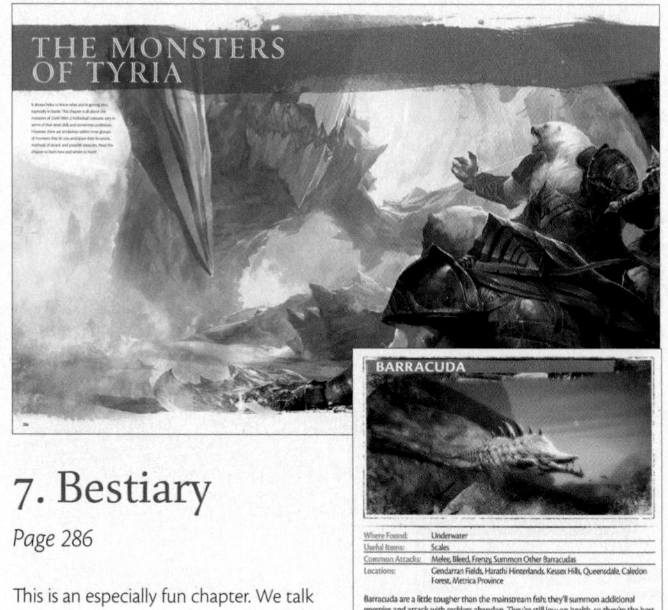

6. Crafting

Page 278

The crafting chapter is for people who like to make their own equipment. In *Guild Wars 2*, everyone can harvest the ingredients needed for crafting. So, the only people who need to pursue the actual crafting skills are those who plan to do the work. Read this chapter to learn which crafts are right for you and how to progress within these trades.

7. Bestiary

Page 286

This is an especially fun chapter. We talk about the major groups of enemies, their strengths and weaknesses, and what treasure you get from defeating the creatures. Anyone hunting for specific item types should go here to see what to hunt and where to find their quarry.

8. Player vs. Player (PvP)

Page 304

Much of this guide is devoted to the environments of Tyria and its various hazards. The PvP chapter focuses on fighting between players, whether in smaller matches or in the large-scale World-versus-World battles (sometimes called WvWvW, WvW, or World PvP). When you're ready to take your fight to the masses, go here and learn how to prepare your character for the greatest challenge in the game.

9. The World

Page 322

Here we start to guide you through Tyria's overland regions. We talk about level ranges, harvesting locations, monsters, and events for as much of the world as we can fit into one book. Think of this as a walkthrough for the cities and regions, helping you find and master all of the available content. If you feel overwhelmed by the size of *Guild Wars 2*, this is a perfect chapter for you. Pick the region where your character begins, turn to that section of the chapter, and let us guide you through the leveling process.

10. Dungeons

Page 492

Dungeons are some of the most challenging areas in the game. Player versus Player (PvP) tests your ability to fight other players. Dungeons are where you go to prove your Player-versus-Environment (PvE) mettle, meaning you face the meanest monsters and the toughest events. You should have a group of five people before you enter one of these. Consult this chapter to find out where the dungeons are located and to gain some tips for defeating them!

GLOSSARY

A

Add
An extra monster that has joined an existing battle.

Alt
A character on your account other than your main character. A secondary character.

AoE
Area of Effect. Often used to talk about abilities that damage enemies in groups.

AE
Area Effect (see **AoE**).

Aegis
A boon exclusive to guardians. The next attack by the affected target is blocked.

AFK
Away From Keyboard. Used to show that players aren't at their computers.

Aggro
A monster's aggressive attention. "That Ooze is aggroing on you. Look out!"

Aggro Radius
The radius around monsters that determines their aggression. You will be attacked if you step within their aggro radius.

AH
Auction House (see **Trading Post**).

Asura Gate
A purple-hued gateway that connects major areas of the world. These are often found in capital cities, such as Lion's Arch.

Attribute
A modifier that affects a character's performance in combat. Four attributes are shared across all professions: Power, Precision, Toughness, and Vitality. Power and Precision modify offense; Toughness and Vitality affect your character's survival.

B

Bank
A place of storage found in each major city in the game. All of these are connected, and the items you place in the bank are available to each of your characters. Some player guilds will also have a guild bank for additional storage.

Bleed
A condition that causes the affected target to lose a constant amount of health over time. Bleed is a stackable debuff.

Blind
A condition that causes affected targets to miss their next attack.

Boon
One of various positive status effects associated with skill use or attacks. Boons include Aegis, Fury, Might, Protection, Regeneration, Rejuvenation, Retaliation, Stability, Swiftness, and Vigor. For negative effects, see **Condition**; see **Positioning Effect** for effects related to movement.

Buff
A beneficial effect put on a player or monster. (See **Boon**).

Burning
A condition that causes the affected target to lose a constant amount of health over time (due to being on fire). Burning is a stackable debuff for duration, but not for damage delivered.

C

Caster
A character or monster that uses magic-based skills, often at range.

CC
Crowd Control. The use of skills designed to temporarily incapacitate or slow down an enemy. Cripple, stun, and knockback are all examples of this.

Champion
An extremely tough monster. Champions should be approached cautiously and preferably fought only by a group; they are tougher than Veterans (see **Veteran**).

Channel
Term for skills that require several seconds of focus to complete. Your character usually has to stand still during this time, but some skills allow movement even while channeling.

Cheese
To exploit an imbalance in the game.

Chilled/Frozen
A condition that causes the affected target to move 66% slower and become unable to dodge. Skills also take 66% longer to recharge.

Combat Pet
A creature controlled by a player that assists during combat. These can come from your utility skills or as a result of being a ranger or necromancer.

Combo
Short for "combination." This is an interaction between skills, resulting in added damage or other effects. Combos are determined by combo fields and combo finishers. The fields set up the opportunity for the finishers. When a skill with a finisher interacts with a field, the attack takes on a property of the field.

Condition
One of various negative status effects associated with skill use or attacks. Conditions include Blind, Burning, Chilled, Confusion, Cripple, Daze, Fear, Immobilize, Poison, Stun, Vulnerability, and Weakness. For positive effects, see **Boon**; see **Positioning Effect** for effects related to movement.

Confusion
A condition that deals damage to the affected target every time a skill is activated. Confusion is a stackable debuff.

Cripple
A condition that causes the affected target to move 50% slower and have a visible limp. Dodging speed is affected as well, though you can still use this mechanic.

Critical Hit
An attack that deals 50% (or more) bonus damage. The chance of scoring a critical hit is based on your character's precision, skills, and active boons.

D

Daze
A condition that interrupts and keeps the affected target from using skills.

DD
Direct Damage. This is a skill that inflicts all of its damage in one hit rather than spreading its damage over time.

Debuff
A negative effect placed on a target that makes it less powerful. (See **Condition**.)

Defense
A measure of a person's armor quality. Raise this to improve your character's resistance to damage.

DMG
Damage. Also listed as DPS at times, even though that technically means Damage Per Second.

Dodge
A sudden burst of movement (in any direction). This is used to avoid enemy attacks. It uses endurance and cannot be spammed, so timing is critical.

DOT
Damage Over Time. This often refers to an effect that "ticks" frequently, applying damage each time there is a tick. Example: Bleed.

Downed
In *Guild Wars 2*, your character doesn't automatically die at zero health. Instead, you drop to the ground and can fight for survival. This state is called the downed state. Rallying is when you defeat an enemy and get back on your feet.

DPS
Damage Per Second. This concept allows one to evaluate weapons and skills of different speeds. It's also used as a generic term for damage output. "Need more DPS," means that we need to concentrate more damage on this target.

Duration
The amount of time it takes for an effect to wear off.

Dye
Colors that are used to personalize the look of your armor/character. Many of these are available by default, and more can be found as you explore the world.

E

Elite Skill
The tenth skill slot on each character's bar. This is gained at level 30 and often involves very powerful abilities.

Endurance
An indicator of a character's energy. It is used to dodge incoming attacks by double-tapping in a given direction (or using the Dodge key while pressing in any direction).

Event
Something that is occurring in the local area. Completing these repeatable missions is worth experience, gold, and karma. They can be completed multiple times. See also **Group Event** and **World Event**.

Experience (XP/EXP)
A stat that rises from exploration, killing monsters, crafting, and completing tasks. The accrual of experience increases a character's level and grants him or her access to traits and stronger attributes.

F

Fear
A condition that causes the affected target to run directly away from the caster, often for a very short duration.

FTL
For The Lose, or For The Loss. An Internet or sports term that implies that a strategy, concept, or action is weak.

FTW
For The Win. This means that something is powerful or useful.

Fury
A boon that causes more of the affected target's attacks to score critical hits.

G

Gem
A form of currency purchased with real money or via gold in the Gem Store. You use gems to upgrade your *Guild Wars 2* account or to purchase a number of temporary boons.

Gem Store
The place where you make gem purchases. Look on the top portion of your screen to find the icon for this store.

GG
Good Game. Most often used after a PvP engagement to thank other players for contributing, or when someone is about to log off.

Griefer
A person who purposely tries to annoy or anger other players.

Grinding
To repeat any activity to achieve a conclusion through sheer effort. "I'll keep fighting these centaurs to grind out this level."

Ground-targeted
Skill effects may target areas instead of monsters. These effects are said to be ground-targeted. They normally create a circle on the ground that you can move around until you click a second time; the second click triggers the actual skill effect.

Group
A team of up to five characters that join together to take on a dungeon or a particularly tricky event.

Group Event
An event that is much higher in difficulty, often requiring several cooperating players to complete.

Guild
An organization of players established to support each other in PvP, exploration, fighting, or just for kicks.

GW2
Guild Wars 2.

H

Healing Skill
All characters have the ability to heal themselves and potentially others, as well. Characters start with one default Healing Skill. Up to three others can be purchased and selected through the Skill menu. These skills are bound to key "6" on your keyboard.

Heart
A local event or mission; see **Task**. Hearts that are open signify tasks that can still be completed. Solid Hearts are ones you have already done. These are also called Renown Hearts.

HP
Hit Points or Health. This is a measure of a character's survivability. It is affected by vitality.

I

Iconic
Extremely important racial NPCs that are critical to the *Guild Wars 2* story. Example: Logan Thackeray.

Immobilize
A condition that hinders affected targets, making them unable to dodge or move.

Incoming (INC)
This means an attack is imminent.

Instance
A copy of an area available only to a specific individual or group. The world is not instanced. Dungeons, home areas, and personal quest events have many copies; these are instances.

K

Karma
A tangible reward for your good works in the world. You gain karma primarily by completing repeatable events.

Kiting
A style of combat in which players stay out of combat range from their enemies, usually by running away from them while simultaneously causing damage to them.

Knockback
A positioning effect that pushes targets back and interrupts them.

Knockdown
A positioning effect that forces affected targets to the ground. This interrupts the targets and causes them to be unable to move or use skills for a short duration.

L

Launch/Blowup
A positioning effect that interrupts affected targets and whips them into the air.

Leap
A positioning effect where the user moves rapidly forward over a short distance.

LFG
Looking For Group.

LFM
Looking For More. This implies that an existing group has open slots and wants to get more people before starting a dungeon run or difficult event.

Log
When you log off/disconnect from the game.

LOL
Laughing Out Loud. An Internet term expressing humor.

LOS
Line of Sight. Often used as a warning. "Break LOS" means you should get your character behind cover to avoid a target's attention or attacks.

LOS Pull
To hit a monster at range and then run behind cover so the monster has to come all the way to you. It's a way to start an encounter in the place where you feel safest.

Loot
To take the treasure from a chest or to get the items from a slain monster.

Merchant
A computer-controlled character that sells some type of equipment or items. Merchants are often willing to give your character money for items you no longer want. Karma merchants sell special rewards for karma instead of gold.

M

Might
A stacking boon that increases the damage of the affected target's attacks. Might raises power.

MMO
Massive Multiplayer Online.

MMOG
Massive Multiplayer Online Game.

MMORPG
Massive Multiplayer Online Role-Playing Game.

MOB
An old programming acronym of "Mobile Object Block." Mobs are computer-controlled characters (usually monsters) in the game.

MOG
Massive Online Game.

N

Nerf
To downgrade, to be made softer, or to make less effective. "X has been nerfed because it was way overpowered."

Newbie
A new player.

Newb/Noob
Short for newbie, but more often used as a pejorative.

NP
No Problem.

NPC
Non-Player Character. An in-game person who is controlled by the server, such as a task giver or someone who assists during your personal story.

P

Pat
A patrolling monster. This may be exclaimed as a warning that said creature is coming your way. "PAT!"

PBAoE
Point Blank Area of Effect attack. An AoE that targets the area around your character in a 360-degree circle.

PC
Player Character. This is you, or the real people you interact with in-game.

Personal Story
A series of quests that are given to your character throughout the leveling process. The choices you make and the background of your character determine the progression of this chronicle, so it's a highly personal sequence. You can bring allies into your story, but it's always up to you (no one can simply wander in).

Pet
A creature controlled by a player, such as a moa, skale, and so on. Some professions get combative pets, and everyone can collect mini pets.

Poison
A condition that causes the affected target to lose health over time. Poisoned characters receive less health from healing effects.

Positioning Effect
An effect caused by an attack or skill use that changes the affected target's location. These effects include knockback, knockdown, launch, leap, pull, retreat, and teleport.

Power
An offensive attribute that quantifies your character's raw damage output. The higher your power, the more damage you can inflict.

Precision
An offensive attribute that affects your critical hit rate. The higher your precision, the greater your chance of performing a critical attack.

Proc
An effect that randomly triggers from time to time. An example of a proc is a rune that grants a weapon a chance to heal its user when it critically hits a target.

Profession
What your character specializes in (his or her class). The eight professions include: guardians, warriors, engineers, rangers, thieves, elementalists, mesmers, and necromancers.

Protection
A boon that increases the defense of the affected target. The affected target then takes less damage from incoming attacks.

PST
Please Send Tell. This indicates that the person wants to hear back regarding a certain sale or issue.

Pull (action)
The act of heading out, getting attention from a monster, and bringing the fight back to a group.

Pull (effect)
A positioning effect, caused by some skills, that shortens the distance between users and their targets.

Puller
A character that goes out and gets monsters for the party, controlling the way a battle is initiated.

PvE
Player vs. Environment. Combat between players and computer-controlled opponents.

PvP
Player vs. Player. Combat between players.

R

Rally
Killing an enemy (or being aided) while you're downed, and then getting back on your feet.

Regeneration
A boon that causes the affected target to heal over time.

Res/Rez/Revive
The act of reviving a character. "I need a rez. I'm dead."

Respawn
When monsters (or NPCs) reappear after being dead for a short time.

Respec
The act of resetting and redistributing your trait points. This is done by talking with your profession trainer and paying the associated fee.

Retreat
A positioning effect where the user of a skill rolls or jumps directly backward.

RP/RPing
Role Play. To interact with the game and players as though you *are* your character.

S

Skill
An ability used by your character. Skills are determined according to the weapon(s) you use, as well as your character's profession and race.

Stack (Items)
A number of identical items placed in a single inventory slot to conserve space. Not every item can be stacked.

Stack (Effects)
To apply boons or conditions multiple times on the same target to achieve a cumulative effect. For example, stacking Might raises power each time a new Might effect is placed on the character. Not all boons and conditions are stackable. Also, the effects of stacking max out at 25 applications in a given instance.

Stun
A condition that interrupts, immobilizes, and incapacitates the affected target for a short duration.

Swiftness
A boon that increases the affected target's movement speed.

T

Task
A local mission. Tasks are shown by hearts on your map. Tasks are given by specific individuals in the world, and finishing a task yields experience and money. You can complete each task only once with a given character.

Teleport
A position effect where the user of a skill instantly moves from one location to another.

Toughness
A defensive attribute that quantifies your ability to withstand damage. The higher your toughness, the greater your armor. Toughness is particularly effective at eliminating damage from numerous small hits.

Trading Post
A place where players buy and sell items.

Trainer
An NPC that allows players to alter their trait selections.

Trait
An ability, chosen by the player, that provides passive, ongoing effects. Traits can boost a character's attributes, improve the effects of skills, or reduce the effects of conditions.

Trait Book
These books unlock the various tiers of traits. Your profession's trainer sells these books for a moderate amount of gold.

Trait Line
The set of traits along a specific path.

Twink
A low-level character possessing the absolute best gear, often through guild assistance or money/equipment sent down by a higher-level character played by the same person.

TY
Thank You.

U

Über (or Uber)
German slang for "super." This is a common gamer term for something that is impressive.

Utility Skills
Skills that you choose, purchase, and equip. These depend on your character's profession and race. They are bound to keys "7," "8," and "9" on your keyboard.

V

Vendor Trash
An item that only a merchant would buy. These icons are shown in grey.

Veteran
A tougher monster. Any fight with a Veteran is harder than normal. While most are soloable, a partner or a group makes things much safer.

Vigor
A boon that increases endurance regeneration.

Vitality
A defensive attribute that quantifies your character's maximum health. The higher your vitality, the greater your hit points.

Vulnerability
A stackable condition that causes the affected target to take more damage from attacks.

Waypoint (or WP)
Waypoint. A magical means of instantaneous travel throughout the world.

Weakness
A condition that reduces damage from non-critical hits by 50%. This also slows endurance regeneration.

Weapon Skill
A skill associated with the weapon(s) you currently wield. Skill slots 1-5 are determined by weapon choice.

World Event
A region-wide event. World Events require certain listed conditions to be completed as the event proceeds. These constitute opportunities for everyone in the entire zone to work together to achieve a common goal.

WTB
Want to Buy. Shorthand for saying that someone is looking to purchase something, often listing his or her intentions afterward.

WTS
Want to Sell. Shorthand for saying that someone has something to sell, often listing his or her goods afterward.

YW
You're Welcome.

REGIONS AND RACES

The world of Tyria is a rich and exciting place. It's separated into several major regions: Kryta, Ascalon, the Tainted Coast, and Orr. The regions are bound by the natural barriers of the Steamspur and Shiverpeak Mountains. To the south lies the Sea of Sorrows, with the city of Lion's Arch occupying its northern shore. The shoreline of the far west, along the Strait of Malchor, is known as the Tarnished Coast. The far east ends at the Blazeridge Mountains and what lies beyond is only mystery.

The Regions

Lion's Arch

Lion's Arch, once the capital of Kryta, is now a power in its own right. This multiracial city is a primary gathering point for traders, explorers, and adventurers. From here, the Lionguard battle myriad threats facing Tyria, and their forces can be found wherever tranquility and stability are threatened.

Kryta

The green and fertile lands of Kryta offer the perfect location to settle down, grow a few crops, and raise a family. From Divinity's Reach, the new Krytan capital, the Seraph military works tirelessly to try and defend those traveling through Queensdale, Kessex Hills, Gendarran Fields, and Harathi Hinterlands. It's a region worth fighting for, and it's the last chance for many humans to live a life of peace. Whether the centaurs will give them that chance is still uncertain.

The Tarnished Coast

All of the peninsula is a vast and verdant jungle, but while the wastes have completely dried and are uninhabitable, the Tarnished Coast has maintained its wildland of tropical trees. It is here that the asura and sylvari races have made their homes (from their capitals of Rata Sum and the Grove, respectively). Metrica Province and Caledon Forest collectively pour into the Brisban Wildlands, and later into more cultivated territory.

Shiverpeak Mountains

The northern and southern Shiverpeaks cut through the lands of Kryta and Ascalon. These rugged and foreboding mountains are the domain of the norn. From their capital of Hoelbrak in the (slightly gentler) Wayfarer Foothills, the norn have claimed and now protect the regions of Snowden Drifts, Lornar's Pass, Dredgehaunt Cliffs, and Frostgorge Sound. They're threatened by the mole-like dredge, the mighty jotun, and from internal strife because of the Sons of Svanir.

Steamspur Mountains

The Steamspur Mountains mark a natural barrier between Ascalon (to the east) and Orr (to the south, across the sea). The high elevations of Timberline Falls and Mount Maelstrom soon give way to the swamps of Bloodtide Coast and Sparkfly Fen. These mountains may offer salvation: they provide a natural barrier against the undead making their way inland, through the marshes.

Ascalon

Ascalon is the domain of the charr. Their capital of the Black Citadel sternly rises over the Plains of Ashford, proclaiming the might of the Legions. Ascalon is a land that has long known war, and the regions of Diessa Plateau, the Fields of Ruin, Blazeridge Steppes, Iron Marches, and Fireheart Rise have been marked by scorched vegetation and dry savannahs. It is a tough land but a strong one. How fitting for the dauntless charr. They fight against Ascalonian ghosts, human separatists, and members of the renegade Flame Legion.

Orr

The sunken land of Orr has returned from the watery depths, and with it, the populace of the destroyed land. The Orrian undead now plod inexorably along the Cursed Shore, past Malchor's Leap, and through the Straits of Devastation. Much of the region is coastal, with large expanses of water punctuated by islands and shore-lined hills. There are few bastions of safety, with only a few forts trying to stem the tide of living dead. Even the large expanse of sea isn't safe; undead wildlife and the risen Orrian navy patrol the ocean. Dark times indeed.

Races

Humans

Humans were once the dominant race in Tyria, but now they hold only one region as their own. As such, Kryta is a land of refugees and survivors; it has a diverse populace, composed of people from all over the world. Humans have a large variety of skin, hair, and eye colors, with a wide range of heights and body shapes. As a culture, humans tend to be spiritual, and they look to their gods for guidance and morality. Their faith has bolstered them in dark times, and although the gods may be silent now, that hasn't stopped humans from standing firm against evil. They possess abundant determination, cleverness, and courage. This will serve them well in the trials to come.

Norn

Norn are built in proportions similar to humans, but they stand larger and stronger. These 9-foot-tall people can withstand great hardship and cold temperatures. As a culture, the norn prize skill, personal achievement, and prowess in hunting and battle; success is the greatest measure of worth. Still, the norn are a tolerant group. When the hardest test is survival, it doesn't help to get hung up on trivialities. When they aren't focusing on individual accomplishments, norn spend their time warming up with their companions around a good fire, drinking beer, and telling stories of renown.

Charr

Fierce, strong, and cunning, the cat-like charr are made for war. Standing slightly taller than humans, the charr usually settle into a hunched posture, but they will drop to all fours while running. They have tails and short fur, in a variety of colors and patterns (like those of tigers, leopards, lions, and cheetahs). Their elongated muzzle hides sharp, long, canine teeth. While charr do have retractable claws, they prefer to fight with weapons. With their ferocity and intelligence dedicated to battle, the charr may find it more challenging to adapt to peace.

Asura

Small, wide-eyed, and quick, it might be tempting for the uninformed to think of the asura as whimsical or saccharinely cute. Nothing could be further from the truth. A closer look demonstrates how the asura have been marked by their subterranean origins. Their small stature and fast movements allow them to traverse tunnels, and their wide eyes let them see in the dark. Any lingering doubts about "adorableness" can be dispelled by the asuran smile: they possess a mouth with abundant, small, shark-like teeth. And while the asuran temperament does value some level of lightheartedness, behind it all is the keen calculation of a researcher. These tiny geniuses have supreme confidence in their intellect and the use of applied intelligence. They are not shy or modest about their skills, and the path of the world has no choice but to be shaped by their will.

Sylvari

The sylvari are a race of humanoid plants. Slightly shorter and more "willowy" than humans, the sylvari have a fey cast to their features, with pointed ears and tilted eyes. Instead of hair, they have leaves or petals; some of them even have bark-like skin. Sylvari come from large seed pods on the Pale Tree. The first 12 sylvari emerged about 25 years ago, with more arriving as the years went on. They are a young race in Tyria, and they are still trying to find their way in the world. Although a bit naïve, sylvari culture prizes the search for knowledge and an individual's quest to find a well-developed morality. Through it all, they look toward friendship and joy. In a dangerous and dark world, they offer light and a happy spirit.

THE HISTORY OF GUILD WARS

The origins of the world of Tyria are lost in time and shrouded in myth. They are also colored by cultural perceptions, bias, and mysticism. But if we can't have facts, at least we can have *stories!* This section of our book is about the time before *Guild Wars 2*, from the formation of the world to the events that took place in the original *Guild Wars* and its expansions.

Cosmology and Geography

The Mists constitute the fabric of time and space. Within the Mists are worlds, each with their own realities and histories, floating as islands in the ether. Some worlds are enormous, such as the Underworld, the home of the dead; others are simply residences for powerful spirits or deities. At the center of the Mists is the Rift, and within the Rift is the Hall of Heroes, the final resting place of powerful and virtuous souls.

Tyria is only one world among many in the Mists. It is a very large world, but history has only chronicled events that have taken place on three major continents; these continents are Tyria (named for the world), Cantha, and Elona.

For a long time, only events on the continent of Tyria were known to historians (the primary storyline of *Guild Wars: Prophecies* takes place there). Through the subsequent *Guild Wars* expansions, people began to learn about events in other parts of the world. Tyrian history and human culture are both heavily represented in this, but the other races have many of their own stories and legends to add.

The Creation of the World

Tyria is said to be over 11,000 years old, but its primordial history is still mostly shrouded in mystery. The earliest lifeforms on Tyria were the Elder Dragons, who spent much of their time in hibernation, and the Giganticus Lupicus, a race of giants that are now extinct.

There is a 7,000-year gap in the timeline of the world, for unknown reasons. The ancient *Tome of the Rubicon* mentions several races: the dwarves, the mursaat, and the seers. It also states that the mursaat and the seers warred with each other, but the reason why and the resolution of the conflict are unrecorded. Of course, the *Tome of Rubicon* is a dwarven book, and its prophecies and histories are far more concerned with dwarven matters.

At some point in prehistory, beings of enormous power, knowledge, and magic walked and lived upon the land. In the religion of the humans, they are called the Old Gods, or the True Gods:

> **Dwayna**, Goddess of Life and Air (Leader of the Pantheon)
> **Balthazar**, God of Fire and War
> **Lyssa**, Twin Goddess of Beauty and Illusions
> **Melandru**, Goddess of Nature and Earth
> **Abaddon**, God of Secrets and Water
> **Grenth**, God of Death and Ice

The earliest scriptures tell of another God of Death, Dhuum, but he was overthrown by Grenth for being unjust. Dhuum was imprisoned in the Underworld. Abaddon, as well, may have had a predecessor, but that is a matter of debate by the priesthood.

In the tales, the gods created the world, shaping the lands, forming the plants and animals, and breathing life into the various races. Others say that the gods were caretakers of Tyria, and that they brought other spirits to the world.

Tyria flourished under the protection and care of the gods. To aid them and serve as caretakers, the gods had servants—a race of serpentine creatures, now called the Forgotten. The Forgotten were meant to shepherd, teach, and care for the growing world, as well as for the other beings that were to come.

It wasn't long before Tyria was home to many: the charr, tengu, minotaur, dwarves, centaur, and others. Finally, another race came to Tyria, and they brought with them a desire for domination. They were humans.

The Power of Magic

Humans quickly spread and began to conquer all the lands they encountered. They had a thirst for knowledge and technology, combined with overwhelming ambition. They saw the world as something to be mastered, and they changed the world to accommodate their desires.

It wasn't long before human cities dominated the landscape. From these centers of power, humanity attempted to tame the world to suit their desires. The cities were bastions of learning and culture, with libraries, schools, and trading opportunities, but they were also military outposts. Not content with conquering their own lands, humans began moving into the lands of other races. They clearcut jungles, preyed upon other creatures, and invaded the domains of the other races. This was when the humans drove the charr from their homeland, the region of Ascalon.

The Forgotten, charged with upholding the balance of Tyria, were completely ousted. Loath to fight a bloody battle against the humans, and realizing the simple peace of the old times would never return, they withdrew to a remote region, the Crystal Desert. Over time, all knowledge of them faded, and they became part of history and half-remembered stories.

But even with their servants gone, the gods continued their work with the world. They crafted a marvelous gift, which Abaddon brought forth and gave equally to all the races of the world: the power of magic. It was meant to aid in the struggle of existence, to help provide shelter and healing in a difficult world, and to provide a form of stability.

Instead, magic was almost immediately used as a weapon.

Tyria was consumed by war and devastation. The magical races tore at themselves and each other. Warlords rose to subjugate territories and the less fortunate, and nations embroiled themselves in a race for dominion. For some, it was a chance to settle old grudges, and the humans found themselves heavily outmatched by the enemies they'd made. So great was the destruction caused by the newfound power of magic that some races faced extinction.

Eventually, the remaining human cities united under one ruler, King Doric. In desperation, Doric traveled to the holy city of Arah, on the Orrian Peninsula, where the gods made their home. Begging an audience with the gods, Doric pleaded with them to take back their gift, to reclaim magic as their own. Without this, Tyria would never know peace and tranquility again.

The gods granted his request. They took back magic from the races and crafted it into a gigantic stone. The stone was then broken into five parts. Four parts corresponded to the schools of magic (Preservation, Destruction, Aggression, and Denial), and the last part was a keystone. Without the keystone, the other four parts could never again be reassembled. Magic would remain in the world, but it would never be entirely under the control of a single entity.

Because King Doric had made the plea, he and his descendants were charged with protecting the stones. They were then sealed with a drop of Doric's blood (and hence known as the Bloodstones) and hurled into a volcano off the shore of the kingdom of Kryta.

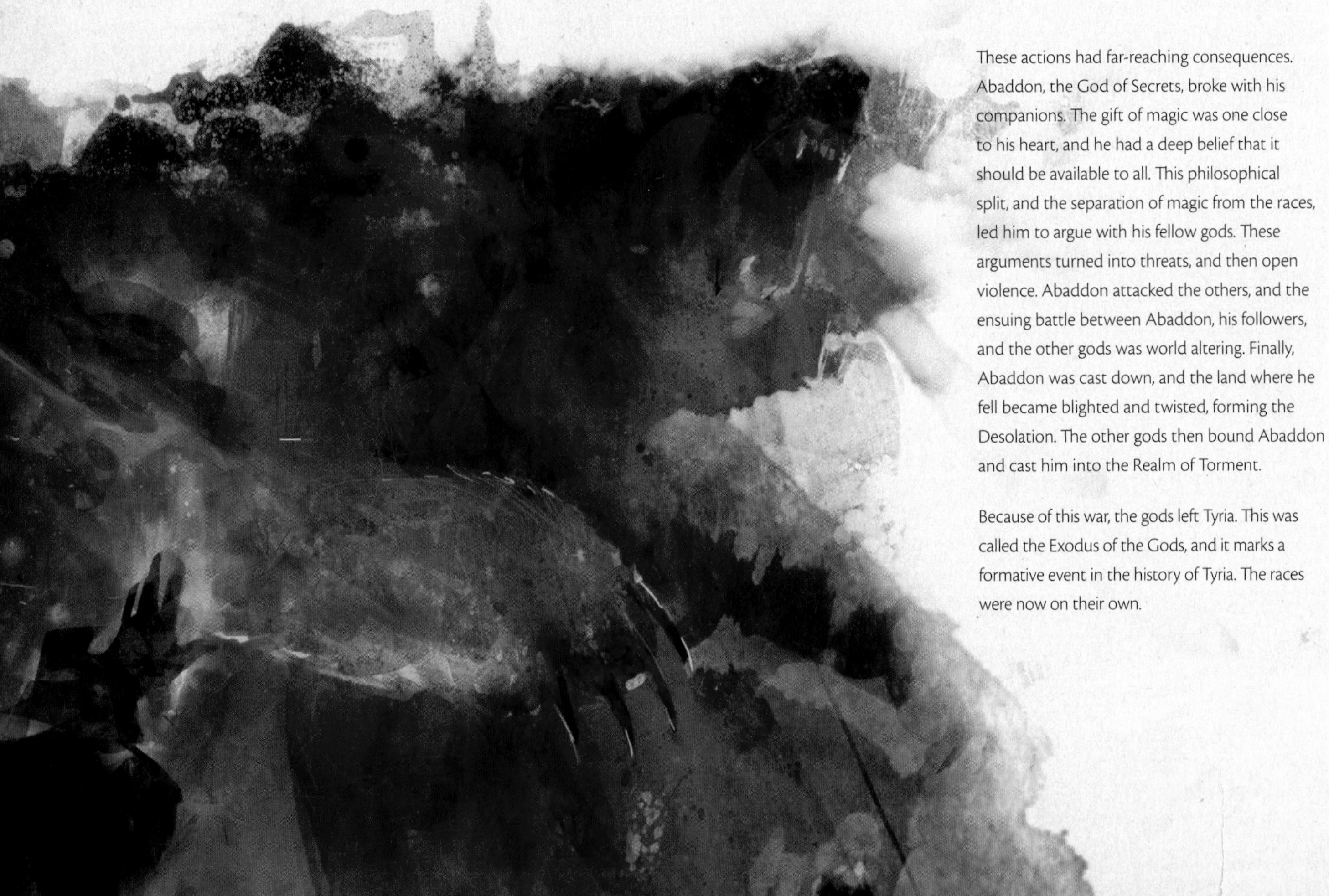

These actions had far-reaching consequences. Abaddon, the God of Secrets, broke with his companions. The gift of magic was one close to his heart, and he had a deep belief that it should be available to all. This philosophical split, and the separation of magic from the races, led him to argue with his fellow gods. These arguments turned into threats, and then open violence. Abaddon attacked the others, and the ensuing battle between Abaddon, his followers, and the other gods was world altering. Finally, Abaddon was cast down, and the land where he fell became blighted and twisted, forming the Desolation. The other gods then bound Abaddon and cast him into the Realm of Torment.

Because of this war, the gods left Tyria. This was called the Exodus of the Gods, and it marks a formative event in the history of Tyria. The races were now on their own.

Human History

The Rise of the Human Nations: Kryta, Ascalon, and Orr

The next 100 years were a time of peace and prosperity, especially for the various human nations. Three powerful countries emerged: Kryta, Ascalon, and Orr. Each of these nations was home to its own dynasties, politics, and cultures, but no single country was seen as dominant.

Instead, this was a time of invention and trade. Connections and opportunities led to the creation of guilds. At first, these were economic organizations, a means for merchants to meet, disseminate goods, and set prices. However, the guilds grew beyond the bounds of mere trade. Soon there were guilds geared toward warfare, religion, magical ability, and even social concerns—in short, any purpose that would bring together a group of people.

Because the guilds fostered communication as well as economic prosperity, they transcended borders. For instance, a guild that held sway in Kryta might also have chapters in Orr and Ascalon. They also began to dominate the political arena. A king or council might make a law, but it was the military guilds that were responsible for enforcing the proclamation. In essence, guilds began to hold the real power of human society.

The Guild Wars

Change came in the form of an enormous natural disaster. The volcano off the Krytan coast, which had been used to contain the Bloodstones, erupted. The stones were scattered throughout the land, and the magic they contained seeped into whatever they touched.

Once humanity realized what had occurred, and the potential inherent in the Bloodstones, they attempted to possess them. However, because so much power was held by the guilds, they used their influence over the human nations to vie for control. It became an enormous game of power, prestige, and guile, with countless guilds each struggling to claim the Bloodstones.

This period of strife and warfare was called the Guild Wars.

The Guild Wars lasted for decades. It was not comprised of any single campaign; instead, it encompassed a long-term struggle between a number of distinct factions. Over time, with no clear victor, the quest for dominance embroiled all the human nations. Ascalon, Orr, and Kryta declared war on each other, which caused constant fighting, manipulation, and the deaths of many.

The Guild Wars came to an abrupt and brutal end by the emergence of an even greater threat. The charr invaded the human kingdoms, and they brought with them such brutality and ferocity that all the other conflicts paled in comparison. The charr military was a force the human lands were not prepared for; they were used to human tactics and human sentiments. The charr were another force entirely. They looked at the human countries, weakened by war and infighting, and saw lands ripe for conquering and subjugation.

The Charr Invasion and Its Aftermath (Events of *Guild Wars: Prophecies*)

The Fall of Ascalon

Ascalon was the ancestral seat of the charr and a primary focus of the charr military force. The humans took shelter behind the Great Northern Wall as a barrier against their foes, but the charr shamans of the Flame Legion had powerful magics at their disposal. Using the Cauldron of Cataclysm and the power of the Titans (powerful spirits worshipped as gods), the shaman Jaw Smokeskin unleashed a devastation known as the Searing. Burning crystals of flame fell from the skies, igniting all that they came in contact with. The spell was as powerful as a natural calamity; it changed the very land itself, creating craters and fissures in the ground and even making the rivers flow with tar and lava. Countless lives were lost.

In the Ascalon capital city of Rin, the royal family tried to give strength and resolve to the people. However, there was a deep divide over how this should be accomplished. While King Adelbern believed that the humans should concentrate on rebuilding the city, his son, Prince Rurik, vehemently disagreed, feeling that the humans should strike back at the charr and take the offensive.

Against his father's wishes, Rurik led a small force to the remnants of the Great Northern Wall. There he witnessed the sheer numbers of charr amassed to take the human lands. It was obvious to Rurik the wall would soon fall; he then ordered a retreat of the human defenders. Before he left, however, Rurik found an unexpected artifact during a rescue mission: the mouthpiece of the legendary warhorn Stormcaller. He then undertook a quest to restore Stormcaller, convinced it was the only thing to save his people. This quest was ultimately successful.

With Stormcaller complete, Rurik attempted to return to the capital, but his arrival found the city in flames. The charr legions were successful; they were in the process of burning and razing the city. Prince Rurik let loose the magic of Stormcaller. At the sounding of the horn, the skies clouded over. Soon, a gentle rain pattered forth. The fires of the burning city were put out, and the remaining citizens were able to flee from the charr.

With Rin fallen, the Ascalonians faced a difficult decision. The neighboring nation of Kryta had extended an offer of aid; they were willing to allow the entrance of Ascalonian refugees and provide additional support to the military effort. Prince Rurik was heavily in favor of this course; he knew what the charr were capable of and how hopeless it would be to fight the charr without this aid. However, the Guild Wars had eroded any trust between the human nations. King Adelbern refused to accept the offer. He outright forbade the Ascalonians to leave the country. Finally, after Prince Rurik vehemently argued against this, Adelbern cast him out, banishing his son (and his followers).

With nothing to stop the charr advance, the legions began to move on to the territories of Orr and Kryta.

The Sinking of Orr

The Orrian military had been tested in the battles of the Guild Wars, and the inhabitants of the city-state were confident they could defend themselves against the charr.

They had no idea what would befall them.

The charr forces overwhelmed the defenders and marched to the holy city of Arah, where the gods had once walked Tyria. The Orrians scattered and died before the legions. But Orr was an old land, a powerful land—and a land of secrets. The king's personal advisor, a man versed in the mystical arts, crept into a warded vault deep in the catacombs of Arah. There, he unrolled the Lost Scrolls and uttered a spell that would be the doom of all in Orr.

An enormous explosion rocked the continent, and the lands of Orr shuddered and collapsed. Arah, and all the country around it, began to sink. Where there was once a countryside of invading armies, scattered villages, and fertile woodlands, there was now only an expanse of sea and water.

Few humans or charr lived through the event. It was known as the Cataclysm.

The Path of the Exiled

With no hope of relief from Orr, Prince Rurik looked to Kryta. However, the journey from Ascalon to Kryta was a difficult and dangerous crossing, with the foreboding Shiverpeak Mountains between them. Rurik, now an outcast, was joined by a number of supporters; he resolved to lead them over the mountains, where they could find sanctuary.

As the group traversed the mountains, they found themselves caught in another conflict. The Shiverpeaks were the domain of the dwarves, and they themselves were embroiled in a civil war. The Deldrimor dwarves were friendly to the refugees, but the opposing faction, the dwarves of the Stone Summit, believed in the innate superiority of dwarves over all other races. The Stone Summit made it a mission to destroy the Ascalonians as they moved through the harsh Shiverpeaks. It was only through the actions of Prince Rurik and his most trusted allies that the refugees were able to survive. It was not without cost; Rurik sacrificed himself at the Frost Gate, and the Ascalonians were left to face their future without the bravery of their prince.

Arrival at Kryta: A Dangerous Homecoming

Kryta offered a chance for many Ascalonians to find a new home and a new life, but it was not the bastion of security the refugees believed it to be. The country had its own problems: it was beset by undead led by a horrific figure known only as the Lich Lord.

However, the Ascalonian survivors were hardy and stalwart folk. After crossing the Shiverpeaks, they were inured to hardship. Faced with an undead attack, they repelled them, smashing the foul creatures. Because of their courage, the White Mantle, which was the governing body of Kryta, offered them the rights to settle north of Lion's Arch, the capital.

For many refugees, this was the end to their story, an opportunity for them to resume a simple life. However, Prince Rurik's loyal followers were not content. When they were given an opportunity to assist the White Mantle, they gladly accepted. During one of the missions, these loyalists saved the leader of the White Mantle, Confessor Dorian. They also helped him to acquire a powerful artifact, the Scepter of Orr, stymieing the undead that were also attempting to obtain it.

As a reward for their service to the White Mantle, these Ascalonians were given the honor of being admitted to the order. They were also given a responsibility: to administer the Test of the Chosen to the people along Divinity Coast. The Test of the Chosen was an annual event organized by the White Mantle in which a magical object, the Eye of Janthir, was taken to villages on the Summer Solstice. The Eye had the ability to distinguish the Chosen from the rest of the populace. The Chosen were then taken from their homes and escorted to a White Mantle stronghold, the Temple of the Unseen. There they would learn under the Grand Masters.

However, in the course of following their duties, the new Ascalonian members found out their Chosen had been kidnapped. The culprits appeared to be a rebel group: the Shining Blade. The group was asked to find out where the Chosen had been taken, retrieve them, and destroy the Shining Blade abductors.

Between the White Mantle and the Shining Blade

The Ascalonians tracked down the Chosen and confronted the Shining Blade, but in doing so they learned a strange truth: the Shining Blade was attempting to *save* the Chosen from the White Mantle. The group found evidence that the White Mantle murdered the Chosen, as a sacrifice to their masters (known as The Unseen Ones). The group was marked as traitors by the White Mantle, and the Order went to great lengths to both discredit and eliminate them. The White Mantle enlisted a spy from within the Shining Blade and used the information gained from their informant to get the upper hand in the struggle.

Evennia, the leader of the Shining Blade, knew it was only a matter time before the conflict would worsen. She sought a fortified location from where her forces could fight against the White Mantle. After much thought, she asked the Ascalonians to help her take a settlement called the Henge of Denravi. From this base, the Shining Blade was able to form new allies, principally a man known as Vizier Khilbron. However, Khilbron would only commit to the cause if he were given a powerful magical talisman, one encountered by the Ascalonians before: the Scepter of Orr.

The group was successful in gaining the Scepter of Orr. In the course of this mission, they found out about the White Mantle spy. They were able to meet with Vizier Khilbron and give him the scepter, but the meeting was known to the White Mantle. During the rendezvous, Evennia was captured, the Shining Blade was scattered, and the Ascalonians left to find their own path of action. Under the advice of Khilbron, they traveled to the Crystal Desert, a wasteland. It was Khilbron's wish that the group attempt the Rite of Ascension, a means to gain the attention and blessings of the gods. According to Khilbron, it was only through that power the group could succeed in overthrowing the mastery of the Unseen Ones.

The Quest for Ascension

In the Crystal Desert, the group completed many deeds of great renown. They found the Vision Crystal, an artifact meant to gather the gaze of the gods. They helped their guide, a spirit named Turai Ossa, assume the Throne of Pellentia. This also gained them access to the Temple of Ascension. At the Thirsty River, they defeated waves of creatures known as the Forgotten, which helped them prove their worthiness to Ascend. Finally, they faced a test where they confronted their own doppelgangers. This let them enter the Dragon's Lair, the final step toward their goal.

Perhaps not surprisingly, Dragon's Lair was the abode of a dragon named Glint. She was not only a powerful magical creature but also a prophet. Her visions were recorded in the *Flameseeker Prophecies*, and Glint was willing to share her knowledge with the group. Through her, they learned the identity of the treacherous informant (a man named Markis) and the true identity of the Unseen One. A long time ago, before humanity appeared, there was a race strong in the magical arts, known as the mursaat. The Unseen Ones were all that remained of them.

Glint counseled the party to travel to the southern Shiverpeak Mountains, where they could rescue captured members of Shining Blade and perhaps reveal more information.

Return to the Shiverpeak Mountains

Fortunately, the party had allies in the Shiverpeaks. The Deldrimor dwarves, led by King Jalis Ironhammer, offered assistance to the group. The first goal was to rescue the leader of the Shining Blade, Evennia. This was accomplished in short order. It was during this mission the group learned of a horrifying ability possessed by the mursaat: Spectral Agony. It was capable of killing nearly everything in its path, and the group was helpless against it.

To combat this, the dwarves suggested that the group seek out a creature known only as the Seer. This mysterious being lived deep in the mountains, and it was said to be one of the last of a line of an ancient people. After meeting with the Seer, the group learned the Seer's people were once at war with the mursaat. The Seer's people had perfected a way to combat the mursaat's power of Spectral Agony, through a process called Infusion. Despite this, the Seer's people lost the war with the mursaat, and they eventually dwindled over time, leaving nothing but ruins. The Seer taught the seekers how to Infuse their armor, finally giving them a way to destroy the mursaat.

Now protected, the group attacked the Iron Mines of Moladune, a mursaat stronghold. There, they killed Markis, avenging the comrades they lost due to his treachery. They were met with terrible news upon their return: the Deldrimor capital of Thunderhead Keep had fallen to the Stone Summit dwarves. To make matters worse, the White Mantle forces and mursaat were amassing to assault the city. Together with King Ironhammer, the group was successful in driving off the invading dwarves and, in a devastating blow, they killed Confessor Dorian, leader of the White Mantle.

With the city of Thunderhead Keep now significantly safer, the group earned a chance to rest and recover. Unfortunately, this was not to be; Vizier Khilbron arrived, and he brought with him a means to strike back at the mursaat. An island chain known as the Ring of Fire, south of the Tarnished Coast, held the key.

Secrets and Treachery Revealed

The Ring of Fire islands comprised the resting place of one of the Bloodstones. At the center of the islands was an enormous volcano, called Abaddon's Mouth. The volcano was the access point to the Door of Komalie, where a weapon against the mursaat could be found.

The group was able to fight through the mursaat to finally unseal the Door of Komalie. It was at that moment they made a terrifying discovery: they had been betrayed. Vizier Khilbron was no helpful benefactor. He had been responsible for a number of horrific acts in the past. In his early days, he was an advisor to King Reza of Orr. However, with the charr invasion, and under the influence of a demon sent by the fallen god Abaddon, Khilbron unleashed the dark magics that sunk Orr. The Cataclysm that followed killed thousands, including Vizier, but it had not destroyed him. Instead, he was transformed into an Undead Lich, and his evil continued. As the Lich Lord, he led armies of the undead into Kryta, but his plans extended far beyond.

Behind the door was a threat to all existence: the Titans. Using the Scepter of Orr, Khilbron was able to control the Titans, and he led them forth to conquer Tyria.

The End of the Threat of the Titans

The Lich Lord's advance was stopped at Hell's Precipice. After a climactic battle, the group was finally able to kill the Lich Lord. Without his guidance, however, the Titans were free to do whatever they wanted, and they wanted to destroy all of civilization.

This information helped shed some light on earlier events. It seemed the charr had come into contact with the Titans some time ago. The charr shamans were worshipping the Titans as gods, and the Titans' influence had encouraged the charr to attack the humans of Ascalon.

With Glint's help, the group was able to mobilize and defend several important locations: the dwarven town of Droknar's Forge, their homeland of Ascalon City, the Shining Blade stronghold of the Henge of Denravi, and finally the Krytan capital of Lion's Arch.

With the knowledge gained from their encounters with the Titans, as well as Glint's advice, the group determined the location of the Titans' high command. In Ascalon, deep within lands claimed by the charr, was the Titan Source. From there, three mighty Titan Lords and representatives of the charr military sent forth orders. The only chance to free Tyria was for a small group to travel there and eliminate the Titan Lords.

This pivotal battle had the desired effect. The Titan Lords were defeated. The charr were thrown into disarray. Civilization was saved, and many attempted to return to a peaceful existence.

The Mysterious Lands of Cantha (Events of *Guild Wars: Factions*)

Cantha is an old land, and one that has been occupied by humans from their first days on Tyria. In fact, the northern coastline of Cantha is the earliest known location of human settlements. Cantha could be called humanity's birthplace—at least until more evidence comes to light. While Cantha has its own rich and well-developed history, it has also been gripped with periods of isolation.

Cantha has mostly been ruled by a single empire, called the Empire of the Dragon (or, alternatively, the Empire of Cantha). A direct descendant of the empire's founder still rules the continent today.

The Jade Wind

The Jade Wind was a formative event in Canthan history. It occurred when one of the emperor's most honored bodyguards, Shiro Tagachi, assassinated his master, the 26th emperor of Cantha, Angsiyan. Shiro was a formidable warrior in his own right, but he also performed a number of dark rituals in preparation for his actions.

Shiro did not live long after committing the murder. Three of the emperor's guard, the Luxon spearmaster Archemorus, the Kurzick Saint Viktor, and the assassin Vizu, attacked him. In a climactic battle, Archemorus and Viktor were able to wrestle Shiro's swords from him and, turning them against their wielder, nearly slice him in two. In Shiro's final moments, he called upon dark powers and sucked out the fallen emperor's very soul. Tagachi's death cry released the foulest of magic, a horrific wail that rose like a gale over the land. This Jade Wind spread from the temple, turning the sea into solid jade and petrifying everything it touched (trees, animals, and people) within Echovald Forest.

The newly crowned monarch, Emperor Hanjai, Angsiyan's son, took the throne. The next summer, he instituted the Dragon Festival. It was meant to commemorate those who had lost their lives in the Jade Wind, unite all denizens of the empire, and celebrate the establishment of a community on Shing Jea Island. It also symbolized the survival of the Empire of the Cantha in the face of calamity.

A Mysterious Plague and the Return of an Ancient Evil

One hundred years after the Jade Wind, events occurred that revealed Shiro Tagachi's evil was not fully destroyed. The Heroes of Tyria joined forces with Emperor Kisu, his half-brother Master Togo, and Togo's former student, Brother Mhenlo.

The journey began with the appearance of a horrible plague, which turned the victims of the disease into violent creatures, called the Afflicted. After researching the disease, the group found evidence of Shiro Tagachi, a man long dead. However, beings from the afterlife, called envoys, told them that Shiro was turned into a spirit. The envoys' task, as penance for crimes committed in life, was to guide the souls of the dead. Instead, Shiro was corrupting the spirits, merging them with magical constructs (the Shiro'ken), and building an army.

The group attempted to destroy Shiro, but they were unsuccessful. They needed allies. Emperor Kisu was easy to convince; the Oracle of the Mists, Suun, also contributed valuable knowledge. After several negotiations, they convinced the Canthan vassal states of Luxon and Kurzick to join them. The dragon Kuunavang taught them valuable skills and agreed to fight alongside them.

Finally, the group ascertained Shiro's final goal. He was trying to return to life, and he only needed one more thing: to spill the blood of a member of the imperial bloodline. Togo, Mhenlo, and the Heroes wasted no time in returning to the palace, but they only arrived at the last second. Battling their way through the Shiro'ken, the group reached the Imperial Sanctum to find Shiro standing over Emperor Kisu, about to give the final strike. Master Togo, in a desperate act, rushed to his half-brother, taking the blow. The emperor was saved, but Togo sacrificed himself—and Shiro, with his quest now complete, had achieved his goal. The betrayer left to complete his spell, leaving the survivors behind to mourn a great man.

In an attempt to avenge his teacher, Mhenlo rushed into the Imperial Sanctum to confront Shiro, and the group followed him. They found Shiro Tagachi fully restored, a deadly and formidable assassin—but, once again, a mortal one. A terrible battle ensued, but the party was able to bring down Shiro. As Shiro lay dying, the Oracle Suun appeared, using his power to encase Shiro's body in solid jade. The envoys also arrived, seeking Shiro's soul. The last remnants of Shiro Tagachi were consigned to a special place in the Underworld, where his spirit was imprisoned and forced to answer for his many crimes.

Elona: Land of Secrets (Events of *Guild Wars: Nightfall*)

Humans appeared in the lands of Elona at roughly the same time as they did in Tyria. They found a land rich in natural resources; warm winds created a temperate climate, and the savannahs and forests were home to a variety of wildlife. Rivers flowed into the interior, bringing with them the potential for rich farmland, trade, and plentiful fishing. The glory of Elona soon gave it a notable title: the Land of the Golden Sun.

The Primeval and Margonite Dynasties

It was on the island of Istan, the largest of the island masses on the west of Elona, that the first notable human civilization was founded. From the city of Fahranur, the Primeval Kings conquered their island and moved on, spreading their culture to the mainland, through the present-day lands of Kourna and Vabbi, and even moving as far as Tyria (into the Crystal Desert region) and Kryta. In fact, Kryta was originally an Elonian colony during the time of the Primeval Dynasty. However, the Krytans rebelled and seceded from the union, gaining their independence.

As the Primeval Empire spread, it came into contact with another civilization, that of the Margonites. The Margonites were a seafaring people, and their homeland was somewhere in the Unending Ocean. They were worshippers of Abaddon, the God of Secrets. Though they sometimes created settlements, they lived more on their ships than on the coastlines. For some time, the Primeval Kings ruled the lands of Elona and the Margonites held the entirety of the Unending Ocean.

The face of Elona, however, was drastically changed by the creation of the Bloodstones. The Margonites, as followers of Abaddon, rose with their master to challenge the other gods. They lost. They were imprisoned with Abaddon in the Realm of Torment, and their exposure to the god corrupted them into demons. The destruction of the Margonites, and the obliteration of all traces of their existence, have led some scholars to question whether the Margonites were ever really a separate people or if they came into being when Abaddon created them (beginning with the first Margonite, Lord Jadoth).

The Forging of a Great Alliance

In contrast, the end of the Primeval Dynasty came not through war, but by sickness. The Scarab Plague swept through Elona, infecting and killing a huge swath of the population. The Royal House was totally wiped out, and the island of Istan itself was abandoned. The only remnants of the Primeval Empire were scattered monuments, ruins, and ancient mausoleums. The Tomb of the Primeval Kings, where the royal family had been buried for eons, was left as a grim testament to what remained. In years to come, it would be a place of great significance, where mortal adventurers could travel into the Mists and prove themselves. But that is a story for another time.

This fall of the Primeval Dynasty left a power vacuum that many tried to fill. Eventually (after the rise and fall of the Great Dynasty and the subsequent Pretender Wars), three allied provinces emerged, which still exist in the present day: Kourna, Istan, and Vabbi. Calling for an end to the bloodshed, they dedicated themselves to rebuilding and healing their populace.

The Scourge of Vabbi and the Founding of the Order of Whispers

The next challenge to the people of Elona came during an invasion from the Desolation. From his Bone Palace in the Desolation, the necromancer Palawa Joko employed dark rituals to bring forth an army. His forces swept into the northern province of Vabbi, butchering and consuming all before them. This act earned Palawa Joko the cursed title of "The Scourge of Vabbi." The Scourge's power was so overwhelming that he was able to conquer most of Elona, subjugating the provinces. He was finally defeated when a great Kournan general, Turai Ossa, challenged him to single combat during the Battle of Jahai. The necromancer was defeated, but he was so powerful that many feared his reach would extend beyond death. Instead, he was sealed beneath the sands, and Turai Ossa's elite bodyguards were tasked as wardens; they would later be known as the Order of Whispers.

Turai Ossa himself became the king of all Elona. However, obsessed with the gods, he eventually gave up the crown. He was last seen leading a pilgrimage into the Crystal Desert. Some say his spirit resides there still.

The Ascension of a God

Kormir was the spearmarshal of the Order of Sunspears, and she was one of the most dedicated of them all. The Order of Sunspears was charged with protecting all of the united provinces; their duties included fighting off the pirate Corsairs, investigating crimes, and maintaining the defense of Elona. Kormir and her group were based in Istan, where an excavation of the First City, Fahranur, was ongoing. When an archeological crew was killed, it was up to Kormir and her group to uncover what happened. The mystery deepened when all they could discover were undead creatures and prophecies related to the "Coming of Nightfall."

Things became more dangerous when the Elonians were betrayed by those meant to protect them. Warmarshal Varesh Ossa, a descendant of Turai Ossa, was just as obsessed with the gods as her forebear, but her ways took a darker turn. She was influenced by her mentor, General Kahyet—who happened to be an ardent worshipper of Abaddon. Varesh and Kahyet were systematically weakening the bonds of allegiance among the provinces, first by allying with the Corsair pirates and then by leading the Kournan military against Istan. It was Varesh's ultimate goal to release Abaddon from his prison, and she didn't care if that meant sacrificing her homeland.

The final stage of Varesh's ritual took place at the Mouth of Torment in the Desolation—the very place where the gods struck down Abaddon. During their journey there, Kormir was separated from her group; the same disruption unleashed Palawa Joko, another ancient (albeit lesser) evil, back into the world. Unfortunately, Palawa Joko was probably the only being that could give the group directions on how to cross the Desolation, and they were forced to make a deal with him: his freedom and aid in reclaiming power in exchange for directions for safe passage. With those conditions in place, the group helped Palawa Joko reclaim his Bone Palace. In return, he taught them how to ride great wurms and make their way through the Desolation.

The group arrived as Varesh was finishing her rites. Even though they were able to defeat her, they could not escape the results of the ritual. They were pulled through a dark vortex into the Realm of Torment, into the domain of a dark and powerful god. However, they also found an unexpected friend: Kormir. She'd learned that anyone who came into contact with Abaddon or his minions would be pulled into the Realm of Torment, if it were allowed to remain open. The group had to find a way to close the portal, and that meant defeating the God of Secrets.

Mere mortals could not hope to accomplish such a thing without aid from the other gods. The group fought its way to the Temple of the Six Gods, defeating several noteworthy foes from the past that allied themselves with Abaddon, including the Lich Lord and Shiro Tagachi. Once the group arrived at the Temple of the Six Gods, Kormir pleaded with the gods to offer their assistance. And they answered.

The gods gave Kormir a gift. They said it was one that only a mortal could use. The gods chose not to fight Abaddon directly, and said that the Heroes had all that was necessary within them. With that, the gods departed, leaving Kormir and her supporters to defeat a deity.

Confused but determined, Kormir and the party traveled to Abaddon's Gate. There, they fought a titanic battle against the god. Though weakened by imprisonment, Abaddon was still a powerful force to be reckoned with, and he did not go easily into the Mists. When Abaddon was finally destroyed, his mystical energies threatened to destroy the entire realm. As the power began to engulf the world, Kormir realized what the gods' gift was meant to do.

Throwing herself into the void, Kormir sacrificed herself for Tyria. In doing so, she left behind her mortal body and assumed the power of a deity. When all was done, Kormir had become the sixth god: Goddess of Truth, Knowledge, and Secrets. Abaddon was usurped!

Elona was battered but not defeated, and its people had been safeguarded. Kormir dedicated herself to continuing the duties she once had as part of the Order of the Sunspears: to defend the innocent and uphold the values of truth, knowledge, and clarity. Now she did that for the whole world.

Return to Tyria (Events of *Guild Wars: Eye of the North*)

History is a continuous stream, and events in Tyria did not cease simply because momentous happenings occurred in Cantha and Elona. It didn't take long before worship of Kormir had spread to the human lands of the Tyrian continent. And they needed any relief that their renewed faith in their gods could bring.

Stirrings Within the Earth

A series of earthquakes heralded the beginning of a new threat. Within their subterranean tunnels, the asura took notice. Their researchers determined that something was deeply wrong. While some were assigned to explore the matter further, the asuran government decided on a safer, more conservative approach. They moved the asuran populace to the surface, to the new city of Rata Sum. They brought with them technology never before seen on Tyria: the ability to travel quickly between distant areas. These were known as the Asura Gates, and they revolutionized movement within and between the countries of the world.

In the dwarven realms, the Deldrimor dwarves also felt the earthquakes. To some, these movements in the earth were a sign of ancient prophecies coming to fruition. Their stories tell of the patron deity, the Great Dwarf. In the ancient days, the Great Dwarf used his strength and power to create all the other dwarves; he also forged great weapons and armor for them. With these items, the Great Dwarf battled against the Great Destroyer. To defeat this foe, he stole its name and sealed it within the *Tome of Rubicon*. When he left Tyria, the Great Dwarf traveled into the Rift, where he now resides in the Great Forge. No living dwarf had ever seen the Great Dwarf, but they still believed in his existence. And some believed in the Great Destroyer, as well.

Civil War in Kryta and the Rule of Queen Salma

Lion's Arch, the capital of the nation of Kryta, was still held by the remnants of the White Mantle. When the charr invaded, the ruling house, led by King Jadon, fled the city, and the White Mantle assumed control. The king left behind an illegitimate daughter; the child he had with a priestess of the Temple of Ages. Her name was Salma, and she had a strong claim to the throne of Kryta. She was the former betrothed of Prince Rurik of Ascalon, until he met his courageous end.

The Shining Blade discovered Salma's existence and rallied to her cause. With their efforts, Salma, Evennia, and the forces of the Shining Blade took Lion's Arch and overthrew the White Mantle. Queen Salma was crowned to the applause (and relief) of the Krytan people.

Ascalon's Last Stand

In Ascalon, King Adelbern still ruled over what was left of the human nation. He called upon Ebonhawke, the last free city of Ascalon, to answer his warbanner. The Ebon Vanguard answered by sending a force to assist the king. Renamed the Ascalon Vanguard, they were assigned to the Shiverpeaks. They took the fight to the charr homeland, to the Shiverpeak Mountains, and then beyond.

A Gathering of Allies

In the Shiverpeaks, the dwarf Ogden Stonehealer and the asuran Vekk were constructing an Asura Gate through the underground depths. They were forced to flee through it by a destroyer attack. (Destroyers were something only spoken of in legend and were said to be the heralds and minions of the Great Destroyer itself.) The unlikely pair of heroes arrived at Boreal Station in the Shiverpeaks, where they encountered Jora, a norn, and later Gwen, a member of the Vanguard. Gwen was stationed at the Eye of the North, a tower fortification overlooking the snowy peaks. This team would make a huge impact on the world if they could learn to work together.

All of the members of the gathering were concerned with their own conflicts. The asura were the easiest to aid; they simply wanted to maintain the safety of their new territory. Once that was taken care of, they joined the effort.

Jora was on an important hunt. She'd lost her reputation as a warrior and could no longer "become the bear." Jora and her brother, Svanir, were hunting along the Drakkar Lake, but something had corrupted Svanir. He'd heard a calling, which led him to join with a dark presence. Time would reveal the presence was that of the Elder Dragon Jormag, who was waking from his hibernation. The event transformed Svanir into a monstrous nornbear. Jora was seriously injured during this event, and it cut her off from the spiritual energies of her people. The Heroes helped Jora find her brother, and, when he could not be healed, they killed him. The event renewed Jora's spiritual bond, but Svanir's story became a disturbing foreshadowing of things to come.

With Gwen's assistance, the group made their way through the Shiverpeaks and into the charr lands. It was there that the humans had their first glimpse of hope in their war against the charr: the legions weren't united any more. The Fire Legion, led by the shamans, had been a decisive force driving the war effort. They worshipped the Titans as gods, but with the defeat of the Titans, the other charr rebelled against them. If the charr were in the midst of a civil uprising, that could open several possibilities. The party rescued many captive members of the Ascalon Vanguard and regrouped at the Shiverpeaks.

The Last Battle Against the Great Destroyer

With the Great Destroyer awakening, the dwarves were faced with a battle against their ancient foe. Using a powerful artifact, King Jalis Ironhammer performed a ritual. At the end of his rite, the majority of the dwarves were transformed into stone through the power of the Great Dwarf. Now stronger than before, the dwarves made their way into the darkness to battle the Great Destroyer.

They were aided in their effort by norn warriors, asuran mages and golems, and the Ebon Vanguard. Although the Great Destroyer had powerful abilities and could summon lesser destroyers, it was eventually defeated. This loss signaled the end of the destroyer threat. Ogden, was left to carry on the final legacy of his people.

Between Then and Now (Events Leading Up to *Guild Wars 2*)

Contact Lost Between Tyria and the Other Continents

The people of Tyria were now on their own. In Cantha, the new emperor, Usoka, had finally unified his continent into the Empire of the Dragon. His armies conquered the vassal states of Kurzick and Luxon, making his power absolute. These efforts were supported by the Ministry of Purity, which was originally established by Reiko Murakami to combat the Afflicted. Emperor Usoka had begun to purge the lands of rebels, the sick, and any non-humans; it wasn't long before his embassies started to follow isolationist policies. There was currently no diplomatic contact with Cantha.

In Elona, things were even more dire. Palawa Joko, now freed from his captivity and in control of an undead army, had captured most of the continent. Vabbi, Istan, and Kourna had fallen. The last stories out of Elona were ones of horror and terror. Few knew what transpired there.

The Last Stand of Ascalon and the Foefire

King Adelbern's reign had come to an end. Faced with the destruction of his line, the defeat of his people, and the fall of Ascalon City, Adelbern resolved to take the charr with him in defeat. In the last battle for Ascalon City, Adelbern used the power held in his ancient sword, Magdaer, a relic left from the time of Arah. With his sword aloft, standing on the highest tower in the city, King Adelbern let loose a gout of flame. A white, burning heat swept the streets, immolating Ascalonian and charr alike. But only the Ascalonians arose as ghosts to continue the battle.

The spirits of the dead drove the charr from the city, forcing them to abandon the area.

However, even the Foefire could not stop the charr forever. The legion regrouped and fought their way through the spirits of the dead. The fortress of the Black Citadel now stood on the ruins of the Ascalonian capital of Rin. Outside, charr warbands held the territory from the ghosts, which they could disperse but not fully defeat.

The Founding of Durmand Priory

Many records from the past were destroyed by the horrible events of recent times. The Foefire, Searing, and Cataclysm were all tragic in their loss of life, but there were some who mourned the loss of books, records, and knowledge, as well. A group of monks and scholars came together to protect knowledge and lore during these hard times. They located and protected the monastery of Durmand Priory; it held a wealth of material from the past. These scholars named their organization after the building that gave them something to fight for.

The scholars of Durmand Priory were some of the most knowledgable and dedicated in the world. Their most practical contribution was the creation of the New Krytan alphabet, which soon spread through the known world. This language allowed communication between all countries, cultures, and races.

Because of its philosophies and ideals, the Durmand Priory was one of the first organizations to accept members from all races.

The End of the Flame Legion

The legions of the charr were divided into four distinct groups: the Iron Legion (engineers), the Blood Legion (warriors), the Ash Legion (scouts and assassins), and the Flame Legion (the shamans and spiritualists). However, the Flame Legion assumed power over the others when they discovered the Titans.

With the defeat of the Titans, the Flame Legion went into disarray. The rest of the legions took their chance to move against the Flame Legion. Led by Kalla Scorchrazor, the charr revolted. They were successful in the final battle, eventually casting out the Flame Legion (now renamed as the pejorative "Gold Legion" for their weakness). After this, charr females were liberated and were allowed to serve in the legions once more. It also marked an end to charr invasions. With the Flame Legion no longer in charge, there was an opportunity for the charr and humans to have lasting peace.

Primordus Awakens

In the Depths of Tyria, the Elder Dragon Primordus had been slumbering. The stirrings of his sleep sent forth the earthquakes that rocked the continent, and the time of rest had come to an end.

While he had not yet emerged from underground, the signs of Primordus' awakening were apparent. The stone dwarves were gone; they had moved deeper into the depths to fight the Elder Dragon. The surface was suddenly home to races that once only inhabited tunnels. The skritt, fleeing from the minions of Primordus, were trying to survive the best they could. The dredge, now wholly free from dwarven slavery, could find no safety deep underground. Their autonomous collective tried to find shelter in its own way, by holding territory in the mountains.

The Deceit of Jormag

The Elder Ice Dragon Jormag was responsible for more subtle attacks on the world. His corruption infected Svanir, a champion of the norn people. Devotees now espoused the lies and treachery of the Elder Dragon. The Sons of Svanir were a group of norn who worshipped the Elder Dragon, and they brought their voice to the Hoelbrak, hoping to gain additional support.

It was the awakening of Jormag that forced the norn from their ancestral reaches and into the Shiverpeak Mountains. They took some of the former territory held by the dwarves and were attempting to carve a new place for themselves. Hardy and resilient, the norn were also a surprisingly tolerant people. They were willing to lend their aid against the Elder Dragons, but some were undecided about what should be done.

Zhaitan, Master of the Orrian Horde

Far below the ancient city of Orr, the Elder Dragon Zhaitan once slept. Insidiously, its power and energies infested the wreckage of the once-great nation. When Zhaitan awoke, Orr did as well. The undead dragon rose and brought with him the city of Orr, pulling itself from the ocean floor. The dead came with it! Now the Orrian undead were seeping into the lands to the north, infecting all with decay and sickness.

The undead armada, a navy composed of former Orrian ships, holds the coast. They have blockaded the Tyrian continent. The Elder Dragon itself is found in what remains of the holy city of Arah, deep within the Orrian Peninsula.

The Deep Sea Dragon

Very little is known about this Elder Dragon. It resided deep underwater, probably somewhere in the Unending Ocean. Its awakening wreaked havoc on the undersea races of the quaggan and krait, but its influence on land has been minimal. Still, there is no way this Elder Dragon intends good for anyone.

Kralkatorrik's Birthing

Once mistaken for a mountain in the charr homelands, Kralkatorrik emerged from the rubble when this mountain exploded. The dragon flew over Blazeridge Steppes, and its passage left behind a devastated swath of land known as the Dragonbrand. Crystalline formations and corrupted creatures now patrol the area, and the charr are attempting to keep them in check. They are joined by the Vigil, a multiracial military organization dedicated to defend those in need, fight against the darkness, and offer help to all.

No one knows where the Elder Dragon flew or where it now makes its abode.

The Order of Whispers

Once based in Elona, the Order of Whispers has spread out from that continent. Their agents were the first to discover that the Elder Dragons were awakening, but they believed their information would be discounted. Instead, they began to gather members from all the peoples of the world and educate them about the danger.

Today, the Order of Whispers is a multiracial group that works against the forces of darkness wherever they are encountered. They prefer the way of the stealthy and subtle over direct combat, but they are fully capable of defending themselves if the need arises. The agents of the Order of Whispers may have a reputation as sneaks, assassins, or spies, but they also are fervently dedicated to standing against evil in all its forms.

The People of Tyria Respond to the New Threat

The Tentative Yet Relentless Spread of the Asura

With the earthquakes and direct devastation caused by the Elder Dragon Primordus, the asura abandoned the underground. They moved to the Tarnished Coast of the Maguuma Jungle, where they constructed the enormous floating city of Rata Sum. This is where the majority of the asuran populace lives, although asuran researchers can be found throughout the world.

Although the asura prize neutrality, they have cautiously allowed other races access to the Asura Gates, permitting unprecedented travel across regions. The knowledge of how to construct and manipulate gate energies is a zealously guarded asuran secret.

In recent years, the asura have had some disturbing internal problems. There is a major philosophical split between influential members of the primary asuran laboratories (krewes). This has led to the rise of the Inquest, a meta-krewe that believes the entire world is a machine that can (and should) be run. The Inquest defy many traditional asuran ethics. Led by a former student of Snaff (a founding member of Destiny's Edge), the Inquest won't allow its members to leave. They may be the cause of the first asuran civil war.

Divinity's Reach

Soon after the awakening of Zhaitan, Lion's Arch and much of the human lands were flooded. Torn by warfare, and desperate for civilization, the survivors of many engagements ended up in the Krytan province of Shaemoor. There they founded Divinity's Reach, a city that would be home to refugees from all the human civilizations. Everyone could have a chance to start again.

Currently, Divinity's Reach is ruled by the young Queen Jennah, a direct descendant of Queen Salma and (significantly farther back) King Doric. She is supported by the senators of the city and by her loyal Seraph, headed by Commander Logan Thackery, a former member of Destiny's Edge. The city has its work cut out for it. They face problems of internal corruption and hostile attacks by bandits and centaur, and there is still the overwhelming threat of the Elder Dragons.

Lion's Arch

Zhaitan's rising flooded the city but did not destroy it. After much of the populace fled, Corsairs moved into the ruins. As the ruins dried, the Krytans wanted their territory back. They fought the Corsairs and drove the pirates out, reclaiming the old capital.

As a central location, Lion's Arch exists now as a nexus of travel and home to all the races. The city holds a number of Asura Gates, connecting it with all the various capitals of Tyria, and it stands as a beacon against the Elder Dragons' evil. The Lionguard helps to patrol the roads and give stability to the region, and there are many who owe their lives to this military organization.

The Emergence of the Sylvari

The roots of the sylvari go deep, but they're still considered a new race in Tyria. Many years ago, a human Shining Blade soldier named Ronan found a fist-sized seed in a cave. When he returned home from his battles, he found his home on the Tarnished Coast had been destroyed by the mursaat. At that point, he planted the seed on his family's graves and vowed never to fight again. He was later joined by a centaur named Ventari, someone who had seen the devastation of war and its effects on his people. The two formed a friendship based on mutual respect and shared pacifistic ideals. The two nurtured the seed Ronan planted, and it grew into a pale sapling and then a tree.

Ronan and Ventari's views soon attracted a number of followers who formed a Sanctuary of Peace at the foot of the Pale Tree. As time moved on, Ronan passed away; Ventari followed him, but before he died, the centaur carved all the accrued wisdom of his life into a tablet, which was placed at the foot of the Pale Tree.

More than 100 years later, the Pale Tree flowered and then formed golden fruit. When the fruit opened, the first sylvari emerged. The 12 firstborn of the sylvari found Ventari's Tablet, and, impressed by the knowledge imparted by it, chose to revere Ventari and Ronan and their teachings. The firstborn taught the sylvari who followed them about Ronan's bravery and Ventari's wisdom, with the goal of following these ideals and morality.

All sylvari are connected to each other through the Dream, a spiritual bond. However, there are those among the sylvari who have a shadow over their heart. They have rejected the teachings of Ventari, seeing them as a shackle holding their people back. These sylvari are trying to corrupt the Pale Tree. Under their influence, the Dream would become a Nightmare. Sylvari who follow this way of thinking are known as members of the Nightmare Court.

Destiny's Edge

Destiny's Edge was an adventuring guild famous for its deeds throughout Tyria. They were dedicated to stopping the Elder Dragons and their minions, and they achieved unprecedented success in many of their battles, even confronting two of the dragons face to face. However, their last battle, against the Elder Dragon Kralkatorrik, went badly. One of the members, Logan Thackery, left right before the confrontation, weakening the group significantly. Perhaps as a result of this, another member died in the fight. Destiny's Edge disbanded soon afterward.

The following were the known members of Destiny's Edge:

Eir Stegalkin is a norn ranger who lives with her wolf Garm. Eir was once the leader of Destiny's Edge and is still well known for this. A visionary, tactician, explorer, and sometimes artist, Eir has returned to her norn people in Hoelbrak. While the norn respect her abilities, Eir seems to have lost a great deal of her vibrancy and momentum after the defeat of Destiny's Edge. There are now some who doubt her abilities.

Logan Thackery is a human guardian and the current Commander of the Seraph at Divinity's Reach. Logan is the son of the Heroes Gwen (of the Ebon Vanguard) and Lieutenant Keiran Thackery. He once had an older brother, Dylan. When Dylan died, Logan accepted his brother's swords and the ideals of being a Hero. As a young man, Logan became enthralled by Queen Jennah and made a pledge to serve her. She shared his feelings but felt compelled by duty.

Together, they shared a magical bond, which allowed Logan to know if Queen Jennah were ever in danger so he could come to her. This bond was the downfall of Destiny's Edge. Just as the group was about to fight Kralkatorrik, Jennah summoned Logan to defend her in Ebonhawke from the dragon's minions. He came to his Queen's defense and saved her, but at a cost. One of Destiny's Edge, the asuran Snaff, was killed, and the Elder Dragon was victorious. There are those in Destiny's Edge who hold Logan indirectly responsible for Snaff's death, and these are feelings that Logan shares. However, loyalty (and love) for his Queen is his first concern. He currently holds a position as her personal champion in Divinity's Reach.

Caithe is a sylvari thief and is one of the firstborn. As a member of Destiny's Edge, Caithe was adept at helping the group find its way through the shadows, and many of the sylvari characterize her as being drawn to and understanding the darker ways of the world. This has followed in her personal affairs. Caithe was once a lover of Faolain, the Grand Duchess (and current leader) of the Nightmare Court. When Caithe left her, unable to support Faolain's descent into despair, Faolain didn't take it well. She continues to haunt Caithe, attempting to draw her into the Nightmare. Caithe, however, has a strong will and believes in her own ideals. As such, she remains resolved in the fight against the Elder Dragons, and her wish is the restoration of Destiny's Edge and the continuation of their work.

Rytlock Brimstone is a charr warrior. Rytlock is a member of the Blood Legion and is one of the best-regarded charr of the Black Citadel, where he holds the position of Tribune. He wields the artifact sword Sohothin, once the sword of Prince Rurik and twin to the blade Magdaer, which was used by King Adelbern to cause the Foefire. Once a close friend of Logan Thackery, the two are now estranged due to the events of the final battle against the Elder Dragon. Lately, some charr have attempted to diminish Rytlock's accomplishments, calling him "strange" and citing his former friendship with a human. This has only fueled Rytlock's temper, but he has tried (somewhat) to focus it against the myriad enemies the world faces.

Snaff was an asuran golemancer. Snaff was a highly regarded magical theorist and inventor before he encountered Destiny's Edge, but the group helped him develop and hone his talents even more. Snaff specialized in the creation of enormous combat golems, but many of his smaller inventions focused on using telepathic control instead of machinery. In the final battle against Kralkatorrik, Snaff grappled with the mind of the Elder Dragon directly; he was even able to successfully control it for a time. However, the minions of the Elder Dragon attacked him, and, because he was poorly defended, they succeeded in killing him. Destiny's Edge dissolved soon afterward. Snaff is regarded as a major hero, and the asura dedicated a memorial laboratory to him. This is the highest honor that the asura bestow on anyone.

Zojja is an asuran elementalist and golemancer, and she's also a former apprentice of Snaff. Zojja remains devoted to his memory and ideals. She followed Snaff into Destiny's Edge, regarding him as a genius. He felt the same way about her (which is a distinct rarity, as most asura never admit to having intellectual equals). When Snaff died, she attended his cremation and returned his ashes to the asuran capital of Rata Sum. She is now a member of the College of Synergistics, where she helps guide young asuran inventors. Her snarky attitude and vivacious nature have won her both admirers and detractors, and while she has adjusted to her current position, there is a part of her that longs for the time she spent with Snaff and Destiny's Edge.

MULTIPLAYER ONLINE GAME BASICS

Suppose that you're not only new to *Guild Wars 2* but new to massively multiplayer online games (MMOs) in general. Well, this is the section for you! Here, we'll talk about common concepts in all MMOs, how they relate to *Guild Wars 2*, and how you interact with an online environment like this one.

Compared with Single-Player Games

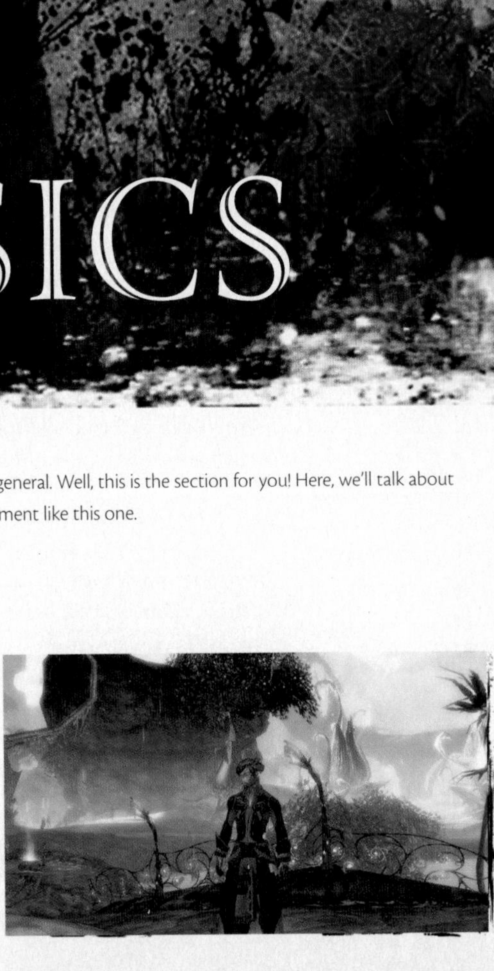

MMOs are a completely different experience than general single-player games. Most single-player games have well-defined boundaries; as you play them, you are guided through a storyline with a set beginning and end, and you don't socially interact with other people. Your character's progression is determined solely by decisions you make (through skills/levels), but the characters themselves are defined through a static pool of traits. With the exception of the occasional gameplay patch, the characters (and the world they inhabit) don't change in terms of gameplay or effectiveness.

MMOs aren't like that. First, because they are fully online, they are dynamic. What you experience in terms of gameplay, character progression, and social interactions can change depending on what server you join, who you meet, and what you determine to be important.

Try this example. In a single-player game, the end of the game is the end of the plotline. However, in an MMO, you have a lot of input regarding what you consider the "end" of the game. Is it when you hit the events in the highest-level regions? How about when you discover all the crafting recipes? Or, is it when your gear is the best it can be? What about once you've completed every single task available or discovered every single exploration point? The answer depends on what you want, and you don't have to pick only one! Make up new ones as you go.

A Story All Your Own

Many people's enjoyment of a game depends greatly on how they relate to the story. They look for a vibrant world with well-developed characters and imaginative plotlines. It's even better when they get to contribute to the environment they inhabit.

Many MMOs have been criticized for not having a story or plotline that relates to a player, that the player in an MMO doesn't have an effect on the world. This isn't the case with *Guild Wars 2*.

All players have their own personal story. This story depends on choices you make, from your character's creation to decisions other characters ask you to make. What you decide changes what missions become available to you and how the story progresses. Your race, character background, affiliations, and morality all play a major role in the epic quest that unfolds.

Your Place in the World

In addition, we mentioned that *Guild Wars 2* is very dynamic, right? Things happen in the world when you aren't there, and it changes according to what you do (or don't do). You may find a fort filled with hostile centaurs that attack you the moment you get close. The defenders of the area are all gone or dead, and you have to decide to help or just move on. If you help, you can fight the centaurs back, revive the guards, and restore the fort. Soon afterward, you might see a merchant show up. The next person to arrive will find a well-defended bastion in the wilderness, complete with protection and opportunities to buy, sell, and repair. How's that for having an effect on the world?

Developing Your Character

Character progression is a defining trait of MMOs. Because what is important varies from player to player, there are numerous paths to power. Here, we'll take a look at the various ways characters can progress, from rising in level to gaining equipment to crafting and beyond.

Remember, this is a chapter on MMO basics. We're only going to cover these topics in a general manner. For more information, and especially how they relate to *Guild Wars 2*, read our chapter How to Play *Guild Wars 2*.

Leveling Characters

The most rudimentary means of character progression is leveling. As you play your character, you gain experience, which raises your character's level. Higher levels increase your character's stats, and hence effectiveness.

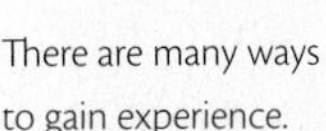

There are many ways to gain experience. Killing monsters is the most obvious way, but there are more. Exploring the world itself, completing your personal story events, finishing renown tasks, and participating in dungeon runs are all ways to acquire experience. You can even gain experience by crafting, and by harvesting the ingredients for crafting. The most effective way to gain experience in *Guild Wars 2* is to do a number of these things during a play session.

RENOWN TASKS AND NPCs

For an easy way to tell where you should explore, look at the renown hearts while you walk through each region. Highlight these hearts on your map to see their level; even at range, this lets you know if you're in a place with monsters that are appropriate for your character to fight. Let the hearts be your guide to the world! Complete the tasks that NPCs associated with renown hearts give to earn experience, gold, and sometimes gain access to special vendors!

Participating in Events

For many MMOs, characters gain experience by completing quests. These are activities offered by non-player characters (NPCs) that players accept and perform. They include killing a set number of monsters (kill quests), picking up items from the ground (groundspawns) or from bodies (gathering quests), or protecting an NPC or group of NPCs from enemies as they move through the wilderness (escort quests).

Guild Wars 2 handles these activities differently. As you enter a region and move around, you'll encounter events, which encompass just about anything that's going on in the area. New events occur regularly, and they're heralded by a message across your screen. In addition, if you look on your minimap, there are icons indicating event locations.

A standard event in *Guild Wars 2* would be to go over to, say, a dam and drive out harpies. The harpies have a concentration of force over the dam, and they have strong morale. As you kill the harpies, their morale decreases, and once enough of them have been defeated, the rest of the flock scatters and runs. You get experience from killing the monsters and from completing the event!

Events that require gathering materials from the ground or bodies are easier to complete than the typical MMO model. Instead of having to find an NPC and have them ask you to do something, you have more control over how much you want to help and where you go. First, the NPC is clearly marked on your minimap (by an asterisk), and most of the time you don't even have to talk to them to start participating. As you move around or defeat foes, you pick up the materials. Once you feel like you've gotten enough, then you talk to the NPC and drop off the stuff. The event meter tells you how much you contributed and how close the event is to completion. You can choose to stay and complete the event or go on your merry way; you will always get some reward for your trouble, but the more you help, the better the reward.

Escorts are marked by shield symbols on the minimap. Generally, you talk to the NPC and offer to help them by protecting them (and/or their group or beast of burden) as they go between locations. This gives you an opportunity to see more of the world and can lead you to new and interesting locations (with new and interesting events in them).

COME ONE, COME ALL

Events in *Guild Wars 2* are open to everyone. All it takes to join the event is simply to be in the area. Killing one enemy (or even just hitting several as you run by) can help to complete the event and gain you a little bit of a reward. Even if the event fails, you'll get *something*. And this works for escorts and gathering events as well. If you're in the area, all you have to do is walk for a few feet and help protect a caravan; if you have a gathering item, all you need to do is pass one to the NPC for it to help. There is no reason *not* to chip in on an event!

Conversely, there's no penalty for not doing the event. You won't miss out on subsequent follow-up events or a vital piece of rare equipment. You simply won't get the rewards (money, experience, or karma) associated with the event's completion.

Getting Better Equipment

Gaining more powerful or higher-level equipment is a huge focus of character progression in MMOs, and *Guild Wars 2* has a number of ways for you to get nice stuff.

THE EQUIPMENT RAINBOW

The color of an item gives a quick indication of how powerful it is. The rarer the quality of an item, the stronger it is. Exceptional items (such as those of exotic or rare quality) have higher stats and more powerful sigils; common items have lower stats and minor or no sigils. Sigils are added benefits you gain by equipping the particular item to which the sigil is attached.

The easiest way to find weapons and armor is as loot from killing monsters. If an enemy's body is glowing, there's loot for you to pick up. If you're in a party and you see a glowing corpse, that loot is for you and only for you, and no one else in the group will ever see what you've acquired. Monsters drop a wide variety of items, and you can usually keep yourself moderately equipped with what you find.

There are periods when you haven't found something you need in quite a long time or you want something special. In general, it's more prudent to keep your weapon up to date than your armor; after all, if you kill something quickly, you won't have to worry about it hitting you! Still, if you're running around with the same gloves you had at level 5 and now you're at level 30, it's time for a change.

At the Trading Post, you can find anything that other players feel is worth putting up for auction. These include weapons, armor, and runes, as well as containers (bags, packs, etc.), dyes, and crafting components. Trading Posts are found in every major city, and in major settled areas around the world.

Another way to gain equipment is through crafting. Crafting is a means of making your own equipment by combining the raw materials (like thread, cloth, metal) at a specific location (such as a forge or loom). Crafting can be very addicting and satisfying, but it does require a time, money, and material commitment. If you want to know more about crafting, see the Crafters and Their Fine Goods chapter.

You can also buy equipment directly from vendors. Vendors are found in all the capital cities and scattered throughout the world. In fact, sometimes they even appear after you have successfully reclaimed an area in an event. Most armorsmiths and weaponsmiths sell gear at 5-level intervals (you gain access to new gear at levels 5, 10, 15, and so on). Thus, the majority of vendor equipment can fill out any gaps in your character's gear that you haven't been able to satisfy in other ways or if you simply don't feel like going back to the Trading Post.

You accrue karma while completing various renown tasks and events. You can spend this resource to purchase higher quality equipment. Look for karma vendors as you explore. Sometimes these are unlocked by completing renown tasks and talking to the NPC around which the task centered (they're still marked with a heart on your map). See if they have anything fun to purchase.

Fighting Monsters

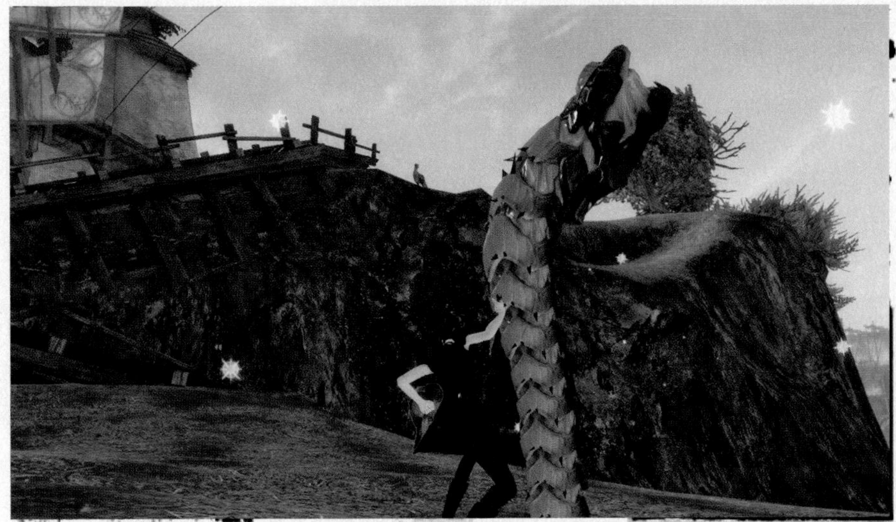

If you're playing an MMO, you're going to be fighting a lot of monsters. That's the way it is! But there are all sorts of ways to fight those monsters, and how you accomplish these engagements depends on your playstyle, the profession of your character, and what monsters you're fighting.

Getting a Monster's Attention

In a simple battle, getting a monster's attention is pretty easy. Basically, you hit it with something. Your autoattack (number "1" on the keyboard) hits the creature with an attack or spell. After starting your autoattack, let the blows rain down until the target falls.

WHAT'S IN A MONSTER'S NAME?

The color of the name above enemies or characters gives you a quick assessment of how aggressive they are. Here's the breakdown.

- **GREEN:** Friendly NPCs or characters.
- **BLUE:** Other player characters.
- **LIGHT BLUE:** Player characters in your party.
- **GREY:** Wildlife that won't be worth experience.
- **YELLOW:** Neutral creatures that only attack when provoked.
- **RED:** Hostile targets that will attack on sight.
- **GOLD:** Other players in the same guild.

The majority of enemies you'll encounter have a standard level of power. They can hurt your character but shouldn't be able to overwhelm you without help from their allies, siege equipment, or more powerful units. Some enemies are listed as veterans or champions. These are stronger and more powerful than others in the area. Veterans have greater health and more brutal attacks, and champions are even worse!

While you can take down veterans on your own (with some luck and skill), don't attempt to bring down a champion. Look around for other people to help! What you can't do by yourself may be easily accomplished with the aid of others.

Using advanced tactics, you can often kill enemies that would destroy you in a standup fight. These techniques are more efficient, and if you handle combat well you won't have to worry about waiting around for your health to come back; instead, you'll be out there spreading healthy anarchy.

Stand and Fight

All right, so you've walked up to your monster and hit it with an attack. What attack do you want? Every attack is a bit different, and what you decide could influence the course of the fight. Take your time and look over your skills as you get them. Experiment with them and see which ones work best together and which ones you like (or don't). In many MMOs, you don't have to move around very much during combat. In *Guild Wars 2*, moving your character to avoid attacks is an important way to survive. The more you play, the more you learn to avoid damage through careful movement and positioning your character. Skills and armor help you in every fight, but quick thinking, dodging, and tactics take you to the next level!

Pulling

There are times when the monster you want is surrounded by other enemies, and if you wander too close, you know that you'll be overwhelmed by their numbers. Or, maybe you don't feel like wandering over that ledge for one monster, or you want to use some abilities that require a lot of room and distance. What do you do? You pull the monster back to the area where you want to fight it.

AGGRO

Getting a monster's attention is also known as getting aggro. This is a more advanced game concept and is explained throughout the guide. For a general idea, consider that your enemies sometimes have multiple targets to attack. Will they go after you, your guardian buddy, or someone else?

To decide this, enemies quickly think about which target is closest to them, which one is inflicting the most damage, and whether any opponents are trying to revive allies. If you want monsters' attention, move into close range and hit them hard. To avoid aggro, let others get the first hit, keep yourself at range, and back away when something starts to run toward you. Give your allies a chance to lure the monster's attention back onto themselves—or to kill the beast, slow it down, or otherwise delay the enemy's attack.

Pulling consists of using an ability at range and having the monster come to you. This is a staple for ranged attack users, and all professions have abilities to pull.

This technique is particularly effective in dungeons, which have large numbers of nasty, high-damage enemies. One person picks a target, goes out, hits the target, and runs back to the group. The target follows, and the group then falls upon it and takes it down, giving the group much more safety than if they had all gone into a room filled with brutal foes.

Line of Sight Tricks

Pulling enemies that have ranged attacks can be tricky. After all, why would they come over to your group when they can sit still and shoot arrows into your head? Try this: attack the enemy or get him to aggro on you, and then hurry behind cover. As soon as you break line of sight, the enemy is forced to stop attacking. He needs a new angle to get line of sight back. So, the creature moves forward. When the monster gets to your hiding spot, jump out and beat it down.

Kiting

Kiting is a combat technique that lets you kill enemies over time. You control the position of your foes, and prevent them from closing to use their best attacks. You want to keep the enemy at a distance while still doing full damage to it.

Pick a ranged ability, preferably one that also slows or impedes your target's movement with Cripple or Frozen effects. You fire with that first, and when the target beelines toward you, run to the side and keep moving. The enemy keeps trying to reach you to attack, but you stay out of its range because you're moving faster than it is. You still attack as you move, but have a positional attack ready when the monster reaches you. Using skills that cause conditions such as Poison or Burning are particularly effective, as they inflict damage even after the initial attack ends. Knock the enemy back, Immobilize it, or do something to get away from it again and resume the kiting. If you want to exploit this style of fighting to its fullest, find items, sigils, and traits that help your character get more and more condition damage!

If the target completely catches up with you, dodge to the side to avoid whatever attack is coming your way. Come out of the roll and keep moving, using your best attacks to slow the monster again and get back to long range.

Area-of-Effect Attacks: Killing Monsters en Masse

We've talked about how to fight one monster at a time, but suppose you want to fight many of them. This is where you use area-of-effect (AoE) attacks. AoEs are abilities with a ground-targeted radius or a blast that centers around your character or the target. Anything within that radius gets hit by the skill's effect. Some AoEs are damaging enough that they outright kill anything in the circle, but they can also merely injure a large number of foes or put damaging conditions (status effects) on them.

Have a few characters work together with AoEs to burn down entire groups of enemies in short order.

Interacting with Other Players

The most fundamental distinction between single-player games and MMOs is the multiplayer component: you're playing the game with other people! For some, this is the sole reason they picked up the game in the first place: all their friends are playing it. For others, the addition of a social component adds flavor, volatility, and an opportunity to interact with the game in a different way. There are also people who aren't really that engaged with the social aspect; there are other reasons they like MMOs, and they prefer to play on their own.

BENEFITS OF SOLOING VS. GROUPS

This list is by no means exhaustive, but it does give an idea of why people choose the playstyle they do.

Soloing

- You alone decide your course of action.
- You can change your mind whenever you want.
- You can complete tasks, events, and other goals at your own pace.
- It can be a relaxing and quiet time.

Grouping

- You can take on events, enemies, and dungeons that would be impossible to complete on your own.
- You gain the protection of a group.
- You can talk, roleplay, and interact with other people.
- There is an increase in useful loot drops because you are killing more things faster.
- It adds a level of excitement and strategy to a play session.
- Guild groups contribute toward the progression/special abilities of their guild.

Making Friends

Because you interact with so many people, MMOs offer a great opportunity to make friends. People from all over the world, from all ages and all walks of life, have come together to play the same game. This means you have an instant ice breaker: you have the common experience of playing *Guild Wars 2*. You could meet your best friend for life or your prospective spouse. Or you could find great companions for regular dungeon runs, or simply a helpful acquaintance who helps you finish a one-time event. You never know.

We'll talk more about ways to converse with fellow adventurers in the Game Mechanics chapter, just a bit farther into this book. For now, look at your text window on the lower-left side of the screen. That's where you can read messages from guild members, players in your current region, or people who are trying to message you from afar. In return, you can type messages to others using commands like "/say Hi" (which would deliver your greeting to nearby heroes).

A NOTE ABOUT ETIQUETTE

Etiquette in any MMO can be boiled down to one simple rule: treat other people as you'd like to be treated. You'll rarely upset people by treating them respectfully. If you're friendly, most people will respond in kind.

Here are some general guidelines that can help in your interactions with other people.

- If you need help with something, ask someone openly and deferentially.
- Say "please" and "thank you."
- Apologies go a long way toward smoothing ruffled feelings.
- If you've finished a good event/dungeon run, let people know you appreciated their time and work.
- Ask before you put someone on your friends list or before you offer a guild invitation.
- Be responsible for your own progression (e.g., don't beg strangers for cash or items).
- Keep your public interactions friendly but to the point (e.g., don't clog up chat channels with useless or rude comments).
- Your thoughts on politics, religion, and racial or gender dynamics are private.
- If you can't say something nice, don't say anything at all.

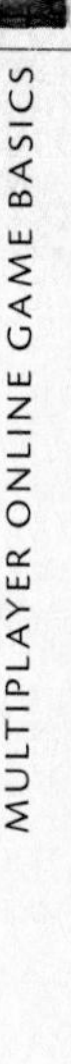

THIS TIME IT'S PERSONAL

You may end up meeting individuals who are simply offensive, for whatever reason. And maybe they also can't take a hint (or even a direct order) to stop their behavior. You are under no obligation to group with them or respond to such people. Most of the time, the best course of action is to try to step back, not take it personally, and ignore it. Proceed with your game and leave them to their own mess.

For truly nasty behavior, you can report them to a *Guild Wars 2* representative.

Watch Your Language

People of all ages and all walks of life are playing this game with you. Therefore, it's a good rule of thumb in your interactions with other people to watch your language.

The obvious part of this is not to use foul language in general speech in chat channels or in group. There is a filter (in your Options menu) that edits language. It edits out the majority of bad words and keeps them from being posted. However, if you're worried about being offensive in a public forum, it's the best course of action to be practical and not use terms that might upset people (or introduce younger players to terms that aren't relevant to their gaming experience).

This includes negative language relating to racial descriptions and sexual orientation. Using those terms simply isn't cool. Using these words can alienate you from mature groups, leading to lost opportunities for fun, better loot, and greater experience.

Interacting with Others in the World

As you move around the world of Tyria, you'll meet tons of people on a completely casual, random basis. You'll see them running around cities, completing all sorts of events, and exploring the wonderful places this world has to offer.

In many ways, *Guild Wars 2* has made it exceptionally easy to interact with people in ways that tangibly benefit you without forcing you to do anything. In addition, the game excels at not limiting resources, so people don't feel as possessive or selfish about going after what they want or need. We'll explore this below in greater detail.

Group Loot

Most games show what everyone in the party is looting. This causes occasional drama because someone will beg for, or outright demand, an item. The system in *Guild Wars 2* keeps things private by making all loot personal. You won't have to deal with "loot ninjas" or other treasure issues while grouping with strangers.

No Tapping: Everyone Gets Credit

Most MMOs have an attack system where a given monster is linked with a specific player or group after they attack it. This is called "tapping" a monster. When a monster is tapped, any loot and experience gained after the monster has been killed belongs to that player/group. This has led to the following situation: someone hits a monster, tapping it, and then runs off. The monster follows him and bumps into you. You defend yourself, killing the enemy, but you don't get any reward, experience, or loot. The coward gets to prosper at your expense, and you did all the real work. It gets even worse if this wasn't an accident and the person keeps doing it repeatedly.

A second consequence of the tapping system is that certain rare or important enemies were the focus of negative competitions between players. Some quests would only give credit if you killed a special creature. Because these rare monsters would only appear in special locations or after a long interval had passed, there would either be queues of polite groups waiting to attack them or a rush of constant area-of-effect attacks by multiple groups within an area, with each group vying for who got to be the one to tap the enemy.

Guild Wars 2 avoids the entire quagmire. Everyone who deals a non-trivial amount of damage to a target gets credit for the kill. You have a chance to loot, score experience when the creature dies, and contribute toward any events in the area. You can effectively act as a group with strangers even if you're only passing each other during a few fights. It's that intuitive. Cooperation has no downsides, and competition has no teeth.

I WAS JUST TRYING TO HELP

Even though the game allows (and even encourages) you to help other people in their battles, it's possible that players will take offense with you "butting in" on their action. They might not understand how the system works, or they might be enjoying the challenge of one-on-one combat. The wise course is to apologize, move on, and put some space between you and them.

And if you see players that look like they're in trouble, help out! You won't be taking anything from them, and you might have just saved their lives. Most players appreciate the assistance, even if they aren't in as much trouble as it appeared.

All Your Resources Belong to Us

In the sense that monsters can't be claimed by one person, all of the resources in the world work the same way. If you see an ore vein, a fruitful sapling, or a tasty herb patch, harvest it! In fact, everyone can (and should) do the same thing. Resources in the world are available to everyone. When the resource disappears from your game, it will still be there in the world for someone else. So, you won't be taking it away from anyone.

To harvest these items, make sure your character has the proper tools. For a small amount of money, you can secure tools for foraging, logging, and mining. Merchants in town sell these, and you use them each time you harvest items from a node. Eventually, your items wear out and you have to purchase more of the tools.

The expense of keeping your tools up to date isn't a major hardship. The profit from selling harvested items, or the money you save by grabbing them yourself instead of using the trading post, is often quite substantial. Be sure to harvest when you can, for free experience, future profit, or to help crafters (and yourself) make better items.

IT'S THERE TO BE HARVESTED

Every time you harvest a resource, be it wood, metal, vegetables, whatever, you get a small bit of experience in addition to the harvested items. This means that a whole party can gather around the harvesting point and gain benefits!

Death and Aiding the Fallen

A world filled with adventure, by necessity, is also a place of great danger. Monsters are extremely tough if you aren't careful, and some creatures are so powerful that even the best players are likely to go down fighting them.

Do not fear this! The game does not punish you excessively when your character falls. Reaching zero health puts your character into a downed state. You can't access many skills in this position, but you can still fight and attempt to heal yourself a little. Should you regain decent health or kill one of your enemies, your character rallies and resumes the engagement. Underwater, you can also choose to swim for the surface to try and heal and rally.

Take too long to rally, and your downed character will be defeated. This is still not the end. You just have to teleport to a waypoint of your choice and resume exploring. Some of your equipment is damaged in the process, but the monetary hit from repairing isn't meant to cripple you. It's just a light penalty. Feel free to take risks and have fun out there.

Guild Wars 2 also rewards people for bringing back the dead! Every time you revive someone (by interacting with his or her body) you gain a reward. Players are worth experience, many NPCs are worth credit toward local tasks, and so forth.

THOSE ZANY DEAD PEOPLE

If you look on your minimap, you can see the location of downed characters. There's a circle icon with a small skull. The color denotes who's died:

- **Blue:** A slain player
- **White:** A dead NPC

The Concept of Griefing

By rewarding beneficial activities and limiting negative ones, *Guild Wars 2* has created a system that discourages griefing. What is griefing, you might ask. Griefing is deliberately annoying or upsetting other players. Griefing is a true nuisance in most MMOs, mostly because griefers don't care about completing in-game goals. Mostly, they're in it for attention.

By opening up the battle system and by individually assigning loot and resources, *Guild Wars 2* keeps most griefing activities to a minimum. No one can steal your loot or your monster. Everyone gets access to all harvesting points. These things make for a much better gaming experience.

Travel and Exploration

Getting around the world is important if you want to explore, find new challenges, and meet new allies. *Guild Wars 2* provides a few ways to do this, and some of them might be totally new to you. Walking around is easy enough. You just put one foot in front of the other and see where the road takes you.

But as you travel, you'll start to see new things. Points of interest are special locations that you encounter. Visit each one you find for experience and map completion—when you complete a full tour of the area, you get an additional reward.

If you see a diamond-like icon on the map, go toward it. It's a waypoint. These travel hubs are essential for getting around quickly. As long as you've visited a waypoint location at least once and have a few coins to spare for the travel fee, your heroes can teleport to any waypoint that isn't contested by monsters. The gentle tinkling sound of a waypoint lets you know when it's close even if you aren't looking at the map.

Vistas are locations with beautiful scenery or important locales. These also show up on your map. The icon looks like a green pair of triangles.

For fast travel between major cities, use the pinkish/purplish Asura Gates. They're an ideal way to get to places even if you've never been there before. Approach the gate in your city and get close enough to see where it leads. Walk through the shimmering gate to see what's on the other side. There is no fee for doing this, so get out there and meet new people.

Help

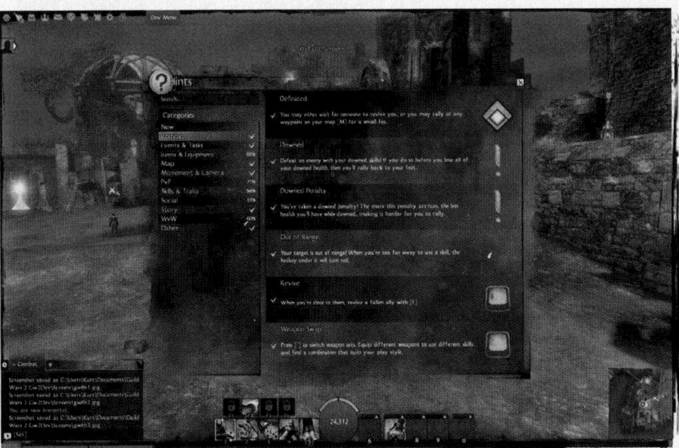

If you'd like to learn more about the game's mechanics, you don't have far to look. There is a help system built into *Guild Wars 2*. Sometimes the game will detect that you're having trouble with a specific concept. In response, it might pop up a helpful window to explain something new.

To review hints that you've seen previously, click on the gear at the top-left side of your screen. This opens the help system and lets you browse or directly search for tips about a variety of the game's functions. Typing "/help" also gets you to the same window.

CHARACTER CREATION

Your first step in exploring the beautiful and exciting lands of *Guild Wars 2* is to create a character. This chapter will walk you through the process. It will also give you an idea of just how many options for self-expression and variety are available to you in this system!

STARTING THE PROCESS

After you have logged on, you'll find yourself in the character screen. There are a number of empty boxes at the bottom of the screen, along with three buttons (Play, Create, and Delete). When you're ready to make your character, click on an empty gray box and select "Create."

I REGRET NOTHING!

There are 10 character creation screens, and you can return and change things at any point during the process until you actually finalize your character. All you have to do is hit the "Back" button at the bottom of the screen to rewind through your selections and review your decisions.

CHOOSING YOUR RACE

There are five playable races in *Guild Wars* 2: charr, human, norn, asura, and sylvari. Each of them has a rich and colorful history in the world, and we encourage you to take a look through this guide to learn more about them.

Once you have a race that suits your character's personality, choose it and go forward.

THE RACES (IN SHORT)

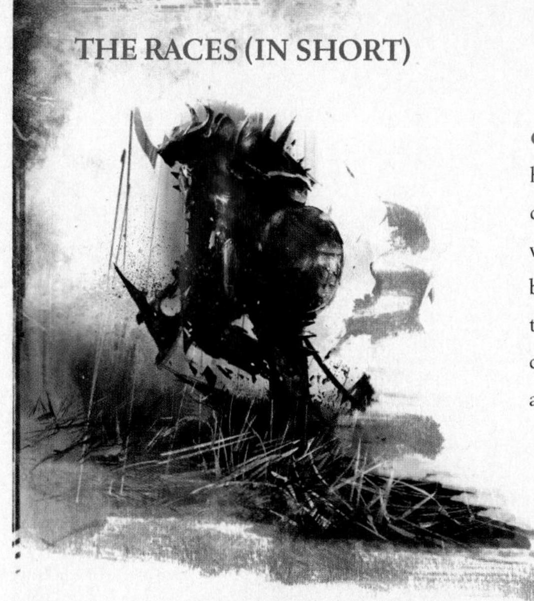

Charr: Feline-like humanoids. The charr are focused on war and dedicated to battle. They have a tendency to rush into confrontations and ask questions later.

Humans: The humans in *Guild Wars 2* are quite diverse and come from a variety of cultures. They are a spiritual people renown for their courage and ability to conquer adversity.

Asura: Short goblin/gnome-like people. The asura are dedicated artisans and geniuses. Their egos are inversely proportional to their size.

Norn: Giant humanoids. The norn are a bit rough around the edges, but they value fellowship, deeds of heroism, and celebration of good times.

Sylvari: Fey-like plant people. The sylvari are adventurers and philosophers; each of them is searching for their place in the world.

In terms of character statistics, there aren't any differences between the races. Choose whichever race appeals to you. The more you enjoy your characters, and the more you relate to them, the more you'll love playing them!

No one in *Guild Wars 2* is going to be laughed out of a dungeon group for any combination of race, sex, or profession. All of the options are similarly balanced, with only minor skill differences between them.

CHOOSING THE SEX OF YOUR CHARACTER

The next decision you'll make is whether to play as a male or female. Technically the sylvari, being plants, aren't either, but they still have male or female characteristics. As a point of interest, the world of *Guild Wars 2* is strongly egalitarian. There are prominent male and female heroes and villains, and the diversity even extends to monsters.

Your character's base statistics are not affected in any way by which sex you choose. So, decide what appeals to you. The voice acting is different with either choice, so factor that in when you're considering your character as well.

YOUR PROFESSION

This is one of the most important decisions you have to make. Your profession determines how your character interacts with the world and how you engage in combat. It's worth taking some time to figure out what profession appeals to you the most. We encourage you to look through the Professions chapter, which goes far deeper into each profession's mechanics, skills, and weapons.

PROFESSIONS IN SHORT

Elementalists: Direct-damage casters that specialize in elemental abilities (fire, water, air, and earth). They wear light armor and use primarily ranged magic weapons.

Warriors: Fighters focusing on direct-damage combat. Warriors wear heavy armor and use a wide variety of weaponry, including both melee and ranged weapons.

Guardians: Fighters focusing on protective and defensive abilities. Guardians wear heavy armor and use primarily melee weapons. They're great in groups but still fight reliably on their own.

Engineers: Do damage through mechanical contraptions, mitigate damage through elixirs, and put negative conditions on enemies. Engineers wear medium armor and use primarily ranged weapons and tools of their own creation.

Rangers: Attack enemies with their pets and traps. Rangers wear medium armor and use a mix of melee and ranged weapons. They're ideal for killing enemies over distance and time.

Necromancers: Use summoned creatures, poison, bleeding attacks, and negative conditions. Necromancers wear light armor and use mixed melee/ranged magic weapons. They're surprisingly hard to kill, cloaking themselves in the power of death.

Thieves: Mobile attackers with the advantages of stealth, traps, and both melee and ranged weaponry. Thieves wear medium armor and are able to move around the battlefield like few others.

Mesmers: Scholars who use illusions to confuse and damage opponents. Mesmers wear light armor and are challenging to keep alive. Though tricky to play, their abilities are both flashy and effective.

CHOOSING YOUR APPEARANCE

After you've selected your race and profession, it's time to customize your character's appearance. There's an enormous amount of variety available to you. The choices in this section let you alter and perfect your character's size, shape, and features, as well as the colors of his or her default armor.

GETTING A BETTER LOOK

Underneath your character are buttons allowing you to remove or restore your character's armor and to zoom in or out. If you want a better view of your character as you customize his or her appearance, simply click on the relevant button. This helps a great deal when, for example, you want to see different charr fur patterns or judge differences in physiques.

BODY FEATURES

This portion of the appearance menu lets you decide your character's height and physique. It also allows you to alter race-specific features of your character.

For height, the guide on the right side of the screen gives you a sense of scale and the height range available to your character. The slider shows where your character lies in terms of the average height for that race. Move the slider up to make your character taller and down for shorter.

The next choice is physique. Look at the menu to the right; there are a number of different physique selections, ranging from heavy to light. Select the one you think best reflects your character.

The last section of the body features menu has race-specific features. Charr have fur patterns, norn have colorful tattoos, and asura and sylvari can change their skin markings. Feel free to tinker with the various sliders and menu options until you find just what you're looking for.

HEAD OPTIONS

This part of the appearance menu lets you select from a series of default faces, hairstyles, and sex- and race-specific characteristics (facial hair, horns, ears). It also allows you to customize your skin tone and hair color. As you can see, there's a nice amount of customization. Don't rush through this in an attempt to get into the game sooner. You might be playing this character for years. Make sure you get the appearance just right.

In general, the default face options are a stepping stone to save time for some players, and they give a good general starting point (for things such as age and general bone structure). There's a lot more that can be done with your character's facial features, such as those in the next set of options.

FACE DETAILS

These options allow you to tinker even more with the facial features of your character. Eyes, eye colors, nose, mouth, chin and jaw, ears—all of these can be shifted and adjusted so you have even more control over what your character looks like. Have fun!

ARMOR DYES

Now that you've completed your character's body and face, it's time to move on to clothing. There are three customizable sections of armor: upper, lower, and footwear. Each of these has three separate dye channels, which alter different parts of the respective armor section. Click around and choose what you think your character looks best in.

The dye selections you make will carry through as you find new armor in the world. So, if you put on a new chestpiece, the dye selections you made for your starting armor will still color your new piece. Pieces that weren't part of your starting equipment (gloves, shoulders, etc.) can be dyed through your Hero screen at any time in the future, so you aren't locked into any specific color scheme.

To do this once you're in the game, press "H" to bring up the Hero window. Then, click on the small eyedropper (at the top of the screen, just to the right of your armor). This opens the dyes available to you. You acquire new dyes within the game by bringing colorful seeds to your home and getting a dye merchant to help grow them.

BACKGROUND

The next few pages offer you selections to customize your character's personality and backstory. These primarily affect your character's personal story. They offer greater depth and development to your character.

PROFESSIONAL AFFINITY

This question lets you decide what the most important factor is in your profession.

Elementalist	Elemental Affinity (Water, Fire, Earth, Air)
Warrior	Helm
Guardian	Armor piece (pauldron or helm)
Engineer	Favorite tool (universal multi-tool, eagle-eye goggles, panscopic monocle)
Ranger	Favorite pet companion (devourer, stalker, drake)
Necromancer	Facial markings (trickster demon, skull, ghostly wraith)
Mesmer	Mask (harlequin's smile, phantasm of sorrow, fanged dread)

PERSONALITY

This gives you an opportunity to decide how your character handles problems: through charm (heart), dignity (crown), or ferocity (fist). These come up through conversations with nonplayer characters. The choice you make here is reflected in your Hero screen, at the top right, next to your profession. The one you pick gets the highest starting bar. This may change over the course of the game if you use the other techniques more often. Your character grows and changes over time, based on your roleplaying interests.

PERSONAL HISTORY

The next three questions examine where your character fits in relation to his or her people and culture. It also affects how other nonplayer characters relate to you during your personal story.

YOUR PAST

Charr	Your Legion (Blood, Ash, Iron)
Human	Your upbringing, where you were raised (in the streets, by common folk, among the nobility)
Norn	The most important quality of a hero (strength, cunning, instinct)
Asura	College (Statics, Dynamics, Synergistics)
Sylvari	Vision quest spirit (White Stag, Green Huntsman, Shield of the Moon)

MEMORABLE PERSON/EVENT

Charr	Sparring partner (Maverick, Euryale, Clawspur, Dinky, Reeva)
Human	Missed opportunity (I've never searched for my true parents; I never recovered my sister's body; I passed up an opportunity to join the circus)
Norn	Actions at a recent celebratory moot (passed out, got in a fight, lost an heirloom)
Asura	Your first invention (the VAL-A golem, a transatmospheric converter, an infinity ball)
Sylvari	The most important of Ventari's teachings (act with wisdom, but act; all things have a right to grow; where life goes, so should you)

CHARACTER DEVELOPMENT

Charr	Your sire's history (Loyal Soldier, Sorcerous Shaman, Honorless Gladium)
Human	Blessing of which god (Dwayna, Grenth, Balthazar, Melandru, Lyssa, Kormir)
Norn	The spirit of the wild that calls to you (Bear, Snow Leopard, Wolf, Raven)
Asura	Your first advisor (Bronk, Zinga, Blipp, Canni)
Sylvari	The time you were awakened by the Pale Tree (Cycle of Dawn, Cycle of Noon, Cycle of Dusk, Cycle of Night)

CHARACTER NAME AND REVIEW

The final part of character creation lets you review the choices you made. Look at your character and read through the answers to the questions provided. If you've changed your mind about anything, go back and make a different selection. Otherwise, sign your name at the bottom of the page. This will be your character's name in game, so make it memorable and exciting.

WHAT'S IN A NAME?

Your name can be up to 21 characters in length. The system lets you create middle and last names too, so there's considerable variety. Pick whatever you want! That said, it's usually best to use something that you'll easily remember and that won't be too hard to type.

ROLEPLAYING CONVENTIONS FOR NAMES IN *GUILD WARS 2*

Many people are interested in naming their character something that "fits" with the world and cultures of *Guild Wars 2*. This is particularly true for roleplayers. Here are some suggestions, though you're free to go off on your own.

Charr: They usually have Roman (or Grecian) first names. Their last names feature their warband name and then an additional word or two to reflect their more ferocious or warlike nature.

Humans: Have a huge variety in names, but those in Kryta have European/English/American first and last names. General fantasy names work as well.

Norn: Most norn have Northern European or Viking-style first names. Their last names are usually patronymic or matronymic (father/mother's first name followed by "son" or "dottir").

Asura: Usually have a very short name (one or two syllables). Their last names are usually their job title, their krewe name, or an honorific.

Sylvari: Have a number of Celtic/Irish names, mostly without last names. However, general fantasy or elven-styled names follow their theme.

HOW TO PLAY GUILD WARS 2

This chapter covers the fundamental game system of *Guild Wars 2*. We help you understand character control, the game's economy, equipment upgrades, leveling, fighting, and so forth. Even if you're familiar with existing online games (or the original *Guild Wars*), this is still a great place to learn this game's specifics.

THE INTERFACE

Before we delve into anything complex, let's discuss the game's interface. After you create a character, you gain access to the game's features and options. Though there is a brief tutorial adventure for each character, this doesn't last long, and you're then thrown into the open world of Tyria.

THE CHAT PANEL

Take a look at your screen. A huge amount of information is available in various windows and secondary screens. The lower left is the default location for text. You can see what NPCs are saying, listen to other characters, and so forth.

You can also add new windows to the chat panel by selecting "+" or "New Tab." These new tabs can be renamed to reflect their function at any point, and you can cycle through them easily. Make a window for Combat information if you want to review damage done (and received). This is useful for people who are vigorously testing their characters and want to find out what's working and what isn't.

The wheel on the window's left side opens a set of options. You can adjust the filter for language there. Set it to none if you're not easily offended, or set it to maximum if you have kids playing or just want to keep things in the PG range.

Change text size if you have trouble reading text in the window.

Each tab has its own options too. For instance, clicking the down arrowhead next to each panel title opens up the Tab Options menu, which lets you toggle the messages that are displayed. Turn off anything that distracts you, but be sure to toggle those back on later if they become important. We suggest you leave on essential messages, such as Party/Guild/Squad. You don't want to miss warnings, tactics, or questions from people who are trying to help you!

EVENT LOG

The screen's right side lists the current story event you're working on. It also dynamically displays events close enough for you to participate in, including renown tasks, normal events, group events, and world events. Each listing conveys the event's level and a basic description of what you should do to complete it.

Events often list a quantity of items to gather, or kills you have to make. Look here to find out about your progress and whether various actions have a major impact on the event.

Left-click on events to open or close their information listings. If you aren't working on one that's listed, go ahead and close it to allot more space to the other events.

THE MINIMAP

Look in the lower right for your minimap. It offers a great view of the area surrounding your character. Event goals appear on it, and pretty much any detail from the full map is there as well.

Use the "+" and "-" buttons around the minimap to zoom in or out. Pull out to find crafting resources from a considerable distance away. Zoom in to gain more accurate information about your immediate surroundings and facilitate navigation. The minimap's zoom has four settings, and you can click on them individually if you know exactly what you want.

The map can be set to rotate with your character, so that the top of the minimap always faces in the same direction as your character. Or, if you prefer, use the arrow on the right side of the minimap interface to toggle between that setting and an "always north" style.

That interface area also has an icon to take you to the full map (also accessed if you press "M"), as well as an icon that focuses the minimap on your current story goal. This is helpful if you're a little lost and want a quick reminder of where you're heading.

HEALTH, SKILLS, AND EVERYTHING ELSE

The bottom of the screen has almost everything else you need. The red globe has your character's health listing. As your health falls in battle, the circle empties until there is nothing left. When that happens, your character goes down and has to fight for survival until he or she rallies or is killed.

Above your health globe is your endurance meter (in yellow), showing how much endurance you have for dodging enemy attacks. The left side has profession-specific meters or skills.

Boons and conditions are shown to the right of the health circle. Highlight these icons to find out what each one means. These icons are coded by color so you quickly know whether something is good or bad. Boons show up as golden icons; they're always good! Conditions show up in red, and they're bad for your character in a variety of ways. If a boon or condition has a number associated with it, that's telling you multiple copies of the effect are stacking, multiplying their potency.

The number and skill icons show the available skills for your character. The numbers below correspond to the keys you press to activate each skill. Yellow skills have a target that is within range. Red ones do not. Watch these to know exactly when your targets come into range.

Skills that are cooling down are shown in black and can't be used until they're ready.

The arrows above healing, utility, and elite skills let you switch to other skills of the same type. This can't be done during battle, but it's possible to do at any other time (as long as the original skill is not cooling down currently). If that's the case, wait until the ability is available again and then switch it for another skill.

To the left of your weapon skills is a button for swapping weapons. You can also press "~" to accomplish the same thing.

PAGES AND WINDOWS

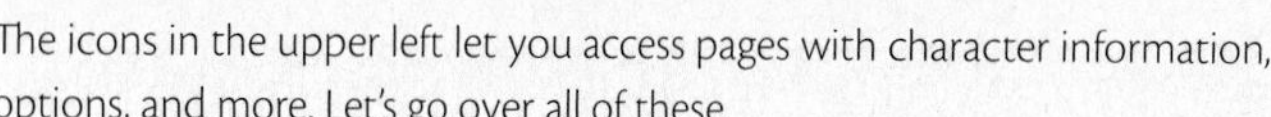

The icons in the upper left let you access pages with character information, options, and more. Let's go over all of these.

HERO PAGE [H]

The shield and sword icon is the first in the lineup. It takes you to the Hero page, where there are tabs with equipment, skills and traits, your story, crafting, and achievements.

- **EQUIPMENT TAB:** Switch gear, look at your stats, adjust the look of your armor, and change into town clothes instead of your combat gear
- **SKILLS AND TRAITS TAB:** See information about weapon skills, slot skills to purchase, and traits (you get to start grabbing these after reaching level 11)
- **STORY TAB:** Goes over the events your character has completed in his or her personal story
- **CRAFTING:** Shows all of the recipes your character has unlocked
- **ACHIEVEMENTS:** Gives you information about daily, monthly, and permanent achievements
- **PVP:** Allows you to enter the Heart of the Mists at any point, letting you participate in Player-versus-Player battles

INVENTORY [I]

Press "I" to look at your character's bags. The circular gear icon in the upper right lets you compact the gear in your bags to keep the screen from getting cluttered. You can also move items around manually by left-clicking on items and dragging them to wherever you'd like.

If you release an item outside of the window, you're given the option to destroy it. This is a good way to get rid of event items you no longer need. Another way to accomplish this is to right-click on the items and select "Destroy."

Right-clicking on items gives you all pertinent options for the object in question. This is used to equip gear, mail things to other players, and so on. Note that you cannot make armor or weapon changes during combat (with the exception of switching between weapon sets that are already equipped).

Crafting items have two more options involving the Trading Post. You can choose to sell the material through the Trading Post or buy more of it. So, if you aren't interested in crafting or acquire a large amount of stuff for a craft you aren't pursuing, you can make some quick gold and clear out your inventory easily. By the same token, if you are a crafter and want to get materials while you are out adventuring, you don't have to stop and visit a Trading Post in town at inconvenient times.

You can also send crafting materials directly to your personal Bank. Selecting the "Collectible" option removes the item from your inventory and shifts it to your Bank. Once you're at the Bank, choose the "Collections" option to access your materials. The collections are organized by the type of material and rarity. You can also look through your selection of minis here.

PARTY [P]

The Party window lets you create or leave groups and squads. Groups are used for dungeon runs, having fun while exploring the world, or simply for palling around in town. Squads are used in World versus World (sometimes called WvW, WvWvW, or World PvP) to provide a level or organization for larger forces that are fighting together.

You don't need to use the Party window to start a group. If you're exploring and others ask to join you, go ahead and click the character and then right-click on their portrait. This gives you the option of starting a group with them without needing to type in their name or worrying about inviting someone with a similar name.

When friends are in your contact list or guild, you can also invite them into groups from those pages.

CONTACT PAGE [Y]

The Contact Page has a listing for several types of social groups that you're a party of.

> **FRIENDS:** Allows you to invite people to be your friends;also shows friends you've made and whether they're online, which region they're in, and their achievement totals

> **LOOKING FOR GROUP:** Helps you find allies for more difficult events and dungeon runs

> **FOLLOWERS:** Lists people who have added you to their friends list but you have not yet added as a friend.

> **BLOCKED:** Allows you to type in names of people you don't want to hear from anymore; it also keeps a tally of the players you've blocked

Use the friends list to keep track of people you really enjoy playing with in *Guild Wars 2*. The system tracks your friends by account, so even someone who creates alts constantly can be kept track of.

Hopefully you won't have to do much blocking. That's reserved for times when someone is hassling you or trying to grief your character. Type their name in and block the player's account. You can always change your mind later and unblock the person if you think the trouble has passed.

MAIL

The primary way to send money and equipment between characters is to use the mail system. This is accessible from anywhere in the world, so you don't have to go and "check your mail" to get the items involved. Also, there isn't an appreciable transit time, so you can get things to friends without any delay.

Just type in the name of your recipient and drag items from your inventory into the mail (or right-click on them and add the items to the letter; that's easier). Type a subject line and message to let people know what's going on, and then send the mail when you're done. It's pretty darn simple.

If you're just trying to send a short message, you can also /whisper to a person to communicate with them directly. This is easier than mail if the subject is short. Example: */whisper Emil [tab] AFK for a few minutes.*

Messages for you arrive in your inbox. These can be from your buddies, the Trading Post, or grateful NPCs. Clicking on a given letter allows you to remove its contents. You can also choose to reply to the sender, return the materials to the sender, or delete the letter.

Note that at this time, you cannot mail letters to yourself (either your current character or alts). If you want to pass materials between your characters, use your Bank.

BLACK LION TRADING COMPANY [O]

The Gem Store is next. That's where you go to buy and sell gems, and purchase all sorts of rewards. Gems are the micro-transaction currency in *Guild Wars 2*. These go toward helping the developers maintain the game, and you get all sorts of goodies for playing with them. Because this is somewhat involved, we'll talk more about it later in the chapter.

In short, the first tab is where you find the rewards that are purchased with gems. The second tab is the Currency Exchange, and that's the place where you buy or sell gems.

This is also how you get to the Trading Post (to buy or sell items), and where you can look over your transactions and collect profit and purchases.

PVP

Guild Wars 2 has a clear separation between content against the world and its monsters (Player versus Environment) and content against other players (Player versus Player). When you want to step into PvP, go to your Hero window and click on the PvP tab. PvP is very challenging and exciting. It's best if you learn the basics of *Guild Wars 2* before delving into this area of competition!

GAME MENU [ESCAPE]

The Game Menu has a number of additional options to alter your gameplay in *Guild Wars 2*. This is also the place that you go to edit your account, log out of the game, or quit your session outright.

GAME MENU CHOICES

SELECTION	FUNCTION
Return to Game	Closes the window
Options	Brings up the options menu
Edit Account	Loads the account webpage in your browser
Log Out	Returns you to the load-in screen (this is the best option for switching characters)
Exit to Desktop	Takes you back to your desktop

HINTS

The Hints page lets you search for topics on a variety of game systems. Type in something you'd like to know more about and watch the system shift the text below around to show what you're looking for. If there are any terms or concepts that you hear about and don't understand, just come here to find out more about them.

OPTIONS MENU

Go to this when you want to modify your game's graphics, sound, and controls. There are also some very interesting gameplay toggles in here. Many of these settings are a matter of personal preference, but we'll still mention a few of the choices.

Double-Tap to Evade should be checked for most players. It's a very useful way to avoid danger.

Auto Targeting is player-specific. Some players like to attack and let the game figure out which monster they were going after. This option is good for them. Players who want extremely specific targeting should leave this off. If you find that you're shooting the wrong targets or starting fights you didn't intend to get into, switch this off.

Autoloot should almost always be checked. This lets you loot corpses very quickly. It's essential in groups when people don't want to wait around.

If you have a sluggish framerate, make sure to set your options and possibly your resolution down a tad. It's more important to have a smooth framerate if you want to ensure maximum effectiveness in combat, and a more enjoyable game experience.

The control tab has bindings for your keyboard and mouse. Modify these until they suit your playstyle perfectly. You're going to be putting a lot of hours into this game; there's no reason to play with the default layout unless you absolutely love it.

MOVEMENT

Movement is quite simple and intuitive in *Guild Wars 2*. It's handled in the same way as many other games of its type, so veterans of other online games will take to it quickly.

Look through the key bindings and make sure you're happy with the settings as they stand. You need to have a layout that lets you move forward, backward, strafe left, and strafe right as easily as possible. Some people turn left and right with their keyboards as well, though we recommend you handle that with your mouse instead. Let your keyboard hand control the direction of movement, while your mouse hand adjusts your view (and thus the orientation of your character).

This makes it easier to dodge to either side when facing an enemy. Strafing is a powerful defensive option for avoiding ranged attacks and abilities. If your settings allow dodging by double-tapping your movement keys, this is even better. Double-tap while strafing to leap out of the way from incoming enemy attacks that would otherwise hit you hard. Any time you see an enemy charging up before an attack, get ready to dodge!

"Endurance regenerates quickly. Don't be afraid to dodge roll!"

—*Peter Larkin*

MOVING AND ATTACKING

Many games don't let you use your best attacks while moving around. Characters have to plant their feet and spend time casting their spells or using their powers. *Guild Wars 2* breaks from that mold and lets you use the vast majority of your skills while running at full speed. This opens the way for more tactical and involved combat. You can get away with fighting some monsters in a traditional way; walk up, hit them with your weapons, and wait for them to die. But smarter enemies (like centaurs) are going to run circles around your heroes, making it harder to win if you wait for a standup fight.

Other players are even more likely to take advantage of this. They'll try to avoid your best attacks, run around behind your character, and use abilities to slow or disrupt your movement while seeking every opportunity to cut you down.

Fight fire with fire! Learn to attack while you're on the move so it's harder to nail your character with ground-targeted skills, charged attacks, and so forth. Combine this with dodging so you can string melee enemies along and force them to waste time catching your hero. Every second that an enemy can't attack is time that you get to keep your health at full.

"Don't stand in red circles, bad things happen."

—*Hugh Norfolk*

WHAT IS DODGING?

We've mentioned dodging already, so let's talk about what this command actually does. Dodging is a sudden roll in any direction. You can use the dodge key and a movement key together to determine the direction, or simply double-tap where you want to dodge. This fast evasion requires endurance (there's a bar for that above your health, at the bottom of the screen).

Dodging is incredibly powerful. Avoiding major attacks isn't the only thing it does. You can dodge through groups of enemies while fleeing to give yourself time to escape. Some characters learn attack abilities that trigger when they dodge, so it can be an offensive option as well. Endurance regenerates automatically, so you don't lose anything by dodging. It won't tax your attack skills or cause your character to slow down or be exposed afterward.

Endurance is meant to be used, so use it well! Dodge backward when an ettin comes in for a heavy pounding. Dodge to the side when a centaur lancer tries to knock you back. Dodge forward through a ranger's AoEs and get that much closer to your quarry while avoiding their attacks.

By default, your hero can dodge twice in a row before depleting his or her endurance. It then takes a short time to let your endurance regenerate before you can make even a single dodge. There are boons that increase the rate of your endurance regenerations, while conditions can slow the rate too. Expect to see these much more often in PvP matches than in most fights against monsters. Slowing players' movement and stopping them from dodging is incredibly useful for controlling a fight. Hit people with attacks that apply frozen or cripple to your victim to do this. Weakness is also a major factor in stopping enemy dodging.

JUMPING

Yes, you can jump in *Guild Wars 2*! Keep this key bound near your movement hand so it's easy to jump while moving. It's often possible to leap up rocky inclines by jumping repeatedly and looking for a climbable path. Try this out to cut down on travel time or to enter areas from an angle that gives you an advantage over the players or monsters guarding it.

UNDERWATER ENVIRONMENTS

There are quite a few lakes and rivers in *Guild Wars 2*, and your heroes can even swim in the ocean. Down in the depths are hidden treasures, monsters, and events you can uncover if you aren't afraid to swim around and look for them. Air isn't an issue because all characters have items that allow them to survive indefinitely while submerged. You only have to worry about monsters!

Each hero is allowed to equip one or two types of underwater weapons. These have different attack skills than your terrestrial weapons, so it takes time, practice, and kills to unlock and master these new techniques. Elementalists have different spells when they're underwater, because their abilities interact with the water around them. It's really awesome to watch, so don't be shy about jumping in and trying things out.

While swimming, you need to move three-dimensionally. The normal motion keys work as they do on land, but jumping causes you to swim up. Angle your character down and move forward to descend.

Characters can still dodge when they're underwater, so keep that in mind while you're fighting. Don't let yourself fall into the "stand and fight" mentality, because it's a major weakness against most enemies.

EXPLORING THE WORLD

Tyria is a big place, and you can spend days exploring it while only finding a portion of what it has to offer. *Guild Wars 2* rewards exploration in a variety of ways. You get experience for finding new places, but that isn't the only benefit. Explore to find additional skill points so your character becomes more complex and more flexible in handling battle. Look for materials to harvest so you or your friends can craft new items. Or, wander the world for the sheer joy of seeing new places.

Guild Wars 2 lowers your character's effective level if you enter a region that is beneath your current power. This means you'll never wander through areas while ignoring all of the monsters and challenges. Wherever you go, there are threats and obstacles worthy of your attention. That makes exploring a lot more fun. It's also much more dangerous, so watch out!

READING YOUR MAP

The game map gives you a fair amount of information to process. When you're looking at the world map, you can see the names of greater regions (like Kryta or Ascalon), regional names, points of interest, waypoints, level ranges, renown tasks, and more. Consult the table on the next page to learn what the map icons mean.

IN-GAME MAP ICON LEGEND

NAME	ICON	PURPOSE
Renown Task		Marks an important event in the area
Completed Renown Task		Marks an event that you have completed and cannot repeat
Waypoint		A waypoint you haven't visited
Unlocked Waypoint		A waypoint you can teleport to or from for a nominal fee
Contested Waypoint		A waypoint you cannot currently use because there is an event going on in that area
Undiscovered Point of Interest		An interesting location on the map you haven't yet found
Discovered Point of Interest		An interesting location on the map (shows name of the location)
Skill Challenge		A place where your hero can pick up a skill Point
Completed Skill Challenge		Marks a skill challenge you've already beaten
Asura Gate		Location of Asura Gate, which allows travel between major cities
Personal Story Marker		Go here to continue your personal story (either its exact location or closest point in the zone)
Bank		Go here to access your personal Bank or Guild Bank
Trading Post		Go here to access the Trading Post to buy or sell materials
Repair Merchant		Go here to repair damaged or broken equipment
Merchant		Go here to sell items or buy general supplies
Armorsmith		Go here to sell items or buy armor
Weaponsmith		Go here to sell items or buy weapons
Leatherworking Station		Go here to practice the Leatherworking craft
Huntsman's Station		Go here to practice the Huntsman craft
Artificing Station		Go here to practice the Artificing craft
Weaponsmithing Station		Go here to practice the Weaponsmithing craft
Jeweling Station		Go here to practice the Jewelworking craft
Armorsmithing Station		Go here to practice the Armorworking craft
Tailoring Station		Go here to practice the Tailoring craft
Cooking Station		Go here to practice the Cooking craft
Scout		Talk to this NPC to find out about renown tasks in the area
Trainer		Talk to this NPC to buy training manuals and re-spec your traits
Guild Registrar		Talk to this NPC to create and manage a guild
Fallen Ally		An NPC needing to be revived
Fallen Player		A player needing to be revived
Powerful Enemy		Go here to fight a strong foe
Elevator (Up, Down, Up and Down)		Shows an elevator between levels
Stairs		Shows stairs between levels
Cave (Entrance, Exit)		Shows a cave entrance/exit
Vista		An interesting location on the map that triggers a cutscene when the player interacts with it

Zoom in and out with your mouse wheel to get an idea of the big picture or to see just the area that your character is exploring. Level ranges are based by region, and you can even get an idea of their progression by looking at the surrounding maps. The easier end of a region is often the one that butts up against lower-level neighbors. Example: The northern side of Kessex bumps into Queensdale, the first region for human players. Thus, the northern end of Kessex is going to have weaker enemies than the southern region.

For more information, highlight the hearts associated with renown tasks in each area. Even across the map, you can see the difficulty level of a task by highlighting its heart.

Left-click and drag the world map around to see different parts of it. Only areas that your character has explored will be visible. Unlocked waypoints are used by clicking on them and teleporting to that area.

If you need to see terrain above or below your character, use the panels on the lower-right side to shift between underground, surface, and upper-level versions of each map.

The top left of the map is a measure of your map's completion. There are two main sections: the world (as a whole) and the region. Underneath each section are statistics showing how many renown tasks you've completed, waypoints you've opened, points of interests you've found, and skill challenges you've beaten. To help you with this, the total number for each is shown.

Note that harvesting nodes don't appear unless your character is reasonably close to them. You can't look at the main map and simply beeline toward whatever node you'd like. Finding the best places to mine, harvest plants, and chop down trees requires exploration. When you see rock piles, bushes, and trees on your map, that's what they refer to. Harvest these by equipping the proper tools and interacting with the nodes as your hero passes through each area.

WALKING AROUND

The most basic and common means of travel is walking around. You don't need mounts in *Guild Wars 2* because initial exploration of an area is meant to be challenging. Your heroes have to face monsters, avoid obstacles, and find new areas and adventures. Along the way, you're rewarded with waypoints that let you travel instantly back to areas you've already explored. So, you spend more time up-front learning an area, but afterward it's really easy to get wherever you want to go.

There are ways to speed up your normal movement. If you're planning a major exploration run, choose skills that aid your character's running speed (we'll talk about skill choices later in this chapter). Skills that grant swiftness are a huge benefit if you're trying to get around the maps at high speed. Other useful skills include banners that can be carried to aid a group's speed, and any passive trait that increases your pace.

Though unconventional, another technique for faster travel is to use your attack abilities to jump ahead. Many characters have attacks that push them forward quickly to close the gap against distant enemies. You can often use these even when you don't have a target, creating a form of simple travel power. This won't make a massive difference, but it's worth doing if you're with a group that is bent on getting somewhere as soon as possible!

WAYPOINTS

Those waypoints we mentioned are all over the world. You find more than a dozen of these in most regions. They're inside dungeons, capital cities, and some of your story events.

Waypoints look like diamonds on your map and minimap. All you need to do to unlock one is to walk close to it. A tinkling noise sounds, and the icon changes to show you've unlocked the area. To return to that location at any time, open your map and click on the waypoint icon.

Every waypoint has its own unique name. This makes it a lot easier to organize group meetings ("Everyone go to Shaemoor waypoint in Queensdale!") and helps you remember where merchants are.

Waypoint travel usually costs money (travel within and between cities does not). This cost is not a major burden in any way, and it goes toward maintaining the highest standards of asuran craftsmanship in your local communities.

WAYPOINTS MAKE YOU MONEY

This seems like a good time to address the myth that waypoints cost "a lot of money." You'll hear some players say that, and that they sometimes walk between areas to save their hard-earned cash. This is a penny-wise but dollar-dim argument. Sure, you save on the initial cost of the waypoint, but let's look at this closely.

Let's say you save ten minutes jumping between maps with your waypoints. These quick travel options cost more money the farther you go, so any travel that was shorter than that would cost only a trivial amount of money.

So you might spend several silver (at most) to jump down to a high-level region. Use that time to complete a single event and you've paid for the trip. The rest of that time and any loot you get from monsters while fighting is yours to keep. It's possible to fight while traveling, but that's going to make the trip even slower. It's tough' to keep up with the fighting and event completion rate of someone who jumps to a waypoint ahead of you.

In reality, waypoints don't cost you money. They MAKE you money by letting you spend your time killing monsters and completing events instead of walking.

ASURA GATES

Asura Gates are swirling purple portals of energy. They're made and maintained by the asura, using radically advanced technology. Asura Gates are free to use, and each pair links two specific areas of the world. The capital cities connect to Lion's Arch, so that's the game's biggest hub. If you're trying to enter a new region that isn't anywhere close to a place you've explored, try going to a capital city that's in the same part of the world. Instead of walking across three or four regions to get where you're going, you might only have to go through one!

Some people like to use the Asura Gates early on to visit every capital city, to unlock waypoints for future travel. This tourist romp costs you nothing and is a great way to see where and how each of the races lives.

WHERE TO GO AND WHAT TO SEE

Let's talk about the places that make up the world of Tyria.

CAPITAL CITIES

There are six major cities in the game right now. Each race has its own capital city as well as a place where everyone comes together.

CITY	LOCATION	RACE(S) ASSOCIATED WITH THIS CAPITAL
Rata Sum	Tarnished Coast	Asura
Black Citadel	Ascalon	Charr
Divinity's Reach	Kryta	Human
Hoelbrak	Shiverpeak Mountains	Norn
The Grove	Tarnished Coast	Sylvari
Lion's Arch	Tarnished Coast	All races are present here

Asura Gates connect these cities so you can travel between them without having to spend an hour wandering through the wilderness to meet your friends. This makes it easier to create groups of heroes with real-life buddies and still meet up without needing to wait. As soon as you finish your respective starting areas, everyone can decide on a city and meet there. Thus, you can spend levels 2-80 with all of your friends. Awesome!

REGIONS

Outside of the capitals, there are large regions that have their own names, level ranges, and stories. These regions interconnect, but each has its own map and requires loading into the area. You can't wander back and forth between regions seamlessly, so you need to look for gateways between the areas. These show up as swirling circles of energy, and they're almost always found on the edge of the maps. Walk through these portals to go between areas.

Here is a list of the zones in *Guild Wars 2*, along with their level ranges. You're never locked into a single area because of your racial choice or story, so it's fun to jump back and forth between different regions to mix up the creatures you're fighting and the stories being told.

REGION NAME	LOCATION	LEVEL RANGE
Queensdale	Kryta	1-15
Kessex Hills	Kryta	15-25
Gendarran Fields	Kryta	25-35
Harathi Hinterlands	Kryta	35-45
Metrica Province	Tarnished Coast	1-15
Caledon Forest	Tarnished Coast	1-15
Brisban Wildlands	Tarnished Coast	15-25
Bloodtide Coast	Tarnished Coast	45-55
Sparkfly Fen	Tarnished Coast	55-65
Timberline Falls	Steamspur Mountains	50-60
Mount Maelstrom	Steamspur Mountains	60-70
Plains of Ashford	Ascalon	1-15
Diessa Plateau	Ascalon	15-25
Fields of Ruins	Ascalon	30-40
Blazeridge Steppes	Ascalon	40-50
Iron Marches	Ascalon	50-60
Fireheart Rise	Ascalon	60-70
Wayfarer Foothills	Shiverpeak Mountains	1-15
Snowden Drifts	Shiverpeak Mountains	15-25
Lornar's Pass	Shiverpeak Mountains	25-40
Dredgehaunt Cliffs	Shiverpeak Mountains	40-50
Frostgorge Sound	Shiverpeak Mountains	70-80
Straits of Devastation	Orr	70-75
Malchor's Leap	Orr	75-80
Cursed Shore	Orr	80+

POINTS OF INTEREST

Each region is marked by dozens of points of interest. These are named areas that have their own flavor and problems. Many of them have events your characters can participate in to make the place a bit better. Search for points of interest to fill up the world map, get bonus experience, and see all that Tyria has to offer.

LEARNING ABOUT THE SKILL BAR

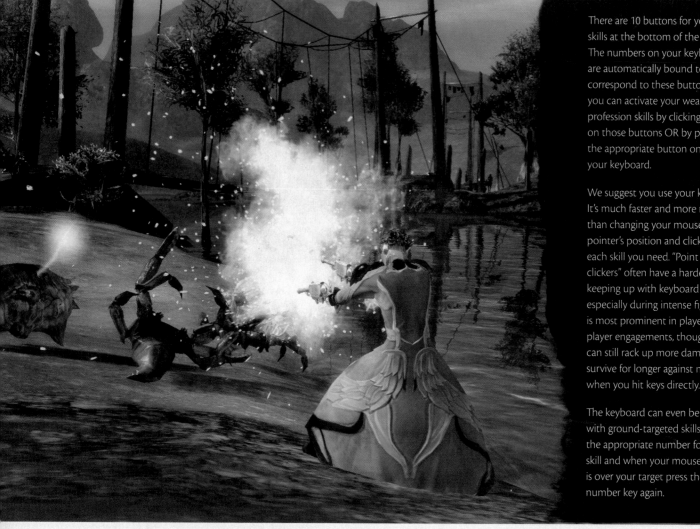

There are 10 buttons for your skills at the bottom of the screen. The numbers on your keyboard are automatically bound to correspond to these buttons, so you can activate your weapon and profession skills by clicking on those buttons OR by pressing the appropriate button on your keyboard.

We suggest you use your keyboard. It's much faster and more reactive than changing your mouse pointer's position and clicking on each skill you need. "Point and clickers" often have a harder time keeping up with keyboard users, especially during intense fights. This is most prominent in player-versus-player engagements, though you can still rack up more damage and survive for longer against monsters when you hit keys directly.

The keyboard can even be used with ground-targeted skills. Press the appropriate number for the skill and when your mouse pointer is over your target press the number key again.

SKILL BAR ASSOCIATIONS

NUMBER(S)	SKILL TYPE
1-5	Weapon
6	Healing
7-9	Utility
10	Elite

All characters begin with the ability to learn their weapon skills in addition to a default unlocked healing skill. That means your character can have up to six skills to use during battles as early as level two. As you continue to adventure, utility skills and other healing skills are unlocked. These fill out your profession by providing options for survivability, increased damage, pet summoning, boons, and more.

Elite skills are the most powerful ones in the game. They're also the last slot that gets unlocked, so you won't have to worry about them until level 30. Most elite skills provide a powerful series of effects that change the entire nature of a battle but can only be used once every few minutes.

SKILL BAR UNLOCKS

SKILL SLOT	UNLOCKED AT CHARACTER LEVEL
1	Automatically Unlocked
2-5	1 (But Requires Weapon Kills)
6	Automatically Unlocked
7	5
8	10
9	20
10	30

BUYING SKILLS

Skill points are found all over the world. They have a chevron icon when you're searching on the map, and you stumble over them in all sorts of locations. Complete the skill challenges at each location to grab a point for your character. These are spent in the Hero screen to learn healing, utility, and elite skills.

You also get skill points while leveling up, so even people who haven't explored the world yet have a few points to spend here and there. Go into the Hero screen, highlight skills that look fun and read about them, and then click on the ones you want. Confirm your choices to buy these skills and then they're available to you for the rest of your career.

Even after reaching level 80, your hero learns more about him- or herself and about the world. Experience at that lofty height still goes onto your bar, eventually leading to new "levels" that grant free skill points. You won't rise above the level cap, but these points let you learn new skills or buy items that are used with the powerful mystic forge recipes.

SWITCHING SKILLS

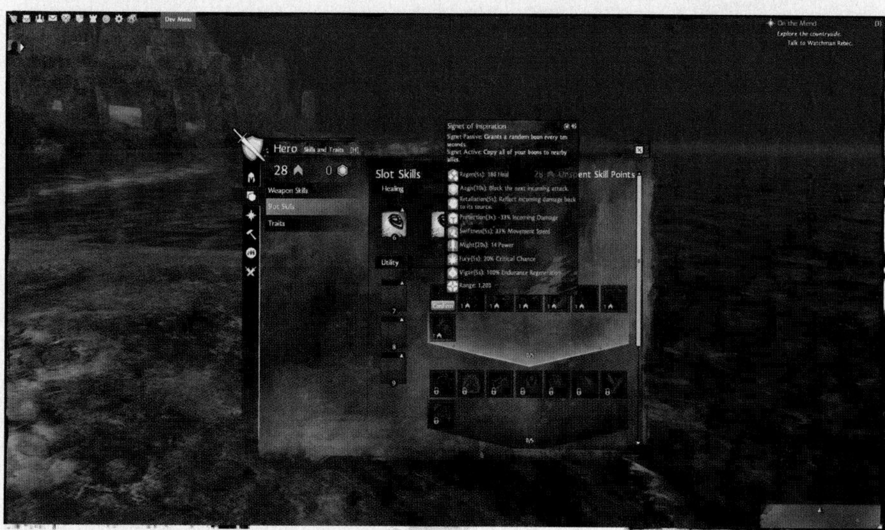

Once you've learned a skill, move the arrow over the pertinent skill's slot (the healing, utility, or elite slot). This opens a window with all of the skills you've learned in that field. Choose the one you want and it'll be installed into that slot. This works whether you're in the Hero screen or out in the world using the interface on the bottom.

This isn't a game where you choose a skill for your character and have to live with that as a major component of play for the rest of eternity. All heroes have the ability to learn all of their skills. This takes time, and you have to get a considerable number of skill points to do it. However, it's rare that you'll be forced to use any specific skill you don't like or don't need.

You might be confused at first, because it doesn't seem like there are many skill slots. Your weapons knock out half of them, and that means you only get to choose from the other five, right?

Well, yes and no. It's true that you only have those five slots to play around with at any given time. But, you can switch your healing, utility, and elite skills around whenever your character isn't in battle. As long as the skill in that slot has finished its cooldown, you can put something new in its place.

That means you actually get a huge pile of skills to play around with. There are 10 skills available at the beginning of each fight, and even that isn't a real limitation. Through weapon swapping (or the changing of elements/tools) you get even more skills.

The system is so much deeper than it first appears. You can learn the basics in a few minutes, but mastering the skill system takes genuine work and love.

CUSTOMIZE YOUR SKILL BAR FOR THE TASK AT HAND

All of this comes together when you start figuring out times and places for each skill. Something that seems awesome when you're soloing in the wilderness might stink in a dungeon group. The same situation might make another skill go from being tepid to saving the lives of your entire party.

Don't slot your favorite skills and forget about the rest of the ones you've learned. Almost everything has an ideal use. Reconfigure your skill bar constantly, as a matter of habit. Example: "These enemies are a pain in the rump; they have stuns and knockbacks all over the place. I need to slot something with stability."

> "Don't be fooled; any class can be very durable and/or very fragile."
>
> —*Hugh Norfolk*

Think about what you're facing during each event, dungeon, and encounter. Changing skills can turn battles from defeat into victory.

WEAPON SELECTION AND USE

During your travels, you meet some people and monsters that don't quite agree with you. This causes fights from time to time, so be ready to defend yourself.

CHOOSE A WEAPON

All professions have a selection of weapons they're allowed to equip. If your profession can't use a given type of weapon, it's thoroughly useless to you (and will have red text in its description to let you know why the weapon won't equip).

If your profession can use a weapon, right-click on the item in your inventory and choose to equip it. Or, go into your Hero screen and double-click on the weapon in question on the left side of the panel. Weapons and armor that are level- and profession-allowable for your character show up there.

The weapon or weapons you currently have equipped are what determine skill slots 1-5 on the bottom of your screen. Two-handed weapons have five skills each. Single-handed weapons have two or three each, so your five skills are determined by the combination of skills on your primary and secondary weapons.

WHICH SKILLS CAN I USE?

Look in your Hero screen, go to the skills area, and view weapon skills. This window shows you the skills for your profession based on every weapon type you can equip. It also tells you more about each skill and whether it's unlocked for your hero.

UNLOCKING WEAPON SKILLS

Your characters start with only one skill for each weapon type. This is always an autoattack that doesn't have a cooldown or cost of any sort. You can wail away with your autoattack until the cows come home. However, these attacks don't have many particular strengths.

To get more skills, kill enemies with each weapon group. Every kill counts toward your total, and soon more and more skills begin to open up. These go in order from two to five. In the case where you're dual wielding, primary weapon skills are always unlocked before the secondary weapon's skills have a chance.

TO BE FAIR

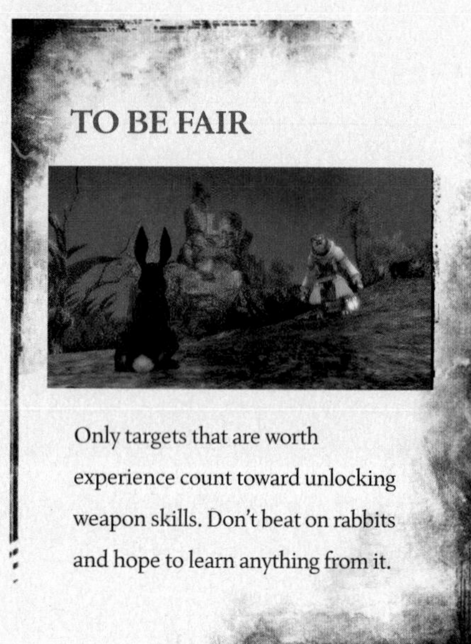

Only targets that are worth experience count toward unlocking weapon skills. Don't beat on rabbits and hope to learn anything from it.

Weapon swapping is similar to dodging in that new players won't take as much advantage of it as they will later on. Advanced players learn their weapons so well that they can use multiple attacks from one weapon and then switch to the second set to exploit the advantages gained by their early attacks. They effectively have access to ten weapon skills at a time!

Even if you don't master that level of weapon switching, consider a basic layout where you have a ranged weapon and a melee weapon. If enemies run away from you or are throwing down too many AoE attacks, break out your ranged weapon and punish them. When the monsters catch up to you, switch to melee and burn them down.

The best way to learn new skills is to go to a lower-level region and kill enemies with low health that are found in large groups. Packs of wolves or schools of barracuda are good for this, but anything will do. The faster the kills, the sooner you get your skills. Having a group makes the process faster and more enjoyable because you only need to hit the target a few times for it to count, so you learn based off of the group's kill rate rather than just your own.

SWAPPING WEAPONS

Once you get past the first few levels, most professions unlock a second set of weapon slots; engineers and elementalists do not, due to their existing variety of attacks.

Put a complementary set of weapons into these slots and then use the tilde key ("~"), or whatever key you bind, to switch between these sets. There isn't a cooldown for this if you're outside of battle. During fights there is a cooldown, though it gets better as you level through traits you choose.

WEAPON RANGES

Because it's possible to attack without an enemy targeted, you might be confused about weapon ranges early on. When a character attacks an enemy that's too far away, the attack automatically misses. This can be frustrating because you might not know your exact weapon range until you've worked with the weapon for a good while.

That's why it's important to look at your skill bar. Each button at the bottom of the screen is shown in red when there isn't a viable target selected within range. These turn yellow when you acquire a target. Use this as a way to figure out what is and what isn't inside your weapon's attack range.

Not all skills have the same range, even on the same weapon type for the same profession! Watch the differences to learn which skills you can use farther off.

Some "melee" weapons have ranged attacks, so don't assume that a greatsword is a close-range weapon for all professions at all times. In fact, mesmers use greatswords as ranged weapons exclusively. They're better at maximum range than they are up close.

HUNTING MONSTERS

It's hard to be a hero without fighting a few monsters, eh? There are plenty of them in Tyria, so it's essential to learn how to fight. Melee, missile attacks, magic, and healing are all a part of this. Most importantly, you need to use your head and think about what you're doing. Mindless killing won't get you very far!

BASIC COMBAT

Select a target by left-clicking on it or using one of the targeting keys, such as "Tab." Make sure the monster doesn't sound too tough for your hero to handle, and then press one of your weapon skill buttons once you've closed to an appropriate range.

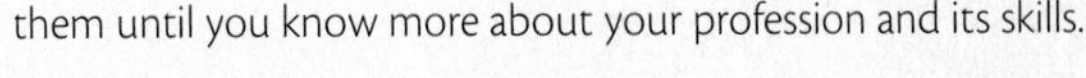

At first, you won't know which skills to use and in what order. That's fine. For easy fights, your hero will be safe even if he or she uses skills awkwardly. Weak single enemies can't kill you without a lot of luck. Only veteran and champion enemy units pose a threat by themselves, and you won't face any of them until you know more about your profession and its skills.

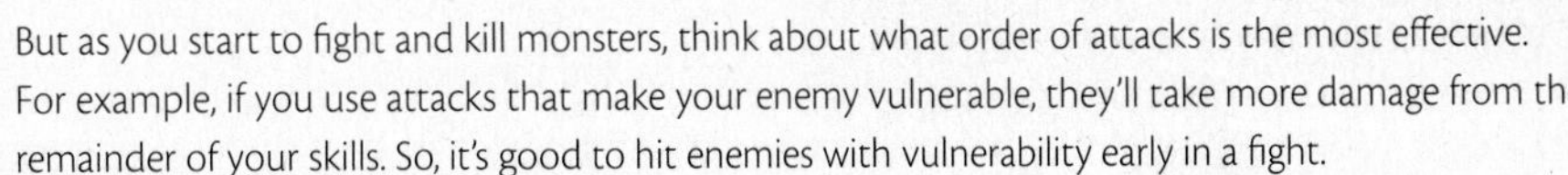

But as you start to fight and kill monsters, think about what order of attacks is the most effective. For example, if you use attacks that make your enemy vulnerable, they'll take more damage from the remainder of your skills. So, it's good to hit enemies with vulnerability early in a fight.

> Don't tap your autoattack button repeatedly. It's unnecessary because your character automatically continues to move through his or her autoattack sequence as long as it's active and there is a target in range.

"Don't be afraid to swap out your utilities and major traits to prepare for a difficult fight. You can change them any time you're out of combat."

—Peter Larkin

Our profession write-ups help you by discussing all of the weapon skills and how they relate to each other. Even without those, you should be comfortable exploring each attack. Highlight skills with your mouse, read the information about those attacks, and try them out on their own to see the specific damage numbers and effects that pop up. Trial and error can still teach you a huge amount about how to play your character well.

GROUP TARGETING

Because there aren't macros in *Guild Wars 2*, you can't make a simple assist routine and have the rest of your party attack the same target all of the time. It takes more skill to stay on the right enemies in this game. That said, you still have a tool to help alert group members when you have an important enemy targeted. Use "Control + T" to send an alert to the group. They can then press "T" to instantly change to the target you want them to kill.

This isn't important in most events or small fights. Save it for dungeon groups when you're facing extremely dangerous enemies. Assign an experienced player to call out the targets that are going to go down first, and then everyone can focus their damage output on those enemies. Killing individual enemies quickly is a very important way to mitigate extreme damage output or disruptive abilities.

GETTING UP TO SPEED

Once you figure out the basics of combat, start using your abilities while on the move. Because most skills can be used while mobile, your character shouldn't have to stand still very often. Use that to your advantage, because many of the world's monsters have attacks that force them to stand still. Run around behind moas, ettins, basilisks, and similar enemies that blast whatever is in front of them. Dodge heavy attacks and come back swinging. With practice, it's possible to avoid many of the heaviest attacks in your enemy's lineup.

If you have a ranged weapon, don't let enemies get close to you. Run to the side to stay at full speed, and go in a circle around your victims while slamming the fools with cripple, frozen, or immobilization to prevent them from reaching you. When they do, use attacks that stun, launch, or knock around the monsters and then continue the game.

When you're the melee character, use the same techniques to prevent enemies from doing that to your hero. Keep the victims slow or immobile so your best close-range attacks hit home every time. Don't let mobile enemies like centaurs have fun at your expense.

SKILL TIMINGS

As you use more and more skills, you may notice that some of them activate in different ways. A skill might activate instantly, during a short animation, or the ability could be channeled for several seconds. Learn the difference between these so you know when to use each skill to its fullest.

"Pay attention to your enemy's animations. You can predict some devastating attacks by watching for cues from your opponent."

—*Peter Larkin*

INSTANT SKILLS

> You can move, dodge, or use other skills while activating these.

Skills that activate instantly start their cooldown as soon as you touch them. Signets are a great example of these abilities. You can toss them out at any moment, making them great reaction abilities. "I need some damage NOW." Hit the signet. "Crud, I'm stunned." Hit the signet to break out of that.

Instant skills have massive advantages because they can even be used while you're in the middle of other attacks. You can be channeling one skill, see an opportunity, and then exploit that with your instant abilities without having to cancel anything. Pretty cool, indeed!

NORMAL SKILLS

> Your character can move and activate these skills, but dodging disrupts them.

The average skill isn't as flexible as those instants. They take a moment to animate, and during that time you can't use other abilities. Pressing the buttons for them just queues the next skill your hero will try to use. Your hero can move normally without disrupting these skills, but dodging will cancel them (and put the skill onto a short cooldown if it was in progress). The majority of attacks and healing skills fall into this category.

HEALING PRECEDENCE

Attack skills won't overwrite each other. As we said, if you hit one skill while a first one is animating, the second ability queues up and triggers as soon as the first one finishes. However, there is an exception. Most healing abilities have precedence and try to activate as soon as you hit them. Your current attack disengages and the healing skill tries to activate as soon as it possibly can.

CHANNELED SKILLS

> Even normal movement might disrupt a channeled skill.

Abilities that take a few seconds to complete show a progress bar at the bottom of your screen. You can't use other non-instant skills while channeling them, and you might not be able to move around without disrupting your ability. Test each channeled skill you have to find out whether you can move while using it. Disrupted channeled skills enter their full cooldown phase because you technically were using the skill already, even though you didn't get the full benefit from it.

Unlike normal skills, you can shift into other attacks at almost any time while channeling. If you hit the new attack skill, your channeled ability ends and the new attack triggers. Autoattacks often work this way. They act like a channeled ability until another attack gets precedence.

HIGHER-LEVEL MONSTERS

This game's dynamic level adjustment system levels you down to deal with easier content. That way, nothing gets stale or imbalanced just because you're over-leveled for a region. However, that won't protect you from facing high-level enemies if you explore areas before your time.

Look at monsters before you fight them, and be very careful if the targets are more than three levels above you. Things hit extremely hard when they're higher level. Two heroes working together can combat this fairly well, and a full party can do even better. Even five heroes shouldn't try to attack an area where the enemies are six or more levels above your people. Incoming damage gets so high that characters are downed constantly, and people won't have as much fun. It's good to challenge yourself, but be careful not to take it too far!

SINGLE-TARGET KILLING VS. AOEs

At its most simple level, you have two ways to deal with groups of enemies. Single out the weakest target, kill it, and move on to the next weakest enemy. Or, try to take out everything at once with area-of-effect attacks. Both of these are viable methods, so it's wise to look at the pros and cons of each.

At its most simple level, you have two ways to deal with groups of enemies. Single out the weakest target, kill it, and move on to the next weakest enemy. Or, try to take out everything at once with area-of-effect attacks. Both of these are viable methods, so it's wise to look at the pros and cons of each.

SINGLE-TARGET KILLING

> Is easier to do, is more reliable, and puts one enemy out of the fight quickly.

> Can be done by almost any character.

> Is safer.

AREA-OF-EFFECT FIGHTING

> Has more risk, but offers faster experience gain and more money per hour.

> Requires a loadout of skills capable of hitting multiple targets.

> Can be quite a bit of fun.

It doesn't take long to explain single-target methods. Find enemies, attack them, and kill them with whatever does the most damage. Heal when you need to restore health, and run if you bite off more than you can chew. Your goal should be to attack only an enemy or two at a time because extra targets just mean you'll take more damage over the course of the fight.

AoE characters and groups have a different way of looking at the world. They're trying to find clusters of enemies that are quite large. You want areas where there are groups of enemies within short range of each other. It's best if the enemies use melee attacks, which makes them easier to group together. You and any allies stay almost on top of each other, and that brings the foes together. Then, use as many AoEs as you have to kill everything in a blaze of glory.

When working with an AoE group, you can assign specific characters to different roles. A common trick is to have a ranged character ignore the AoE damage output and spend his or her time pulling enemies over to the group. This puller wants to have the longest range possible, and it's better if he or she is experienced enough to know when to stop grabbing enemies.

Ideally, you want to learn both methods of killing so you can switch between them at leisure. When you face lots of mobile enemies, use single-target methods. If the area has groups of enemies, it's AoE time. Use techniques that fit the event and area at hand.

WHICH PROFESSIONS ARE THE "BEST" FOR AOE GROUPS?

The answer is, "All of them!" Every profession has weapons and skills that are well suited for area-of-effect fighting—melee characters, ranged characters, casters, and brutes alike. Two-handed weapons are usually superior for this because of their increased swing range/attack radius. Look at greatswords, hammers, staves, and longbows. This isn't a hard and fast rule, but it's a good place to start.

EVAC!

No matter how good you are at this game, there will come a time when things go wrong. You might take on too many enemies, or attack something that's way too tough for your level, skill loadout, etc. If you watch the action closely, it's possible to see the way things are going before it's too late to do something about it.

This is why it's good to have at least one skill for getting out of trouble. Many professions have things that give them greatly reduced damage taken for a short time. Damage immunity is even better! Hit these skills once you know things are going south and then run in the opposite direction from the majority of enemy combatants. When your damage reduction/immunity falls, start to use your dodges in the direction you're already heading. This helps to avoid a few ranged attacks and anything swung by your closest pursuers. After your endurance is out, make sure you don't have a target and then use any skills that cause your character to charge ahead. Lacking those, use skills with swiftness to get an edge.

While evacuating the area, look ahead and see if there are pockets of aggressive monsters. Avoid those even if it means slowing down a little, because you can't afford to attract even more enemy attention when you're already in trouble. Running into friendly NPCs is a good thing, whenever possible, because they can help to distract your pursuers.

Don't run through real players. It's considered bad form; if the people want to help, they'll come on their own. If they don't, you really shouldn't make their fights any worse because of your failed battle.

TETHERING

The good news is that enemies won't chase you for too long. All foes have an area they consider home, and they won't want to stray too far from it. The farther away you get, the safer you'll be. Don't run in a circle while trying to shake enemies off your back. Not only is this foolish since the enemies catch up sooner, but it's also not going to cause them to tether.

Players who kill enemies from range should remember this too. You have to stay close to the enemies' home while killing them over time because you won't want them to tether. Enemies that head home will heal themselves to full health very quickly, and that's always a shame when you put in the time to kick them around in the first place.

GETTING AGGRO

"Getting Aggro" is what people often say when they talk about getting a monster's attention. In a group, you want the person with the best armor and health to have aggro as often as possible. This reduces the amount of damage coming at the party because that character is better able to mitigate the damage. It's also beneficial because that character is prepared for the damage, so he or she will be fighting with a higher number of defensive skills.

Getting aggro isn't always a simple process. *Guild Wars*, as a series, is known for having a very interesting aggro system. Proximity to the monsters and damage output are the two biggest factors in aggro generation. Monsters like to attack closer targets first! This is NOT common in other games, despite the fact that it's very intuitive. Any character that is supposed to tank and get aggro should be at the front and ready to attack enemies as soon as they approach.

Characters that are reviving fallen allies get extra aggro. Be aware of this before you try to revive someone when your health is already low. It's usually better to finish off targets and then save your friends. Besides, they might rally off of the slain enemies.

COMBOS AND COMBO FINISHERS

Some skills have Combo Fields or Combo Finishers in their descriptions. At first, you're probably confused by these. What do they mean?

Combo abilities place some type of effect in an area. For instance, you might put up a field of smoke with a skill. That field affects some types of skills that pass through it. Enemy projectiles that pass through smoke end up missing as if the attacker had been blinded. Isn't that awesome!

These can be offensive or defensive. A field of fire helps your side's ranged attackers. Their projectiles catch on fire and end up burning enemies that are struck. See the table to get an idea what types of combos are possible.

FIELD	MULTI-PROJECTILE	PROJECTILE	LEAP (SELF)	BLAST (AOE)	WHIRL
Fire	20% Burning	100% Burning	Self Fire Aura	AoE Might	Fire Bolts
Water	20% Regen	100% Regen	Heal Self	AoE Heal	Water Bolts
Lightning	20% Vulnerability	20% Vulnerability	Self Shocking Aura	AoE Swiftness	AoE Sparks
Ice	20% Freeze	100% Freeze	Self Frost Aura	AoE Frost Aura	Ice Bolts
Poison	20% Poison	100% Poison	Weakness after hit	AoE Weakness	Poison Bolts
Smoke	20% Blind	100% Blind	Stealth after hit	AoE Stealth	Smoke Bolts
Light	20% Removal	100% Removal	Self Retaliation	AoE Retaliation	Light Bolts
Dark	20% Lifesteal	100% Lifesteal	Blind Target	AoE Blind	Dark Bolts
Chaos	20% Confusion	20% Confusion	Daze target on next hit	AoE Daze	Chaos Bolts

USING CONDITIONS AND POSITIONAL ABILITIES AGAINST YOUR FOES

Direct damage isn't always the way to go. Some enemies have a huge amount of armor, or they have so much health that you need to keep your damage output high for more than a short burst. Conditions give you a way to deal with these situations. Use poison to hurt enemies over time while damaging their ability to heal themselves. Bleeding doesn't do much up front, but stack a dozen bleeds on someone and watch him take constant damage.

Look at your profession's abilities and see if there's anything you can gain from adding conditions to your attacks. Not all of these options are found in your weapon skills. Make sure to look at your utility slots and traits as well. Many professions have the option to add conditions to their critical hits; if you're a character with a high precision, this is a wonderful way to make yourself deadlier without any change in playstyle.

CONDITIONS

EFFECT	WHAT IT DOES
Bleed	Damage over time, highly stackable
Blind	Enemies miss their next attack
Burning	Damage over time
Confuse	Targets lose health if they use their skills
Cripple	Slows the target
Fear	Causes the victim to flee uncontrollably
Frozen	Slows targets and increases their cooldown times
Poison	Damage over time and reduces the effectiveness of healing
Vulnerability	Reduces the target's defense
Weakness	Slows endurance regeneration and causes fumble (which reduces damage of non-critical attacks)

STATUS EFFECTS

EFFECT	WHAT IT DOES
Daze	Prevents the enemy from using abilities
Float	Underwater effect that causes you to lose control of movement and skills while also rising
Immobilize	Locks victims in place, though they can still act
Knockback	Throws the target away from the attacker
Knockdown	Knocks the victim to the ground
Launch	Launches the target into the air
Pull	Brings an enemy over to your character
Sink	Underwater effect that causes you to lose control of movement and skills while also descending
Stun	Stops movement and actions for a brief period

** Note that traits and effects that add to conditions only affect actual conditions (and not status effects).*

It's a lot to take in, isn't it? All of these effects are powerful and useful, so you have to learn when and where to use each. The simple version is to group them into general categories. Bleed, poison, confuse, and burning are on the damaging side. Use them for faster kills. Blind, daze, fear, knockback, knockdown, launch, and stun are for crowd control; they mitigate enemy damage in various ways and keep your hero safe. Cripple, frozen, and immobilize are for inhibiting movement, when you want to control your enemy and determine where a fight occurs.

Use the effects that accentuate your playstyle. Crowd control is for safety, for you and your allies. Movement inhibiting lets you kite enemies around and kill them slowly but surely. The deadly abilities simply let you bring down targets as soon as possible.

BOONS, BUFFS, POSITIVE POSITIONAL EFFECTS

Boons are the opposite of conditions. They make your hero more effective for a short duration. Buffs are effects that assist your character and give him or her an edge over enemies. Things that improve your character's boons do not contribute toward buffs.

BOONS

EFFECT	WHAT IT DOES
Aegis	Blocks the next incoming attack
Fury	20% critical chance
Might	Raises power (increasing all types of damage output)
Protection	Raises defense (decreasing incoming damage)
Regeneration	Restores health over time
Retaliation	Reflect damage back at the attacker
Swiftness	Improves movement speed by 33%
Vigor	Increased endurance regeneration

BUFFS

EFFECT	WHAT IT DOES
Invisibility	Hides your character from sight
Invulnerability	Damage immunity for a short time
Quickness	All actions and animations are twice as fast
Stability	You can't be affected by positional abilities, such as Launch, Knockback, etc.

POSITIVE POSITIONAL EFFECTS

EFFECT	WHAT IT DOES
Leap/Charge	Moves quickly toward your target
Retreat	Causes your character to move backward suddenly
Teleport/ Shadowstep	Instantly moves you to the target's position

Vigor, protection, and regeneration raise hero survivability in a long-term way. They reduce the chance of your death out in the field, but they don't offer sudden protection against spikes in enemy damage. Invulnerability is what you need for that. Abilities with invulnerability are excellent for getting out of trouble.

Fury and might are your damage dealers. They raise critical rates and direct damage, respectively, and they are both quite important for offensive characters. These boons help melee, missile, and magic equally, so every attacker wants them.

Leap, retreat, swiftness, and teleport are positional effects that help you in getting to or away from enemies. They're superb for kiting and anti-kiting, so slow-killing ranged characters or melee-only heroes should use them often.

ITEMS THAT HELP YOUR CHARACTER

If you're looking for another type of boon, seek items that provide long-lasting bonuses for your hero. Many karma items (and some that are bought with gems) give your character an hour of increased potential. They may help your might, add protection, or increase the rate of magical item drops, for example.

To get items with karma, talk to the NPCs that give you renown tasks after completing your work. These people often offer rewards, including such things as karma-purchasable items and boons. Very nice!

Or, look at the Gem Store to find these and see if any of them interest you. They can be quite powerful.

CHARACTER TRAITS

Each profession has five lines of traits. Characters don't start getting trait points until level 11, and after that they get one every level until capping at 80. This means you end up with 70 points for traits and can spread them around however you wish.

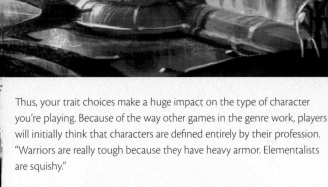

Each trait line has 30 points to unlock. Go to your profession trainer and buy a book to unlock the first tier (that covers 10 points of traits in every line). At levels 40 and 60 you have to come back and get new books to reach the second and then final set of traits.

Because of this system, you're forced to spread trait points around during your early leveling. That's good, since you won't know what works best for your character until you've played around with a little bit of everything.

Though the trait lines are profession-specific, there is a general style to them. Three of the lines focus more on damage output, while one centers around healing, and another is for outright survivability. Characters that go after all three damage lines end up being horrifically destructive. They're also made of paper and can drop quickly in a fight that goes the wrong way. Those with a heavy investment in healing and survival can take much more damage, even if they're wearing lighter armor.

Thus, your trait choices make a huge impact on the type of character you're playing. Because of the way other games in the genre work, players will initially think that characters are defined entirely by their profession. "Warriors are really tough because they have heavy armor. Elementalists are squishy."

The thing is, that's not always the case. Playstyle, equipment choices, and trait selections can turn these preconceived notions on their heads. You can make a warrior with damage that a thief and elementalist would drool over, but you're going to pay for it one way or another. By the same token, it's easy to make hardy and survivable characters regardless of the base armor in any profession.

TRAIT SELECTION WHILE LEVELING

If you don't have a strong notion of what to do with your character while leveling, consider an aggressive configuration. Though slightly harder to play at first, characters with the bonus power, precision, and critical damage from offensive traits can kill faster. This leads to higher income, slightly faster leveling, and the ability to finish most events quickly.

The trade-off is that you die more than hardier characters, and challenging events may be impossible to solo (whereas a really tough character might be able to beat the same content after ten minutes of trying).

But that's just our suggestion, if you don't have an idea what you want. If you know that healing and group support are important to you, then put points in your healing line. You'll still be able to kill enemies and win the day. Nobody is a backline healer in *Guild Wars 2*; the choices just define what abilities you are best at using. You're still going to use everything at your disposal.

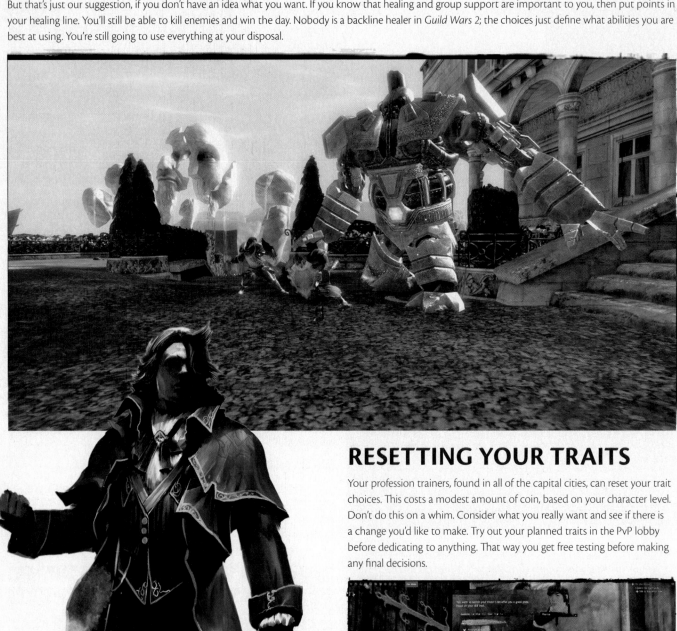

RESETTING YOUR TRAITS

Your profession trainers, found in all of the capital cities, can reset your trait choices. This costs a modest amount of coin, based on your character level. Don't do this on a whim. Consider what you really want and see if there is a change you'd like to make. Try out your planned traits in the PvP lobby before dedicating to anything. That way you get free testing before making any final decisions.

EQUIPMENT AND VISUAL CUSTOMIZATION

Your character is able to mitigate incoming damage by having good armor. Good weapons help you deal damage to enemies and have access to a wide array of attacks. That's all rather obvious, so let's talk about the more subtle aspects of equipment collecting.

ITEM LEVEL AND RARITY

Everything you look for in *Guild Wars 2* is going to be defined by its level range, rarity, and stats. The level range is the easiest to understand. Equipment (whether we're talking about weapons, armor, or accessories) can only be used once your hero reaches a minimal level. That could be anything from 1 to 80. Equipment rises in power throughout the levels, so something that's ideal at level 15 will be weaker at 20 and darn near useless if you're still holding onto it at 36! That's because enemies get tougher as you level, and having access to level-appropriate gear is the way to counter these new challenges.

Equipment rarity gives you a quick idea of how good an item is for its actual level. Items of equal level but varying rarity have a substantial difference in their stats. This isn't as big a jump as you'd see in most games from this genre, but it's still important to try and find better equipment whenever you can.

EQUIPMENT COLOR AND RARITY

RARITY	COLOR	GENERAL STATS
Basic	White	85%
Fine	Blue	100%
Masterwork	Green	105%
Rare	Yellow	110%
Exotic	Orange	120%
Legendary	Purple	120%

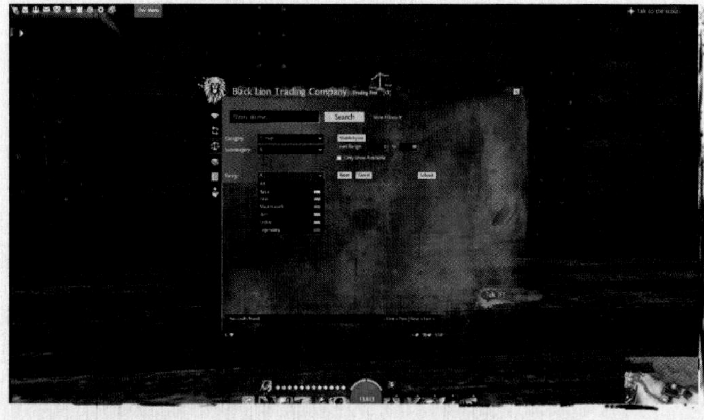

This means that items of the same level will be substantially better if you make sure to find versions of higher rarity. Fine items are the baseline. They're easily purchased or found while exploring and killing enemies. They don't cost much to get from the Trading Post, and you can always commission something better from a crafter.

Getting masterwork items (the green ones) gives you a little more power. If you look at the equipment closely, you'll see that a green item is often three or four levels stronger in terms of stats when compared to a blue. Don't fall into the trick of going by color rather than stats. Some people deck themselves out in green or yellow gear and then don't bother looking at blues that drop. If your yellow gear is ten levels old, those blues are probably on par or better than what you have!

Don't expect to find many exotic items while you're leveling up. These pieces are quite hard to find, and their value is considerable. Even if you find one, think about whether it's worth keeping. Selling these pieces on the Trading Post can net you a substantial amount of money.

SPECIFIC STATS

So you found an item your character can use, that is level appropriate, and it has a decent rarity. Does that mean you've found the perfect fit? Well, maybe not. There's still the issue of the stats on the item. If you found a piece with bonus healing and toughness, you might not be as happy as if you found the same item with power and precision. It's all about the focus of your character.

Going after specific stats is important if you want your character to be exceptional at a given type of play. Jack of all trades characters can grab a bit of everything, and they're cool too (as long as you're happy).

The best killers should look at maximum weapon damage, power, precision, condition damage, and critical damage. Survivability is based on defense, toughness, and healing.

Upgrading your items with sigils and runes that focus entirely on damage, survivability, or group utility is another way to advance your character. That's easier to control than what gear you find.

> "Equip weapon runes to complement the weapon. For example, add a chill or cripple effect to your melee weapon set to keep your enemy from getting away!"
>
> —*Andrew Freeman*

In case you're wondering about the difference between exotic and legendary equipment, here's how it all works: Legendary weapons have the same basic stats as exotic versions. However, they have a different appearance and a powerful-looking set of visual effects. These weapons are created at the mystic forge. It takes serious time and effort to put them together, but the result is a weapon with top-notch power and serious credibility. You'll look great wielding them.

There aren't legendary armor pieces, so exotic armor is the top of the line, both visually and in terms of direct power.

GETTING THE BEST GEAR

If you have loads of money, use the Trading Post for all of your acquisitions. But most of us aren't laden with constant cash, so there have to be other ways, right? Here's what you do: get a group together. Groups of players are able to kill more enemies in the same amount of time. That means you have more chances for magical items to drop. In addition, parties have a hidden bonus to their drop rates, so you end up finding even more items than if you killed the same number of enemies while soloing.

Because loot is individualized, you don't lose anything by having allies around. They're getting tons of loot, and so are you. For an even better experience, get together with friends or guild members. This raises the chance of people hooking you up with equipment that dropped for them. "Hey, I got this heavy armor, and I don't need it. Do you need X?"

Trading items makes the group system even more efficient. You can have your character set up with level-appropriate items in no time, and without spending a single copper. You even make money while doing it, because the group is blowing through events and monsters at a speedy clip.

VISUAL MODIFICATIONS

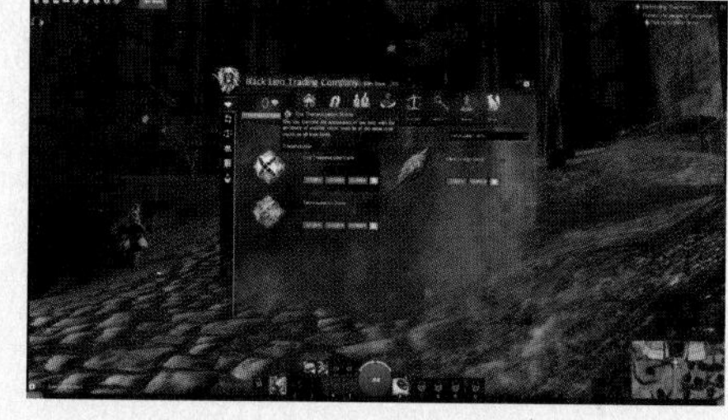

"But wait," some say. "I found the coolest armor ever, and I don't want to leave it behind just for some better stats." Don't worry about that. *Guild Wars* 2 wants you to look your best. There is a system in place to let you have the best of all worlds. You can keep the look of one item and combine it with the stats of another. This is as awesome as you'd hope.

To do it, go into the Gem Store. There are Transmutation Stones in that section. Buy a stone that is higher level than the items you're combining. But don't spend extra for one that's too much higher; you only need it to be equal to or above the higher item's level. The Fine Transmutation Stones are only needed for top tier items.

Once you have the stone, use it to take the appearance, stats, and upgrades for the two items and choose the best from each category. You end up with the desired piece of equipment, and that's that. These stones cost a bit, but it's not a punitive amount.

CHANGING COLORS

If you don't like the default coloring of your equipment, that's modifiable as well. Go into your Hero screen and look for the eyedropper above your armor. Click on that and look at the dyes your character has unlocked. Play around with these to change the default look of your character; the changes even apply if you switch armor around, so there's no need to take time out of adventuring every time you find an upgrade.

"Right-click a dye to set it as a favorite so you can get to your more commonly used dyes faster."

—*Bob Green*

The system is quite flexible, and every piece of armor has a few different areas to color in. Make the hero that you see in your mind and have him or her come to life.

GETTING NEW DYES

To get even more color choices, you need to find more dyes. These can be obtained by drops in the world (called Unidentified Dyes), purchased on the Gem Store, or crafted. When you purchase Dye Packs from the Gem Store, you get a variety of common and rare dyes with one simple purchase. This is a very good way to get more colors without spending any time.

TOWN CLOTHES

For another change of appearance, use the classy town clothes symbol on your Hero page to switch into casual gear. Your character swaps back to combat clothing when you use the armor toggle nearby or when he or she takes any damage.

New sets of town clothing can be purchased at the Gem Store. The alternatives cost a fair bit, but they're all pretty darn cool.

COLLECTING SETS OF EQUIPMENT

Dungeons have their own weapon and armor rewards,' themed to match the dungeon they come from. If you want a really stylish look, run through the exploration mode of a dungeon enough times to get a complete suit of armor, and then transmute future upgrades so your stats stay current but your visual appearance retains that awesome look you worked for.

This is more popular with higher-level characters because they don't upgrade equipment as often (so they don't have to use gems constantly to keep their gear looking great).

EXPERIENCE AND LEVELING

Your journey from level 1 to 80 is going to be adventurous, and it's up to you to decide how you go about it. Many of *Guild Wars 2*'s activities provide experience. This allows you to level in a number of different ways.

GAINING EXPERIENCE

At any time, you can look at the bottom of your screen and see your character's visual progress toward the next level. In addition to the bar that fills up as you gain experience, you can highlight the area to see the exact numbers as well. As soon as you reach the specified number, the bar empties and the process begins anew.

ACTIVITIES THAT AWARD EXPERIENCE

- **Killing monsters**
- **Exploring new areas of the map**
- **Daily achievements**
- **Finishing renown tasks and events**
- **Working on your character's personal story**
- **Crafting items**

You can also get bonus experience by buying boons from the Gem Store or by building guild rewards that yield temporary experience boons.

KILL XP

You won't get the majority of experience by killing monsters unless you consciously decide to slow down and just slaughter for fun. This isn't a fast way to advance in your profession, though it's decent for getting treasure.

Higher-level monsters, compared to your hero, are worth more than anything below your level. For maximum experience, find monsters that have low health and are a couple levels above you. Monsters with high health, nasty condition effects, and positional attacks are the worst for experience because they draw out their fights or cause you to have more downtime due to low health.

Kill experience is much higher in a good group than it is while soloing. Make sure everyone in the group is hitting each target, and watch the kills pile up.

EXPLORATION

Uncovering new parts of the map awards experience based on your character's current level. This means that a high-level person gains levels just as quickly while exploring as a new character would. You don't have to explore high-level areas to get full credit. Anywhere your character hasn't been will count toward your exploration credit. Take a look around starting zones for other races for a relaxing time. This isn't fast for leveling, but it gets you waypoints and skill challenges, and it's pretty fun.

DAILY ACHIEVEMENTS

Daily Achievements are awarded for a number of activities. Completing these help your characters to level quickly. Monster kills, kill variety, harvesting materials, and completing events help to fulfill these goals. Even if you can get on for only half an hour or so a day, you can make considerable progress for your character by collecting these rewards.

If your hero completes all of his or her daily achievements, an additional chest of money and experience appears. Heck yeah!

EVENTS

All forms of events are worth major chunks of experience. The best combination is to find events in the same area as a renown task you haven't completed. Work on both goals at the same time to get a heavy helping of experience and loot.

The more events you complete per hour, the faster you'll level. It's as simple as that.

CRAFTING

Crafting a few items here and there won't get you too much experience. It's more a bonus than a means of advancing your character quickly. However, guild crafters supported by a full team of harvesters can get bursts of leveling done because they have so many materials to work with at each tier.

PACING YOUR STORY

With so many choices, it can be hard to figure out what to do next. Groups have their own momentum, and you can often just follow other people around and have fun doing whatever comes up. When you're soloing, you have to decide on something for yourself! One method to advance quickly and have fun is to jump between story quests and the events out in the world. Your character's personal story awards a hefty amount of experience, and that combines well with the amount you get from normal events. Gain a level out in the field, then do a story mission. Switch back and forth like this and you'll always be doing something a little bit different.

"If you run your personal story with a party of other players, the enemies will become more challenging and numerous based on the party size. Party members who are on the same story step as you can choose to count your story step completion as their own, reaping the same rewards and enabling them to advance to the next step with you."

—*Rob Thody*

This is far superior to leveling up and then running through your story all at once. Doing things that way wastes all of the bonus experience you get from beating sections of your story. It also ruins the fun of being taken to new areas; your hero's personal story matches the game's progression in a good way. If you stay current on your story, it'll take you to new places at the perfect time to match your hero's levels.

THE LEVELING PROCESS

Most games have a leveling treadmill that really slows down as you reach the mid- to later levels. That isn't so with *Guild Wars* 2. Character progression has a much gentler curve. You won't have to invest 10 hours in a level, even if you're almost at cap.

If you're a speed leveler, the way to gain power quickly is to race through as many events as possible. The bonus experience you get from completing events is quite major. Killing monsters and exploring get you supplementary experience, but it won't easily beat events unless you have a very specific group to work with. Even then, a group that can AoE kill at a ludicrous rate should find an area with events that allow them to kill enemies for additional credit.

Completing events that are well beneath your character's level won't get you as much experience. It's better to challenge yourself and face higher difficulty content whenever you're up to it. This is yet another area where groups make a huge difference. Because groups can survive higher-level engagements, it's easier for them to complete a wide range of events.

> **Leveling with allies is almost universally faster than soloing, across all character builds and professions.**

DYNAMIC LEVEL ADJUSTMENT

Guild Wars 2 is set up to give players massive freedom in exploration and the ability to play and group with friends. The game lets you experience lower-level content without feeling overpowered, but that's not all it does. If your hero visits lower-level areas, his or her levels are automatically adjusted so that content is still exciting and challenging. You can play with your friends even if they aren't as high level as your character. You still get a fair amount of experience when you complete events, which means you'll level up despite being in a region with weaker enemies.

Though it's true that you can level faster by taking on higher-end content, the ability to join with others and help them through the game more than makes up for a minor experience penalty.

As an additional incentive and reward for doing this, the loot system sometimes gives you items for your character's real level (instead of the adjusted level). This isn't a bug! It's a reward for helping friends and strangers alike.

DEATH AND TAXES

You can't win every fight, and you can't always escape. Sometimes the bad guys win. When that happens, your character is going to take too much damage and go down when your health bottoms out. That isn't the end of your story. You get a chance to rally and keep up the good fight, and even after that you have a few options.

DOWNED STATE

Characters with zero health fall to the ground and enter a downed state. They're still conscious but are too badly injured to fight properly. Each profession has four abilities they can use while downed. Your goal is to kill an enemy and rally yourself—or, if all of the enemies have been chased off already, to heal yourself back to the point where you rally on your own.

Immediately switch targets to find the weakest enemy within weapon range. Downed characters have a modest ranged attack, so anything that's attacking you is probably fair game.

If you have a group, let them know you're in trouble. Someone can race over to heal you (by interacting with your character). This provides a fast heal that can get your character up in just a few moments.

When PvP opponents try to rally, you have the option of running over to stomp on them (to make sure they die and stay dead). Don't assume they are out of the fight just because they fall; many abilities can restore downed opponents.

THINGS GET HARDER

If you fall in battle a single time, your character starts the downed state with a moderate amount of health. It's harder for enemies to completely kill you. However, this amount will be less if you fall again within the next few minutes. Eventually, your character will need to have pretty much instant healing or a kill, or they'll die just after going down.

Avoid combat for a few minutes to clear this condition from your character, or work very hard to stay up in the first place—not that you always have a choice!

To check on your downed penalty, look for a skull icon at the lower-left side of your health meter. Once that fades, you're back to your normal state.

UNDERWATER COMBAT

Downed characters in the water can fight while they're under the surface or swim to the top to begin healing. Be careful about the latter option, because you can only heal at the top (you can't fight back). If your enemies chase you up there you'll face a long, lingering war between your healing and the enemies' damage output. Only go to the top if you think you're in the clear.

DEATH

Long falls or defeat from your downed state both lead to character death. Other players can slowly restore you to life by interacting with your corpse, but it's hard to do in battle. Plus, there might not be anyone around to help you. But that's still not the end of the road! You just have to select a waypoint and teleport there. Your character arrives with health and life restored. You don't face many penalties from this, but there is a financial burden. One piece of your equipment is damaged in the process. If all of your armor is damaged already, due to repeated deaths, then a piece of armor will break.

Damaged armor functions normally. Broken armor loses all of its stats and won't show up on your character. You don't want to run around without any defense (or clothing), so something has to be done about this.

Look for a repair merchant. These NPCs are found in cities and towns around the world. They have their own distinct red icon and can be seen from quite a distance away. They'll fix you right up for a modest fee.

Make a habit of repairing whenever you see these guys so you don't forget and end up having your equipment break. Damaged and broken armor can be repaired fully, so you never have to lose items as a result of character death.

YOUR CHARACTER'S STORY

We've talked about your character's personal story tangentially, but let's focus on what that actually means. All heroes in *Guild Wars 2* have a series of personal quests that lead them through the game and develop their own saga. The events you experience are not determined by any sole factor, so most players are going to have different experiences in their stories.

Your race plays a major factor, but the decisions you made during character creation and the choices you make while dealing with NPCs over the course of your story are also critical.

A green star marks the location for personal story goals. These missions take place all over Tyria, often going back and forth between cities and dangerous parts of the wilderness.

Completed sections of the story provide massive infusions of experience, and there are sometimes monetary and equipment rewards as well.

Expect other long-term changes based on the things that happen in your story. If you take one route as opposed to another, there may be changes in your home (the part of your hero's city that is instanced specifically for him or her).

If you forget what's going on with your story or would just like to see what you've accomplished, go into your Hero screen and look at the story tab. There is information about all of the deeds you've accomplished throughout the story.

RENOWN TASKS AND EVENTS: A SHIFT IN THE WAY YOU ADVENTURE

While your persona story is an epic quest, the rest of *Guild Wars 2* is dominated by events. You don't walk up to quest givers, receive a specific assignment, and then get to work. Instead, you are told about events as they unfold. These events are based on the area you're traveling through, and completing them is often intuitive.

You don't need to start most events or stop to turn them in. It all happens automatically, and you're a participant in the process just by doing anything in the area that moves the event forward.

For example, a town may come under attack. The right side of your screen updates to show that there are enemies doing this, and as you rush to fight them their morale falls. When it reaches 0%, the event concludes and you're given money, karma, and experience as a reward.

OPEN WORLD ACTIVITIES

- **Renown Tasks**
- **Normal Events**
- **Group Events**
- **World Events**

RENOWN TASKS

Renown Tasks are an interesting case because they differ from events. You find tasks on the map quite easily; they show up as hearts that are visible from a fair distance off. Scouts in each area direct you toward these hearts, making them even easier to uncover.

Renown Tasks are not public in the way that events are. Think of these hearts as the micro stories of the world. Each task has a specific area that deals with the problems of that location. When you adventure there, you help to make the place better. You might do this by killing enemies, finding items for people, helping children, or whatever. There are often many ways to complete a renown task, and all of them show up as progress on the task bar that appears on your screen.

When the renown task completes, you get your reward (and a letter in the mail with some money). Once a task is done, it's done forever. You've helped that area, and they don't need any further help from you. It's possible to help other people with renown tasks whether you're done or working on the same thing.

Sometimes there are special rewards for completing a renown task. The task-giver may turn into a karma merchant with special items to purchase. Make sure to check on these NPCs to see if there is anything fun to get from them.

"By helping NPCs with various renown tasks, they will sometimes sell you more advanced gathering tools that have a higher chance to find rare materials."

—*Aaron Sebenius*

EVENTS

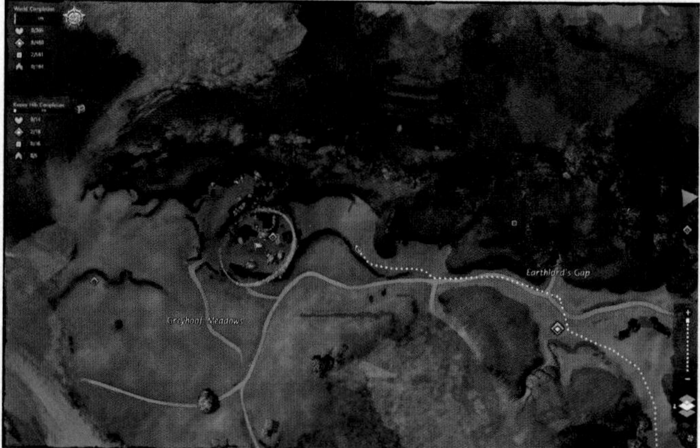

Events pop up whenever something critical happens in an area. If you're close enough to be a part of the event, the game updates your log on the right side of the screen and says what's going on. The map also updates, showing orange icons to let you know where the event is taking place and what to focus on when you get there.

Shield icons mark things that should be protected for the event. Skulls indicate specific enemies that must be killed. The area involved is often circled to mark the event's outer boundaries. Gear icons show items of interest.

All events are public. Your work combines with all of the other heroes in the area, and together you form a team (even if you never group up or even fight the same enemies at the same time). It's still a community effort to help one cause or another. Content scales for the majority of events, so having more people around makes the activity more fun without trivializing the challenges. More enemies show up to fight the extra heroes, and more items are needed when people are collecting things.

TRIGGERING EVENTS

In some cases, NPCs hold off on their own events until you're ready for them. Escorts are the most common case for these. You'll find them with an orange icon over their head. Talk to them and let them know you're up for the challenge and they'll start the event. Other NPCs might alert you toward events in the area, so it's always good to talk to everyone you meet. You learn about the backstory of the region and find even more of the content there.

GROUP EVENTS

Group events have the same general dynamic. You're told something is happening, you go there, and then work together on a common goal. The difference with these challenges is that they're tough! A single player will often get killed trying to do these alone. You should find a team of people willing to hit the event together. Groups of four or five have a good time with these events, though the more the merrier.

"Events are never about competing with other players. Each player gets their own reward regardless of others' actions, so work together!"

—*Peter Larkin*

WORLD EVENTS

World events cover the major story arcs and problems of a given area. They encompass multiple events that dynamically shift as the forces of an area battle against each other. Multiple groups of heroes can work together (or independently) to complete various goals while leading to a greater victory.

Many regions have world events. They're often a superb source of experience and gold. Expect heavy fighting, interesting stories, and some very epic monsters. Because portions of these events reset quickly, your group can dash between several areas in the map and battle constantly to hold back the tide of monsters dominating the area.

THE KARMA SYSTEM

Characters purchase items and services with gold at most merchants, but there is another currency of a sort. Karma is awarded when you finish most events. Karma cannot be traded nor purchased, so it's entirely based on the work you've put into your character.

Karma merchants show up with a purple icon when you're looking at the map. They sell a huge range of rewards, including weapons, armor, temporary boons, and services. Talk to these merchants to find out what specific rewards they give.

EVENT GOALS

Just look on the right side of your screen when an event is within range. The game always tells you the basics of what needs to be done to complete local events; this is true both for renown tasks and your personal story.

KILL ENEMIES OR DEPLETE ENEMY MORALE

A common goal is to destroy monsters. This is quite direct because you get used to combat very quickly. When you have a kill task, go over to the area and see which monsters affect your goal. If there are bandits, boars, and grubs in the area, kill at least one of each and see if the renown task or event progresses. Sometimes a variety of monsters influences the event, so you should treat all members of those groups as targets of opportunity. Kill them on sight!

It's a little bit harder if you have to deplete the area of enemy forces. Sometimes the creatures you're attacking get reinforcements, restoring some of their lost numbers. If that's happening, you have to hustle and kill quickly enough to bring their forces down to zero. Heal during battle to reduce downtime, and use the most aggressive weapons and skills you have to ensure that fights don't take very long. It's riskier fighting this way, but you're more likely to succeed!

CAPTURE AN AREA

A section of territory is outlined in red, and you're tasked with seizing and holding that spot. To do this, move into the region and kill all active enemies within the circle. The area turns blue when you succeed, and it begins to convert to your team or group. Progress is shown on the right, but this stops if there isn't at least one player still inside the circle's radius at all times. It also stops if any monsters come into the area to reinforce their fallen buddies.

Whenever possible, have your group defend the major chokepoints leading into the territory. Most monsters have to come forward naturally (instead of respawning in the midst of your group). If players stand on the edge of the circle and engage monsters before they break the perimeter, it avoids losing progress. Have one person stay inside the circle while others try to intercept and defeat incoming enemies.

COLLECTING GOODIES FOR AN NPC

Someone is looking for mining tools, siege weapon parts, or who knows what else. The log on the right lets you know that an NPC is collecting items, and the progress text lets you know how many you've turned in. This makes it easy to tell when a collection event is starting.

Look on the map for a circle that identifies the area where these items appear. It's not always next to the event NPC, so don't assume anything. Go to the marked location and scour the ground for sparkling objects. Interact with them to pick up the piece of whatever you need, and bring these back to the NPC; they're also marked on your map, so it's easy to find them.

Some events like this demand that you carry heavy objects, like barrels of ale! You won't be able to grab more than one at a time, so your character has to run back and forth between the items' locations and the NPC, handing the goodies over as you go. Other events look for smaller objects. When that happens, get eight to ten pieces at once before making the trek back to the event NPC. This is more efficient and lets you finish on your first or second turn-in.

Most collection events conclude with a timer that lets other people hurry back to hand in the leftover pieces still in their inventory. If someone else completes the event, run back to the NPC and hand in whatever you have left. This gets the materials out of your inventory AND increases your contribution toward the event.

Also, watch for secondary events. Not all collection events chain into something else after they're completed, but enough of them do that it's worth sticking around for a moment after you beat the initial scenario.

Renown tasks may have a collection aspect worked into their overall goals. If you get credit for picking up an item during your task, look for the heart icon on your map. NPCs managing the renown task are often where you turn in any collectible items associated with said task. You'll get credit for grabbing the item AND for handing it over to the NPC.

BREAKING STUFF!

Everybody loves to smash things. Some events send you into enemy camps and ask that you break their siege weapons, supplies, weapon racks, or whatever the bad guys care about. Items you need to break can be targeted normally, and all of your attacks are likely to affect them.

If your character has a weapon that deals area-of-effect damage, try to fight enemies near their equipment so your attacks smash the place up even when you're engaged. This makes the fighting more efficient (and more fun).

INTERACT WITH VARIOUS ENVIRONMENTAL OBJECTS

Some events have more complex goals. Stomp mounds of dirt, search through bushes, put out fires, and so forth. When the text indicates something more involved, stop for a second and look for the objects related to the event.

Move your mouse over the area and click on objects that might be useful to you. Once you find something to interact with, the event quickly becomes intuitive. "There's grain over here. I'm supposed to interact with that to pick it up, and then I interact with a cow to feed the cow. That's easy!" You get the idea.

YOU'RE BEING GRADED

Each person's contribution toward an event is tracked by the server. If you only kill a single enemy or grab one item before the event completes, you're not going to get full credit compared to a player who has been there the entire time.

The quick and simple rule is that the amount you contributed toward the event's progress is going to determine your tier of reward. Work hard and you'll get a gold reward icon; this is almost always the case if you're one of the only people in the area. The more players there are, the more likely it is for you to get a silver or bronze. This reduces the experience, gold, and karma you receive for participating in an event. Still, being involved with other players gets events done sooner and frequently leads to increased experience, gold, and karma per hour of play. So don't avoid events that other people are working on, even if they've gotten a head-start.

HOW TO GET THE BEST EVENT REWARDS

Kill enemies quickly with the most damaging weapons you have. Don't try to kite or kill single enemies over time unless you can't win without doing so. Take on multiple opponents at once and storm the area if you're up to the challenge. This has the added benefit of giving you practice for more challenging PvE content, like dungeons. Learn how much your character can handle, and practice using your skills to their best advantage.

Also, push for higher-level events whenever you can. Groups of skilled players slamming through content two or three levels above their characters often rake in the rewards.

> "You get XP for reviving a downed player. And, you get another ally to help you out!"
>
> —*Peter Larkin*

Even tiny contributions are rewarded well. Participate in a single fight during an escort event: you'll get credit for that event, even if someone else takes the NPCs all the way to their goal (or gets them killed).

BANKS, BAGS, AND ITEM SPACE

Item storage is always a big deal because your characters pick up all kinds of things as they adventure through the world. *Guild Wars 2* defaults to giving your people one large bag and four slots to additional bags. Four-slot bags are purchasable from a number of vendors, and they drop commonly in the low-level areas. However, they aren't of much use after you've gotten a little ways into the game. You're going to want a lot more space than that!

First off, each account has a bank vault with additional storage. Go into any major city and look for the bag icon. That's where the bank is located. You can access the bank out in the wilderness if you have an Asuran Bank Portal (purchasable with gems).

Store crafting ingredients and equipment for the future in your bank. Don't carry everything around or you won't have as much room for treasure! That's bad because you end up leaving items on corpses and losing money over time because of it. Take notice if your character fills up on treasure too quickly, and try to compensate by visiting towns more often to sell items and by upgrading your storage capacity.

ASSET MANAGEMENT

Right-clicking on Crafting Ingredients opens up several options to help you manage your assets. If you don't want the material, you can send it directly to the Trading Post and put it up for sale. If you do want it (but don't want to carry it around), selecting the Collectible option sends the stuff directly to your personal Bank. The ingredients are then found in the Collections section and are sorted by material and rarity.

You can keep an eye on what you have and how much space is available for treasure in your bags pretty easily. The Inventory screen has a number of management tools. First, you can see how many open bag spaces are available out of the total number. You can also compact your inventory using the available icon to fill up bag slots sequentially (instead of spread throughout the various bags). In addition, if you want to collapse the individual bag separations to create a seamless storage window, you can do that. Finally, if you want to search your bags for something specific, there's even a handy search feature!

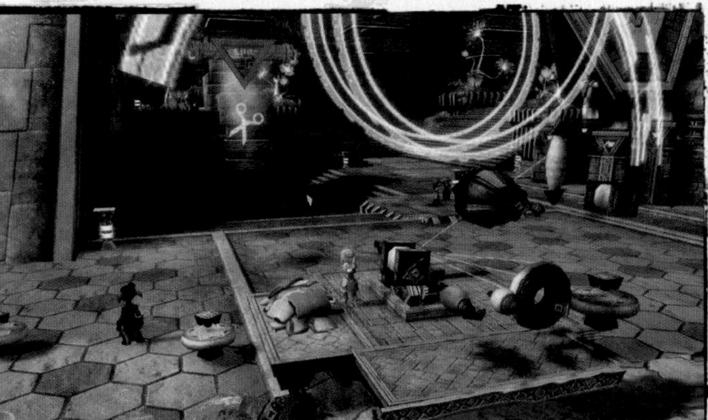

GETTING BIGGER BAGS

Bigger bags make a tremendous difference in your ability to carry around a ton of fun stuff. Many crafts are involved in making larger bags, boxes, and packs. You should look for (or learn how to become) an armorsmith, tailor, or leatherworker. All of them know how to make better storage items. Inexperienced craftsmen might only be able to make eight-slot items, but things go up quickly from there. They can eventually make awesome items that store as much as your starting pack.

These upgrades cost money because they require a fair number of ingredients to make. Remember that better storage makes you more money in the long term by saving on trips into town and avoiding wasted loot. Don't be afraid to invest some of your cash in better bags.

MORE BAG SLOTS

Another way to get more space is to buy bag slots so your character can carry even more bags of whatever size. There is a Gem Store upgrade that costs a few hundred gems. Your other characters do not get this benefit, so be careful which hero buys the upgrade!

MORE SPACE IN THE BANK

Another Gem Store upgrade is to purchase additional tabs in the bank vault. All of your characters share their space in the bank, so everyone benefits from having additional tabs.

GIVE IT TO THE GUILD

Guilds that have unlocked a shared vault can save a huge amount of personal space by giving common items to the guild's major crafters. Donate cloth, ore, wood, trophies, and other crafting items and then you won't have to worry about them. In return, you can get help equipping your characters and getting those large bags we talked about!

THE POWER OF GROUPING

Parties form when players want to adventure together. It's as simple as clicking on people, right-clicking on their picture when it appears, and inviting them into a group. Add more fun people while you play, and that's all there is to it. You're in a group, you're hacking through enemies, and a good time will be had by all.

PROS OF BEING IN A GROUP

- **You get a higher percentage of magical treasure.**
- **Experience per hour is generally much higher.**
- **Full guild groups earn much more influence for events they complete.**
- **The social aspect of play can be rewarding unto itself.**
- **Challenging content is more accessible.**

CONS FOR BEING IN A GROUP

- **At worst, someone could be a jerk.**

In truth, there aren't any cons as long as you play with people you like. The game rewards group play again and again. Soloing is always possible, and you aren't penalized for choosing it. However, groups have a higher kill rate and they finish more events per hour. That puts them hand and fist above soloers. In addition, *Guild Wars 2* doesn't knock your kill experience for having buddies around. Thus, you won't get one fifth of your experience by being in a full group. You still get plenty of experience for each kill, even if you inflict only a portion of the damage against the creature.

TAP EVERYTHING?

Some groups get a bit compulsive and try to divvy up their fighting so everyone gets to take on each monster, grab every item, and so forth. This is done with the idea that it maximizes experience and event completion. That's fairly true. Groups are at their "best" rates when everyone is able to hit all targets. More experience comes in, and events complete sooner because everyone is getting credit for each action.

However, getting too concerned about this is bad for most groups. Not all players are obsessed with perfect efficiency and completion rates. They're here to enjoy a game, and groups are already able to level quickly and burn through huge numbers of enemies. There's no need to boss everyone around toward one style of play.

If you like power leveling at maximum speed, find a few other people who enjoy that style of gaming. Have a blast! If you're more the type who wants to relax and ease through content, search for likeminded players. Don't mix and match unless you're not concerned and could go either way.

ALL THINGS FOR ALL PEOPLE

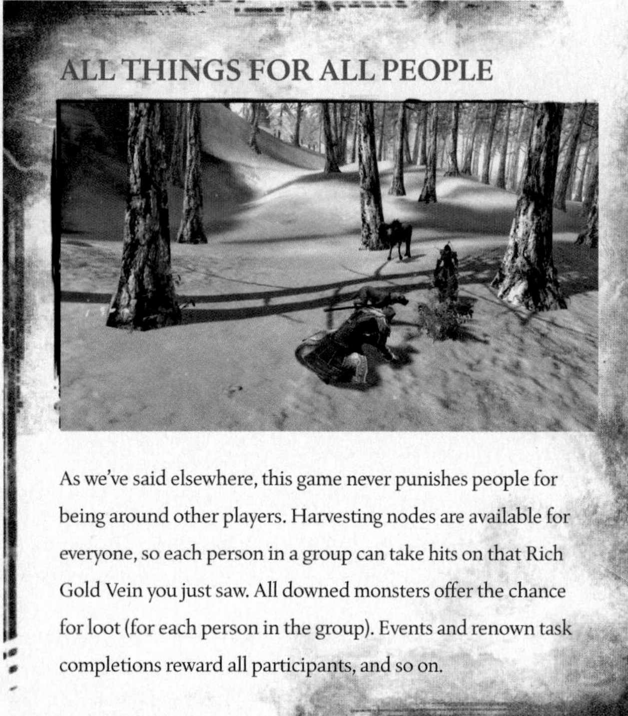

As we've said elsewhere, this game never punishes people for being around other players. Harvesting nodes are available for everyone, so each person in a group can take hits on that Rich Gold Vein you just saw. All downed monsters offer the chance for loot (for each person in the group). Events and renown task completions reward all participants, and so on.

HOW MANY PEOPLE DO WE NEED?

Soloers can level from 1-80 without a hitch, but they can't see the entire world and all of its events and content. Most regions have a few areas that are a bit tougher. You find group events (some of which can still be soloed), or more challenging areas where the monsters are thick and ready to mash anyone who comes near.

So how many players does it take to conquer the world?

- **Almost all standard events:** 1+ players
- **Group events:** Vary greatly, but many are possible with 3+ players
- **Dungeons:** Full groups of 5 players are usually required
- **Special World Events:** May take 10 or more players to defeat!

Most content in the game is made to scale based on how many people are participating. Standard events are made to be doable by a single person. They just get a bit harder as more and more players arrive, and you face additional enemies or are required to complete more objectives.

Group events scale this way too, but they assume a baseline that's balanced for a minimum of several characters. Thus, a soloer faces the same enemies as a small group, making it very hard to complete the event.

Dungeons do not scale because they're entirely balanced for five-person teams. An extremely skilled group can go in with fewer people, but it doesn't make sense to do so. There's nothing gained by heading into a place understaffed.

Scaling for most events can head all the way into the stratosphere. A number of world events can have 50 people (or more!) working together and still have the challenge shift appropriately.

WHAT TO DO IN A GROUP

Don't be anxious about joining others. The standards for play aren't that high; people won't expect you to be the god of the game. As long as you follow a few basic rules, you won't upset many people.

BASIC GROUP RULES

- **Be friendly.**
- **Watch your minimap and follow the group so people mostly stick together.**
- **Attack what other people are attacking.**
- **Don't act like a maniac and get killed constantly and then yell for people to come and save you.**

If you can handle those rules, you'll get along with the vast majority of players. This isn't a game where people need to assign healing duties, tanking, offtanking, aggro rules, and the like. Extremely high-end dungeon groups talk more about tactics before their fights, but even there the game demands a high level of personal skill in one's profession and not much in the way of meta gaming.

You can group with members of the same profession without being unbalanced. You can have entire teams of people in light armor without getting torn in half.

Other games have said, "Bring the player, not the class." It's entirely true in *Guild Wars 2*. Be a good player or just a friendly person and you're going to be fine.

THE TRADING POST

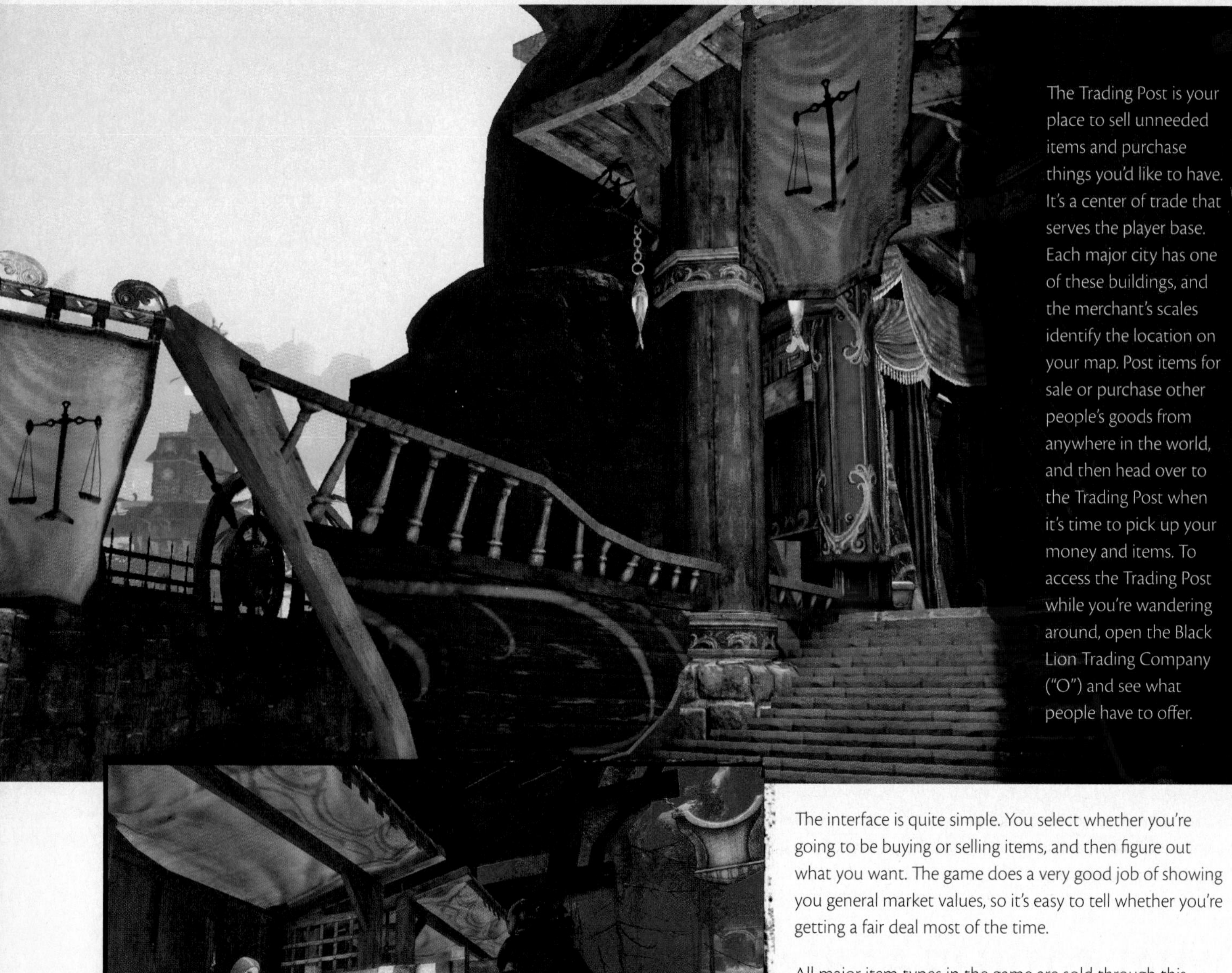

The Trading Post is your place to sell unneeded items and purchase things you'd like to have. It's a center of trade that serves the player base. Each major city has one of these buildings, and the merchant's scales identify the location on your map. Post items for sale or purchase other people's goods from anywhere in the world, and then head over to the Trading Post when it's time to pick up your money and items. To access the Trading Post while you're wandering around, open the Black Lion Trading Company ("O") and see what people have to offer.

The interface is quite simple. You select whether you're going to be buying or selling items, and then figure out what you want. The game does a very good job of showing you general market values, so it's easy to tell whether you're getting a fair deal most of the time.

All major item types in the game are sold through this interface. The listings are shown across all of the cities, so you won't have to worry about posting something in any specific location. Something listed in Hoelbrak is available in Divinity's Reach and other locales.

Items and money that are exchanged at the Trading Post stay there. When you want to collect them, go to the building in one of the major cities and switch to the Pick Up tab to get your stuff. Or, buy a Black Lion Trader Express from the Gem Store. This is extremely convenient and you're quite far away from the capitals (and don't have the time to drop whatever you're doing).

Because *Guild Wars 2* doesn't have a personal trading system, this is the only way to sell items between players; you can always trade freely through the mail system, but if you need money for your items and want to make sure you get it, the Trading Post is your solution!

USING FILTERS

Inside the Trading Post system, you can type in the name of the item you want (with the search bar up top), and that immediately takes you to any sales for that item. However, you might not know what you're looking for. That's where filters come in.

Click on the filters selection and then you can browse for materials by type, rarity, level, and so on. It really helps to let you search for a variety of weapons, armor pieces, and other goodies.

The categories for items include the following:

- **Armor:** Defensive equipment
- **Bags/Containers:** Storage items for your character
- **Consumables:** Armor dyes and other short-term usable items
- **Crafting Materials:** Items needed for creating weapons, food, armor, and bags
- **Gathering:** Items that allow you to gather resources from harvesting nodes
- **Gizmos:** Treasure chests
- **Minis:** Collectible creatures
- **Tools:** Salvage kits
- **Trinkets:** Accessories that augment your character's stats
- **Fine and Rare Crafting Materials:** Pieces of monsters that are used in crafting
- **Upgrade Components:** Usable items that attach to equipment to improve their stats
- **Weapons:** Offensive equipment

You can limit the level range of items that are displayed so you 'don't see anything too far below (or above) your character. This helps limit the massive selection of items so you're only seeing viable equipment pieces.

Search when you've finished making your filter selections, and then organize the items shown on the main page. Click on the categories at the top to sort the items by that listing: Item Name, Level, Price, Rarity, and # Available.

SELLING

When you select the Sell tab, the Trading Post shows you the items from your inventory and lets you know if there are any current offers for those items. In *Guild Wars 2*, it's possible to put a request out for an item even if it isn't listed at the time. If you see that your items are needed, look at the price and fulfill those orders for some quick cash.

Crafters should scour these "work for hire" type of bids to see what they can do. It's a wonderful way to get paid more while raising your skills and earning experience. Otherwise, click on the items you want to sell and then choose a price and quantity for your sale. People in a hurry can click "Match Lowest Seller" so they follow the trending market price instead of taking the time to figure out whether something should be undercut or ignored. You can also add items to an older listing if you're just contributing more of the same and want to match your existing offer.

It's a rather convenient system, and it doesn't take long to get used to it. Try it out with smaller sales at first, and soon you won't have to worry about whether you're messing anything up.

THE GEM STORE AND CURRENCY EXCHANGE

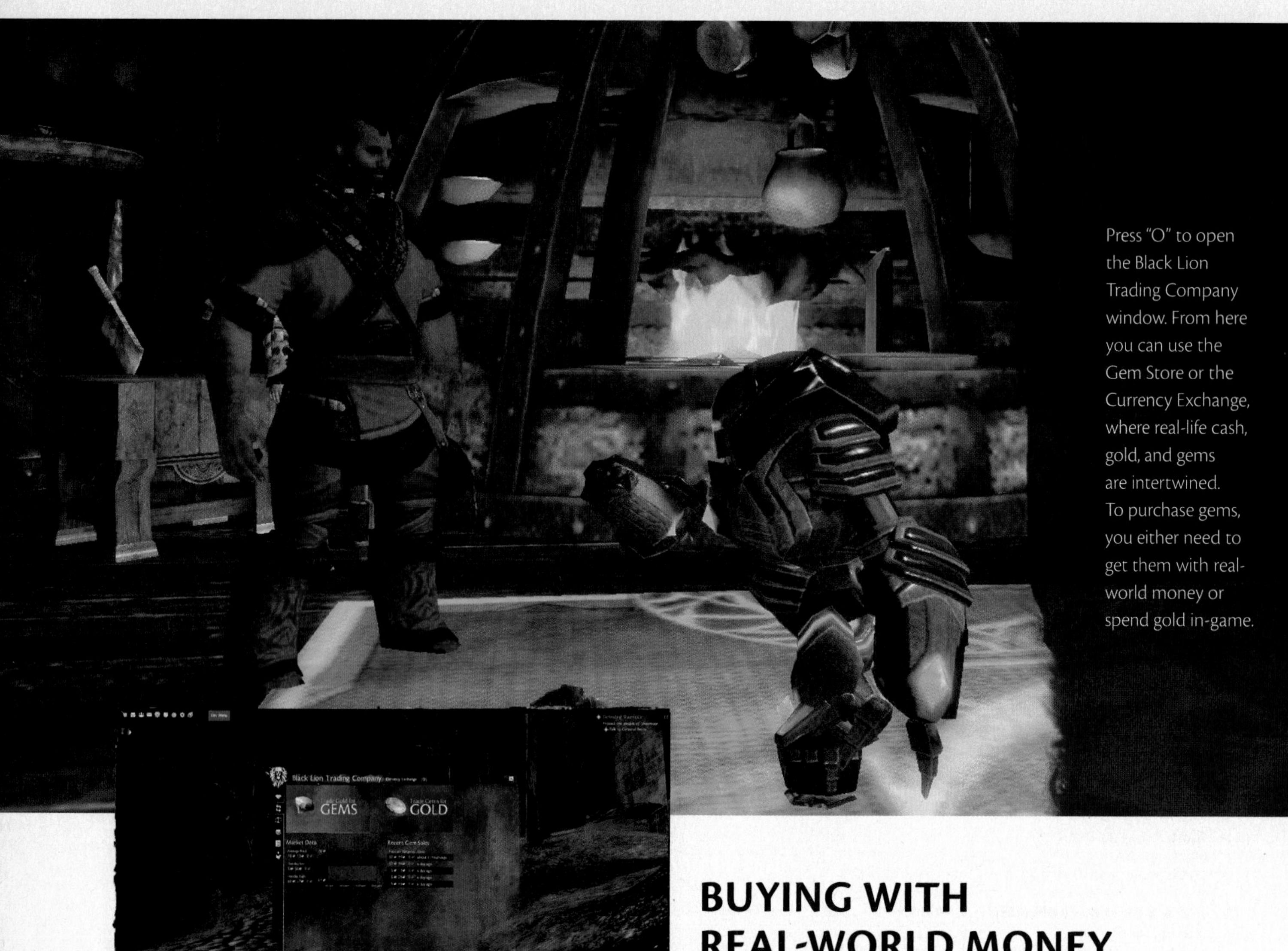

Press "O" to open the Black Lion Trading Company window. From here you can use the Gem Store or the Currency Exchange, where real-life cash, gold, and gems are intertwined. To purchase gems, you either need to get them with real-world money or spend gold in-game.

To buy gems with gold, go to the Currency Exchange and select "Trade Gold for Gems" to sell your money and collect gems. If you reverse this process, you can get gold by selling off gems. Buying during off periods and selling gems for gold during peaks is a good way to make money if you're willing to take some risk!

The in-game price of gems floats, based on how much demand there is for them. As more and more people purchase gems with in-game gold, the price of these items rises substantially. If you watch trends carefully, you can avoid paying quite as much gold for them by buying during periods of low sales. These times vary, but the system tracks the peaks and troughs so you can get an idea of when it is usually safer to buy (or sell) gems.

BUYING WITH REAL-WORLD MONEY

Real-world money, in-game gold, and gems are almost fully intertwined. Money can be used to purchase gems (and thus in-game gold as well). Gold can buy gems and thus buy anything else that gems have to offer, including the ability to convert them back into gold at a later point. Timed well, this earns you a profit for buying gems when they're cheap and selling them when they're expensive.

The only part of the system that is a one-way street is the use of real-world money. You cannot sell gems or gold for real-world cash.

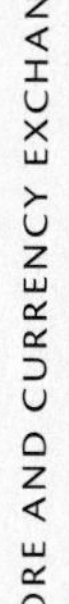

PLAYING THE ECONOMY

You can make speculative purchases through this system. If you think the price of gems is going to go up by a substantial amount, you're entirely free to buy a fair number with your gold and then sell the gems back for gold when the prices are higher. An example: Christmas is coming up, and you think there is going to be an infusion of new players. You deduce that some of them will be buying gems as soon as they can. You purchase a number of gems before the holiday hits, and then you sell them in the week following Christmas during a particularly high spike in gem valuation.

If you're into economics, this can be fun. It's a little game within a game for you, and making a profit is always a good thing. What's cool about the system is that you don't have to realize a loss even if you screw up and buy when the gems are higher than usual. Gems are always going to be useful for something, so holding onto an imprudent purchase isn't that painful. Just use the gems for fun and learn from the experience.

ITEMS ON THE GEM STORE

By now you're wondering what is available on the Gem Store. Let's get into that! Here are the general categories of items on the store.

GEM STORE CATEGORIES	TYPES OF ITEMS INCLUDED HERE
Promotions	Special Deals
Style	Town Clothes (Cool Non-Combat Outfits)
Consumable	Dyes, Chest Keys, Fun Effects
Support	Access to Banks, Trading Post Items, Bag Slots, etc.
Account	Bank Slot Upgrades, New Character Slots
Boosts	Temporary Boons (Crafting, XP, Etc.)
Minis	Collectible Creatures

Temporary boons last through death, so you won't lose your gems needlessly. Feel free to buy them any time you think they'd be useful. The items are delivered to your mailbox, and you can carry them around until it's time to use them. The buffs' timers don't start until they're used, so hold off on activating them. Wait for a major event, battle, or group to form. That's when you use buffs. You get the most out of them that way.

Account upgrades are permanent. They're often a very good use of your time and money.

Town clothes have no tangible benefit, but they're fun for roleplaying or goofing around.

Transmutation Stones let you combine the visual appearance, stats, and upgrades from two different items. They're an exceptionally good way to give your character a unique look without sacrificing damage, survivability, or utility. Get the equipment you like from special events, dungeon runs, etc., and then combine that item's appearance with the stats from higher-level equipment that you find or purchase.

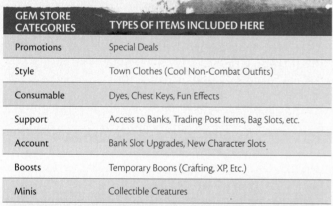

MINIS

Minis are found at the Black Lion Trading Company and represent cool creatures from all over the world. You can travel with these buddies or keep them in your collection to see how many you can find.

To use minis, put them in your inventory and right-click on the pet that you want to bring out. Select "Use" and watch the creature come out. If you want to send it back home, you can deposit it in your collection at any time (also by right-clicking).

ACHIEVEMENTS

Bring up your Hero window ("H") and then look at the achievements tab. This is where you find information about daily, monthly, and permanent achievements. You get to see your current point total (a sum of the achievements you've earned across all of your characters).

The front page lists your daily total, which is important for grabbing bonus experience. That isn't tracked by account; it's character based, so you're able to switch between your characters and grab daily achievements for each. We'll get into that in just a moment.

To learn about the various achievements, click on the major categories on the left side of the screen. The page switches to display all of the achievements within that category, the points you've earned, and the progress you've made.

If you complete enough types of achievements, you unlock titles that can be selected from this screen. Find one that suits your character and go after it!

DAILY ACHIEVEMENTS

Daily achievements are available every 24 hours for each character you play. When you reach each tier of performance in the daily categories, you receive bonus experience. The amount you get is based on the level of your character, so the effect scales well over the course of your leveling.

Daily achievements aren't a necessary part of improving your character, but they're fun and easy to accomplish. These are awarded for types of play that you're going to be interested in anyway: killing enemies, gathering crafting items, and so forth.

DAILY ACHIEVEMENT CATEGORIES

- **Kills**
- **Kill Variety**
- **Gathering (Wood, Metal, Cooking Ingredients)**
- **Completing Events**

Daily achievements aren't worth many points toward your overall score, but they add up well over time. Players who are heavily involved with multiple alts end up having a hefty score.

MONTHLY ACHIEVEMENTS

Monthly achievements are tracked by account, so your participation in WvW and events contributes toward your total even if you have a variety of alts doing the work. You get rewards for these achievements too, though it takes more time to unlock them. It's better to let the goals accrue naturally rather than to focus on a specific type of play you don't normally enjoy.

That said, it's a fun challenge to work on the Exp Survivor achievement. You can have a good time forcing yourself to play with that air of wariness. "If I die, I'll lose my progress." It might be frustrating to some players, but for others it's a great way to ratchet up the intensity for their fighting. It makes the consequences a little more tangible.

MONTHLY ACHIEVEMENT CATEGORIES

- **WvW Player Kills**
- **Event Participation**
- **Salvage Kit Uses**
- **Exp Survivor**

PERMANENT ACHIEVEMENTS

All other groups of achievements are long-term goals. They are account-based and you're encouraged to work on them with multiple characters, though most can be accomplished with just a few.

PERMANENT ACHIEVEMENT CATEGORIES

- **Slayer**
- **Hero**
- **PvP Conqueror**
- **Tradesman**
- **Explorer**
- **Fashion**
- **Weapon Master**
- **Community**
- **Hall of Monuments**

Many achievements complete even when you aren't trying to work on them. Almost all of the things you do as a character are tracked, so casual, hardcore, and compulsive players alike reap the benefits of whatever they enjoy doing.

For the most points, make sure your characters cover all five races and each of the crafts, and that you have someone who can use each type of weapon. Together, this gets you a massive number of achievement points. Split up your heroes while leveling so you conquer different regions. This is fun because you get to see more of the game world, and it also gets you additional points because you are rewarded for exploring more places!

COMMUNICATING WITH OTHER PEOPLE

Social games reward social people in a variety of ways. Though you're free to go out on your own, it's fun and often useful to have allies around. Let's talk about the ways you can coordinate with other players to form groups, maintain a guild, trade equipment, and roleplay.

CHATTING AWAY

Using the /local channel is the most basic form of communication. If your hero is in the local channel, you can type text and any players relatively close by in the same region can see it.

"Would you like to form a group?" "Thanks for helping me!" "Your hammer is sick, where did you find that?"

Whatever you want to talk about, local speech is only limited by distance and good manners.

When you're looking for a group to help with difficult content, this is a valuable tool. Ask around in your guild, if you have one, but also look for allies working in the same area as your character. They're going to benefit from having another hero around, so it's often in their best interest to form a group with you.

You can switch chat channels by clicking on the small area where it says "/local" in the lower left side of the screen. This channel also changes if you type **/local, /guild, /party, /squad, /team,** or ***/whisper***. All of these commands let the game know you're trying to talk to different people in different ways.

TYPES OF SPEECH

COMMAND/ CHANNEL	HOW YOUR CHARACTER SPEAKS
/guild	Only characters in the guild you're currently representing can hear you; distance is not a factor
/local	Local players can hear you, and distance is the only factor in who can see what you're typing
/party	The other members of your party can see what you're typing, regardless of distance
/squad	Members of your PvP squad can see what you're typing, regardless of distance
/team	Everyone on your team can see what you're typing, regardless of whisper
/whisper	This sends a private message to one named character on your server (Example: **/whisper Emil I'm killing Centaurs in Kessex**)
/map	A region-wide message to all allies; use this sparingly

There are other ways to communicate. If players are offline when you want to message them, consider sending some mail. The mail system lets you send text, money, or items to other players, even if they aren't on to receive the letter.

MAIL CALL

Click on the mail icon at the top of the screen. Write a message by clicking "Compose" in the lower part of the window. Choose a character's name before you do anything else. This determines where the mail is going. Messages are account based, so it's easy to use the shortest name of the person you're messaging. If someone's characters are named Galondasthrek, Pillbugason, and Trey, then go ahead and message Trey even if you usually group with Galondasthrek. It's just easier this way, and the letter still goes where it needs to go.

Trading items and equipment via mail is a great way to enhance the utility of groups. Make an agreement to freely trade useful equipment and then send the items you find to each other so everyone gets equipped as quickly as possible. The money you forfeit in lost sales pales in comparison to the amount you save by getting constant blue and green quality upgrades for your character.

Don't bother sending every item as soon as you find it. It's best to wait until people are repairing and selling. That way you won't fall behind and get attacked while you're halfway through your mail.

GUILD CHAT

Each guild has its own style and flavor when it comes to chatting. You might be in a mature guild where people are pretty formal, talk about what they need, and that's about it. Quiet, eh? Or, you could be surrounded by a raucous bunch that jokes and talks constantly (about everything under the sun).

As we always suggest: find the guild that matches your personality. People can learn how to play their professions better over time. They can discover the best ways to find loot or beat events in *Guild Wars 2*. But they won't change much as people. Look for a group that fits who you are and it'll be much more enjoyable to spend days, weeks, months, or even longer hanging out with them!

Always read or listen to the guild officers' rules of conduct for the guild. Avoid language that is forbidden in public channels.

YOUR CONTACT LIST

Press "Y" to open your contact list. This system makes it easier to find friends when they're online, especially if they don't join the same guild. When you have a good time with others, ask if you can put them on your friends list, and then group with them in the future.

Similarly, you should block anyone who really upsets you. There is no need to get into fights and deal with major problems when you're trying to have fun at a game. If there are people you just can't stand, block them and enjoy the sound of silence. It's better than causing guild drama or looking like an idiot by arguing with someone who won't listen to you anyway!

FINDING AND DEVELOPING A GUILD

Starting a guild is simple. When you want to form one, open the Guild Window ("G") and select a name and an abbreviation for your guild. You won't need to visit a city and register until it's time to deal with emblems, guild banks, and other guild services that take time to unlock. In the beginning, you just need a name that is catchy, fun, and will draw in the right kind of people (ones you enjoy playing with).

But you don't have to start your own guild. If you'd prefer to be a follower instead of a leader, find someone cool who seems to be good at taking care of things. When you have fun grouping with that person, ask about the guild he or she is in. You might get an invite that easily, or find a way to apply over the next couple of days.

In most cases, it's not hard to find or create a guild. The real issue is how to develop things once you're there.

GUILD FEATURES

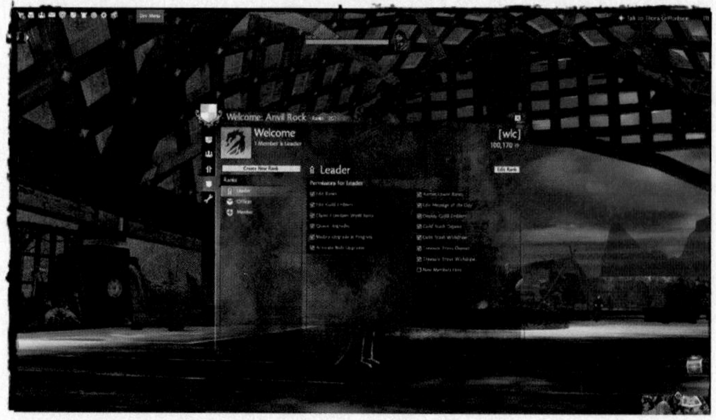

Once you're in a guild, the Guild Window brings up new choices. The default is to look at the history for your guild—things that have happened recently to affect its members.

Using the tabs on the left side of the window, you can switch to other pages. The roster tells you who is in the guild, what levels and skills they have, and where they are. Upgrades shows the temporary boons and permanent bonuses available to guild members. We'll talk more about those shortly. Finally, there is a page for guild ranks so you can see who is permitted to do what.

Permissive guilds might allow all but the most recent members to freely use the guild bank, chat with each other, do as they please, and work with guild influence. Other guilds reserve many organizational aspects of guild play for officers, and their rank and file members are free to relax and just play the game.

In general, the larger the guild, the more restrictions you need to have (for everyone's protection). It's usually possible to guarantee that everyone in a 10-person guild of real-life buddies will behave. You can't make that promise with 40 players who have barely met. Make sure the rules for your guild match the level of trust and comfort that players have for each other. It's in everyone's best interest.

GUILD INFLUENCE

Guilds have their own progression in *Guild Wars 2*. There are many special perks they unlock by spending influence. Guild influence accrues when members of the guild complete events out in the world. Solo characters get a tiny amount of credit for everything they do. Guild groups get FAR more points for each event, making it possible to purchase upgrades much more often.

Having a larger guild makes this process easier, by nature of having more people online throughout the day. However, an organized guild can outperform a large guild that doesn't work together (up to a point).

The best way to get influence is to have members stick together in small groups of guildies. Have them level, get money, and do whatever they want to do while hanging out with each other. This lets the guild bond while the points fly in.

Dungeon runs in guild groups are quite lucrative as well, though they're harder to put together than a small event party. Make sure people who are forming dungeon runs are fair about starting times, group goals, and so forth. If you have a guild website, consider having members post there so they can organize and keep their in-game time free to have fun instead of hanging around in guild chat getting people together.

TYPES OF GUILD UPGRADES

Once your guild has some influence, invest it in something that most (or all) of your players would enjoy. There are four categories of upgrades: Politics, Art of War, Economy, and Infrastructure.

Politics help your guild strut their stuff around other people. You can make an emblem, show off how cool your guild looks, summon public boons to aid non-guilded players, and so on. If you want to have a big guild and draw in lots of followers, this is a decent path.

Art of War is purely for guilds that enjoy PvP. A huge number of boons are waiting here. They make it easier to dominate in WvW encounters.

Economy upgrades help your guild members accrue karma, gold, magic items, and experience. While leveling or farming for cash, these are the best upgrades around. PvE guilds enjoy these benefits tremendously.

Infrastructure upgrades are convenient. They help the guild trade items through a guild bank. You can also unlock an ability to research multiple upgrades simultaneously, and that's rather useful for large guilds that have a lot of influence to spend.

SPENDING THE POINTS

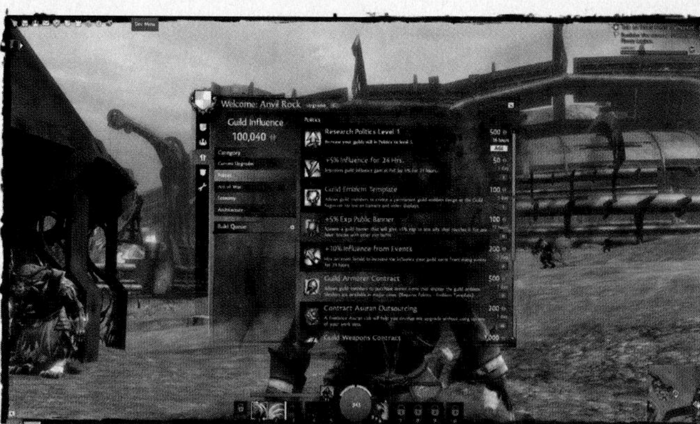

The guild leader and his or her officers are going to make most of the choices for influence upgrades. Expect most guilds to talk about the direction of the upgrades publicly; there might be a vote, a general discussion, or whatever. When a decision is made, someone queues research and a timer starts.

Most guild upgrades take hours to complete. The influence cost is deducted immediately, but it's possible to cancel the research and get a full refund at any time before the process completes.

Permanent upgrades take effect as soon as the research is done. Temporary buffs don't work that way. Instead, they complete and become available to the guild. The timer on those boons won't start until someone activates the boon. You won't have to worry about timing research so it finishes at the optimal time. Go ahead and queue things overnight, over multiple days, or whatever.

TIERS OF RESEARCH

You can't have your guild go after all of the best items until everyone has paid his or her dues. Each category of guild upgrades is divided into tiers. The best research choices are often in the higher tiers, and you have to purchase each tier in turn before getting all the way up.

All categories have five tiers, and your guild starts at level zero! Allocate influence for advancement and for the boons you need.

CRAFTING

Each character can learn two crafts that take basic items and turn them into useful equipment. There are eight crafts in the game, so it's possible to learn them all with four characters. You can switch between crafts with even a single character if you find that one doesn't suit you, but there is a modest penalty if you do this. Your old skill won't be deleted, but you can't access it without returning to a trainer and retaking the craft (and dealing with the financial penalty yet again).

CRAFTS IN GUILD WARS 2

SKILL	PURPOSE
Armorsmiths	Make heavy armor
Artificers	Create magical weapons (staves, focuses, scepters)
Cooks	Prepare food for temporary boons
Huntsmen	Craft ranged weapons (torches, warhorns, bows, and pistols)
Jewelcrafters	Improve gems to upgrade existing equipment and craft rings and necklaces
Leatherworkers	Create medium armor
Tailors	Make light armor
Weaponsmiths	Craft a variety of melee weapons

We've devoted an entire chapter in this book to crafting, so we don't want to go over everything just yet. The basic idea is that each craft has basic recipes you learn by working with your trainer and leveling the skill, and you need to unlock more advanced recipes through discovery.

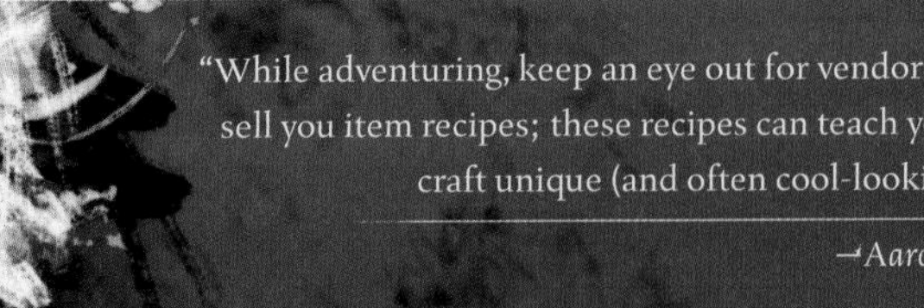

"While adventuring, keep an eye out for vendors who will sell you item recipes; these recipes can teach you how to craft unique (and often cool-looking) gear!"

—*Aaron Sebenius*

Discovery is a process where you combine simple crafted items and sometimes trophies you get from killing monsters. Trophies are made into insignias, and those become major pieces for crafting higher quality equipment.

This sounds rather complex—and it is, at first. You need to have a massive amount of storage space, some spare cash, and plenty of time to get good at crafting. Don't stress yourself out about leveling crafting quickly to keep up with your main character. That's often quite difficult to do. Instead, think of crafting as a way to help your secondary character (and other people).

Leveling crafting at its own speed takes off so much pressure and gives your character permission to level at any speed while having a good time and getting more money. The spare cash you make with a high-level primary character opens many doors for your future crafting.

WHAT ARE SALVAGE KITS?

These kits are purchased from merchants in many cities and towns, and they can be found on specific karma vendors. Salvage Kits break down many types of equipment or salvageable gear you find while fighting monsters. Double-click on the kit in your inventory and then click on the item(s) you wish to break down into their components. This is an extremely good way to get materials for your crafting efforts. Though you lose money on the Salvage Kit and the depletion of sellable loot, you save more money by avoiding Trading Post prices for your raw materials!

DID I JUST LEVEL UP?

Crafting gives you experience for each item you create. More involved items are worth even more experience. Just as your crafting skill increases, so does your character's knowledge of the world. Extremely dedicated crafters might even use crafting as their primary means of leveling. People who have a guild to support their advancement (or other characters that feed them items) can go pretty much all the way to the cap by switching between all of the trades and learning each in turn!

DUNGEON DELVING

This is another advanced concept that gets its own chapter later in the guide. Dungeons are areas that only allow a single group of heroes to enter. Thus, you end up with one to five characters facing off against some of the toughest challenges in the game. It's like an extended group event that is tied into a complex story. There are a number of these throughout the world, and each has several versions.

The Story Mode of each dungeon is the first version of it that you encounter. Story Modes are easier because you get walked through the dungeon with some form of assistance. These versions of the dungeons are also a little bit lower level, often being five levels before the Exploration Mode of the same dungeon.

Once you complete Story Mode, you unlock Exploration Mode for that dungeon in the future. Enemies are tougher, the dungeon itself changes, and new choices you make will define which bosses you'll encounter. It's all quite interesting and makes the dungeons much more replayable than they would be in other games.

SIMPLE DUNGEON RULES

Always have access to close-range and long-range weapons. Don't come to a dungeon with a single weapon set and think you're good to go. There are various challenges to face, and you don't want to be the player who says, "I can't do this." Come to dungeons with several sets of weapons. Preferably, have something for crowd control to keep enemies stunned. Have a set for ranged combat and kiting. And also keep a set for pure damage output. Depending on your profession, something for survivability sure wouldn't hurt either!

"Consider equipping a mix of ranged and melee weapons if your profession can weapon swap. Some enemies are easier with a ranged weapon equipped."

—*Peter Larkin*

Repair everything before you go inside. You don't want your gear to break as soon as your character dies. It's easy to get killed in dungeons, especially when you're learning each new area.

In the same way, make sure that your inventory is fairly open. You don't want to miss out on a great new weapon because your bags were full and you stopped looting! Or, you don't want to hold up the group because you have to go through your bags and decide what to keep or destroy after something especially nice drops.

Try new things and new ideas. If a fight seems way too difficult, you're probably not fighting optimally. Try spreading out and using attacks that give the party maximum survivability. Or push everyone's damage against a single enemy and see if it can be burned down before the fight gets too intense. Look for specific problems during the battle; if you can identify the source of your character's deaths, it'll help immensely. "That guy has a damage shield, and we're all killing ourselves on it." Ha! So stop damage against that creep while his damage shield is up.

We'll go over these tricks, and quite a few more, in the future.

FIGHTING AGAINST OTHER PLAYERS

You already know what we're going to say here, don't you? This too is a subject that demands much more attention than we can afford to give it here. *Guild Wars 2* tests your skills considerably. PvP only has a few ways to get an edge in this game without having practice and raw skill. Gear only gets you, well, not very far at all. PvP is about picking the best mix of skills for the fight at hand and using those skills to perfection.

Structured PvP is a carefully measured challenge to ensure that competitive teams have the most professional environment possible. Leveling, PvE gear, expensive potions, and other unbalancing elements are *not* a part of this. *Guild Wars 2* wants to see who can play the best, not who can spend the most time and money on his or her character.

World versus World (WvW, or WvWvW) is more open to participants who want to play as part of a larger team. Instead of battling other small groups, there is the potential to take entire keeps, scour multiple maps of territory, and procure benefits for your server along the way.

Gear is a factor in WvW, so lower-level players are at a disadvantage, but that doesn't stop people from being able to contribute. It just provides incentive to acquire higher-end PvE gear and thus be well-equipped for both types of play.

When you're ready to jump into this side of the game, go to the PvP tab in your Hero window and come into the Mists. From there you can configure your hero's settings and PvP equipment.

"If you want to try out different specs and see all of your traits, press 'H' and go to the mists! Re-speccing is free and all abilities and traits are available right away."

—*Chris "Cool Guy" Roberts*

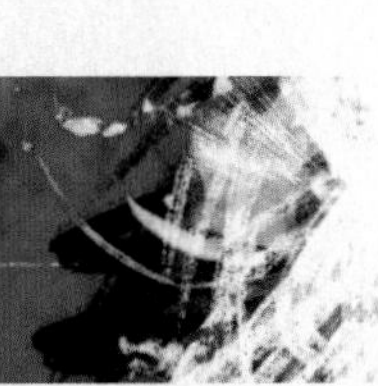

FIRST EXPERIENCES

Once you've created a character, the game places you into a short instanced area. This begins your character's personal story while introducing you to some of *Guild Wars 2*'s concepts and enemies. We'll quickly walk you through these to help get things going.

ASURA

The asuran people have been driven to the surface of Tyria. There isn't time or reason to lament this fact. It's better to find solutions! Your people have been busy at work creating new golems and machines to help with living on the surface. It's gone well for the most part, yet there are occasional slips. Today, there has been such an accident, and mad golems are suddenly running amok. Someone has to stop them, and at least you're carrying a weapon.

EXPLOSIVE INTELLECT

Your hero stands in an open pavilion, near another asura. Talk to your buddy there (Robb) and see what's going on. Right-click on nearby NPCs to hear what they have to say. After hearing about the golems, you're asked to find the Peacemakers (as if they'd know what to do).

FIND PEACEMAKER GEZZI

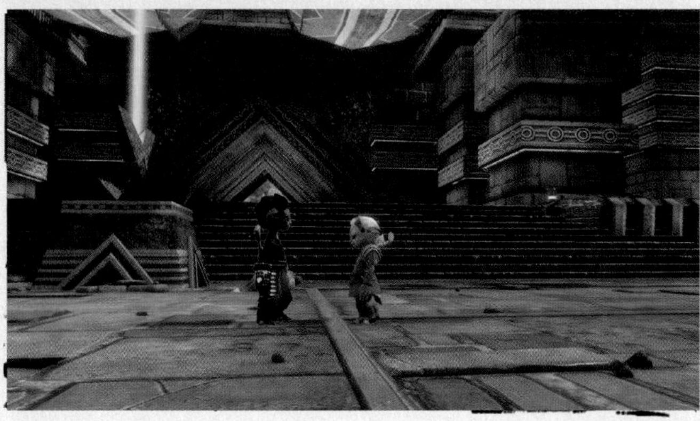

A green icon moves east on your minimap to show this new goal. The minimap is at the bottom right side of the screen. It shows the region around your character, and story goals always appear in green (either as a direction to travel or as a specific target if you get close enough).

Run through the golem-infested area toward that goal. You don't have to fight these aggressive golems, but it's a good way to start practicing with your weapons. You learn weapon skills by killing enemies with different varieties of weapons. Each kill unlocks a percentage of the next available skill, and you can check on your progress by highlighting the skill in question.

Peacemaker Gezzi isn't far away. Talk to him and see if you can lend your assistance. An asuran woman named Zojja has taken the lead in stopping this golem uprising. She's farther southeast, but Gezzi has his hands full with the golems that are already here. Step up and help out! Zojja is a major figure in Rata Sum, and getting to know her could help your career.

FIND THE PORTAL TO THE GOLEMAGICAL INSTITUTE

Fight your way to the southeast. Attack golems that are already in battle to have an easier time raking in kills. During these early encounters, it's fine to walk up to your targets, press "1," and let the autoattack do its work. This doesn't kill targets quickly, but it's very easy.

LEARNING TO FIGHT

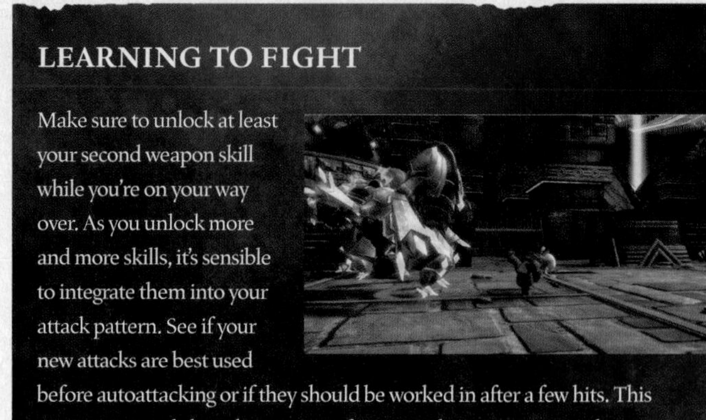

Make sure to unlock at least your second weapon skill while you're on your way over. As you unlock more and more skills, it's sensible to integrate them into your attack pattern. See if your new attacks are best used before autoattacking or if they should be worked in after a few hits. This varies immensely based on your profession and current weapon choice.

SHINY!

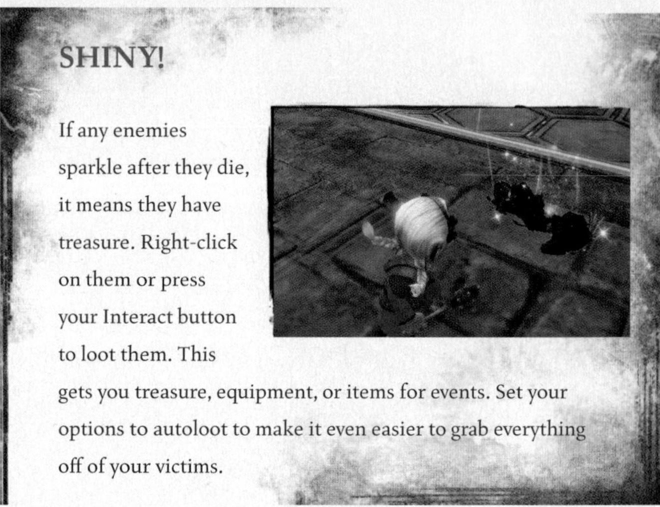

If any enemies sparkle after they die, it means they have treasure. Right-click on them or press your Interact button to loot them. This gets you treasure, equipment, or items for events. Set your options to autoloot to make it even easier to grab everything off of your victims.

When you arrive in the southeast, another asura tells you that Zojja has gone through a portal into the Golemagical Institute. Follow her through the pink gateway and teleport to the institute.

DESTROY THE INQUEST GOLEMS

Approach Zojja on the other side of the portal. She is in the middle of a confrontation. She and some Inquest operatives are staring each other down. The Inquest krewe is a group that has been destabilizing asuran politics lately. They have some pretty radical ideas (and not in a good way).

A fight soon begins. You can tell this because the text on the right side of your screen updates, and there is a telltale "ding" noise to get your attention.

You have to fight five waves of Inquest golems and operatives. Use "Tab" (or whatever button you've assigned) to target the enemies in the open room ahead. Approach and attempt to kill them while Zojja and her golem assist. Stay near these allied NPCs to ensure you have a safer time in this long fight.

HEALING SKILLS

Your health shows up in red at the bottom of the screen. If it gets all the way to zero, your character will collapse and be at risk of dying if he or she can't defeat an enemy or receive help in short order. It's better to keep your health near its full value whenever possible.

Look at the skill assigned to number "6" on your keyboard. This is your profession's default healing skill. Use this during fights to keep your health as high as possible. Over time, you'll earn skill points and get to unlock other healing abilities, but the default ones are often quite good in a variety of situations.

Keep blasting through Inquest targets until five waves of the enemies have fallen. This triggers a new event, as a prototype golem begins to activate. The fight just got a whole lot bigger!

PROTOTYPE X

This new golem type is impressive. It has arm cannons for ranged fighting, it can pound anything close by, and the sucker can sure take some punishment! During tougher encounters like this, you might collapse at some point. If that happens, you have to rally by healing yourself (with the "4" key once it becomes available).

Ranged heroes should watch the ground while attacking Prototype X. When the golem starts marking spots in red, that's a sign to close in toward the golem. You can avoid the ranged attacks as the enemy spins around and shoots at everything farther off. Back away afterward to avoid the golem's melee attacks.

Melee characters don't have to worry about the ranged weaponry, but they take damage somewhat consistently throughout the fight.

If you have a melee weapon, use your healing skill as often as possible to keep yourself in good shape. Back away if your health gets too low at any point, and give your healing skill time to cool down. Use it and return to the fight when you're ready.

You can target most parts of Prototype X's body, and the damage still goes to the core of this creature. You won't waste your damage by hitting it on the arms or wherever you target. Just make sure you're hitting the golem and continue to do so until it breaks down.

Afterward, a short scene plays and then you're taken out of the instance. You gain level 2 and enter Metrica Province. That's the low-level zone for starting asuran characters. You'll meet other players, see a huge range of events, and get to continue your story (whenever you want, and at your own pace).

The portal behind your hero leads into Rata Sum, the capital city of your people. Go in there now, or after some adventuring, to get waypoints, see the sights, and use the city's many merchants.

To learn more about Metrica Province, and about the other regions of Tyria, see our World chapter. We'll walk you through many more events.

CHARR

You've joined the legion! This isn't some gentle human army. You're going to fight for a living. Hell, you're going to fight just to live. There are Ascalonian ghosts all over the place, and who knows what else will stand in the way of charr supremacy. The gods are dead. Let's see if we can put the Elder Dragons down next.

FURY OF THE DEAD

The Ascalonians are restless again. From the ground itself they surge, fighting the legionnaires without any way to settle the battle permanently. Your charr starts near the site of the conflict. Look for your map on the lower right side of the screen. The green symbol directs you toward Legionnaire Tosia Domesplitter. Walk southeast until you meet her.

Right-click on Tosia to talk to her. She'll let you know what to do next, and a new waypoint appears on your map immediately afterward.

FIGHT YOUR WAY TO THE FRONT

Continue southeast into Vir's Gate. There are Ascalonians and charr everywhere. Kill the pale spirits as you go, and practice your combat techniques.

THE HEART OF A CHARR

Whether you use magic, blades, or technology, you are a fighter. Charr are born for struggle and glory. Kill Ascalonians and use this practice to learn new weapon skills. Watch them unlock at the bottom of the screen, where your number keys are listed. Each kill gets you closer to the next skill for your current weapon set.

Try to have at least your second skill unlocked before you get to the end of Vir's Gate.

THE SPOILS OF WAR

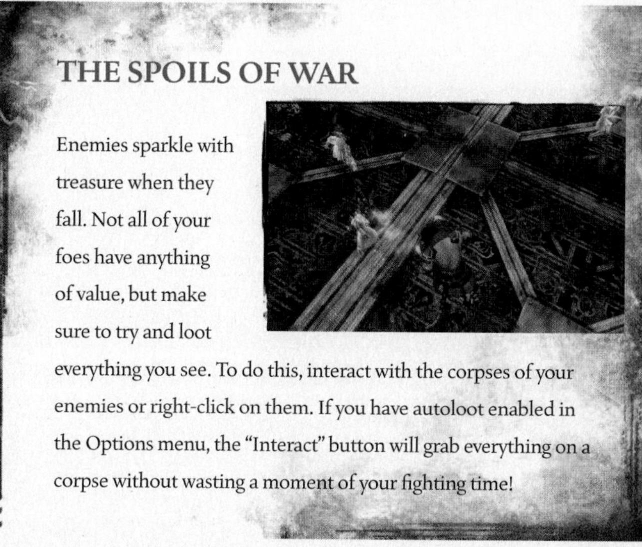

Enemies sparkle with treasure when they fall. Not all of your foes have anything of value, but make sure to try and loot everything you see. To do this, interact with the corpses of your enemies or right-click on them. If you have autoloot enabled in the Options menu, the "Interact" button will grab everything on a corpse without wasting a moment of your fighting time!

Centurion Gracchus Krysknife has been injured. Talk to Gracchus and learn more about this battle. The centurion is too badly injured to go on, and you must take up the call to arms.

GET INTO THE CRYPT GATE

Leave the centurion and make for the crypt to the east. A powerful human spirit is down there, and he's leading these ghosts in their fight. Destroying the lord offers only temporary respite, but it must be done!

Use the mortars nearby to clear out a few spirits if you think that's fun, or just kill your way down the path ahead. There are more than enough targets to keep you entertained.

A MOMENT'S REST

Characters heal naturally if they stay outside of battle for more than a few moments. When that isn't an option, use the skill linked to number "6" on your keyboard. This is always a healing ability; these work quite well to stave off death when you're in the thick of battle. All professions have healing skills.

JOIN RYTLOCK BRIMSTONE IN BARRADIN'S VAULTS

The great war hero Rytlock Brimstone is already down in the crypt vaults. Hurry into the depths and follow him. There are enough charr already fighting here that you can rush past almost all of the Ascalonians if you're itching to meet up with Rytlock.

When you meet the hero at the back of the crypt, he's already engaging the ghosts. Help him fight four waves of the spirits, including Duke Barradin, when the dead leader of the troops manifests. He'll be the fourth wave of the fight. Once he's badly injured, the duke retreats to the back of the room and possesses the statue above a tomb. Now the fight is truly epic!

DUKE BARRADIN

The statue gives Duke Barradin far more power and protection, so he won't be dispersed without taking some punishment. Rytlock and the other charr attack him directly. The ghost uses fear, melee attacks, and sometimes a more distant strike to knock down his enemies.

Early in the fight, your hero goes down from the ghost's sudden onslaught. This is a way to show you what happens when your character goes into a downed state. To rally out of it, wait until the skill under ability "4" lights up, and use that to heal yourself. This rallies your character and gets you back into the engagement. Killing enemies with the "1" key would have done the same thing. Do that if any of the ghosts attack your character while you're healing.

Now you're ready for blood!

To melee the ghost, jump onto his tomb and attack directly from there. You can watch the statue's health fall while you do this. If you're using a ranged weapon instead, stay slightly to the side so you aren't hit by as many of the ghost's melee attacks.

Ascalonians are summoned to aid their duke throughout the fight. Kill most of them, but always leave one alive and injured. If you go down during any portion of the engagement, kill the lone spirit to rally yourself and return to the fight.

Use your healing skill often to stay in fine fighting form. Soon enough, the duke will fall back into the ether.

After this victory, your charr goes to the village of Smokestead, on the western side of the Plains of Ashford. You're now in the main portion of *Guild Wars 2*. The portal to your west goes to the charr capital city (the Black Citadel). Everything to the east is filled with events and adventure! Go out and meet friends, gain levels, and continue your personal story whenever you wish.

Look up the Plains of Ashford in our World chapter if you'd like to keep going with this walkthrough. Or, you can explore and do whatever you like. You're a charr; you only follow the legion's orders.

HUMAN

Kryta was the only human nation in the land that did not fall under the shadows of the charr invasion and the resulting times of destruction. Holed up in Divinity's Reach, the people of Kryta are still fighting just to survive. Though the charr legions no longer press west through the Shiverpeak Mountains, the centaurs are now becoming just as great a threat. Heroes have to stand tall against the darkness to protect what is left of humanity in Tyria. A new battle in that war is just about to begin.

THE DEFENSE OF SHAEMOOR

You begin in the village of Shaemoor, outside the capital city. Centaurs have been increasingly bold in approaching Divinity's Reach with their raiding parties, and the region has been overrun by their forces. Talk to Corporal Beirne (by right-clicking the soldier) on the road into Shaemoor, where you begin. He'll urge your hero to get to the village inn, where the defenders are rallying.

Follow the road south and look at the bottom of your screen. On the right side is your minimap. A green arrow leads your hero toward the inn. Go inside as soon as you find it, and look for Sergeant Walters at the back of the building.

Sergeant Walters has too much on her hands. She's organizing the defenders here, but there are civilians to protect. When the call comes in to help the soldiers at the garrison, she doesn't have anyone to spare. It's your turn to step up.

DEFEND THE GARRISON

Agree to go to the garrison in the sergeant's place. Fight your way out of the inn, and take the eastern road toward the garrison.

TAKE THE BATTLE TO THEM!

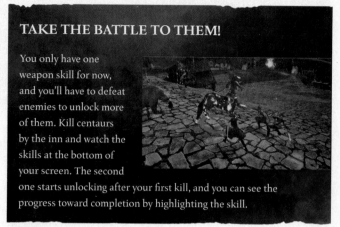

You only have one weapon skill for now, and you'll have to defeat enemies to unlock more of them. Kill centaurs by the inn and watch the skills at the bottom of your screen. The second one starts unlocking after your first kill, and you can see the progress toward completion by highlighting the skill.

SEE IF THE RAIDERS HAVE ANYTHING USEFUL

Fallen centaurs sometimes sparkle. That means they have treasure for your hero. Interact with the body or right-click on the fallen enemy to get their treasure. This is the same way you interact with items that spawn on the ground (for events and such).

Use the autoloot selection from the Options menu to ensure that you grab treasure from your enemies without wasting any time.

There's a bridge at the end of the eastern road. Cross it to enter the garrison and expect a large assault shortly after you arrive. Logan Thackeray and his troops are holding the line against the approaching centaurs, but they'll sure appreciate the help. Attackers are using the southern bridge to enter the fort. Stay near the bridge and hit the centaurs as they come in.

There are several waves of these troops, and then champion Modniir High Sage attacks. He's the leader of the centaur raiding party. Join the human defenders and pile on against the champion. Bring him to low health with your attacks, and don't be surprised when he turns tail. The champion flees back across the bridge and summons a mighty earth elemental.

PROTECT YOURSELF AS WELL AS THE VILLAGERS

If you're injured while fighting the centaurs, use the skill tied to the number "6" key on your keyboard. That is the default healing skill for your profession, and it allows your character to restore health during battle or between fights. The cooldowns for healing abilities are substantial, so you can't spam them to keep yourself at full health forever. Wait until you're around half health to use most of them, and see if that works well for your given profession.

Cross the bridge and enter the southern field. That's where the earth elemental rises. It has smaller elementals to support its attack, but you have Logan and his soldiers at your side. You must not fail!

EARTH ELEMENTAL

Your character falls to the ground shortly after the battle begins. In this downed state, you only have four possible skills. Use the one under skill "4" to heal your character and rally. Killing enemies is another way to rally while you're in a downed state.

Once you rally, take the fight to the earth elemental. Attack it by targeting any portion of its body. The gigantic monster requires quite a few hits to destroy, but the other soldiers are doing enough damage that the creature will eventually die even if you don't intervene.

Stop attacking if you see any of the smaller elementals nearby. Kill them to prevent your hero or the soldiers from taking much damage. Use your healing skill to restore lost health throughout the fight, and be patient.

If too many of the soldiers fall in battle, interact with their bodies to revive them and get them back into the conflict. They'll give the little elementals more targets to attack, so it's in your best interest to have the soldiers live to the end of the battle.

Though wounded in the battle of Shaemoor, your character has survived the encounter. Now a hero in every right, you have the privilege and responsibility to continue your efforts for Divinity's Reach.

Your hero's story continues in the area around Shaemoor and in Divinity's Reach (to the north). Read through the Queensdale entry in our World chapter if you'd like to continue this journey with a bit of help.

NORN

I am norn, hunter of the wild, born of the free and rugged Shiverpeak mountains.

The norn haven't been broken by their defeat. Though cast out of their homeland by the Elder Dragon Jormag, the norn are still able to hunt, build, and celebrate! This is the time of a great hunt, when young and veteran hunters alike can meet and prove themselves. Join them, and see if you can raise your standing among the people of Hoelbrak.

THE GREAT HUNT

Your hero begins in Snowlord's Gate, a small town to the east of Hoelbrak. The drinking and merrymaking is already getting underway, but you have even more exciting things to do. Talk to Thora Griffonbane, on the northern side of the road. Interact with Thora or right-click on her to start the conversation. She'll direct you to gather a trophy from a great monster in the area.

It's your choice whether to go after a dire boar, sire griffon, or minotaur bull. All three of these enemies are found to the south, in the forest. If you get close to any of these animals, the target will be marked on your minimap (that's on the bottom right side of the screen).

To kill the creatures, approach them and use your autoattack. Press "1" to start using that skill, and your character will continue to hit the monster as long as it stays within weapon range. Kill the first great monster you see, and bring back a trophy from the kill.

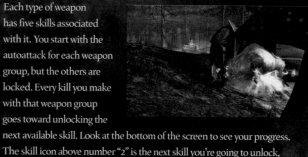

PRACTICE MAKES PERFECT

Each type of weapon has five skills associated with it. You start with the autoattack for each weapon group, but the others are locked. Every kill you make with that weapon group goes toward unlocking the next available skill. Look at the bottom of the screen to see your progress. The skill icon above number "2" is the next skill you're going to unlock, and it only takes a few kills to do this. Some of the lesser beasts in the forest make good targets for this type of hunting.

AH, RICHES!

Watch when you fell each beast. Creatures that sparkle have treasure for your hero. Right-click on enemies to loot them, or use the "Interact" button to accomplish the same result. That's how you pick up the trophy you need. Use the autoloot selection from the Options menu to make the process easier and faster.

BRING THE TROPHY TO IDO THE TANNER TO ENTER THE GREAT HUNT

Walk back to Snowlord's Gate and look for a man named Ido. His location is marked on your map, so it shouldn't take long to find him. Ido is a tanner, and he can prepare the trophy you just earned. It'll make a perfect item to boast about later. Use it to impress the other norn and enter the Great Hunt!

Eir is a legendary hero of your people, and she's leading the hunt this year. Meet her on the steps to the north of Snowlord's Gate. Talk to Eir and follow her up to the top of the area. Norn warriors follow, as they also wish to participate.

The mighty wurm Issormir is at the top of the mountain. Its small offspring cover the area. Issormir won't come out until you've given her sufficient motivation. Go with the warriors and start to kill the smaller wurms.

DON'T LET YOUR WOUNDS FESTER

The sixth ability on your skill bar is for healing. Use it whenever your character takes more than a trivial amount of damage. This will be quite important during the fight with Issormir!

When enough of the lesser wurms are slain, Issormir rises from the snow and readies her attack. Have no fear! You're one of the norn's greatest young hunters, and Eir is still at your side.

ISSORMIR

This wurm is a heck of a lot bigger than the others. She'll take a long time to defeat, and most of the warriors won't be around to help. Keep your distance from any smaller wurms that pop up during the fight so you can focus entirely on Issormir. If she knocks your character back, race forward to reengage her as soon as possible.

When you get splattered on the ground, switch targets and attack the lesser wurms to try and rally (this gets you back on your feet as long as you can kill the enemy before your character dies). If none of the lesser enemies are close by while you're downed, use "4" to heal yourself and rally on your own.

When fighting, use your healing skill to stay alive, and back off from Issormir if you need to catch a breath. Stand back, wait for your healing skill to cool down, and then come back to the fight after you've healed.

Other than that, you just need to pound the wurm until she can no longer fight. This ends the Great Hunt and gives you a keen victory for your name and your legend.

The next stage of your story begins after the Great Hunt is won. Your hero stands at the northwestern end of the Wayfarer Foothills. The northwest road takes you into Hoelbrak, the capital. It's where you'll go to access the Bank, Trading Post, meet other players, and generally hang out. The lands to the east have many tasks and events to help you rise in glory and renown.

To find out more about the region, use our World chapter to look up the Wayfarer Foothills. The descriptions in that chapter help you run through the area, find enemies, and complete the events.

SYLVARI

Your story begins before you even wake in the world of Tyria. While still within the Dream, your hero is summoned by a spirit. The Dream is a place where the sylvari watch the events of the world before they become a physical part of it. Something dark is stirring within that place of rest.

FIGHTING THE NIGHTMARE

Look around in the Dream. Not far away from your hero is a spirit named Caithe. Her position is shown on your minimap, on the lower right side of the screen. Approach Caithe and then right-click on her (or use your "Interact" button to accomplish the same thing). This starts a conversation.

Caithe wants you to travel south. There are shadows of the real world bleeding through into the Dream. You cannot affect these, but there are also nightmares here. They manifest as mastiffs that attack anything that gets close to them. You must defend yourself.

"ACT WITH WISDOM, BUT ACT"

This is a time of struggle and loss. You're going to have to kill, regardless of your feelings about violence. Choosing not to fight would mean that others would be killed, and you can't allow nature or innocent people to be harmed.

Kill the mastiffs and learn from them. Each time you kill an enemy, you work toward learning new weapon skills. These are shown at the bottom of your screen. The skill marked with a "1" is unlocked automatically, and you use that to fight initially. Once you've killed several foes, the second ability lights up as well.

"ALL THINGS HAVE A RIGHT TO GROW"

There's no reason to waste what the creatures possessed. When enemies are slain, look at their bodies and loot the ones that sparkle. Interact with the bodies or right-click on them. Use the autoloot option to make the act as fast and painless as possible.

Kill the mastiffs as you look for Caithe again. She'll be standing near a small path. Talk to her and then continue south on that path.

FIND AND PROTECT THE BRIDGE

There are only a few more mastiffs on the way up to the bridge. Fight them while observing the dreaming people on the sides of the path. When you reach the top, Caithe is there. Go with her across the bridge and attack the mastiffs beyond.

"WHERE LIFE GOES, SO TOO SHOULD YOU"

If your hero is wounded during these fights, press "6" to heal yourself. Watch the cooldown for this skill closely; it should be used often when you're doing heavy fighting. It's also possible to heal your character by staying outside of battle for a short time.

An alarming number of the mastiffs have gathered on the other side of the bridge. Caithe doesn't know what they're here for, but it's got to be something bad. Start to kill the mastiffs, and stay close to Caithe. She can manifest here, and that lets the two of you support each other during the fighting.

When enough of the mastiffs have been slain, a shadow emerges from the mists of the Dream. Whatever evil it represents, you must stop the creature.

SHADOW OF THE DRAGON

This monster is immense. Before long, it will knock down your character unless you're careful. While downed, you can't fight back normally. Left with only a few skills, you can rally by healing yourself (with the "4" key). When that's done, get up and fight back!

Target the shadow's forelegs and start attacking immediately. Watch the ground for red circles, and avoid these whenever they show up. The shadow attacks in bursts, and you can avoid most of the damage by retreating during these phases.

Only Caithe is here to help you, so the fight takes quite some time. Rely on your healing skill to recover from any mistakes, and keep at least one mastiff around at all times. They're summoned throughout the fight, but it's not bad to have one nearby. Attack the mastiffs if you're downed again. Killing them in this state rallies your character instantly.

Maintain your assault on this monster until it is driven away. Whether this is a temporary victory is irrelevant. It had to be done either way.

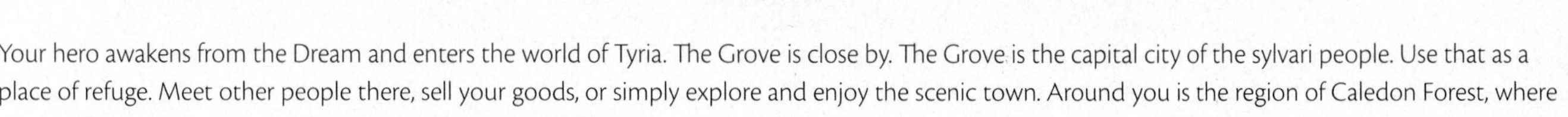

Your hero awakens from the Dream and enters the world of Tyria. The Grove is close by. The Grove is the capital city of the sylvari people. Use that as a place of refuge. Meet other people there, sell your goods, or simply explore and enjoy the scenic town. Around you is the region of Caledon Forest, where you can fight other monsters that are a threat to the world.

To learn more, switch to the World chapter and read about Caledon Forest in greater detail. We'll walk you through the events and challenges of that area (and more).

PROFESSIONS

Professions define your weapon and skill choices for a character. Though *Guild Wars 2* allows ample leeway in what you can accomplish within a given profession, it's still essential to find what works best for you as a player. This chapter explains the strengths and limitations of every profession in the game. We discuss their armor choices, weapons, skills, and general playstyles. Even if you know the original *Guild Wars* like the back of your hand, this is an important chapter to examine. Many professions have changed since their first iterations, and you might be surprised at what they can do now!

INTRODUCTION

Before we look at each profession individually, let's talk about their universal aspects. Every profession has an armor type: light, medium, or heavy. Each profession has at least one special skill that's linked with the function keys. Keys F1 through F4 are dedicated to these, so your profession might have as many as four additional skills that are not slotted or determined by your weapons.

Not all skills are dictated by profession. Naturally, racial skills are determined by the race of your character. They're independent of your profession, so norn get the same skills whether they're warriors, thieves, or whatever you'd like to play. We'll examine the pros and cons of racial skills soon.

Attribute Choices

Professions influence your character's attributes in many ways, including trait availability, synergy between skills and attributes, and so forth. It's important to know that no attributes are profession-dependent. This isn't a game where you can say, "Don't raise X attribute; my class doesn't use that at all." All classes use all of their attributes. Whether you go for health, survivability, damage output, or critical hits for burst damage, your character will benefit from everything.

Attribute	Effect	Used For
Power	Raises damage output	Higher sustained damage
Precision	Raises critical hit rate	Getting more procs (e.g. critical hits)
Toughness	Reduces incoming damage	Survive normal incoming damage
Vitality	Increases your health	Survive condition damage
Healing	Improves the amount healed by healing skills	Maintaining health during challenging fights

What's more, you won't necessarily choose the same style of attributes as someone else who's playing the same profession. One warrior can maximize damage output by getting as much power and precision as possible. Another might make a survivable character with toughness and vitality. You can mix three or even all four attributes, or stack as much as possible on a single type.

Racial Skills

Racial skills add variety to the game and accent the differences between the five playable races that dominate Tyria. Sometimes these help fill out your builds, providing skills that are wildly different from what your profession already has.

Note that racial abilities aren't balanced around their PvP utility. As such, they aren't allowed in fights against other players. This avoids arguments about which race is best for which professions in PvP.

Asura

PAIN INVERTER

Damage:	N/A
Effect:	Retaliation (30 Seconds)
Cooldown:	90 Seconds

This ability lets you throw damage back at your enemy, hurting him every time he attacks. Use this to mess with groups of enemies while you're tanking and using AoEs.

TECHNOBABBLE

Damage:	N/A
Effect:	Daze (3 Seconds)
Cooldown:	120 Seconds

When asura try to explain things to non-asura, it can get a little weird. Over time, asura have found that this unsettling effect can be used in combat. Use Technobabble to shut down single, powerful opponents. Wait until they're winding up their best attacks and stop them cold for a few seconds. This can provide time to escape, continue attacking, or whatever else you'd like to try.

7-SERIES GOLEM (ELITE)

Damage:	N/A
Effect:	Summon Golem (30 Seconds)
Cooldown:	180 Seconds

When you want an aggressive pet, why not create one for yourself? Asura with non-pet classes stand to gain the most from this. You get 30 seconds with your buddy, so be sure to wait until combat with a high-end target is already underway.

SUMMON POWER SUIT (ELITE)

Damage:	Special
Effect:	Change Weapon Skills
Cooldown:	180 Seconds

The power suit is a long-lasting elite skill that summons a suit of armor into which your asura can climb. It has melee and ranged attacks, can knockback foes, and repair itself. You must try this skill; it's absolutely amazing.

D-SERIES GOLEM (ELITE)

Damage:	N/A
Effect:	Summon Golem (30 Seconds)
Cooldown:	180 Seconds

Defensive Golem is very similar to Offensive Golem. Use the other version if you're contributing more toward a group's damage. Use this one if you're trying to tank for the group and want to share the incoming damage.

Charr

BATTLE ROAR

Damage:	N/A
Effect:	Fury (15 Seconds), Might (x3) (15 Seconds)
Cooldown:	30 Seconds

If you want to raise general damage and burst DPS for your group, this is a good skill to take. It raises your group support potential and gets better and better the more allies you have.

HIDDEN PISTOL

Damage:	Low
Effect:	Combo Finisher (Projectile), Backward Evade
Cooldown:	15 Seconds

Players who want more defensive options should invest in Hidden Pistol. Though its outright damage is low, the back step you get can save your hero when endurance runs out and major attacks are coming in. Ranged characters should find this especially useful, as it provides yet another way to get away from targets.

ARTILLERY BARRAGE (ELITE)

Damage:	Moderate-to-High
Effect:	AoE Damage
Cooldown:	240 Seconds

Artillery Barrage is awesome! If you like AoEs and want to have another at your disposal, choose this. The attack's duration is long, so you contribute quite a bit of damage over time, especially if quite a few enemies are fighting in your area.

WARBAND SUPPORT (ELITE)

Damage:	N/A
Effect:	Summon Allies (30 Seconds)
Cooldown:	240 Seconds

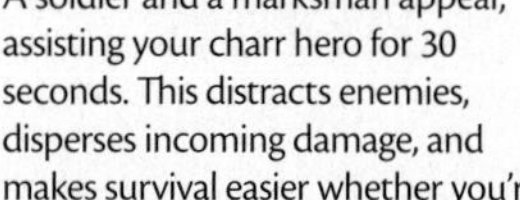

A soldier and a marksman appear, assisting your charr hero for 30 seconds. This distracts enemies, disperses incoming damage, and makes survival easier whether you're facing a single foe or a large group. If you don't know what type of encounter is looming, this is a solid default because it's always useful.

CHARRZOOKA (ELITE)

Damage:	Special
Effect:	Five New Weapon Skills (60 Seconds)
Cooldown:	180 Seconds

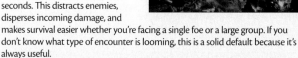

The legendary Charrzooka replaces your current weapon with a ranged, explosive gadget that rocks the house. Expect high damage, agonizing Burning effects, and a good time to be had by all. The extended duration means you get to have fun for a good while.

If you need intense ranged damage, effects to knock around enemies, and high damage output over time, this is a perfect elite skill.

Norn

CALL OWL

Damage:	Extremely High
Effect:	Bleed
Cooldown:	20 Seconds

Call Owl quickly summons a creature to attack your foe, dealing high damage and then putting a nasty Bleed effect on the victim. Use this to augment your character when damage is a high priority.

CALL WURM

Damage:	Low But Consistent
Effect:	Summon Wurm (60 Seconds)
Cooldown:	90 Seconds

This skill calls a pet that uses its ranged attacks to help you in combat. The wurms aren't powerful enough to blow through enemies on their own, but they add moderate damage over time to your encounter. They're at their best when you fight in a region with many enemies over time, such as when you defend a control point during a PvE event.

BECOME THE WOLF (ELITE)

Damage:	N/A
Effect:	Shift into Wolf Form for 30 Seconds
Cooldown:	240 Seconds

This form gives your norn an entirely new series of attacks, and you visually transform as well. Your wolf can attack to Bleed enemies, steal their health, or knock them down. You also get a fear skill that sends your foes running for the hills.

For group utility, this form also provides a buff, giving you and nearby allies fury and regeneration!

Use wolf form when you want to support a group in a challenging encounter. Disable the enemies, keep yourself alive, buff others, and enjoy the benefits of this mixed series of attacks. It's a good blend of survivability, support, and offense.

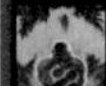

BECOME THE BEAR (ELITE)

Damage:	N/A
Effect:	Shift into Bear Form for 30 Seconds
Cooldown:	240 Seconds

Bears are all about the damage, baby. This form doesn't have much to control your enemies, but you can kill them outright without too much work. Your new form gives characters a knockback, a might buff, and a charge. But mostly, the raw damage stats are what you get from the bear. Use this when you want to lay into an especially powerful target: veterans, champions, etc.

BECOME THE RAVEN (ELITE)

Damage:	N/A
Effect:	Shift into Raven Form for 30 Seconds
Cooldown:	240 Seconds

Raven form lays into groups of enemies without much difficulty. You can use projectiles and a charge when targets are distant or spread out. You also have a Daze and a Bleed when you're looking for pure damage. This is a good form for AoE fights.

BECOME THE SNOW LEOPARD (ELITE)

Damage:	N/A
Effect:	Shift into Snow Leopard Form for 30 Seconds
Cooldown:	240 Seconds

The snow leopard form kills single targets with high reliability. Its considerable damage works well with condition skills that add weaken and cripple to your enemies. To catch targets, you also have the power to dash after them, or use stealth to get the upper hand.

Human

PRAYER TO DWAYNA (HEALING)

Damage:	N/A
Effect:	Moderate Self-Heal
Cooldown:	30 Seconds

Humans get an extra healing ability. Prayer to Dwayna features a moderate cooldown and middle-of-the-road healing. It's most useful when you don't have a traditional, straightforward healing skill (e.g. engineers).

PRAYER TO KORMIR

Damage:	N/A
Effect:	Removes 3 Conditions
Cooldown:	40 Seconds

Most condition-removing abilities strip off only one or two of these status effects. Removing three of them at once is a big deal, making this a powerful ability when you face dungeon bosses or champions prone to dishing out the conditions. This isn't a skill to keep on your bar permanently, but it's a wonderful situational tool to have at your disposal.

PRAYER TO LYSSA

Damage:	N/A
Effect:	Random Boon for You, Random Condition for an Enemy
Cooldown:	30 Seconds

Prayer to Lyssa is like being a mesmer for a brief moment. You get to grab a free boon and lay down a condition on an enemy—if you have one targeted. This isn't an exceptionally powerful trick because it's hard to plan any tactics around two random effects. Use these more for fun than for survival.

REAPER OF GRENTH (ELITE)

Damage:	N/A
Effect:	Transformation (10 Seconds), Chill (3 Seconds), Poison (3 Seconds)
Cooldown:	180 Seconds

For a brief time, this elite skill turns your character into the personification of Grenth. While transformed, you Chill and Poison all enemies that get too close to your character. This is a useful trick against healing or kiting enemies.

AVATAR OF MELANDRU (ELITE)

Damage: Special

Effect: Transform (20 Seconds), Stability (20 Seconds)

Cooldown: 180 Seconds

This elite skill is extremely powerful, especially in groups. Your character takes on the power of Melandru. While transformed, you gain new weapon skills and can damage and disrupt enemies, clear conditions from yourself and nearby allies, and heal those around you. For serious party support, you can't do much better than this. It's wonderful in dungeon runs or larger group events.

HOUNDS OF BALTHAZAR (ELITE)

Damage: N/A

Effect: Summons 2 Pets (30 Seconds)

Cooldown: 240 Seconds

If damage and personal survival are more important than party support, slot Hounds of Balthazar. Human players love this skill for its ability to augment damage output, distract enemies (by giving them more targets), and for the awesome look of the two hounds it summons. When you aren't sure which elite to buy first, consider this one. It's great for solo players, and it still stands up well in groups.

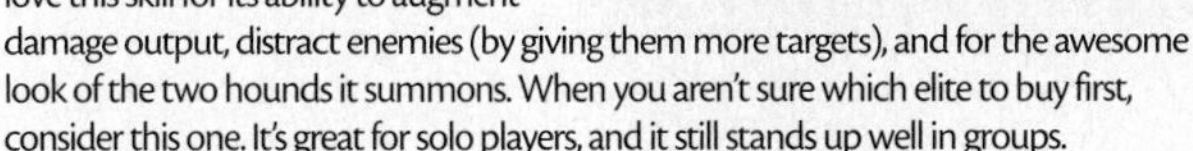

Sylvari

HEALING SEED (HEALING)

Damage: N/A

Effect: Deploys a Healing Plant

Cooldown: 45 Seconds

If you want health restoration over time for a group, use Healing Seed. This skill summons a plant that appears near your hero. The plant heals itself and all nearby allies for the duration of the effect. The effect lasts for a decent portion of the cooldown, so you can use Healing Seed fairly often.

Avoid taking Healing Seed for encounters with high burst damage. The little plant can't heal through things of that nature. That's not what it's made for.

GRASPING VINES

Damage: High (Over Time)

Effect: Immobilize

Cooldown: 45 Seconds

This skill calls forth a set of vines to grab your targeted opponent. The binding roots that erupt from the group immobilize the victim and deal damage over time to it. Grasping Vines is a wonderful ability, especially if you have a ranged weapon to exploit your foe's hapless condition.

SEED TURRET

Damage: High (Over Time)

Effect: Summon Turret (30 Seconds)

Cooldown: 60 Seconds

Turrets are always fun. They're immobile pets that shoot at any monster in the area. Use them to improve your damage output or to give monsters one more thing to peck at. Seed Turret is ideal for holding territory during events where enemies spawn and come at you. In a pinch they're also useful in escort events or in entering areas where you can pull multiple monsters back to your turret.

SUMMON FERN MASTIFF (ELITE)

Damage: High

Effect: Summon Fern Mastiff (30 Seconds)

Cooldown: 240 Seconds

The Fern Mastiff is a single pet with high survivability and darn good damage output. The beast poisons its targets and can hold monsters to protect your hero. Between this and Seed Turret, you can easily give your hero more time to fight (or run), even during the most intense encounters.

TAKE ROOT (ELITE)

Damage: Psychotic

Effect: Summon an Army of Seed Turrets

Cooldown: 600 Seconds

This elite skill's huge downside is that you can use it only once in a blue moon. However, Take Root is so powerful that it's worth getting once you can afford the skill points. When cast, Take Root summons Seed Turrets all over the area. They help you overwhelm anything short of a full invasion. Veterans and champions are much easier to defeat with this skill in your arsenal. Have an ally start the fight while you get close to the enemy and summon your little friends. The rest is pure enjoyment.

SUMMON DRUID SPIRIT (ELITE)

Damage: High

Effect: Summon Pet (60 Seconds)

Cooldown: 360 Seconds

The problem with most pets is that they don't last very long. This elite skill is noteworthy because it gives you more time with your new friend. The extended cooldown somewhat balances that, but think about the advantages. Having a pet for a longer encounter means you're much safer for twice as long. The Thorn Wolf is better for fast events where you frequently need a little help. The Druid Spirit is better for larger events, big battles, and major make-or-break situations for you and your party.

ELEMENTALIST

Elementalists are powerful and versatile spell casters that specialize in magical (elemental) damage. Although they wear light armor, they have potent healing and boon abilities that give them respectable survivability. Their use of potent direct-damage spells combined with condition damage makes them formidable adversaries. The breadth and depth of spells available to an elementalist is enormous, and you'll find something to suit any playstyle.

As soloists, elementalists can cast a large number of fast, deadly spells. Their mix of direct-damage and area-of-effect abilities allows them to decimate their foes. In a pinch, they can switch over to defensive and healing abilities, letting them live through battles that other professions wouldn't survive. And don't think that just because you're a light-armor-wearing caster you have to whittle targets down from range—a dagger-wielding elementalist gets right up in his or her enemies' faces and cuts them down in melee.

Group work offers elementalists an opportunity to play with their heavy area-of-effect damage. They have a number of powerful, wide-range targeted spells; being in a group means you have the time to cast them to their full effect. Elementalists also offer a number of group-friendly traits and slot skills, which can impart a wide array of boons to your party. Finally, a staff-wielding elementalist using Water spells is the closest thing you'll find to a specialized healer. This is exceptionally nice to have in a group, but don't think for a moment that your only purpose in the party is to sit in the back and heal! Even at your "healiest" you can inflict decent damage. The moment you want to unload on your hapless foes, all you have to do is tap a button and let loose with your strongest spells.

Profession Stats

Attribute	Starting Stats	Naked at Level 80
Power	24	1216
Precision	24	1016
Toughness	24	1016
Vitality	24	1016
Attack	160	1216
Critical Chance	4%	9%
Armor	83	1091
Health	245	11,805

The preceding stats give you an idea of what to expect from your character. They show elementalist progression through examples taken at the beginning and end of leveling. Your actual stats will likely vary from this.

Weapons and Weapon Skills

Elementalists master spells based on Fire, Water, Air, and Earth. At first, you have only Fire and Water open to you, but the others appear in short order—you'll have everything by level eight.

Elementalists cannot swap weapons in combat. Like engineers, they can wield only one weapon at a time. To compensate for this, elementalists can switch between their elemental attunements. Use function keys F1-F4 to do this. Switching attunement puts your older element into a cooldown period so you can swap between elements rather quickly. However, you have to give ones that you use about 15 seconds to restore themselves.

Fire-based spells concentrate on inflicting direct- and area-of-effect damage. Many of them also put a Burning condition over an area. They contribute to fire-based combos. Fire is a powerful and destructive force in the hands of an elementalist, and it's a wonderful means of laying waste to enemy groups.

Water-based abilities are more defensive. A number of spells combine damage and healing, both for you and for allies. Water-based spells also have a means to remove conditions. Many Water abilities impart the Chill condition, making it a strong means of disruption and crowd control.

Air is the place to find single-target damage. Some area-of-effect spells are here, as well, along with a good mix of defensive conditions (Blind, Vulnerability, and Stun). But Air's real glory lies in its movement effects. If you want to disrupt your foes by knocking them around (great for PvP) or if you love casting while on the move, Air is exactly what you need.

Earth might not be as flashy as Fire or Air when it comes to its damage spells, but don't be fooled. Real potency is here, both in terms of direct damage and some area-of-effect attacks. Also, you can deliver a huge amount of easily stackable Bleed damage. The damage mitigation you gain from Earth is phenomenal, as well; damage shields and even limited invulnerability are in its lineup.

As main-hand weapons, elementalists can use daggers (short range), scepters (medium range), or staves (long range). As off-hand weapons, elementalists must decide between daggers (for more damage) or focuses (for defense). Staves are two-handed weapons, so you can't wield an off-hand weapon with them. In terms of underwater weapons, elementalists use tridents.

Daggers (Main Hand)

A stereotypical melee weapon like a dagger may seem an odd choice for a caster. Yet, elementalists are versatile magic users, and daggers don't change that. You can cast any number of elemental attacks and switch between the four elements to balance damage, conditions, and healing. The downside is that daggers have very limited range; you have to be very close to your enemy before you can hit him. If that's not a problem, use a dagger in your off hand, as well. Or, to mitigate the range problem, use a focus in your off hand.

Daggers are great weapons to use as a soloist. You can get up close and personal with your target and lay into him with speed. Daggers also look extremely cool!

 DRAGON'S CLAW (FIRE)

Damage: High
Effect: None
Cooldown: None

This basic Fire attack spreads a claw-shaped blast of flame at your foe. It's quick and delivers high damage, and it looks beautifully violent. While this attack lacks the Burn condition that a number of other fire attacks have, the high damage more than makes up for it. The only downside is its close range. You have to be right in front of a target, and that's a dangerous place. If you're at point blank, the attack hits a target multiple times, making the skill much more efficient at killing its prey.

DRAKE'S BREATH (FIRE)

Damage: Very High
Effect: Channeled, Burning (3 Seconds)
Cooldown: 5 Seconds

Drake's Breath is a channeled ability that has you breathe a gout of flame over your foe. At the end of the flame spray, your enemy Burns, taking nasty damage over time. This attack is powerful, but it requires a bit of a commitment. Because you have to dedicate time to channel it, you open yourself up to other attacks, especially ones that knock you down or launch you. While you can move around while casting the spell, if you get disrupted, it still breaks the channeling. It's best to open a fight with this spell. The Burn effect will scorch your enemy, and you can keep moving.

 BURNING SPEED (FIRE)

Damage: Moderate
Effect: Burning (1 Second), Combo Field (Fire)
Cooldown: 15 Seconds

This attack causes your hero to sprint forward. As you move, a wave of fire radiates outward, causing Burning to foes nearby. This attack helps to offset the short range of your dagger attacks. Pick your foes, use Burning Speed to reach them, and then hit them with Dragon's Breath or Dragon's Claw. As an added bonus, you can help with some combo damage. Anyone who attacks through your flame trail gains Fire elemental damage.

VAPOR BLADE (WATER)

Damage: Low
Effect: Vulnerability (6 Seconds)
Cooldown: None

This autoattack doesn't do much damage, but it weakens your opponents' armor ratings. They take more damage from your next few attacks. Vapor Blade is pretty much a bread-and-butter attack; it wears down your foes, and you keep nailing them with it until they're gone. The vulnerability makes it a good opening to the battle. Another perk of this attack is that it has surprisingly good range. Use it to soften targets that kite your hero, or before enemies reach you for melee combat.

CONE OF COLD (WATER)

Damage: Low

Effect: Channeled, Heals

Cooldown: 10 Seconds

Cone of Cold sprays ice in a forward cone. This damages any foes in the area and lightly heals allies. While you don't see high damage numbers using this attack, it adds group utility to your dagger skills.

FROZEN BLAST (WATER)

Damage: Low

Effect: Area-of-Effect Damage, Chilled (3 Seconds)

Cooldown: 15 Seconds

This low-damage AoE attack also chills your enemies. It's very nice for making sure enemies don't run away from you, and it keeps them from using their skills against you as quickly. If you're surrounded by enemies, and the one you've been slamming turns to run, hit him with a Frozen Blast and then follow with Vapor Blade.

LIGHTNING WHIP (AIR)

Damage: Low

Effect: None

Cooldown: None

It has to be said: Lightning Whip simply looks awesome! You create a wave of electricity that slices into enemies. This autoattack is *slightly* stronger than those of the other elements, but its real glory is speed. You can lash your foes with it until they fall, and look good doing it.

LIGHTNING TOUCH (AIR)

Damage: Low

Effect: Area-of-Effect Damage, Vulnerability (6 Seconds)

Cooldown: 6 Seconds

A cone of electricity bursts forth, shocking your foes. This makes them vulnerable, exposing them to more damage from your attacks. It's a good mix with your Lightning Whip, and the short cooldown lets you add it whenever you want. You really can't go wrong with it.

SHOCKING AURA (AIR)

Damage: None

Effect: Duration (5 Seconds), Stun (1 Second)

Cooldown: 25 Seconds

You form an electrical field that stuns anyone who attacks you. Use this defensive ability just before you engage a target, or when you see an enemy telegraphing a powerful attack. The stun doesn't last long, but it's disruptive. With the enemy stunned, take the chance to lay on damage with Lightning Touch or Lightning Whip.

IMPALE (EARTH)

Damage: Low

Effect: Bleeding (8 Seconds)

Cooldown: None

An enormous spike of earth bursts out of the ground, impaling your enemies and causing them to Bleed. This autoattack has the potential to inflict more damage than it first appears; there's no cooldown and the Bleeds stack, so you can hit your foes again and again and have them Bleed away.

RING OF EARTH (EARTH)

Damage: Moderate

Effect: Area of Effect, Bleeding (12 Seconds)

Cooldown: 6 Seconds

Ring of Earth can hit multiple enemies, causing all of them to Bleed. Combine this with Impale to get enemies' health to drop as quickly as possible. If you're fighting a group, it's a good way to inflict some damage to all the targets as you lay into one unlucky enemy.

MAGNETIC GRASP (EARTH)

Damage: Low

Effect: Immobilize (2 Seconds)

Cooldown: 12 Seconds

This attack mitigates the dagger's major drawback: its short range. Choose your target, grapple to him with Magnetic Grasp (immobilizing him), and then slam into him with any of your Bleed-damage attacks. The cooldown is just the right duration (more or less) to use it to start the next fight.

Dagger (Off Hand)

Equipping a dagger in your off hand gives you even more damaging attacks and crowd-control abilities. Many of these have area-of-effect damage, letting you dish out unhappiness to a number of foes.

RING OF FIRE (FIRE)

Damage:	Low
Effect:	Area-of-Effect Damage, Burning (5 Seconds), Combo Field (Fire)
Cooldown:	15 Seconds

This spell damages any enemy near your hero and Burns anything that passes through it. This nice, simple attack spreads decent damage to a number of foes, and it's good to use as often as it becomes available. It pairs well with Dragon's Claw/Drake's Breath (if you have a dagger in your main hand) or Flamestrike/Dragon's Tooth (for a scepter).

FIRE GRAB (FIRE)

Damage:	High
Effect:	Area-of-Effect Damage
Cooldown:	45 Seconds

Fire Grab hits enemies in a forward cone; enemies that are already Burning take additional damage from the attack. A large number of Fire elemental attacks place Burning effects on targets, and you can add even more utility skills that do the same thing. So, Burned enemies aren't hard to find. All you have to remember is to use Fire Grab later in the fight, after your enemies are on fire.

FROST AURA (WATER)

Damage:	None
Effect:	Chilled (1 Second), Duration (7 Seconds)
Cooldown:	40 Seconds

You surround yourself with a sphere of frost that lasts for seven seconds. Any foes that hit you during that time are Chilled. This defensive spell is best to use with a scepter in your main hand. Scepters allow medium-range attacks, and the Chilling effect keeps your enemy from closing in on or running away from you while you hit him with Ice Shards or lay a Shatterstone in front of him.

 CLEANSING WAVE (WATER)

Damage:	None
Effect:	Area of Effect, Healing (Self and Allies), Removes a Condition
Cooldown:	40 Seconds

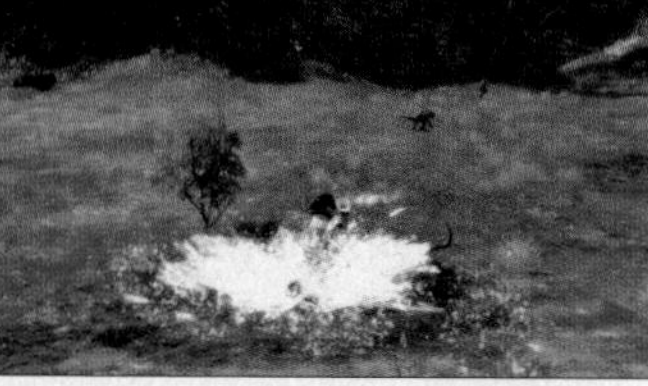

This spell offers dagger wielders the ability to heal themselves (and others) while removing conditions. The supplemental healing is always welcome, and the ability to take out a condition means you also get to mitigate damage or other disabilities. Cleansing Wave's long cooldown means you can't cast it as much as you'd like, so make sure to wait until you need its healing and condition removal.

RIDE THE LIGHTNING (AIR)

Damage: Moderate
Effect: Area-of-Effect Damage, Teleport
Cooldown: 15 Seconds

Ride the Lightning shoots a distant foe and then teleports your hero to the target. When you reach your enemy, the lightning blasts outward, damaging all nearby foes. If you have a dagger in your main hand, this spell is brilliant! It completely changes your range of combat from very short to long range. Choose your targets, Ride the Lightning to them, and then continue with your nastiest attacks. As a bonus, you even get to inflict a little damage to a group. The reasonable cooldown time means you can use it to start the next fight.

UPDRAFT (AIR)

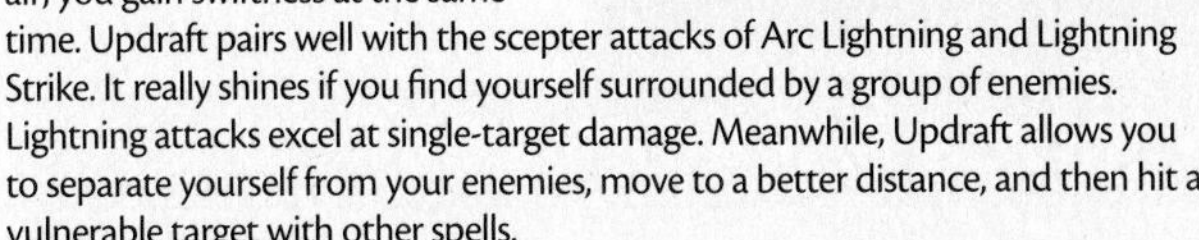

Damage: None
Effect: Swiftness (10 Seconds), AoE Launch
Cooldown: 40 Seconds

This attack slams into a group of enemies and launches them into the air; you gain swiftness at the same time. Updraft pairs well with the scepter attacks of Arc Lightning and Lightning Strike. It really shines if you find yourself surrounded by a group of enemies. Lightning attacks excel at single-target damage. Meanwhile, Updraft allows you to separate yourself from your enemies, move to a better distance, and then hit a vulnerable target with other spells.

EARTHQUAKE (EARTH)

Damage: High
Effect: Knockdown (2 Seconds), Combo Finisher (Blast)
Cooldown: 45 Seconds

This is a fun one! You set off an earthquake that knocks down your enemy and hits him for high damage. This offensive spell is a "use it whenever you can" ability. You can't go wrong with knockdown and easy damage.

CHURNING EARTH (EARTH)

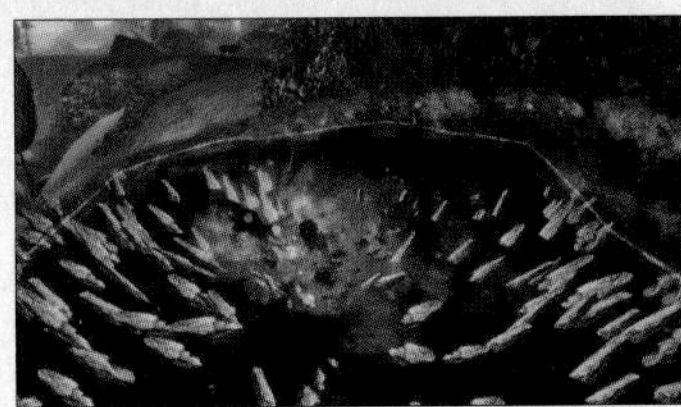

Damage: Very High
Effect: Channeled Area-of-Effect Damage, Cripple (1 Second), Bleeding (8 Seconds), Combo Finisher (Blast)
Cooldown: 30 Seconds

This channeled spell lets loose a crumbling circle of churning earth. Those within the area are afflicted with Cripple and Bleeding in addition to direct damage. This attack takes a long time to complete, so be careful not to use it when enemies are highly mobile or have a good chance to counter you. Use a knockdown attack or something else that's disabling to leave enemies exposed ahead of time. This makes it easier to get the most out of this awesome spell.

Scepter (Main Hand)

Scepters provide elementalists with sustainable medium-range damage options and the ability to lay down some nasty conditions. They're a solid main-hand choice, especially for group work. This is because they allow you to stay out of your enemy's reach and control the fight on your terms. Pair Scepters with a dagger in the off hand for more offensive attacks or for a focus on defensive/damage-mitigation abilities.

FLAMESTRIKE (FIRE)

Damage: Low
Effect: Burning (2 Seconds)
Cooldown: None

This autoattack sends a small ball of fire at an enemy, Burning him. It's a solid damage spell as your basic attack, and the Burning is a nice touch.

DRAGON'S TOOTH (FIRE)

Damage: High
Effect: Area-of-Effect Damage, Burning (3 Seconds), Combo Finisher (Blast)
Cooldown: 6 Seconds

Ah, what isn't there to love about Dragon's Tooth? Though the skill takes a while to cast, it slaps enemies for high damage, hits other targets, and causes Burning. Its low cooldown makes the spell a constant damage dealer.

PHOENIX (FIRE)

Damage: High
Effect: Area-of-Effect Damage, Targeted Circle of Effect, Vigor (10 Seconds), Combo Finisher (Blast)
Cooldown: 20 Seconds

This skill rakes all foes in a forward line and then explodes, inflicting damage. The Phoenix returns to your hero afterward, granting vigor and removing conditions. While it may sound complex, this spell provides modest area-of-effect damage, and you control the targeted area. Once you set the spell free, let it take care of itself—move on to another attack while the Phoenix does its work.

ICE SHARDS (WATER)

Damage: Low to Moderate
Effect: None
Cooldown: None

This autoattack sends an arc of three ice shards into your target. It's a simple attack to use mainly when your heavier spells are on cooldown.

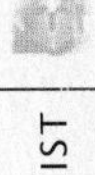

SHATTERSTONE (WATER)

Damage: Moderate

Effect: Area-of-Effect Damage, Vulnerability (15 Seconds)

Cooldown: 2 Seconds

You place a large shard of ice in a circle, it grows for two seconds, and then it explodes. Anything it hits becomes vulnerable. Because the Shatterstone has a delay between when you place it and when it explodes, it's good to use at the start of a fight, particularly if you're facing a group of foes. The vulnerability lasts a long time, so you can systematically attack targets and deliver extra damage for most of the engagement.

WATER TRIDENT (WATER)

Damage: Low to Moderate

Effect: Area-of-Effect Damage, Healing

Cooldown: 20 Seconds

You form a trident made of water and throw it into an area. The trident hurts enemies in the target zone, but allies are healed. This scepter attack provides good group utility (as healing), and it lets you stay at a distance while you assist your compatriots. It isn't as useful when you're soloing, because of its relatively low damage output. Save it to use after Shatterstone.

ARC LIGHTNING (AIR)

Damage: Moderate

Effect: Channeled (3 Seconds)

Cooldown: None

Arc Lightning channels for three seconds, dealing damage the entire time. It hits only a single target, but the total damage output is reasonable for a basic autoattack. While you're channeling Arc Lightning, you can also use Blinding Flash and Lightning Strike, increasing your character's damage output and survivability.

LIGHTNING STRIKE (AIR)

Damage: Moderate

Effect: None

Cooldown: 5 Seconds

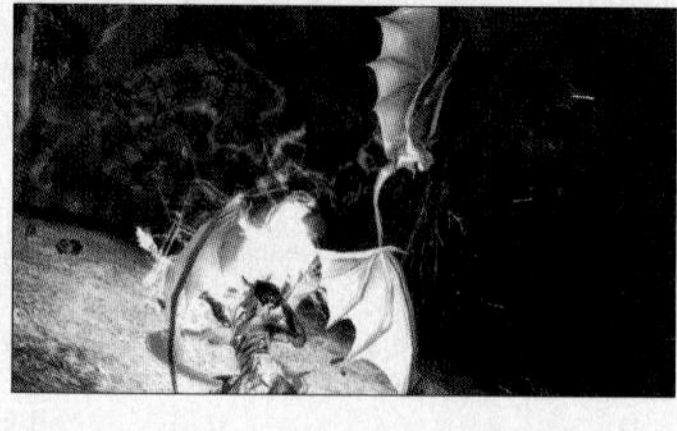

You strike your target with a large bolt of lightning. This single-target damage spell is another solid addition to your Air elemental arsenal. It's easy to incorporate into your attack lineup, and it provides a good power base for your Air attacks if you're using a focus in your off hand. Focuses are a bit more defensive, so the extra damage is nice to fall back on.

BLINDING FLASH (AIR)

Damage: None

Effect: Blindness (6 Seconds)

Cooldown: 10 Seconds

You create a ball of light that flashes to Blind your opponent. This doesn't do any damage, but your enemy misses with his next attack. It's good to use just as your foe telegraphs a big attack, like when that ettin starts its windup.

STONE SHARDS (EARTH)

Damage: Low

Effect: Bleeding (6 Seconds), Combo Finisher (Physical Projectile)

Cooldown: None

This is a lovely autoattack. Your hero fires three waves of pointed shards. The projectiles are pretty close together, and they perforate their target, causing Bleeding damage. To kill a single target over time, stack the Bleeds and use Rock Barrier to outlast your enemy in a war of attrition.

ROCK BARRIER (EARTH)

Damage: Minimal to Moderate

Effect: Create Armor (30 Second Duration)

Cooldown: 15 Seconds

You surround yourself with a barrier of five stone shards that improve armor. This barrier's duration is 30 seconds, after which time all the shards disappear. The stone shards themselves can be hurled at enemies as an attack. Once all shards are depleted, Rock Barrier is gone and begins to recharge. Cast this just before you start any engagement.

DUST DEVIL (EARTH)

Damage: Low

Effect: Area-of-Effect Damage, Blindness (10 Seconds)

Cooldown: 15 Seconds

You send a small tornado of sand through a line of foes, blinding them in the process. This attack lets you exert a bit of crowd control, and it's nice to mitigate damage against you or your allies. Lining up your enemies can be a little difficult, so back up or go around corners to force them into a tighter cluster before you cast Dust Devil.

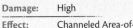

Staves

These two-handed weapons provide long-range attacks. A number of area-of-effect damage spells and healing abilities are in the lineup. The condition damage isn't bad, either! Staves are at their best when you're in a group. Your hero can hit a number of targets at once while staying safely away from combat. A quick switch to Water adds wonderful party healing.

FIREBALL (FIRE)

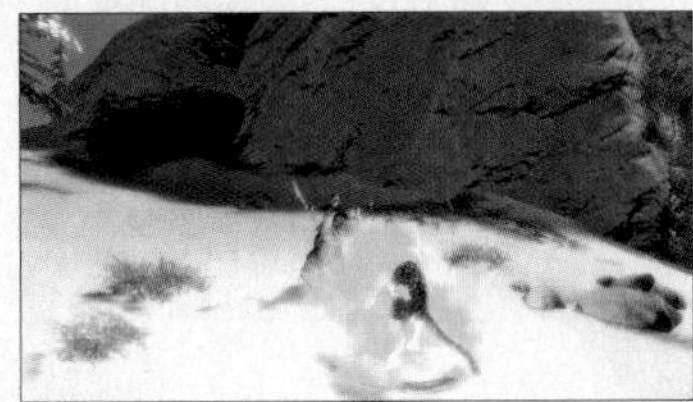

Damage: Moderate

Effect: Area-of-Effect Damage

Cooldown: None

A fireball explodes within the area of effect, hitting anything in its radius. This is exactly what you'd expect from a Fire elemental attack: solid damage, fast cast time, and the ability to hit multiple opponents.

LAVA FONT (FIRE)

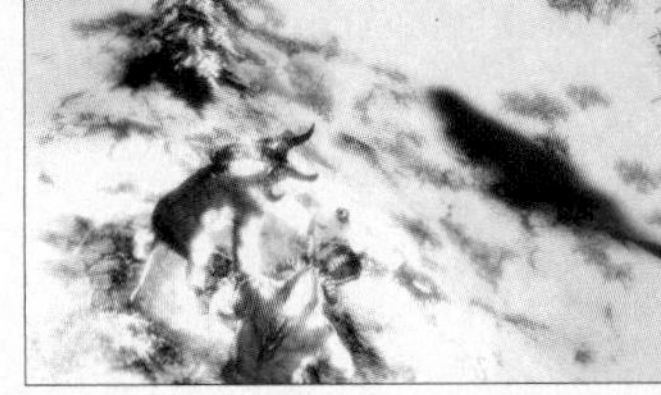

Damage: Moderate to High

Effect: Area-of-Effect Damage, Duration (4 Seconds), Combo Field (Fire)

Cooldown: 6 Seconds

Lava erupts within the targeted area. The attack inflicts decent damage to anything in its radius. Anyone in your party who attacks through the field of fire has a chance to get a Fire effect on their victims.

FLAME BURST (FIRE)

Damage: N/A

Effect: Area-of-Effect, Burning (5 Seconds)

Cooldown: 10 Seconds

Any enemies within the region are set alight, Burning them over time. Pair Flame Burst with Lava Font to continue laying down elemental damage.

BURNING RETREAT (FIRE)

Damage: Low

Effect: Burning (1 Second), Combo Field (Fire), Duration (6 Seconds), Retreat from Enemy

Cooldown: 20 Seconds

You quickly roll backward, leaving behind a trail of burning, fiery death. This is a mixed offensive/defensive ability. Use it to avoid damage from oncoming enemies and to maintain distance. If the targets follow, they'll have to eat Burn damage.

If you have a lot of ranged allies, one trick is to roll in a horizontal line in front of them. This creates a wall of fire through which your comrades can shoot. This looks cool and gives your ranged buddies some extra damage.

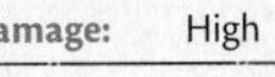

METEOR SHOWER (FIRE)

Damage: High

Effect: Channeled Area-of-Effect Damage

Cooldown: 30 Seconds

Meteor Shower creates a substantial AoE that hits anything in its path. This is a channeled spell, and it takes a few seconds to cast. The payoff is the huge amount of damage delivered to anything in its radius. It's best to use this spell when you (and your group) fight a large number of enemies. Wait until targets are caught in battle so you don't waste the spell on mobile enemies.

WATER BLAST (WATER)

Damage: Low

Effect: Healing

Cooldown: None

Your basic Water autoattack inflicts light damage but also heals you a small amount. Your elementalist gets plenty of range, so it's a good spell for starting fights and staying away from enemies. The healing effect, though modest, affects your allies, as well.

ICE SPIKE (WATER)

Damage: Moderate to High

Effect: Area-of-Effect Damage, Vulnerability (x3) (10 Seconds)

Cooldown: 4 Seconds

A giant spike of ice falls from the sky, impacting anything in its area and causing Vulnerability. This is *the* damage spell for Water-based staff attacks. Use it as soon and as often as you can.

GEYSER (WATER)

Damage: None

Effect: Area of Effect, Healing, Combo Field (Water), Duration (2 Seconds)

Cooldown: 20 Seconds

You create a small geyser of water that pours over a small area, healing anyone nearby. This spell provides modest supplemental healing to you and your allies. It's good to keep in reserve for emergencies or anytime the group can stand together for a short period.

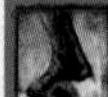

FROZEN GROUND (WATER)

Damage: None

Effect: Area of Effect, Chill (2 Seconds), Combo Field (Ice), Duration (5 Seconds)

Cooldown: 40 Seconds

You coat the target area with a field of ice. Any enemies within the ice field become Chilled, and any allies within it gain ice combo potential. Because you control the region the spell affects, you can keep enemies far, far away from you. This keeps them in close range of your allies (if applicable) and gives you time to keep them in range of your damage spells, like Ice Spike.

HEALING RAIN (WATER)

Damage: None

Effect: Area of Effect, Regeneration (4 Seconds), Healing, Removes Conditions (Every 3 Seconds), Combo Field (Water), Duration (9 Seconds)

Cooldown: 45 Seconds

Rain falls over a large circle for nine seconds, healing everyone within it, giving them Regeneration, and removing conditions once every three seconds. This is healing at its best! The area of effect is so wide that a large number of people can be affected, and the benefits are very nice. The only drawback is the spell's long cooldown.

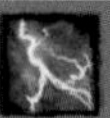

CHAIN LIGHTNING (AIR)

Damage: Moderate

Effect: Area-of-Effect Damage, Maximum Targets (3 Within 10 Seconds)

Cooldown: None

Chain Lightning hits multiple targets over a moderate area of effect. This is your basic Lightning attack. It's all about dealing decent damage whenever you need it.

LIGHTNING SURGE (AIR)

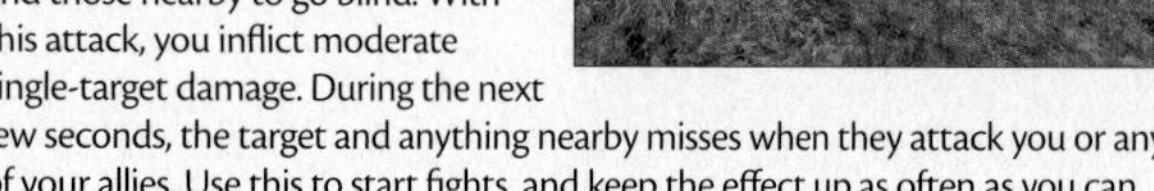

Damage: High

Effect: Area of Effect, Blindness (5 Seconds)

Cooldown: 10 Seconds

Lightning Surge causes your enemy and those nearby to go blind. With this attack, you inflict moderate single-target damage. During the next few seconds, the target and anything nearby misses when they attack you or any of your allies. Use this to start fights, and keep the effect up as often as you can.

GUST (AIR)

Damage: None

Effect: Area of Effect, Knockback

Cooldown: 30 Seconds

Gust is all about disruption. Instead of inflicting damage, it knocks everything away from your caster. This is great in a number of situations: it keeps you from getting overwhelmed; you get to cast from long range; and your enemies are disrupted. The PvP implications are pretty obvious, also. The only thing you have to be careful of is working with group members who love melee range; they won't appreciate you knocking away their targets.

WINDBORNE SPEED (AIR)

Damage: None

Effect: Swiftness (10 Seconds), Removes Cripple, Immobilize, and Chill

Cooldown: 30 Seconds

Windborne Speed functions as a situational ability and a marvelous travel spell. The situational aspect is that it removes movement-impairing conditions, restoring full mobility to you and your allies. In addition, it's easy to cast this spell outside of combat to gain a good speed boost. You and your group can then move quickly over territory, helping you get where you need to go. This is enjoyable in PvE, but it can be downright crucial for PvP, where movement speed and territory control are vital.

STATIC FIELD (AIR)

Damage: Low to Moderate

Effect: Area of Effect, Stun (3 Seconds), Combo Field (Lightning), Duration (4 Seconds)

Cooldown: 40 Seconds

This skill summons a static field that Stuns anything that crosses it. Stuns completely disable foes throughout their duration, so they're one of the best possible crowd-control abilities. This is not a high-damage attack, but you can work into other group-damaging attack spells (e.g. Chain Lightning and Lightning Surge). It becomes more useful in PvP, where you can keep a number of opponents from attacking.

STONING (EARTH)

Damage: Low

Effect: Weakness (1 Second), Combo (Physical Projectile)

Cooldown: None

You create a huge rock and throw it at your foe, Weakening the enemy. This is a useful autoattack for mitigating enemy damage. Choose the most dangerous enemy on the field and keep him weakened for as long as possible.

ERUPTION (EARTH)

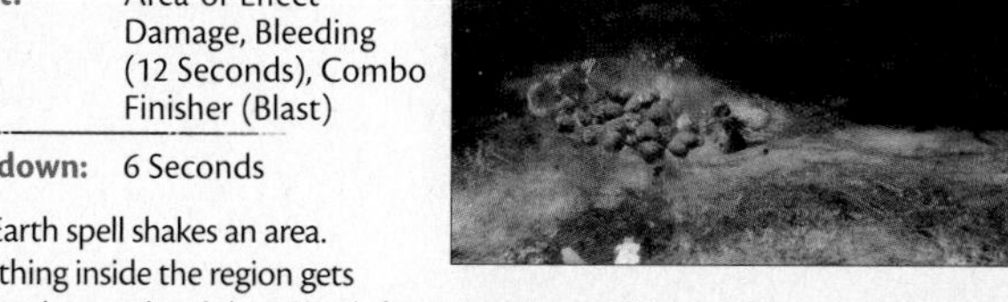

Damage: High

Effect: Area-of-Effect Damage, Bleeding (12 Seconds), Combo Finisher (Blast)

Cooldown: 6 Seconds

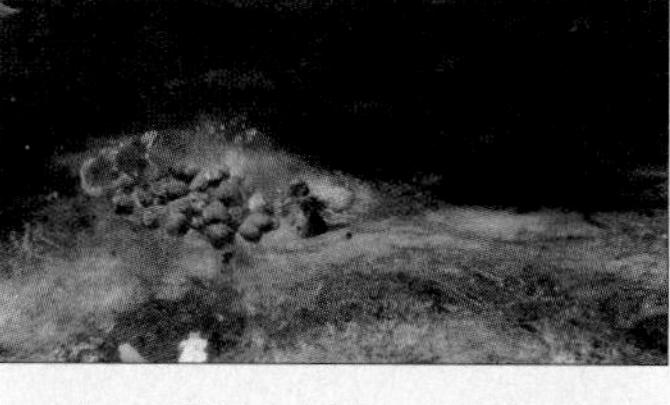

This Earth spell shakes an area. Everything inside the region gets slammed around and then Bleeds from the mix-up. This is a solid damage attack that you can cast very often.

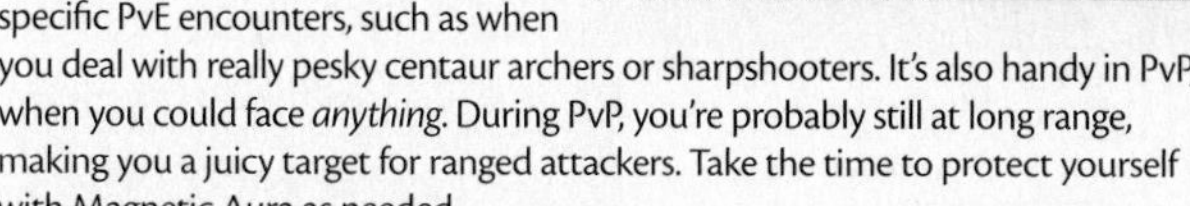

MAGNETIC AURA (EARTH)

Damage: None

Effect: Reflect Projectiles, Duration (5 Seconds)

Cooldown: 30 Seconds

For five seconds, magnetic energy reflects any projectiles fired at you. This situational spell is useful in specific PvE encounters, such as when you deal with really pesky centaur archers or sharpshooters. It's also handy in PvP, when you could face *anything*. During PvP, you're probably still at long range, making you a juicy target for ranged attackers. Take the time to protect yourself with Magnetic Aura as needed.

UNSTEADY GROUND (EARTH)

Damage: Very Low

Effect: Area-of-Effect Damage, Cripple (2 Seconds)

Cooldown: 30 Seconds

This spell forms a line on the ground; any enemies in the area of effect take light damage and are Crippled for two seconds. Use this to disrupt mobile forces and gain a chance to stay at range while they try to close with you. It works best as a fight opener in PvE, keeping attackers at a distance. In PvP, use it to kite enemies that can't attack you at long range.

SHOCKWAVE (EARTH)

Damage: Moderate

Effect: Bleed (20 Seconds), Immobilize (2 Seconds), Combo Finisher (Physical Projectile)

Cooldown: 30 Seconds

You let loose a shockwave that Bleeds and Immobilizes your enemy. This single-target ability is potent. Your hapless foe takes nasty damage and then has to contend with being Immobilized and Bleeding (also not fun). Combine Shockwave with Eruption to double down on the pain!

Focus (Off Hand)

Focuses are off-hand weapons that add to an elementalist's survivability. A lot of damage mitigation is here, in addition to damage output. This works well with both main-hand weapons: daggers and scepters. Daggers rely on close-range attacks, and scepter users need something to hit foes that close in on them.

FLAMEWALL (FIRE)

Damage: Low

Effect: Area-of-Effect Damage, Burning (1 Second), Combo Field (Fire), Duration (8 Seconds)

Cooldown: 20 seconds

This skill creates a wall of fire at a targeted location. Anything that crosses it starts to Burn. Thus, you work to protect yourself and inflict damage, both directly and over time. You can also lay down a combo field through which allies can fire. Because you choose where the wall goes, you can put it between your character and your foe, between the battle and a group member (say, a ranger or engineer), or even directly on top of an enemy.

FIRE SHIELD (FIRE)

Damage: None

Effect: Burning (1 Second), Duration (3 Seconds)

Cooldown: 40 seconds

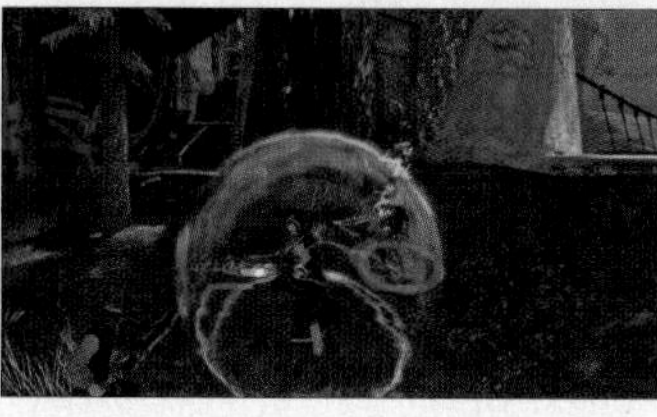

An orb of fire surrounds you for three seconds. Anything that hits you during this time gets scorched. If you have a main-hand dagger, use Fire Shield as your opening move in a battle. You get to lay down fast Burn damage, and the cooldown allows you to start with it for the next fight. If you have a scepter, hold off on Fire Shield until your enemies get a bit closer to you. Use it at the same time as Dragon's Tooth and Phoenix to take full advantage of area-of-effect damage.

FREEZING GUST (WATER)

Damage: Low

Effect: Chilled (3 Seconds)

Cooldown: 25 seconds

Cracks your foe with freezing water, Chilling him briefly. This spell is meant to serve two purposes: either to keep foes from getting to you (perfect for scepter users), or to keep them from running away from you (for dagger users). It works as a wonderful anti-kiting spell.

COMET (WATER)

Damage: High

Effect: Area-of-Effect Damage, Daze (2 Seconds), Combo Field (Blast)

Cooldown: 25 Seconds

This spell creates a large ice comet that falls on your foes. Anything the comet hits is Dazed. This area-of-effect attack helps round out your Water-based spells, letting you inflict respectable damage while stopping enemy attacks for a short time. Wait until enemies are clustered to use this high-end attack.

 SWIRLING WINDS (AIR)

Damage: None

Effect: Area of Effect, Destroys Projectiles, Duration (6 seconds)

Cooldown: 30 seconds

A swirling wind surrounds you for five seconds, deflecting enemy projectiles. This is a situational defense in PvE, but it's very useful in PvP. This is especially true for scepter users, who sometimes operate a bit further back from combat, making them tempting targets for snipers. If you notice yourself getting pecked by distant attacks, tap Swirling Winds to save yourself.

GALE (AIR)

Damage: None

Effect: Knockdown (2 Seconds)

Cooldown: 50 Seconds

Send forth a wind blast that knocks down your enemies. This hits multiple targets if they're close together, allowing decent disruption and mitigation of enemy damage. Because the spell has a long cooldown, you should save it for moments of great necessity, when enemies are really threatening your hero or your party.

 MAGNETIC WAVE (EARTH)

Damage: Moderate

Effect: Area of Effect, Remove Conditions, Reflect Projectiles, Combo Finisher (Blast), Duration (3 Seconds)

Cooldown: 25 seconds

Magnetic Wave damages foes, gets rid of pesky conditions, and keeps projectiles from hitting you. Use this after Ring of Earth (for dagger main hand) or a basic attack, such as Impale or Stone Shards.

 OBSIDIAN FLESH (EARTH)

Damage: None

Effect: Invulnerability (4 Seconds)

Cooldown: 50 Seconds

For four seconds, your hero becomes invulnerable, wrapped in stony armor. Use this time to survive intense bursts of enemy damage, to gain a chance to heal yourself, or to flee from whatever is kicking your butt around the field. Because Obsidian Flesh's cooldown is so long, avoid using it casually. Wait until you're in real danger before you tap this skill.

Trident (Underwater)

The elementalist's underwater weapon is the trident. It's a long-range weapon, allowing you to keep your distance and cast at enemies with impunity. Spell effects are especially awesome underwater, and you still have access to all four elements. Play around with each until you master all underwater skills. By then, you'll have many tools to survive aquatic engagements.

 MAGMA ORB (FIRE)

Damage: Low

Effect: None

Cooldown: None

This skill shoots small blobs of magma that explode after a short delay. Magma Orb provides steady damage whenever you need it, and it's a perfectly good standby.

 BOIL (FIRE)

Damage: Moderate

Effect: Duration (4 Seconds)

Cooldown: 10 Seconds

For four seconds, the water around your target boils. The damage from the attack is adequate, and the spell's visual effect is awesome.

 STEAM (FIRE)

Damage: Low

Effect: Blindness (5 Seconds)

Cooldown: 25 Seconds

You hit your foes with superheated water, Blinding them with flash-created steam. The attack isn't that deadly, but the Blindness is a nice touch whenever you need to mitigate enemy damage.

LAVA CHAINS (FIRE)

Damage: Moderate

Effect: Cripple (6 Seconds)

Cooldown: 30 Seconds

Chains of lava form around your enemies, Crippling them. This spell also looks great, and it has wonderful utility. The damage is perfectly respectable, and it has a long duration. Impede enemies and maintain range against them while you move back to direct damage spells.

HEAT WAVE (FIRE)

Damage:	High
Effect:	Burning (3 Seconds), Vigor (5 Seconds)
Cooldown:	40 Seconds

You Burn your enemies with a blast of heat. Any nearby allies are filled with Vigor, making this a solid PvP ability for the few areas that feature underwater combat. In PvE, the Vigor helps your hero dodge around and avoid even more attacks from enemies that close the distance.

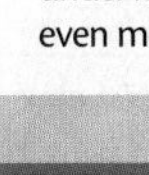

WATER MISSILE (WATER)

Damage:	Low
Effect:	None
Cooldown:	None

You launch a slow-moving ball of ice. This basic attack is pretty much what you'd expect: a standard, direct-damage ability.

ICE GLOBE (WATER)

Damage:	Very High
Effect:	None
Cooldown:	10 Seconds

You shoot a slow-moving globe of ice that can be detonated for higher damage. This attack takes a little practice to master, but it's worth the investment. If you just hit the enemy with the ice globe, the damage by itself is good. However, detonating the attack ahead of time is even more lethal.

ICE WALL (WATER)

Damage:	None (Detonate: Very High)
Effect:	Explosive Barrier, Duration (10 Seconds)
Cooldown:	20 Seconds

A wall of ice forms for 10 seconds. This wall can be shattered to deliver high damage to nearby enemies. Block approaching targets with Ice Wall, and then smash the wall before its duration expires.

UNDERCURRENT (WATER)

Damage:	Low
Effect:	Regeneration (5 Seconds)
Cooldown:	25 Seconds

You guide a current of water that damages nearby enemies while healing your allies. The supplemental healing for your party is always welcome, and you get to inflict a little damage in the process. Undercurrent is a weak attack spell, so we recommend saving it for its regenerative effects.

TIDAL WAVE (WATER)

Damage:	Moderate (Wave Damage: High)
Effect:	Light Healing, Teleport
Cooldown:	30 Seconds

Tidal Wave sends your hero darting forward through the water. You reach your targets quickly, hitting them as a wave follows you from behind. The wave heals allies and then crashes into your targets, hurting them even more. Tidal Wave is an excellent water attack, and you should use it heavily. In a pinch, this doubles as an underwater travel power, letting you scoot forward inside or outside of battle.

FORKED LIGHTNING (AIR)

Damage:	Low
Effect:	Area-of-Effect Damage
Cooldown:	None

You cast a bolt of lightning that forks on impact, hitting multiple foes. The autoattack does sustainable damage to a group of enemies. It's weak against single opponents.

ELECTROCUTE (AIR)

Damage:	Moderate
Effect:	None
Cooldown:	5 Seconds

The water around your foe becomes charged with electricity. Electrocute is a single-target attack with a short cooldown. Cast it often for decent damage when you're down to a single opponent.

AIR POCKET (AIR)

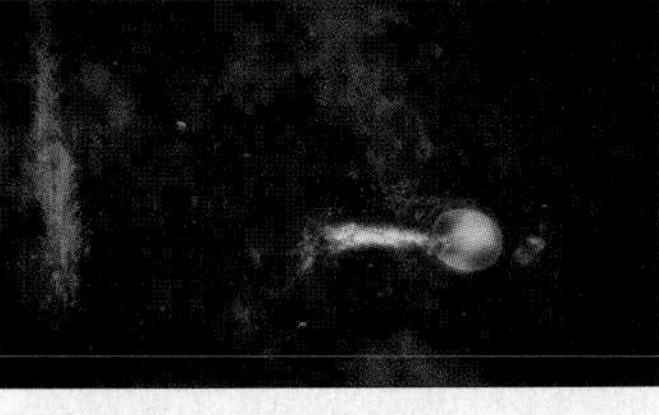

Damage:	Moderate
Effect:	Teleport
Cooldown:	12 Seconds

Your hero releases a slow-moving air pocket. The pocket explodes when it hits a target, dealing damage and causing your elementalist to teleport over to the victim. This attack requires some practice to master. Try not to become disoriented when your position changes, and don't cast it when you're trying to maintain ranged attacks against your enemies.

AIR BUBBLE (AIR)

Damage:	None
Effect:	Float (2 Seconds)
Cooldown:	40 Seconds

Your target becomes trapped in an air bubble. The attack immobilizes the enemy and floats him helplessly to the surface. This is a good disruptive ability. And, because the trident uses long range, you get to continue attacking your foe the entire time. If you want to follow the target upward, hit him with Air Pocket when he's near the surface.

LIGHTNING CAGE (AIR)

Damage:	Low
Effect:	Stun (3 Seconds), Duration (5 Seconds)
Cooldown:	30 Seconds

You create a cage of lightning, stunning any foes that cross it. This is a close-range disruptive attack against multiple targets. It's meant to keep an enemy group from overwhelming you. If you find yourself surrounded, put down your Lightning Cage, get to range, and resume your assault.

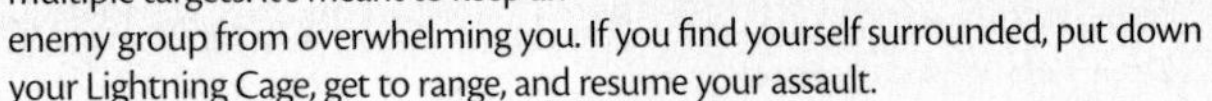

ROCK BLADE (EARTH)

Damage:	Low
Effect:	Bleeding (1 Second)
Cooldown:	None

This autoattack delivers a surprising amount of damage once you factor in the stacking Bleed condition. It has decent range, as well, and you can bring down enemies without resorting to more complex skills or tactics.

ROCK SPRAY (EARTH)

Damage:	High
Effect:	Area-of-Effect Damage, Bleeding (10 Seconds)
Cooldown:	12 Seconds

When you want to inflict Bleed on more targets, there's always Rock Spray. You fling a cone of gravel through the water that impacts multiple targets. Partner this with Rock Blade to stack on the condition damage.

MAGNETIC CURRENT (EARTH)

Damage:	Moderate
Effect:	Pull Yourself, Immobilize (2 Seconds)
Cooldown:	18 Seconds

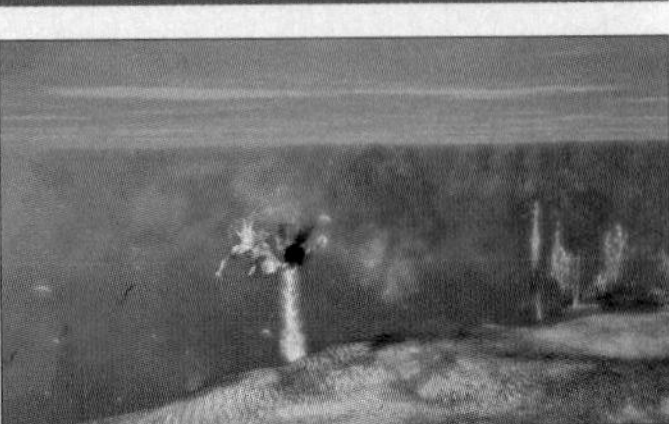

A magnetic attraction forms between you and your foe. Your hero is pulled over to the target, and the enemy is suddenly immobilized. This attack is great to keep your enemies from swimming away in PvP. It is also an ideal way to close gaps against targets if you're worried about being kited or want to nail enemies with Rockspray.

ROCK ANCHOR (EARTH)

Damage:	None
Effect:	Sink (2 Seconds)
Cooldown:	35 Seconds

A stony anchor draws your enemy down into the depths. This is a disruptive ability that buys you time to flee or pile on free damage.

MURKY WATER (EARTH)

Damage:	Low
Effect:	Area-of-Effect Damage, Blindness (1 Second), Duration (6 Seconds)
Cooldown:	45 Seconds

This attack creates a screen of debris-filled water, blinding any nearby enemies. This attack is useful in longer or larger fights to help mitigate damage. It can keep you from being overwhelmed by an enemy force.

Downed Skills

On the Ground

Elementalists have a lot of tricks and survivability on their side, but sometimes their light armor doesn't give them much durability. Fortunately, they can fall back on an array of spells if they're downed. Even fallen elementalists are formidable opponents, and they'll use everything at their disposal to regain their footing.

DISCHARGE LIGHTNING

Damage: Low
Effect: Vulnerability (10 Seconds)
Cooldown: None

This fast spell gives you an opportunity to bring down a foe and rally. In addition to winnowing down your enemies' health, it slams them with Vulnerability, reducing their defensive potential. Always target the enemy with the lowest health; it's your best chance to score a kill. If you have allies nearby, focus on whatever they're attacking to further improve your odds.

GRASPING EARTH

Damage: Low
Effect: Channeled, Immobilize (1 Second)
Cooldown: 10 Seconds

If you're worried about enemies running away just before you can bring them down, Grasping Earth lets you immobilize foes. They can't run, and they can't dodge, either. Use this only for holding enemies in place; stick with Discharge Lightning if you're simply trying for a basic kill.

VAPOR FORM

Damage: None
Effect: Invulnerable, Duration (5 Seconds)
Cooldown: 20 Seconds

You become an invulnerable mist, preventing any damage to you and allowing you to move, possibly away from enemies or toward friends. Follow this with Bandage to get some health after you scoot into a better position.

BANDAGE

Damage: N/A
Effect: Self-Heal
Cooldown: 5 Seconds

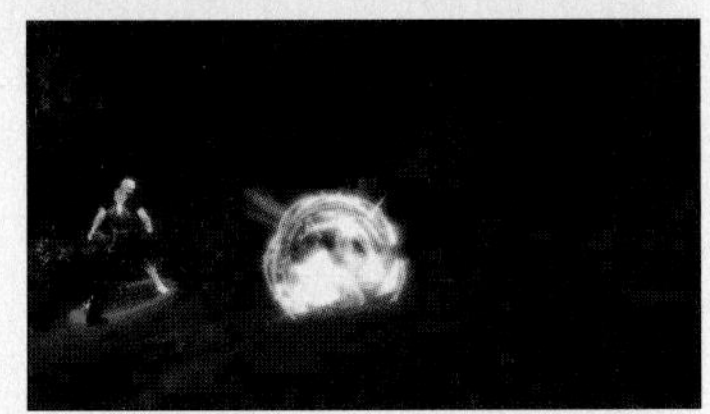

Use this ability when no enemies are attacking you. Your hero heals a small amount over time. The healing is interrupted the moment you take damage. You have to heal your character all the way to full before rally triggers, so this works only if there aren't any enemies coming after you. Otherwise, it's there just to give you a little health, possibly allowing you to last that much longer as you attempt to score a kill.

Underwater

New skills are available to elementalists if they encounter trouble underwater. Unfortunately, none of them inflicts a huge amount of damage. Fight your hardest, hope for the best, and swim to the surface if you don't think you can kill any of your enemies before death veils your eyes.

WATER FIST

Damage: Low
Effect: None
Cooldown: None

You throw a fist of water at your enemy. This low-damage attack gives you a chance to kill your target and rally. You can use it while you're moving, so swim upward while you execute it. As in any downed situation, target the enemy with the lowest health for your best chance of recovery.

STONE KICK

Damage: Moderate-to-High
Effect: None
Cooldown: 6 Seconds

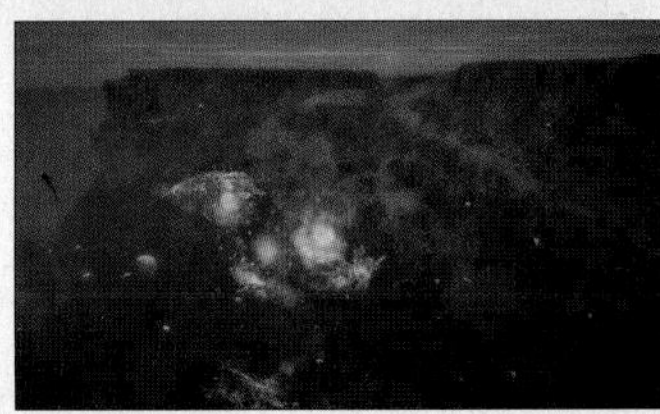

You wrap your foot in stone and kick your enemy. This delivers decent damage. Use it whenever the cooldown expires.

STEAM VENT

Damage: Low
Effect: Speed to Surface, Blindness (3 Seconds), Burning (3 Seconds)
Cooldown: 15 Seconds

You burst to the surface, leaving enemies behind your character Blind and Burning. If you can't rally without fleeing, this is the best way to gain distance and steal some time up top to heal before enemies catch up and hurt you.

BANDAGE

Damage: None
Effect: Self-Heal
Cooldown: 5 Seconds

This works the same way as Bandaging yourself on land.

Slot Skills

Healing

Several healing options are open to elementalists through their weapon skills alone. Because of this, it's wise to take a solid self-healing skill for most of your career as an elementalist. Make sure you can support yourself during solo and group engagements.

GLYPH OF ELEMENTAL HARMONY

Effect: Self-Heal, Gain Boon

Cooldown: 20 Seconds

You start the game with this skill, and it never becomes obsolete. Your elementalist restores a fair amount of health when you cast this, and then you also get a boon. What boon you receive depends on the element to which you are attuned.

- **Fire:** Might (20 Seconds)
- **Water:** Regen (10 Seconds)
- **Air:** Swiftness (10 Seconds)
- **Earth:** Protection (10 Seconds)

The Quick Glyph Air trait reduces the already fast recharge time of your healing skill and any Glyph utility skills you want to take.

ETHER RENEWAL

Effect: Self-Heal, Remove Condition

Cooldown: 15 Seconds

This is a decent healing skill for PvE, but it really shines in PvP. Most enemies in PvE don't stack on a number of conditions. However, the moment you move over to fight with players, they pile on conditions. Ether Renewal's short cooldown means you can use it every fight or two. This makes it a wonderful spell when you don't know what's coming up in the next set of events.

SIGNET OF RESTORATION

Effect: Passively Restores Health, Activate for Self-Heal

Cooldown: 40 Seconds

This is a great healing skill for defensive players, particularly those roaming around the world in a group. Every time you cast a spell, you get a little boost of health. It isn't much, but it adds up, and it'll keep you in fighting trim. If you ever get into trouble, you can activate the skill for a stronger boost.

Utility

Elementalists have a huge variety in their utility skills. They range from direct damage, area-of-effect attacks, defensive abilities, guaranteed condition damage, conjured weapons, and summoned creatures. There isn't a right or wrong choice here. Instead, choose the skills that match what you love for a given situation. Don't be afraid to branch out and try something different. Many of these utility skills supplement an elementalist's magical repertoire, but they do so in unique ways.

TIER 1

ARCANE BLAST

Effect: Single-Target Damage, Combo Finisher (Physical Projectile)

Cooldown: 15 Seconds

You shoot your target with a bolt of arcane energy. This single-target spell delivers high damage, and it recharges pretty quickly. You can use it fight after fight (or even within a battle) as needed. Many traits improve the effects of arcane spells, so look through your options in the trait lines if you like specializing in arcane spells.

ARCANE WAVE

Effect: AoE Damage, Combo Finisher (Blast)

Cooldown: 20 Seconds

This skill hits nearby foes with AoE damage. Anything within the area gets a wave of energy to the face. If you need more close-range damage, this is good for your lineup. Dagger elementalists already do well in this area, but having even more AoE potential is nice for inflicting high burst damage.

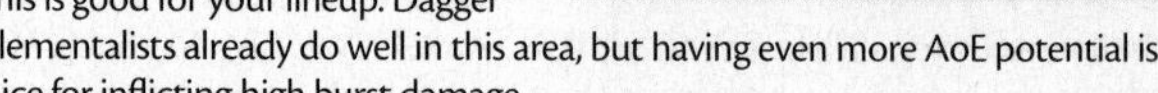

GLYPH OF ELEMENTAL POWER

Effect: Causes Condition

Cooldown: 45 Seconds

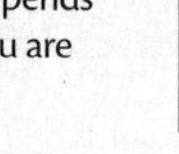

For 30 seconds, you get a chance for all your spells to impart a condition. What condition is added depends on the element to which you are attuned.

- **Fire:** Burning (3 seconds)
- **Water:** Chilled (2 seconds)
- **Air:** Weakness (6 seconds)
- **Earth:** Cripple (5 seconds)

This spell is good for people who love cycling through their elements and want to add some condition damage to everything. It also has benefits in PvP, as you can lay down several different area-of-effect spells while you're putting on those conditions.

GLYPH OF STORMS

Effect: AoE Damage

Cooldown: 60 seconds

This skill creates a huge elemental storm over a targeted area. This looks great, and it delivers high damage. Glyph of Storms is exceptionally good for supportive elementalists who'd like to have damage potential even when they're attuned to Water (or one of the other supportive configurations).

SIGNET OF FIRE

Effect: Passively Raise Your Critical Chance; Actively Adds Burning (9 Seconds)

Cooldown: 20 Seconds

Simply slotting Signet of Fire increases your chance to make critical hits. That's a decent way to raise your character's base damage and burst potential. But that isn't all it does! If you activate this signet, you lose the passive effect but can inflict Burning on your target, no matter what your attunement.

ARMOR OF EARTH

Effect: Break Stun, Gain Protection (8 Seconds), Stability (8 Seconds), Duration (12 Seconds)

Cooldown: 90 Seconds

This cantrip encases your hero in earth for 12 seconds. You break out of stuns and can't be knocked around or restunned for the duration of the effect. Slot this skill before going into PvP or facing off against bosses in group events. You don't have to wait for a stun to activate this; the spell's protective elements are just as important, and your hero can survive far more damage while the armor is up. Use this to endure burst damage from the most fearsome enemies.

CONJURE FLAME AXE

Effect: Summon Weapon

Cooldown: 60 Seconds

This skill equips you with an axe made of lava and manifests a second axe at the targeted location. The lava axe has 15 charges and the following abilities:

- Lava Axe: Throws the axe at a target for moderate damage.
- Explosive Lava Axe (5-second cooldown): Throws the axe, which explodes for very high damage.
- Burning Retreat (15-second cooldown): Retreat and cause Burning for 1 second to anything that follows.
- Ring of Fire (15-second cooldown): Creates a ring of fire that Burns targets for 5 seconds and deals additional damage.
- Flaming Leap (20 seconds): Your hero leaps forward and hits foes for high damage and Burning (5 seconds).

It's best to use Conjure Fire Axe in a group situation, as both you and a group member get a very powerful weapon. The group member gains access to the same weapon skills listed above. It's also most useful in a PvE situation, where people have a bit more freedom and time to experiment with their new weapon. You can also use it just before you fight a major boss in a dungeon.

This skill works well for support elementalists who want some type of damage mode when all of their other slots are filled with utility, healing, and survival abilities.

TIER 2

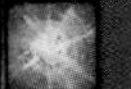

ARCANE POWER

Effect: Your Next Few Attacks do Critical Damage

Cooldown: 45 Seconds

This skill is absolutely wonderful. Guaranteed critical hits essentially add free burst damage to your lineup. You can activate Arcane Power before a fight or during the engagement. Use your best high-damage spells afterward to ensure you get the most out of this. High-damage AoEs are the best of all.

Arcane Power has a long cooldown time, but this can be shortened by Arcane Mastery (in the Arcane Magic trait line).

GLYPH OF LESSER ELEMENTALS

Effect: Summon Pet

Cooldown: 45 Seconds

For 60 seconds, you get a pet elemental. The elemental summoned depends on your attunement. You can't directly control your elemental, but it will attack your enemies and deal damage, and it is hard to kill. This distracts enemies from going after your elementalist, so the extra damage is combined with increased survivability for your caster.

SIGNET OF WATER

Effect: Passively Removes a Condition (Every 10 Seconds); Actively adds Chill (4 Seconds)

Cooldown: 30 Seconds

This is a wonderful PvP skill. Removing conditions is essential for PvP or battles against higher-level PvE monsters because many of them expose your character to increased damage and attack. Having the option to slow enemies and reduce their damage output makes Signet of Water even better for that environment. When you hit your enemy with the active Chill effect, it even does modest damage.

SIGNET OF AIR

Effect: Passively Grants a 10% Increase in Movement Speed; Actively Imparts Area-of-Effect Blindness (5 Seconds)

Cooldown: 20 Seconds

This signet is equally pleasing in PvE and PvP. The movement buff is at its best when you're crossing large distances in the Eternal Battlegrounds, or while you hunt for monsters and resources throughout Tyria. When you need a sudden chance to escape from enemies, use the signet to blind them, and flee while they whiff for their next attack. Use the signet at the start of a major engagement to give your group a big edge. The damage isn't very high, but it's pretty much free when you're using it to blind the enemy.

SIGNET OF EARTH

Effect: Passively Improves Toughness; Actively Imparts Immobilize (3 Seconds)

Cooldown: 30 Seconds

Signet of Earth doesn't give you much of a defensive bonus, so consider it a minor benefit. Its strong option is the Immobilizing effect against a target. If you're a dagger wielder, use this when you're kiting with ranged spells or catching up to enemies.

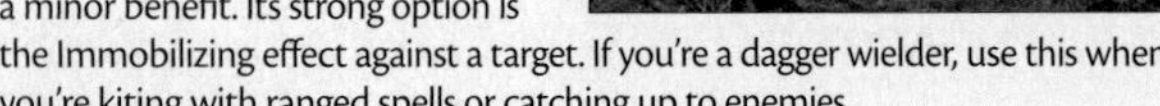

CLEANSING FIRE

Effect: Breaks Stun, Remove Conditions (3), AoE Burning (3 Seconds)

Cooldown: 50 Seconds

If you don't know what's coming up, Cleansing Fire is a safe skill to slot. Though it's not as powerful at any individual effect as some other utility skills, this choice has a bit of everything. Use this cantrip to get out of trouble and leave everyone behind you on fire.

CONJURE FROST BOW

Effect: Summon Weapon

Cooldown: 60 Seconds

This skill equips you with a bow made of frost and manifests a second frost bow at the targeted location. The frost bow has 15 charges and the following abilities:

- Water Arrow: Inflicts low-ranged damage while healing your hero and nearby allies.
- Frost Volley (8-second cooldown): Fires quickly, inflicting low damage and Vulnerability on your foes.
- Frost Fan (15-second cooldown): Fires arrows in a forward cone. Each deals low damage and Chills foes for 3 seconds.
- Ice Storm (20-second cooldown): Targets an area for high damage and causes Confusion to struck enemies.
- Deep Freeze (30-second cooldown): Blocks enemies with a wall of ice that can be shattered for high AoE damage.

It's best to use Conjure Frost Bow in a group situation, which lets both you and a group member get the weapon. People familiar with your play style benefit the most because they'll understand what's going on. It's not as useful if you're playing with random buddies during an event.

Use these frost attacks when your character suddenly needs decent range. It's a good skill for dagger users that find themselves caught in combat (and thus unable to switch weapons). With this, they get the range they need to counter kiting tactics.

TIER 3

ARCANE SHIELD

Effect: Blocks Damage; Deals AoE Damage

Cooldown: 75 Seconds

This spell protects your caster for three attacks and then explodes. The blast trashes nearby enemies for high damage. This arcane spell is equally good in PvP and PvE. It's especially useful against melee enemies, whether you're a ranged character or a close-up caster.

GLYPH OF RENEWAL

Effect: Revive Ally

Cooldown: 105 Seconds

Cast this to immediately raise a fallen group member or allied NPC. This comes up often in certain events, when it's great to have allies distracting enemy attention. It's also a godsend in PvP, when stopping to revive a fallen buddy is quite dangerous.

When Glyph of Renewal is activated, each attunement has a secondary effect.

- **Fire:** Grants a passive buff that revives you the next time you are downed.
- **Water:** Your revived ally comes back with full health.
- **Air:** Teleports the revived ally to your location.
- **Earth:** Revives up to three nearby allies.

Be certain to change your attunement based on what you need the most. If multiple allies are down, Earth is by far the best thing you can do for them. This gives the whole team a second wind.

MIST FORM

Effect: Breaks Stun, Invulnerability (3 Seconds)

Cooldown: 75 Seconds

For three seconds, you turn into vaporous mist. During this time, you are Invulnerable but cannot use weapons or skills. Use that time to flee, get to range, avoid heavy channeled attacks from enemies, or simply buy time when cooldowns are progressing.

LIGHTNING FLASH

Effect: Breaks Stun, Teleport

Cooldown: 60 Seconds

Use this cantrip to jump away from enemies or to move quickly toward a new target. Lightning Flash gets you out of trouble nicely. If you pair it with other cantrips, your caster can use multiple ways to escape to range. This makes it very hard for kiting characters to catch you. They have to do it time and time again before their abilities start to stick.

CONJURE LIGHTNING HAMMER

Effect: Summon Weapon

Cooldown: 60 Seconds

This skill equips you with a hammer made of lightning and manifests a second lightning hammer at the targeted location. The lightning hammer has 15 charges and the following abilities:

- Lightning Swing: Deals moderate melee damage.
- Lightning Leap (6-second cooldown): Leaps forward to hit enemies for moderate damage.
- Wind Blast (18-second cooldown): Knocks your targets around, disabling them for a brief time.
- Lightning Storm (20-second cooldown): Hits up to five enemies for low damage.
- Static Field (25 seconds): Inflicts low damage to clustered enemies and Stuns them, as well!

Like the other elemental summonings, this tool gets the most use when you have a buddy ready to assist. When you're soloing, these elemental weapons augment the play styles you use the least. Lightning doesn't do much damage, but it's good for harassing powerful targets you need to take out of the fight with crowd control. It's most useful when you have additional characters to focus on damage output while you lock down the enemy.

CONJURE EARTH SHIELD

Effect: Summon Weapon

Cooldown: 60 Seconds

This skill equips you with a shield made of earth and manifests a second earth shield at the targeted location. The earth shield has 15 charges and the following abilities:

- Shield Smack: Deals moderate melee damage.
- Crippling Shield (8-second cooldown): Cripples enemies in a line; the effect lasts for 2 seconds.
- Magnetic Surge (12-second cooldown): Deals low damage and dazes your enemy for 2 seconds.
- Magnetic Shield (25-second cooldown): Pulls enemies toward your character, immobilizes them, and deals low damage.
- Fortify (45-second cooldown): Makes your hero Invulnerable for 6 seconds.

For bursts of survivability, Earth is the element you want to summon. Whether during intense group events or PvP, your character must sometimes face enemy parties that are too much to handle. Shield of Earth can buy you time to escort, get reinforcements, or allow others to rally.

Elite

Elite skills are powerful and complex, especially in the hands of elementalists. Take Glyph of Elementals to start with something that's easy to integrate into your routines. Then branch out from there to see everything the profession has to offer. They're all good skills.

GLYPH OF ELEMENTALS

Effect: Summon Pet (60 Seconds)

Cooldown: 120 Seconds

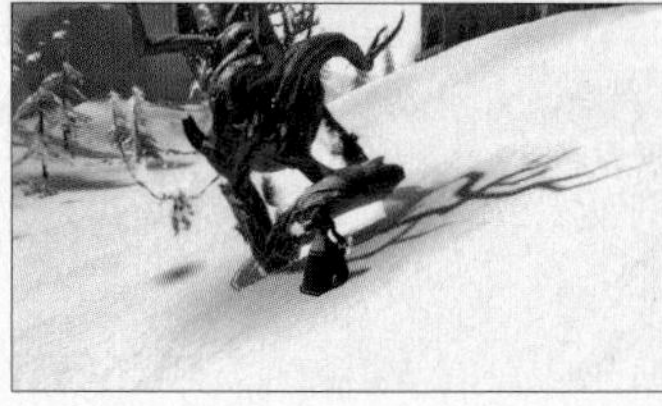

You summon a large elemental. The type of elemental is based on the element to which you are attuned. They elementals are capable of the following:

- **Fire:** Deal heavy damage.
- **Water:** Fight and heal.
- **Air:** Stun enemies.
- **Earth:** Survive an epic beatdown.

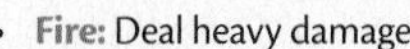

These elementals look great, last quite a while, and can keep enemies off your back, making fights easier to win. You cannot go wrong in choosing this skill.

CONJURE FIERY GREATSWORD

Effect: Summon Weapon

Cooldown: 180 Seconds

This skill equips you with a greatsword made of fire and manifests a second fiery greatsword at the targeted location. Additionally, the second blade Burns the area where it appears, damaging enemies in the process. The fiery greatsword has 15 charges and the following abilities:

- Flame Wave: Throws fireballs into your foe, dealing moderate damage.
- Fiery Eruption (5-second cooldown): Burns nearby enemies, setting each of them on fire for 3 seconds.
- Fiery Whirl (5-second cooldown): Deals AoE damage and Cripples enemies for 3 seconds.
- Fiery Rush (10-second cooldown): Charge toward your target, doing moderate damage and leaving a trail of flame.
- Firestorm (15-second cooldown): Summons a story of fire for moderate damage to all enemies near the targeted area.

Use Conjure Fiery Greatsword when you're paired with another character to deal moderate damage to entire groups. This elite skill is at its best when you're with another character possessing primarily non-damaging spells. It's nice to convert two people into damage mode for a short time. Characters with heavy loadouts of damaging skills don't need this nearly as much; they may even inflict less damage with it than they would without it.

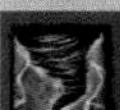

TORNADO

Effect: Gain Stability (15 Seconds), AoE Damage and Launch

Cooldown: 180 Seconds

This is a great elite skill for PvP. You shapeshift into a swirling tornado. As you whip through the area, you damage all enemies you encounter and launch them into the air. Your path of destruction cannot be stopped by movement-impairing conditions.

Traits

Fire Magic (Raises Power and Condition Duration)

REWARDS

Points Invested	Ability Gained
5	20% chance to cause Burning whenever a foe attacks you in melee
15	Deal damage at your location when attuned to Fire
25	Inflict 5% more damage to a Burning foe

SKILL OPTIONS (GAINED EVERY 10 POINTS)

ADEPT TIER

- Lava Tomb: Create a lava font when downed.
- Burning Fire: Cleansing Flame, Signet of Fire, Conjure Flame Axe, and Conjure Fiery Greatsword gain 3 seconds of Burning.
- Ember's Might: You gain Might for 30 seconds whenever you are set on fire.
- Spell Slinger: Cantrips grant you 3 stacks of Might when activated.
- Burning Precision: 20% chance to cause Burning on a critical hit.
- Internal Fire: Deal 10% more damage when attuned to Fire.

MASTER TIER

- Pyromancer's Alacrity: All your Fire weapon skills recharge 20% faster.
- Conjurer: Conjured weapons have 10 more charges.
- Fire's Embrace: When you activate a Signet, you gain a fiery aura for 3 seconds.
- One with Fire: Your flame barrier's chance to Burn foes increases the longer you are attuned to Fire.

GRANDMASTER TIER

- Persisting Flames: Fire fields last 30% longer.
- Pyromancer's Puissance: Each Fire spell you cast adds Might for a short time.

Air (Raises Precision and Critical Damage)

REWARDS

Points Invested	Ability Gained
5	Move 10% faster while attuned to Air
15	Strike your target with a bolt of lightning when attuned to Air
25	60% chance to cause Vulnerability on critical hits

SKILL OPTIONS (GAINED EVERY 10 POINTS)

ADEPT TIER

- Tempest Strength: +5% damage while moving.
- Zephyr's Focus: Your endurance regenerates 100% faster while channeling skills.
- Quick Glyphs: Glyphs recharge 20% faster.
- One with Air: You move faster the longer you are attuned to Air.
- Soothing Winds: 5% of your Precision is converted to healing.
- Bolt to the Heart: +20% damage to a foe with less than 25% health.

MASTER TIER

- Arcane Lightning: You have 3% more critical damage for each arcane skill equipped.
- Inscription: Grant a boon associated with your current attunement when you cast a Glyph.
- Aeromancer's Alacrity: All your Air weapon skills recharge 15% faster.
- Air Training: +10% damage while attuned to Air.

GRANDMASTER TIER

- Zephyr's Boon: Auras grant Swiftness and Fury when applied.
- Grounded: +20% damage to stunned or knocked-down foes.

Earth Magic (Raises Condition Damage and Toughness)

REWARDS

Points Invested	Ability Gained
5	Gain extra armor when attuned to Earth
15	Damage and Cripple foes when attuned to Earth
25	+10% damage when your endurance is full

SKILL OPTIONS (GAINED EVERY 10 POINTS)

ADEPT TIER

- Obsidian Focus: Gain Toughness when using a channeled skill.
- Signet Mastery: Signets recharge 20% faster.
- Earth's Embrace: Gain Armor of Earth when health reaches 50%. This effect cannot trigger more than once every 90 seconds.
- Salt Stone: You deal 5% damage against Bleeding foes.
- Serrated Stones: Bleeds you apply last 20% longer.
- Stone Splinters: 5% damage while within melee range of your opponent.

MASTER TIER

- Strength of Stone: +10% damage while attuned to Earth.
- Elemental Shielding: You gain protection when applying an aura to an ally or yourself.
- Geomancer's Freedom: All conjure skills break Stun.
- Geomancer's Alacrity: All your Earth weapon skills recharge 30% faster.

GRANDMASTER TIER

- Rock's Fortitude: Grant Stability to nearby allies when attuned to Earth.
- Written in Stone: You don't lose the passive effects of signets when you activate them.

Water Magic (Raises Healing and Vitality)

REWARDS

Points Invested	Ability Gained
5	Regenerate health when attuned to Water
15	Heal nearby allies when attuned to Water
25	+2% damage for each boon on you

SKILL OPTIONS (GAINED EVERY 10 POINTS)

ADEPT TIER

- Cleansing Water: Whenever you grant regeneration to yourself or an ally, you also remove a condition.
- Shard of Ice: Arcane and Signet skills cause Vulnerability when activated.
- Soothing Disruption: Cantrips grant you Vigor and Regeneration.
- Piercing Shards: While attuned to Water, your spells deal 20% more damage against Vulnerable foes.
- Cleansing Wave: Remove a condition from you and your allies when attuned to water.
- Vital Striking: Deal extra damage when health is above 90%.

MASTER TIER

- Aquamancer's Alacrity: All your Water weapon skills recharge 15% faster.
- Icy Mist: Cause Chill, Vulnerability, and damage to nearby foes while in mist or vapor form.
- Cantrip Mastery: Cantrips recharge 20% faster.
- Soothing Wave: Mist Form and Signet of Water grant 2 seconds of regeneration.

GRANDMASTER TIER

- Stop Drop and Roll: Dodge-rolling removes a condition.
- Powerful Aura: Auras apply to nearby allies.

Arcane Mastery (Raises Boon Duration and Attunement Recharge Rate)

REWARDS

Points Invested	Ability Gained
5	Attunement bonuses linger for 5 seconds
15	Grant yourself Fury on attunement
25	Skills have a chance to apply a condition on critical hit

SKILL OPTIONS (GAINED EVERY 10 POINTS)

ADEPT TIER

- Arcane Mastery: Arcane skills recharge 20% faster.
- Arcane Resurrection: When you resurrect an ally, you and the resurrected ally gain an aura based on your attunement.
- Arcane Retribution: Gain Arcane Power at 75% health.
- Final Shielding: Create an Arcane Shield when health reaches 25%.
- Elemental Attunement: You and all nearby allies gain Might when attuned to Fire, Regeneration when attuned to Water, Swiftness when attuned to Air, and Protection when attuned to Earth.
- Renewing Stamina: You have a 33% chance to gain Vigor on critical hits.

MASTER TIER

- Vigorous Scepter: Endurance recharges faster while wielding a scepter.
- Blasting Staff: Area attacks are larger when wielding a staff.
- Windbourne Dagger: Move 15% faster when wielding a dagger.
- Arcane Energy: Your Arcane and Signet skills restore 25% endurance when used.

GRANDMASTER TIER

- Evasive Arcane: Create an attunement-based spell on dodge.
- Elemental Surge: Arcane spells gain Burning when attuned to Fire (5 seconds), Chill when attuned to Water (3 seconds), Blindness when attuned to Air (5 seconds), and Immobilize when attuned to Earth (1 Second).

Elementalists in PvE

Elementalist is a wonderful profession for someone simply to pick up and play. It's easy to understand and relate to many of their abilities, and they don't require intricate positioning or balancing to be effective. It's an excellent profession for exploring and getting to know the world of *Guild Wars 2*. Their utility and versatility allow them to rise to any challenge they encounter.

Indeed, elementalists' power lies in their flexibility. Their ability to shift almost effortlessly between damage dealing, healing, and buff/debuffing is second to none. Even in the middle of a fight, you can switch from high area-of-effect damage to keeping everyone healed, and then back to wholesale destruction.

Also, you don't need to keep as many weapons up to date. Because elementalists don't switch weapons during combat, they tend to carry fewer weapons and stick more to whatever combination they love the most.

If you're on your own, figure out whether you like close-range (dagger main hand) or medium-range fighting (scepter main hand), and invest strongly in your weapons. If you find that you want more survivability, add a focus. If you crave damage potential, take a second dagger for your off hand. Either way, your primary goal is not to have long fights. You don't have the defense or armor to withstand that sort of barrage.

For group work, the scepter/focus combination is valid, and staves are brilliant. The ability to hit large numbers of enemies at range lets you contribute to any tasks you encounter. You also don't have to worry about being overwhelmed, and you have reliable control over the battle's progression. If anything unfortunate happens, switch to Water spells and pull your group's butt out of the fire. No one—absolutely no one—can heal like a staff-wielding, Water-casting elementalist.

Keep your main weapon up to date at all times. You're a light armor wearer, and that means you never want to stand still and take hits. You want power and precision to lay waste to your foes. Some condition damage is nice, especially if you like Earth abilities, but direct damage will usually be more prominent.

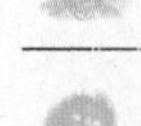

To this end, some utility skills come into play. Arcane Power deserves special mention because it gives you guaranteed critical hits over your next few attacks—you can't go wrong with that! The passive effects from a number of your signet abilities can be very good, as well: Signet of Fire gives you a boost to your critical chance, and Signet of Water can free you from worrying about nasty condition damage for long. Finally, try out Glyph of Elemental Power and Glyph of Lesser Elemental. Elemental Power ensures you always have some sort of condition damage active. Lesser Elemental grants you a pretty strong pet to help in your battles.

Also, when you fight, keep in mind that you don't have to stand still to cast your spells (unlike in many other games). Unless you're in a specific channeling spell, you have complete freedom to move around, dodge, strafe, or jump up and down—all while launching your attacks. This makes things much safer for you and lets you control a fight much more easily.

Elementalists in PvP

Elementalists in PvP fall into three major roles: those who want large-scale AoE damage, those who want to heal their side as much as possible, and those who work on damage mitigation (buff your team, debuff the opposing team). You can find something for each of these roles in the elementalist's lineup.

For AoE damage, Fire spells are the key. Rain down as much fiery destruction as possible over a large, targeted area. If you like healing, go for Water and take a staff with you. You won't deliver much damage (although you can do some), but you can heal like nobody's business. If you like buff/debuff work, Air and Earth both have good sets. Air's abilities harp on positioning and movement-altering effects. Earth can help you and your team be more defensive while weakening the other side with condition damage.

Skilled elementalists learn to shift between elemental attunements as soon as a need for something new arises. If there's a lull in the battle, switch to Water and top off wounded allies. Big push? It's Fire time! Is one guy being a pest? Give him Earth or Air, depending on your setup.

Because the dagger's close range is a significant liability in PvP, take a staff or scepter as your main-hand weapon. In terms of your armor, your choices are more varied. While you still benefit from Power and Precision, you can make stronger gains in Toughness and Vitality. The trait skills you get from those lines help you add base conditions to your spells, and they make those conditions even more damaging.

A number of slot skills work well in PvP. Of note, the signet and cantrip spells give you massive options for getting around the field and controlling fights. Signet spells give you fabulous passive abilities combined with conditions that disrupt your enemies. Cantrips break Stun and help your elementalist stay three steps ahead of your rivals.

When it comes to elite skills, you really have to love Tornado. The idea that you can move around, hitting and sweeping people away, is just perfect.

ENGINEER

Engineers are versatile and survivable combatants with medium armor and a general focus on ranged combat (but the profession has a few close-range options). Armed with a shield, these characters can mitigate damage with stuns and knockbacks. With a rifle or dual pistols equipped, engineers are able to deal damage while keeping their foes at a distance.

Engineers often get their group utility from elixirs, which can be thrown or fired from the elixir gun, to grant helpful boons to allies or harmful conditions to enemies. You're more than just a long-range damage dealer. Everybody appreciates extra healing and boons.

If you like variety, this is your profession. You can toss bombs and elixirs, shoot flames, set up turrets, or surprise your foes with a rocket-boot kick or wrench to the face.

Profession Stats

Attribute	Starting Stats	Naked at Level 80
Power	28	916
Precision	28	916
Toughness	28	916
Vitality	28	916
Attack	177	916
Critical Chance	4%	4%
Armor	89	916
Health	316	15,082

These stats give you an idea of what to expect from your character. They show engineer progression through examples taken at the beginning and end of leveling. Your actual stats will likely vary from this.

Weapons and Weapon Skills

Engineers have a short list of standard weaponry they can use. Instead of variety, each weapon set has the skills that fill the engineers' needs. Pistols are multitarget-focused, shields add survivability, and rifles have great burst damage.

Pistols (Main Hand)

Pistols focus on damage over time and combat with multiple enemies. They don't burst very well, but their total output gets fairly high once you've nailed the target with poison. The second ability mitigates damage from multiple targets.

EXPLOSIVE SHOT

Damage: Low

Effect: Bleed (4 Seconds), Combo Finisher (Physical Projectile: 20% Chance)

Cooldown: None

Your basic autoattack with the pistol is packed with goodness. Not only do you make your target Bleed, but any enemies standing nearby gain the condition as well.

POISON DART VOLLEY

Damage: Moderate

Effect: Poison (2 Seconds)

Cooldown: 10 Seconds

You fire five poison darts at your foes in rapid succession. There is a chance that a bullet or two might miss, but the poison condition makes up for it. Shooting at a group of enemies is even better since you can spread the poison around.

STATIC SHOT

Damage: Medium

Effect: Blind (3 Seconds), Confusion (3 Seconds)

Cooldown: 15 Seconds

This shot fires a burst of static electricity that jumps between enemies. The initial struck enemy misses on his next attack, and the next four enemies nearby are confused. This sometimes bounces between targets, hitting individual enemies multiple times. Use Static Shot to mitigate some damage and force enemies to hold off on their own moves or damage themselves if they persist.

Pistols (Off Hand)

Equipping a pistol in your off hand continues the theme of area-of-effect attacks and dependable damage gained from the main hand. With the second pistol, you acquire a much-needed crowd control ability and a cone attack.

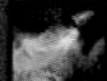

BLOW TORCH

Damage: Low to Medium

Effect: Burning

Cooldown: 18 Seconds

This shoots a cone of fire from your pistol, harming enemies and setting them aflame! Burning is a strong damage over time condition, and it gets better the closer the target is to you. Use this right before your Glue Shot when an enemy gets too close. Follow it up with Dart Volley and let the conditions do the work for you.

GLUE SHOT

Damage: None

Effect: Immobilize (1 Second), Duration (6 Seconds)

Cooldown: 30 seconds

The main-hand pistol's abilities are for fighting multiple targets, but what can you do to keep the bloodthirsty hordes at a distance? This ability spreads an area of sticky glue on the ground. Enemies stuck in it take no damage, but you get a few seconds to attack from safety.

Shield (Off Hand)

Placing a shield in your off hand lowers your damage output but raises your survivability. As a wearer of medium armor, PvP opponents may see you as a soft target. In PvE, you may find yourself under heavy ranged attack, or melee enemies might get too close for comfort and you don't have enough endurance to evade. Grab a shield to increase your defensive options to negate or mitigate damage.

MAGNETIC SHIELD

Damage: Low

Effect: Ranged Attack Deflection and an Area-of-Effect Launch

Cooldown: 35 Seconds

Sometimes a good offense is a good defense. This ability magnetically charges your shield to deflect ranged attacks for 3 seconds. Select the shield again to release the charge to launch enemies. Taken together, you get a short respite from damage and a method to kite melee attackers.

STATIC SHIELD

Damage: None

Effect: Stun (3 Seconds), Daze (2 Seconds)

Cooldown: 40 Seconds

When the going gets tough, engineers electrify their shields. The next enemy to hit you gets stunned! Select this ability again to release the charge and have it daze enemies as the energy flies out and boomerangs back. Aligned properly, you can restrict a large number of enemies from using their special abilities.

Rifle (Two-Handed)

Rifles fire slower but hit harder than pistols. Another difference is both of the rifles' crowd control abilities are single target. The focus is burst damage rather than conditions or damage mitigation. It's much easier to control and take down a single target with a rifle than with a pistol.

HIP SHOT

Damage: Medium

Effect: Combo Finisher (Physical Projectile: 20% Chance)

Cooldown: None

Hip Shot is the basic automatic attack with the rifle. Attacks from this skill pierce targets, allowing you to damage an entire line of enemies as long as you keep them lined up in front of your hero. Back away from enemies while you fire to keep them in a roughly straight path as they follow you.

NET SHOT

Damage None

Effect: Immobilize (2 Seconds)

Cooldown: 10 Seconds

This shot fires an enveloping net at a single enemy. Although this does no damage, you can get in a few free hits or make it to safety while your enemy is trying to break free. This ability's short cooldown means it's almost always available.

BLUNDERBUSS

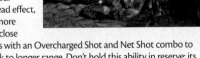

Damage: Very High

Effect: Closer Targets Take Increased Damage

Cooldown: 10 Seconds

Fire a spray of buckshot at your enemies! Because of the spread effect, enemies closer to you take more damage. Let your target get close and then follow Blunderbuss with an Overcharged Shot and Net Shot combo to give yourself time to get back to longer range. Don't hold this ability in reserve; its cooldown is nice and short.

OVERCHARGED SHOT

Damage: High

Effect: Launch Enemy and Knockback Self

Cooldown: 20 Seconds

You can overload your rifle with a powerful shot to knock your enemies back and yourself away from them. Followed by a Net Shot, this can grant you valuable space and time. Be aware of your surroundings. Knocking an enemy off a cliff or into an ally's attack is a big advantage. Conversely, blasting yourself into a wall or off a cliff will do you no good.

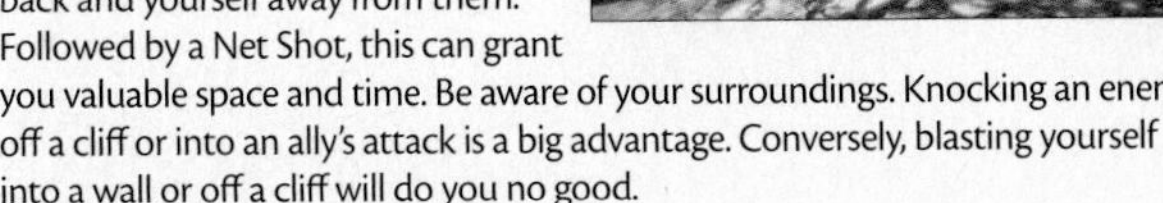

JUMP SHOT

Damage: Very High to Extreme

Effect: Launch Yourself Up and Damage the Area Where You Land, Combo Finisher (Leap)

Cooldown: 20 Seconds

This high-damage attack is very fun to use. Firing a blast at the ground, you launch yourself into the air, slamming into the ground when you land. There are two major strategies for this ability. The first is to aim at your feet. You do damage when you take off and when you land, so the combination of the two punishes any enemies caught in the blasts. The second way is to use it to add to your mobility. If you find yourself surrounded, pick a point a good distance away and blast your way out of danger with some damage as a parting gift.

Harpoon Gun (Underwater Weapon)

The Harpoon Gun mixes multitarget damage with distance-retaining options. Your abilities spread damage around and keep your enemies at long range.

TORPEDO SHOT

Damage: Moderate

Effect: N/A

Cooldown: None

This ability fires a shot that homes in on your target.

SCATTER MINES

Damage: Very High

Effect: N/A

Cooldown: 5 Seconds

Tossing these mines out is great when your other abilities are on cooldown. This ability becomes available again pretty quickly, so don't hesitate to use it. Three mines spread out ahead of you to hit multiple targets. Once the mines are on their way, select the attack again to detonate the mines.

RETREATING GRAPPLE

Damage: Low

Effect: Retreat, Pull Foe

Cooldown: 18 Seconds

Often, your survival in underwater combat depends on your ability to stay mobile and kite. With this ability, you can fire a line behind yourself and pull yourself backward. This quick ability lets you scoot out of your enemies' reach, allowing you vital space to attack. Once at range, you pull your foe over to your new position. If you want to isolate an enemy and get them away from an ally, this is especially helpful.

TIMED CHARGE

Damage: Very High

Effect: Delayed Area of Effect

Cooldown: 18 Seconds

With this ability, you fire a harpoon with an explosive charge attached to it. This explosive goes off several seconds later, and enemies nearby take damage from the blast. The delayed area of effect helps you to space out your damage and keeps you from acquiring too much attention in a group situation.

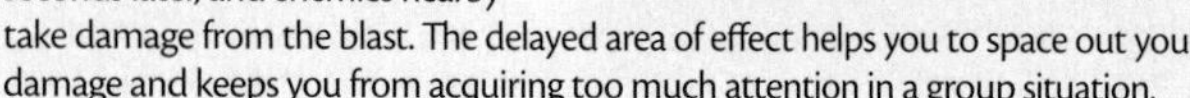

NET WALL

Damage: None

Effect: Immobilize (3 Seconds)

Cooldown: 25 Seconds

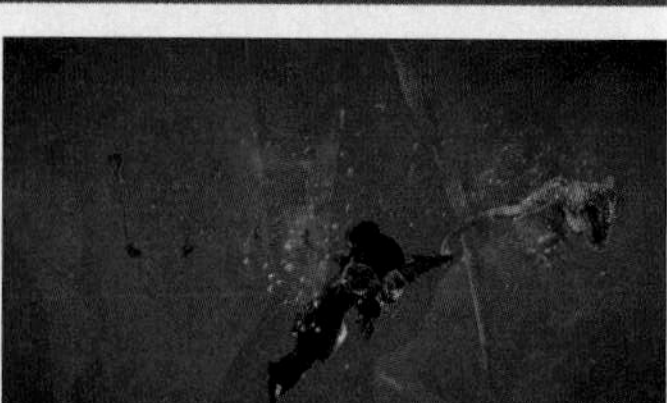

The Harpoon Gun shoots out a net that spreads out ahead of you to catch enemies. Use this ability at the start of a fight to tie up an entire group of enemies. You can then follow this up with mines to really damage your helpless foes.

Downed Skills

When your health is reduced to zero, you still have a chance to fight back. While you are in the downed state, these abilities are available.

THROW JUNK

Damage: Very Low

Effect: Random Effect (Bleed, Frozen, Weakness for 3 Seconds)

Cooldown: None

Finding yourself in a desperate situation, you grab whatever you have nearest at hand. This ends up being all the spare parts you carry around with you. The conditions your attacks apply do more to increase your survivability than increase your DPS.

GRAPPLING LINE

Damage: None

Effect: Pulls an Enemy Toward You

Cooldown: 10 Seconds

Usually engineers like to keep danger at a distance. Things are different when you are downed. The Grappling Line is used to pull enemies over to your character. Pulling in a vulnerable ranged enemy can give you an easy target for a quick second wind. Close range combat also means the enemy is in range of your Booby Trap attack. You don't have much time in your current state, so you need to bring all of your damage to bear.

BOOBY TRAP

Damage: Very High

Effect: Launch Enemies

Cooldown: 20 Seconds

Engineers always have one more trick up their sleeves. Just when your foes think they have you down, set off an explosive Booby Trap to harm multiple targets nearby. Use this when there are many enemies around and you don't have time to target one specifically to bring it down. Use the attack as soon as it finishes its cooldown, so that you can take advantage of its considerable power.

BANDAGE

Healing: Low to High Over Time

Effect: Channeled Self-Heal

Cooldown: 5 Seconds

While the most common way to rally yourself from the downed state is to kill an enemy, sometimes there aren't any in range or you don't want to grab more attention. Activate and channel the Bandage ability to heal yourself in increasing amounts until you are back in fighting shape. If an enemy strikes you, the action will be interrupted and you'll have to wait for the cooldown before trying again.

Drowning Skills

FLOATING MINE

Damage: Low

Effect: Area of Effect

Cooldown: N/A

This skill tosses a mine into the water that detonates for low but acceptable damage. Engineers don't have anything else with which to hurt foes when they're drowning, so this is all you have. Use it or lose it!

ANCHOR

Damage: Very Low

Effect: Sink (3 Seconds)

Cooldown: 10 Seconds

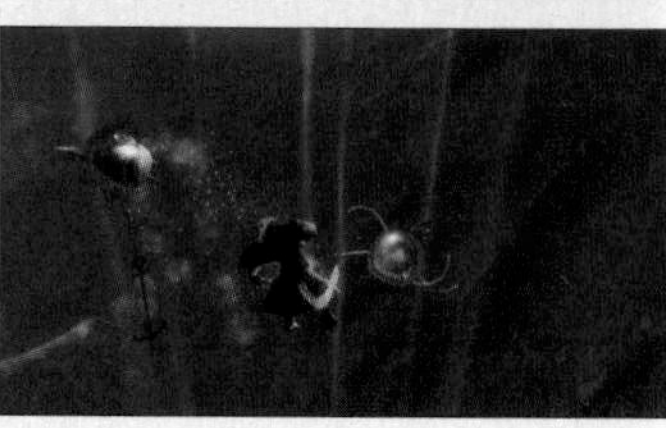

Disable a single enemy by weighing them down. Though the damage from this is laughable, it's a good way to prevent especially powerful enemies from damaging you while you're drowning. This is excellent to use before swimming to the surface if you plan on fleeing in that manner.

BUOY

Damage: N/A

Effect: Floats You to the Surface

Cooldown: 15 Seconds

Buoy gives you a rapid escape toward the surface of the water. Anchor your most dangerous foe and then get out of there as quickly as possible.

BANDAGE

Healing: Low to High Over Time

Effect: Channeled Self-Heal

Cooldown: 5 Seconds

This is the same as the terrestrial version of Bandage. Use it to improve your hero's health. If you get your bar fully recharged, your character rallies even without killing any targets.

Slot Skills

Healing

Engineer healing abilities are very party friendly. Even the default self-heal skill has a secondary option to grant boons to allies.

ELIXIR H

Effect: A Large Self-Heal that Applies One of Three Boons (Protection [5 Seconds], Regeneration [10 Seconds], or Swiftness [10 Seconds])

Cooldown: 30 Seconds

Elixir H is the default engineer healing skill. It's perfect for times when you don't know what to expect. The cooldown is short, so it's effective for keeping your health high. Soloers love it because it has the highest healing and all of the boons are good. You can't go wrong with this one.

- Toss Elixir H: Throw the elixir to grant a small heal to the affected allies and grant Protection, Regen, or Swiftness.

MED KIT

Effect: Allows You to Place Med Packs on the Ground

Cooldown: None

Use this ability to equip a medical bag as a kit. Your normal weapon abilities are replaced with the ability to drop Bandages that heal and grant boons. Allies can grab the packs by walking over them. In addition to the health-restoring functions, you can remove conditions or provide very nice boons: Fury and Swiftness. Use this healing skill when you want party healing to be your main focus.

- Drop Bandages (x3): Drops a pack of bandages that provides a little healing (15-second cooldown).
- Drop Antidote: Drops a vial of antidote that removes conditions (15-second cooldown).
- Drop Stimulant: Drops a stimulant that grants Fury and Swiftness for 10 seconds (20-second cooldown).

HEALING TURRET

Effect: AoE Healing, Regeneration (8 Seconds)

Cooldown: 20 Seconds

This places a turret that releases a healing mist. This is most effective with groups or escorts that stay in the same spot. It is also effective in situations where you need consistent healing over time (such as fighting enemies that use damage over time conditions like Bleed). Use it again to cleanse conditions off of your group. Its secondary ability is to self-destruct, which removes the turret.

- Cleansing Burst: Releases a burst of increased healing that removes conditions for yourself and nearby allies (60-second cooldown).
- Detonate Healing Turret: Healing Turret self-destructs, damaging nearby enemies (30-second cooldown).

Utility

Engineer utility skills add even greater variety. Many of these skills are gadget kits of equipment that change your normal weapon attacks. Whether they are equipped or not, each skill's secondary ability is always available. By selecting and equipping the right skills, you can fill different party roles and overcome challenges.

TIER 1

RIFLE TURRET

Effect: Places a Rifle Turret that Fires on Enemies at Range

Cooldown: 20 Seconds

This skill is incredibly effective for the skill point cost and should be one of the first ones you pick up. Once placed, the Rifle Turret fires for low to medium damage on all aggressive enemies or structures until it is destroyed. When it is active, you have the ability to enhance it with Automatic Fire to greatly increase its damage for a short period. Like all turrets, its secondary ability is to be detonated, which damages all enemies nearby. Putting down turrets increases your damage output without attracting attention to yourself. Many tasks require that you guard or control a large area; turrets let you project damage over distance and multiple directions.

- Automatic Fire: Increases the firing rate of the turret by 50% and adds Bleed (30-second cooldown).
- Detonate Rifle Turret: Rifle Turret self-destructs, damaging nearby enemies (30-second cooldown).

FLAME TURRET

Effect: Summon Fire Turret

Cooldown: 40 Seconds

This turret functions much like the Rifle Turret except instead of projectiles, it fires a cone of flame. The nice thing about fire is that it can hit multiple enemies and applies Burning to all of them. When it is active, you have the ability to enhance it by having it release smoke that blinds enemies. The turret does enough damage that you can either gain enemy attention or use the smoke to protect yourself. Like all turrets, its secondary ability is to be detonated, damaging enemies nearby. Place the Flame Turret near other turrets so they can support each other and create a kill zone.

- Smoke Screen: Releases a blinding cloud of smoke (30-second cooldown). Combo Field: Smoke.
- Detonate Flame Turret: Flame Turret self-destructs, damaging nearby enemies (30-second cooldown).

ELIXIR B

Effect: Grants Might (30 Seconds), Fury (10 Seconds), and Swiftness (10 Seconds)

Cooldown: 40 Seconds

This elixir gives you buffs to your Power, Precision, and running speed all in one dose. This effect improves your chance to critically hit monsters as well as the total damage done with each attack. You can't go wrong with this elixir.

This skill also puts the same boons on any ally in the area-of-effect radius. Swiftness reduces travel time while exploring, and no one is going to complain about more damage output in fights.

ELIXIR U

Effect: Randomly Apply One of Three Different Utility Skills from Another Profession (Haste, Frenzy, or Quickening Zephyr for 5 Seconds) to Yourself

Cooldown: 60 Seconds

Elixir U is a potion that is most useful in PvP matches. Using it on yourself applies Frenzy, Haste, or Quickening Zephyr. All of these are powerful during intense encounters where high burst damage is essential for your survival and victory.

GRENADE KIT

Effect: Turns Your Weapon Skills into Grenade Attacks

Cooldown: None

Equip this kit to gain access to a set of grenade attacks. Each attack is a ground-targeted area-of-effect strike. In addition, each grenade has a different effect: damage, damage over time, damage mitigation, and crowd control. While you can select and target your attacks with the mouse, it's much faster to use your keyboard. Aim with your mouse and double tap the button to quickly toss grenades. The secondary ability tosses a Grenade Barrage. This kit is great in dungeons or in any situation where you have multiple foes that stay clustered together at a distance. Here are the grenades in your kit:

- Grenade Barrage (30-second cooldown): Throws several high-damage grenades at once.
- Grenade: Medium-damage attack within a radius.
- Shrapnel Grenade (5-second cooldown): Causes medium damage and applies Bleed (12 seconds) in a radius.
- Flash Grenade (10-second cooldown).: Affects targets in a radius with Blind (5 seconds)
- Freeze Grenade (15-second cooldown): Medium damage and applies Chilled (3 seconds).
- Poison Grenade (15-second cooldown): Releases a cloud of poisonous gas that applies Poison (5 seconds).

THROW MINE

Effect: Throws a Mine to Damage, Remove a Boon, and Knock Back Enemies (Combo Finisher: Blast)

Cooldown: 18 Seconds

This gadget skill tosses a mine at your enemy. When it lands, the mine explodes and deals modest damage to all nearby targets. Affected enemies are thrown back, and each one loses a single boon (if applicable). Throw Mine is excellent for disruption, even though its direct damage is only decent. Use it to distract, delay, or debuff enemies.

UTILITY GOGGLES

Effect: Break Stun, Gain Fury, Immunity to Blind (10 Seconds)

Cooldown: 40 Seconds

If you love your critical hits, this is a great skill choice. Your increased critical chance and protection from being blinded greatly increase your damage for the duration. Further increase your output by using the Analyze ability. Taken together, this makes any other weapon or skill you use better. Keep in mind that the cooldowns for each are long. Use them when you can and make each hit count!

- Analyze (40-second cooldown): Causes Vulnerability (x5: 10 seconds).

TIER 2

NET TURRET

Effect: Fires a Net that Immobilizes Targets at Range (3 Seconds)

Cooldown: 30 Seconds

While not as flashy as the other turrets, the Net Turret does have utility. If your playstyle focuses on turrets, the additional crowd control can keep enemies out of capture zones or melee range. Select the skill again to enhance the turret to fire Electrified Net, which stuns the target. Use the secondary skill to detonate the turret when you are done with it.

- Electrified Net (30-second cooldown): Overcharges your turret to fire an electrified net that Stuns and Immobilizes your target.
- Detonate Net Turret (30-second cooldown): Net Turret self-destructs, damaging nearby enemies.

ELIXIR S

Effect: Shrink Yourself (4 Seconds), Evade, Break Stun

Cooldown: 60 Seconds

This elixir is geared for survivability in PvP. If you find yourself surrounded and low on health, use it to escape from further harm. At your new size, you are freed from crowd control effects, but you are too small to harm others until you return to your normal size. Use the secondary ability to toss the elixir at allies to protect them from stun, knockdown, and launch. Sometimes a PvP victory is gained simply by staying on your feet longer than the other team.

- Toss Elixir S (60-second cooldown): Affected allies grow and gain Stability for 6 seconds.

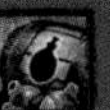 BOMB KIT

Effect: Changes Your Weapon Skills into Bomb Attacks

Cooldown: None

This weapon kit requires some courage to use, but it is undoubtedly effective. With the right traits selected you even have the ability to heal your allies. Instead of attacking at range, each attack places a bomb at your feet that explodes in a few seconds. Thankfully, the blast will not harm you or your allies.

This opens up useful strategies. You can drop the bombs while retreating to harass anyone in pursuit. The Glue Bomb is especially effective for this. Or, you can go all out and run into a group of enemies and be the Evil Midnight Bomber What Bombs at Midnight. Use the Concussion and Smoke Bombs to help you survive. The secondary ability is the Big Ole Bomb, which has a longer fuse but a much larger boom. The blowout knocks enemies away, giving you breathing room. Speaking of which, ranged attackers can be a problem when using the Bomb Kit. Use the Glue Bomb to stop them from running, or switch to another weapon if they try to kite you.

- Big Ole Bomb: Massive damage in a wide radius and launches enemies.
- Bomb: An area-of-effect damage bomb that does decent damage in a small radius.
- Fire Bomb (10-second cooldown): Low damage to foes and applies Burning within a radius.
- Concussion Bomb (18-second cooldown): Low-damage attack that Dazes enemies in a radius.
- Smoke Bomb (25-second cooldown): Blinds enemies (5 seconds) in moderate radius, smoke lasts 3 seconds.
- Glue Bomb (25-second cooldown): Bursts and spreads sticky glue in a moderate area that immobilizes enemies for 1 second.

 FLAMETHROWER

Effect: Changes Your Weapon Skills into Flame Attacks

Cooldown: None

Put on this kit and set the world on fire! The wide range of abilities you gain from this kit makes it useful in just about any situation. The Flamethrower really shines when you're with a fast-moving group fighting multiple enemies. The secondary ability is Incendiary Ammo. Activate this any time you can; it makes all weapons better.

Try the following powerful combo. Start the fight with Flame Blast and pull your foes forward with Backdraft. Put down Napalm where they land and spray them with Flame Jet. If they are not dead by the time Napalm dies out, knock them back with Air Blast so they are in range of another Flame Blast. Laughing maniacally is optional.

- Incendiary Ammo (60-second cooldown): Burns foes with your next three attacks.
- Flame Jet: Shoots a cone of fire for high damage.
- Flame Blast (6-second cooldown): Fires a gout of flame that explodes in a radius for medium to high damage.
- Air Blast (15-second cooldown): Launches foes.
- Napalm (30-second cooldown): Target the ground and set a wall of flame that applies burning for 1 second, Combo Field (Fire).
- Vent Smoke (40-second cooldown): Blinds all nearby enemies.

 ELIXIR GUN

Effect: Changes Your Weapon Skills into Elixir Attacks

Cooldown: None

This kit brings elixirs' party utility into one complete package. Equip this when you join a group to disable enemies and boost your friends. The secondary ability is a small pointblank area-of-effect heal, available even if you don't have the kit equipped. Your damage isn't as high as other weapon kits, but you definitely turn the tide in your party's favor.

- Tranquilizer Dart: Does low damage and applies Weakness and Bleeding (3 seconds), Combo Finisher (Physical Projectile).
- Elixir F (5-second cooldown): Shoots a projectile that bounces between friends and foes; does medium damage to foes and Cripples them (5 seconds); for allies, it adds Swiftness (5 seconds).
- Fumigate (10-second cooldown): Sprays elixir fumes in a cone pattern, Poisoning and inflicting Vulnerability on enemies (1 second).
- Acid Bomb (15-second cooldown): Leap back, blasting the ground with acid, moderately damaging any foes that touch it.
- Super Elixir (20-second cooldown): Shoots an elixir orb that heals allies on impact for a small amount and creates a healing area for 10 seconds.

 ROCKET BOOTS

Effect: Break Stun, Fly Backward, High Damage, Combo Finisher (Blast)

Cooldown: 30 Seconds

Give melee attackers a nasty surprise with this skill. If your playstyle depends on having a safe distance from your enemies, this is perfect because it sends you back even farther than Overcharged Shot. Start by using the Rocket Kick's secondary ability and then use the boots to break any stuns and escape. As you fly away, you do high damage and apply Burning. Arm yourself with a rifle to completely frustrate your target with your kiting ability.

- Rocket Kick (20-second cooldown): Kick your enemy in the face for high damage and apply Burning (5 seconds).

 PERSONAL BATTERING RAM

Effect: Launch an Enemy Using a Concealed Battering Ram

Cooldown: 45 Seconds

If you're tired of enemies getting in your face, add this skill to your bag of tricks. Even if you don't need to reposition your foes, they can't attack if they're airborne. You can launch enemies a substantial distance to get some personal space. If your targets are at range, use the secondary attack to fire the ram's head and knock them down. Either way, it comes in handy in many situations.

- Launch Personal Battering Ram (18-second cooldown): Does low damage and Cripples enemies (5 seconds), Combo Finisher (Physical Projectile).

TIER 3

 THUMPER TURRET

Effect: Summon Thumper Turret

Cooldown: 50 Seconds

This turret both gives and takes a pounding. It's most useful when you know an enemy will be standing at a certain point. The Thumper's range is limited to a minimal area of effect, so bad placement can render it useless. It's best to put it down where your enemy has to go through a door or arch, interact with an object, or fight you in melee. In PvE, it can pull aggro and act as a tank for you and other turrets. In PvP, you'll have to be a bit smarter and use it as a damaging obstacle to enemy movement. Once placed, activate the turret again to Thump and launch enemies away. Its secondary ability is to self-destruct. Use it to cause some parting damage before it is destroyed or to remove it so you can place it in a better spot.

- Thump (30-second cooldown): Overcharges your thumper turret to Launch foes.
- Detonate Thumper Turret (30-second cooldown): Thumper Turret self-destructs, damaging nearby enemies.

ROCKET TURRET

Effect: Summon Rocket Turret

Cooldown: 60 Seconds

One of the most powerful turrets available. This skill is useful in a wide variety of situations. Each rocket that it fires does high damage and applies Burning. The active ability of the turret (Explosive Rockets) provides a sudden surge in damage output that is useful against clustered enemies or powerful single targets.

- Explosive Rockets (20-second cooldown): Overcharges your turret to fire heavy-damage explosive rockets.
- Detonate Rocket Turret (30-second cooldown): Rocket Turret self-destructs, damaging nearby enemies.

 ELIXIR C

Effect: Converts Conditions into Boons, Duration (5 Seconds)

Cooldown: 60 Seconds

Turn the tables on your enemies with Elixir C! It's most useful in PvP, where getting conditions is common. Just when your enemies think they have you debilitated, you can bounce back stronger than ever. Throw the elixir to have the same effect on your allies. Keep yourself and your teammates fighting at full strength with Elixir C. Now with more sodium!

- Toss Elixir C (30-second cooldown): Throw to convert one condition to a random boon.

ELIXIR R

Effect: Break Stun, Refills Endurance

Cooldown: 45 Seconds

Elixir R is a powerful PvP and dungeon skill. Any ability that breaks crowd control can determine the difference between victory and defeat. The secondary ability revives downed allies and removes harmful conditions from them. You become a literal lifesaver to your allies. It's a massive boon during boss fights, PvP matches, and large-scale events.

Try to use Elixir R after you've already pushed your endurance to its limits. Dodging twice, using Elixir R, and then being able dodge even more can get you out of some serious trouble.

- Toss Elixir R (85-second cooldown): Throw to remove conditions and revive allies within the area of effect.

 TOOL KIT

Effect: Changes Your Weapon Skills to Tool-Based Attacks

Cooldown: None

The Tool Kit is a unique armed kit that gives you a fun change of pace for both PvE and PvP. It equips you with a set of melee skills rather than ranged attacks. In fact, the only ranged attack is a secondary ability, Throw Wrench. This changes your strategy from "keep everyone away" to "pull everyone in." Use Magnet to pull enemies in and Box of Nails to keep them from escaping. If the enemy charges up a big attack, it can be blocked with Gear Shield or interrupted with Pry Bar. Otherwise, have fun beating things about the head and neck with your wrench, using the Smack ability.

- Throw Wrench (20-second cooldown): Boomerang throw your wrench at your target and back, hitting foes for high damage each way and repairing your turrets if they're nearby.
- Smack: Strike your foe with a wrench for medium damage. Multiple strikes with Smack form a combo that inflicts Vulnerability on your target.
- Box of Nails (10-second cooldown): Scatters nails in a pointblank area of effect that applies Bleed and Cripple (2 seconds).
- Pry Bar (45-second cooldown): Confuses your enemy.
- Gear Shield (20-second cooldown): Blocks incoming attacks.
- Magnet (20-second cooldown): Pulls enemies toward you.

SLICK SHOES

Effect: Knockdown Foes (on Land), Blinds Foes (in Water)

Cooldown: 60 Seconds

Use this quirky gadget to kite your enemy or escape from combat. Its primary use is for solo PvE or PvP survival. Enemies stepping on the oil do a comical slip and fall. If you are fighting underwater, the oil Blinds enemies for a short time. Use the Slick Shoes' secondary ability to gain a boost of speed for fleeing encounters or advanced kiting.

- Super Speed (45-second cooldown): Run at double speed (5 seconds).

Elite

Engineer elite skills vary quite a bit in what they do. Let's discuss each in turn.

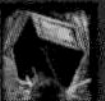 SUPPLY CRATE

Effect: Stun Enemies (2 Seconds), Deploy Turrets, Deploy Bandages

Cooldown: 180 Seconds

Supply Crate is an elite party support skill. Drop a piñata of pain to do heavy damage and stun enemies within the targeted area. Med packs and random turrets are spread around, making it a safe place for allies to heal and recuperate. It's handy in any group situation, for PvP or larger events.

ELIXIR X

Effect: Random Morph (20 Seconds)

Cooldown: 150 Seconds

This powerful elixir is made of fresh snake tears, hen's teeth, and a single split second that was divided by zero. Like many of your gadget kits, this elixir will replace your weapons skills, but it will also block the use of your other skills while it is active. This means you can't let the power go to your head because you have no ability to self-heal while the elixir is active. Have no fear of crowd control abilities when you drink Elixir X. Each form gives you stability, which protects you from movement—and action-impairing conditions.

Rampaging Brute: Become a monstrosity of destruction. Watch your health while in this form. You can dish out damage, but you are also a big target. Use Dash to get into the fight and Kick, Stomp, and Throw Boulder to knock enemies around. Use Smash when the other abilities are on cooldown.

- Smash: A direct high-damage attack.
- Kick (6-second cooldown): A heavy damage knockback.
- Dash (8-second cooldown): Charges at your target for high damage, Combo Finisher (Leap).
- Throw Boulder (12-second cooldown): Knock an enemy back.
- Stomp (15-second cooldown): Stamp on the ground for high damage and launch enemies into the air, Combo Finisher (Blast).

Tornado: Change into a howling windstorm. Bowl through enemy formations and throw them into chaos. The range of all your abilities is limited to physical contact, so get moving.

- Electrified Tornado: Harms any enemies you come into contact with by using Bleed (6 seconds).
- Dust Tornado: Blinds any enemies that touch you.
- Debris Tornado: Cripples your foes and poisons them whenever they touch you.

MORTAR

Effect: Summon Usable Mortar

Cooldown: 120 Seconds

The Mortar elite skill has situational uses. Using it while solo is difficult, because of its minimum firing distance. Dungeons are a little claustrophobic for its use. Instead, it's perfect for taking or defending a specific piece of territory in PvP. Put it down outside the fray and you or an ally can rain damage, conditions, and heals within a large radius.

- Launch Mortar Shot (2-second cooldown): Fires a high damage mortar shot into a radius.
- Launch Caltrops Mortar (12-second cooldown): Applies Cripple (2 seconds) and Bleed (12 seconds) to all enemies in a small radius.
- Launch Elixir (15-second cooldown): Give allies a small heal in a large area.
- Launch Ice Mortar (30-second cooldown): Chills enemies (1 second), Combo Field (Ice).
- Launch Concussion Barrage (30-second cooldown): Extreme damage shells causing knockback to enemies.

Traits

Explosives (Raises Power and Condition Duration)

REWARDS

Points Invested	Ability Gained
5	Creates a bomb when you dodge
15	Releases a number of timed mines when you hit 25% health
25	Explosions cause Vulnerability

SKILL OPTIONS (GAINED EVERY 10 POINTS)

ADEPT TIER

- Explosive Elixirs: Thrown elixirs explode when they land.
- Shrapnel: Explosions have a 6% chance to cause Bleeding.
- Forceful Explosives: Bombs and mines have a larger explosion radius.
- Empowering Adrenaline: Get a 5% damage bonus when endurance is not full.
- Incendiary Powder: All explosions cause Burning on critical hits.
- Exploit Weakness (15-second cooldown): Applies Cripple to enemies that you hit when they are below 25% health.

MASTER TIER

- Throwing Arm: Improved range for grenades and mines.
- Short Fuse: 10% reduced recharge for bombs and grenades.
- Accelerant-Packed Turrets: Turrets explode when killed; when this happens, they push enemies back.
- Big Grenade Pouch: Gives you a 50% chance to throw extra grenades when using a Grenade Kit.

GRANDMASTER TIER

- Explosive Powder: Improves damage from explosions by 10%.
- Elixir-Infused Bombs: Bomb explosions heal allies.

Firearms (Precision and Condition Damage)

REWARDS

Points Invested	Ability Gained
5	Chance to cause Bleeding on critical hits
15	Gives a 10% increased critical hit chance against enemies with low health
25	Adds 5% damage against Bleeding enemies

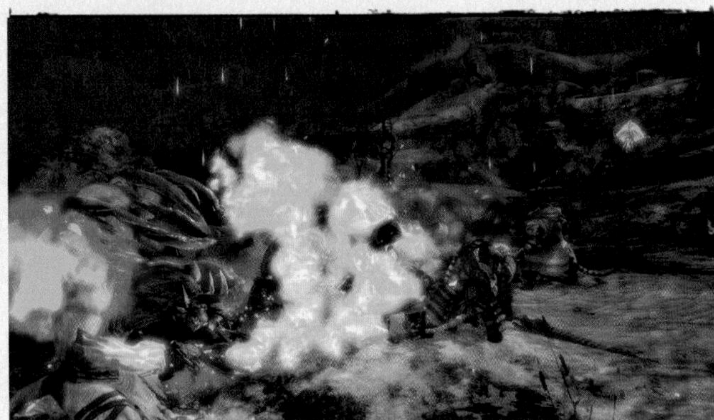

SKILL OPTIONS (GAINED EVERY 10 POINTS)

ADEPT TIER

- Knee Shot: Cripples targets when you Immobilize them.
- Sitting Duck: Deals 5% extra damage versus Immobilized enemies.
- Infusion Precision: 50% chance to gain Swiftness on critical hits.
- Rifled Barrels: Improved rifle, pistol, Harpoon Gun, and Elixir Gun range.
- Precise Sights: Adds a 33% chance to cause Vulnerability on critical hits.
- Hair Trigger: Rifle, pistol, and Harpoon Gun skills recharge 20% faster.

MASTER TIER

- Napalm Specialist: Adds a 25% chance to cause Burning (1 second) on critical hits with a Flamethrower.
- Fireforged Trigger: Flamethrower and Elixir Gun skills have a 20% shorter recharge.
- Rifle Mod: Improved rifle and Harpoon Gun damage.
- Go for the Eyes: Critical hits with rifles gain a 33% chance to Blind targets.

GRANDMASTER TIER

- Juggernaut: You move 50% slower when wielding the Flamethrower, but gain Stability and Toughness (2 points per level).
- Coated Bullets: Pistol shots pierce.

Inventions (Raises Toughness and Healing)

REWARDS

Points Invested	Ability Gained
5	Heal Stat increased when below 25% health
15	All healing skills recharge when you reach less than 25% health (can only trigger once every 90 seconds)
25	20% of Healing is added as bonus Power

SKILL OPTIONS (GAINED EVERY 10 POINTS)

ADEPT TIER

- Protective Shield: Gain Protection when you rally (5 seconds).
- Explosive Descent: Release a barrage of grenades when you take falling damage; take only 50% of normal falling damage.
- Metal Plating: Turrets take 15% less damage.
- Stabilized Armor: Take 5% less damage when your endurance bar is full.
- Power Shoes: 10% faster movement speed in combat.
- Cloaking Device: You become Invisible when Immobilized.

MASTER TIER

- Reinforced Shield: Increased armor with shields; shield skills recharge 20% faster.
- Protective Turrets: Gain 30 Toughness for each deployed turret (Supply Crate turrets do not count toward this).
- Elite Supplies: The Supply Crate has extra Med Packs and a Rifle Turret.
- Deployable Turrets: Turrets are ground targeted, so you can place them more cautiously.

GRANDMASTER TIER

- Electromagnetic Mines: Explosions from your mines remove boons from enemies.
- Rifled Turret Barrels: Increases attack range and damage for all types of turrets.

Alchemy (Raises Vitality and Boon Duration)

REWARDS

Points Invested	Ability Gained
5	Drink an Elixir B at 75% health
15	3% chance to convert incoming conditions to boons
25	Deal extra damage for each boon on your character

SKILL OPTIONS (GAINED EVERY 10 POINTS)

ADEPT TIER

- Invigorating Speed: When you gain Swiftness you gain Vigor (5 seconds).
- Fast-Acting Elixirs: Elixir cooldowns recharge 20% faster.
- Acidic Coating: Adds a 10% chance to inflict Poison (3 seconds) when your hero is struck in melee.
- Self-Regulating Defenses: Drink an Elixir S at 25% health.
- Blood Injection: 10% of your Vitality is converted into bonus condition damage.
- Protection Injection: Gain Protection (3 seconds) whenever your character is Stunned, Dazed, Feared, or Launched/Knocked.

MASTER TIER

- Deadly Mixture: Deal extra damage with Flamethrowers and Elixir Guns.
- Potent Elixirs: Increases Elixir durations.
- Backpack Regenerator: Gain Regeneration when using a kit.
- Cleaning Formula: Throwing/consuming elixirs removes conditions from those affected.

GRANDMASTER TIER

- H.G.H: Elixirs give Might (20 seconds).
- Automated Response: Become immune to conditions when health is below 25%.

Tools (Raises Critical Damage and Tool Belt Recharge Rate)

REWARDS

Points Invested	Ability Gained
5	Using tool belt skills restores 10% of your endurance
15	When health reaches 25%, all tool belt skills are recharged
25	Increases damage by 10% when endurance is full

SKILL OPTIONS (GAINED EVERY 10 POINTS)

ADEPT TIER

- Always Prepared: Drop a Flamethrower or Elixir Gun when downed.
- Static Discharge: Cause Vulnerability (10 seconds) when you block an attack.
- Speedy Gadgets: Gadget recharges are reduced by 30%.
- Kit Refinement: Equipping a kit creates an attack or a spell.
- Adrenal Implant: 25% faster endurance regeneration.
- Speedy Kits: Reduced cooldown on swapping kits.

MASTER TIER

- Packaged Stimulants: Med Kit skills can be thrown.
- Power Wrench: Doubles the turret healing of your tool kit.
- Crippling Wrenches: Hits with toolkit wrenches cripple your target.
- Leg Mods: Move faster while using an unarmed kit.

GRANDMASTER TIER

- Armor Mods: +90 Toughness while a Device Kit is equipped.
- Autotool Installation: Turrets are self-repairing.

Engineers in PvE

Engineers are all about versatility, and you can start to get a feel for that from the beginning of your career. Once you're level five or so, hit a capital city and buy two pistols, a rifle, and a shield. Gaining all the weapon skills won't take long and this practice helps you figure out your playstyle. You might find that you're especially happy with one weapon type over another, even if the abilities didn't sound that much better initially.

During this period, make sure to explore the world thoroughly. Gaining skill points is quite important because you want to develop a library of awesome utility skills. The bigger your bag of tricks, the more situations your engineer will be able to handle. Get skills that aid you in soloing early on. More challenging group content is out there, but the really hard stuff doesn't come up until you're at least level 30. That's more than enough time to get your soloing skills developed.

Select your traits with an eye toward your favorite activities. If you like healing, for instance, make sure you think about how your traits and skills interact. Select the Elixir-Infused Bombs trait, and you can start healing parties with the Bomb Kit! That type of synergy is what makes engineers both strange and exciting.

Engineers have to be smart when they're fighting. The majority of your attacks and skills have area-of-effect damage and effects. As a wearer of medium armor, this may get you more attention than you want. Practice your crowd control skills to control your enemies' positions, whether you want them to be near or far. Have fun trying out different combinations of weapons, skills, and traits. With an armed kit, Elixir B, and the Rifle Turret, you are ready for just about anything.

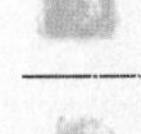

Take the turret skills to keep your foes distracted and to control the terrain. It takes skill to have proper placement of your turrets, but you can create deadly killzones once you're used to these weapons. Grab enemies' attention and pull them back into your turrets. This makes the most of your goodies without having to wait for cooldowns for every single fight.

Turrets help when you're trying to capture or defend territory. Spaced-out turrets soften targets while you're occupied elsewhere. Put down the Rifle, Flame, and Rocket Turrets to create deadly ground. Equip a shield and take the Protective Turrets trait and you become considerably harder to kill. Trait points in Inventions and Firearms are the most effective for this style of play.

Elixirs increase the survivability of both you and your allies. Elixir B is a great tool for exploring and solo survival. Equip the Elixir Gun and you get a whole suite of helpful skills with short cooldowns, some damage, and group utility. Put your trait points into Alchemy and Inventions and put anything left over into Tools. These traits give you the skill options and stats to boost your party support effectiveness. Look for equipment that has high Vitality to increase boon duration.

Explosives are very fun. Use mines to lay traps for foes. Grenades are great for ranged area-of-effect damage. The Bomb Kit has the highest damage, but it's also the riskiest kit. The Flamethrower has damage and control abilities, so it's the complete package. Perk explosives and put some points into both Inventions and Alchemy to help you survive. Choose equipment with both Power and Vitality if you're going down this road.

Practice switching between weapon kits. Just because you put one on doesn't mean you're stuck using it for an entire fight. If your group isn't in danger, switch from the Elixir Gun to the Grenade Kit. If you're running around solo, use the Magnet ability from the Tool Kit to pull enemies in and then switch to the Bomb Kit to blast the gathered victims. Make sure you're willing to change skills any time your situation changes. "Here are my group tools, here is my setup for really tough events, and this is my fun and fast soloing set." That way, you don't have any wasted utility skills at any time.

Soloers should use equipment that has a balance of Power, Precision, and Vitality. Engineers don't kill things fast enough to rely entirely on damage output.

When you're in a group, consider gear with Vitality and Toughness. Not only do you gain more fortitude, but your boons and healing become stronger. You also survive a lot longer, even if things turn sour and enemies come after you directly.

Engineers in PvP

In PvP, many of your neglected skills come to the forefront. Tossing Elixir R and Elixir C lets you turn the tables in PvP by removing conditions and breaking stuns. The Med Kit and the Packaged Meds trait keep your allies fighting as long as possible. The Elixir Gun lets you spread boons, conditions, and healing. Drop Supply Crates to make an instant battle station.

If you want to do more damage, equip the Grenade Kit and Flamethrower. The Flamethrower is great when you have to keep up with a fast-moving group. In situations where you don't want to get too close to the fighting, use the Grenade Kit's range to your advantage. If you aren't moving around as much, turrets and the Mortar are fun. Support your team by bombarding the enemy with damage and conditions.

For close-in fighting, use the Tool Kit. Or, use the Bomb Kit to help take out structures and clusters of enemies. Activate the abilities of the Utility Goggles to boost the damage of any of your weapons or skills. Elixir X has the ability to catch the other team off guard and gain the advantage by changing you into one of three overwhelming forms. It's chancy because you can't plan what form you'll take, but all of them are powerful.

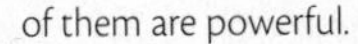

If you ever get into trouble, you have several options to protect yourself. When you just need a little room, the Personal Battering Ram is good. Its sudden strike can shake an attacker's confidence. Movement conditions and stuns are often a death sentence if you can't avoid them; Elixir S lets you slip away from these dangers. When enemies are chasing your hero, use Slick Shoes. Super Speed Boost and Rocket Boots are also good ways to escape and either continue kiting (or come back from another angle, where it's safer).

GUARDIAN

Guardians are frontline combatants who use heavy armor and can perform either as ranged or melee fighters. Their high survivability and numerous boons and healing powers make them fantastic support characters in any group. You're most likely to enjoy this profession if you enjoy melee combat or supporting your teammates through healing and boons. This is one of the best professions for pure and easy survivability, so that is a draw as well. If you're looking for something tough and accessible, you've found the right place.

As soloers, guardians are hardy. They can't be killed easily, and their most damaging weapons keep the kills flowing. You won't be disappointed in the profession in any way. However, you miss out on the glory of guardians in a larger group. That is the situation where these characters go from good to stunning. Many guardian abilities make allies better in a variety of ways. You'll find a huge amount of synergy in parties that have a guardian around. They're the epitome of team players, especially if you choose your traits and slot skills to accentuate that aspect of play.

Don't fall into the trap of thinking guardians are "tanks," "healers," or whatever other archetypes come to mind. As with all *Guild Wars 2* professions, you can make a number of decisions to influence how your character performs. Guardians can be pushed to excel at damage, survivability, group healing and survival, or whatever else you desire. The world is your oyster.

Profession Stats

Attribute	Starting Stats	Naked at Level 80
Power	24	1216
Precision	24	916
Toughness	24	916
Vitality	24	1166
Attack	158	1216
Critical Chance	4%	4%
Armor	106	916
Health	268	13,305

These stats give you an idea of what to expect from your character. They show guardian progression through examples taken at the beginning and end of leveling. Your actual stats will likely vary from this.

Weapons and Weapon Skills

Guardians have a great lineup of weapons they can use. Each weapon has a different specialty that helps the guardian perform well in combat. Standard groupings include area-of-effect damage (mace/torch and greatsword), boons (mace/shield), conditions (sword/focus), or a single target assault (sword/shield). Guardians can be prepared for almost any situation.

Virtues

Virtues are a special set of guardian powers that make it much easier for you to dominate your enemies. These three abilities are given to all guardians, regardless of the traits you choose and the weapons you wield. Virtues have two states: passive and active. If you don't click on the virtues, they'll each add a minor power to your character (extra damage, passive health regeneration, and a blocked attack every 40 seconds). When you engage these abilities, their respective passive boons fall, but a great power replaces them temporarily.

You can activate one, two, or even all three virtues simultaneously. They're all at your disposal unless any of the abilities are still on cooldown from being used recently.

Let's talk about the virtues in greater depth.

VIRTUE OF JUSTICE

Damage: Special

Effect: Burning

Cooldown: 30 Seconds

Justice normally operates by giving your guardian a burning attack with every fifth swing of their weapon. Burning attacks hit with a moderate damage over time bonus that sets the enemies on fire. When activated, Justice makes your next attack (and those of any nearby allies) a guaranteed blast of fire five times as powerful as the normal Burning effect. It's amazing in groups. Watch veterans, champions, and other high-end targets get walloped!

VIRTUE OF RESOLVE

Damage: N/A

Effect: Regenerate Health

Cooldown: 60 Seconds

Resolve gives your character a minor amount of health regeneration that ticks every few seconds. It's not enough to help you survive under all conditions, but the free health makes it easier to solo longer, endure long battles of attrition, and so forth. When used actively, Resolve throws a powerful healing spell on your guardian and every ally nearby. That's a major boost during battles where your party is under heavy fire.

VIRTUE OF COURAGE

Damage: N/A

Effect: Block an Attack

Cooldown: 90 Seconds

Courage gives your guardian an Aegis every 40 seconds. The Aegis blocks the next attack levied against your hero. When used actively, the virtue gives your hero and every nearby ally a free Aegis. Save this for times when a powerful enemy is about to launch an extremely potent attack, especially if it's an area-of-effect blast you don't think your party can avoid or survive. Hit Virtue of Courage and give your people the chance to make it through unscathed.

Sword (Main Hand)

For guardians, swords focus on quick melee strikes that inflict conditions and use traits that emphasize critical hits. These weapons use both AoE and single-target attacks, and are an excellent way to quickly use your Virtue of Justice to great effect. Damage from sword skills is generally low, but their ability to blind opponents and provide projectile blocking trades damage for added survivability.

SWORD OF WRATH

Damage: Medium

Effect: Special

Cooldown: None

This basic sword attack rotates between Sword of Wrath, Sword Arc, and Sword Wave. These are cone attacks that strike up to three targets for decent damage.

FLASHING BLADE

Damage: Low

Effect: Blind (3 Seconds)

Cooldown: 10 Seconds

Flashing Blade allows you to teleport into combat or catch up to foes and strike them with a small area attack that blinds all enemies right next to your hero. Use this to get into combat fast, or even as an escape route if you find yourself surrounded. The Blinding effect helps to mitigate damage during dangerous fights, so that's when Flashing Blade is most effective.

ZEALOT'S DEFENSE

Damage: High

Effect: Multi-Attack, Blocks Projectiles (3 Seconds)

Cooldown: 15 Seconds

Zealot's Defense is an indispensable attack for a sword user. It combines a short-range projectile attack with the ability to automatically block other incoming projectiles while it is in effect. Employ this to attack projectile users, allowing you to defend yourself and attack your enemies at the same time. Use this after a Flashing Blade to move in quickly and damage ranged foes before they can hurt you. Even while in melee, this power should be used regularly, because you block projectiles, and each projectile you send out also counts toward your Virtue of Justice.

Hammer (Two-Handed)

The hammer is a slow, high-damage, area-of-effect weapon. Its basic attack hits multiple foes per swing, and its other skills involve crowd control and group support.

HAMMER SWING

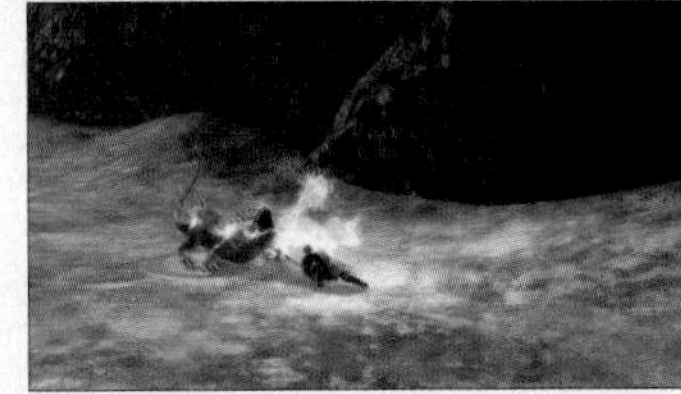

Damage: Moderate

Effect: Chain Attack (Symbol of Protection), Area Damage

Cooldown: None

Hammer Swing is a chain attack that boasts decent damage. Its third hit creates a symbol that grants protection to you and your allies. Use this power as often as possible in melee to keep protection up for your party. Hammer Swings strike everything in front of your guardian, so they're very effective against groups close to your character.

MIGHTY BLOW

Damage: Very High

Effect: Area Damage, Combo Finisher (Blast)

Cooldown: 8 Seconds

Mighty Blow is a forward-facing area-of-effect attack. It has a very wide range, so use this ability whenever you are in melee combat with more than one enemy nearby. The main benefit of Mighty Blow is its sheer damage output.

ZEALOT'S EMBRACE

Damage: Moderate

Effect: Immobilize (2 Seconds)

Cooldown: 18 Seconds

This attack Immobilizes an entire line of enemies. Use this before strafing around your targets so they can't set up a good counterattack against you.

BANISH

Damage: High

Effect: Blowout

Cooldown: 35 Seconds

Banish smashes enemies for high damage and hurls them backwards a huge distance. This power is fantastic for both PvP and PvE. Use it to hurl your enemies away, mitigate their damage for time, interrupt them, or just use it for the damage and fun. Save Banish for important enemies; don't waste it on foes that would die in just a few hits.

RING OF WARDING

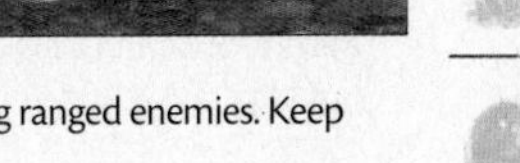

Damage: N/A

Effect: Creates a Wall

Cooldown: 45 Seconds

This skill creates a circular area around you that cannot be crossed by enemies. Use this power to prevent melee attackers from reaching you, or to trap an enemy so he can't get away from your hero. The latter is wonderful in PvP for grabbing ranged enemies. Keep them from kiting you by encircling them.

Greatsword (Two-Handed)

Greatswords are one of the deadliest weapons in the guardian's arsenal. Every attack hits hard and affects a relatively wide area. This makes the greatsword an ideal weapon when you're fighting groups of enemies, especially if you don't need to rely on crowd control to survive their attacks. The only downside of greatswords is they lack subtlety and versatility. Make sure to pair them with something that gives you either range, freedom of movement, or crowd control capabilities. Mace + shield in one slot and greatsword in the other is a perfectly fun example of this.

STRIKE

Damage: High

Effect: Chain Attack

Cooldown: None

The basic attack of the greatsword hits all enemies in a large frontal arc, finishing the chain with a very high-damage line attack. The large area affected and the greatsword's decent speed make this a brutal attack, especially for something that doesn't have a cooldown. Use this as your default damage-dealing skill and save your other attacks for appropriate situations. Because the final attack in the combo grants Might for each target you hit, Strike encourages very aggressive play. Lure enemies into tight areas so you can hit as many foes as possible for high damage and free boons!

SYMBOL OF WRATH

Damage: Moderate to High (Depending on Number of Targets)

Effect: Area Damage, Retaliation (2 Seconds), Combo Field (Light)

Cooldown: 15 Seconds

The Symbol of Wrath deals damage over time to all enemies in its area and grants 2 seconds of Retaliation to you and any allies in its area. This power is best paired with other damage symbols. Save this for fights against larger groups; Symbol of Wrath doesn't pay for itself well against single targets but quickly becomes impressive when there are more opponents to retaliate against.

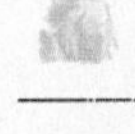

WHIRLING WRATH

Damage: Very High

Effect: Area Damage, Throws Projectiles, Combo Finisher (Whirl)

Cooldown: 10 Seconds

Whirling Wrath causes the guardian to spin in place, dealing damage to all opponents near him while hurling additional projectiles to strike distant enemies. The accuracy of this skill isn't good at long range, but with proper positioning you can strike two or three enemies with both the weapon and the projectiles, improving the damage you deal. Use this power whenever you are surrounded by enemies and want to hit targets in front of and behind your guardian.

LEAP OF FAITH

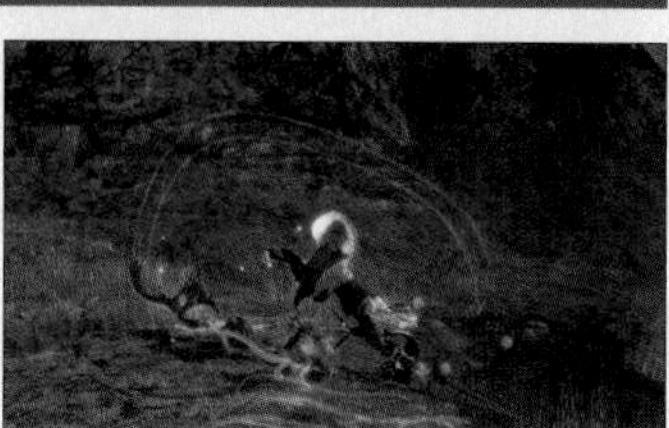

Damage: Moderate to High

Effect: Area Damage, Blindness (3 Seconds)

Cooldown: 20 Seconds

Leap of Faith jumps toward your target while making the attack, so this skill helps your guardian get into position against groups of fleeing or ranged enemies. This power is one you should use as often as possible. It has a large area of effect, and enemies you strike are blinded for several seconds.

BINDING BLADE

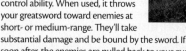

Damage: Moderate to High

Effect: Chain Attack, Pull Enemies

Cooldown: 30 Seconds

Binding Blade is a great crowd control ability. When used, it throws your greatsword toward enemies at short- or medium-range. They'll take substantial damage and be bound by the sword. If you press the button again soon after, the enemies are pulled back to your guardian, and then it's time for area-of-effect slaughter. Use this to prevent enemies from running away or to stop their ranged assault on your party.

Mace (Main Hand)

The mace is one of the guardian's most versatile tools; it pairs well with almost any weapon setup. Maces boast a large variety of effects: boons, conditions, group healing, and decent damage output. Maces have it all, and they fit a large number of themes.

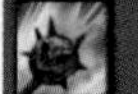

TRUE STRIKE

Damage: Moderate to High

Effect: Area Healing

Cooldown: None

True Strike delivers a series of three blows. The third strike does higher damage and heals you and your allies for a small amount. This makes the mace an invaluable survival tool, especially if you have high healing bonuses because of traits or equipment choices. Though True Strike doesn't heal for much health, the lack of cooldown makes it fairly effective for topping off your group's health.

SYMBOL OF FAITH

Damage: Low Per Target

Effect: Area Damage, Regeneration (1 Second), Combo Field (Light)

Cooldown: 8 Seconds

This symbol provides respectable damage and decent healing output for the guardian. When traited, it affects a large area and lasts as long as its cooldown. Combine this with True Strike or another damage symbol, such as the one from Greatsword, to quickly kill any enemy foolish enough to stand in the way.

PROTECTOR'S STRIKE

Damage: High

Effect: Counterattack (Area Damage) or Protection (3 Seconds), Combo Finisher (Whirl)

Cooldown: 15 Seconds

Protector's Strike channels a shield around you and your allies, and if an attack penetrates it, you unleash a shockwave that deals very high damage. If you are not attacked, this ability grants protection to you and all allies. This skill is best used when currently under attack to make maximum use of its high area-of-effect damage.

Scepter (Main Hand)

Scepters are guardians' best condition-afflicting weapons. They're an excellent choice for killing over time, ranged attacks, and for maximizing your survivability against extremely dangerous opponents. The trade-off here is that they have a slightly lower kill rate compared to maces, greatswords, and hammers.

ORB OF WRATH

Damage: High

Effect: N/A

Cooldown: None

Orb of Wrath is a decent damage skill. This attack does an acceptable job of knocking foes around while Smite is on cooldown. Orb of Wrath has very good range and can be used on the move to kite enemies.

SMITE

Damage: High

Effect: Area of Effect

Cooldown: 6 Seconds

Smite strikes multiple opponents in a close area. Each blow is quite low on damage, but the total output of the attack is more reasonable. This is especially true if Virtue of Justice is on passive mode. Having the Burn attacks trigger every fifth blow is nice when you use this attack (Smite tosses out many hits over time).

CHAINS OF LIGHT

Damage: N/A

Effect: Immobilize (2 Seconds), Vulnerability (x3) (6 Seconds)

Cooldown: 20 Seconds

This skill is a basic Immobilizing effect. Use it to halt fleeing or kiting enemies in their tracks. Alternatively, cast it to stop melee enemies that are trying to catch up to your guardian when you are the one doing the kiting. Make them work for it! The Vulnerability this adds lets you punish the enemies afterward, so use this before hitting Smite to make the attacks that much better.

Staff (Two-Handed)

The staff is a great back-up weapon for situational use. Though it isn't the ultimate damage solution for guardians, its skills have a little bit of everything: afflicting and removing conditions, hitting a wide area, and healing.

WAVE OF WRATH

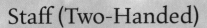

Damage: Medium

Effect: Area Damage

Cooldown: None

This is a straightforward attack. It hits up to five different enemies in a wide frontal cone. Use this while standing back from a large melee so you can support your allies while remaining a safe distance away.

ORB OF LIGHT

Damage: High

Effect: AoE Damage or Healing

Cooldown: 3 Seconds

Orb of Light fires a glowing sphere that does damage to enemies it hits and any of their buddies nearby. If you press "2" while the orb is in the air, the sphere detonates and heals your allies. This skill is thus quite flexible in giving you AoE damage or healing, depending on the need of your group. The area of effect from Orb of Light is impressive, so it isn't hard to affect multiple targets even when things are hectic.

SYMBOL OF SWIFTNESS

Damage: Low

Effect: Area Damage, Swiftness (2 Seconds), Combo Field (Light)

Cooldown: 15 Seconds

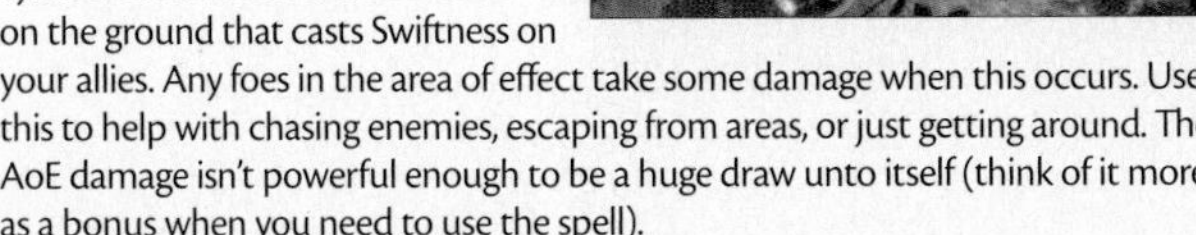

Symbol of Swiftness creates a circle on the ground that casts Swiftness on your allies. Any foes in the area of effect take some damage when this occurs. Use this to help with chasing enemies, escaping from areas, or just getting around. The AoE damage isn't powerful enough to be a huge draw unto itself (think of it more as a bonus when you need to use the spell).

LINE OF WARDING

Damage: N/A

Effect: Summon Wall (5 Seconds)

Cooldown: 45 Seconds

Line of Warding creates a long wall in front of the player that prevents all enemy movement across it. Use this power when facing a large number of melee foes, especially in PvE, because enemies who attempt to cross are knocked back and stunned, giving you time to soften them up from range with the ability of your choice.

EMPOWER

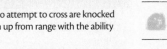

Damage: N/A

Effect: Might (x6) (12 Seconds), Healing

Cooldown: 20 Seconds

This skill is a channeled healing ability. You and your allies gain many stacks of Might for a considerable duration. At the end of the channeling, all your people also get a decent chunk of their health restored. Use Empower between waves of a fight. You don't want to use it when enemies are right on top of you; they'll interrupt you too often. Instead, wait until you have a moment of spare time to whip out the Might and help keep your group alive.

Focus (Off Hand)

Focus is a pure defensive weapon. Use it to protect yourself and others from damage and conditions. This is a good tool for prolonged fights with higher survivability. It's not a wise choice if you need fast kills!

RAY OF JUDGMENT

Damage: Low

Effect: Regeneration (5 Seconds), Blind (5 Seconds), Bounces Between Targets

Cooldown: 25 Seconds

Ray of Judgment isn't the most accurate skill. It bounces around after striking targets, and you can't control the spell. However, it makes up for that by being a good melee healing ability. Enemies take damage from it and miss their next attacks, while the spell comes back to you and regenerates some of your health. The mix of mitigation and healing make it very hard for enemies to kill you without a fight. Use Ray of Judgment when you need to buy time for your healing ability to cool down.

SHIELD OF WRATH

Damage: Varies

Effect: Block, Area Damage, Combo Finisher (Blast)

Cooldown: 45 Seconds

Shield of Wrath helps you hold the line during a sudden rush of attacks. The skill blocks the next few blows, mitigating a huge amount of damage. If the shield isn't fully expended, it detonates at the end of a few seconds and damages all enemies nearby. Use this when your guardian is rushed by a large group of enemies. This is a nifty skill for PvP and heavy WvW engagements. These largest battles ensure you use the shield to its fullest and have the best chance to mitigate major damage. Enemies pile on to avoid the shield's detonation. That buys your allies time to heal, regain their footing, and turn the tables on a superior force.

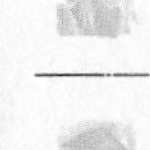

Torch (Off Hand)

We know you like setting things on fire. What guardian doesn't? Torches give you a couple of damage over time abilities that are extremely fun to use. You get to hit multiple targets and leave them burning for more. While lacking a focus' survivability, torches compensate with faster kill potential.

CLEANSING FLAME

Damage: Light

Effect: Channeled, Removes Conditions, Unblockable

Cooldown: 15 Seconds

Cleansing Flame deals moderate damage while being channeled. Though each hit is low on damage, the cumulative effect is adequate. You get to set your enemies on fire, so Virtue of Justice kicks in well due to the volume of attacks. Cleansing Flame removes one condition from each ally in the area as well, so this attack has a defensive aspect.

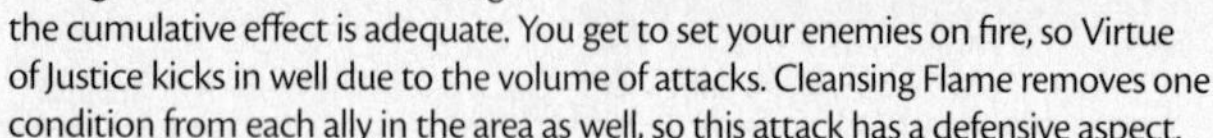

ZEALOT'S FLAME

Damage: Medium to High

Effect: Instant Cast, Burning (3 Seconds), Duration (10 Seconds)

Cooldown: 20 Seconds

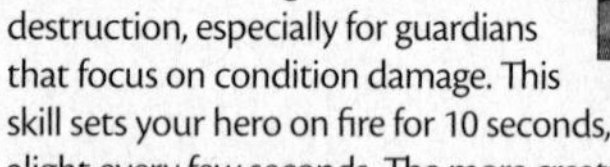

Zealot's Flame is a good source of AoE destruction, especially for guardians that focus on condition damage. This skill sets your hero on fire for 10 seconds, and nearby enemies keep getting set alight every few seconds. The more creatures you're fighting, the better the spell gets. If you're fighting someone especially nasty, press "5" again before Zealot's Flame wears off to burn a single target for even more damage.

This spell is cast instantly, so use it while you're autoattacking or channeling something else.

Shield (Off Hand)

Shields specialize in protection, both for you and your party. They provide Aegis, block projectiles, and generally make it easier to survive for as long as possible. Take this over a focus if you want to have even more damage mitigation.

SHIELD OF JUDGMENT

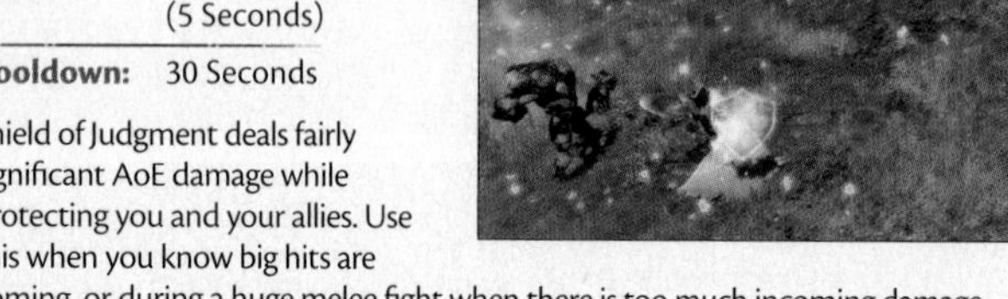

Damage: Moderate

Effect: Protection 33% (5 Seconds)

Cooldown: 30 Seconds

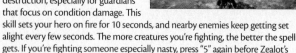

Shield of Judgment deals fairly significant AoE damage while protecting you and your allies. Use this when you know big hits are coming, or during a huge melee fight when there is too much incoming damage for players to handle. The protection affects you and every friendly target in the area, so it's great to have in dungeons, PvP, or in group events.

SHIELD OF ABSORPTION

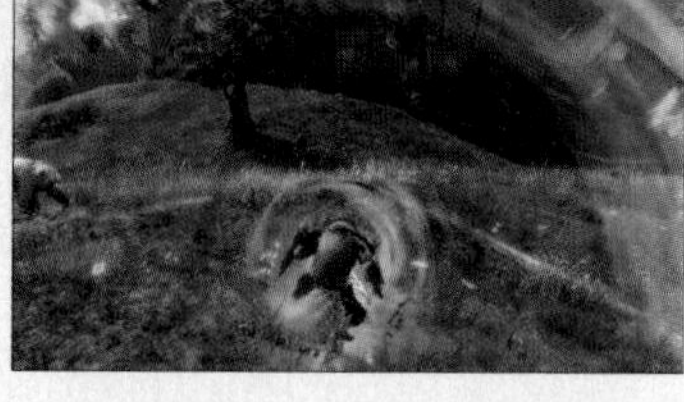

Damage: N/A

Effect: Knockback, Projectile Protection, Duration (4 Seconds)

Cooldown: 40 Seconds

Shield of Absorption is a great way to control your enemies and block projectiles. When used, any enemies within the area are pushed back and knocked down, and the barrier itself blocks all enemy projectiles that come into contact with it. This is versatile because you can hit Shield of Absorption for its crowd control or its anti-ranged properties. Either way, you're mitigating damage by disrupting nearby and distant enemies.

Spears (Two-Handed)

Spears are underwater weapons that give guardians a considerable amount of stopping power. They have high damage output on almost all of their attacks, but they aren't made for kiting or long-term survival. Get in there and kill quickly; otherwise you're going to get eaten up.

SPEAR OF LIGHT

Damage: Moderate

Effect: Vulnerability (5 Seconds)

Cooldown: N/A

This autoattack is wonderful because it does reliable damage and leaves your foe vulnerable to future attacks. Lead with Spear of Light and use it in between special attacks to keep that condition on your targets.

ZEALOT'S FLURRY

Damage: High

Effect: Pure Damage

Cooldown: 6 Seconds

Zealot's Flurry starts a chain of fast attacks that rip through anything in front of your guardian. It's a great way to follow through on the Vulnerability caused by Spear of Light.

BRILLIANCE

Damage: High

Effect: Blindness (5 Seconds)

Cooldown: 15 Seconds

Mitigate damage from enemies close to your hero by blinding them. They'll take enough damage that you aren't wasting any time or slowing down the fight while you're keeping yourself safe. Use Brilliance whenever its cooldown expires, especially if there are two or more enemies still engaging your hero.

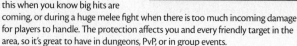

SPEAR WALL

Damage:	Moderate
Effect:	N/A
Cooldown:	20 Seconds

Spear Wall creates a line that damages any enemies that pass through it. Position your guardian just a bit behind the wall so every enemy that comes forward ends up swimming into the area of effect when they engage you.

WRATHFUL GRASP

Damage:	Extremely High
Effect:	Burning (5 Seconds), Pull Target
Cooldown:	25 Seconds

Bring fleeing, ranged, or distant targets over to your guardian while doing very high damage to them. The hapless foe is set on fire while this happens, making the attack even more effective. Use this any time you're dealing with a tough target or something that is hard to engage in melee. If an enemy is avoiding your Spear Wall, use Wrathful Grasp to yank him through the area of effect. It's a dirty trick, but a fun one.

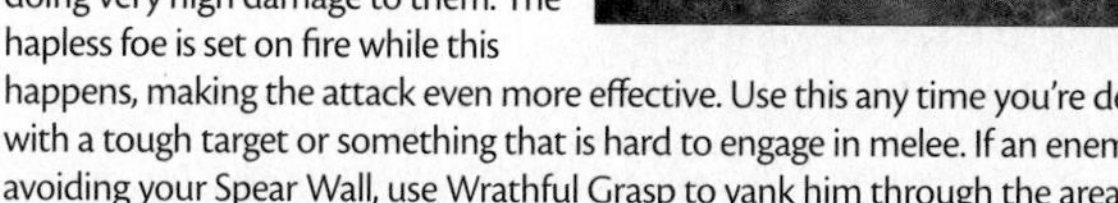

Tridents (Two-Handed)

Tridents give guardians much more survivability during aquatic battles. You can't rival spears' damage output, but the skills here have more healing and mitigation. Use the spears for easier fights to end them quickly. Use tridents when things get tough so your guardian doesn't go belly up.

LIGHT OF JUDGMENT

Damage:	Moderate
Effect:	Minor Healing, Bounces Between Targets
Cooldown:	N/A

This skill fires a projectile that heals nearby allies and wounds enemies. The healing effect is minor, so think of this as a means of surviving attrition rather than making it through burst damage. You still need healing with fair frequency.

PURIFY

Damage:	Very High
Effect:	Remove Conditions, Burning (5 Seconds)
Cooldown:	12 Seconds

Cast Purify to launch a sphere that can be detonated mid-flight by pressing "2" again. The sphere removes conditions as it passes through allies, and does so again when it's detonated. Enemies caught in the final blast radius take a massive amount of damage, making this the cream of the crop for trident burst damage.

PILLAR OF LIGHT

Damage:	Very High
Effect:	N/A
Cooldown:	8 Seconds

The other solid trident attack skill is Pillar of Light. It pulses in the area where you summon it, dealing damage to the enemies there. Though this isn't high burst damage, it adds up well over the 5-second duration of the skill.

REFRACTION

Damage:	Varies
Effect:	Retaliation (5 Seconds), Duration (7 Seconds)
Cooldown:	25 Seconds

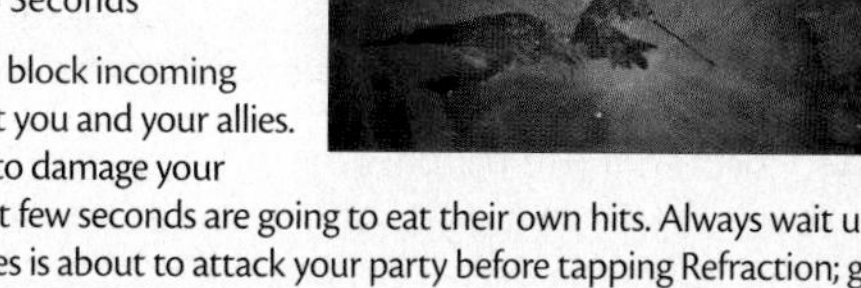

Use this attack to block incoming projectiles against you and your allies. Enemies that try to damage your group for the next few seconds are going to eat their own hits. Always wait until a group of enemies is about to attack your party before tapping Refraction; good timing turns this into an amazing skill.

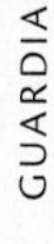

WEIGHT OF JUSTICE

Damage:	N/A
Effect:	Sink (2 Seconds)
Cooldown:	20 Seconds

Disrupt a single enemy for 2 seconds, giving you time to swim away, reposition, start a major attack, or do whatever you need to do. Though you can't kill anything with Weight of Justice, it's nice to have options.

Downed Skills

On the Ground

Guardians are almost as tough on the ground as they are on their feet. These heroes won't take death lightly; they'll fight until the end once they're downed. Guardians use a bit of healing and delaying tactics to stave off their enemies in this state. They don't have much direct damage, so it's easiest to survive when you're in a group.

WRATH

Damage: Low
Effect: N/A
Cooldown: N/A

This simple attack does a little damage while you're lying there, hoping to score a kill (any kill) to try and rally. Always target the enemy with the lowest health. This gives you your best chance to survive the encounter.

WAVE OF LIGHT

Damage: Moderate
Effect: Knockback
Cooldown: 15 Seconds

Wave of Light throws enemies away from your guardian. This buys you time to heal or finish off a weakened enemy before the enemies kill your hero. Use this attack if too many targets get close to your guardian.

SYMBOL OF JUDGMENT

Damage: High
Effect: Healing, Combo Field (Light)
Cooldown: 20 Seconds

Use Symbol of Judgment every time it comes up. The skill does fairly high damage to your enemies, so it's much more effective than Wrath. In addition, the skill has a substantial AoE healing effect. You can still help yourself and your group while attempting to recover.

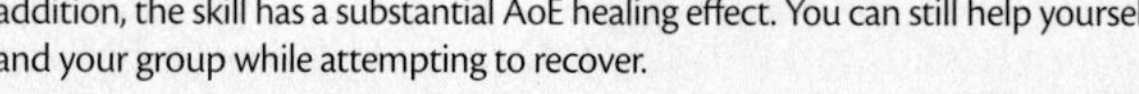

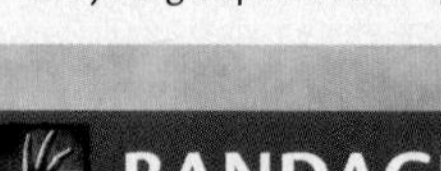

BANDAGE

Damage: N/A
Effect: Self-Heal
Cooldown: 5 Seconds

Use this to heal yourself if there aren't any enemies coming after you. It allows you to recover fairly quickly. If you're attacked, the effect ends and you have to fight for your life once more.

Underwater

To be fair, guardians aren't at their best underwater. Maybe it's the heavy armor! Though they can escape to the surface quickly, there isn't much else these heroes can do to survive. Their aquatic damage output is low when rallying, and there aren't many tricks or traps at their disposal. Try not to go down in the first place, because if you do it's going to be tough times!

SHACKLE

Damage: Low
Effect: Cripple (2 Seconds)
Cooldown: N/A

Shackle is a basic attack that does light damage while you're trying to finish off an aquatic target. If the monster is already low on health, you're likely to succeed. Otherwise, swim to the surface and take your chances there. The crippling effect of this attack slows your enemies' movement, but that's only useful if they're chasing your allies. Ranged targets won't care, and melee targets that take you down are already close enough to be a threat.

REVEAL THE DEPTHS

Damage: Low
Effect: Area of Effect
Cooldown: 5 Seconds

This is an area-of-effect attack that deals light damage to everything near your guardian. It's somewhat useful when you have a few enemies close by that are very low on health, especially if you aren't sure which one will die soonest.

RENEWING CURRENT

Damage: N/A
Effect: Escape
Cooldown: 20 Seconds

Use Renewing Current to swim to the surface quickly. You won't be able to defend your character up there, but healing is automatic. If there aren't monsters nearby, or if you're deep underwater and might escape by going up high enough, this is a good skill.

BANDAGE

Damage: None
Effect: Self-Healing
Cooldown: 5 Seconds

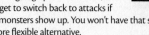

If your hero isn't being attacked directly while you're down, use this skill to start healing. This lets you rally without going up to the surface, and you get to switch back to attacks if any monsters show up. You won't have that same option on the surface, so this is a more flexible alternative.

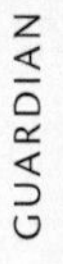

Slot Skills

Healing

Guardians have excellent healing abilities, from a large self-heal with a block effect, to a condition removing signet, to an excellent group heal that's channeled. No matter which one you choose, you'll get good mileage out of it. Switch between them to match whatever situation you're heading into.

SHELTER

Effect: High Self-Heal, Blocks Attacks While Casting

Cooldown: 45 Seconds

Shelter is your first heal, and if you never take any other healing ability, this one will still serve you well. It's a 2-second cast that blocks all attacks hitting you until you finish casting—so not only is it good as a healing spell, in a pinch it can be used to block an incoming high damage attack.

SIGNET OF RESOLVE

Effect: Passively Removes Conditions (Once Every 10 Seconds), Heals on Activation

Cooldown: 30 Seconds

This signet removes a condition from you once every 10 seconds, plus it acts as a strong heal when activated. This doesn't heal as much as Shelter, though they're very close. Signet of Resolve is still ideal when you're fighting enemies that rely on conditions. It's great in dungeons and during PvP encounters.

HEALING BREEZE

Effect: AoE Healing

Cooldown: 40 Seconds

This heal affects both you and any allies in a narrow cone in front of your hero. Slot this skill if you're in a group with professions that have less of an ability to heal themselves. Healing Breeze is best slotted in mid- to large-sized groups.

Utility

Almost all guardian utility skills are group friendly. They encourage guardians to group with others to make maximum use of their abilities. Every category of guardian utility has at least one party-friendly ability. Some, like the shouts and signets, are used almost exclusively for group effects. Many of these provide boons that can turn the tide of a battle in an instant.

TIER 1

HAMMER OF WISDOM

Effect: Summon Hammer (20 Seconds)

Cooldown: 45 Seconds

This spirit weapon has excellent damage per hit. While slow, it strikes in an area and also knocks enemies away from you each time it attacks. Like all spirit weapons, it has an activated ability that consumes the summon for an extremely high damage smash. For the Hammer, this lets you knock down your opponent for two seconds. Use Hammer of Wisdom for spare damage to keep enemies off your hero, and to mitigate some of their attacks.

SWORD OF JUSTICE

Effect: Summon Sword (30 Seconds)

Cooldown: 30 Seconds

The Sword of Justice is a spirit weapon that normally attacks a single enemy. When its special skill is activated, it strikes the ground near the targeted foe and deals massive area-of-effect damage. Since it hits a wide area, this skill is better at dealing AoE damage compared to the other summoned weapons. It's great in large battles!

BANE SIGNET

Effect: Passive Might Buff, Active (Knockdown Target) (2 Seconds)

Cooldown: 45 Seconds

This signet gives a mild boost to your guardian's damage, making it a decent skill to hold onto. Its activated ability is best used to interrupt or stun a foe. Improve your ability to solo high-end targets with that attack.

SIGNET OF JUDGMENT

Effect: Passively Reduces Incoming Damage, Active (Retaliation for Hero, Weakness for Enemies) (5 Seconds)

Cooldown: 20 Seconds

This signet is amazing! Its passive defense boost is already good enough to warrant keeping it around. Then, the active ability helps you reflect damage back at opponents. The cooldown for this isn't even that long.

RETREAT

Effect: Aegis (5 Seconds), Swiftness (15 Seconds)

Cooldown: 60 Seconds

Retreat, despite its name, is useful in many ways. First, as a means of mitigating the initial damage you take when entering combat. Those early seconds are often the highest damage output times for your enemies. Hit Retreat to mitigate the next attack coming at you. Your allies get the same buff, so this can stop a huge amount of total damage.

Also, you can use Retreat to quickly close with an enemy in PvP. In a pinch, the skill gives you medicine to get out of trouble. Keep your health up for longer while fleeing at maximum speed before enemies take down your hero.

WALL OF REFLECTION

Effect: Summon Wall (10 Seconds), Reflect Projectiles, Combo Field (Light)

Cooldown: 40 Seconds

The Wall of Reflection does exactly what its name implies. It creates a wall that reflects projectiles, causing them to go flying back toward the enemy who fired them. Obviously, this is a good power to bring with you if you expect to see a lot of projectiles aimed at you. When fighting ranged opponents, such as centaurs, this is quite effective. Used in conjunction with other projectile-blocking abilities, such as Shield of Absorption, you make it very hard to kite your character successfully.

SMITE CONDITION

Damage: Medium or High

Effect: Remove Condition

Cooldown: 20 Seconds

Smite Condition tries to remove a condition from your guardian. If it cannot, it deals moderate damage to all nearby enemies. That's not bad, is it? But if you do have a condition harming your character, the damage from the attack is doubled. Now you're cooking with heat!

TIER 2

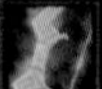

BOW OF TRUTH

Effect: Summon Bow (20 Seconds)

Cooldown: 60 Seconds

This spirit weapon periodically fires a bolt of energy at someone in the party, removing a condition from him or her. These attacks also heal your hero for a minor amount, making it easier to survive light damage over time. The shots are slow and there are better condition removers for guardians, but during times of heavy condition fighting you can stack the skills together. The active ability for the bow creates a rain of healing arrows at its location. Use that when the bow is about to expire so you get some extra love from it.

SIGNET OF WRATH

Effect: Passively Improves Condition Damage, Active (Immobilize) (3 Seconds)

Cooldown: 30 Seconds

This is a good PvP Signet because Immobilize is often needed to kite or stop kiting enemies. You can't go wrong with it, and having better burning damage is a good thing too. Immobilize your foes and unload with your most damaging attacks when you know enemies won't be able to flee and save themselves.

"SAVE YOURSELVES!"

Effect: Draw Ally Conditions, Gain Boons

Cooldown: 60 Seconds

This useful ability rips conditions off of allies so they can fight at their best. Your hero pulls these conditions into him, but also gains a number of boons to help compensate for this danger. When you're alone, "Save Yourselves" is a great way to give yourself a sudden huge influx of boons. In a party, it's a lifesaver to stave off the effects of condition-based enemies.

STAND YOUR GROUND

Effect: Stability (3 Seconds)

Cooldown: 30 Seconds

Stand Your Ground grants a buff that prevents you from being Knocked Down, Chilled, Crippled, Feared, Stunned, or Launched. While not useful all the time, it is definitely effective against some of the bigger group event bosses who have a tendency to use Launch and Knockdown abilities. It's also essential for PvP, where you can protect yourself and your squad from being knocked around constantly. Even a few seconds of immunity to this can change the course of a battle, and the cooldown isn't bad at all.

PURGING FLAMES

Effect: Burning (5 Seconds), Remove Conditions, Combo Field (Fire)

Cooldown: 40 Seconds

Use Purging Flames to strip conditions off of you and your allies while torching any enemies that try to get close to your characters. This is especially effective if you have allies with ranged projectile weapons that can shoot through the fire and pick up its attributes for fast combos. The one-two punch here is that your ranged characters get to have fun, and enemies either have to play their game at a distance, or charge forward and eat all the fire damage from the circle itself.

CONTEMPLATION OF PURITY

Effect: Remove Conditions, Gain Boons, Break Stun

Cooldown: 60 Seconds

This power removes all conditions from your hero and turns them into boons instead. For example, if you remove Bleeding or Burning, you'll get Regeneration. If you remove Vulnerability, you will gain Protection, and so on. This is a fantastic ability to bring with you in PvP or into dungeons and high-end encounters. It's least useful when you're soloing; the long cooldown doesn't work well, especially if you're facing foes that are only going to slap one or two conditions on you rather than a whole menagerie of pain.

JUDGE'S INTERVENTION

Effect: Teleport, Burning (3 Seconds), Break Stun

Cooldown: 45 Seconds

This flexible skill has offensive and defensive benefits. The fast teleport lets you catch ranged enemies, flee targets, and kite opponents without delay. As you arrive, a shockwave of fire sets nearby targets alight, so there is damage as well as utility. Because the ability lets you break out of Stuns too, it's even a way to combat opponents with crowd control by turning their best abilities into an excuse for you to hurt them.

TIER 3

SHIELD OF THE AVENGER

Effect: Summon Shield (20 Seconds)

Cooldown: 60 Seconds

This spirit weapon periodically creates a shield around an area; the shield blocks projectiles from entering the space. Its cooldown is such that the shield is up most of the time. The shield's active ability causes it to fly at several enemies, striking each of them once and causing Weakness before dissipating. Take this power with you if you know you'll be fighting a lot of ranged attackers.

SIGNET OF MERCY

Effect: Passively Improves Healing, Active (Revives an Ally)

Cooldown: 240 Seconds

This signet boosts your healing. When activated, it revives a downed friendly target. This is a major benefit when grouping with others, doing group events, going into dungeons, or holding areas in PvP. You can last that much longer by raising a downed friend without needing to expose yourself.

"HOLD THE LINE!"

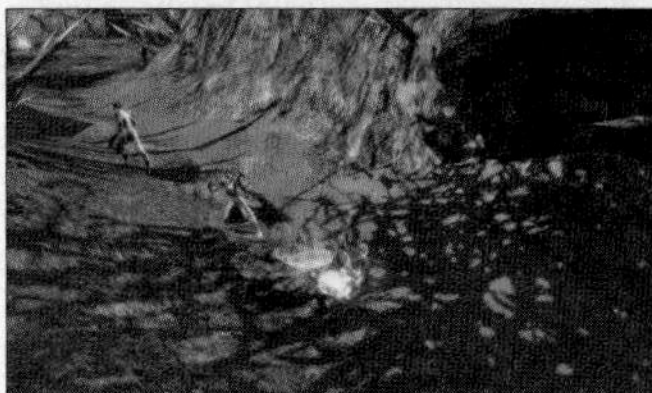

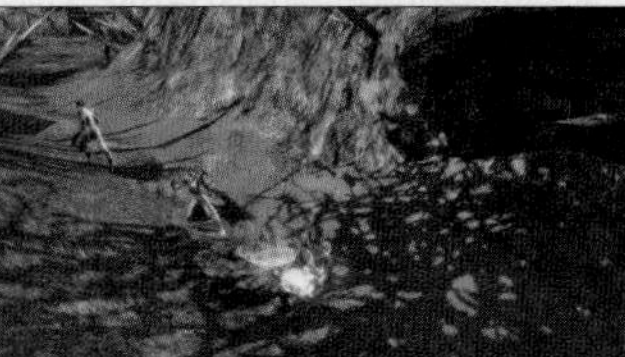

Effect: Protection (3 Seconds), Regeneration (6 Seconds), Break Stun

Cooldown: 35 Seconds

This shout is one of the best support abilities a guardian can bring to a group. It has a large range, can affect up to five targets, and mitigates damage while it heals. This ability goes especially well with any group that makes use of pets, like rangers or necromancers. More challenging content such as group events, dungeons, and PvP all encourage abilities of this nature.

HALLOWED GROUND

Effect: Stability (10 Seconds), Combo Field (Fire)

Cooldown: 80 Seconds

Hallowed Ground gives you and your buddies 10 seconds where no one can be Stunned or knocked around. It's a great way to handle a charge from dungeon bosses with those abilities, group events, or PvP opponents who are likely to use Stuns to great advantage. Because this skill has a long cooldown, it's highly situational. You should slot it only when you know a specific battle is ahead that will require that level of defensive play.

SANCTUARY

Effect: Form Barrier (10 Seconds), Heal Allies

Cooldown: 120 Seconds

Sanctuary is another defensive skill that protects you and your party. For 10 seconds, no enemies can approach or leave the area near your hero. Projectiles are also affected, so ranged enemies are useless against you during this time. Also during this 10-second window, you and your allies are healed as long as they stay within the area of effect.

Though extremely powerful and long lasting for effects of this type, Sanctuary has a long cooldown and should be reserved for large group play. The more allies you have, the more of an advantage you buy with this skill.

MERCIFUL INTERVENTION

Effect: Teleport, Healing Aura

Cooldown: 80 Seconds

This skill automatically teleports you to the nearest ally with low health and starts forming a healing aura to help him or her recover. If you want to support your group, especially in a dungeon environment, this is wonderful.

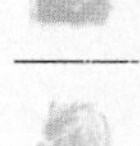

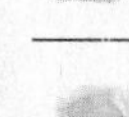

Elite

Guardian elites give your character powerful options for heavy offense or support. Your choices are quite involved, so it's wise to read all of them thoroughly before you dedicate any skill points to any of them.

TIER 1

TOME OF WRATH

Effect: Special

Cooldown: 180 Seconds

This elite skill switches your skillbar to include a number of new powers. Use your best normal weapon skills before activating Tome of Wrath so you get the best of both worlds and can have your cooldowns take place while you're doing other things.

If you're transforming to do damage, first try Zealot's Power, then Judgment, and then switch to an alternating pattern of Affliction and Conflagrate for the remainder of your time.

- Conflagrate (no cooldown): Deals decent damage and inflicts burning on your victims for 2 seconds.
- Affliction (3-second cooldown): Afflicts Weakness and Cripple to your targets. This attack hits quite hard and cools down quickly. Try to get at least a couple uses out of it during this period.
- Smiter's Boon (5-second cooldown): Grants Swiftness and Might to your hero and any allies in a forward cone. This doesn't do any damage to your enemies, so only use it if you have a ton of buddies ahead of your character. Otherwise, wait until you've put almost everything else on cooldown.
- Zealot's Fervor (10-second cooldown): Gives Fury to your hero and nearby allies. This raises the chance for a critical hit by 20% for 5 seconds. If you're alone, it's useful but not a major focus. If you're in a group, it's the first thing you want to use.

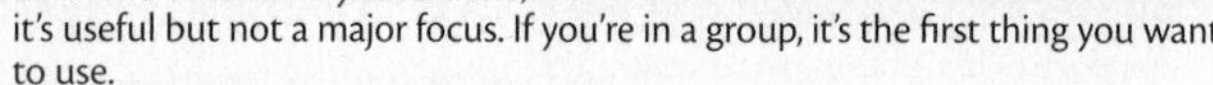

- Judgment (30-second cooldown): There isn't enough time to use this twice during your transformation, but even a single use is wonderful. Judgment knocks down up to five enemies and leaves them on the ground for 2 seconds. They'll take agonizing damage in the process, so this ability is as good offensively as it is defensively.

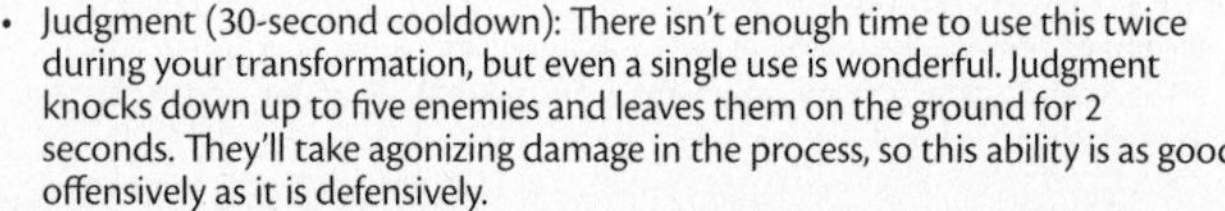

RENEWED FOCUS

Effect: Recharge Virtues, Breaks Stun, Invulnerability

Cooldown: 180 Seconds

Renewed Focus is a simple elite skill that restores your virtues instantly, leaves you immune to damage during the channeling of the skill, and breaks your hero out of Stun. Use all of your virtues ahead of time so you get the benefit of their active powers, and then you can enjoy either their passives or a second wave of active use. You can work Renewed Focus into soloing, group events, and PvP interactions. There's no "bad" time to use it.

TIER 2

TOME OF COURAGE

Effect: Special

Cooldown: 180 Seconds

This is another elite skill that switches your skills around. Blow your best attacks early in a major fight and then tap Tome of Courage to get a number of awesome support abilities. Learn all of them ahead of time so you're not just mashing buttons during your transformation.

When you activate the tome, use Protective Spirit ("3") and then start spamming Heal Area. That's your non-situational ability. Throw in Purifying Ribbon ("2") if conditions start to hurt your group. Use "4" to stop enemy damage for a few seconds. Save that for a time when things are looking bad, and use "5" to heal everyone to full health just before the tome finishes its duration OR if someone in the group is about to die.

- Heal Area (no cooldown): Heals your character and allies. Because this doesn't have a cooldown, you can spam the healing to really keep your party alive through some serious trouble.
- Purifying Ribbon (3-second cooldown): Use this skill to remove conditions from allies. The ability bounces between them, cleansing wherever it goes.
- Protective Spirit (15-second cooldown): For 5 seconds, you and your allies are affected by Protection and Regeneration. Hit this as soon as its cooldown ends to mitigate as much damage as possible for as long as possible. When combined with Heal Area, this helps your group tremendously.

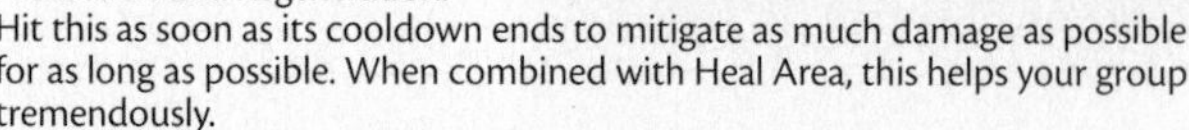

- Pacifism (20-second cooldown): Dazes enemies around your group for 3 seconds. This is another ideal way to mitigate damage when it's coming in too quickly to heal through. Watch for enemies that are charging up or channeling their best attacks so you can use Pacifism at just the right time.
- Light of Deliverance (30-second cooldown): When everything is about to go pear-shaped, this skill fully heals up to five allies. This is one of the most amazing skills in the game. You can turn a major fight around instantly, whether in PvE or PvP.

Traits

Zeal (Raises Power and Condition Duration)

REWARDS

Points Invested	Ability Gained
5	Creates a Symbol of Wrath when your health dips below 25% (30-second cooldown)
15	Your symbols apply Vulnerability to enemies
25	Increases the Power of your symbols

SKILL OPTIONS (GAINED EVERY 10 POINTS)

ADEPT TIER

- Binding Jeopardy: Immobilizing a foe also applies Vulnerability to it.
- Fiery Wrath: You deal 10% more damage against Burning foes.
- Protector's Impact: Creates a Symbol of Protection when you take falling damage; falling damage is reduced by 50%.
- Revenge of the Fallen: Deals 50% increased damage when downed.
- Shattered Aegis: Your Aegis Burns enemies when they're removed.
- Spirit Weapon Mastery: Spirit weapons cool down 20% faster.

MASTER TIER

- Greatsword Power: Adds 5% to greatsword damage.
- Focused Mastery: Focus skills recharge 20% faster.
- Scepter Power: Adds 5% to scepter damage.
- Eternal Spirit: Your spirit weapons are not consumed when commanded.

GRANDMASTER TIER

- Wrathful Spirits: Spirit weapons do 10% more damage.
- Zealous Blade: Your greatsword attacks heal you.

Radiance (Precision and Condition Damage)

REWARDS

Points Invested	Ability Gained
5	Nearby enemies are blinded when you activate Virtue of Justice
15	Virtue of Justice is renewed every time you kill an enemy
25	Your hero deals more damage against foes that are afflicted with conditions

SKILL OPTIONS (GAINED EVERY 10 POINTS)

ADEPT TIER

- Healer's Retribution: Gain 3 seconds of Retaliation whenever you use a heal skill.
- Signet Mastery: 20% faster signet cooldown.
- Shimmering Defense (60-second cooldown): Blind foes when your health reaches 25%.
- Inner Fire: Your hero gains Fury whenever he or she is set on fire.
- Searing Flames: When you apply Burning to an enemy, there is a 25% chance to strip away one of his boons.
- Blind Exposure: Applying Blind to an enemy also applies Vulnerability.

MASTER TIER

- Radiant Fire: Torch skills recharge 15% faster.
- A Fire Inside: Your spirit weapons cause burning.
- Inscribed Removal: Using a signet also removes a condition from your character.
- Powerful Blades: Adds 5% to sword and spear damage.

GRANDMASTER TIER

- Right-Handed Strength: +15% chance to critically hit with one-handed weapons.
- Perfect Inscriptions: All of your signets' passive effects are improved.

Valor (Raises Toughness and Critical Damage)

REWARDS

Points Invested	Ability Gained
5	You gain Aegis when your health reaches 50%
15	Virtue of Courage is recharged whenever you rally
25	Blocking attacks grants your character Might

SKILL OPTIONS (GAINED EVERY 10 POINTS)

ADEPT TIER

- Meditation Mastery: Your meditations recharge 20% faster.
- Defender's Flame: When blocking, your hero has a 20% chance to burn attackers.
- Strength of the Fallen: You lose health 33% slower while downed.
- Strength in Numbers: Gives +30 Toughness to nearby allies.
- Purity: You cleanse a condition from yourself every 10 seconds.
- Retributive Armor: 10% of your Toughness is also added to Precision.

MASTER TIER

- Mace of Justice: Adds 5% to mace damage.
- Defender's Shield: Gain +90 Toughness as long as you are wielding a shield.
- Honorable Shield: All shield skills cool down 20% faster.
- Focused Mind: Meditation skills become instant.

GRANDMASTER TIER

- Altruistic Healing: Applying a boon to an ally heals your character.
- Monk's Focus: You are healed whenever you use a meditation skill.

Honor (Raises Vitality and Healing)

REWARDS

Points Invested	Ability Gained
5	Gain a second of Vigor whenever you critically hit an enemy
15	Dodging heals nearby allies
25	Your hero does more damage when his or her endurance is low

SKILL OPTIONS (GAINED EVERY 10 POINTS)

ADEPT TIER

- Protective Spirit: Aegis grants protection if it expires without activating.
- Superior Aria: Shouts recharge 20% faster.
- Writ of Exaltation: Symbols have a larger area of effect.
- Protective Reviver: You and your ally gain Aegis when you revive someone.
- Resolute Healer: Generates a Shield of Absorption when you start to revive an ally.
- Pure of Heart: Aegis heals when removed.

MASTER TIER

- Writ of Persistence: Your symbols last longer.
- Empowering Might: Nearby allies gain Might (5 seconds) when you land a critical hit.
- Two-Handed Mastery: Two-handed weapon skills recharge 20% faster.
- Writ of the Merciful: All symbols heal allies.

GRANDMASTER TIER

- Pure of Voice: Your shouts convert one condition into a boon (for yourself and allies).
- Battle Presence: Nearby allies gain your passive Virtue of Resolve.

Virtues (Raises Boon Duration and Virtue Recharge Rate)

REWARDS

Points Invested	Ability Gained
5	Virtues grant additional boons (Justice gives Might, Resolve adds Regeneration, and Courage grants Protection)
15	You gain Retaliation after activating a virtue
25	Each boon increases the damage you deal

SKILL OPTIONS (GAINED EVERY 10 POINTS)

ADEPT TIER

- Justice's Wrath: The burn duration is increased when you activate Justice.
- Vengeful: Retaliation effects last 50% longer.
- Consecrated Ground: Consecrations become ground-targeted.
- Courageous: Your passive Aegis triggers every 30 seconds.
- Resolute: The passive effect from Resolve is strengthened.
- Fearless: Virtue of Courage grants Stability (3 seconds).

MASTER TIER

- Elite Focus: Elite skills last longer.
- Purity of Resolve: Activating Virtue of Resolve removes three conditions from your hero.
- Improved Spirit Weapon Duration: Summoned spirit weapons last 50% longer.
- Master of Consecrations: Your consecrations recharge 20% faster.

GRANDMASTER TIER

- Extended Consecrations: Your consecrations last longer.
- Judgmental: Virtue of Justice causes burning every four attacks (instead of every five).

Guardians in PvE

Professions are well balanced in *Guild Wars 2*, yet we still have to highlight guardians as one of the most powerful options for new players. If you look at their skills and traits, it's clear these guys were meant to be highly flexible. They have a wide range of healing and support skills, some weaponry with major firepower, and heavy armor as well. Other professions certainly reach the same level of prowess once you master them, but a new player can reach that point on the power curve sooner while playing a guardian.

But why? The major reason is guardians don't need as many active tricks from the player to be at their best. A strong foil would be the thieves. They're deadly, too. Once you learn to evade like a pro, and master the timings of your enemies, thieves are horrifying and joyous at the same time. But getting them just right takes weeks or months of practice.

Guardians don't need to have impeccable timing. Primarily, they need to understand their weapon selections, bring the right tools for the right battle, and let loose.

That's a good and a bad thing. Players who want extremely active combat might be happier with a warrior; they're also heavy armor wearers, so they have some of the same flavor. Guardians pound down their opponents and pick up their whole group to move on and repeat the process. If that doesn't sound crazy enough for you, then try something else before you dedicate to the guardian profession.

The other angle is guardians just get better and better in large groups. If you love playing by yourself, you won't get to see your guardian at his best. Close? Sure. Soloing guardians shred the field. But they're even better if you have four other friends to buff.

Once you've decided guardian is right for you, start looking for weapons. As we suggested, a greatsword and a mace and shield make for a terrific default weapon set. Greatswords, hammers, and maces are all quite enjoyable for killing enemies.

When you start to get interested in group events or dungeons, make sure to branch out and take more alternative weapons. Scepter and focus, or a good staff, are fun for these outings. Make sure to practice the new techniques for each combination. Guardians feel like an entirely different class when you switch to their more magical skills. Get used to the slower attack timings and range.

Early in your career, you won't use virtues quite as well. That's normal, because they're one of the few hard aspects of the class. They're happy to help you with their cool passive benefits, but deciding when to activate each virtue is a challenge. Don't blow all three at once just because you get into a tough fight. That's a normal urge ("Get all of my goodies up NOW!"), but hold off on that.

Use Justice only when you face off against a group's toughest enemy. Don't waste such a nice burn attack on some weakling that's about to drop from your normal hits.

By the same logic, you want to wait on Courage until your normal Aegis falls. Buffing the rest of your group with an Aegis is worthwhile by itself, but the free shield should go to you too. Wait until a few moments after a large fight begins, and then use Courage to protect your party.

If you have a really good sense of timing, you can even hold off for the exact moment when Courage will get the optimum use. Delay until something big and damaging is about to go off in a few seconds. Using Courage at that time can save lives instead of simply mitigating a bit of damage.

Guardians don't have many abilities that let them fly around the wilderness. They're not mobile like thieves, rangers, some warriors, or others. That means you have to learn how to fight against kiting enemies. See which weapons and slot skills are necessary for beating centaurs, fleeing bandits, PvP enemies, and so forth. Make the most use of skills like Judge's Intervention so you can reach enemies when things get desperate!

One way to catch ranged enemies is to force them to come to you. Guardians have many skills that block projectiles or set up barriers. If you're having trouble at range, use these toys to force ranged enemies into your world. When they don't approach, you get the time to flee and come back better prepared. If they change their mind and come forward, cut them down.

Make sure to switch your slot skills over when you're shifting roles from personal battle (where mobility and damage output are your best friends) into something that augments the group.

Tome of Courage, Shield of Judgment, Signet of Mercy, Retreat, Hold the Line, and quite a few others give you the ability to mitigate or outright avoid damage for your team. Switch to Healing Breeze and double up on non-combative weapon sets to complete your transformation from battle platform to group-supported.

And it doesn't matter if you've invested in traits that are initially damage focused. Even a Zeal and Radiance type of guardian can swap around their abilities to ensure they are still viable in group defense.

Guardians in PvP

To master PvP as a guardian, you need to define your intentions. When assaulting points in a smaller squad, you might want to stick with maximum damage output and play as a damage-oriented character. But as the groups get bigger and bigger, you start to have more influence as a healing and boon/condition character. Guardians have so many powerful boons to offer it's painful to pass them up when you're able to buff large groups. Making five people hard to kill, healing them, and then adding direct damage and boons that raise their damage is a game changer.

The same is true in reverse! If you're a group healer and protector, don't believe you can't do other things. When smaller combat erupts, be ready to break out the hammer and lock down the one annoying sucker that keeps getting away.

MESMER

Mesmers are light-armor-wearing casters that weave and spin illusions to damage and disrupt their enemies. They offer a mixture of magic and melee, with an emphasis on supplementing their attacks with strong boons for themselves and condition damage to their foes. They also create their own followers, in the form of independent copies of themselves (clones) and stronger phantasms. This helps them survive frontline combat and gives enemies something to focus on if they attack at range.

If you're interested in group play, either PvE or PvP, you'll enjoy being a mesmer. In addition to their illusions, mesmers are powerful buffers and debuffers. They also take buffs away from their enemies and remove conditions from their allies. In terms of soloing, mesmers concentrate on tearing down their foes, using a mixture of steady attacks, assistance from their illusionary compatriots, and burst damage from their powerful Shatter skills.

Of all the professions, mesmers are the most difficult to fit into a stereotypical MOG class. Their combination of magic, illusion creation, and weapon combat abilities is both interesting and refreshing. The profession has a lot to offer players, making the experience a unique and enjoyable one.

Players who are newer to online gaming, and to *Guild Wars 2* specifically, should consider trying another profession before getting heavily invested in mesmers. Though awesome and fun to watch, this profession requires a higher level of skill, timing, and comfort with the game. They're not the easiest choice for newcomers.

Profession Stats

Attribute	Starting Stats	Naked at Level 80	Geared at 80
Power	24	1216	2219
Precision	24	1066	1066
Toughness	24	916	1571
Vitality	24	916	1571
Attack	158	1216	3336
Critical Chance	4%	11%	11%
Armor	83	916	2508
Health	258	15,082	21,632

These stats give you an idea of what to expect from your character. They show mesmer progression through examples taken at the beginning and end of leveling. Your actual stats will likely vary from this.

Weapons and Weapon Skills

You might be surprised by the weapon selections available to mesmers. Though these characters look like pure casters, they can use an interesting assortment of melee and ranged weapons.

Shatter

Mesmers have four special skills. All of them Shatter their illusions (both clones and phantasms) and produce an immediate and powerful effect. It's best to wait until you have a couple clones and/or a phantasm out before triggering a Shatter skill; the next ability you cast should be a clone-creating spell, to help protect yourself while preparing for the next Shattering.

The majority of Shatter skills cover an area of effect, and they provide burst damage, damage mitigation, or crowd control. This is particularly useful for mesmers because most of their skills hit only a single target. We'll talk more in detail about each Shatter skill below.

MIND WRACK

Effect: High AoE Damage

Cooldown: 15 Seconds

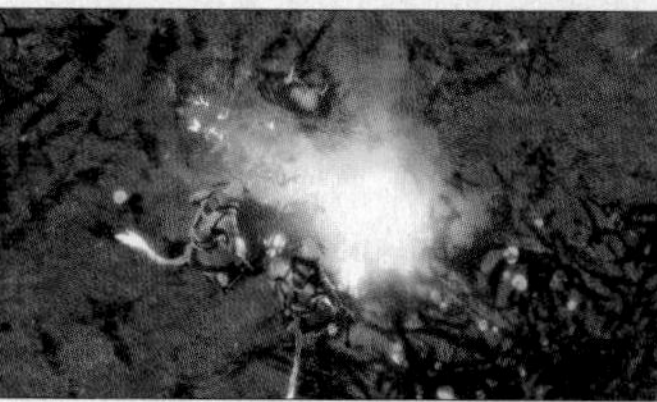

Mind Wrack destroys your illusions in favor of an area-of-effect damage attack. This skill is a reliable damage-dealing ability with great general applicability, but it's particularly effective for soloists. Not surprisingly, it gives a mesmer burst potential, and it's a wonderful fight ender. The short cooldown allows it to be triggered multiple times throughout the battle, as desired.

CRY OF FRUSTRATION

Effect: Moderate Damage, Confusion (4 Seconds)

Cooldown: 30 Seconds

Cry of Frustration does AoE damage in two ways. Not only are enemies hit initially by the attack, but they are confused for several seconds. During that time, the mesmer's attacks cause enemies to take damage. This is a deterrent for enemy attacks in PvP, and it's a good way to hurt foes even more in PvE.

DIVERSION

Effect: Daze (1 Second)

Cooldown: 45 Seconds

Diversion destroys your illusions to inflict Daze on nearby targets. This is a strong damage mitigation ability, and it works wonders in PvP. Use Diversion to slip away from combat or to keep from being overwhelmed when attacked by an enemy group. If the attack persists (and there are enough illusions), let loose with Cry of Frustration or Mind Wrack.

DISTORTION

Effect: Distortion (1 Second); Longer Distortion for Each Illusion Shattered

Cooldown: 60 Seconds

Distortion is mesmers' last-ditch survival ability, and it allows them to evade all incoming attacks (for a period of time dependent on the number of destroyed illusions). While Distortion is active, you can take the time to evacuate from the battle or start generating as many illusions as possible.

Sword (Main Hand)

Swords are wonderful melee weapons for mesmers. They provide high damage and are easy to use. However, they are close-range weapons, and that makes them a bit risky. Have a longer-range weapon (like a greatsword or staff) as a secondary choice. Open fights at range and then switch to swords when the enemies close.

MIND SLASH

Damage: Moderate

Effect: Chains, Vulnerability (5 Seconds)

Cooldown: None

Slash your foe with three attacks (Mind Slash, Mind Gash, and Mind Stab). The last hit causes Vulnerability. This autoattack is a great stand-alone ability, and the additional Vulnerability gives it even more combat utility.

BLURRED FRENZY

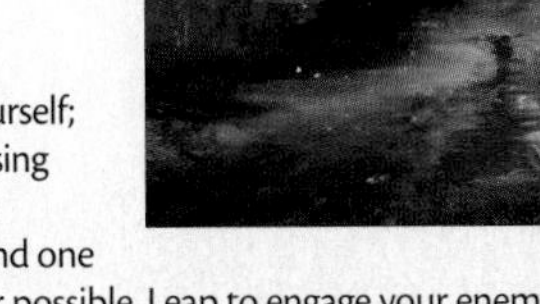

Damage: Very High

Effect: Evasion (2 Seconds)

Cooldown: 10 Seconds

Strike with a flurry of attacks, distorting the area around yourself; the distortion cloaks you, causing your enemy to miss. This is an extremely damaging attack, and one that should be used whenever possible. Leap to engage your enemy, and then immediately use Blurred Frenzy as a follow-up.

ILLUSIONARY LEAP

Damage: Low

Effect: Clone, Combo Finisher (Leap)

Cooldown: 12 Seconds

This skill summons a clone that leaps at your target and attacks it. Its initial hit Cripples targets, and then future attacks add Vulnerability to your enemy as well. As this happens, your skill toggles to a new power. Use Illusionary Leap again to swap places with your clone to Immobilize the target and get up close and personal with it.

Sword (Off Hand)

Off-hand swords are meant for close-range defense. They provide a means for damage mitigation in addition to a helpful ally.

ILLUSIONARY RIPOSTE

Damage: None

Effect: Clone, Block Duration (2 Seconds)

Cooldown: 15 Seconds

Illusionary Riposte blocks your enemy's next attack and generates an illusion when it does so. This is a nice damage mitigation ability, and the addition of a clone makes it even more useful. After it is used, Illusionary Riposte toggles into a new function. Press the same key during this time to launch an attack that Dazes targets in a line. This skill works especially well after Illusionary Leap (main-hand sword) or Illusionary Counter (main-hand scepter).

PHANTASMAL SWORDSMAN

Damage: Very High

Effect: Phantasm, Combo Finisher (Leap)

Cooldown: 15 Seconds

Phantasmal Swordsman creates a phantasm who proceeds to attack your target. The phantasm isn't under your control, but he directly damages your opponent and stays throughout the battle. This ability has a low cooldown time, so use it frequently. The swordsman has an evasive attack, making it hard for most enemies to defeat him without some serious investment.

Greatsword (Two-Handed)

In the hands of a mesmer, greatswords are long-range powerhouses. Most people wouldn't think of greatswords as ranged weapons, but that's exactly how they function here, and they are certainly effective. Make sure to pair them with something to aid against close-range combat. Main-hand swords paired with either a second sword or a torch are great for this.

SPATIAL SURGE

Damage: Very Low to Medium

Effect: None

Cooldown: None

Spatial Surge is an odd ability in that its damage is dependent on your distance from your enemy. The farther away you are, the more damage it does. Because of that, it's a sure-fire fight opener. However, once your enemy is near you, the damage drops significantly. Because the distance-damage effect is so pronounced, one perfectly valid technique is to stay at long range as long as possible. Strafe to stay mobile and keep your enemy from closing quickly. Continue attacking, evade if the enemy gets close enough to attack, and swap to a melee weapon set if you can't get away.

MIRROR BLADE

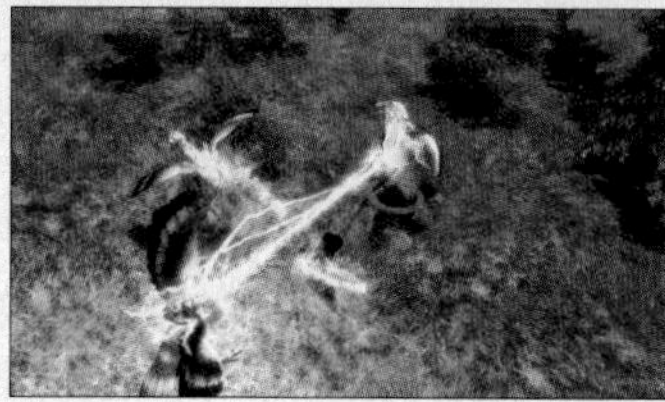

Damage: High

Effect: Clone, Might (5 Seconds), Combo Finisher (Physical Projectile)

Cooldown: 8 Seconds

Mirror Blade is an archetypal mesmer ability. The greatsword bounces between you and your enemy, causing you to receive Might and them to take damage. At the end of the exchange, a clone appears. Use Mirror Blade when your enemy gets to midrange. Your clone will be ready when the target arrives. This skill is even better when there are small groups of enemies. The thrown blade bounces in between the targets and hits up to four of them.

MIND STAB

Damage: High

Effect: Vulnerability (x5) (6 Seconds)

Cooldown: 12 Seconds

Thrust the greatsword into the ground, causing a powerful attack that damages foes and inflicts Vulnerability on all of them. Use Mind Stab once the enemy is in melee range. Afterward, your target will be much easier to kill for a short time, so immediately follow with another high-damage attack.

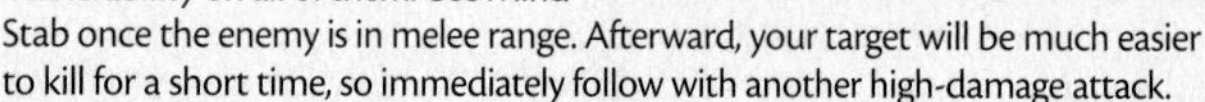

PHANTASMAL BERSERKER

Damage: High

Effect: Phantasm, Cripple (2 Seconds)

Cooldown: 20 Seconds

Phantasmal Berserker summons a phantasm that Cripples your target. This is another melee-range ability designed to help bring down already wounded enemies. Cripple assists in keeping them from ditching the fight, and the additional ally swipes them down as necessary.

ILLUSIONARY WAVE

Damage: Low

Effect: Area-of-Effect Knockback

Cooldown: 30 Seconds

Illusionary Wave creates a cone of energy that launches back anything it impacts. This is a marvelous ability because it gives you some time and space to continue your kiting and ranged combat. Throw your enemies back and retreat while continuing your assault.

Pistol (Off Hand)

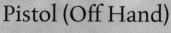

Pistols are off-hand weapons that give the mesmer a fighting chance against groups of enemies. They also summon allies, providing extra damage and distractions for your foes.

ILLUSIONARY DUELIST

Damage: Moderate

Effect: Phantasm

Cooldown: 15 Seconds

Illusionary Duelist creates a phantasm who immediately unloads a pistol barrage against your foe. Phantasms are always powerful allies, and the duelist is no exception. After the pistol barrage is over, the duelist stays to help end the battle.

MAGIC BULLET

Damage: Low

Effect: Maximum of Three Targets, Stun (2 Seconds), Daze (2 Seconds), and/or Blindness (5 Seconds)

Cooldown: 25 Seconds

Magic Bullet is an ability designed to fight groups of enemies. It hits up to three targets: the first target is Stunned, the second is Dazed, and the third is Blinded. It's a useful ability, especially because mesmers aren't very strong in the area-of-effect department. Because you can't control the targeting perfectly, avoid shooting at enemies who are near other monsters that aren't attacking. You might aggro additional enemies by firing Trick Shot at the wrong time.

Scepter (Main Hand)

Scepters embody the magical nature of mesmers, and they focus on medium-range attacks. These weapons pair moderate-damage abilities with damage mitigation (through conditions). This functions to slowly wear away your enemies while keeping them from effectively attacking you.

ETHER BOLT

Damage: Moderate

Effect: Chain, Confusion (3 Seconds)

Cooldown: None

Ether Bolt chains into Ether Blast and Ether Clone. Both Ether Bolt and Ether Blast create confusion for your target, and Ether Clone grants you an illusionary clone of yourself, which uses Ether Bolt attacks. It's a strong attack that generates a large number of illusions, making it perfect to use with Shattering.

ILLUSIONARY COUNTER

Damage: None
Effect: Clone, Block (2 Seconds)
Cooldown: 12 Seconds

Illusionary Counter blocks the next attack from your enemy and creates a clone. This ability can be used at any range, and the short recharge time makes it useful for any fight. After it is used, Illusionary Counter toggles into a new effect. Press the button again to attack and Blind everything in a line. Use Illusionary Counter when you expect an especially heavy attack from your opponent. Careful timing pays for itself well.

CONFUSING IMAGES

Damage: Moderate
Effect: Channeled, Confusion (5 Seconds)
Cooldown: 15 Seconds

This ability channels a beam of light that damages and Confuses your foe. Because of the channeling aspect, use it as your enemy approaches to attack. Follow it with a phantasm-creating ability from your off-hand weapon (to help you do damage).

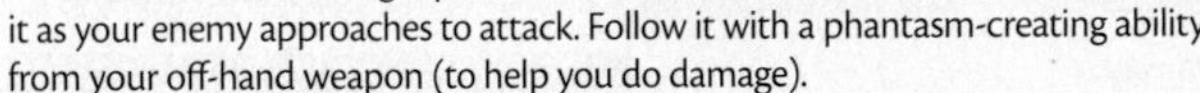

Staff (Two-Handed)

Staves are long-range magical weapons that are perfect for mesmers in groups, especially in PvP. They don't do high damage, but they are perfect for buffing and debuffing multiple targets. Pair them with a set of weapons for melee damage (sword/sword) or something with crowd control (focus, torch, or greatsword).

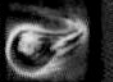

WINDS OF CHAOS

Damage: Low
Effect: Random Boon, Random Condition
Cooldown: None

Winds of Chaos creates an orb of energy between enemies and allies that applies random boons to allies and random conditions to enemies. It provides enough damage to slightly assist with the fight, but its major strength is in combined buff/debuff work.

PHASE RETREAT

Damage: Low
Effect: Clone, Teleport Away, Combo Finisher (Leap)
Cooldown: 10 Seconds

This skill lets mesmers retreat from combat, teleporting away from their foe. This creates a clone who immediately leaps forward to attack the target with Winds of Chaos. The Clone provides something for your enemy to focus on while you move to long range, away from melee damage. Anything that keeps mesmers out of close range while giving them a means to do damage is a good thing.

PHANTASMAL WARLOCK

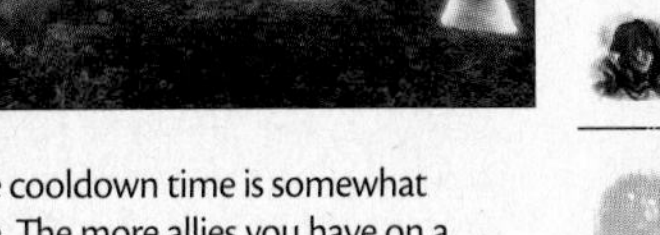

Damage: Varies
Effect: Phantasm
Cooldown: 18 Seconds

Phantasmal Warlock creates an illusion that does extra damage for each condition on the target. As a soloer, it's difficult to slam down that many conditions to rack up high damage, but in a group it's a whole lot easier. The cooldown time is somewhat short, making this ability a vital part of any battle. The more allies you have on a single target, the better and more powerful this skill becomes.

CHAOS ARMOR

Damage: Moderate
Effect: Random Boon, Random Condition
Cooldown: 40 Seconds

For 5 seconds, the mesmer is surrounded by Chaos Armor. When attacked, the mesmer is granted a random boon, and the enemy has to contend with damage and a random condition. This defensive ability provides protection and some solid buff/debuff work. Use it when your enemy gets into melee range. It's even more effective if you get jumped by a group of enemies. Hit Chaos Armor and then tap Phase Retreat to get out of there.

CHAOS STORM

Damage: Low
Effect: AoE Damage, Random Boon, Random Condition, Combo Field (Ethereal)
Cooldown: 40 Seconds

Chaos Storm creates a low-damage blaze of energy over a targeted area. Enemies within the storm are hit with a random condition, and allies are granted a random boon. The bigger the fight, the better this ability becomes. It shines in WvW and dungeon battles.

Focus (Off Hand)

Focuses rely on close-range defensive abilities combined with group utility. They work to protect the mesmer from incoming damage and assist with damage mitigation. They are also potent anti-kiting weapons, which makes them good PvP weapons.

TEMPORAL CURTAIN

Damage: None
Effect: Cripple (5 Seconds), Swiftness (10 Seconds), Combo Field (Light)
Cooldown: 25 Seconds

Temporal Curtain creates a wall of energy that inflicts Cripple on enemies and grants Swiftness to allies who cross it. Before melee is engaged, place the wall in an area where enemies and allies are about to collide. The curtain can also function as an anti-kiting and a movement-assisting ability. Place it in front of your enemies to Cripple them, or in front of yourself to give Swiftness and move out of combat range.

MESMER

PHANTASMAL WARDEN

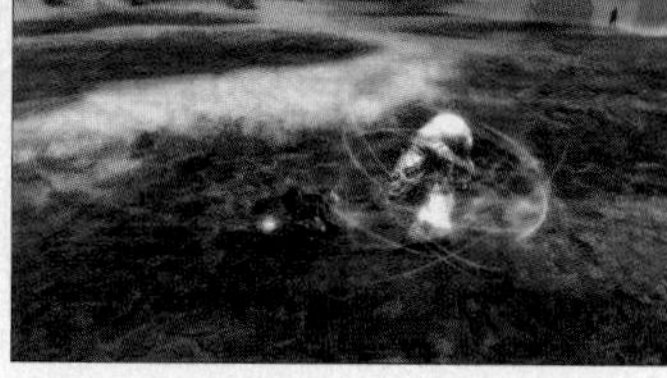

Damage: Very Low

Effect: Phantasm, Deflect Projectiles

Cooldown: 25 Seconds

Phantasmal Warden creates a defensive phantasm. The phantasm deals damage, but its primary ability is to form a defensive bubble around the mesmer and allies; this deflects incoming projectiles. It's a wonderful protective ability to have for PvP engagements at long range. The mesmer helps protect long-range allies while switching between secondary damage-dealing weapons (greatswords and staves).

Torch (Off Hand)

Torches are incredibly fun to use. They're applicable to a number of situations, with both soloing and group utility. These are the weapons you take when you don't know what you'll be facing.

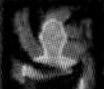

THE PRESTIGE

Damage: Moderate

Effect: Invulnerable Form, Blindness (5 Seconds), Burning (3 Seconds)

Cooldown: 30 Seconds

Prestige is a good evacuation ability. The mesmer disappears in a cloud of smoke, letting the hero move around the area of battle. After 3 seconds, the mesmer reappears, spreading burning flames around. This is something to use to get out of trouble fast, particularly when surrounded by a group of enemies. It's also a good damage opener in melee combat; the Burning condition is quite potent, especially if it's hitting a huge group of enemies.

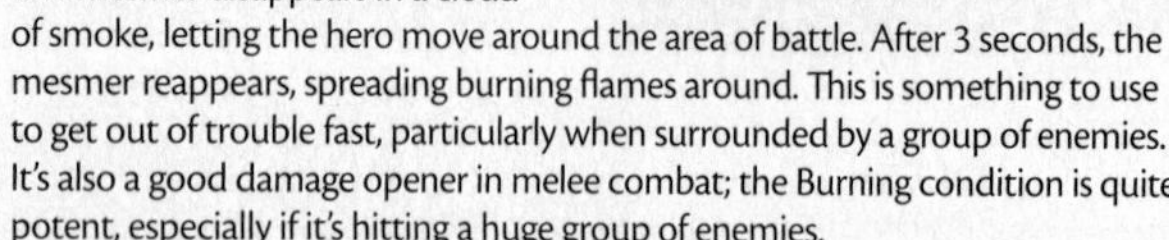

PHANTASMAL MAGE

Damage: High

Effect: Summon Phantasm, Confusion (9 Seconds), Retaliation (3 Seconds)

Cooldown: 30 Seconds

Phantasmal Mage creates a phantasm that does high damage and inflicts Confusion on enemies. Allies gain Retaliation for a few seconds, turning a rush of enemy attacks back on themselves. The best case scenario is to use this in a group, but it provides solid benefits even for a solo mesmer.

Spear (Underwater, Two-Handed)

Spears are close-range, high-damage weapons. They're wonderful for underwater solo encounters. Mesmers retain their ability to create phantasmal allies even while under the waves. With spears, they also have crowd control to fall back on.

STAB

Damage: High

Effect: Chain

Cooldown: None

Stab is a series of attacks for the spear, providing high damage. It's a valid and brutal technique to sit back and keep stabbing your enemy to death. The final strike in this trio has an evade worked into it, so you end up avoiding a moderate amount of enemy damage while you lay into your target.

FEIGNED SURGE

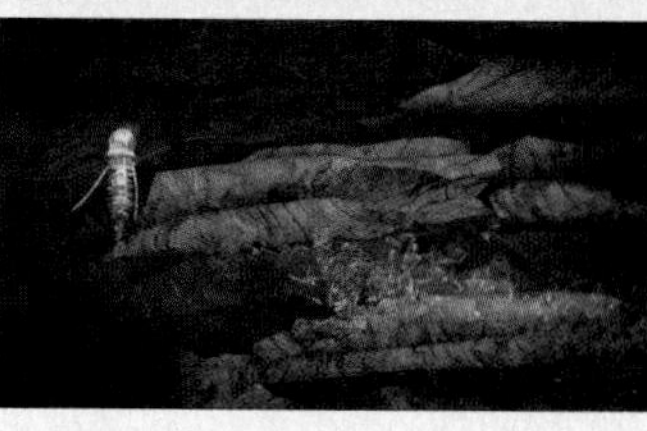

Damage: High

Effect: Clone, Charge, Teleport

Cooldown: 8 Seconds

Feigned Surge is a joy to use. It slams into anything in front of your hero with a powerful attack. Afterward, your character teleports back to the starting location. It also creates a clone, which immediately engages your enemy. The only downside is it can be somewhat disorienting due to the teleportation.

ILLUSIONARY MARINER

Damage: Very High

Effect: Phantasm

Cooldown: 20 Seconds

Phantasmal Mariner creates an underwater phantasm to fight alongside you. The phantasm wields a spear and delivers a flurry of blows to a single target. It also represents something else for your enemy to attack (which is always nice). Use this skill early in a fight and then hit Feigned Surge. Your enemy ends up attacking the phantasm, while your hero is left safe and sound.

SLIPSTREAM

Damage: None

Effect: Charge, Push Back

Cooldown: 25 Seconds

Slipstream creates a current in front of mesmers that rapidly propels them forward and pushes back any foes that enter. This ability splits a group of enemies, allowing mesmers to focus their attacks on one at a time. Combine it with Feigned Surge and Vortex to twist and turn around in the water, leaving any enemies puzzled and open to high-damage attacks.

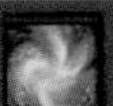

VORTEX

Damage: Moderate
Effect: Pull
Cooldown: 40 Seconds

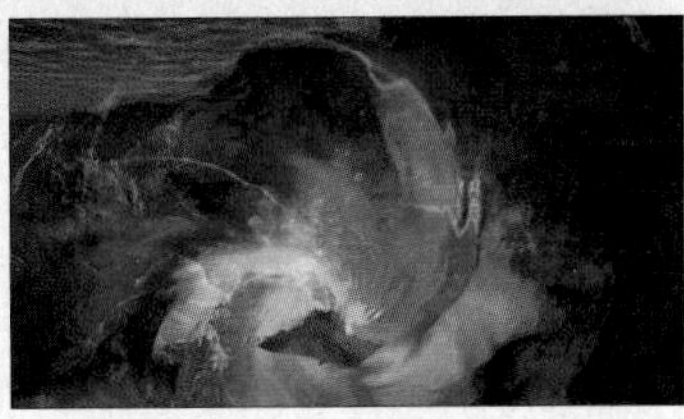

Vortex creates a whirlpool at your location, pulling any nearby enemies toward you. It's disruptive to their attacks and allows great range control in a fight. Paired with Feigned Surge and Slipstream, enemies won't know where their target is supposed to be or how to attack! As with many mesmer skills, this is even more effective in PvP. The disruption has a lasting effect on human opponents because they need to figure out what's going on. AI enemies react much faster.

Trident (Underwater, Two-Handed)

Tridents are long-range weapons that provide mild healing and damage mitigation abilities. They're the perfect thing for group underwater engagements. The ranged aspect of these weapons allows a mesmer to keep sight of their party while doing damage and casting conditions. In addition, tridents have several area-of-effect condition spells that help to keep the mesmer from being surrounded and overwhelmed.

SIREN'S CALL

Damage: Moderate
Effect: Confusion (3 Seconds), Light Healing
Cooldown: None

Siren's Call creates a ribbon of energy that bounces among enemies, confusing them. It also provides minor healing, topping off lightly wounded characters.

INEPTITUDE

Damage: High
Effect: Blindness (4 Seconds)
Cooldown: 12 Seconds

Ineptitude smacks into your foes with high damage and a flashing light that causes Blindness. It's a great contribution to any fight, so use it as often as you can. The only downside is that sometimes neutral creatures add to a fight if they're near your target. Still, the long range of the trident combined with its area-of-effect damage keeps that from being too dangerous a threat.

SPINNING REVENGE

Damage: None
Effect: Clone, Retaliation (3 Seconds)
Cooldown: 15 Seconds

Spinning Revenge creates a clone to aid your hero; it also grants a Retaliation boon. This is a good spell to trigger once your enemy has gotten close to you, after Siren's Call and Ineptitude have done their work. The clone always appears nearby, and they'll move to engage the enemy without delay.

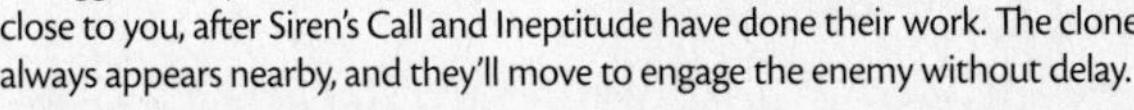

ILLUSIONARY WHALER

Damage: None
Effect: Phantasm, Bleeding (5 Seconds)
Cooldown: 20 Seconds

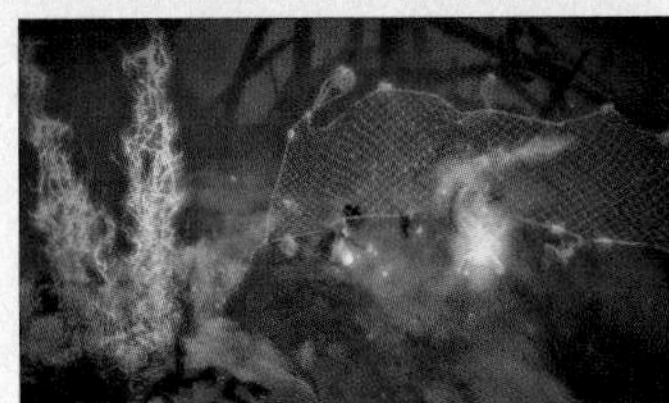

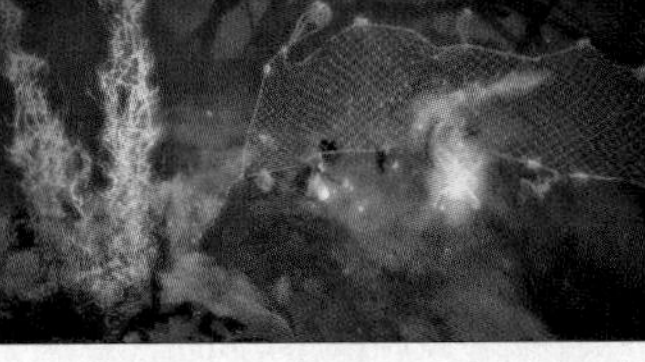

Illusionary Whaler is the phantasm creator of the trident lineup, but this illusion comes complete with a bleed-inducing harpoon gun! The Whaler appears next to you, so use this skill when your enemy is somewhat close by. Pair this attack with Spinning Revenge to have an entire pack of ethereal companions.

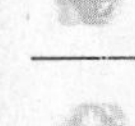

MESMER

ILLUSION OF DROWNING

Damage: High
Effect: Sink (2 Seconds)
Cooldown: 18 Seconds

Illusion of Drowning forms a translucent anchor that wraps around enemies, dragging them painfully to the bottom. They *can't* move, and you get to slam them from a distance. This is a great way to discourage underwater enemies from following you and impeding your travel.

Downed Skills

On the Ground

Mesmers still have a few tricks up their sleeves if they fall in battle. Using damage mitigation and their powers of illusion, they can find their feet and rally once again. They can even skip away from their foes and take advantage of their enemies' inattention.

MIND BLAST

Effect: Low Damage, Confusion (5 Seconds)
Cooldown: None

Mind Blast creates an energy surge that damages and confuses your targets. This is the basic damage-dealing attack in your downed state. Target enemies with the lowest health and start the barrage. It doesn't matter if they're attacking you; the confusion hurts them as long as they're attacking something (anything).

DECEPTION

Effect: Clone, Vengeance (10 seconds)
Cooldown: 10 seconds

Deception summons a clone that attacks your enemy. This grants your character Vengeance and gives you some damage output while trying to recover. Combine this with Phantasmal Rogue to really burn down a weakened foe and rally as soon as possible.

PHANTASMAL ROGUE

Effect: Phantasm, Blindness, Very High Damage

Cooldown: 20 Seconds

Phantasmal Rogue creates an ally that fights any attacking forces and limits their effectiveness. This serves to protect downed mesmers and helps them rally by killing something. The phantasm appears next to you, and you can't control it. It's most effective when you've been brought down by a single foe.

BANDAGE

Effect: Channel, Light Healing

Cooldown: 5 Seconds

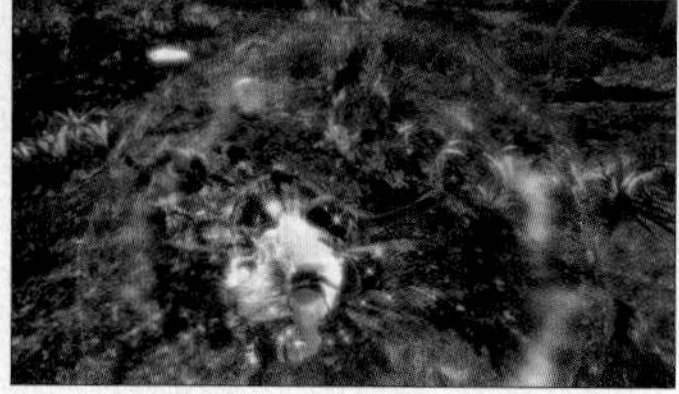

Bandage is a channeled ability that restores health over the course of the channel. Any damage taken interrupts the channeling, disrupting the ability. Use it when there aren't any enemies nearby, or if your group members are handling the fight and you have time to recover.

Underwater

Mesmers have the exact same functionality underwater that they do on land. They can Mind Blast to damage enemies, summon a Phantasmal Rogue for assistance, or use Displacement to Teleport away from trouble. Bandaging is done normally.

Slot Skills

Healing

Mesmers have strong healing abilities that complement the general dynamics of the profession well. These skills have impressive PvP utility. As a bonus, mesmer cooldown times are very short, letting them cast their spells quickly and easily. Note that all of their healing abilities are self-heals; group healing is mainly done through a mesmer's utility skills.

ETHER FEAST

Effect: Healing

Cooldown: 20 Seconds

Ether Feast is the mesmer's catch-all, every-situation healing skill. It provides a strong amount of healing by default. The more illusions you have out at the moment, the higher this gets. This is the best PvE and solo healing ability for the profession.

MIRROR

Effect: Reflect Projectiles, Healing

Cooldown: 30 Seconds

Mirror creates a shield that reflects incoming projectiles while healing your mesmer. It's a skill geared toward PvP and specific PvE situations. Use it when you expect combat to be range-based, such as during castle sieges or events with monsters that use missile weapons.

MANTRA OF RECOVERY

Effect: Channel, Healing

Cooldown: 8 Seconds

Mantra of Recovery is a healing skill. It has an exceptionally short cooldown. Use this mantra in a group environment (in either PvP or PvE) or between battles. For even greater benefits, consider adding the Inspiration trait skill of Restorative Mantras (all mantra effects also apply to allies).

Note that Mantras are charged ahead of time by using the skill a single time. Once it's ready, press the skill button again to trigger the effect. This lets you frontload your ability, allowing you to trigger it when you're in the middle of using other skills.

Utility

Mesmers fill out their repertoire with utility skills that accentuate several aspects of play. As with all professions, signets have minor passive bonuses and more powerful active effects. Mantras are extremely powerful but take more time to cast and prepare. Various illusory spells give mesmers even more variety in what they have access to, regardless of weapon choice.

TIER 1

SIGNET OF INSPIRATION

Effect: Passively Grants a Random Boon Every 10 Seconds; Actively Copies All of Your Boons to Nearby Allies

Cooldown: 45 Seconds

Signet of Inspiration allows a mesmer to fight more effectively while adding some group benefits. Once activated, the passive effect is lost. It's a good basic skill for PvE in and of itself (used entirely for its passive effect), but it really shines in group play. All you need to do is wait until you have an exceptionally nice boon to spread. Use this with a staff to make the signet even more powerful because you'll have more boons to hand off.

SIGNET OF DOMINATION

Effect: Passively Improves Condition Damage; Actively Stuns (2 Seconds) Your Foe

Cooldown: 45 Seconds

Signet of Domination is another skill applicable to a large number of situations. Mesmers use a lot of condition damage, so the passive effect does a great deal for them. The active effect works as a "get out of trouble" ability, giving a means of damage mitigation or escape. As always, the passive effect is lost when the ability is activated.

MANTRA OF PAIN

Effect: Channel, Direct Damage

Cooldown: 1 Second

Mantra of Pain is a single-target attack with decent damage. It's an ability geared for group play, where mesmers can take the time to channel without opening themselves up to damage. The good news is that the cooldown is extremely short, so it can be used again and again to wonderful effect. It's perfect for dungeon runs, allowing the mesmer to stay at range and contribute damage at any time.

Note that Mantras are charged ahead of time by using the skill a single time. Once it's ready, press the skill button again to trigger the effect. This lets you frontload your ability, allowing you to trigger it when you're in the middle of using other skills.

MANTRA OF DISTRACTION

Effect: Channel, Daze

Cooldown: 15 Seconds

Mantra of Distraction causes a single target to be Dazed. This skill is at its best during dungeon runs, when consistently taking down enemy damage is a very big deal.

Note that Mantras are charged ahead of time by using the skill a single time. Once it's ready, press the skill button again to trigger the effect. This lets you frontload your ability, allowing you to trigger it when you're in the middle of using other skills.

BLINK

Effect: Teleport, Break Stun

Cooldown: 30 Seconds

Blink is a manipulation/misdirection skill that teleports mesmers to a position behind their original location. It also breaks Stuns, giving it even more PvP utility. Blink provides a quick means of escape and helps with battle control. Use this to stay at long range against melee or medium-range opponents.

PHANTASMAL DISENCHANTER

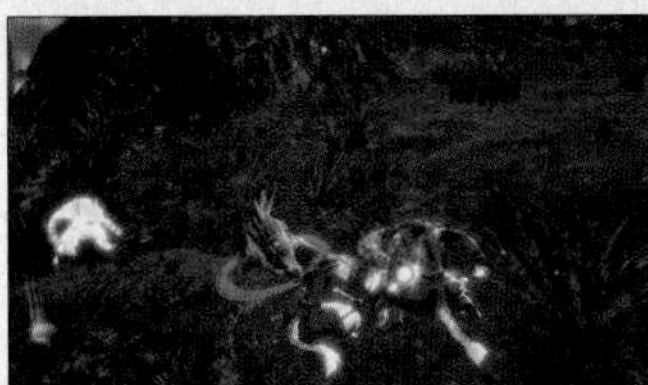

Effect: Phantasm, Remove Boons from Enemies, Remove Conditions from Allies

Cooldown: 30 Seconds

A slot skill with a free phantasm? Yes! Phantasmal Disenchanter creates an illusion that removes boons from foes and conditions from allies, and it's a beautiful defensive PvP skill. Summon this ally to distract enemies, to keep your group safe, and to limit enemy boons and ensure that your side keeps the advantage.

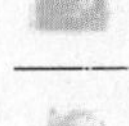

NULL FIELD

Effect: Remove Boons, Remove Conditions, Combo Field (Ethereal), Duration (7 Seconds)

Cooldown: 45 Seconds

Null Field is a glamour spell that creates a field of energy for 7 seconds. This energy field removes all boons from enemies and conditions from allies. Save this for WvW, dungeon battles, or large events where you can affect the most targets. It has only limited value in soloing or small group events.

TIER 2

SIGNET OF MIDNIGHT

Effect: Passively Improves Boon Duration; Actively Blinds (3 Seconds) Nearby Foes, Break Stun

Cooldown: 35 Seconds

Signet of Midnight has a very potent passive ability; mesmers can gain a number of boons based on their traits and utility skills. Having an AoE blind is a big deal because it gets your mesmer out of serious trouble. It's even better for sword-using mesmers, who seem to get into trouble even more often than most.

MANTRA OF RESOLVE

Effect: Channel, Removes All Conditions

Cooldown: 15 Seconds

Mantra of Resolve removes all conditions from the mesmer. This mantra is more PvP friendly, where the conditions fly fast and free.

ARCANE THIEVERY

Effect: Transfer Conditions, Steal Boons

Cooldown: 90 Seconds

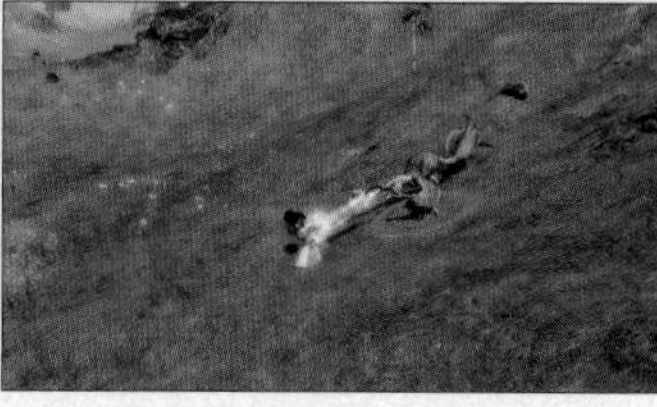

Arcane Thievery is a nasty little piece of work. This spell strips conditions off of your mesmer, gives them to a targeted foe, and then grabs their boons for yourself. It's a perfect spell when dueling high-end targets, especially in PvP. Time this so that you use it right after enemies nail you with their worst conditions or use their best buffing abilities. Once you get the hang of it, this gets pretty brutal.

ILLUSION OF LIFE

Effect: Revive Ally

Cooldown: 135 Seconds

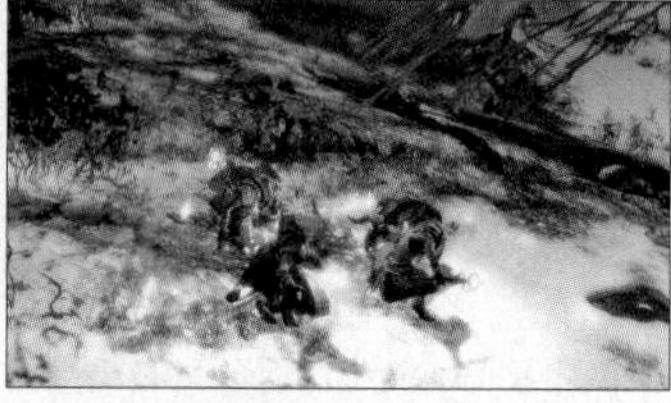

Illusion of Life is a manipulation spell that functions like an extended rally attempt. Downed allies within the targeted location are temporarily restored to battle, and they become fully revived if they kill a foe. Illusion of Life is the only means that mesmers have to revive allies (outside of manually helping them), so this ability is paramount in dungeon runs.

DECOY

Effect: Clone, Stealth (3 Seconds), Break Stun

Cooldown: 40 Seconds

Decoy summons an illusion to attack your foe; at the same time, the mesmer becomes invisible. This works exactly as you'd expect, with the enemy attacking the decoy clone. This is a protective ability for when things get *way* too serious. It works exceptionally well with mantra spells, with stealth earning you free time to begin your powerful new attack.

PHANTASMAL DEFENDER

Effect: Summon Phantasm

Cooldown: 30 Seconds

Phantasmal Defender is a superior mitigation skill. The Phantasm it summons is able to redirect half of your incoming damage onto itself. This greatly extends the amount of time you can survive when focused on by a dangerous enemy, whether in PvE or PvP. When you're guarding areas or trying to complete high-end events, this is an ideal skill to slot.

FEEDBACK

Effect: Shield (6 Seconds), Reflect Projectiles, Combo Field (Ethereal)

Cooldown: 45 Seconds

Feedback is a defensive AoE designed for PvP and PvE group play. It works differently than most barriers in that it creates a dome around your enemies that reflects projectiles. Allies fighting within the shield gain ethereal combo potential.

TIER 3

SIGNET OF ILLUSIONS

Effect: Passively Grants More Health to Your Illusions; Actively Recharges Your Shatter Skills

Cooldown: 90 Seconds

Signet of Illusions is a soloing mesmer's dream. A soloing mesmer relies on clones and phantasms to deal damage to foes and to distract enemies. Getting more health for your illusions is a nice way to increase your hero's survivability when soloing. The active use of this signet lets you pop Shatter skills far more often in a single fight. Use them, hit the signet, and do it again once you have some illusions back up. Swap weapons to make this process even faster.

MANTRA OF CONCENTRATION

Effect: Channel, Stability, Break Stuns

Cooldown: 20 Seconds

Mantra of Concentration breaks Stuns and adds stability so mesmers can't be nailed with crowd control skills for a short time. The short cooldown makes it possible for mesmers to consistently have an edge when kiting and fighting against other kiters.

MIMIC

Effect: Absorb Projectile, Redirect Damage, Duration (4 Seconds)

Cooldown: 15 Seconds

This manipulation spell should be cast when you know an enemy is going to hit you with some serious projectile damage. Not only will this protect your mesmer from the attack, it also toggles the skill when you absorb an attack. Press the skill's button again to throw that damage back at your victim. Because you only have 4 seconds to work with, it's very important you hold this skill until you're right in the thick of a ranged engagement.

MIRROR IMAGES

Effect: Clones (x2)

Cooldown: 45 Seconds

Send in the clones! Mirror Images creates two clones who join the battle immediately. This is a wonderful PvE spell. Use it to have more damage in battle and then Shatter these allies toward the end of their duration to get the most out of them.

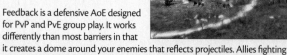

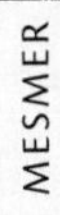

PORTAL ENTRE

Effect: Area-of-Effect Teleport

Cooldown: 60 Seconds

Portal Entre is a movement-altering ability that allows a mesmer to create two portals; the entry portal is located at the mesmer's feet, and the exit portal is at the targeted location. The portals exist for 60 seconds. Press the skill's button a second time to connect the two portals. Use Portal to escape trouble, get past defensive forces, confuse enemies, and so forth.

VEIL OF INVISIBILITY

Effect: Stealth (4 Seconds), Curtain (8 Seconds), Combo Field (Light)

Cooldown: 90 Seconds

Veil of Invisibility creates a curtain of light that grants Stealth to the mesmer and nearby allies. Use this period to revive fallen allies, heal, get behind cover, or otherwise turn the tide of a battle that isn't going your way.

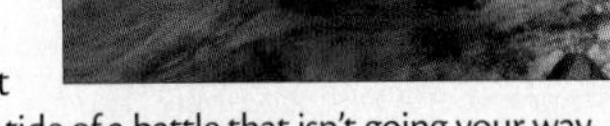

Elite

Elite mesmer skills continue the trend of having high group utility or PvP potential. The more people you have around, the better most of these abilities become.

TIER 1

MOA MORPH

Effect: Transformation (10 Seconds)

Cooldown: 180 Seconds

Moa Morph turns your enemy into a Moa! This is a great elite ability for dungeon runs, effectively hampering your enemies (and their damage output). It's also a very amusing ability, so people who like to get a laugh out of things will be happiest.

TIME WARP

Effect: Quickness (1 Second), Combo Field (Ethereal), Duration (10 Seconds)

Cooldown: 210 Seconds

Time Warp creates a field that lasts for 10 seconds, granting mesmers and their allies Quickness. It's geared for group play and especially for PvP, dungeon runs, and large group events. If you want direct power, this is the best elite skill to use as a starter.

TIER 2

MASS INVISIBILITY

Effect: Stealth (5 Seconds)

Cooldown: 90 Seconds

Mass Invisibility does exactly what it says: mesmers and their allies are gifted with full Stealth for a short time. Use this and then Veil of Invisibility as a double whammy to surprise your opponents.

Traits

Domination (Raises Power and Condition Duration)

REWARDS

Points Invested	Ability Gained
5	Cause a 5-second Vulnerability when you interrupt a foe
15	Dazes you inflict also cause Vulnerability (3 Seconds)
25	5% increased damage to inactive foes

SKILL OPTIONS (GAINED EVERY 10 POINTS)

ADEPT TIER

- Mental Torment: Mind Wrack causes 20% more damage.
- Halting Strike: Deal damage when you interrupt an enemy.
- Empowered Illusions: 30% increased illusion skill damage.
- Rending Shatter: When you Shatter, it causes Vulnerability to nearby enemies (8 Seconds).
- Crippling Dissipation: Clones Cripple nearby foes when they are killed.
- Shattered Concentration: Shatter skills remove a boon on hit.

MASTER TIER

- Confusing Enchantments: Glamours Confuse foes who enter or exit their areas (5 Seconds).
- Signet Mastery: The recharge on your signets is reduced by 20%.
- Cleansing Conflagration: Torch skills remove conditions.
- Greatsword Training: +50 Power while wielding a greatsword.

GRANDMASTER TIER

- Harmonious Mantras: You can activate mantras twice before having to channel them again.
- Confounding Suggestions: 50% chance to cause a 1-second Stun whenever you Daze a target.

Dueling (Raises Precision and Critical Damage)

REWARDS

Points Invested	Ability Gained
5	Gain 1 second of Vigor when you critically hit an enemy
15	Create a clone at your current position when you dodge
25	Your illusions cause 3 seconds of Confusion when they are killed

SKILL OPTIONS (GAINED EVERY 10 POINTS)

ADEPT TIER

- Far-Reaching Manipulations: The range of your Manipulation skills is increased.
- Phantasm Fury: Your phantasms have Fury.
- Retaliatory Shield: Gain 3 seconds of Retaliation when you block an attack.
- Mantra Mastery: Recharge on mantra skills reduced by 20%.
- Desperate Decoy: Cloak and leave a clone of yourself Blinded at 25% health.
- Sharper Images: Illusions cause Bleeding with critical hits.

MASTER TIER

- Empowering Mantras: Increased damage for each readied mantra.
- Furious Interruption: Gain 3 seconds of Fury when you interrupt a foe.
- Duelist's Discipline: Increased pistol attack range, including illusion pistol attacks.
- Blade Training: +50 Precision while wielding a sword or a spear.

GRANDMASTER TIER

- Blurred Inscriptions: Activating a signet grants you 1 second of Distortion.
- Protected Mantras: Increased armor while casting mantras.

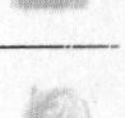

Chaos (Raises Toughness and Boon Duration)

REWARDS

Points Invested	Ability Gained
5	Gain 10 seconds of Regeneration when your health reaches 75% (30-second cooldown)
15	Gain Protection (2 seconds) when you gain Regeneration
25	5% of your Toughness is given as a bonus to condition damage

SKILL OPTIONS (GAINED EVERY 10 POINTS)

ADEPT TIER

- Chaotic Revival: Gain 5 seconds of Chaos Armor when you rally.
- Descent into Madness: Create a Chaos Storm when you take falling damage; falling damage is also reduced by 50%.
- Reviver's Retribution: Grants 5 seconds of Retaliation to you and your allies when you revive them.
- Illusionary Defense: 3% reduced damage for each illusion you have in the world.
- Debilitating Dissipation: Clones apply a random condition to nearby foes when they are killed.
- Retaliatory Demise: Gain 5 seconds of Retaliation when you are downed.

MASTER TIER

- Master of Manipulation: Manipulation skills have 20% shorter recharges.
- Chaotic Interruption: Apply a random condition when you interrupt an enemy.
- Bountiful Interruption: Apply a random boon to yourself when you interrupt an enemy.
- Chaotic Dampening: +50 Toughness while wielding a staff or trident.

GRANDMASTER TIER

- Cleansing Inscriptions: Activating a signet removes a condition.
- Prismatic Understanding: Cloaking skills last 1 second longer.

Inspiration (Raises Vitality and Healing)

REWARDS

Points Invested	Ability Gained
5	Phantasms have Retaliation
15	Phantasms grant Regeneration to nearby allies
25	Phantasms deal 25% more damage

SKILL OPTIONS (GAINED EVERY 10 POINTS)

ADEPT TIER

- Medic's Feedback: Create a Feedback bubble while reviving an ally (10-second cooldown).
- Glamour Mastery: Recharge for Glamour skills is 20% faster.
- Vigorous Revelation: Grants Vigor to nearby allies when you Shatter your illusions.
- Mender's Purity: Remove a condition when you heal.
- Persisting Images: Phantasms have 20% more health.
- Compounding Celerity: Move faster for each active illusion you've summoned.

MASTER TIER

- Malicious Sorcery: +50 Malice when wielding a scepter.
- Warden's Feedback: Focus skills Reflect projectiles.
- Temporal Enchanter: Your Glamour skills last longer.
- Shattered Conditions: Using a Shatter skill removes a condition from you.

GRANDMASTER TIER

- Restorative Mantras: Heal allies when you cast a mantra.
- Restorative Illusions: Heal a small amount when you Shatter illusions.

Illusions (Raises Condition Damage and Shredding Recharge Rate)

REWARDS

Points Invested	Ability Gained
5	10% faster cooldown on all illusion summoning skills
15	All Shatter skills add Confusion
25	Shattering illusions gives you Might

SKILL OPTIONS (GAINED EVERY 10 POINTS)

ADEPT TIER

- Precise Wrack: 10% increased critical hit chance with Mind Wrack.
- Confusing Cry: Cry of Frustration grants Retaliation.
- Compounding Power: 3% extra damage for each of your active illusions.
- Masterful Reflection: Distortion also grants Reflection.
- Master of Misdirection: Confusion you apply lasts 33% longer.
- Illusionary Invigoration: Recharge all of your Shatters at 50% health (90-second cooldown).

MASTER TIER

- Illusionary Elasticity: Bouncing attacks yield an additional bounce.
- Dazzling Glamours: Glamour skills Blind foes at target location.
- Blinding Befuddlement: Cause Confusion when you Blind an enemy.
- Phantasmal Haste: Your summoned phantasms have faster skill recharges.

GRANDMASTER TIER

- Illusionary Persona: When Shattering illusions, cause the Shatter effect on yourself as well.
- Imbued Diversion: Diversion hits multiple targets.

Mesmers in PvE

Mesmers fall into the challenging category for starting players. They aren't easy powerhouses for novices, and their light armor means there isn't as much wiggle room for errors. It takes a while to figure out the best time to trigger your Shatter skills, when to summon phantasms, and when to switch into secondary weapons. Mesmers really shine in group situations, and not everyone begins the game with an established set of friends to adventure with.

What mesmers offer is an entirely unique play experience. They're a hybrid class in that they mix together magic and melee, and they have a wide range of boons and conditions available to them. They also have a special form of pet, in terms of their clones and phantasms. As a mesmer, you never have to face a battle alone—you summon companions to fight with you in every engagement.

Things get even better for mesmers when they join in groups. This offers them a world of freedom to do long-range damage, buff their allies, and disrupt enemy parties.

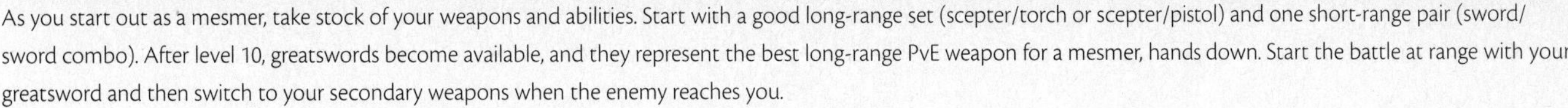

As you start out as a mesmer, take stock of your weapons and abilities. Start with a good long-range set (scepter/torch or scepter/pistol) and one short-range pair (sword/sword combo). After level 10, greatswords become available, and they represent the best long-range PvE weapon for a mesmer, hands down. Start the battle at range with your greatsword and then switch to your secondary weapons when the enemy reaches you.

Your weapons are your lifeblood, and you need to keep them as up-to-date as possible. Wearing light armor means you're going to get smacked around *if* you get hit; it's more important to do damage fast and take out your target.

The way a battle progresses is exceptionally important, and you want to control it as much as possible. Every weapon set has both a clone and a phantasm ability. By the time an enemy gets to you, you want to have at least one illusion ready to attack it. If you have several, take advantage of your Shatter skills, and pop another illusion up at the next opportunity.

In terms of slot skills, Ether Feast is a wonderful healing spell, and you'll usually have a number of active illusions around you to take full advantage of it. You can't go wrong with Mirror Images; having two clones right off the bat is sweet. Check out the signet spells as well. Their passive abilities (especially Signet of Illusion) are worth it on their own, and the active ones can really get you out of trouble.

The Domination, Dueling, and Illusions trait lines offer a lot of potential, in terms of helping to raise your attack strength and the destructive capabilities of your clones and phantasms. If you're not sure what to grab, take traits that make your illusions stronger/do more damage.

One of the exceptionally nice things about mesmers is they have less to worry about from kiters. They're more damaging at long range (because of their greatsword's distance-based attacks). And if anything gets in close, well, that's what their secondary weapons, illusions, and slot skills are for!

Mesmers in PvP

Mesmers have a huge range of tools for PvP (whether small-scale or WvW). They're really at their best in this group environment, and players with an interest in this mode of competition will be much happier with the profession. Mesmers fare best when facing real human opponents.

Left on their own, mesmers strip away any boons on the enemy team, leaving them with no protection and no chance of damage augmentation. At the same time, they keep their allies safe and healthy, taking away any harmful conditions. This is augmented by their control over boons and conditions; mesmers have a wide variety of both to throw at enemies and to aid allies. A huge number of slot skills specialize in boon/condition modifications, and it's best to experiment and see which ones really click with your playstyle.

Mesmers also have access to the most powerful transportation and point control abilities in the game. They are able to teleport themselves and others, in addition to two forms of mass-target invisibility. These are battle-changing abilities, and ones that make mesmers strong defenders on the field of battle, as well as a powerful means to take and hold positions.

The Chaos trait line really comes into its own during PvP. The additional toughness is well appreciated, but the real gem is Prismatic Understanding, which lets all Cloaking skills last 1 second longer. That extra second could mean the difference between a prolonged battle and one handily won.

NECROMANCER

Necromancers are dangerous spellcasters with higher survivability than you might expect. Though limited to light armor, their abilities frequently steal life from enemies to keep themselves alive. In addition, these scholars specialize in conditions that prevent enemies from performing at their best. A happy mix of poison and fear makes everyone's life a bit shorter!

When soloing, necromancers have a huge array of mindless pets to draw on. These help to distract enemies or even beat them down. In a group, necromancers disable targets and deal considerable damage over time.

Area-of-effect attacks are common for these foul casters. They can drop areas of poison and plague on the ground and hurt everything that stays close. This is useful in large fights and in PvP, when chokepoints can be exploited to hurt many characters simultaneously.

In addition, necromancers have a special ability called the Death Shroud. This is an alternate state for the casters; they build life force to go into their Death Shroud mode by killing their opponents. Under the effect of Death Shroud, necromancers can deal considerable damage while protecting themselves from harm.

Profession Stats

Attribute	Starting Stats	Naked at Level 80
Power	24	1729
Precision	24	916
Toughness	24	1571
Vitality	24	1571
Attack	165	1729
Critical Chance	4%	4%
Armor	83	1571
Health	268	24,922

These stats give you an idea of what to expect from your character. They show necromancer progression through examples taken at the beginning and end of leveling. Your actual stats will likely vary from this.

Weapons and Weapon Skills

Necromancers use axes, daggers, scepters, staves, focuses, and warhorns to do most of their direct damage. Many of these provide ranged attack skills, so the profession is primarily able to deal damage to enemies without closing on them.

Because necromancers quickly learn to wield two sets of weapons, you're encouraged to get a few weapons that provide options for several types of combat. For example, take an area-of-effect set and a single-target pair that disables powerful enemies.

Death Shroud (Burst Special Form)

All necromancers have access to Death Shroud as an ability on their function bar. Press "F1" to surround your hero with dark energies, to protect from damage. While in this mode, you have access to several new attacks. These are unlocked just like normal weapon skills (in that you have to kill enemies while in Death Shroud to gain access to the more powerful attacks).

DEATH SHROUD ON LAND

Here are the moves you gain in Death Shroud when you're on land:

Life Blast	Direct attack that deals more damage if you have a higher amount of life force
Dark Path (15-second cooldown)	Shadowstep toward your targets the next time they attack your hero; Chill them and any enemies nearby when you arrive (5 seconds)
Doom (20-second cooldown)	Make the target flee in fear (1 second)
Life Transfer (40-second cooldown)	Point-blank attack that sucks the life out of nearby enemies and turns that energy into life force

Life force is the power that lets you stay in this form. As we said earlier, this resource is gained when you kill your enemies. Watch the bar rise and then enter the form when you're surrounded by foes. This buys you time to survive difficult encounters while your healing skill is on cooldown. Hit Life Transfer to steal additional life force from enemies and prolong this mode.

The Soul Reaping line of traits has some awesome abilities for improving your Death Shroud powers. Take a look at them if you're interested in making the most of this potent ability.

DEATH SHROUD UNDERWATER

Here are the aquatic abilities you learn with Death Shroud:

Life Blast	Still a basic, direct attack; similar to the terrestrial version
Dark Water (15-second cooldown)	A low-damage area-of-effect attack that Blinds enemies (3 seconds) and Poisons them (7 seconds)
Wave of Fear (25-second cooldown)	Deals moderate damage and terrifies all foes in front of your necromancer (2 seconds)
Gathering Plague (30-second cooldown)	Gathers conditions from all of your allies and stacks them onto your necromancer, also inflicting Weakness on your hero

These must be unlocked separately from the terrestrial powers.

The aquatic powers aren't as dangerous as their above-water equivalents, but they have a number of useful functions. Dark Water is beautiful for messing with groups of enemies. Being able to land Blind on multiple enemies is a very big deal because it's a lot of mitigation for a single ability. Wave of Fear has more duration than Doom, and it does damage, too. Both of these abilities are very nice.

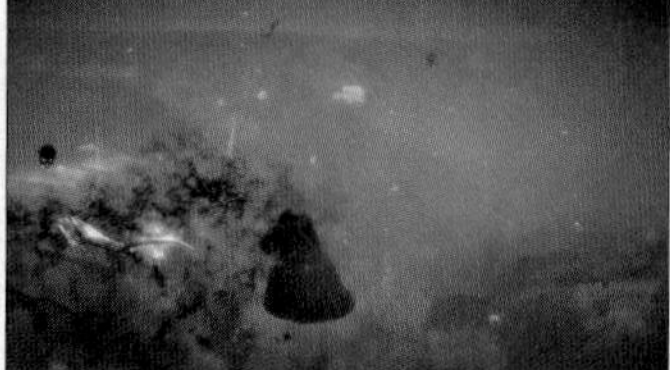

Gathering Plague is the very definition of a situational ability. Do it in a group to help your friends if they're in a bad place. You can gather their conditions and then use utility skills to toss them at your enemies when you come out of Death Shroud. If you don't have the utility skills to do that, try Consume Conditions; it's a healing skill that restores your health for each condition it cleanses.

Axe (Main Hand)

Axes provide solid damage at range for necromancers. Their primary attack gives you decent damage and some Vulnerability for your targets. The other attacks add extra oomph to the lineup and increase the kiting potential.

RENDING CLAWS

Damage:	High
Effect:	Vulnerability (x2) (5 Seconds)
Cooldown:	None

Rending Claws gives your hero a base level of strong damage against single targets. Its moderate range gives you the ability to do some kiting while stacking Vulnerability on your foe.

GHASTLY CLAWS

Damage:	Very High
Effect:	Channeled (3 Seconds)
Cooldown:	8 Seconds

Ghastly Claws is another single-target damage ability. It smacks your target again and again in rapid succession, and the total damage is fairly good. Stack conditions on your opponent ahead of time and then use this as a finishing attack while the damage is already ticking away by your Bleeds or Poison effects. This helps to recharge your life force while staying mobile and at range.

UNHOLY FEAST

Damage:	Medium to High
Effect:	Cripple (5 Seconds), Retaliation (3 Seconds)
Cooldown:	15 Seconds

Unholy Feast is a direct attack that does decent damage. You hit an entire group over a fair area, making it useful for any encounter with multiple enemies. If you're the one doing kiting, then Unholy Feast is a good way to slow down an entire group of foes while you run away and keep hitting them.

Because you gain Retaliation during this time, Unholy Feast is also a key element in AoE fights. If you aren't running away from the enemies, you can instead reflect damage back at them, making the fight shorter and easier to survive.

Dagger (Main Hand)

Daggers give your necromancer fast damage against single targets. They have better survivability than axes because some skills steal life from opponents. The downside of these weapons is that they have little or no range for all of their main-hand attacks. If you like using daggers, make sure to equip something with long range in your secondary weapon set so enemies can't kite you!

NECROTIC SLASH

Damage: Very High

Effect: N/A

Cooldown: None

The fast swing speed of this attack makes it more deadly than it first appears. You lay on the damage quite well with Necrotic Slash, despite a lack of Bleed or Poison effects. This trio of attacks builds life force quickly, making it quite useful for necromancers that rely heavily on Death Shroud. Compensate for the short range by slotting skills that keep enemies from avoiding your melee attacks: Signet of Spite, Spectral Grasp.

LIFE SIPHON

Damage: Moderate

Effect: Steals Health

Cooldown: 12 Seconds

Life Siphon is a channeled skill that takes several seconds to complete. It has more range than Necrotic Slash (but not much). You're still limited to close range. Though the damage dealt is rather poor compared with your other attacks, the health stolen lets your hero survive for much longer during long fights. This won't help you survive spikes of damage like a healing skill, but it's useful for maintaining a higher level of health.

If you're already topped off, don't use this ability. It's less useful for its pure damage, so don't throw it into your rotation unless you've taken a few hits.

DARK PACT

Damage: Moderate

Effect: Immobilize (3 Seconds)

Cooldown: 25 Seconds

Dark Pact locks your enemies in place, making it easier to catch up to them and get some damage done. Slap this on enemies that are trying to kite your hero. Immobilize them for a few seconds and lay into them with some damage before they can run away. It's still better to have anti-kiting weaponry or skills at your disposal, but if you're waiting to swap weapons, this is a great skill against kiters and mobile targets.

Dagger (Off Hand)

Daggers in your off hand provide damage mitigation. Blindness and Weakness are both major assets for necromancers who want to live a bit longer. In addition, both of these dagger skills have AoE potential, making them better when you want to fight against enemy groups.

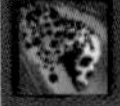

DEATHLY SWARM

Damage: Moderate

Effect: Transfers Conditions, Blind (6 Seconds)

Cooldown: 18 Seconds

Deathly Swarm gives your necromancer the option to get rid of conditions that are giving you trouble. If someone tries to stack damage-over-time effects or something that slows you down, slap him or her with Deathly Swarm. Successful attacks pull the conditions off of your hero and inflict them on the target instead!

Also use this if you're facing enemies with heavy, slower attacks. Blinding them is a good way to reduce incoming damage. Don't use Deathly Swarm for its raw damage output; save it for times when it's going to help you with its secondary effects.

ENFEEBLING BLOOD

Damage: Moderate

Effect: Weakness (10 Seconds), Bleed (10 Seconds)

Cooldown: 25 Seconds

Enfeebling Blood is a ground-targeted spell that doesn't do much damage up front. Instead, it does a fair amount of damage over time. It's intended for disrupting enemies. They won't be able to dodge as well or as often, so it's quite a good PvP spell for taking away enemy options. Because Weakness also debuffs an enemy's damage output, this is also a valuable tool against veterans, champions, and groups of monsters during AoE encounters.

Scepter (Main Hand)

Scepters have more range than axes and daggers, so they're pretty darn effective for necromancers that want to do their own kiting. In addition, these weapons are loaded with condition potential. You get to hurt your foes over time and finish them off with a skill that deals extra damage against enemies that have multiple conditions. Scepters are an excellent secondary weapon for melee necromancers.

BLOOD CURSE

Damage: Moderate

Effect: Bleed (7 Seconds)

Cooldown: None

Blood Curse doesn't have much initial strength as an autoattack. However, its combination of damage over time and long range makes it an essential tool for cutting down single enemies that can't close the gap with your character. Slow the victim with Grasping Dead and then run around, watching him bleed to death without being able to catch you. The third attack in this combo causes Poison, making the attacks even better for kiting!

GRASPING DEAD

Damage: Moderate

Effect: Bleed (5 Seconds), Cripple (5 Seconds)

Cooldown: 10 Seconds

Grasping Dead is a ground-targeted spell that lets you start Bleeding your enemies early in a fight. The fact that it also slows them down is wonderful, making this an ideal battle opener. Use Grasping Dead every time it finishes its cooldown so your enemies are moving slowly during half of the fight. This attack is immensely frustrating to fight against in PvP.

FEAST OF CORRUPTION

Damage: High

Effect: Gain Life Force, Bonus Damage (Per Enemy Condition)

Cooldown: 10 Seconds

Feast of Corruption should be used later in a fight, when enemies are filled with conditions from you and your allies. This attack does more damage when the enemy has conditions in effect.

Staff (Two-Handed Weapon)

Staves are similar to scepters, but they push the kiting function of those weapons even further. With this set of weapons, you get a combination of long range, damage over time, and unrelenting kiting potential. For longer fights that are ludicrously balanced in your favor, choose a staff. Though their attacks deal very little damage at first, the constant damage over time mixed with an area of effect means you can still get a decent kill rate if you're skilled. Either way, your enemies will have a heck of a time trying to catch you.

NECROTIC GRASP

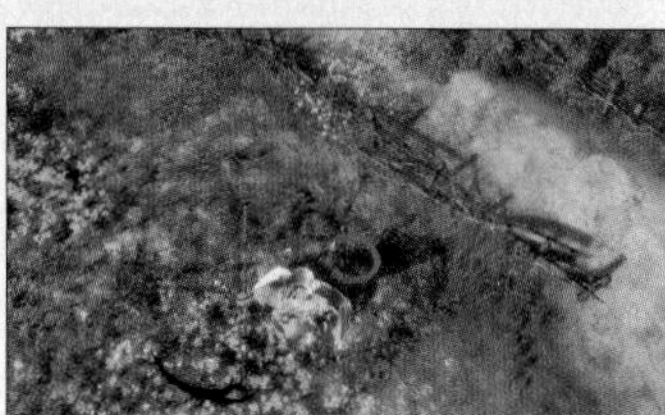

Damage: Moderate

Effect: Life Force Gain, Combo Finisher (Physical Projectile: 20% Chance)

Cooldown: None

This autoattack has considerable range, and it hits enemies in a line between you and the target. Use it to restore life force and to kite enemies while your greater skills are on cooldown.

MARK OF BLOOD

Damage: Low

Effect: Regeneration (6 Seconds), Bleed (x3) (8 Seconds)

Cooldown: 10 Seconds

Mark of Blood is a ground-targeted spell. You can cast it at an existing enemy or group of enemies. Or, you can leave it by your necromancer and wait for the spell to trigger when an enemy enters the area of effect. Both are viable and effective. The latter is better when you're setting up for a major fight because it'll save you casting time and allow your necromancer to lay in with other attacks as the enemy comes to you.

The actual spell puts a long-lasting Bleed on the enemy while regenerating health for your necromancer and nearby allies. As with Life Siphon, this is a great way to sustain your health over the course of longer fights. The difference is this skill does enough damage with its Bleeding that you should use it even if you don't need the health. Target large groups to get everyone Bleeding as soon as possible; that'll make your work easier when you target each enemy in turn.

PUTRID MARK

Damage: High

Effect: Transfers Conditions, Combo Finisher (Blast)

Cooldown: 15 Seconds

Putrid Mark is yet another ground-targeted area-of-effect attack. This one delivers major damage (a rarity for staff attacks). It also cleanses conditions from your allies and nails your targets with the same effects. If you're in a situation where your group is being hit with conditions quite commonly, save this attack until the conditions are stacked high and then use it to protect your group. The damage isn't as important as the cleansing of conditions in that circumstance.

CHILBLAINS

Damage: Moderate

Effect: Chill (4 Seconds), Poison (6 Seconds), Combo Field (Poison)

Cooldown: 20 Seconds

Chilblains is your fight starter for most encounters. It disrupts enemy movement and is ground targeted, so you can hit several foes with it if they're grouped together. Slap this down and cast Reaper's Touch a moment later to get yourself moving while the enemies are still moving and attacking at reduced speed.

REAPER'S MARK

Damage: Low

Effect: Fear (1 Second)

Cooldown: 45 Seconds

Use Reaper's Mark to scare away enemies and give yourself time to flee, get back to ideal kiting range, or just to blast away at someone. This keeps your character safe while disrupting enemies whether in PvP or PvE. In addition, this is a ground-targeted spell, so you can hit several enemies at once.

Focus (Off Hand)

Take a focus on your off hand if you want to mess with enemies. The direct damage output isn't very high with a focus, but the number of conditions you can stack on targets is quite reasonable. Having access to Chill and Vulnerability is quite versatile. This aids in kiting or in catching mobile enemies. It's an intuitive pairing with the scepter if you want to keep dropping constant conditions on your enemies. Paired with the axe, it's a good tool for keeping enemies disabled while the axe skills do the real damage. Daggers are the most unconventional choice to pair with focuses because you're still not going to kite enemies while wielding daggers. If you hate swapping weapons, dagger + focus helps to catch up to enemies, but that's about the most you get from them.

REAPER'S TOUCH

Damage: Low

Effect: Swiftness (5 Seconds), Vulnerability (x2) (10 Seconds)

Cooldown: 18 Seconds

In case it wasn't clear enough already, this skill makes staff users into supreme kiting champions. It boosts their movement rate (and that of allies, as well) and the targets are exposed to greater damage. The attack can bounce between enemies up to a few times, so Reaper's Touch is quite useful for aiding in AoE fights.

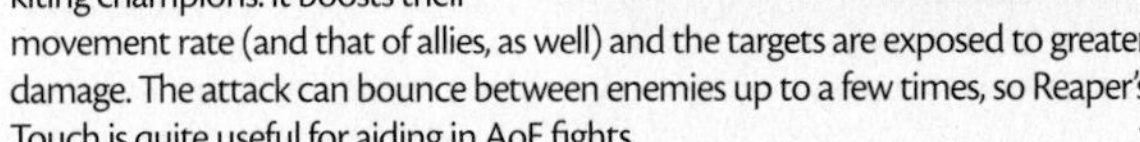

SPINAL SHIVERS

Damage: Low

Effect: Chill (5 Seconds), Remove Boons

Cooldown: 25 Seconds

Spinal Shivers slows targets down and makes them take longer to attack even if they have ranged weapons. This skill also reduces enemy damage potential because it can strip off up to three boons from a powerful opponent. This is a good attack in PvP or in battles against high-end single targets.

Warhorn (Off Hand)

Warhorns are excellent off-hand weapons for additional damage and the ability to Daze your enemies. They're easy to use and are one of the few necromancer weapon choices that don't require good use of ground targeting. If you're someone who likes simple weapons that are still effective, warhorns are perfect for you. Though powerful, the one disadvantage of these weapons is that they have long cooldowns and are anything but spammable. You'll want to have a weapon in your main hand that has much shorter cooldown times. We suggest axe + warhorn as a combo for solid damage and sheer fun.

WAIL OF DOOM

Damage: Moderate to High

Effect: Daze (2 Seconds)

Cooldown: 30 Seconds

Wail of Doom hits hard in a cone in front of your character. Everyone struck suffers from Daze, buying you some time to keep hitting targets when they can't strike back. Obviously, Wail of Doom is better when you can hit even more targets with it, but even against single enemies it's a perfect tool for slipping in damage while disrupting your enemies.

LOCUST SWARM

Damage: Low

Effect: Cripple (1 Second), Swiftness (10 Seconds)

Cooldown: 30 Seconds

Locust Swarm is a spell that stays around your character and hits enemies periodically, dealing light damage to all nearby targets. You won't have to sacrifice additional casting time, and the speed bonus it grants lasts for a good while. All of these perks add up to make the damage and utility of this skill better than it seems (especially if there are several enemies close to your character).

Spear (Aquatic Weapon)

Necromancers use spears as high-damage melee weapons with a fair number of positional abilities. They can pull enemies toward them or pull themselves over to enemies. This makes it harder to kite spear users, and easier for necromancers to choose the range they like for their battles.

CRUEL STRIKE

Damage: Moderate to High

Effect: N/A

Cooldown: None

This series of melee attacks deals considerable damage and ends the trio with an area-of-effect lifesteal. This helps keep your hero's health topped off.

WICKED SPIRAL

Damage: Very High

Effect: Vulnerability (6 Seconds)

Cooldown: 10 Seconds

Use this as your bread-and-butter damage ability when you're underwater. Wicked Spiral hits hard and leaves enough Vulnerability on your target to follow up with another nasty strike or two. Use this early in a fight and then hit it again every time the cooldown expires.

DEADLY FEAST

Damage: Low

Effect: Light Healing, Swiftness (6 Seconds)

Cooldown: 18 Seconds

Deadly Feast is more situational. It gives your necromancer a movement boost for a short period, and the healing isn't a bad thing either. It's just that the effect isn't that extreme, and the basic damage of the attack is fairly low. Save this for times when you really need to get to (or get away from) an enemy.

DEADLY CATCH

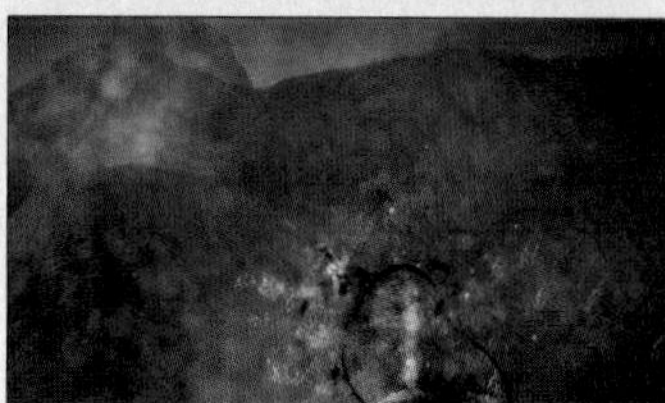

Damage: N/A

Effect: Cripple (3 Seconds), Combo Finisher (Whirl)

Cooldown: 25 Seconds

Use Deadly Catch to grab enemies trying to stay at range. Your hero can close the gap and keep the enemy slowed for a short time.

DARK SPEAR

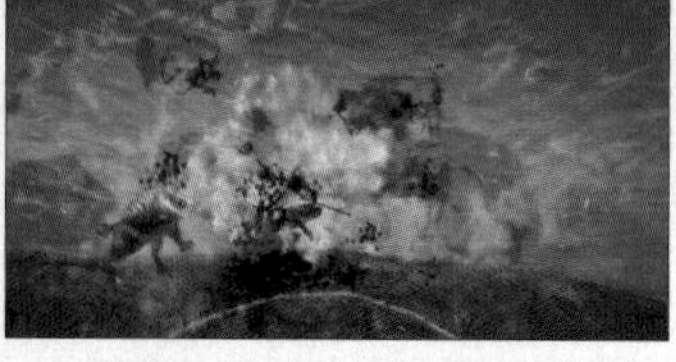

Damage: High

Effect: Bleed (x5) (8 Seconds), Charge

Cooldown: 25 Seconds

Dark Spear is a great fight opener because it gets you into melee range in the blink of an eye. When you need to rush a target, it's the best choice. The skill's high damage and Bleeding effect make it a superior choice even when you don't need it for closing the gap with a victim.

Trident (Aquatic Weapon)

Tridents aren't as melee-centered as spears, but they still aren't much of a ranged option. Attacks with these weapons are either melee range or have just a little more distance to offer. You lose the spears' direct damage, but tridents make up for it with their disabling conditions.

The real trick is to avoid the tradeoff entirely. Spears are a better weapon most of the time. Their skills do more damage and offer better control over your position. However, tridents have a godly fifth slot attack. Keep a good spear for most fights, and break out the trident when you need to disable enemies or hit them with Frozen Abyss for some noteworthy area-of-effect damage.

CRIMSON TIDE

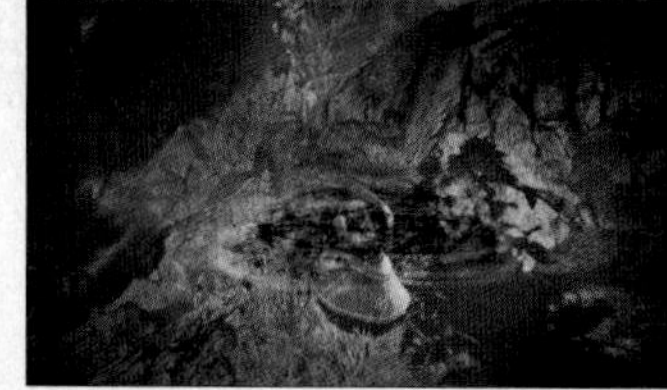

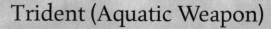

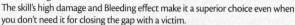

Damage: Low

Effect: Bleed (5 Seconds)

Cooldown: None

Crimson Tide has a modest range. It's still not enough for proper kiting unless you're really facing a weak enemy. Instead, it's more of a skill to pull enemies away from their original locations (if there are too many foes close together and you're worried about getting into a big fight).

FEAST

Damage: Moderate to High

Effect: Weakness (5 Seconds), Life Force Gain

Cooldown: 12 Seconds

This AoE damages nearby enemies, reduces most of their damage output, helps you gain life force, and makes it harder for enemies to dodge as often. It's a little bit of everything without a high price or cooldown.

FOUL CURRENT

Damage: N/A

Effect: Poison (4 Seconds)

Cooldown: 15 Seconds

Your necromancer darts through the water, Poisoning everything in your wake. Use the attack to close the gap toward distant enemies, to escape from your current fight with the sudden burst of speed, or to Poison groups of enemies lined up in front of you. Because the attack doesn't hit for any initial damage, the Poison is all you get out of Foul Current. It's not worthwhile against single opponents unless you'll benefit from the change in position.

SINKING TOMB

Damage: None

Effect: Sink (2 Seconds)

Cooldown: 20 Seconds

Sinking Tomb causes targets to Sink for 2 seconds, briefly leaving them defenseless against your attacks. Use this to stop enemies if they're charging up for something dangerous. Or, rely on it for basic damage mitigation if you're having trouble timing the move.

FROZEN ABYSS

Damage: Extremely High

Effect: Chill (1 Second)

Cooldown: 25 Seconds

This is the gem of the trident lineup. Everything else is too low damage to really shine, but Frozen Abyss blasts everything near your character for oodles of damage. Use the spear skills during most fights, but swap to a trident when there are several aquatic enemies going after your hero. Toast them with this skill and swap back to your spear soon afterward.

Downed Skills

On the Ground

Necromancer downed abilities are all about extended survivability. You can't do immense damage from the ground, but you can steal life, scare enemies away, and heavily mitigate their damage. Hold on until you can get help from friends or slowly win a war of attrition against your opponent.

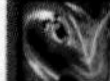

LIFE LEECH

Damage: Low

Effect: Health Steal

Cooldown: N/A

Life Leech steals health to heal your necromancer while you're trying to kill the most injured enemy within range. It's not a fast killer, but the added survivability is of great use.

FEAR

Damage: N/A
Effect: Fear (2 Seconds)
Cooldown: 10 Seconds

Scare an enemy away from you to buy your necromancer time to Bandage.

FETID GROUND

Damage: Very High
Effect: Poison (x5) (3 Seconds)
Cooldown: 20 Seconds

Fetid Ground damages nearby foes over time. Use this the moment any targets come into range, and put it back up as soon as it recharges.

BANDAGE

Damage: N/A
Effect: Self-Heal
Cooldown: 5 Seconds

Use this to heal yourself if there aren't any enemies coming after you. It allows you to recover fairly quickly. If you're attacked, the effect ends and you have to fight for your life once more.

Underwater

As on land, necromancers won't die without giving it their best. Use Life Leech to restore health, keep Feeding Frenzy going, and buy time with Death Curse. Only swim to the surface if you're being overwhelmed by groups of enemies. These abilities don't handle that very well.

LIFE LEECH

Damage: Low
Effect: Health Steal
Cooldown: N/A

This is the same as its surface variant.

FEEDING FRENZY

Damage: Low
Effect: Summon Fish
Cooldown: 5 Seconds

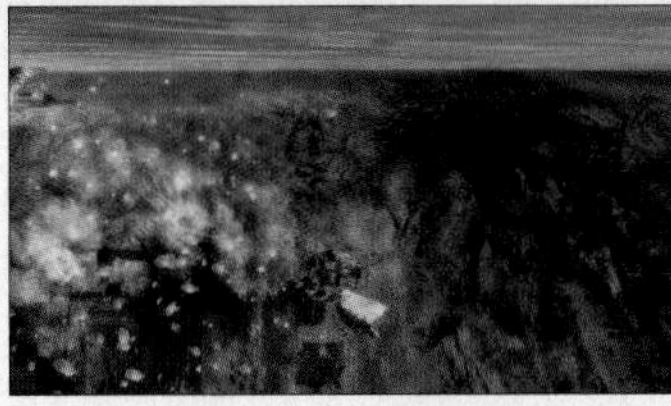

Feeding Frenzy calls over a school of hungry fish to nip at your enemies while you try to recover. Call them early in the fight and restore them every few seconds, between Life Leeches.

DEATH CURSE

Damage: Low
Effect: Fear (2 Seconds), Poison (5 Seconds)
Cooldown: 20 Seconds

Though slow to cool down, this powerful ability is a major asset when you're underwater. Death Curse not only sends enemies swimming for their lives, but its Poison is enough of a damage over time effect to make a decent difference in your rally attempt. Instead of using it on secondary enemies to give yourself more time, hit your primary target with Death Curse to hasten their demise.

BANDAGE

Damage: N/A
Effect: Self-Heal
Cooldown: 5 Seconds

If your hero isn't being attacked directly while you're down, use this skill to start healing. This lets you rally without going up to the surface, and you get to switch back to attacks if any monsters show up. You won't have that same option on the surface, so this is a more flexible alternative.

Slot Skills

Healing

Necromancers have really cool healing skills. They can summon a pet that heals, clean their conditions, or even raise a well that heals an entire group. Nifty stuff!

SUMMON BLOOD FIEND

Effect: Creates a Healing Pet
Cooldown: 20 Seconds

This spell creates a Blood Fiend that will follow your necromancer around and attack whatever you're fighting. Every time the Blood Fiend hits a target, your necromancer gets a little bit of health. You won't survive spiky damage very well this way, but it's good for taking care of low-level damage. In a pinch, you can also sacrifice the Blood Fiend for a bit of extra health. The creature can be summoned again about 20 seconds after the sacrifice. Use the sacrifice function when you're about to go into Death Shroud or when a battle is just about to end. That way you get the health and can still summon another Blood Fiend when you get to the next fight.

CONSUME CONDITIONS

Effect: Removes Conditions
Cooldown: 25 Seconds

This is an extremely powerful healing ability. Not only can it help you overcome sudden spikes in damage fairly well, but the chance to get rid of nasty conditions should never be ignored. Expect this to be an extremely common choice for soloers. You get bonus health for each condition the spell removes, making this a wonderful PvP/WvWvW skill choice.

WELL OF BLOOD

Effect: Heals Yourself and Nearby Allies (10 Seconds)

Cooldown: 40 Seconds

The Well of Blood is your best group healing option. The well has an initial heal for your hero, and then everyone nearby gets health for the next 10 seconds. Put this down when your group is starting a nasty encounter and let the healing give everyone more time before they have to start popping their best "get out of trouble" abilities.

Utility

Necromancer utility skills are often centered on combative pets, spreading conditions around, and poisoning the world. There's a lot of fun in there. Wells create area-of-effect benefits for your caster (or peril for your enemies). Summon spells spawn mindless pets that follow you around and attack whatever gets too close to them. Signets have minor passive effects that always aid you and then can be activated to provide a short-term effect that is even stronger.

TIER 1

WELL OF SUFFERING

Effect: Moderate Damage, Weakness (3 Seconds), Combo Field (Dark), Duration (8 Seconds)

Cooldown: 60 Seconds

Well of Suffering creates an area of effect where enemies take reasonably high damage and are afflicted with Weakness, making it harder to dodge as often or do consistently high damage. This is a helpful AoE or PvP ability to use early in a large battle; your allies have a better chance of pounding their targets with additional area-of-effect attacks.

SUMMON BONE MINION

Effect: Summons Minions (x2)(No Duration)

Cooldown: 20 Seconds

Bone Minions are small creatures that add into fights and help your necromancer by attacking anything hostile. You can't order them around specifically because they're undead, but you can blow them up to deal sudden high damage to your targets. Think of these guys as expendable friends. Leave them behind to tie off pursuing monsters, or detonate them when you need damage the most.

SUMMON BONE FIEND

Effect: Summons Fiend (No Duration)

Cooldown: 30 Seconds

Bone Fiends are nastier than Bone Minions. You only get a single creature, but it's much harder to kill, so you won't have to resummon it very often. In addition, the Bone Minion has an Immobilizing attack that locks it in place but also prevents the enemy from moving for a short time. If your necromancer likes to kite enemies, the Bone Fiend is helpful for grabbing more powerful targets and keeping them from getting to you. Though the cooldown on the attack is fairly long, this is one more "get out of trouble" item in your arsenal.

SIGNET OF SPITE

Effect: Passively Improves Power, Can Be Used to Inflict Bleeding, Blind, Cripple, Poison, Weakness, and Vulnerability on Your Target

Cooldown: 90 Seconds

Signet of Spite is a lethal single-target attack that drops a wave of conditions on your enemy and deals damage to them at the same time. It's a wonderful attack, especially against other players, veterans, or champion monsters.

SIGNET OF THE LOCUST

Effect: Passively Increases Movement Rate (10%), Can Be Used to Steal Health from Nearby Enemies

Cooldown: 60 Seconds

When you're traveling around the world, Signet of the Locust is one of the best skills in your grimoire. The boost to your hero's movement rate is of constant benefit, almost paying for the skill by itself. Then you add the area-of-effect health stealing; this is wonderful in pivotal battles because you can get a fair heal off of it while hurting everything that's attacking you. It's perfect for exploring new areas, fighting large groups of monsters during events, and it's not bad in WvWvW either (when you have to cross large distances).

SPECTRAL GRASP

Effect: Pull Foe, Chill (4 Seconds)

Cooldown: 40 Seconds

The targeted enemy is pulled over to your necromancer and then hit with a 4-second Chill effect. This is an anti-kiting ability. Most necromancers are mobile and have plenty of their own ranged attacks, but dagger users can really appreciate this skill because they're usually the ones who have to close the distance. Use this to stop mobile enemies from getting away from your hero and to keep them close-by for a few seconds while you unload on them.

CORROSIVE POISON CLOUD

Effect: Weaken Self (6 Seconds), AoE Poison (3 Seconds), Vulnerability (15 Seconds), Combo Field (Poison), Duration (15 Seconds)

Cooldown: 40 Seconds

Use this skill to create a cloud of poison around yourself. Enemies that approach are going to take damage and lose some of their healing efficiency, and the cloud doesn't go away quickly. Gather enemies with your ranged attacks and bring them together for area of effects in the middle of the cloud. Though this attack Weakens your character, the skill's long duration and conditions make it highly valuable when you're facing large groups of opponents.

EPIDEMIC

Effect: Self Vulnerability (x3) (6 Seconds), Spreads Conditions

Cooldown: 15 Seconds

This awesome attack skill lets you turn your conditions into more of an area-of-effect attack. Lay into one enemy with as many conditions as you can, and use Epidemic when the poor fool is about to die. The conditions spread, and the cooldown is short enough that you can use the attack again just a few kills later (at most).

Your hero takes more damage when using Epidemic, but your enemies die much faster. It's often worth the price.

TIER 2

WELL OF CORRUPTION

Effect: Convert Enemy Boons, Duration (8 Seconds)

Cooldown: 60 Seconds

This area-of-effect attack periodically converts enemy boons into conditions over the 8-second duration of the well. This is effective against both players and monsters, especially when fighting enemies that are prone to giving themselves multiple stacks of boons.

WELL OF POWER

Effect: Convert Ally Conditions

Cooldown: 60 Seconds

Well of Power goes the other way; it aids your allies by removing their conditions and turning them into something positive. It's easier to use Well of Power than Well of Corruption, because you often have a good idea of your group's status. Look at your character's conditions and the portraits of your party members to see when it's a good time to cast Well of Power.

SUMMON SHADOW FIEND

Effect: Summons Shadow (No Duration)

Cooldown: 30 Seconds

Shadow Fiends are dark spirits that attack your enemies with slow, powerful melee hits. If you use their special attack, it Blinds the enemy for a few seconds. Shadow Fiends help the most against single, potent targets. They're fun for bringing down veterans and champions, or for times when you're facing smaller numbers in PvP.

PLAGUE SIGNET

Effect: Passively Removes Ally Conditions and Places Them on Your Necromancer, Can Be Used to Send Your Conditions to a Foe

Cooldown: 60 Seconds

Plague Signet loses most of its utility if you're soloing. Being able to throw conditions back at your enemy is okay, but the long cooldown limits the skill. However, a large party makes this ability much more effective. You end up protecting your group from conditions, and then having far more oomph when you unleash these effects on tougher enemies. Plague Signet also works well with Epidemic. Nail your enemy with conditions and then immediately hit Epidemic to spread the suffering to additional targets.

SPECTRAL ARMOR

Effect: Break Stun, Life Force Gain, Protection (6 Seconds)

Cooldown: 90 Seconds

Spectral Armor is a get-out-of-trouble card for your hero. The damage reduction, Stun breaking, and boost to life force all make it easier to survive during difficult fights. This is a small-scale PvP ability, or a strong tool for soloers who like to evacuate when everything goes wrong. While still useful in a group environment, Spectral Armor doesn't have much utility for allies and is only necessary if you're getting way too much attention from the enemies.

CORRUPT BOON

Effect: Self-Poison (6 Seconds), Convert Foe Boons

Cooldown: 25 Seconds

Though most generic enemies don't have many boons, you get a lot out of Corrupt Boon when fighting against especially powerful veterans, champions, or single players. This is more of a PvP (as opposed to WvWvW) ability. It's hard to see when to break it out in massive battles, but when you're only fighting a few people it's more obvious who to rip the boons off of. When opponents' bars start filling up with goodies, ruin their day.

TIER 3

WELL OF DARKNESS

Effect: Blinds Enemies (Every 2 Seconds), Combo Field (Dark)

Cooldown: 60 Seconds

This area of effect surrounds your character with a field that Blinds enemies, causing them to miss their attacks. As with all wells, the area of effect itself lasts for 8 seconds, so enemies can be disrupted for quite some time. This is an excellent way to mitigate damage against your hero or your entire group. It's useful in dungeons or PvP. For dungeon use, make sure your group pulls the enemies into a tight spot. That way, all of them are affected and can be blown down with area-of-effect assaults while their attacks miss again and again.

SUMMON FLESH WURM

Effect: Summon Wurm (No Duration)

Cooldown: 40 Seconds

A single Flesh Wurm burrows up from the ground when you summon it. These creatures do fairly low damage with their attacks, but they have a powerful secondary ability. You can teleport to your Flesh Wurm, sacrifice it, and Poison enemies nearby. This makes Flesh Wurms useful as an ally for the early part of a fight and then as a free area-of-effect attack when they start to take some damage. In addition, the Teleport can be used to get your necromancer out of trouble if you're fighting elsewhere on the field.

 SIGNET OF UNDEATH

Effect: Generate Life Force, Break Stun, Revive Allies

Cooldown: 180 Seconds

Use the signet to break yourself out of Stuns and to revive group members, especially if there aren't any wounded targets for them to rally off of. This lowers the chance that anyone will be defeated outright. The life force generation of the signet is of benefit, but there are many superior ways to accrue life force (so think of that as a secondary use of the skill).

 SPECTRAL WALL

Effect: Protect Allies (5 Seconds), Vulnerability for Foes (x3)(10 Seconds), Duration (9 Seconds)

Cooldown: 45 Seconds

This skill creates a wall on both flanks of your hero. Allies standing there take reduced damage for a short time, and all enemies in the area are slammed with Vulnerability. Because the area of effect isn't terribly large, you get the most from this skill when you work with people who know your profession and can keep enemies in the right position. For example, teams that work over a voice communication program get more from Spectral Wall because the necromancer can tell everyone "Line up for Spec Wall." Done correctly, this is a very powerful ability in tricky events or dungeon encounters. It's harder to use in PvP, where fights are much more chaotic.

SPECTRAL WALK

Effect: Swiftness (10 Seconds)

Cooldown: 60 Seconds

Spectral Walk is made for battle. Give yourself tons of speed for kiting enemies. At the end of the duration, the ability snaps you back to your point of origin. This confuses other players, giving you time to plan a new assault. Enemy monsters are disrupted as well because they still have to turn around and get back to you.

It is possible to cancel this effect and use Spectral Walk purely for its movement boost. When you do that, you suffer from Vulnerability for a few seconds, so watch out for doing this during an intense fight. Only do it if your opponent has already turned around to go and catch you (i.e., if they turn around to get back to your point of origin prematurely). This won't happen often, so don't plan on doing it frequently.

BLOOD IS POWER

Effect: Moderate Damage, Self-Bleed (x2) (10 Seconds), Bleed (x2)(30 Seconds), Gain Life Force

Cooldown: 30 Seconds

Blood is Power puts a Bleed effect on your necromancer while savaging your targets. They get hit with long-term Bleeding, which will make a nice difference in slow encounters. Use this against dungeon bosses, veterans, champions, or enemy players who are trying to kite or fight slowly (those with heavy armor, defenders, and so forth).

Elite

Have you ever wanted to be a lich? Sure, we all have. Let's look into necromancer elites!

TIER 1

PLAGUE

Effect: Plague Form (20 Seconds)

Cooldown: 180 Seconds

This elite skill is weak against single targets and small groups; it's made to cause massive devastation when your necromancer is in the middle of a huge fight. Slot this elite when you expect to be facing major numbers in WvWvW or events that have monsters running in all the time. The more targets you have, the better this ability becomes.

SUMMON FLESH GOLEM

Effect: Summon Golem (No Duration)

Cooldown: 60 Seconds

Flesh Golems are yet another summonable monster in the necromancer lineup. These guys are hard to kill, attack quickly, and cripple their victims so your hero can kite them even more easily. It's a pretty brutal combination, and every 40 seconds you can order them to charge and rip through everything in front of them. If you like having pets around, Flesh Golems are the bomb. Also, it's nice to have an elite skill that is always active. Though not as powerful with bursts of aggression as some of the other elites, this ability provides a constant bonus for your hero.

TIER 2

LICH FORM

Effect: Transform into Lich (30 Seconds)

Cooldown: 180 Seconds

Assume the form of an undying lich. Your necromancer loses existing weapon skills, but in their place you gain a variety of potent new attacks. For most situations, this is a superior elite skill compared with Plague. The mix of damage and conditions here are well suited for fights against single targets, small groups, and either human or AI-controlled enemies.

- Deathly Claws (no cooldown): Deal direct damage.
- Marked for Death (10-second cooldown): Does damage and hits targets with Vulnerability.
- Chilling Wind (20-second cooldown): This is a crowd control ability that combines Knockback and Chill.
- Mark of Horror (25-second cooldown): Summons five Jagged Horrors to distract enemies and contribute additional damage for a short time.
- Grim Specter (30-second cooldown): Does heavy damage while removing boons from your enemies and conditions from allies.

Your character stays a lich for long enough to use all of these attacks and then come back for more with the ones that cool down faster. Because all of the abilities are powerful, you should try to use each one as soon as it refreshes. Don't use Deathly Claws unless everything else is already on cooldown.

You have 30 seconds to enjoy life as a lich. Make the most of it!

Traits

Spite (Raises Power and Condition Duration)

REWARDS

Points Invested	Ability Gained
5	You gain health whenever you kill something
15	5% of Power is converted into a Healing bonus
25	Gain Might if you're hit at under 25% health

SKILL OPTIONS (GAINED EVERY 10 POINTS)

ADEPT TIER

- Death's Embrace: Your hero deals 50% more damage when in a downed state.
- Spiteful Talisman: Increased range for focus skills.
- Spiteful Removal: When you kill a foe you lose a condition.
- Signet Mastery: Signet recharges are reduced by 20%.
- Spiteful Spirit: Gain Retaliation when entering Death Shroud.
- Reaper's Might: Life Blast and Plague Blast grant Might for 15 seconds.

MASTER TIER

- Spiteful Marks: Marks deal more damage.
- Signet Power: Activating a signet gives you Might.
- Spiteful Vigor: Gain Retaliation when you heal.
- Training of the Master: Minion damage is increased by 30%.

GRANDMASTER TIER

- Axe Training: Bonus damage with axe skills.
- Chill of Death: Cast Chilblains when you're hit below 25% health.

Curses (Precision and Condition Damage)

REWARDS

Points Invested	Ability Gained
5	Critical hits cause Bleeding (so awesome!)
15	Gain Fury when entering Death Shroud
25	Increased damage for each condition on a foe

SKILL OPTIONS (GAINED EVERY 10 POINTS)

ADEPT TIER

- Toxic Landing: Creates a poison cloud whenever your hero takes falling damage; falling damage to you is reduced by 50%.
- Hemophilia: 20% increased Bleeding duration.
- Pitch Black: When you Blind a target, you also cause Confusion.
- Weakening Shroud: Cast Enfeeble when entering Death Shroud.
- Reaper's Precision: 33% chance to gain life force when you land a critical hit.
- Terror: Fear does damage.

MASTER TIER

- Master of Corruption: Corruption recharges are reduced by 20%.
- Deep Breath: Warhorn skills recharge 15% faster.
- Focused Rituals: Wells become ground targeted.
- Spectral Attunement: Spectral skills have longer duration.

GRANDMASTER TIER

- Lingering Curse: Conditions from specter skills last longer.
- Withering Precision: Chance to cause Weakness on critical hits.

Death Magic (Raises Toughness and Boon Duration)

REWARDS

Points Invested	Ability Gained
5	Gives a chance to summon a Jagged Horror whenever you kill an enemy
15	+20 Toughness for each summoned minion
25	10% of your Toughness is also added to Power

SKILL OPTIONS (GAINED EVERY 10 POINTS)

ADEPT TIER

- Dark Armor: Gain armor when channeling.
- Greater Marks: Increase the area of your marks.
- Minion Master: Minion recharges are reduced by 20%.
- Ritual of Protection: Wells apply Protection when cast.
- Close to Death: Increases damage by 10% to enemies that are below 50% health.
- Shrouded Removal: Lose a condition when you enter Death Shroud.

MASTER TIER

- Staff Mastery: Staff skill recharge 15% faster.
- Fateful Marks: Marks are unblockable.
- Death Shiver: Apply Spinal Shivers to enemies near you when entering Death Shroud.
- Flesh of the Master: Minions have 20% more health.

GRANDMASTER TIER

- Death Nova: Whenever a minion dies, it explodes in a cloud of Poison.
- Necromatic Corruption: Minions have a 10% chance to remove a boon when they attack.

Blood Magic (Raises Vitality and Healing)

REWARDS

Points Invested	Ability Gained
5	Gain 5 seconds of Regeneration when your health reaches 90% (30-second cooldown)
15	Siphon health whenever you hit an enemy
25	+90 Power whenever your health is above 90%

SKILL OPTIONS (GAINED EVERY 10 POINTS)

ADEPT TIER

- Dagger Mastery: Dagger skills recharge 15% faster.
- Bloodthirst: Siphoning health is more effective.
- Mark of Evasion: Leave a Mark of Blood when you dodge.
- Ritual of Life: Create a Well of Blood whenever you revive an ally.
- Vampiric Precision: Siphon health whenever you critically hit.
- Transfusion: Life Transfer heals nearby allies.

MASTER TIER

- Vampiric Master: Minions siphon health and transfer it to you.
- Ritual Mastery: Well recharges are reduced by 20%.
- Deathly Invigoration: AoE heal when you leave Death Shroud.
- Quickening Thirst: Move faster while wielding a dagger.

GRANDMASTER TIER

- Fetid Consumption: Minions draw conditions.
- Vampiric Rituals: Wells also siphon health.

Soul Reaping (Raises Critical Damage and Life Force Pool)

REWARDS

Points Invested	Ability Gained
5	Life force fills faster
15	Gains Spectral Armor at 50% health (60-second cooldown)
25	Gains Power the more life force your character has (+100 Maximum)

SKILL OPTIONS (GAINED EVERY 10 POINTS)

ADEPT TIER

- Fear of Death: Apply Fear to enemies when you are downed (90-second cooldown).
- Vital Persistence: Life force drains slower while in Death Shroud.
- Mark of Revival: Create a Reaper's Mark while reviving someone.
- Spectral Mastery: Spectral recharges are 20% faster.
- Speed of Shadows: Move faster while in Death Shroud.
- Unyielding Blast: Life Blast pierces.

MASTER TIER

- Path of Midnight: Dark Path recharges 25% faster.
- Decaying Swarm: At 25% health, you become surrounded by a Locust Swarm.
- Master of Terror: Fears you inflict last 50% longer.
- Soul Marks: Marks generate life force when triggered.

GRANDMASTER TIER

- Foot in the Grave: Gain Stability while in Death Shroud.
- Near to Death: Death Shroud recharge is reduced by 33%.

Necromancers in PvE

Necromancers are darn tough, and you won't expect them to survive as much punishment as they take. When you're facing harder battles, it's possible to add minions, life stealing, and traits that give you a number of survivability boosts. Throw in Death Shroud and it seems almost impossible to get your necromancer killed unless you act recklessly (which is fun to do, but that's beside the point).

When soloing, Signet of the Locust is perfect. Using higher movement speed and an area-of-effect lifesteal, you just can't go wrong with it. Once you have more skill points, invest in a tough pet, as well. The Bone Fiend is a great all-weather pet that makes it harder for things to jump on your back without going through something. It's much more of a speed bump than the other non-elite pets.

To deal with powerful single targets, focus on stacking condition after condition on your foes. Necromancers have Bleed and Poison effects all over the place. Make sure Poison is on the target at all times, and then try to get as much Bleeding as you can on that sucker. Though it takes a while to come together, it pays off in massive damage over time.

Practice jumping into and out of Death Shroud at the drop of a hat. Early users have a tendency to use up all of their life force with each Death Shroud run, and that's not optimal. Instead, you want to get in there, use your best abilities and survive sudden bursts in enemy damage, and then drop Death Shroud afterward. That leaves you with more life force for later so you can hop back in when the ability refreshes.

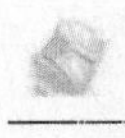

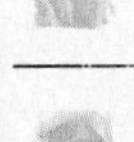

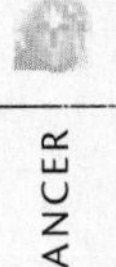

All necromancers should have a kiting set of weapons in either their primary or secondary slots. So many necromancer combinations are effective in this role that you'd be crazy to ignore it. Staves, specter/focus, and axe/dagger are all fun. If you like up-close and personal fighting, keep a set of daggers around. They're your best melee tool, if that's the way you want to play it.

Watch for Condition Damage in addition to outright Power when you're looking to upgrade your damage output. Necromancers get a fair amount of their damage from conditions, so improvements in this area are amplified more than for many other professions.

For a heck of a fun experience, consider the beat squad lineup: Summon Blood Fiend, Shadow Fiend, Bone Fiend, Flesh Wurm, and Flesh Golem. You get to be a walking menagerie! Area of effects blow your entire group in half, so that's bad, but it's great for having a good time against normal enemies. This is doubly the case if you stack Death Magic and Blood Magic traits. Enjoy being hard to kill.

Necromancers in PvP

Necromancers are hard to predict in PvP engagements. Until you engage the individual necromancer, you don't know if your enemy is a glass cannon loaded with attack skills or if your enemy has survival as his or her main focus.

If you're playing a necromancer with a high amount of Power and Condition Damage, you have the potential to drop enemy players quite well. Let other players start engagements whenever possible. You can come in later or from the flanks to clean up by adding massive pressure to individual targets. Though your burst damage isn't as high as it could be, the mix of Poison, Bleeding, and direct damage means that targets are healing poorly and taking a huge amount of total damage over time. Overwhelm them with it!

Use Death Shroud defensively, especially when you're trying to hold an area. Using long-range abilities, kiting tactics, and Death Shroud, you can make it extremely hard for enemies to keep an area—even if they have a couple people trying to fight you. Slow the enemies down with your weapon attacks, and then pop Death Shroud, use Dark Path and Doom, and scuttle off while your enemies are terrified or at least frozen. The longer the fight, the better the chance you'll come out ahead.

Consume Conditions is a wonderful PvP healing ability. Keep that on your bar almost all the time. A mix of this and Plague Signet ensures you won't have as many problems with conditions as your opponents.

Avoid bringing too many minions into most PvP encounters. Your pets are easily killed with area-of-effect attacks, and most of your enemies are going to be well aware of that. They'll have your buddies killed off in no time, and you'll be down a few skills on the exchange. Even when this doesn't happen, you end up losing time and concentration keeping your pets summoned, and the large group you're carrying around makes it possible to spot you from a mile away (even when people aren't looking carefully).

RANGER

Rangers are frontline fighters today, rearline firepower tomorrow, and skirmishers every day of the week. Medium armor keeps them mobile and still able to survive a few hits. A wide variety of weapons gives the ranger the ability to meet enemies on almost any turf. Fighting at range allows the ranger to hit multiple foes from safety, and using melee weapons makes them incredibly mobile and difficult to hit.

Pets are as varied and flexible as the ranger and any enemy that ignores a ranger's pet is in for a world of hurt. Rangers also gain a wealth of group utility from traps and spirits. The spirits increase ally damage, add a new damage type, or even revive fallen allies. Traps slow, Poison, or Burn enemies.

Rangers are the profession for you if you enjoy forcing the enemy to fight on your terms, or if having a smart animal companion sounds really intriguing.

Profession Stats

Attribute	Starting Stats	Naked at Level 80
Power	24	1216
Precision	24	1066
Toughness	24	1016
Vitality	24	916
Attack	24	1216
Critical Chance	4%	11%
Armor	24	1013
Health	258	15,082

The stats listed above give you an idea of what to expect from your character. They show ranger progression through examples taken at the beginning and end of leveling. Your actual stats will likely vary from this.

Companions

As a ranger, you and your companion fight and live side by side. A ranger without a pet is only half a ranger.

Interface and Controls

Rangers have the most versatile and controllable pets in the game. This is very powerful but requires finesse to use a pet to its fullest.

The pet interface is just above your skillbar. The paw-print icon opens the Companion window. The next three icons are your basic controls (detailed in the accompanying table), followed by a portrait of your pet, and then the final button. The red bar beneath all these is your pet's health bar.

Default Key	Action
F1	Attack my target
F2	Pet Special Ability
F3	Toggles between aggressive and passive stance
F4	Switch Pet

Pet special abilities are unique for each type of pet. Learn these abilities so you know which animals are best for a given situation. Attacking your target and toggling between stances is very intuitive. Aggressive stance commands your pet to attack as soon as you take damage or attack a target. Passive stance keeps your pet from attacking or using any abilities unless commanded by you specifically.

Switching pets allows you to swap between two pets during combat. You can change pets outside of combat without trouble, but think of the in-combat switch as being analogous to the weapon swap. This function is very powerful because you can swap a downed pet for a pet with full health. Swapping pets outside of combat has a negligible cooldown, but swapping inside combat starts a 30-second cooldown before you can swap again.

Finding New Companions

All rangers start with a pet, but new pets can be found all over the world (including in WvW areas). Throughout your adventures, watch for Juvenile creatures with their names in green. Approach these and Charm them. This gives you the option to "equip" the pet immediately. This process also gives you a detailed summary of the pet. To give you an idea of what to expect, some of the pets in the game are listed here.

Pet	Type	Highest Stat	F2 Ability	Area to Acquire	Zone to Acquire
Alpine Wolf	Terrestrial	Vitality	Chill	Outcast's Cleft	Wayfarer Foothills (S)
Fern Mastiff	Terrestrial	Vitality	Regen	Sylvari Starter	Sylvari Origin Pet
Hyena	Terrestrial	Vitality	Summon Hyena	Gunbreach Hills	Plains of Ashford (NW)
Red Moa	Terrestrial	Vitality	Fury	Agnos Gorge	Plains of Ashford (N)
Carrion Devourer	Amphibious	Toughness	AoE Poison	Charr Starter	Charr Origin Pet
White Moa	Terrestrial	Vitality	AoE Regen	Vitpeln Hills	Snowden Drifts (N)
Whiptail Devourer	Amphibious	Toughness	Poison	Cadem Forest	Plains of Ashford (E)
Black Bear	Amphibious	Vitality	Weakness/Fumble	Charr's Triumph	Plains of Ashford (W)
Jungle Stalker	Amphibious	Precision	AoE Might	Charr Starter	Charr Origin Pet
Snow Leopard	Amphibious	Precision	Chill	Borealis Forest	Wayfarer Foothills (S)
Flamingo	Terrestrial	Vitality	Daze	Venlin Vale	Brisban Wildlands (SE)
Raven	Terrestrial	Precision	Blindness	Snowlord's Gate	Wayfarer Foothills (S)
Krytan Drakehound	Terrestrial	Vitality	Immobilize	Rurikton	Divinity's Reach (E)
Pig	Terrestrial	Vitality	Improvised Weapon	Ossan Quarter	Divinity's Reach (NW)
Salamander Drake	Amphibious	Vitality	AoE Burning	Relliatus Canyon	Blazeridge Steppes (E)
Owl	Terrestrial	Precision	Chill	Owl's Abattoir	Snowden Drifts (SE)
Eagle	Terrestrial	Precision	Bleed	Sojourner's Way	Kessex Hills (NE)
River Drake	Amphibious	Vitality	Multi-Target Damage	Eastern Divinity Dam	Queensdale (NE)
Brown Bear	Amphibious	Vitality	Remove Conditions	Borealis Forest	Wayfarer Foothills (S)
Jaguar	Amphibious	Precision	Stealth	Akk Wilds	Metrica Province (E)
Blue Jellyfish	Aquatic	Vitality	Chill	Victor's Lodge	Anvil Rock Borderlands (S) WvW
Shark	Aquatic	Precision	Bleed	Viathan Lake	Kessex Hills (E)
Siamoth	Terrestrial	Vitality	Improvised Weapon	Saltflood Mire	Sparkfly Fen (NE)
Warthog	Terrestrial	Vitality	Improvised Weapon	Nemus Groves	Diessa Plateau (E)
Lynx	Terrestrial	Precision	Bleed	Graupel Kohn	Dredgehaunt Cliffs (N)
Forest Spider	Terrestrial	Vitality	Poison	Hellion Forest	Iron Marches (E)

Having the best pet for a given situation is as important as having the right weapons and skills. For example, the White Moa is great for helping tanks stay on their feet. The Golden Moa is excellent for moving a party across terrain quickly. The Krytan Drakehound is wonderful when kiting a powerful enemy with its Immobilize and Knockdown. Experiment and see what works best for you and your allies.

Pet Management

Use the Pet Management window to set pets for above-ground and aquatic use. Terrestrial pets are locked for land use only, while aquatic ones are for water use. There are amphibious pets that can serve you in either environment.

I SHALL CALL HIM MINI-ME

In the Pet Management window you can also rename your pet. Click the icon that looks like a feather pen and start typing! You can rename your pet as many times as you like.

The Pet Management screen gives a full summary of each pet's abilities and stats. Only the first ability can be activated by you (as the F2 ability). The other three are used automatically by your pet. This window also lists where you first encountered the pet in case another ranger asks.

Weapons and Weapon Skills

Rangers have quite a few weapons available. Like many professions, they can have two sets of weapons equipped at any time and switch between those, even during battle. A standard grouping might be a melee mode and a ranged mode (axe/axe and longbow). This allows a ranger to rain death onto enemies until the enemy closes, and then switch to melee weapons to finish off an opponent.

Swords (Main Hand Only)

Swords keep you mobile while slashing away at your opponent. Their damage is fairly high, and nothing is going to get away from you without a great deal of effort. The mobility granted by the sword makes it easy to dodge opponents' more powerful attacks without easing up on your damage.

SLASH

Damage:	Moderate
Effect:	Cripple (2 Seconds), Might (5 Seconds)
Cooldown:	None

The basic sword attack is actually a chain of three hits. The first is a normal attack, the second is a kick that closes short distances and cripples your opponent for a couple seconds, and the third attack is a leaping finish that grants Might to your pet.

HORNET STING

Damage:	Very High
Effect:	Leap Back, Leap Forward
Cooldown:	8 Seconds

Hornet Sting is most useful when an enemy is charging up a point-blank area-of-effect attack. The first use stabs the enemy and jumps you out of melee range (to safety). The second use jumps you back into melee.

SERPENT'S STRIKE

Damage:	High
Effect:	Poison (6 Seconds)
Cooldown:	15 Seconds

Serpent's Strike is all about utility. You jump behind your opponents and Poison them. This moves you away from any frontal AoE attacks and reduces any healing your enemy is using.

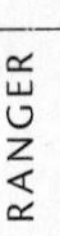

Longbow (Two-Handed)

Longbows are a ranger's best friend. These slender cuts of wood allow rangers to kill enemies at range. Longbows can be fired in melee, but they are far more effective at range. These weapons have Cripple and Knockback to keep enemies where you want them.

LONG RANGE SHOT

Damage: Varies with Range (Modreate to High)

Effect: N/A

Cooldown: None

The basic attack for the longbow shows how you should use this weapon. The damage at maximum range is twice that of a point-blank shot. Because this can be used on the move, you should make your enemies work to get into close range. Keep them Crippled and distant while you plunk arrow after arrow into their midst.

RAPID FIRE

Damage: High

Effect: Combo Finisher (Projectile: 20% Chance)

Cooldown: 10 Seconds

Rapid Fire is a single-target ability. It fires a stream of arrows at your target and can be used while moving! This ability works extremely well with Hunter's Shot. Use Rapid Fire to quickly burn down single enemies that are a threat to your character.

HUNTER'S SHOT

Damage: Moderate

Effect: Vulnerability (x3) (10 Seconds), Pet Swiftness (10 Seconds), Combo Finisher (Physical Projectile)

Cooldown: 15 Seconds

Hunter's Shot should be your first attack in nearly every engagement. The Swiftness gets your pet to the enemy faster while the Vulnerability prepares your enemy for a rain of arrows!

POINT BLANK SHOT

Damage: High

Effect: Knockback, Combo Finisher (Physical Projectile)

Cooldown: 15 Seconds

Enemies will close with you eventually (especially targets with cool skills or high health). Point Blank Shot is a good way to make them do it twice. As they get to melee range, push them away and start the whole dance over again. If you're good enough at kiting to make the process last 15 seconds, you can even repeat the maneuver and continuously throw enemies away from your ranger.

BARRAGE

Damage: Low

Effect: Cripple (1 Second)

Cooldown: 30 Seconds

Barrage is a ground-targeted rain of arrows that Cripples attackers. The skill makes it easier for allies to use their AoEs against the slowed monsters, and the damage gets to be pretty good if you hit enough targets. The only downside to Barrage is that you must plant your feet to use it. Any movement ends the channeling early.

Axe (Main Hand)

Axes are neither subtle nor discriminating. They tend to hit your target and wound anything nearby. Only one of the five attacks is limited to single target damage. All other attacks hit multiple enemies as long as they're clustered together. Wielding axes becomes a delicate dance to position enemies for brutal and unflinching damage.

RICOCHET

Damage: High

Effect: N/A

Cooldown: None

The basic axe attack throws your weapon and hits up to three enemies. Your axe only ricochets to enemies near your target, but they can bounce back to the original enemy for a second smack when there are only two enemies. As this is a thrown attack, use it on your way into a fight as well as at close range.

SPLITBLADE

Damage: Very Low

Effect: Bleed (6 Seconds), Combo Finisher (Physical Projectile: 20% Chance)

Cooldown: 6 Seconds

Splitblade launches a cone of axes toward your target. These pass through the victim and affect all enemies in their path. When fighting one opponent, get very close to them and try to hit the foe with all five axes to stack on the Bleeding.

WINTER'S BITE

Damage: Moderate

Effect: Chill (3 Seconds)

Cooldown: 10 Seconds

Winter's Bite is best used to kite an enemy or flee from a bad situation. The damage is good by itself, and the Chill lets you get some distance. Also, your pet's next hit causes Weakness on the victim, making their endurance return slowly and their normal hits do less damage.

Axe (Off-Hand)

Off-Hand axe skills continue to add damage to your lineup. You get one powerful offensive skill, and a defensive option for blocking ranged attacks from your enemies. These are useful to pair with one single-handed ranger weapon.

PATH OF SCARS

Damage: High

Effect: Combo Finisher (Physical Projectile)

Cooldown: 15 Seconds

Line your enemies up by dragging them around a corner, then introduce them to the Path of Scars. This attack hits every enemy in a line for high damage. It then boomerangs and hits them again on the way back! This is an extremely useful skill for direct damage.

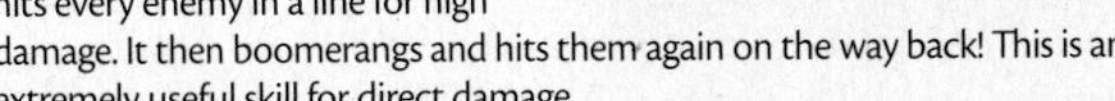

WHIRLING DEFENSE

Damage: Low

Effect: Block Projectile (5 Seconds), Combo Finisher (Whirl)

Cooldown: 25 Seconds

Tight quarters are the playground of Whirling Defense. This skill does low damage to all enemies near your hero while giving you a moment of breathing room against projectiles. These valuable seconds can be used to heal yourself (or others). Or, you can protect yourself and use the time to switch to a long-range weapon for a true reprisal.

Greatsword (Two-Handed)

Greatswords are a catch-all for rangers. There is an evasion attack, Knockback, Charge, Bleed, and a Daze in the lineup. Slash keeps the weapon from being underpowered against large groups, but the wide variety of abilities caters more toward single, high-health opponents.

SLASH

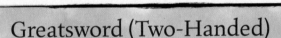

Damage: Moderate

Effect: Evade

Cooldown: None

The greatsword autoattack can be quite confusing to your enemies. During the chain of hits, between the second and third blow, your character evades to the right. You stay in melee range, but any attack the enemy is doing at the time is made useless. The fact that this attack hits multiple targets in front of you is icing on the cake!

MAUL

Damage: Moderate

Effect: Bleed (x3) (4 Seconds)

Cooldown: 6 Seconds

Maul is made for tough opponents. The initial damage is decent, and the Bleeding stacks for fast additional damage. Use this at the start of a fight and refresh it as soon as you can.

SWOOP

Damage: Very High

Effect: Charge, Combo Finisher (Leap)

Cooldown: 12 Seconds

Fly into combat, landing a heavy blow with this ability. It's excellent for beginning a fight and wonderful for changing targets from melee to ranged opponents. There really isn't any reason not to use this ability whenever the opportunity presents itself.

COUNTERATTACK

Damage: Very High

Effect: Block, Knockback

Cooldown: 20 Seconds

Counterattack is situational as it relies on the enemy's attack to do its damage. You block the attack then kick your opponent away from you. If your enemy is preparing a heavy attack, knock him away and follow up with Swoop for massive damage in a short time. As this ability stops your autoattack until the counter triggers, you want to wait until the enemy is just about to hit your hero.

HILT BASH

Damage: Moderate to High

Effect: Daze (1 Second), Stun (1 Second), Pet Damage (+50% For 1 Attack)

Cooldown: 30 Seconds

Hilt Bash is designed for stubborn enemies. Stun targets that are running away when Swoop is on cooldown. Daze enemies that are charging up a particularly nasty attack. The position of your ranger determines which effect hits the enemy, but both are very powerful. Use either to seize the advantage.

Shortbow (Two-Handed)

Shortbows are made for skirmishing. Poison your enemy, then Cripple, Daze, and ditch the opponent if he ever closes with your hero. The biggest advantage to shortbows is their positioning. Keep to the side or behind an opponent when possible to stack Bleeds and split the enemy's attention. This makes shortbows great weapons for group environments or chaotic fights.

CROSSFIRE

Damage: Moderate

Effect: Bleed (3 Seconds), Combo Finisher (Physical Projectile: 20% Chance)

Cooldown: None

Crossfire is your basic attack and is far more powerful if you get behind or beside your target (that is required for the Bleed effect to land). Send your pet in first to try to turn the enemy around. Strafe while attacking if this fails and get into a better position. Crossfire's damage is only moderate, but the Bleeds can really start to stack up.

POISON VOLLEY

Damage: Low

Effect: Poison (2 Seconds)

Cooldown: 9 Seconds

Poison Volley fires several arrows in a forward-facing cone. Any enemies hit by these (they pass through enemies all the way to their maximum range) are Poisoned. Against large groups, this attack can be devastating if you follow it with other AoE damage from allies or additional skills. Against single opponents, save the skill and fire it at point-blank range. This allows all of the arrows to hit the same target.

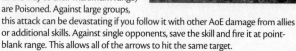

QUICK SHOT

Damage: Moderate

Effect: Retreat, Swiftness (3 Seconds)

Cooldown: 9 Seconds

Quick Shot gets you out of immediate trouble by jumping out of melee range. It gives your hero Swiftness to help reposition quickly and start kiting enemies that are too close. Use this when your enemy catches you so that you can resume the good times.

CRIPPLING SHOT

Damage: Moderate

Effect: Cripple (3 Seconds), Bleed (6 Seconds)

Cooldown: 12 Seconds

Crippling Shot is the mainstay of kiting with a shortbow. The Cripple gives you a few seconds to pull away from your target and lets your pet catch up and start Bleeding the enemy. The fast cooldown on Crippling Shot makes it available almost every time the enemy gets close. Alternate between Crippling Shot and Quick Shot to ensure your ranger always has options for staying ahead of enemies.

CONCUSSION SHOT

Damage: Moderate

Effect: Daze (1 Second), Stun (1 Second), Combo Finisher (Physical Projectile)

Cooldown: 25 Seconds

Don't let ranged opponents opt out of being kited. If enemies switch to a ranged weapon of their own, hit them with Concussion Shot and get a couple seconds of breathing space. You end up getting the Daze off if the enemy is facing you, or a full Stun if the enemy is looking to the side or away from your hero.

War Horn (Off Hand Only)

War Horns are a pleasant balance between damage and group buffing. As they are really the only weapon rangers have that can put boons on your group, they are a strong choice for dungeon and WvW groups.

HUNTER'S CALL

Damage: High

Effect: Channeled

Cooldown: 25 Seconds

Hunter's Call summons a flock of birds to swoop down and peck at your enemy. The damage from a single bird isn't much, but there are a lot of them. This ability is interruptible; any movement or activation of other abilities while this is channeling wastes the ability and puts it on cooldown.

CALL OF THE WILD

Damage: N/A

Effect: Fury (15 Seconds), Might (15 Seconds), Swiftness (15 Seconds)

Cooldown: 35 Seconds

The only bad thing about Call of the Wild is you can't use it more often! This skill buffs any party members near you by increasing critical chance, damage, and movement speed. Use this to help your group catch fleeing enemies in WvW or to help with important battles in dungeon groups.

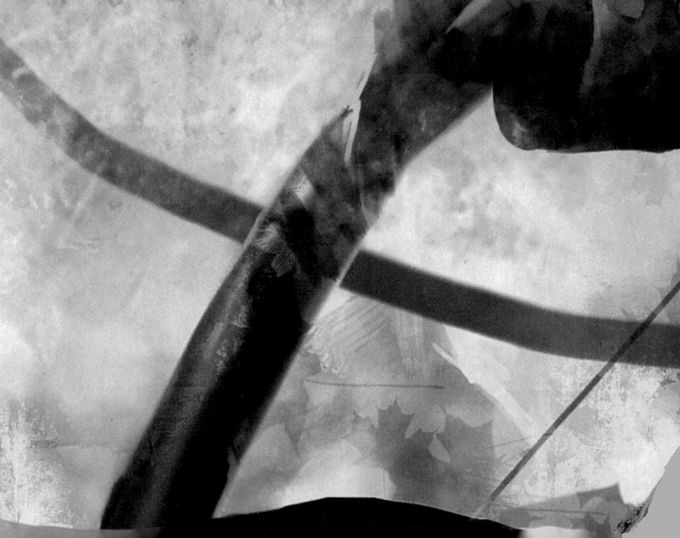

Dagger (Off Hand)

A dagger in your off hand provides powerful options against single targets at close range. Poison, Bleed, and Cripple your opponent before running off. Neither ability does very much initial damage, but both are quite damaging over time.

STALKER'S STRIKE

Damage: Low

Effect: Poison (10 Seconds), Evade

Cooldown: 10 Seconds

Stalker's Strike evades under an enemy attack and Poisons the foe. Use this when an enemy is charging or channeling a heavier attack against you; your character evades after the strike and won't get hit by your enemy's return fire.

CRIPPLING TALON

Damage: High

Effect: Cripple (6 Seconds), Bleed (x3) (8 Seconds), Combo Finisher (Physical Projectile)

Cooldown: 18 Seconds

Crippling Talon is an amazing kiting ability. The Cripple duration lasts for quite some time, putting the enemy at a major disadvantage. The Bleeding does damage while you run around outside of the enemy's range. This ability works extremely well with an axe in your main hand.

Torch (Off Hand Only)

Torches provide an area-of-effect attack and a whole new damage type. There really isn't much to do with a torch aside from Burning your enemies, but sometimes the direct route is the best one.

THROW TORCH

Damage: Moderate

Effect: Burning (6 Seconds)

Cooldown: 15 Seconds

This ranged attack deals heavy damage over time by lighting your opponent on fire. This ability doesn't work well if you are kiting with an axe, as Burning cancels Chill. Otherwise, go after your enemies and watch the world burn.

BONFIRE

Damage: Very Low

Effect: Burning (1 Second), Combo Field (Fire)

Cooldown: 25 Seconds

Bonfire is a bit tricky to use as it is a point-blank AoE. This ability does not do damage to you, but to get the most from it you want a lot of enemies very close to your ranger. Use this in groups by running up with the melee troops and lighting enemies on fire before retreating to the back lines. This skill does not do enough damage to single targets to be worth your time.

Spear (Underwater Weapon)

The spear is your underwater melee weapon. Closing the distance underwater can be a little tricky, as you need to change elevation. Dart gets you to the enemy and Man O' War keeps him from getting away. There is considerable variety in the spear's skill set.

STAB

Damage: High

Effect: N/A

Cooldown: None

Stab is your basic attack with a spear. It does decent damage and doesn't have any major downsides or strengths.

SWIRLING STRIKE

Damage: Very High

Effect: Reflect Projectiles

Cooldown: 8 Seconds

Swirling Strike reflects projectiles while dealing a mighty blow to all enemies in melee range. The damage is high enough that Swirling Strike is decent even against single foes. When fighting groups, it is spectacular and should be used every time it cools down. Swirling Strike is especially fun against enemies that summon pets!

DART

Damage: High

Effect: Charge, Vulnerability (10 Seconds), Bleed (10 Seconds)

Cooldown: 10 Seconds

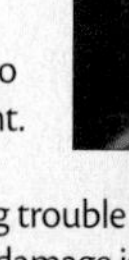

Dart is the fastest and easiest way to close with an underwater opponent. Dart gets your ranger into melee range very quickly. For those having trouble moving around underwater, this ability can't be beat. Over time, its damage is also quite impressive.

COUNTER STRIKE

Damage: Very High

Effect: Block, Knockback

Cooldown: 15 Seconds

Counter Strike is very similar to its above-water counterparts. Once triggered, it causes your ranger to block the next attack an enemy makes, kick him away, and then throw your spear at him. This is a good way to avoid damage and punish your opponent at the same time. Try to time it so Counter Strike is used right before a heavy attack to provide maximum mitigation without causing you to waste much time.

MAN O' WAR

Damage: Massive

Effect: Immobilize (2 Seconds)

Cooldown: 18 Seconds

Man O' War is made for enemies that try to kite you. Dart to them and then use Man O' War to hold them in place. The incredible damage this skill deals makes it a great ability even against enemies that aren't fleeing.

Harpoon Gun (Underwater Weapon)

The harpoon gun is your only ranged underwater weapon. As such, it is your best option for kiting underwater opponents. It doesn't have anything that Chills your enemies, but there are plenty of damage over time abilities—a Cripple, and one retreat. You'll be pretty darn mobile if you use these weapons.

SPLINTER SHOT

Damage: Low

Effect: Bleed (3 Seconds)

Cooldown: None

As a basic attack, Splinter Shot is mediocre against single targets. The damage it does isn't great, but it's something to do while your other shots recharge. Splinter Shot starts really paying for itself when fighting groups of enemies; the Bleed is spread to all targets in a small area, making the attack very efficient to soften an entire group of targets.

CORAL SHOT

Damage: Low

Effect: Bleed (5 Seconds), Cripple (3 Seconds)

Cooldown: 10 Seconds

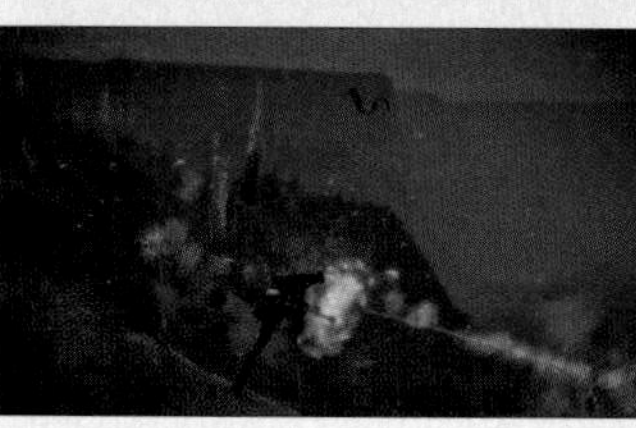

Coral Shot is your primary kiting ability. Combine Bleeding and Cripple so your enemies can't get to you.They take more time in the fight, and they lose health every second. It's a win-win situation for your hero.

FEEDING FRENZY

Damage: Extremely High

Effect: Pet Fury (5 Seconds)

Cooldown: 10 Seconds

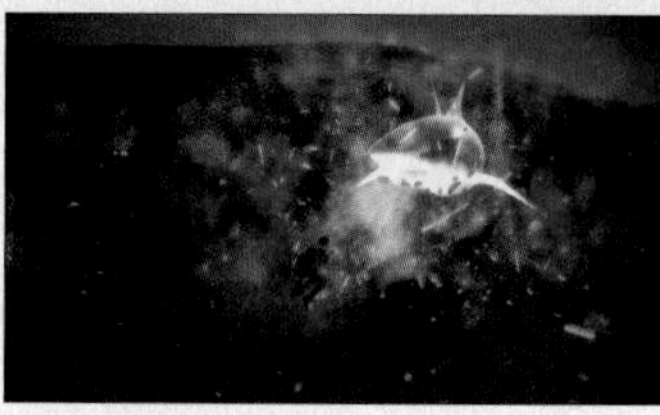

Feeding Frenzy deals substantial damage to your foe. Beyond the immediate burst of damage from the hit, this skill also sends your pet into a Fury. Use this attack every single time it finishes its cooldown.

MERCY SHOT

Damage: High
Effect: None
Cooldown: 12 Seconds

Finish enemies with Mercy Shot. Only use this when the enemy drops below half health, because that's when the damage starts really scaling up. Start fights with Feeding Frenzy, and end them with Mercy Shot.

INK BLAST

Damage: N/A
Effect: Blindness (6 Seconds), Retreat
Cooldown: 18 Seconds

Enemies can't hit what they can't see. Use Ink Blast any time targets close with you. The retreating aspect of the ability helps you get back to kiting and buys your ranger more time for Bleeds to do your dirty work.

LICK WOUNDS

Damage: N/A
Effect: Heal Over Time
Cooldown: 20 Seconds

If your pet is alive and well, it can help revive you by healing you. This is slowed if you are still taking damage, but the amount healed is very high and can often overcome the damage being dealt by one or two enemies.

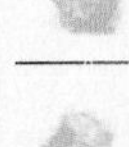

BANDAGE

Damage: N/A
Effect: Self-Heal
Cooldown: 5 Seconds

Use this to heal yourself if there aren't any enemies coming after you. It allows you to recover fairly quickly. If you're attacked, the effect ends and you have to fight for your life once more. If you Call Companion and get threats moved to your pet, you can Bandage without worry.

RANGER

Downed Skills

On the Ground

Ranger downed abilities are often pet based. The ranger can do a little bit of direct damage, but the real trick is to summon pets and get the pets to help with the healing/rallying process. If there's too much heat for your pet to heal through, your ranger is in serious trouble.

THROW DIRT

Damage: Low
Effect: Bleed (2 Seconds)
Cooldown: N/A

This simple attack does a minor amount of damage over time by stacking Bleed and hitting your target. Go after the enemy with the lowest health to dramatically increase your chance to rally before you're defeated.

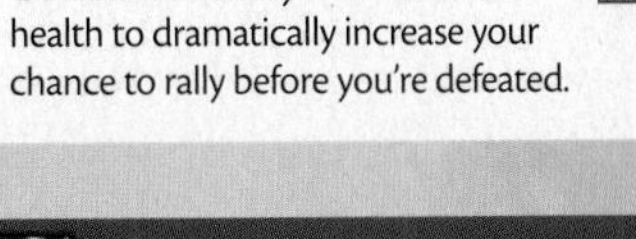

THUNDERCLAP

Damage: N/A
Effect: Summon Pet
Cooldown: 10 Seconds

Bringing down a ranger is only the first step to defeating one. Call your pet to you and use Lick Wounds to heal your ranger, or revive your fallen friend to help finish off the enemy.

Underwater

Underwater abilities work exactly like their above-ground counterparts. Throw Knife is the only exception, and that is explained in just a moment.

THROW KNIFE

Damage: Low
Effect: N/A
Cooldown: N/A

This simple ranged attack is your mainstay while drowning. Use it again and again to deal damage as the cooldowns for the other skills are finishing. As with Throw Dirt, aim for the enemy with lowest health. That's your best chance to rally if your pet can't heal you in time.

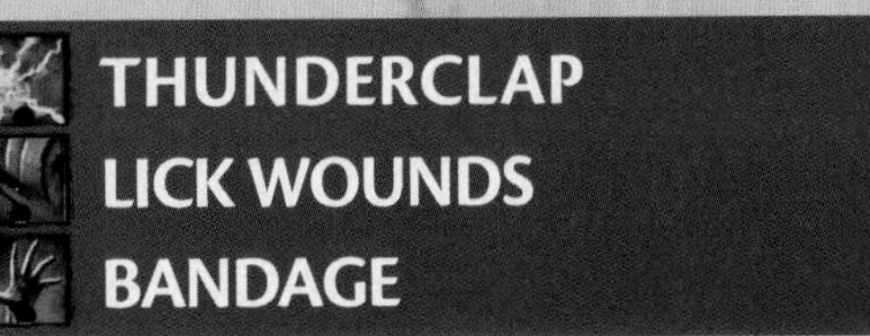

THUNDERCLAP
LICK WOUNDS
BANDAGE

These abilities function in the same manner as their terrestrial versions. Use the same tactics to try and rally yourself, or swim to the surface and attempt to heal yourself there if you think it won't be possible to rally through fighting.

Slot Skills

Healing

Rangers have healing abilities to help themselves, their pets, and their groups. Switch between these to ensure you contribute as much as possible when you get into a larger force.

HEAL AS ONE

Effect: Heal Self, Heal Pet

Cooldown: 20 Seconds

This is the most common ranger healing skill; it heals your ranger and your pet at the same time. Heal as One can be used at range or around corners, so there is little excuse for letting your pet die. This becomes even more useful when you're evacuating an area, as it allows your pet to hold enemies while you get away (you can cast this while running).

TROLL UNGUENT

Effect: Regenerate Health, Duration (10 Seconds)

Cooldown: 40 Seconds

Troll Unguent Regenerates more health than Heal as One, but it has some drawbacks. The longer cooldown is a big one, so it's not as useful when you're topping off your health or helping your pet. In addition, the Regeneration does not affect your pet. The best use for Troll Unguent is at the start of a fight if your ranger is going to be tanking the enemies. Finally, it takes 10 seconds for Troll Unguent to release its healing potential. Thus, Heal as One is better for surviving bursts of high damage.

HEALING SPRING

Effect: Summon Healing Spring (15 Seconds), Regeneration (3 Seconds), Combo Field (Water)

Cooldown: 30 Seconds

Slot this skill if you're joining a dungeon group, and use it to deploy Healing Spring at your feet. Do this when you're standing in the center of the party so everyone benefits from its healing. It's fairly powerful, giving your entire party Regeneration and condition clearing.

Utility

There are a few types of utility skills for rangers. Traps, spirits, and signets are a ranger's bread and butter. Traps make life difficult for enemies, spirits buff party members, and signets help your hero and pet do more damage or survive under harsh circumstances.

TIER 1

SPIKE TRAP

Effect: Low AoE Damage, Bleed (x3) (5 Seconds), Cripple (2 Seconds)

Cooldown: 25 Seconds

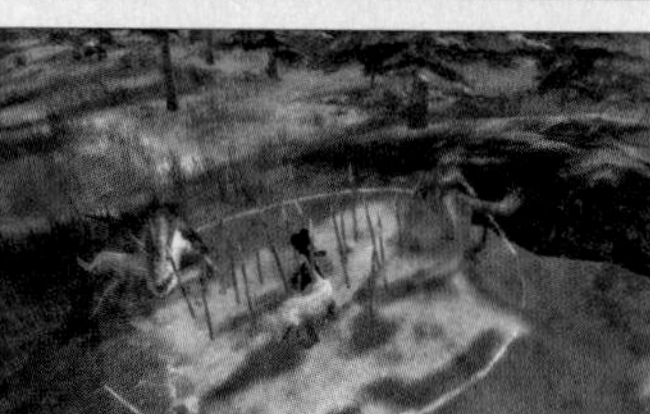

Spike Trap is an excellent way to start a fight. It's also a great way to run from a fight. Pull large groups of enemies through a Spike Trap and you earn a few seconds of free kiting to kill some of them off before they're a threat to you again.

FLAME TRAP

Effect: Moderate AoE Damage, Burning (3 Seconds), Duration (3 Seconds), Combo Field (Fire)

Cooldown: 15 Seconds

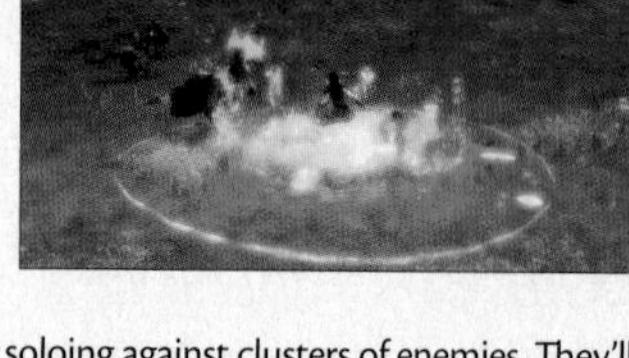

Flame Trap is great when working in a group. Drop the trap under the feet of the tank and watch all the poor monsters burn! It's also useful if you're soloing against clusters of enemies. They'll naturally try to rush you, grouping together near your character. That makes them easy targets for the trap. Chokepoints and corners are often the best areas for this setup.

SIGNET OF RENEWAL

Effect: Remove Conditions Passively, Use to Transfer Conditions to Your Pet and Break Stun

Cooldown: 60 seconds

Signet of Renewal is nearly a must-have for WvW. This ability passively keeps conditions off of your character by removing one every 10 seconds. If used actively, the signet pulls conditions off of you and your allies and throws them all onto your pet. The active use also breaks Stun, giving it even more PvP utility. Swap pets if your animal companion suffers from too many conditions to continue the fight effectively.

SHARPENING STONE

Effect: Cause Bleed (10 Seconds) for 5 Attacks

Cooldown: 45 Seconds

Sharpening Stone works best on single tough enemies and with attacks that hit multiple times. Activate this just before using Splitblade (Axe) to Bleed multiple enemies, or with Rapid Fire (Longbow) to put all five stacks on a single target quickly.

MUDDY TERRAIN

Effect: AoE Immobilize (2 Seconds), Cripple (1 Second)

Cooldown: 30 Seconds

Muddy Terrain is the bane of any group trying to get to you. In WvW, this ability stymies entire enemy groups when used at choke-points. In PvE, this is great against champions when your group needs a breather. The skill Immobilizes enemies when it's first deployed, and it adds Cripple to everything caught in its AoE while pulsing. Rangers already have good kiting abilities, and this pushes them over the top.

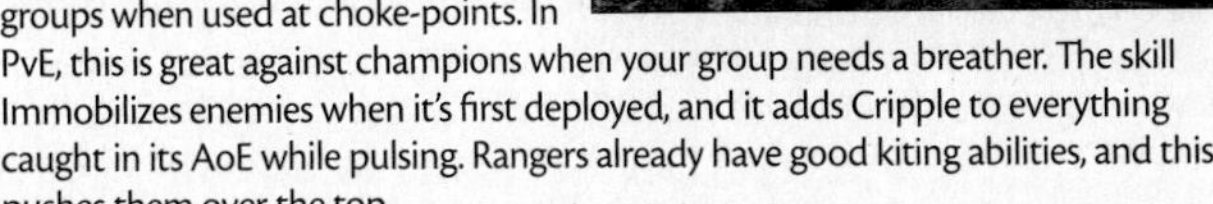

SUN SPIRIT

Effect: Summon Spirit (60 Seconds), Burning (1 Second)

Cooldown: 60 Seconds

Spirits are best used in large parties, as they become far more powerful by affecting more people. Sun Spirit gives all allies a chance to inflict Burning with their attacks. Use Sun Spirit when your allies will be attacking multiple enemies.

"SICK 'EM"

Effect: Buff Pet (Movement and Damage)

Cooldown: 45 Seconds

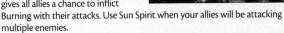

"Sick 'Em" takes away control of your pet but improves its damage and speed. When there aren't many targets to worry about and you just need that one tough enemy dead, you're in great shape with this skill. Or, for fights where you want to throw your pet out there and have it fight until the bitter end, this works too.

Use your pet's F2 power ahead of time, because it won't be available during "Sick 'Em."

TIER 2

VIPER'S NEST

Effect: Poison (3 Seconds)

Cooldown: 20 Seconds

Viper's Nest is a great way to hamper enemy healing in PvP, especially at chokepoints. It's also fun in dungeon groups, where fights are a bit longer; you might even get to use it twice in the same encounter.

SIGNET OF THE HUNT

Effect: Passively Increases Movement Speed, Activate to Increase Damage for Your Pet's Next Attack

Cooldown: 120 Seconds

The increased movement speed of this signet is useful in WvW, general PvP, or while exploring the world of Tyria. The improvement is noticeable and cuts a fair amount of time off of longer trips. Active use gives your pet one big shot, but it's not enough to really turn the tide of battle. Make sure to pop it right before you send your pet in against a new target. That way you get the most for your investment.

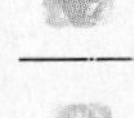

SIGNET OF STONE

Effect: Passively Improves Toughness (Ranger + Pet), Activate to Make Pet Immune to Damage (6 Seconds)

Cooldown: 120 Seconds

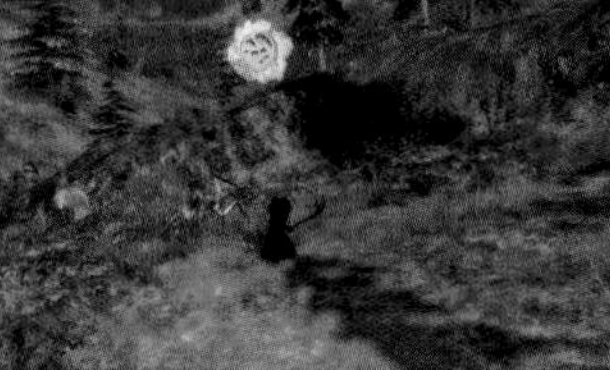

Signet of Stone allows you to stand toe to toe with some of the toughest enemies. Grab this skill and use it as you send your pet in to hold a whole group of targets. Though the cooldown is long, you won't often have to deal with fights that are nasty enough to warrant Signet of Stone. Save it for huge rushes or attacks against especially powerful enemy units.

LIGHTNING REFLEXES

Effect: High Damage, Evade, Vigor (10 Seconds), Break Stun

Cooldown: 45 Seconds

PvP matches are much more difficult without a way to break free from Stun. Lightning Reflexes combines a Stun breaker, an Evade, and Vigor to regenerate Endurance. This skill is most important when you're facing small groups of players that are more likely to use crowd control abilities. This skill also helps immensely when soloing stronger monsters.

STONE SPIRIT

Effect: Protection (1 Second)

Cooldown: 60 Seconds

Stone Spirit grants all allies a chance to gain Protection. This is a wonderful way to help with mitigation in fights that threaten to overwhelm your party. Single enemies of tremendous power and large groups of targets are equally dangerous, and Stone Spirit helps with both.

FROST SPIRIT

Effect: Damage Bonus (10%)

Cooldown: 60 Seconds

Frost Spirit occasionally grants a damage bonus to all nearby allies. This spirit is made for groups that are winning fights already but need to win a little bit faster. When survival is doubtful, use Stone Spirit. When you want to go through easy content even faster, Frost Spirit is your guy.

"PROTECT ME"

Effect: Pet Damage Transfer

Cooldown: 45 Seconds

Your pet stops attacking when this skill is activated. Your loyal pet instead takes damage in your place until the skill ends or your pet dies. When fleeing, tanking enemies for a group, or simply trying to survive, this is a major boost to your longevity.

TIER 3

FROST TRAP

Effect: Chill (1 Second), Combo Field (Ice), Duration (10 Seconds)

Cooldown: 30 Seconds

Frost Trap reduces incoming damage against you, your pet, and any allies. Keep enemies' recharge speed reduced and stop them from catching up to your buddies. This is effective whether you're kiting or tanking the targets.

SIGNET OF THE WILD

Effect: Passively Grants Health Regeneration (Ranger + Pet), Activate to Give Stability and a Damage Buff to Your Pet

Cooldown: 120 Seconds

Signet of the Wild is another tanking skill for pets. The base Regeneration helps with soloing and small fights. It's not enough to make a difference in really brutal encounters, but you'll like it while soloing. The active use is more important. That keeps your pet from being knocked around or hit with crowd control. It also gets a brief damage buff. Combine this with "Sick 'Em" to have your pet become a serious threat to targets.

QUICKENING ZEPHYR

Effect: Quickness (4 Seconds)

Cooldown: 60 Seconds

Quickening Zephyr is made of pure damaging WIN. This skill increases the speed of your abilities and movement (and those of your pet as well). Use this right before a channeled ability and watch the damage go crazy as you channel much faster than normal. Always make sure to plan several seconds of frantic activity to make the most of Quickening Zephyr. Don't waste this on simple autoattacks. Hit every ability you can and lay down the wrath of nature on your opponents.

STORM SPIRIT

Effect: Grants Swiftness (3 Seconds)

Cooldown: 60 Seconds

Storm Spirit isn't for novice groups. Use this in experienced groups in WvW or PvP. By giving allies a chance to gain Swiftness when attacking, you keep your party mobile. That's hard for novices to take advantage of. Kiting groups get the most out of Storm Spirit.

"GUARD"

Effect: Locks Pet in Place

Cooldown: 60 Seconds

This skill commands your pet to stay where it is and rip through any enemies that get too close to it. Set this up near a corner or chokepoint, and lay additional traps down to make the most of this! Another trick is to have your pet guard the area between the melee characters and the ranged attackers in your group. If a foe breaks away from the melee team, your pet will pick it up before it hits the more vulnerable members of the group.

"SEARCH AND RESCUE"

Effect: Revive

Cooldown: 85 Seconds

This skill is quite possibly the most group-friendly ability rangers have. If an ally goes down, hit "Search and Rescue" and kite the enemy away until your pet revives the fallen party member. You benefit heavily from this in events with NPCs, dungeons, and during PvP engagements.

Elite

A ranger and his or her pet already have quite an advantage over most enemies. What happens when the two become the perfect team? Let's find out!

TIER 1

RAMPAGE AS ONE

Effect: Stability (20 Seconds), Fury (20 Seconds), Swiftness (20 Seconds), Might to Your Pet (20 Seconds)

Cooldown: 120 Seconds

When both you and your pet Rampage as One, the enemy cowers. Your ranger and pet ignore control effects, have an increased critical chance, and move faster. And if that weren't enough, you grant Might to your pet every time you attack. Use this during any fight that has large groups or tough enemies, or find any excuse to break out this awesome skill. The boons last for 20 seconds, so you have more than enough time to capitalize on them.

In addition, this skill has a rather short cooldown for an elite skill. This makes Rampage as One extremely tempting as your first elite to purchase. There aren't any bad times to use it.

ENTANGLE

Effect: Immobilize (20 Seconds)

Cooldown: 150 Seconds

Entangle is truly horrific when used in a party of ranged attackers. As the enemy turns toward you, root him in place and let fly with all your attacks. The enemy will be unable to move until the vines are destroyed. This is positively devastating to new players in WvW and PvP who don't know to attack the vines, but even experienced players will be slowed greatly by this.

TIER 2

SPIRIT OF NATURE

Effect: Summon Spirit (60 Seconds)

Cooldown: 240 Seconds

As with all spirits, this is made for use in a group. The Spirit of Nature heals nearby allies and, when commanded, even revives fallen allies and removes conditions. This becomes immensely useful if your group is having trouble with a major event or dungeon boss battle.

Traits

Marksmanship (Raises Power and Condition Duration)

REWARDS

Points Invested	Ability Gained
5	First hit when entering combat causes Vulnerability
15	Your pets also do Opening Strike
25	Opening Strike always lands a critical hit

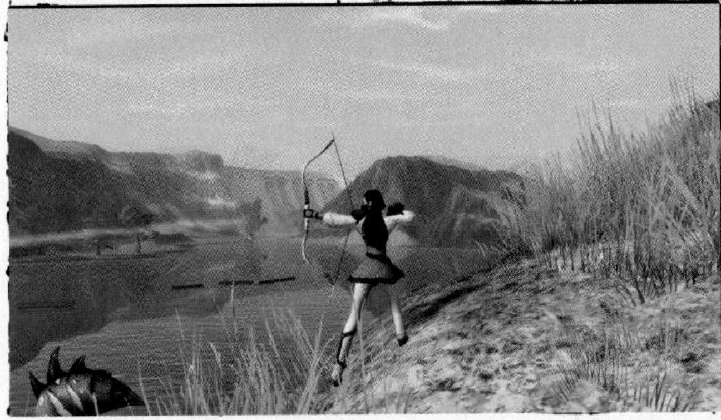

SKILL OPTIONS (GAINED EVERY 10 POINTS)

ADEPT TIER

- Steady Focus: 10% damage bonus when endurance is full.
- Malice Training: Increased duration for conditions applied by your pets.
- Keen Edge: Automatically use Sharpening Stone when health reaches 75%.
- Signet Mastery: Signets have a 20% shorter recharge.
- Predator's Instinct: Apply Cripple to enemies you hit when they are below 25% health (15 second recharge).
- Beastmaster's Bond: Gain Fury and Might when your pet's health reaches 25%.

MASTER TIER

- Long-range Power: Longbow and harpoon gun attacks do 5% more damage.
- Piercing Arrows: All arrow attacks pierce targets.
- Beastmaster's Might: Activating a signet grants Might.
- Eagle Eye: Increased longbow range.

GRANDMASTER TIER

- Signet of the Beastmaster: Active effects of signets affect you as well as your pet.
- Remorseless: Regain Opening Strikes when you kill an enemy.

Skirmishing (Raises Precision and Critical Damage)

REWARDS

Points Invested	Ability Gained
5	You gain Swiftness when swapping weapons in combat
15	You gain Fury when swapping weapons in combat
25	You deal 10% more damage when flanking

SKILL OPTIONS (GAINED EVERY 10 POINTS)

ADEPT TIER

- Pet's Prowess: Your pet's critical hits deal 30% more damage.
- Sharpened Edges: Chance to cause Bleeding on critical hits.
- Trapper's Defense: Create a Spike Trap when reviving an ally.
- Trapper's Knowledge: All traps are larger.
- Companions Might: Critical hits grant Might to your pet.
- Agility Training: Your pet moves 30% faster.

MASTER TIER

- Carnivorous Appetite: Your pet gains health on critical hits.
- Trapper's Expertise: Traps are ground targeted.
- Honed Axes: Axes deal 33% more critical damage.
- Quick Draw: Shortbow skills recharge 15% faster.

GRANDMASTER TIER

- Trap Potency: Conditions caused by traps last twice as long.
- Moment of Clarity: Gain Quickening Zephyr at 25% health.

Wilderness Survival (Raises Toughness and Condition Damage)

REWARDS

Points Invested	Ability Gained
5	You have an additional 50% Endurance regeneration
15	You and your pet gain 2 seconds of Protection when you dodge roll
25	You deal 5% extra damage when your health is above 90%

SKILL OPTIONS (GAINED EVERY 10 POINTS)

ADEPT TIER

- Soften the Fall: Create Muddy terrain when you take falling damage.
- Healers Celerity: Grant Swiftness to you and your ally when you revive someone.
- Master Trapper: Traps recharge 20% faster.
- Vigorous Renewal: Gain Vigor when using a heal skill.
- Expertise Training: Your pets deal extra condition damage.
- Off-hand Mastery: Off-hand skills recharge 20% faster.

MASTER TIER

- Off-hand Training: Off-hand skills have longer range.
- Wilderness Knowledge: Wilderness skills recharge 20% faster.
- Bark Skin: You and your pet take 10% less damage while under 25% health.
- Sword Mastery: Sword skills recharge 20% faster.

GRANDMASTER TIER

- Empathic Bond: Your pet periodically takes conditions from you.
- Hide in Plain Sight: Apply Camouflage at 25% health.

Nature Magic (Raises Vitality and Boon Duration)

REWARDS

Points Invested	Ability Gained
5	You gain Regeneration when your health reaches 75%
15	Any boon you get is shared with your pet
25	You and your pet deal 5% more damage while you have a boon

SKILL OPTIONS (GAINED EVERY 10 POINTS)

ADEPT TIER

- Circle of Life: Create a Healing Spring on death.
- Concentration Training: Boons applied by your pets last longer.
- Nature's Bounty: Regeneration you apply lasts 33% longer.
- Vigorous Spirits: Spirits have twice as much health.
- Strength of Spirit: 10% of your Vitality is given as a bonus to Power.
- Shared Restoration: Heal nearby allies on Revive.

MASTER TIER

- Nature's Vengeance: Spirits activate their toggle skill on death.
- Spiritual Knowledge: Spirit buffs have a 15% better chance of providing their benefits.
- Two-Handed Training: 5% increased damage with greatsword and spear skills.
- Enlargement: Your pet gets Enlarged when you reach 25% health.

GRANDMASTER TIER

- Spirits Unbound: Spirits can move and follow you.
- Evasive Purity: Remove a condition from you and nearby allies on dodge roll.

Beastmastery (Raises Healing and Pet Attribute Bonuses)

REWARDS

Points Invested	Ability Gained
5	You and your pet gain 2 seconds of Quickening Zephyr when you swap pets
15	Cooldowns between pet swaps is shortened by 40%
25	10% of healing is given as a bonus to power

SKILL OPTIONS (GAINED EVERY 10 POINTS)

ADEPT TIER

- Speed Training: Pets have 10% reduced recharge on their skills.
- Master's Bond: Your pet gets attribute bonuses every time your ranger kills something (this lasts until your pet is defeated or deactivated).
- Shout Master: Shouts recharge 20% faster.
- Compassion Training: Your pets heal for more.
- Commanding Voice: Pet activation skills (F2) have faster recharge.
- Mighty Swap: Pets gain three stacks of Might when activated.

MASTER TIER

- Rending Attacks: Drake, Feline, Devourer, and Shark pets Bleed targets when they critically hit with basic attacks.
- Stability Training: Ursine, Porcine, and Armor Fish pets gain Stability (3 seconds) when disabled.
- Intimidation Training: Activated (F2) abilities for Canine and Spiders cause Cripple.
- Vigorous Training: Moa, Bird, and Jellyfish pets grant AoE Vigor (5 seconds) when activated.

GRANDMASTER TIER

- Instinctual Bond: When your ranger is downed, your pet gains Quickness.
- Natural Healing: Your pets have natural health Regeneration.

Rangers in PvE

A well-played ranger is almost impossible for standard enemies to kill. If a fight goes poorly, the ranger's pet can come to the rescue, or the ranger can simply leave and come back later. This flexibility lets a ranger take on tougher opponents with a bit of planning.

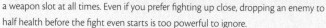

Always be aware of your surroundings. Keep an eye out for terrain you can move over, where cliffs are, and where aggressive and non-aggressive monsters are standing. Kiting is the ranger's most potent weapon. With your complement of Cripples, Chills, Knockbacks, and Bleeds, the only reason to get close to enemies is to loot their corpses. Keep either a longbow or shortbow in a weapon slot at all times. Even if you prefer fighting up close, dropping an enemy to half health before the fight even starts is too powerful to ignore.

Against single targets, stack conditions first (either Vulnerability with the longbow or Poison with the shortbow), then move into your high damage abilities. Keep traps and your pet ready to prevent the enemy from closing with you. Spike Trap and any pet with a Knockdown or Cripple are wonderful for this. As most of your ranged attacks can be used on the run, start strafing away from enemies before they close. By strafing, you keep them in your line of sight. Your ranger can continue firing while running at full speed.

Groups of enemies are more difficult to kite, but the ranger can pull it off. Start the fight with Barrage (longbow) or Poison Volley (shortbow). Marksmanship rangers with Piercing Arrows should keep the farthest enemy targeted (as your attacks will hit everything between you and the actual target). Non-Marksmanship rangers should switch to an Axe as the enemies close. Axes hit multiple targets, and Split Blades provides a multi-target bleed. Lay traps and evade when needed until the final enemy drops.

Swords and greatswords are both good weapons for anyone wanting a closer encounter with an enemy. Fighting at close range has some advantages and a few concerns as well. Your ranger deals much more damage with melee weapons. The primary tradeoff for this is survivability.

Swords have several attacks that also evade. These are very powerful against single, tough opponents. Use a pet with high Vitality or Toughness and watch its health closely. Your pet can keep aggro off you for as long as it lives, so make sure the enemy dies first. Use more damage-focused slot-skills such as Sharpening Stone and Quickening Zephyr. Then, use Heal as One to keep your pet alive. Be ready to swap pets if your primary gets low on health.

In groups, the ranger's versatility truly shines. The ranger can fill almost any role needed in a group. A Wilderness Survival/Nature Magic ranger with a sword and a Vitality pet can absorb quite a bit of damage. Use your Signet of Stone and Signet of the Wild and swap aggro between you and your pet.

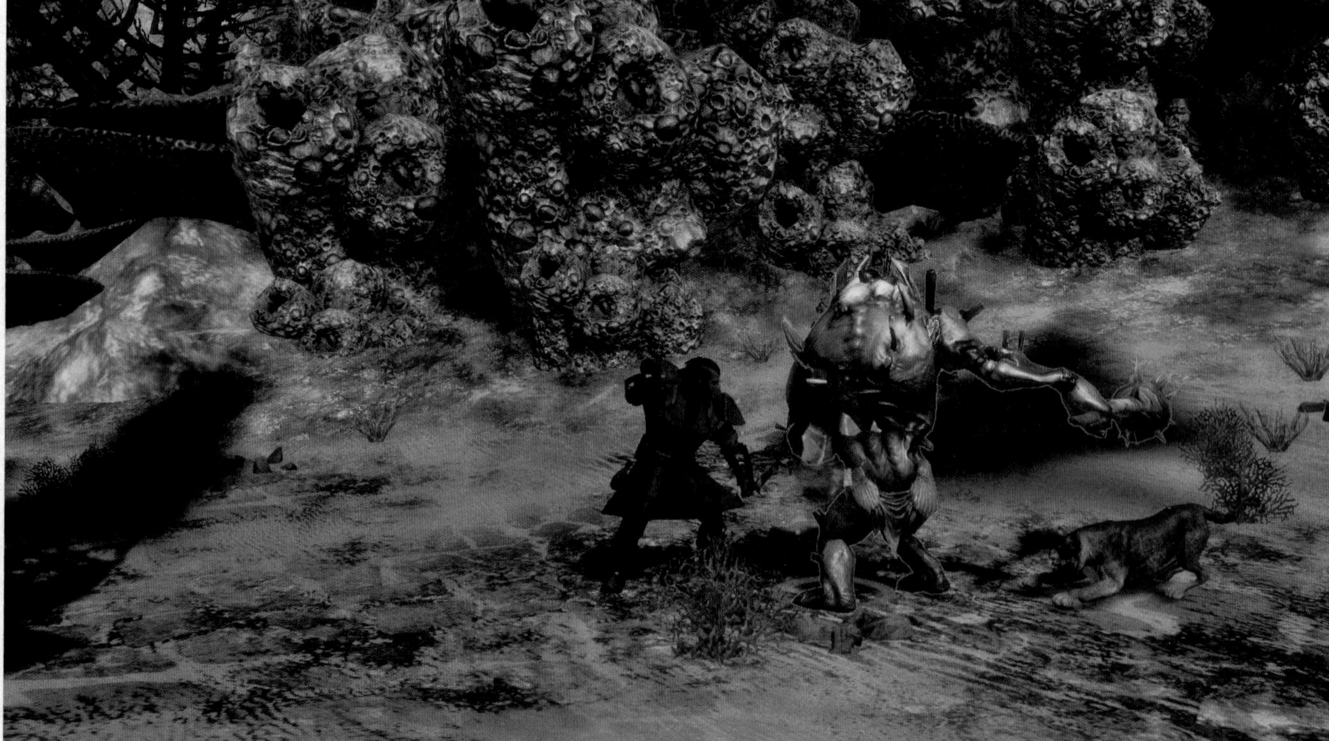

A Beastmastery/Nature Magic ranger with a White Moa, Healing Spring, and Spirit of Nature can fill in as a group healer (while still doing damage). Use Stone Spirit to give your tank protection occasionally. Also use Sun Spirit (when fighting multiple targets) or Frost Spirit (when fighting a single tough enemy) to increase party damage.

Rangers have many choices. Most of them are equally powerful if you tweak your whole character toward a single goal. Don't try to be a jack of all trades, as this will leave you without a clear focus for your character. Instead, play around. Grab new pets, see how they work, and test different combinations of weapons, slot skills, and pets. Rangers can be adapted to almost any playstyle with a bit of work. Go out there and start killing!

Rangers in PvP

Fighting rangers in PvP can be a daunting proposition. With so many ranged attacks and abilities to keep foes at range, rangers make it very hard to close the gap against them. The best way to identify what type of rangers you're dealing with is by looking for their pet. If they have spirits out, they are likely more party-focused. If you see a ranger without a pet, be even more alert so the pet doesn't flank you.

Playing a ranger in PvP can be immensely rewarding and devastating to an enemy group. While rangers are far more powerful in group vs. group engagements, they are more than sufficient at killing people one on one. Equip a sword/dagger combination and a shortbow for some devastating kiting ability and evasion.

Even when you don't kill an enemy quickly, your ranger can ensure that the fight lasts a LONG time. Call for reinforcements so buddies show up just in time to clean up the person who is hassling you.

Stack conditions at range with your shortbow and traps. If you can stay at range and never use your melee weapons, so much the better. Hit Quickening Zephyr early in the fight to cause high burst damage and throw your enemy on the defensive. Swap to your melee set and use the sword's evasion attacks and the dagger's cripples to get back to range quickly if anyone gets close to you. Lightning Reflexes makes this mode of fighting even more enjoyable.

Rangers aren't likely to score as many killing blows in WvW/PvP combat, but the conditions they stack on multiple targets are frightening. Playing defensively gives the ranger the opportunity to choose the terrain for the fight and, more importantly, force enemies to attack through choke-points. Have a Spike Trap at the choke-point, and start raining arrows at them with Barrage (longbow) combined with Sharpening Stone or Poison Volley.

Always look for raised areas that give your ranger a nice vantage point. The more you see, the more you can attack! Many PvP maps have areas that cater to ranged casters and archers. Hunt for these and mix up the ones you use while defending an area. That makes it harder for enemies to sneak up and ambush you.

If there are a lot of ranged damage dealers on your side, drop Healing Spring to keep your allies from suffering from as many conditions as your opponents. Redeploy traps as needed and be ready to kite any enemies that manage to close the distance with you. While spirits have a lot of group utility, they are pretty soft and often die very quickly in PvP. With the proper traits they can be less squishy, but there are far more potent skills to have in those slots.

THIEF

Thieves are an extremely mobile class of melee and missile killers who use Stealth, hit-and-run tactics, and other tricks to kill their enemies. Well versed in traps and subtlety, these characters are best for players who are able to plan ahead and use a bit more guile. Often taken out quickly in a toe-to-toe duel, thieves are forced to use a variety of conditions to give themselves the unfair advantage!

This profession is recommended for the most active players in the game. Thieves spend so much time in motion that you rarely get a moment to stop and think. If you thrive on challenging tactics and get bored with simple characters, you'll be overjoyed with thieves.

Profession Stats

Attribute	Starting Stats	Naked at Level 80
Power	24	2054
Precision	24	1166
Toughness	24	1771
Vitality	24	1571
Attack	156	2054
Critical Chance	4%	14%
Armor	92	1771
Health	245	17,355

The stats listed above give you an idea of what to expect from your character. They show thief progression through examples taken at the beginning and end of leveling. Your actual stats will likely vary from this.

Weapons and Weapon Skills

Thieves have an interesting weapon system for their skills. These aren't entirely determined just by your selection of main hand and off hand weapons. You also get a switch skill in the middle of your bar that is determined by the pairing of your two weapons. Therefore, the third skill for most thief weapon combinations varies if you switch in varying off hand weapon types.

Thieves have a good mix of short- and long-range weapons. You're often well-off with a selection of each, once you get past level seven and can swap between them during battle.

Stealing

Damage:	Random
Effect:	Varies
Cooldown:	45 Seconds

Thieves have a special attack they can use with some frequency. Stealing causes your character to shadowstep to the target, making it possible to dart around the battlefield with almost no delay when you really need to get somewhere. Though the attack has a long cooldown, it's still usable every few fights.

When you get to the target, your hero steals an ability from him. It's easy to think you'll be grabbing his coin purse or something of that nature, so try to think of this more as an attack of opportunity. You're learning how to use a special attack when you steal a random object from your target. Some of these attacks put conditions on your targets, while others are limited AoEs. You don't know what you're going to get until the skill description pops up (after hitting Steal).

So, hit "F1" the first time to shadowstep and steal something from your victim, and hit it again afterward to use the new skill. All of the new skills are one-time deals, so you have to wait until the cooldown refreshes to get another one.

Initiative

All other thief weapon skills work on a special system. Other characters have cooldowns as the limiting factor for their weapon attacks. Thieves don't! They have 12 points of Initiative that act as a resource for triggering your attack skills. You can frontload damage by hitting your best skills several times in a row.

The downside to this is that thieves have a period of lagging damage output after they've expended their initiative. You need to use slot skills wisely to make up for this, and to make every point of initiative count well early in the fight.

Be careful with tapping keys carelessly. Thieves are challenging to play; they have attacks that are quite devastating, but you'll be a sitting duck if you waste your initiative on non-optimal solutions to your problems.

Learn which attacks are best for single targets, AoEs, and longer fights. Use and abuse whatever works best against your current enemy.

Stealth Skills

All weapons have a special stealth skill when a thief wields them. Any time your character goes into stealth (from weapon attacks, healing, or utility skills), your number-one weapon skill changes into something new. These stealth skills are available only until you attack or the duration of stealth finishes.

Stealth skills are often extremely powerful, so make the most of them. If you particularly enjoy these skills, slot skills like Hide in Shadows, Shadow Trap, and so forth, so your thief can use the attacks multiple times in the same fight.

STEALTH ATTACKS

Weapon	Attack Name	Effect
Dagger	Backstab	Very High Damage (even more from behind)
Shortbow	Surprise Shot	High Damage, Immobilize
Sword	Tactical Strike	Very High Damage, Blindness, Daze
Pistol	Sneak Attack	Very High Damage, Bleeding
Harpoon Gun	The Ripper	Moderate Damage, Bleeding
Spear	Deadly Strike	Very High Damage, Weakness
Downed	Venomous Knife	Very High Damage, Bleeding, Poison

Sword (Main Hand Only)

Swords give thieves decent damage and plenty of mobility on the battlefield. They are extremely useful as anti-kiting weapons because of their crippling autoattacks and cheap shadowsteps. Kill ranged enemies reliably with these exciting skills.

SLICE

Damage:	High
Effect:	Cripple (2 Seconds) on Every Third Strike
Initiative Cost:	N/A

This autoattack is a series of three swings. The first two deal basic damage, and the third one is a heavier attack that also slows your victim for a couple seconds. That's more than enough time to be well into your next trio of strikes, so enemies have to work hard to escape. If they do, tap Infiltrator's Strike to catch up and resume the beat session.

INFILTRATOR'S STRIKE

Damage:	High
Effect:	Shadowstep to Target
Initiative Cost:	2/1

Use this attack to quickly close the gap with your target. Your thief blinks over to the victim and hacks at him. If you hit the ability again, your character reverses course and appears back where he or she started. Both features are useful in different ways. Strike and return if you want to hit and run, keeping your enemy off balance. Strike and stay with the target if you're just trying to stick to a kiting or evading opponent.

FLANKING STRIKE (DAGGER AS OFF HAND)

Damage:	Very High
Effect:	Evade
Initiative Cost:	4

Flanking Strike is a sword + dagger skill. It causes your thief to roll around the target, evading any forward-facing strikes during the setup. When you're in place, the thief attacks twice. Total damage output is high, making this a powerful offensive and defensive ability at the same time. Use it to prevent enemies from hitting your thief with predictable attacks, especially if enemies plant their feet and don't turn around while they're attacking.

PISTOL WHIP (PISTOL AS OFF HAND)

Damage:	Very High
Effect:	Stun (1/4 Second)
Initiative Cost:	5

Pistol Whip is available if you pair your sword with a pistol. The attack takes a few moments to complete, but it has decent damage and the ability to Stun targets. This is yet another way for thieves to disrupt enemies. When they go on a major offensive or charge for a big attack, Stun them. If they try to flee, revert to less expensive sword options to stay with them. You control the fight.

STAB (NO OFF HAND CHOSEN)

Damage:	High
Effect:	N/A
Initiative Cost:	4

If you don't have an offhand weapon, your sword gets a simple attack with basic, direct damage. It's quite spammable for adequate damage. You have far more options with a pistol or dagger at your side, so this is more of a choice for characters that are just starting out and don't have good secondary weapons.

Shortbow (Two-Handed)

Shortbows offer a blend of damage and kiting potential for thieves. They lack some of the evil disabling options that pistols have, but they deal very nice damage as long as you're facing small groups of enemies instead of single targets. Fight enemies in groups of two or three to see these weapons at their best.

TRICK SHOT

Damage:	Moderate (Per Target)
Effect:	Can Strike Multiple Enemies, Combo Finisher (Physical Projectile: 20%)
Initiative Cost:	N/A

Trick Shot pegs single enemies for modest damage, but you'll see why it's a great ability once you fight a few targets at once. Your attacks bounce in between the opponents, damaging everything they hit. Use your initiative quickly to get an edge in these fights, and then hit everyone time and time again while your initiative regenerates. Run and dodge while doing this to make it even harder for enemies to lock down your hero.

CLUSTER BOMB

Damage:	High
Effect:	Bleeding (x3) (4 Seconds), Combo Finisher (Blast)
Initiative Cost:	3

Cluster Bomb fires an explosive shot that detonates if you hit the button again while the attack is in the air. Failing that, the shot hits your victim and explodes. Everything nearby takes damage and starts losing health over time for the next few seconds. Get everyone in a group Bleeding and then switch to lighter attacks while the enemies start to drop.

THIEF

DISABLING SHOT

Damage:	Moderate
Effect:	Leap Away, Cripple (2 Seconds), Combo Finisher (Physical Projectile)
Initiative Cost:	3

Some enemies have the audacity to chase you. Disabling Shot is a kiting attack that slows your victims while your hero jumps away from them, getting more safe distance to continue the onslaught. Never use this for raw damage. It's purely an escape maneuver.

CHOKING GAS

Damage:	N/A
Effect:	Poison (5 Seconds), Combo Field (Poison)
Initiative Cost:	4

Choking Gas has no immediate damage, so it's an awful ability to use late in a fight. Instead, hit this early on when fighting either a large group or enemies that rely on healing to keep their health high. This attack is more situational, so it's not one you'd expect to use in smaller fights or against simple monsters.

INFILTRATOR'S ARROW

Damage:	N/A
Effect:	Blindness (5 Seconds)
Initiative Cost:	6

This is a group-friendly attack you should use to mitigate enemy damage. Your thief pops over to targets, Blinds them, and protects herself and any allies from the next attack by those foes. Infiltrator's Arrow is way too expensive to use in normal fights; save this for battles against veterans, champions, and other high damage output enemies.

Dagger (Main or Off Hand)

Close-range damage and group slaughter are the ways of the dagger. These weapons are fun and can rake in the kills for any thief. Their big tradeoffs are a lack of range and defense. You aren't always going to survive when you pull out the daggers, but you're going to take almost everyone with you if you go down! Mwahahaha!

DOUBLE STRIKE (MAIN HAND)

Damage: High

Effect: Weakness (3 Seconds), Vulnerability (3 Seconds)

Initiative Cost: N/A

Double Strike is a melee chain of hits that drops your enemies' defense and makes it hard for them to evade (the third hit from the combo applies Weakness). Use this between your attacks that cost initiative so your enemies suffer from defensive penalties and have trouble getting their endurance back.

HEARTSEEKER (MAIN HAND)

Damage: Varies (High to Scary!)

Effect: Combo Finisher (Leap)

Initiative Cost: 3

Heartseeker is an inexpensive single-target attack that gets better and better as your enemy weakens. Used early in a fight, it's only decent and shouldn't be used against most targets. There are better choices out there. Death Blossom is superior even against a single target! However, Heartseeker comes into its own when enemies fall below 2/3 of their health. When they're down to 1/3, it becomes so powerful that the enemy is just doomed.

In groups, it's highly viable to switch between targets in larger fights and cherry-pick the most injured opponents to burn down with Heartseeker.

DEATH BLOSSOM (DAGGER AS OFF HAND)

Damage: Moderate (High Over Time)

Effect: Evade, Bleeding (x3)(10 Seconds), Combo Finisher (Whirl)

Initiative Cost: 5

If you're wielding dual daggers, this attack becomes available. It's a godsend against almost anything you face. Leaping over your opponents has a defensive benefit because it allows you to stay mobile while attacking. The skill itself does adequate direct damage: hits everything you're close to, and slaps a Bleed on enemies, which seems to last for an eternity. Use Death Blossom early in fights, especially if there are multiple opponents. By the time the Bleeding wears off, everyone is going to be dead or vulnerable to Heartseeker!

SHADOW SHOT (PISTOL AS OFF HAND)

Damage: Very High

Effect: Blindness (5 Seconds), Combo Finisher (Physical Projectile)

Initiative Cost: 4

Shadow Shot has high burst damage potential and mitigates enemy damage as you shadowstep toward targets. They'll miss their next attack, and you get to lay into them in the meantime. If you stagger Shadow Shots, you can knock out three enemy attacks in a fairly short period, all the while doing enough damage to put serious fear into your victims.

TWISTING FANGS (NO OFF HAND CHOSEN)

Damage: Low (High Over Time)

Effect: Bleeding (10 Seconds)

Initiative Cost: 4

Throw long-term Bleeding effects on nearby enemies without investing much time or initiative. The initial damage output isn't very good, but this is an awful attack to use late in the battle. Start with it and let enemies Bleed while you build your initiative back.

DANCING DAGGER (OFF HAND)

Damage: High

Effect: Cripple (5 Seconds), Combo Finisher (Physical Projectile)

Initiative Cost: 3

Dual daggers don't normally have that much range, even with Heartseeker's leap. You need to have something in your arsenal to avoid being kited, and this is that attack. Dancing Dagger slows enemies down and gives you time to catch up to them. Though it can hit multiple enemies, you still do more AoE damage with Leaping Death Blossom. Save this for anti-kiting duties or long-range attacks.

CLOAK AND DAGGER (OFF HAND)

Damage: High

Effect: Stealth (3 Seconds), Vulnerability (x3) (5 Seconds)

Initiative Cost: 6

Cloak and Dagger hits a single target fairly hard and then puts your thief into Stealth. Run around behind the target and nail him with your "1" attack. This transforms into a backstab that does a substantial amount of damage. Cloak and Dagger helps for killing high-end enemies, like veterans and champions. It's fun against real players as well, though skilled opponents can mitigate some damage by rolling away or trying to whirl around so they don't eat the backstab as badly.

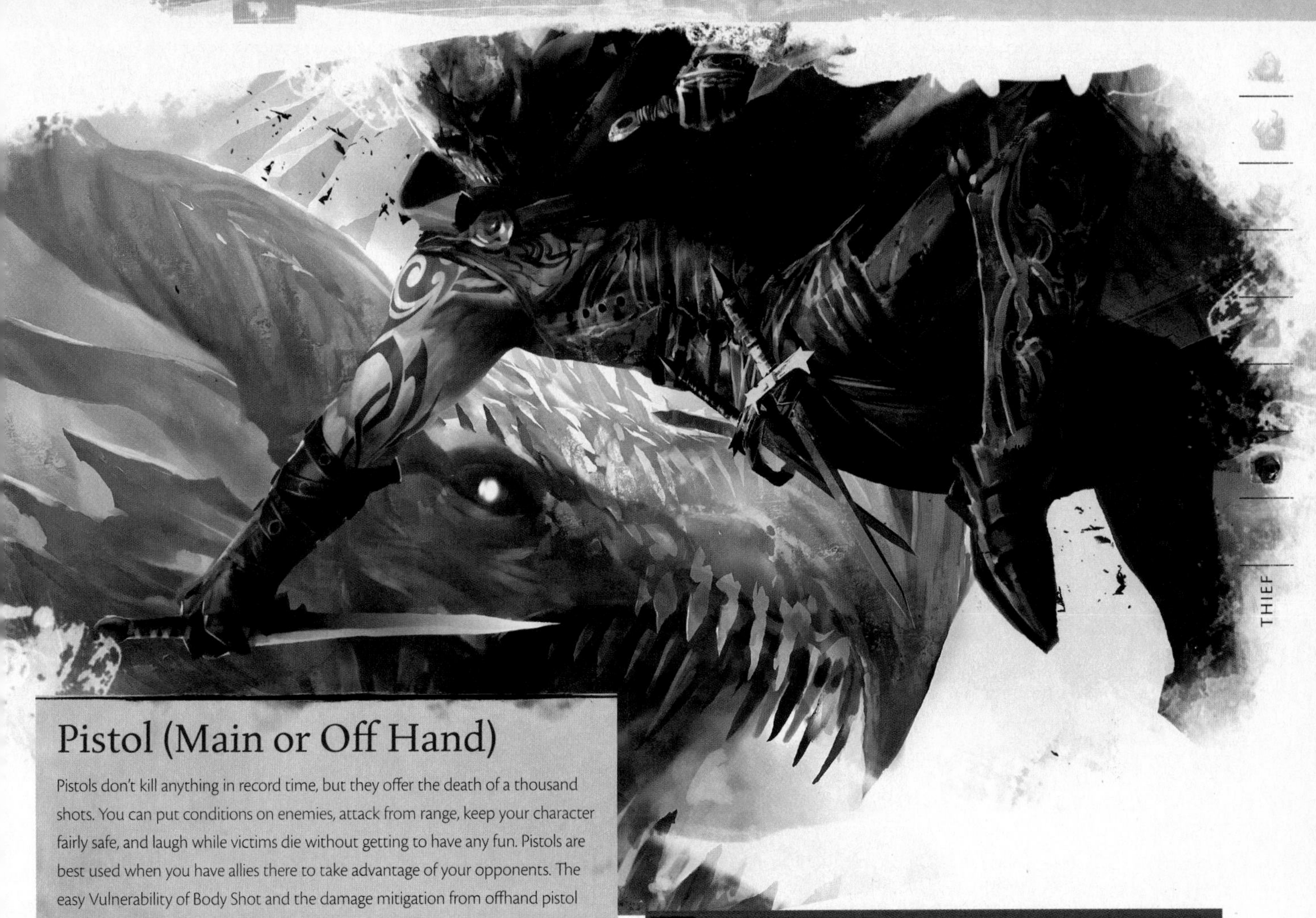

Pistol (Main or Off Hand)

Pistols don't kill anything in record time, but they offer the death of a thousand shots. You can put conditions on enemies, attack from range, keep your character fairly safe, and laugh while victims die without getting to have any fun. Pistols are best used when you have allies there to take advantage of your opponents. The easy Vulnerability of Body Shot and the damage mitigation from offhand pistol attacks are both excellent when you have a friend who knows how to deal real damage. Another fun trick is to bring pistols into your main weapon setup and something especially deadly in your secondary setup. Weaken the enemies early in the fight and then come out swinging with your high-damage gear later on.

VITAL SHOT (MAIN HAND)

Damage:	Moderate
Effect:	Bleed (4 Seconds), Combo Finisher (Physical Projectile: 20% Chance)
Initiative Cost:	N/A

Stack a few gentle Bleeds on your victims while kiting them around. Vital Shot won't kill anyone quickly, but your initiative is saved for attacks that make it hard to catch your thief!

BODY SHOT (MAIN HAND)

Damage:	Moderate
Effect:	Vulnerability (x3)(8 Seconds), Combo Finisher (Physical Projectile)
Initiative Cost:	3

Body Shot throws multiple stacks of Vulnerability on your target, with enough duration to make it count. When you're in a group, this is a wonderful way to boost everyone's damage against a single dangerous opponent. While soloing, it's a good attack to use before tapping Unload.

UNLOAD (PISTOL AS OFF HAND)

Damage:	High
Effect:	Channeled, Combo Finisher (Physical Projectile: 20% Chance)
Initiative Cost:	5

Unload is one of the few damage abilities in the main pistol lineup. Each shot it unleashes is rather weak, but the skill's fast-firing nature rakes in decent damage over the next few seconds. Though the attack is channeled, you can keep moving while unloading on your target. Kite away while your victim gets a face full of lead.

SHADOW STRIKE (DAGGER AS OFF HAND)

Damage:	High
Effect:	Shadowstep Away from Enemy
Initiative Cost:	4

If you're not finished softening an enemy at range, use Shadow Strike to hit him with a dagger attack and then shadowstep back a fair distance. The pistol attack at the end of the animation is where the big damage comes from. This is a useful kiting attack when you want to punish melee enemies for getting too close to your character.

REPEATER (NO OFF HAND CHOSEN)

Damage:	Very High
Effect:	Physical Projectile (20% Chance)
Initiative Cost:	5

Repeater is a single pistol version of Unload. You fire a fair number of shots and do a decent amount of damage. Unload is a lot more fun, so bring another pistol as soon as you can if you're into this type of skill.

HEAD SHOT (OFF HAND)

Damage:	Very Low
Effect:	Daze (1/4 Second), Combo Finisher (Physical Projectile)
Initiative Cost:	4

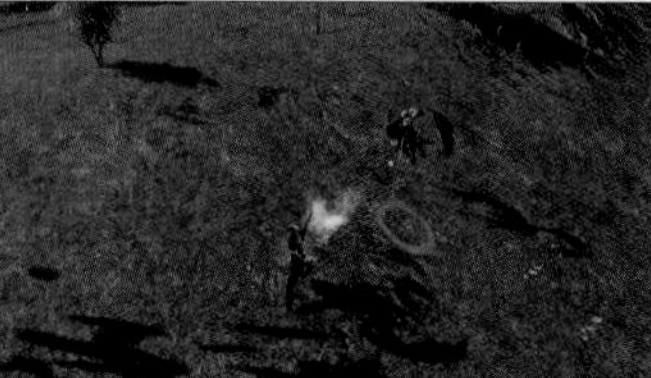

This is another mitigation ability. Head Shot stops single targets from using their attacks for a brief time. Interrupt charging opponents or those channeling attacks of their own. Watch enemy animations carefully so you can judge the optimal time to score a Head Shot.

BLACK POWDER (OFF HAND)

Damage:	Low
Effect:	Blind, Combo Field (Smoke), Combo Finisher (Physical Projectile)
Initiative Cost:	6

Set up a field of smoke with this attack. You and your allies can see through the smoke without trouble, but enemies are Blinded and have trouble landing attacks if they fight through the smoke. Sow confusion and avoid enemy damage with Black

Spear (Two-Handed)

Spears are short-range high-damage weapons in the hands of a thief. Though weak for AoE fighting, they're quite good at taking down single targets. Your thief can hit individual enemies quite hard and usually throw a condition on them to push the fight even more in your favor.

STAB

Damage:	High
Effect:	Poison (3 Seconds)
Initiative Cost:	N/A

The spear autoattack is a trio of short-range blows that eventually lead to a Poison effect. Your damage output is strong with the series, so it isn't hard to take down light targets, even if you're out of initiative.

FLANKING STRIKE

Damage:	Very High
Effect:	Evade
Initiative Cost:	3

Your thief quickly darts to the side and launches a powerful single strike into your target. Use this to avoid heavy attacks from underwater enemies or as a way to get a parting shot while beginning to flee from something.

NINE-TAILED STRIKE

Damage:	High
Effect:	Block, Counterattack
Initiative Cost:	3

This move puts your thief into a defensive stance. If no enemy attacks, you regain initiative after a few seconds. Otherwise, you block and counterattack the next enemy that tries to hit your character. The reprisal is composed of many small strikes that add up to some serious damage. This is your bread-and-butter damage attack with spears, so use it whenever the cooldown expires.

TOW LINE

Damage:	Moderate
Effect:	Cripple (3 Seconds), Pull
Initiative Cost:	4

Tow Line lets you grab distant enemies, whether they're kiting or just out of reach and you're eager to start the engagement. The immediate damage isn't high for the attack, so it's better to save unless you need to close the gap with the target. The Crippling effect makes it easier to keep up with ranged enemies trying to avoid you, so save your initiative for multiple Tow Lines if you simply can't stop your opponent from getting away normally.

SHADOW ASSAULT

Damage:	High
Effect:	Evade
Initiative Cost:	5

Shadow Assault is another attack for pure damage. Use it if Nine Tailed Strike is on cooldown and you're tired of basic Stab attacks.

Harpoon Gun (Two-Handed)

Harpoon guns are long-range underwater weapons. They're an excellent choice for thieves because of their kiting potential, mobility, and decent direct damage. Kiting weapons normally trade a fair amount of their killing potential for the ability to stay at range, but harpoon guns do pretty well with their trade. Spears are much riskier to wield, so if you prefer survival, these guns are the way to go.

Carry a set with each weapon so you can kite enemies with the harpoon gun and switch to spears when you need maximum single-target damage or don't have room to maneuver.

PIERCING SHOT

Damage: Low (Moderate Over Time)

Effect: Bleed (2 Seconds), Combo Finisher (Physical Projectile)

Initiative Cost: N/A

Piercing Shot blows through enemies in a line, giving it basic AoE potential if your enemies are clumped together. Let the Bleeding and direct damage add up after you've used your initiative on other attacks. This makes for great filler in between.

Remember to stay mobile and back away from enemies. Harpoon guns kill well over time, and you benefit heavily from exploiting your range underwater. Many enemies won't be able to hit back until they're in melee range.

DELUGE

Damage: High

Effect: Combo Finisher (Physical Projectile: 20% Chance)

Initiative Cost: 5

Fires a series of spears that do a decent amount of burst damage. Use this as a way to bring targets down quickly. Hit it when enemies are close to you and are low on health.

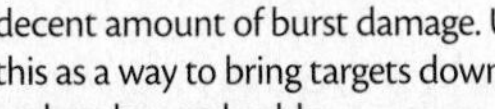

ESCAPE

Damage: High

Effect: Poison (1 Second), Combo Finisher (Physical Projectile)

Initiative Cost: 4

Escape causes your thief to swim backward, away from the target. A poison trail is left in the wake of the shot, so the enemy is forced to eat additional damage over time if he beelines toward you. Only human players avoid this, so AI-controlled enemies get hurt pretty badly. Even most humans won't think to avoid it, and if they do it takes longer for them to catch your thief. It's a win-win situation.

DISABLING SHOT

Damage: High

Effect: Cripple (5 Seconds), Combo Finisher (Physical Projectile)

Initiative Cost: 4

Disabling Shot lets you keep up the kiting for as long as possible. If you're dealing with a fast target or one that can shadowstep or charge into your character, hit him with Disabling Shot to slow him down and give your thief time to flee.

THIEF

INK SHOT

Damage: High

Effect: Blind (3 Seconds)

Initiative Cost: 5

This linear attack blinds everything in its way and then shadowsteps you over toward the target after several seconds. Use Blind to mitigate damage against especially deadly targets underwater. Alternatively, the shadowstep is nice if you want to switch to melee spear attacks. Blink over to the enemy, swap weapons, and then it's time to lay into your victim. Combine Ink Shot and Disabling Shot for a one-two punch of this type. You Blind the foe, slow him, and blink over with your heavier weapon ready to go.

Downed Skills

On the Ground

Thieves do more damage while downed than many professions. Use Venomous Knife and Trail of Knives to hurt your enemies, and then hit Smoke Bomb and Bandage immediately afterward to get some health back. Repeat the process if you can't kill your first target or heal, and hope for the best.

TRAIL OF KNIVES

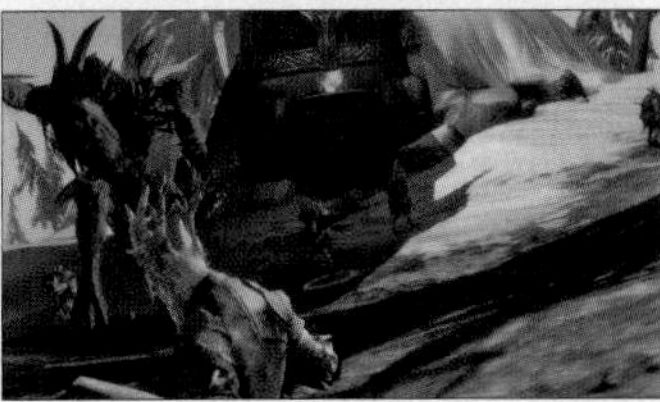

Damage: High

Effect: Cripple (1 Second)

Cooldown: 5 Seconds

Trail of Knives strikes nearby enemies for decent damage. Use this for baseline damage against single or multiple targets, especially if you're trying to slow down enemies to keep them from getting anywhere quickly.

SHADOW ESCAPE

Damage: None

Effect: Teleport

Cooldown: 10 Seconds

This move teleports your thief, so enemies have to find you again to resume their attack. Use Shadow Escape to buy time, hit the targets with Trail of Knives to slow their approach, and then drop a Smoke Bomb as soon as it's available to gain stealth (and access to Venomous Knife, a deadly stealth attack).

SMOKE BOMB

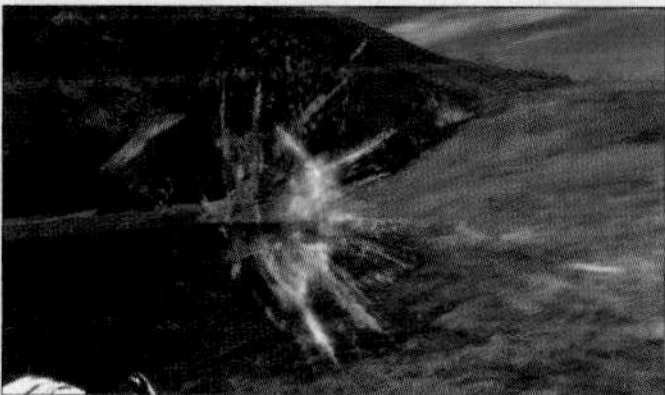

Damage: N/A

Effect: Stealth (2 Seconds)

Cooldown: 20 Seconds

Smoke Bomb buys your thief a few moments of peace. Enemies won't be able to find you. Use Smoke Bomb just before tapping Bandage so you get some extra health before enemies figure out what's going on.

BANDAGE

Damage: N/A

Effect: Self Heal

Cooldown: 5 Seconds

Use this to heal yourself if there aren't any enemies going after your thief. It allows you to recover fairly quickly. If you're attacked, the effect ends and you have to fight for your life once more.

Underwater

When drowning, you only have Diving Knife for any serious damage. Stab targets again and again, and use Cheap Shot to chase them off from time to time. When all of your abilities are ready, try to hide and heal as best you can.

DIVING KNIFE

Damage: Low

Effect: Bleed (6 Seconds)

Cooldown: N/A

This simple attack stabs at your enemy. Use it again and again to deal damage while the cooldowns for the other skills are turning. Alternate between Diving Knife and Cheap Shot to last as long as possible.

CHEAP SHOT

Damage: Low

Effect: Knockback

Cooldown: 5 Seconds

Cheap Shot does less damage than a stab from your Diving Knife, but it throws the target back from your character. Use this to reduce incoming damage from melee enemies while you're trying to rally.

VANISH IN THE DEEP

Damage: N/A

Effect: Stealth (2 Seconds)

Cooldown: 20 Seconds

Use this move to hide from your enemies for a couple seconds. Use Cheap Shot to get them away from your thief, use Vanish in the Deep to hide, and tap Bandage to get as much health as you can.

BANDAGE

Damage: N/A

Effect: Self Heal

Cooldown: 5 Seconds

Bandage yourself underwater just as you would above ground. Adventurers always have some handy waterproof bandages for exactly that type of situation!

Slot Skills

Healing

Thief healing is primarily about defensive options within the context of a healing skill. The two favored skills for more challenging encounters give options for either fast evasion or Stealth, and both of them let you heal your character while avoiding additional damage. Use these skills actively and time them well so you recover while getting away from the nastiest trouble.

HIDE IN SHADOWS

Effect: Regeneration (4 Seconds), Stealth (3 Seconds)

Cooldown: 30 Seconds

Hide in Shadows is an aggressive healing ability. The Regeneration over time is nice, and will help to keep your thief topped off on health, but that's not the only reason you would take this skill. It also puts your thief into Stealth, making it possible to unleash surprise attacks that do major damage. If you think the best defense is a good offensive, then Hide in Shadows is your type of skill.

WITHDRAW

Effect: Backward Roll, Evade, Self-Heal

Cooldown: 15 Seconds

Withdraw is a fast-acting healing skill that gets you out of trouble in the blink of an eye. The backward roll gives you an extra chance to evade when your Endurance is low, and the cooldown is so short that the skill can be used pretty much every time you fight something. This is excellent in small-scale PvP encounters. It's also wonderful when soloing because it can be used so often for health and defense.

When your thief withdraws, any Immobilize, Chill, or Cripple effects on your hero are removed. This is a wonderful survivor's healing skill.

SIGNET OF MALICE

Effect: Passively Grants Health During Your Attacks, Used to Actively Gain Health

Cooldown: 20 Seconds

Signet of Malice is an easier healing skill to use, compared to Withdraw and Hide in Shadows. The other options have more versatility (Stealth and condition removal). However, Signet of Malice isn't situational in any way. The health you get over time from fighting is modest, but it adds up. The active healing is perfectly adequate. If you're still getting used to the other two skills and want something very basic, Signet of Malice is great. Due to its defensive limitations, it's rarely a good choice for PvP.

Utility

Thief utility skills are quite offensive in nature. They're usually going to hit enemies with conditions or damage, and they help you control your fights. You won't get to bring along pets or buff your group well, but the traps, poisons, and maneuvers here are quite deadly.

TIER 1

SPIDER VENOM

Effect: Poison (6 Seconds)

Cooldown: 45 Seconds

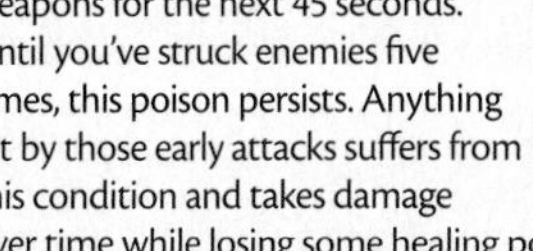

Spider Venom poisons your thief's weapons for the next 45 seconds. Until you've struck enemies five times, this poison persists. Anything hit by those early attacks suffers from this condition and takes damage over time while losing some healing potential. This is a magnificent PvP ability for burning down your opponents.

TRIPWIRE

Effect: Knockdown (3 Seconds)

Cooldown: 30 Seconds

Tripwire sets up a trap that knocks down foes after it's triggered. Knockdowns are worth their weight in gold because they disable enemies' movement and attacks for their full duration. Use Tripwire to limit enemy damage for a short time, buy yourself a chance to escape, or as a way to protect allies from monsters chasing them.

SIGNET OF AGILITY

Effect: Passively Raises Your Chance to Critically Hit, Used to Grant Endurance and Remove Conditions from Yourself and Allies

Cooldown: 30 Seconds

The passive part of this signet adds roughly 2% to your critical hit chance. That's not a ton of extra damage, but it's active all the time and you won't have to worry about when to use it. It's most useful when you're tearing through tons of lighter enemies and don't want to be bothered with more specific attacks.

The active use of Signet of Agility is far more interesting. The endurance boon it provides to your party makes this an extremely viable PvP or "boss fight" ability. Any time your group is running low on endurance, hit Signet of Agility to buy everyone a bit more dodging time.

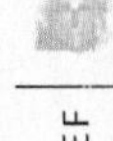

THIEF

ASSASSIN SIGNET

Effect: Passively Raises Power, Used to Deal More Damage for a Single Attack

Cooldown: 45 Seconds

Assassin Signet adds a trivial amount of base damage. It's almost always taken for its active ability; this preps your thief to do as much damage as possible on the next strike. Tap this before backstabbing an opponent and watch your numbers for some new records.

SHADOWSTEP

Effect: Break Stun, Shadowstep, Remove Conditions

Cooldown: 50 Seconds

At first, you would think that Shadowstep is a poor man's Infiltrator's Signet. The long cooldown and lack of secondary powers seem like a big deal, but wait a second before you judge this. First, Shadowstep does have a secondary power (it breaks Stun, saving your butt when fighting other players or especially deadly veterans/champions). Beyond that, the shadowstep from this skill is different than the one you get with Infiltrator's Signet. That skill lets you jump to an enemy. Shadowstep lets you go to a target enemy OR area. It's a free blink to wherever you want to go. That makes this useful for fighting, fleeing, or running through the wilderness.

And after all that, you can use the ability again to return to your starting position and drop three conditions off of your hero. Shadowstep is a PvP gift to thieves.

SCORPION WIRE

Effect: Moderate Damage, Combo Finisher (Physical Projectile)

Cooldown: 30 Seconds

Control the field to win the day. This skill keeps people from kiting your thief. Use it as a sword or dagger fighter to ensure enemies always play by your rules. Pull them, slow the targets down, and waste the fools.

CALTROPS

Effect: Bleed (2 Seconds), Cripple (2 Seconds), Duration (14 Seconds)

Cooldown: 30 Seconds

This skill creates a field of Caltrops that slow down anything that gets too close to your thief. The damage from these Caltrops isn't much, so use this as a disabling attack while kiting enemies, stopping runners, or fleeing from battle.

TIER 2

SKALE VENOM

Effect: Vulnerability (5 Seconds), Weakness (5 Seconds)

Cooldown: 45 Seconds

Skale Venom poisons your thief's weapons for 45 seconds. The next few attacks throw Vulnerability and Weakness on targets, making it harder for the enemies to dodge, and increasing the damage they take. Skale Venom is a general-purpose skill. It's good whether you're fighting monsters or other players.

ICE DRAKE VENOM

Effect: Chill (6 Seconds)

Cooldown: 45 Seconds

Ice Drake Venom, like all thief poisons, lasts for 45 seconds. The next few attacks your thief makes during this time will affect targets by slamming them with Chill. The enemies won't move as quickly, and their recharge times are increased. This is a wonderful skill to use when kiting powerful enemies, such as veterans and champions. It's good against anything, really. The lack of direct damage influence says nothing because this skill lets your character control the fight. Take this as a massive defensive option.

NEEDLE TRAP

Effect: Light Damage, Poison (15 Seconds), Immobilize (5 Seconds)

Cooldown: 40 Seconds

Needle Trap is extremely powerful. When you place the trap, it creates a line on both sides of your character. When crossed, the trap damages, Poisons, and Immobilizes your opponent. Kiting characters get so much out of this because they can drop the trap while fleeing and let enemies race right over it.

SHADOW TRAP

Effect: Stealth (5 Seconds), Shadowstep

Cooldown: 30 Seconds

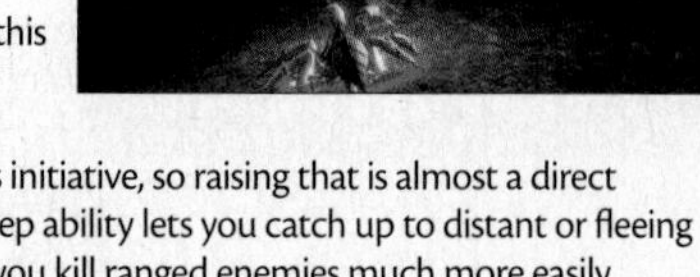

Shadow Trap is interesting—it doesn't function the way most traps do. You're not trying to damage or put conditions on your enemy. Instead, you're giving yourself a chance to ambush the victim. When triggered, the trap pulls your thief back to your victim's location and throws you into Stealth. It's backstab time! Ideal for PvP use when you're guarding a location and want to start a fight entirely in your favor. Lay the trap at a chokepoint when enemies are approaching, and slam them when they step inside.

INFILTRATOR'S SIGNET

Effect: Break Stun, Improves Initiative Regeneration, Used to Shadowstep to Your Foe

Cooldown: 30 Seconds

Melee thieves get quite a bit from this signet. The Initiative Regeneration, though minor, is still a godsend. Almost everything you do requires initiative, so raising that is almost a direct damage boon. Then, the shadowstep ability lets you catch up to distant or fleeing enemies without delay. This helps you kill ranged enemies much more easily. Pop over to them, use attacks that Cripple/Chill them, and the rest is history.

HASTE

Effect: Break Stun, Quickness (6 Seconds)

Cooldown: 60 Seconds

Haste turns a fight around when you're in trouble. For a short time, your character can lay on the damage with blinding speed. The output of your character roughly doubles for 6 seconds, so use your best and most immediately damaging attacks during this time. Make sure your initiative is high before starting Haste so you can throw down whatever you like.

The downside of Haste is that the ability drains your endurance and prevents it from regenerating until the effect runs out. Before you activate Haste, make sure you won't need evasive dodging. And, if something goes wrong, use weapon abilities with built-in evasive aspects to get out of trouble.

BLINDING POWDER

Effect: Blind (5 Seconds), Stealth (3 Seconds)

Cooldown: 60 Seconds

This mitigation ability disrupts enemies by causing all foes nearby to miss their next attack. Meanwhile, you and your allies are Stealthed, so everyone can avoid a little additional damage while they reposition, flee, or reengage. Use Blinding Powder during a major rush of incoming opponents. Many players and monsters use some of their best attacks in the first few seconds, and Blinding Powder can trivialize this sudden burst of damage.

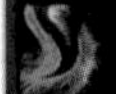

TIER 3

DEVOURER VENOM

Effect: Immobilize (3 Seconds)

Cooldown: 45 Seconds

Your thief's weapons are poisoned for 45 seconds. The next two attacks Immobilize the target for a few seconds. Similar to Ice Drake Venom, this gives you a way to control encounters. It's weak against general monsters in PvE, but powerful against veterans, champions, and human players that rely on melee attacks.

AMBUSH

Effect: Summon Ally (20 Seconds)

Cooldown: 35 Seconds

Ambush sets a trap that creates a short-duration pet for your thief once triggered. You get 20 seconds of increased damage output, and the distraction caused by having a new ally appear in the fight. This is compounded if you follow with an ability that grants Stealth, letting you backstab, flee, or do whatever you want while your opponent focuses on the new threat.

SIGNET OF SHADOWS

Effect: Passively Increases Movement by 25%, Blind (5 Seconds)

Cooldown: 30 Seconds

Slot this skill every time you're exploring or hunting for resources. That 25% movement boon is great, and you'll learn to love it very quickly. In battle, the AoE Blind gives you five seconds to escape from pretty much anything. Use this to disable dangerous targets, or as a way to flee from unwanted encounters. That's yet another way to get around the wilderness quickly and with less hassle!

ROLL FOR INITIATIVE

Effect: Evade, Regenerate Initiative, Remove Stun, Remove Cripple, Remove Chill, Remove Immobilize

Cooldown: 60 Seconds

Except for having a slow cooldown, this is a godly skill. Use it defensively to avoid major attacks when a simple dodge wouldn't get you far away quickly enough. Use it offensively to get back a huge amount of initiative. Or, tap it to ditch conditions that are slowing your character. With great timing, you can get two or even all three of these benefits from the same roll! Rush in, use your best attacks, let the enemy do whatever he's doing, and then Roll for Initiative as soon as the foe readies a major attack. You get to evade it and come back swinging.

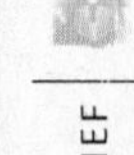

THIEF

SMOKE SCREEN

Effect: Blind (1 Second), Combo Field (Smoke), Duration (7 Seconds)

Cooldown: 30 seconds

Smoke Screen obscures the area, causes enemies to miss while they're inside it, and blocks projectiles that come through. Stand inside or just behind the screen to mitigate enemy damage from a variety of sources. Used in a group, this buys more time for allies to heal and it forces enemies toward your group instead of letting them stay at range.

SHADOW REFUGE

Effect: Area-of-Effect Healing and Stealth (4 Seconds), Combo Field (Dark)

Cooldown: 60 Seconds

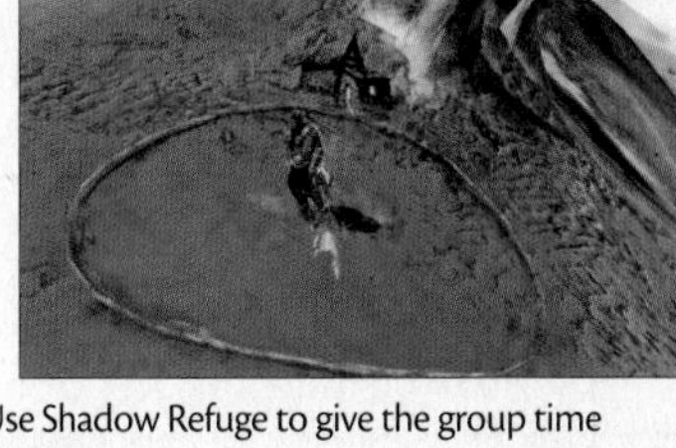

Shadow Refuge heals your thief and any nearby allies. During this time, it Stealths the party and causes monsters to lose interest in the fight. Use Shadow Refuge to give the group time to rally fallen members and get a little healing.

Elite

Thief elites don't have a central theme; they're good for a variety of situations. Take a look at what's available, and choose the one that sounds like it accentuates your playstyle the most. Save up points later for additional elites so you aren't a one-trick character.

TIER 1

THIEVES GUILD

Effect: Summon Thieves (x2)

Cooldown: 180 Seconds

Two other thieves join your party for long enough to help out with a few short fights or one extended encounter. These allies do considerable damage and use common thief attacks to disable enemies. The total damage output from Thieves Guild is quite high, and it's a great choice if you don't know specifically what type of fight you're going to have next. This is a perfect starter elite for that very reason.

BASILISK VENOM

Effect: Turn Enemy to Stone

Cooldown: 45 Seconds

Though initially Basilisk Venom seems like the weakest elite in the lineup, it's very effective once you've tried it out. The short cooldown means it'll be useful for many fights instead of those rare encounters that really test your hero. This venom gives you a way to disable movement and attacks for dangerous single targets. When you're alone, Thieves Guild is still the superior way to survive a fight against a veteran or champion. However, in groups, you use Basilisk Venom against major targets to mitigate the attacks from those enemies. You'll find this to be an enjoyable dungeon elite. You can use it against the primary dungeon encounters, and then switch to Thieves Guild for boss fights. Basilisk Venom's short cooldown means you rarely have to wait long to slot a new elite, so you won't hold up your group.

TIER 2

DAGGER STORM

Effect: Very High Damage AoE, Bleed (5 Seconds), Cripple (2 Seconds), Duration (5 Seconds), Combo Finisher (Whirl)

Cooldown: 180 Seconds

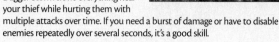

Dagger Storm slows everything near your thief while hurting them with multiple attacks over time. If you need a burst of damage or have to disable enemies repeatedly over several seconds, it's a good skill.

Traits

Deadly Arts (Raises Power and Condition Duration)

REWARDS

Points Invested	Ability Gained
5	Stealing applies Poison (10 seconds)
15	Weaken targets when you Poison them (3 seconds)
25	Deal extra damage (10%) if your target has any conditions

SKILL OPTIONS (GAINED EVERY 10 POINTS)

ADEPT TIER

- Back Fighting: +50% damage while downed.
- Poisonous Traps: Traps apply 10 seconds of Poison when triggered.
- Mug: Deal damage when Stealing.
- Venomous Strength: Gain 2 stacks of Might (20 seconds) when applying venom.
- Potent Poison: Increases Poison duration by 33%.
- Sundering Strikes: 40% chance to cause Vulnerability (5 seconds) on a critical hit (1-second cooldown).

MASTER TIER

- Improvised Venoms: Stealing has a 33% chance to recharge all venom skills.
- Quick Venoms: Venom recharges are reduced by 20%.
- Dagger Training: Dagger damage is increased by 5%.
- Combined Training: Dual skills deal 5% more damage.

GRANDMASTER TIER

- Panic Strike: Strikes you make at under 25% health cause Immobilize (2 seconds), with a 60-second cooldown.
- Residual Venom: Applied venoms last one extra strike.

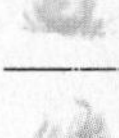

Critical Strikes (Precision and Critical Damage)

REWARDS

Points Invested	Ability Gained
5	Critical-hit chance is increased by 5% while your health is over 90%
15	Critical hits have a 20% chance to restore 1 initiative (1-second cooldown)
25	Higher initiative improves critical damage

SKILL OPTIONS (GAINED EVERY 10 POINTS)

ADEPT TIER

- Furious Retaliation: Gain Fury (10 seconds) when your target reaches half health (45-second cooldown).
- Signets of Power: Gain 5 stacks of Might (5 seconds) when activating a signet.
- Side Strike: +7% chance to critically hit while flanking an opponent.
- Concealed Defeat: Create a Smoke Screen when downed (10-second cooldown).
- Critical Haste: 10% chance to gain Haste on a critical hit (15-second cooldown).
- Executioner: Deal 10% extra damage when target is below 25% health.

MASTER TIER

- Fast Signets: Signet recharges are reduced by 20%.
- Hidden Killer: 50% critical-hit chance while in Stealth.
- Combo Crit Chance: Dual skills have +5% chance to critically hit.
- Pistol Mastery: +5% damage with pistols.

GRANDMASTER TIER

- Ankle Shots: Critical hits with a pistol have a 60% chance to Cripple foes.
- Signet Use: Gain 2 initiative when activating a Signet.

Shadow Arts (Raises Toughness and Healing)

REWARDS

Points Invested	Ability Gained
5	Use Blinding Powder when health reaches 25% (90-second cooldown)
15	Stealth skills last one second longer
25	Gain Might (15 seconds) when in Stealth (triggers every 3 seconds)

SKILL OPTIONS (GAINED EVERY 10 POINTS)

ADEPT TIER

- Cowardly: Regenerate health while in Stealth.
- Reviver's Deception: Grants 2 seconds of Stealth to you and your ally when you revive them.
- Shadow Protector: When you Stealth an ally, they gain Protection for 3 seconds.
- Shadow's Embrace: Remove 1 condition every 3 seconds while in Stealth.
- Infusion of Shadow: Gain 2 initiative when using a skill that Stealths you.
- Cloaking in Shadow: Going into Stealth Blinds nearby foes.

MASTER TIER

- Power Shots: +5% shortbow and harpoon gun damage.
- Master of Deception: Deception recharges are reduced by 20%.
- Leeching Venoms: Venoms steal health when activated.
- Patience: Regain initiative faster while in Stealth.

GRANDMASTER TIER

- Hidden Thief: Stealing grants you 2 seconds of Stealth.
- Venomous Aura: When you use a venom skill, you apply the effects to all nearby allies.

Acrobatics (Raises Vitality and Boon Duration)

REWARDS

Points Invested	Ability Gained
5	Evading grants Swiftness
15	Dodging refunds some of its endurance cost
25	You deal 10% more damage when endurance is recharging

SKILL OPTIONS (GAINED EVERY 10 POINTS)

ADEPT TIER

- Descent of Shadows: Release Blinding Powder when you take falling damage; falling damage is also reduced by 50%.
- Power of Inertia: Gain Might whenever you dodge.
- Vigorous Recovery: Gain Vigor upon healing.
- Assassin's Retreat: Gain Swiftness when you kill an enemy.
- Fleet of Foot: Dodging removes Cripple and Chill from you.
- Fleet Shadow: Move 33% faster while in Stealth.

MASTER TIER

- Master Trapper: Trap recharges are reduced by 20%.
- Pain Response: Gain Regeneration (10 seconds) and remove Bleeding, Poison, and Burning when you reach 75% health (45-second cooldown).
- Quick Recovery: Gain 2 initiative every 10 seconds.
- Martial Agility: Move 10% faster while wielding a sword or a spear.

GRANDMASTER TIER

- Hard to Catch: Gain Haste when you are Dazed, Floating, Knocked Down, Launched, Pushed, Sunk, or Stunned.
- Quick Pockets: Gain 3 initiative on weapon swap while in combat.

Trickery (Raises Condition Damage and Steal Recharge Rate)

REWARDS

Points Invested	Ability Gained
5	Stealing gives you 3 initiative
15	+3 to maximum initiative
25	+2% damage per point of initiative

SKILL OPTIONS (GAINED EVERY 10 POINTS)

ADEPT TIER

- Merciful Ambush: Create an Ambush Trap while reviving an ally.
- Pickpocket's Revenge: Increases damage by 25% with stolen weapons.
- Uncatchable: Leave Caltrops behind when you dodge.
- Flanking Strikes: Increases damage by 5% for flanking attacks.
- Thrill of the Crime: When you steal, you and your allies gain Fury, Might, and Swiftness.
- Long Reach: Increases the range on Stealing.

MASTER TIER

- Bountiful Theft: When Stealing, you and your allies gain Protection (5 seconds) and Regeneration (10 seconds).
- Trickster: Trick recharges are reduced by 20%.
- Initial Strike: Attacks in your initial weapon skill slot (normally bound to "1") have a chance to regain initiative.
- Ricochet: Pistol shots have a chance to bounce to additional targets.

GRANDMASTER TIER

- Hastened Replenishment: You receive 4 initiative when you use a healing skill.
- Sleight of Hand: Stealing also Dazes your target (1 second).

Thieves in PvE

Thieves are a profession that's all about skill—and we don't just mean the skills you learn or select. Thieves are a class that focuses on skilled use of your character. This is one of the worst choices for players who want to pull up to a monster, sit still, and fight it out. Thieves have weak armor, but even worse is the fact that their skills don't give them much additional mitigation without doing active things.

You have to be able to dodge and time evasive attacks properly to get the most out of this profession. They're just amazing once you master these mobile fighting techniques. It's so much fun to play thieves because the fights are dynamic. You're always moving, shifting, and planning. Players who get bored easily should strongly consider thief as their primary profession. To steal a phrase, if you get bored while playing a thief, "You're doing it wrong."

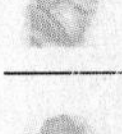
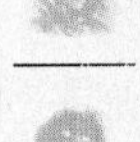
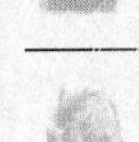

How do people excel in PvE with these characters? First off, make sure to get either two pistols or a shortbow as soon as you can. These ranged beauties are going to be part of your rotation by level seven at the latest. Though lower on damage than daggers or sword skills, ranged combat is a vital part of thieves' language of death. You can't survive easily in prolonged fights without some fun kiting.

An absolutely classic thief combo is double daggers in one slot and a shortbow in the other. Draw enemies out with the bow, pound them while backpedaling to get even more damage against the foes before they can hit back, and then swap to daggers for the mincing action.

Don't assume that power is your only route to deal damage. Thieves want a very high critical rate AND condition damage. You have access to plenty of Poison and Bleeding effects, and it's reckless to ignore that.

For most fights, you should lead with Bleeding or Poison attacks and let the direct damage follow. Many thief weapons have area-of-effect options here and there, so learn what these are. If you're facing multiple opponents, make sure to hit them with condition damage to make the most use of these damage over time attacks while killing your first victim. Death Blossom is a splendid example of this. This dual dagger attack lets you hit everything nearby, Bleed them all, and jump back for a whole second round of pain.

Make the most of your mobility skills. Look at how many thieves have! Stealing is one, and that's available no matter what configuration you're using. There are shadowsteps all over the place and free evades, and even healing skills usually give you either Stealth or a nice dodge. Harp on this advantage. Always try to get to an enemy's sides or rear. That's where you want to attack, even if you don't specialize in flanking damage.

Thieves in PvP

Thieves are masters of the PvP environment. Their traps and venoms are frequently effective against opponents. You get to start fights when and where you want (due to Stealth and the nature of traps). Through high mobility you can guard areas well ***and*** push forward toward new targets at high speed. Avoid fights that aren't in your favor, and always strike when enemies look the most vulnerable.

Guild Wars 2 doesn't let you have the crutch of permanent Stealth. That's a good thing, in a way, because it means that other areas of the profession don't need to be nerfed to make up for such a ludicrous advantage. You can't hide forever, but you won't need to. Race through areas, shadowstep to weak targets, or use evasive maneuvers to get away from people you can't afford to fight. Let mobility serve the same function as Stealth would in other games.

If you're on defense, load up on slot skills that let you draw out the encounters. Bring a ranged weapon, such as double pistols, and make the fights last for an eternity. Kite enemies, Shadowstep away from them if you get Stunned, and use Stealth and barriers that break line of sight to constantly force enemies to chase you without getting anything done. This gives your allies time to swing by and mop up the attackers you're kiting.

On offense, switch to direct damage and lock down enemies with Immobilizing effects of your own. Steal to get close to them, and then unload your slot skills to do as much burst damage as possible while your foe is kept close.

It's harder to backstab real players, but that doesn't mean it's impossible. Practice rushing behind people when you're Stealthed. Assassin Signet, a high critical hit rate, and backstab make for scary burst damage.

And always rely on initiative for that sudden jolt of power. Other professions can't use their best ability again and again. They need to wait for their cooldown. Figure out what you need the most and use it three or four times in a row, relentlessly.

Also, remember to finish off weakened enemies. Several prominent thief skills and traits focus on doing the worst things to injured enemies (e.g., Heartseeker, with double daggers). Don't be shy about jumping in on other people's fights to cherry-pick their victims. You're not stealing their glory; you're freeing them to attack even more targets.

Remember to hit Stability when you attack downed PvPers. That prevents their buddies from interrupting you while you slice down their friends.

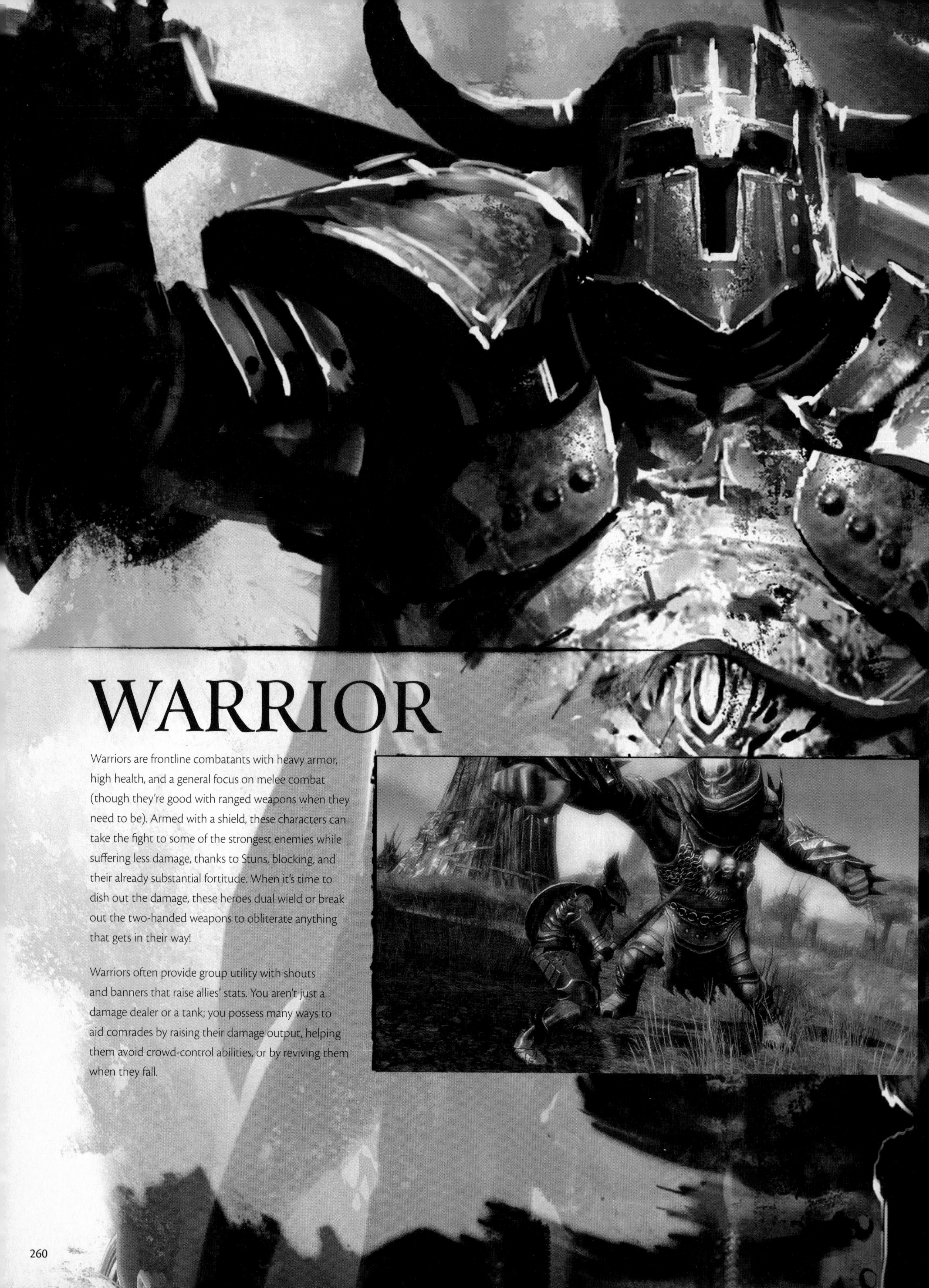

WARRIOR

Warriors are frontline combatants with heavy armor, high health, and a general focus on melee combat (though they're good with ranged weapons when they need to be). Armed with a shield, these characters can take the fight to some of the strongest enemies while suffering less damage, thanks to Stuns, blocking, and their already substantial fortitude. When it's time to dish out the damage, these heroes dual wield or break out the two-handed weapons to obliterate anything that gets in their way!

Warriors often provide group utility with shouts and banners that raise allies' stats. You aren't just a damage dealer or a tank; you possess many ways to aid comrades by raising their damage output, helping them avoid crowd-control abilities, or by reviving them when they fall.

You're most likely to enjoy this profession if you like melee combat, weapon variety, physical attacks (as opposed to magical), or using brute force. Because damage, mitigation, and group support are all available, there's something for everyone as long as you enjoy the preceding styles of play.

Profession Stats

Attribute	Starting Stats	Naked at Level 80
Power	24	1276
Precision	24	1246
Toughness	24	916
Vitality	24	916
Attack	158	1276
Critical Chance	4%	20%
Armor	106	916
Health	268	18,372

The preceding sample stats give you an idea of what to expect from your character. They show warrior progression through examples taken at the beginning and end of leveling. Your actual stats will likely vary from this.

Weapons and Weapon Skills

Warriors can use a massive lineup of weaponry. Like many professions, they can equip two sets of weapons at any time and switch between them even during battle. A standard grouping might facilitate a damage mode and a mitigation mode (e.g. Axe/Axe and Mace/Shield). This allows warriors to fight aggressively in most situations but still have the option to tank up quickly and defend themselves if deadlier opponents emerge.

Sword (Main Hand)

Swords focus on damage over time and high consistency. They don't burst very well, but their total damage output gets fairly high once you nail the target with enough Bleed effects. It's easier to keep up with mobile targets when you use swords; they offer a thrown option, a Cripple effect to slow targets, and an attack that closes the gap between you and your victim.

FLURRY (BURST ATTACK)

Damage: High

Effect: Bleeding (x8) (2 Seconds), Immobilize (2-4 Seconds)

Cooldown: 10 Seconds

Build adrenaline while wielding a sword so you can access this burst attack. Flurry takes a moment to wind up when you hit it, but then it unleashes a number of brutal hits on your target. These attacks pin victims in place and let you smash them to pieces. As with so many sword attacks, Flurry is a wonderful counter to mobile/kiting enemies.

SEVER ARTERY

Damage: High

Effect: Bleed (8 Seconds)

Cooldown: None

The basic sword attack starts the damage-over-time train rolling. It stacks a Bleed effect on your enemy and deals respectable damage. The autoattack is actually a series of blows, with its Bleed effects on the first two strikes, and a major damage boost on the final attack.

SAVAGE LEAP

Damage: High

Effect: Lunge, Combo Finisher (Leap)

Cooldown: 8 Seconds

Savage Leap combines decent damage with fun utility. Your hero leaps across the screen, either jumping forward (if nothing is selected) or toward your target if you have one. Use this to close the gap with enemies that are trying to keep away from you. Or, simply use it to travel quickly and get where you're going even sooner.

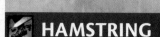

HAMSTRING

Damage: High

Effect: Cripple (7 Seconds)

Cooldown: 15 Seconds

Savage Leap lets you get to your enemies, and Hamstring allows a sword user to keep up with them. Slam evasive foes with this attack to slow them down and make it harder for them to escape. You can use Hamstring to obliterate opponents that try to kite or flee.

Sword (Off Hand)

IMPALE

Damage: Moderate

Effect: Bleeding (x4) (12 Seconds), Combo Finisher (Physical Projectile)

Cooldown: 20 Seconds

Impale is a ranged attack that stacks damage over time on your enemy. Use Impale when enemies take the initiative and try to charge you. Or, use it when Savage Leap is still cooling down, allowing you to still get damage on a target before closing to melee range. Impale is a great fight opener, especially against enemies that don't have the ranged abilities to hit back. Impale, Savage Leap, and then go into your normal routine.

This skill also has a secondary attack. Once it's used, Impale toggles into another ability so your hero can rip the sword out of your victim. Do this for even more damage!

RIPOSTE

Damage: Moderate

Effect: Block, Bleeding (x4) (12 Seconds)

Cooldown: 15 Seconds

Riposte gives you a way to mitigate one enemy attack by blocking it and then turning the blow around on your enemy. You avoid the damage from the next attack and then land a Bleeding effect on your target for 12 seconds. Use this when enemies look like they're winding up for an especially heavy part of their damage routine. Turn that risk into an opportunity!

Riposte is also a toggle skill. Its second version gives your hero adrenaline if no enemies are attacking and you want to prepare for the next part of your battle.

Hammer (Two-Handed)

Two-handed hammers provide high damage and the ability to engage groups of enemies while knocking specific targets around, keeping them off their feet. Hammers aren't quite as deadly as greatswords, but they offer more mitigation through their knockbacks and knockdowns.

EARTHSHAKER (BURST ATTACK)

Damage: High

Effect: Lunge, Stun (1-2 Seconds), Combo Finisher (Blast)

Cooldown: 15 Seconds

Use your adrenaline to activate this burst attack while you wield a hammer. Earthshaker is a ground-targeted AoE, and it hits everything in the affected area for serious damage. The fact that it also Stuns enemies is icing on the cake. Use this to close gaps, disable dangerous targets, or for the raw damage output. If it's easy to group your current enemies together, maneuver them into a single area and then slam the entire group all at once. By the time they recover, the odds will be heavily in your favor.

HAMMER SWING

Damage: High

Effect: N/A

Cooldown: None

Hammer Swing is a series of weapon attacks that puts some damage on any enemies close to your character. This doesn't have any secondary benefits, so it's more of a filler attack when you don't have anything more effective to do. That's fine, because most hammer attacks have a rather long cooldown, so you need something in between for taking out surviving enemies. The third swing in the trio has an area of effect that surrounds your character, making it possible to hit anything (and everything) nearby.

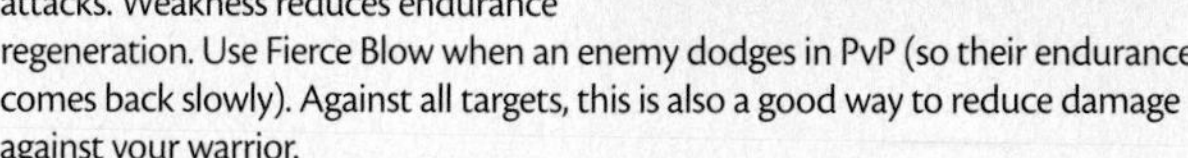

FIERCE BLOW

Damage: Very High

Effect: Weakness (8 Seconds)

Cooldown: 12 Seconds

Fierce Blow is a great way to stop targets from rolling away from your character or generally evading your attacks. Weakness reduces endurance regeneration. Use Fierce Blow when an enemy dodges in PvP (so their endurance comes back slowly). Against all targets, this is also a good way to reduce damage against your warrior.

HAMMER SHOCK

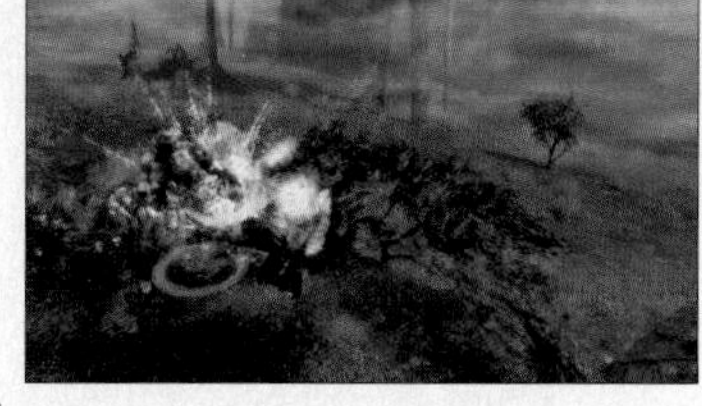

Damage: High

Effect: Cripple (7 Seconds)

Cooldown: 12 Seconds

Hammer Shock is a decent area-of-effect attack for targets in front of your character. Victims are hit for moderate damage and can't flee effectively for 7 seconds. Use Hammer Shock for its raw damage in normal fights with multiple targets. Even better, work in conjunction with another area-of-effect attacker. Get the enemies grouped together, hit them with Hammer Shock, and time it so your ally starts using his or her best AoE at the same time. The enemies can try to flee, but it'll be harder for them to escape.

STAGGERING BLOW

Damage: Very High

Effect: Knockback, Combo Finisher (Whirl)

Cooldown: 20 Seconds

Staggering Blow causes a mild knockback while dealing heavy damage to anything that's close to your hero. Use this to disrupt enemies that are lining up major attacks of their own, or just to slow down incoming damage from clusters of melee attackers. You get to beat on foes, but they have to close with your character a second time while your cooldowns are already progressing nicely.

BACKBREAKER

Damage: Very High

Effect: Knockdown (2 Seconds)

Cooldown: 30 Seconds

Because Backbreaker has such a long cooldown, you don't want to bring out this skill until you can get the most out of it. The attack disables your enemy for a couple seconds, so it's a great way to interrupt targets when they're charging for powerful attacks or using burst/elite skills.

Longbow (Two-Handed)

Longbows give warriors a chance to do damage to multiple targets at range. They're quite different from rifles, which focus on single-target disruption and damage. You can inflict much more damage with melee weapons as a warrior, but your survivability is higher when you stay at range. Use longbows to weaken groups of enemies that stay close together. If they rush you, switch into a melee configuration and chew them up. If they don't, exploit their lack of range by kiting the victims to your heart's content.

COMBUSTIVE SHOT (BURST ATTACK)

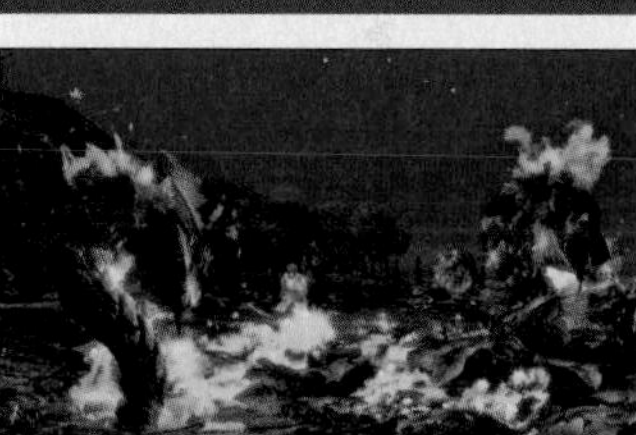

Damage: High

Effect: Burning (2 Seconds), Combo Field (Fire), Duration (4 Seconds)

Cooldown: 20 Seconds

Combustive Shot is the longbow adrenaline ability. It doesn't spike for very much damage, but the damage over time is fairly good. Enemies are engulfed in fire over a designated blast area. If you catch several opponents in it, you'll be quite happy with the results. Use this against targets that aren't moving much. Groups rushing a chokepoint in PvP or clustered enemies make wonderful victims.

DUAL SHOT

Damage: Moderate

Effect: N/A

Cooldown: None

Dual Shot fires two arrows into your target. There aren't any side benefits, and the overall damage isn't enough to kill targets quickly. Use this while you're on the move to kite enemies and deal some damage without letting the targets get to you!

FAN OF FIRE

Damage: Low

Effect: Burning (2 Seconds)

Cooldown: 8 Seconds

Fan of Fire sets targets alight in a forward arc. The damage isn't wonderful, but like all longbow skills, you can use it on the move. Circle around your opponents and stack DOTs on them with this and Incendiary Shot. The longer the fight, the more it plays to your advantage!

WARRIOR

ARCING ARROW

Damage: Very High

Effect: Combo Finisher (Blast)

Cooldown: 10 Seconds

Arcing Arrow takes a moment to activate because you have to select the target area. That's fine, because this skill is worth the extra effort; it's one of your only heavy-hitting attacks with a longbow. Use this as often as possible, even against single targets!

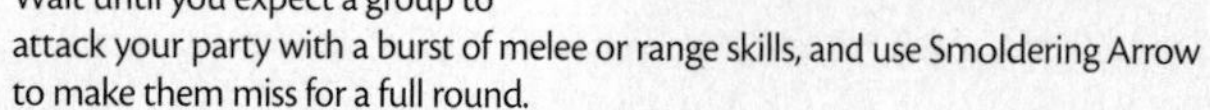

SMOLDERING ARROW

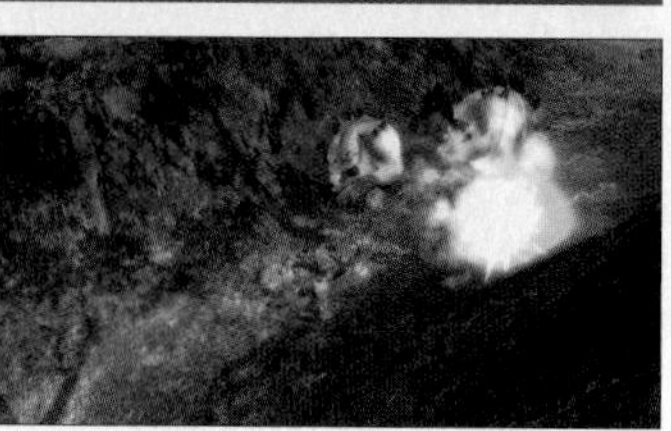

Damage: Low

Effect: Blindness (5 Seconds)

Cooldown: 20 Seconds

Smoldering Arrow is a damage-mitigation ability. Though its damage is low, you can use it to disable a small group of enemies for a short time. Wait until you expect a group to attack your party with a burst of melee or range skills, and use Smoldering Arrow to make them miss for a full round.

PIN DOWN

Damage: Moderate

Effect: Immobilize (3 Seconds), Combo Finisher (Physical Projectile)

Cooldown: 25 Seconds

Save this attack for times when you're kiting enemies. Pin Down stops the target from following you, providing several seconds to get more range or flee to safety. It's weaker as a damaging attack, so avoid using it unless you're stopping foes in their tracks.

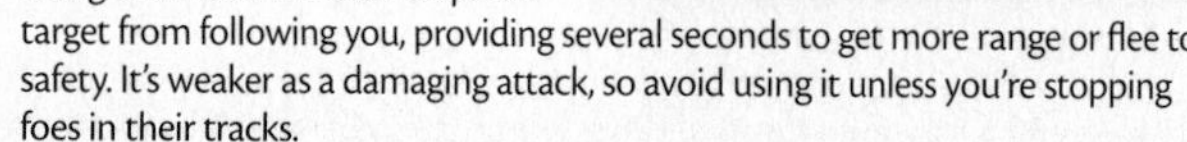

Axe (Main Hand)

Axes are not subtle weapons. You use them to hurt people (or to chop down trees, if that's your thing). If you want spiky damage to overpower adversaries' healing abilities, these are the right tools for the job. A pure DPS warrior can carry a two-handed weapon and an axe set, putting them at their best with group and single-target encounters. Offhanded axes are especially lethal. They don't have many secondary effects, but their damage output is frightening.

EVISCERATE (BURST ATTACK)

Damage: Very High

Effect: Combo Finisher (Leap)

Cooldown: 10 Seconds

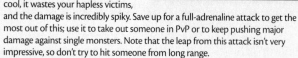

Eviscerate is an adrenaline attack that closes with your enemies and hits them for massive damage. It looks cool, it wastes your hapless victims, and the damage is incredibly spiky. Save up for a full-adrenaline attack to get the most out of this; use it to take out someone in PvP or to keep pushing major damage against single monsters. Note that the leap from this attack isn't very impressive, so don't try to hit someone from long range.

CHOP

Damage: High

Effect: N/A

Cooldown: None

This basic attack hurts enemies at close range. For an autoattack, Chop is pretty good at doing damage. It's also part of a trio that builds adrenaline very quickly. Use this autoattack so your hero can unleash burst skills as often as possible.

CYCLONE AXE

Damage: High
Effect: Vulnerability (x4) (8 Seconds), Combo Finisher (Whirl)
Cooldown: 6 Seconds

Cyclone Axe's short cooldown, decent damage, and ability to weaken enemy defenses make it a staple in any rotation. Don't wait to use this ability unless you're lining up a major AoE attack. It's often best to use Cyclone Axe as soon as it's available so you can keep your enemy's defense on its heels.

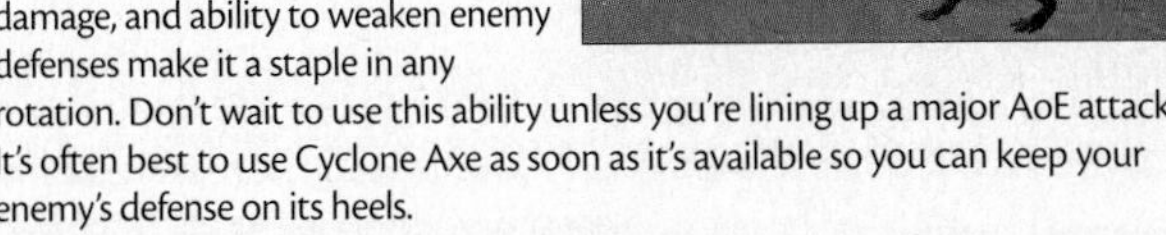

THROW AXE

Damage: High
Effect: Cripple (4 Seconds), Combo Finisher (Physical Projectile)
Cooldown: 10 Seconds

Save this attack to use against enemies that are fleeing or kiting your warrior. Slow them down with it and then rush forward for melee combat. The damage is inferior to Chop, so there's no need to use Throw Axe for its raw damage component.

Axe (Off Hand)

DUAL STRIKE

Damage: Very High
Effect: Fury (2 Seconds)
Cooldown: 12 Seconds

This attack raises your chance to critically hit enemies if one or both of your weapons hit the victim. Even without that buff, Dual Strike is sick and dusting. The damage output is beautiful, so you should use this every time it comes up. Use Dual Strike in combination with boons, such as Fury and Might, so your hero pushes out the maximum possible damage in one sudden burst.

WHIRLING AXE

Damage: Perfect
Effect: Combo Finisher (Whirl)
Cooldown: 20 Seconds

Whirling Axe delivers damage across a small area of effect. Killing enemies is what it does, so the attack fits into the axe lineup quite well. You are allowed to move while the attack is channeled, so walk through enemies, and keep as many targets as possible in front of your hero.

Greatsword (Two-Handed)

Greatswords are the easy choice for area-of-effect damage in a wide variety of situations. It's easy to get close to your enemies and then pound them with autoattacks that cover a huge arc and special attacks that are even more punishing. You won't find many ways to damage enemies over time or disable them; these weapons are all about basic killing power.

ARCING SLICE (BURST ATTACK)

Damage: Very High
Effect: Fury (x3, x6, or x9) (15 Seconds)
Cooldown: 10 Seconds

Arcing Slice is an adrenaline skill that hits your target for a single, heavy blow that deals high damage. Afterward, your hero gains substantial buff to Fury for the next 15 seconds. The more adrenaline you use, the more of a critical-hit bonus you get out of the strike. Use Arcing Slice before you start a chain of major attacks (when cooldowns for your best moves are finishing).

GREATSWORD SWING

Damage: High
Effect: Vulnerability (8 Seconds)
Cooldown: None

The greatsword autoattack is great for weakening entire swaths of enemies. Make sure your character is facing as many targets as possible, and then start ripping through their defenses. When you have allies to exploit this, it's incredibly powerful. Wait for enemies to have a few stacks of Vulnerability, and then switch to Hundred Blades for the *coup de grace*! As a trio of hits, this autoattack lands Vulnerability with the first two strikes, and then finishes with a heavy attack.

HUNDRED BLADES

Damage: Very High
Effect: Channeled
Cooldown: 6 Seconds

Hundred Blades lays into everything in front of your character with a series of lighter attacks. Each blow doesn't deal that much damage, but the number of total hits is daunting. If you have traits that land Bleed or Vulnerability effects on targets, this series of attacks becomes even more effective! Use it often, even against single targets.

The last hit of the sequence deals even more damage, so try to complete Hundred Blades whenever possible. Don't move during this skill's channeling time, as that breaks the sequence.

WHIRLWIND ATTACK

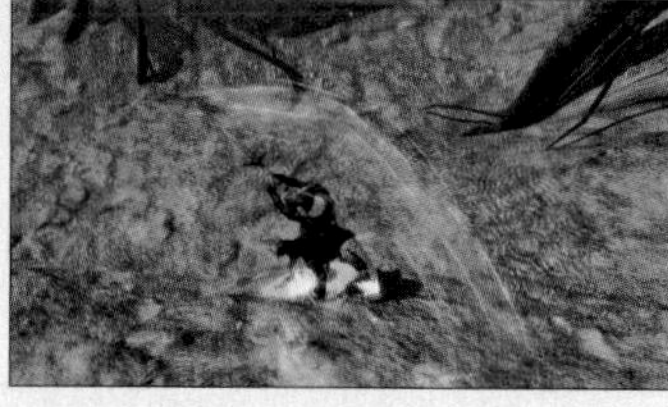

Damage: High
Effect: Combo Finisher (Whirl)
Cooldown: 12 Seconds

Whirlwind Attack causes your hero to charge forward, smashing through anything that gets in your way. The attack even hits enemies that come anywhere near your path, so this AoE does decent damage. If targets are near a wall, you end up hitting them several times because your character continues to spin and attack for a brief period. Another use is to spin away from enemies, hitting them in the process. While spinning, your hero evades enemy attacks, so Whirlwind Attack has a major defensive element as well.

When the animation finishes, turn, throw your greatsword with Bladetrail, and then use Rush to jump directly back into the fray. Enemies often lose their attacks during this sudden maneuver because they have to turn, switch to range, and still hit you.

BLADETRAIL

Damage: High
Effect: Cripple (4 Seconds), Combo Finisher (Physical Projectile)
Cooldown: 20 Seconds

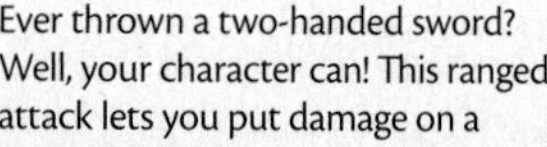

Ever thrown a two-handed sword? Well, your character can! This ranged attack lets you put damage on a target that isn't in melee range yet. Adding Cripple ensures the enemy can't get away from you, so this move is valuable against ranged targets that are attempting to kite you. Always try to throw your sword at enemies in the back of a group; everything the sword goes through takes damage, so this offers a tricky AoE if you pull it off.

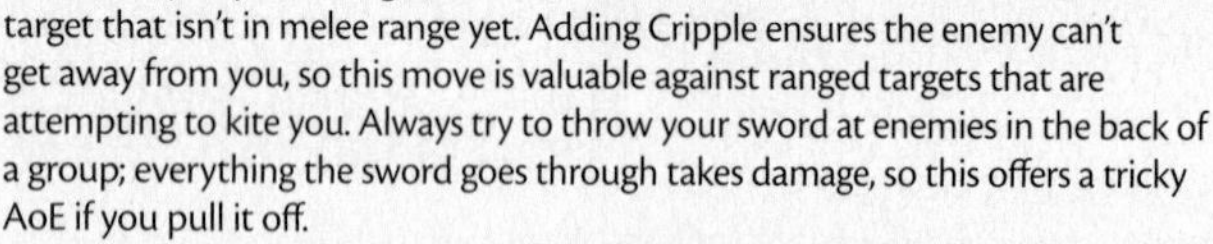

RUSH

Damage: High
Effect: Lunge
Cooldown: 20 Seconds

If you need to get to enemies quickly, Rush is the way to go. Watch the number under your icon. When it turns from red to yellow, you're within range. Rush over and get a free hit against them. This lets you reach kiting foes or ranged enemies, or simply engage a group of enemies sooner than normal. Rush through clusters of enemies to get their attention and start gathering them around your hero. This opens the way for your best AoE attacks.

Mace (Main Hand)

Maces have a strong array of status effects in an arsenal with decent damage. Your hero gains the ability to disrupt enemies while killing them at a moderate pace. You don't have the kill speed of an axe, hammer, or greatsword user, but you'll bring enemies down in relative safety. Mace plus shield gives one of the sturdier groupings in the entire warrior lineup.

SKULL CRACK (BURST ATTACK)

Damage: High
Effect: Stun (1-2 Seconds)
Cooldown: 15 Seconds

Skull Crack uses your adrenaline to stop a target from moving or attacking. Interrupt enemies when they're about to use their most damaging attacks, and use the free time to bash in their heads.

MACE SMASH

Damage: High
Effect: N/A
Cooldown: None

The mace autoattack hits enemies within normal melee range. Try to use Mace Smash in bursts. Its first two attacks are always rather weak, but the third hit of the autoattack is pretty darn good (and causes Weakness on your enemy). The heavy strike is worth your time, so try not to interrupt Mace Smash if you've already dedicated to one or two hits.

COUNTER BLOW

Damage: High
Effect: Block
Cooldown: 10 Seconds

This skill puts your character into a defensive stance for several seconds. You don't make any attacks of your own until an enemy hits you (or the duration ends). When struck, you negate the attack and then brutalize your opponent with an assault that inflicts immense damage. Use this to boost your survivability in a fight, especially if your enemy is using his deadliest attacks in a predictable manner. "Oh, they're charging up for another big attack—hit Counter Blow."

If the attack fails because you aren't attacked, your warrior gets some free adrenaline. This isn't ideal, but at least there is some compensation for your lost time.

POMMEL BASH

Damage: Moderate
Effect: Daze (1 Second)
Cooldown: 15 Seconds

Pommel Bash stops your enemies from attacking for a brief moment. Interrupt heavy attacks when Counter Blow is down, and buy yourself more time in the fight.

Mace (Off Hand)

CRUSHING BLOW

Damage: High

Effect: Vulnerability (x4) (10 Seconds)

Cooldown: 15 Seconds

Crack through an enemy's armor and leave him susceptible to further damage. This attack does enough damage by itself to be useful, so don't hold onto it for special occasions. Use it every time the cooldown elapses.

TREMOR

Damage: High

Effect: Knockdown (2 Seconds), Combo Finisher (Physical Projectile)

Cooldown: 25 Seconds

Tremor is a long-range attack that knocks down enemies. Mace users don't have many ways to rush their enemies, so this skill is essential for disabling foes that are running away from you.

Rifle (Two-Handed)

Rifles are somewhat low-damage standoff weapons for warriors. They target single enemies and disable the foe as much as possible. This is one of the best kiting options for a warrior, a profession that is not especially known for its kiting.

KILL SHOT (BURST ATTACK)

Damage: Varies (High to Very High)

Effect: Combo Finisher (Physical Projectile)

Cooldown: 10 Seconds

Kill Shot charges up and then nails a single target with serious damage. It doesn't have any bells or whistles, but that's kind of a good thing. Rifles need a direct-damage skill, and this is one of the few they get for warriors! When you need your damage to spike, use your adrenaline for a Kill Shot. Whenever you can, use this attack when you already have some range on your victim. You can't move and attack while charging Kill Shot, so your hero is exposed for a couple seconds.

BLEEDING SHOT

Damage: Moderate

Effect: Bleeding (6 Seconds), Combo Finisher (Physical Projectile: 20% Chance)

Cooldown: None

The default attack for rifle users is a ranged hit for modest damage. The Bleeding effect it stacks is a major help in bringing down targets over time. Alternate between Bleeding Shot and your various disabling attacks to keep enemies Bleeding while you kite them around the field.

AIMED SHOT

Damage: Low

Effect: Cripple (5 Seconds), Combo Finisher (Physical Projectile)

Cooldown: 10 Seconds

If you need to slow your victims, hit them with Aimed Shot. Otherwise, save this ability. It doesn't do enough damage to be worthwhile in a DPS rotation. Hold it until you need to stop someone from fleeing or approaching you.

VOLLEY

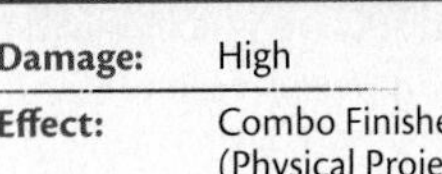

Damage: High

Effect: Combo Finisher (Physical Projectile: 20% Chance)

Cooldown: 10 Seconds

This skill channels for a couple of seconds while firing repeatedly at a targeted enemy. You can still move while attacking, so it doesn't break your kiting routine. This is a decent damage dealer because of the attacks' fast firing pattern. Each hit is only decent by itself, but the cumulative damage is quite good. Use Brutal Shot first to lower the target's defense, and then Volley as a follow-up.

Note that this is the best way to charge your warrior's adrenaline while using a rifle. Never let Volley stay available for long—it's meant to be used frequently.

BRUTAL SHOT

Damage: High

Effect: Vulnerability (x5) (10 Seconds), Combo Finisher (Physical Projectile)

Cooldown: 15 Seconds

Brutal Shot hits targets for adequate damage and then leaves them Vulnerable for a fairly long duration. Use this early in an encounter, and then rely on your most damaging attacks to knock the enemy down a bit faster.

RIFLE BUTT

Damage: High

Effect: Knockback

Cooldown: 20 Seconds

Rifle Butt throws enemies from melee range all the way back so you can keep kiting them. Its damage is very good for a rifle attack, so it's sometimes useful to let enemies close with you just so you can knock them back again, smacking them hard in the process.

Warhorn (Off Hand Only)

Warhorns are offhanded weapons that give warriors more group utility. They're not useful for direct damage. Instead, they Weaken enemies, remove negative conditions, and speed travel.

CHARGE

Damage: N/A

Effect: Swiftness (10 Seconds), Removes Cripple, Immobilize, and Chilled Effects on Your Allies

Cooldown: 20 Seconds

This ability really helps if you're out exploring the world. Having frequent access to Swiftness makes it easier to truck between waypoints without taking as much time. It's also good for harvesting runs, when you run through a region and look for metal, leather, cloth, and wood. In battle, this skill lets you protect your party from a variety of negative effects. If you're facing enemies that frequently use such attacks, Charge is a godsend.

CALL TO ARMS

Damage: N/A

Effect: Vigor (10 Seconds), Weakness (6 Seconds)

Cooldown: 20 Seconds

This ability is quite useful in PvP engagements. Teams like to disable the other players' endurance regeneration. If you can't dodge, you'll eat a lot more attacks. Call to Arms gives your side a major advantage in this. Allies regain more endurance while enemies get less. Larger groups and skilled players get the most out of this. Inexperienced players will find it less powerful because they often don't take advantage of their endurance.

Shield (Off Hand Only)

Shields help your warrior mitigate incoming damage. You hold the shield in your off hand and get skills that either stun your target or block damage directly. Both let you survive longer in whatever manner of encounter you're fighting.

SHIELD BASH

Damage: High

Effect: Stun (1 Second), Combo Finisher (Leap)

Cooldown: 25 Seconds

Bash enemies to interrupt them and keep them in place for a moment. If you time it well, you can stop aggressors in the middle of their best abilities. When targets stop to charge something, that's the time to Shield Bash them! You can also use Shield Bash to keep an enemy exposed for an ally's best attacks.

SHIELD STANCE

Damage: N/A

Effect: Block (3 Seconds)

Cooldown: 25 Seconds

Hunker down and avoid damage for several seconds with this defensive ability. Use it to survive boss' special attacks, charged players' abilities, or anything that just looks scary. Shield Stance is also useful if you need a few seconds before your healing skill recharges.

Spear (Underwater Weapon)

Spears are aquatic melee weapons. They inflict a huge amount of damage and can cut enemies from stem to stern in a matter of moments. Use your harpoon gun in one aquatic weapon slot, and a spear in the other. This way, you always have access to both range and high damage when you're underwater.

WHIRLING STRIKE (BURST ATTACK)

Damage: Extremely High

Effect: Stun (1-2 Seconds)

Cooldown: 10 Seconds

Burn your adrenaline to carve through enemies close to your warrior. Like most spear attacks, Whirling Strike is all about damage output.

STAB

Damage: High

Effect: N/A

Cooldown: None

Stick your enemy with the pointy end of the spear. Rely on this for damage when Mariner's Frenzy and Tsunami Slash are on cooldown. The final attack of this trio ends with a Cripple, so you can keep enemies from retreating.

MARINER'S FRENZY

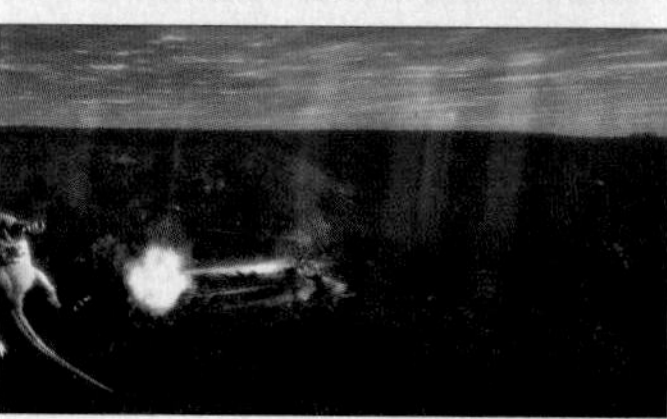

Damage: Very High

Effect: Channeled

Cooldown: 8 Seconds

Your warrior goes all stabby with this channeled skill. The enemies in front of you take major damage from eight rapid hits. You can move while attacking, so keep your enemies in front and watch the damage accumulate.

HARPOON PULL

Damage: High
Effect: Pull
Cooldown: 15 Seconds

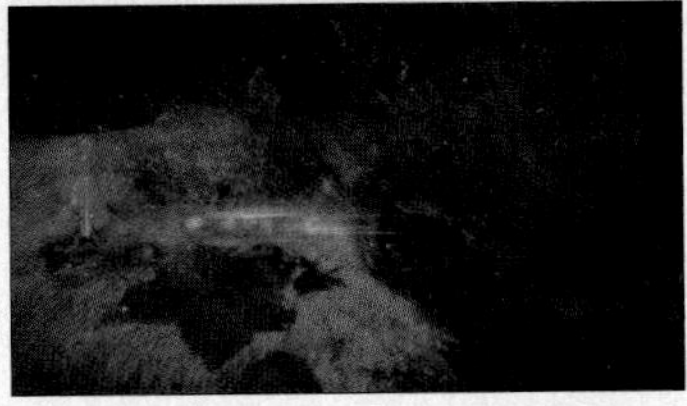

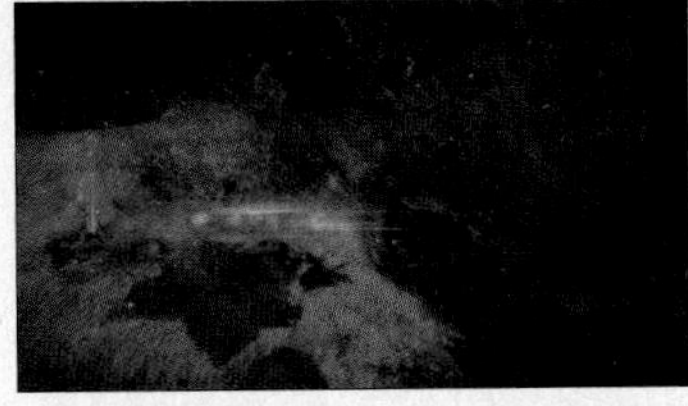

This attack doesn't have as much range as you might expect, so watch the number under the skill closely. Make sure you wait to use Harpoon Pull until the enemy is close enough to grab. Harpoon Pull isn't worthwhile as part of your damage rotation. It's better for pulling fleeing or ranged foes back to your position.

PARRY

Damage: Extremely High
Effect: Block
Cooldown: 15 Seconds

Parry puts your character into a defensive stance. If attacked in the next few seconds, your warrior responds with devastating force. Use Parry to mitigate charged or channeled enemy attacks.

TSUNAMI SLASH

Damage: High
Effect: Channeled
Cooldown: 25 Seconds

Your warrior twirls around and kills everything in sight. This is your bread-and-butter damage ability. Spears are good even without Tsunami Slash, but this attack makes them deadlier against groups or single targets. Save this only if your target is low on health or if you're setting up a bigger AoE in the next few seconds.

Harpoon Gun (Underwater Weapon)

Harpoon Guns don't have the AoE power of a spear, and they aren't as deadly even against single targets. Do you know what they have instead? Unfair, unreasonable amounts of kiting potential. These guns deliver damage to single targets at long range, and they afflict enemies with Bleeding, Immobilization, Knockbacks, and Vulnerability. Harpoon Guns work well in groups because you can support allies without getting into the thick of things. When solo, use these weapons to play keep-away with a victim who never gets a chance to catch up.

FORCEFUL SHOT (BURST ATTACK)

Damage: Varies (High to Very High)
Effect: N/A
Cooldown: 10 Seconds

Your adrenaline is turned into a single-target attack that hits for high damage. The more adrenaline you have, the more damage you inflict.

MARINER'S SHOT

Damage: Varies (Moderate to High)
Effect: Combo Finisher (Physical Projectile)
Cooldown: None

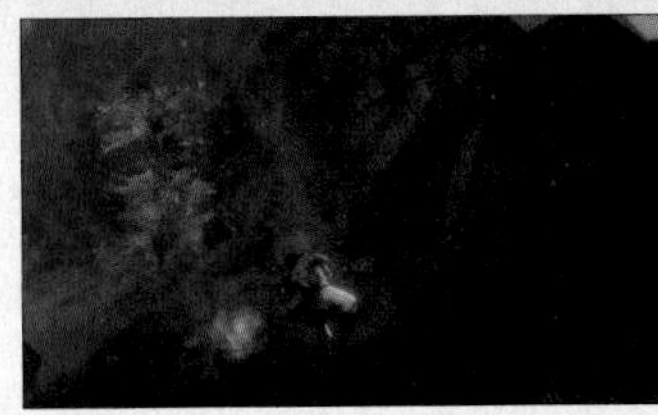

Mariner's Shot does more damage when the target is farther away from your hero. You end up using it a lot because harpoon gun skills have a fairly long cooldown. Hit the enemies with your superior attacks first, and then switch to Mariner's Shot while the others are cooling down. If the enemy catches up to you, switch to your spear.

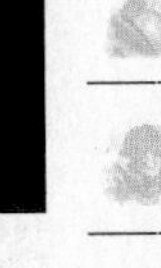

WARRIOR

BRUTAL SHOT

Damage: Moderate
Effect: Vulnerability (15 Seconds)
Cooldown: 3 Seconds

Reduce your enemy's Defense with this attack. It's meant to be used frequently throughout the fight, to keep Vulnerability on your targets.

SPLIT SHOT

Damage: Low
Effect: Bleeding (5 Seconds)
Cooldown: 8 Seconds

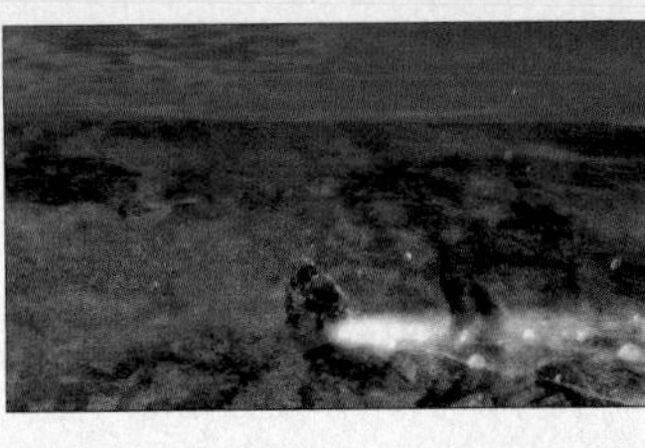

Split Shot shoots a spread of spears into the area. It has the potential to hit multiple targets in front of your warrior, and each one suffers a moderate Bleed effect. The initial damage is quite poor, but the total damage is fairly good, especially if you plan to kite the target anyway.

KNOT SHOT

Damage: Moderate
Effect: Immobilize (2 Seconds)
Cooldown: 25 Seconds

Hold Knot Shot until someone is preparing a major attack or is getting too close to you for comfort. Slap the foe with this for a short reprieve and get some distance between your character and the dangerous enemy. Do not use this as part of your damage rotation. Wait until you need it.

REPEATING SHOT

Damage: High
Effect: Push
Cooldown: 25 Seconds

This channeled attack pushes your enemy away with each hit. Like Knot Shot, it gives you a way to continue kiting a dangerous enemy. Use the two abilities at different times, and keep swimming away from your foe in between.

Downed Skills

On the Ground

Warrior ground abilities are quite simple. Deal damage with Throw Rock and Hammer Toss, Bandage if your enemies are distracted, or hit Vengeance if you're doomed and want to get in some kill time before the inevitable happens.

 THROW ROCK

Damage:	Moderate
Effect:	N/A
Cooldown:	N/A

This basic attack skill tosses a rock at one of your enemies. It has decent range, so you usually have plenty of target options. Try to kill someone with low health so you can rally.

HAMMER TOSS

Damage:	Moderate
Effect:	Knockdown (2 Seconds)
Cooldown:	10 Seconds

Hammer Toss puts a victim down briefly, earning you more time to attack the foe without him returning blows. Use this on your primary victim every time it comes up.

 VENGEANCE

Damage:	N/A
Effect:	Temporarily Rally (15 Seconds)
Cooldown:	30 Seconds

Get back up and fight! Your warrior doesn't stay up for long, but if your group needs you to give it your all, this is the way to step up. Hit Vengeance when you can make a difference and save someone who can revive you afterward.

If you're lucky, you can sometimes "rally" by killing something while Vengeanced. Each kill you make gives your warrior a chance to lose the ability's impending death aspect, so get out there and kill!

 BANDAGE

Damage:	N/A
Effect:	Self Heal
Cooldown:	5 Seconds

Use this to heal yourself if there aren't any enemies coming after you. It allows you to recover fairly quickly. If you're attacked, the effect ends and you have to fight for your life once more.

Underwater

Not much is different under the water. Warriors have a disadvantage in that they're reduced to short-range attacks, but you're allowed to move around underwater. Thus, it's not a big deal. Deal damage with Punch and Kick, heal with Bandage, or hit Vengeance if all is lost. Swim to the surface if you can shake off your enemies and escape.

PUNCH

Damage:	Moderate
Effect:	N/A
Cooldown:	N/A

Punch does exactly what you'd expect. Find a weak enemy and beat on him until he dies!

KICK

Damage:	Moderate-to-Low
Effect:	Push
Cooldown:	5 Seconds

Kick doesn't do much damage, but it gets enemies away from you. If more than one foe is attacking you, Kick the one that you aren't trying to kill so he's out of the fight for a few seconds.

VENGEANCE

Damage:	N/A
Effect:	Temporarily Rally (15 Seconds)
Cooldown:	30 Seconds

Exactly the same as Vengeance's above-ground variant. Your warrior doesn't stay up for long, but if your group needs you to give it your all, this is the way to step up. Hit Vengeance when you can make a difference and save someone who can revive you afterward.

 BANDAGE

Damage:	N/A
Effect:	Self Heal
Cooldown:	5 Seconds

Exactly the same as Bandage's above-ground variant. Use this to heal yourself if there aren't any enemies coming after you. It allows you to recover fairly quickly. If you're attacked, the effect ends and you have to fight for your life once more.

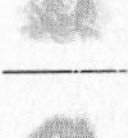
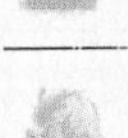

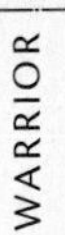

Slot Skills

Healing

Warrior healing abilities are very direct. You use them to restore your health, and that's about it. The side effects are minor and don't heavily alter the way you act within a group. Which one you choose at any given time is mostly a matter of play preference.

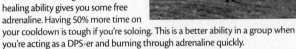

HEALING SURGE

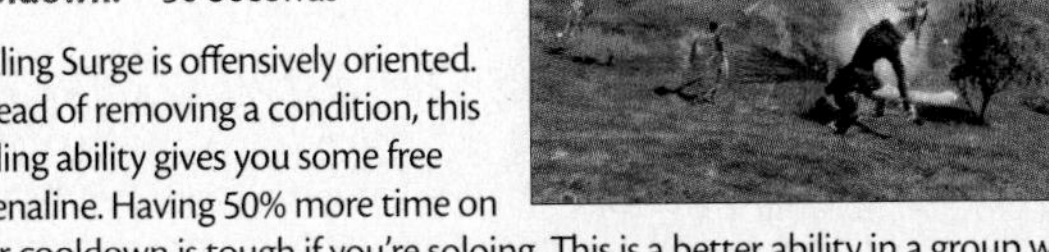

Effect: Moderate Self-Heal and a Boost of Adrenaline

Cooldown: 30 Seconds

Healing Surge is offensively oriented. Instead of removing a condition, this healing ability gives you some free adrenaline. Having 50% more time on your cooldown is tough if you're soloing. This is a better ability in a group when you're acting as a DPS-er and burning through adrenaline quickly.

MENDING

Effect: Heal Self, Remove Conditions

Cooldown: 20 Seconds

Mending is the most basic warrior heal. It's perfect for times when you don't know what to expect. The cooldown is short, so it's effective for keeping your health generally high. Soloers love it because they can purge their negative conditions and heal at the same time. Make this your default healing ability; you can't go wrong with it.

HEALING SIGNET

Effect: Passive Health Regeneration and an Active Self-Heal

Cooldown: 40 Seconds

Healing Signet restores about 1% of your maximum health every three seconds just for having it as your healing skill. When you use it actively, it heals your warrior by a considerable margin. If you're grouped with someone who can remove conditions, this becomes quite a viable healing skill. The regeneration helps keep you topped off during and between battles, and you still have the big heal whenever you need it.

Utility

Warrior utility skills are surprisingly group-friendly. You might expect a variety of attacks, but there are far more ways to buff yourself and allies. Most warrior signets and shouts are fast acting and you can use them during battle without breaking your routine. Banners are summoned and deployed near your character; they are often the source of your group buffs.

TIER 1

KICK

Effect: Knockback

Cooldown: 20 Seconds

This attack pushes an enemy away from your warrior. It's a great complement to bow or rifle skills, and it acts as a way to interrupt enemies even if you're a melee fighter. Is someone charging up for a heavy attack or channeled ability? Kick him away and then use one of your closing weapon attacks to stick with him.

THROW BOLAS

Effect: Immobilize (4 Seconds), Combo Finisher (Physical Projectile)

Cooldown: 20 Seconds

It's no fun to be kited by your enemies. Bolas help level the playing field by stopping your foes for a few seconds. Use this time to get in there and do some real damage. This works just as well if your warrior is the one doing the kiting; hit the enemy with this skill and run away to keep your distance. Either way, you get to control the battle! This is a very good PvP ability. It's decent in PvE, but the attack is more situational (e.g., when you're dealing with single, powerful monsters).

SIGNET OF MIGHT

Effect: Adds a Small Amount of Power to Your Hero All the Time, and Puts on Might (x5) (10 Seconds) When You Use It

Cooldown: 60 Seconds

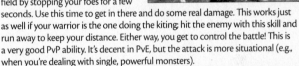

Signet of Might helps your baseline damage. The ability's passive side adds a trivial amount of Power to your character. You'd be better off with the higher critical bonus from Signet of Fury. However, the active Might is much more impressive. If your current weapon setup demands all of your attention, these fast bonuses are better than taking a more active ability, which you might not have time to use.

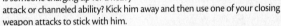

"FOR GREAT JUSTICE!"

Effect: Grants Fury (8 Seconds) and Might (x3)(25 Seconds) for Yourself and All Allies

Cooldown: 25 Seconds

This shout adds Fury and Might to you and your allies. You can't go wrong with this buff. It's decent even when you're soloing. In a group situation, it's a major improvement to the party's total damage output.

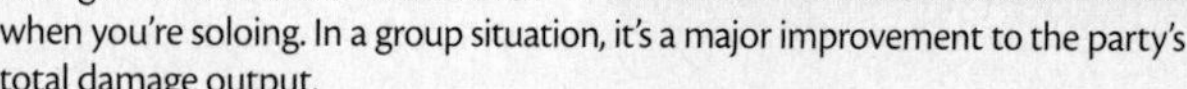

"SHAKE IT OFF!"

Effect: Removes Conditions on Yourself and Nearby Allies

Cooldown: 25 Seconds

This wonderful shout is a lifesaver in PvP or areas where the monsters have powerful conditions to control your party. If you or your allies are getting Stunned or otherwise disabled, shake off the conditions and resume the fight.

BANNER OF DISCIPLINE

Effect: Improves Precision (up to +80) and Critical Damage (+10%)

Cooldown: 120 Seconds

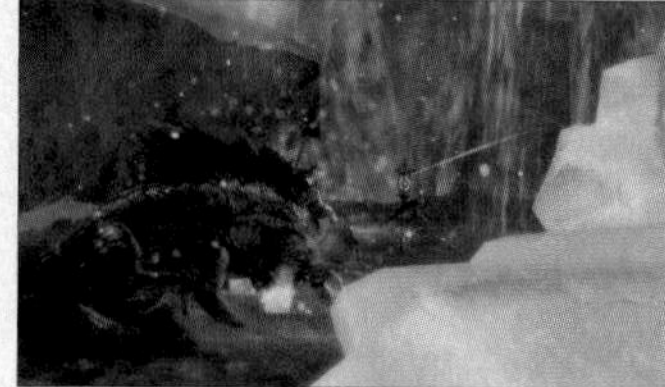

If your warrior's damage output is heavily dependent on critical hits, this is a nice banner. Some builds require criticals to put Vulnerability or Bleed effects on their victims. Deploy this banner during large fights and watch your damage output surge. Combine this with "For Great Justice!" to get as many critical hits as you can.

BERSERKER STANCE

Effect: Gain Adrenaline

Cooldown: 60 Seconds

For 20 seconds, your warrior gains adrenaline just by having this skill active. It's enough that you can gain adrenaline even if you're outside of battle. However, that is not an optimal use because you waste too much of it by being out of combat. Hit Berserker Stance early in a fight to give yourself as much punch as possible.

TIER 2

BULL'S CHARGE

Effect: High Damage, Knockdown (2 Seconds), Combo Finisher (Leap)

Cooldown: 40 Seconds

Bull's Charge is a physical attack possessing several advantages. First, it closes the gap between your hero and the target. Its damage is decent, and then the enemy gets knocked on his rump for two seconds. There are so many times when this ability will save your bacon. It's great against monsters or other players, it counters kiting, and it can interrupt adversaries who are building up their best attacks.

SIGNET OF FURY

Effect: Adds 10% to Your Chance to Critically Hit, and Adds a Full Bar of Adrenaline When Activated

Cooldown: 60 Seconds

Speaking of adrenaline use, Signet of Fury is great if your warrior is dependent on high adrenaline. The passive boost to your critical hit chance is already quite nice. Plus, you can smash down two major burst attacks by using your adrenaline naturally, hitting Signet of Fury, and then nailing your burst attack again as soon as its cooldown finishes. Two full-strength burst attacks in 10 seconds can be pretty powerful. If you have traits to reduce your cooldown on burst attacks, this is even better.

SIGNET OF STAMINA

Effect: Passively Improves Endurance Regeneration and Removes All Conditions When Used Actively

Cooldown: 45 Seconds

This signet focuses heavily on PvP utility. You can use it during PvE encounters if you like dodging often and need the extra endurance. However, you need the combination of that and condition removal the most when you're fighting other players; they use conditions against you more often and require active dodging to defeat.

"I WILL AVENGE YOU!"

Effect: Might, Regeneration, Swiftness (10 Seconds Each), Rallies Fallen Comrades

Cooldown: 85 Seconds

"I Will Avenge You!" does a little bit of everything. It has a short duration, but your hero gains several buffs during that time. If you kill an enemy, any fallen allies nearby are rallied. Wait until you know your buddies are down and one of your targets is low on health. Use this before you finish off the foe to turn the tide of battle completely.

BANNER OF STRENGTH

Effect: Buffs Power and Condition Damage (up to +80)

Cooldown: 120 Seconds

This banner raises baseline damage for your group, though not by a huge margin. If you want to stack as much damage as you can, combine this with a good shout—"For Great Justice!" comes to mind. On its own, there are better ways to pump up your damage. When soloing, avoid this entirely. The ability gets better the more people you use it on. The effect for one person is too low to be worth one of your utility slots, especially with such a long cooldown.

BANNER OF DEFENSE

Effect: Buffs Toughness and Vitality (up to +80)

Cooldown: 120 Seconds

Summon this banner to make you and your allies harder to kill. If you leave the area where it's planted, grab the banner and take it with you—you can do this with all warrior banners. The banner's effect adds several percentage points to your health and defense.

ENDURE PAIN

Effect: Damage Immunity (5 Seconds), Breaks Stun

Cooldown: 90 Seconds

Endure Pain is amazing for a variety of situations. As a soloist, this skill gives you the time to evacuate when things go wrong. It can also give you enough time to win a fight when enemies swarm you and you need to unleash AoE hell to thin their numbers. In dungeons, you can survive when everyone's heals are on cooldown. In PvP, you get to charge through an area, get everyone's attention, and draw fire while your team readies its reprisal. Endure Pain is your best skill for sheer survivability.

TIER 3

STOMP

Effect: High Damage, Launch, Combo Finisher (Blast)

Cooldown: 60 Seconds

Stomp throws your enemies up and away from your character. It's a full PBAoE, meaning you hit enemies even if they're behind your hero. This skill's crowd control aspect is great. You can put an entire team of players or enemies on their butts for a second. That's pretty huge for a single attack. The damage is adequate, but you can't set up for a damaging AoE afterward because the enemies fly off in different directions. So, Stomp is a great defensive ability, but it's tricky to work into a damaging AoE routine.

DOLYAK SIGNET

Effect: Passively Reduces Damage Taken, and is Used for Stability (8 Seconds)

Cooldown: 60 Seconds

Know your enemy! Don't wander around with Dolyak Signet all the time. Add the skill before you fight a specific person or monster that loves to harp on knocking your character around. It's great for certain PvP situations, and fun in places with predictable knockback monsters, like groups of spiders.

"FEAR ME!"

Effect: Fear (1 Second), Combo Finisher (Blast)

Cooldown: 95 Seconds

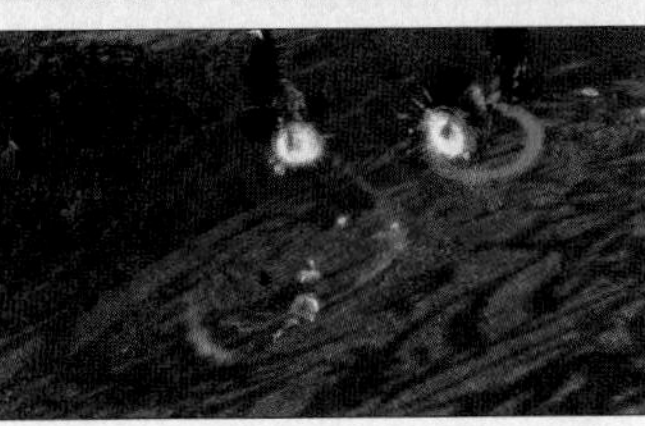

This is another good crowd control skill for warriors. The Fear doesn't last long, so it's more of a way to interrupt enemy actions than to send them screaming over the hills in terror.

BANNER OF TACTICS

Effect: Buffs Healing (up to +80) and Boon Duration (10%), Combo Finisher (Blast)

Cooldown: 120 Seconds

Prolonged encounters demand a great deal from characters' healing abilities. This game doesn't let people simply spam heals and live forever. Drop this banner to help your group survive a battle of attrition. It isn't great for solo or small-group play. It's more of a situational choice for specific dungeon encounters, elite events, or PvP.

BALANCED STANCE

Effect: Stability (8 Seconds), Breaks Stun

Cooldown: 40 Seconds

Similar to Dolyak Signet, this skill lets you avoid a number of crowd-control abilities. It also breaks you out of Stun if you're already affected by it. The cooldown is much shorter and the duration is a little longer. The minor tradeoff is you lose Dolyak Signet's passive benefits.

FRENZY

Effect: Quickness (6 Seconds), Breaks Stun

Cooldown: 60 Seconds

Frenzy breaks your hero out of Stun and puts you into a period of higher damage output. Your warrior moves and attacks like lightning, so use Frenzy when your best attack abilities are ready to go. Frenzy is ideal for offensive warriors in PvP, WvW, and PvE. It's pure liquid damage, ready to serve.

Elite

Warrior elite skills vary quite a bit in what they do. Let's discuss each in turn.

TIER 1

BATTLE STANDARD

Effect: Summon Banner, Stability (3 Seconds), Fury (3 Seconds), Might (10 Seconds), Combo Finisher (Blast), Revive Allies

Cooldown: 240 Seconds

Battle Standard is a superior elite skill for grouped warriors. It lasts longer than Signet of Rage, and the immunity to Stuns and Knockbacks that it provides is almost enough to pay for the skill by itself. You effectively turn an entire fight against your enemies by ensuring your group is the only side that can use much crowd control. That's huge in PvP, and it's pretty darn nice in PvE, as well. Have someone pick up the banner and bring it with your team to keep Battle Standard's effects as long as possible. It's even better if you're defending an area and can force the enemies to come to you!

SIGNET OF RAGE

Effect: You Passively Gain a Small Amount Of Adrenaline; When Used, This Gives You 30 Seconds of Might, Fury, and Swiftness

Cooldown: 120 Seconds

Signet of Rage is a soloist's elite skill. Every few minutes, you get to buff your warrior into a stronger killing machine. The increase in Power and critical hit chance is noteworthy enough. The higher movement rate helps if you're trying to catch mobile prey.

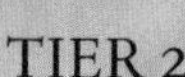

TIER 2

RAMPAGE

Effect: Juggernaut Transformation (20 Seconds)

Cooldown: 180 Seconds

This combative ability changes your warrior into a great monster that can wade through the battlefield. You have 20 seconds to knock your enemies around, gaining a number of crowd-control attacks during this time. Also, you become immune to all forms of crowd control, so no one will stop you until the duration ends, unless your character goes into a downed state. All of your attacks are high damage; here's what they do to their victims:

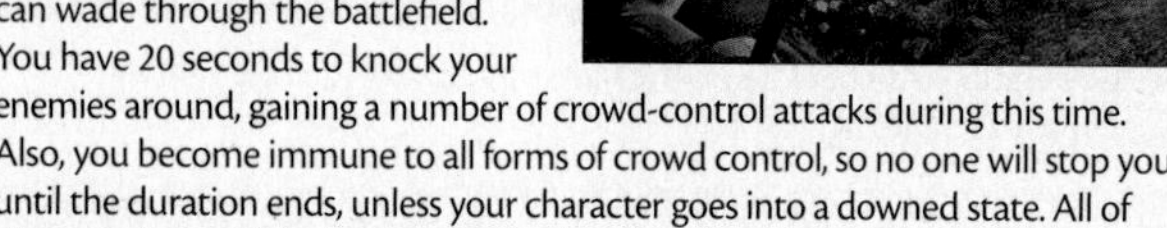

- Smash: A direct-damage attack
- Kick: A heavy Push (6-second cooldown)
- Dash: Charges at your target (8-second cooldown)
- Throw Boulder: Knocks foes down with a hurled stone (12-second cooldown)
- Stomp: Launches foes around your hero (15-second cooldown)

Traits

Strength (Raises Power and Condition Duration)

REWARDS

Points Invested	Ability Gained
5	Damage foes at the end of a dodge
15	Using a burst skill restores endurance
25	Damage is increased when your endurance is recharging

SKILL OPTIONS (GAINED EVERY 10 POINTS)

ADEPT TIER

- Death From Above: Damage and launch enemies when you take falling damage; falling damage is reduced by 50% for your hero.
- Restorative Strength: Using your healing skill removes Cripple, Freeze, Immobilize, and Weakness.
- Great Fortitude: 5% of Power is given as a bonus to Vitality.
- Short Temper: Gain 15 seconds of Might and one strike of adrenaline each time you are blocked.
- Berserker's Power: Increases damage by 2-5% depending on how much adrenaline you have.
- Powerful Banners: Banners deal AoE damage when summoned.

MASTER TIER

- Distracting Strikes: Apply Confusion when you interrupt an enemy.
- Weapon Specialization: Damage is increased by 5% while wielding an axe, mace, or sword in your off hand.
- Slashing Power: Greatsword and spear damage is increased by 10%.
- Physical Training: Increases damage of physical attack skills by 100%. The recharge on your physical attack skills is reduced by 20%.

GRANDMASTER TIER

- Axe Mastery: Improves critical damage by 10% while wielding an axe in your main hand.
- Victorious Might: Gain five stacks of Might (10 seconds) when you kill a foe.

Arms (Precision and Condition Damage)

REWARDS

Points Invested	Ability Gained
5	33% chance to cause Bleeding on critical hits
15	Burst skills have a 10% increased chance to critically hit
25	Increases damage to Bleeding foes by 10%

SKILL OPTIONS (GAINED EVERY 10 POINTS)

ADEPT TIER

- Deep Strike: +40 Precision for each unused Signet that you have equipped.
- Furious Speed: 10% chance to gain Swiftness (3 seconds) on critical hits.
- Deep Cuts: Bleeds you apply last 50% longer.
- Unsuspecting Foe: 50% critical hit chance against Stunned enemies.
- Rending Strikes: 33% chance to cause Vulnerability on critical hits.
- Furious: Critical hits have a 50% chance to grant an extra adrenaline strike.

MASTER TIER

- Gun Mastery: Rifle and harpoon gun skills recharge 20% faster.
- Blademaster: Increases your critical hit chance with a sword by 10%.
- Opportunist: Gain Fury when you Immobilize a target.
- Momentous Greatsword: Gain Might on critical hits with a greatsword.

GRANDMASTER TIER

- Sniper: Rifle and harpoon gun shots pierce.
- Last Chance: Gain Frenzy (4 seconds) when you strike a foe with less than 25% health (90-second cooldown).

Defense (Raises Toughness and Healing)

REWARDS

Points Invested	Ability Gained
5	You gain extra armor when health is above 90%
15	Regenerate health based on adrenaline level
25	10% of Toughness is added as a bonus to Power

SKILL OPTIONS (GAINED EVERY 10 POINTS)

ADEPT TIER

- Embrace the Pain: Gain adrenaline when hit.
- Turtle's Defense: Gain 200 Toughness when Crippled, Chilled, Stunned, or Immobilized.
- Last Stand: Activates Balanced Stance when you are Dazed, Knocked Down, Launched, Pushed, or Stunned.
- Vigorous Return: Increases health on rally.
- Missile Deflection: Reflect missiles whenever you are blocking.
- Shrug It Off: Activates Endure Pain at 25% health.

MASTER TIER

- Blunt Weapon Master: Hammer and mace skills recharge 15% faster.
- Sure-Footed: Increases Stance duration by 25%.
- Shield Master: Gain 90 Toughness while using a shield.
- Cull the Weak: Increases damage to Weakened foes by 5%.

GRANDMASTER TIER

- Merciless Hammer: Hammer damage is increased by 25% when a foe is Knocked Down.
- Sundering Mace: Mace skills cause Weakness (1 second) when dealing critical damage.

Tactics (Raises Vitality and Boon Duration)

REWARDS

Points Invested	Ability Gained
5	Gain 5 Toughness (per level) while reviving
15	Increased revive speed (10%)
25	Grant Might to nearby allies when you revive someone

SKILL OPTIONS (GAINED EVERY 10 POINTS)

ADEPT TIER

- Leg Specialist: Apply Immobilize (1 second) whenever you Cripple a target with a skill.
- Empower Allies: Increases the damage of nearby allies.
- Desperate Power: Increases damage when your health is under 25%.
- Stronger Bowstrings: Increases longbow range.
- Early Escape: Gain Vigor (5 seconds) when your health reaches 90% (30-second cooldown).
- Empowered: Increases damage for every boon on your hero.

MASTER TIER

- Inspiring Banners: Banners apply their bonuses to a larger area.
- Lung Capacity: Shout cooldowns are reduced by 20%.
- Quick Breathing: Warhorn skills recharge 15% faster.
- Burning Arrows: Longbow damage is increased by 10% against Burning foes.

GRANDMASTER TIER

- Inspiring Battle Standard: Banners also apply Regeneration to allies.
- Vigorous Shouts: Shouts heal.

Discipline (Raises Critical Damage and Burst Damage)

REWARDS

Points Invested	Ability Gained
5	Adds five units of adrenaline whenever you swap weapons
15	Decreases the cooldown on weapon swapping by 5 seconds
25	Adds Might (10 seconds) when you swap weapons

SKILL OPTIONS (GAINED EVERY 10 POINTS)

ADEPT TIER

- Mighty Defenses: Gain Might when you block an attack.
- Thrill of the Kill: Gain extra adrenaline for each kill.
- Warrior's Sprint: Run faster while wielding melee weapons.
- Inspiring Shouts: Gain adrenaline when using a shout.
- Heightened Focus: +2% chance to critically hit for stage 1 of adrenaline, 5% at stage 2, and 9% for stage 3.
- Sweet Revenge: It's possible to rally while Vengeanced.

MASTER TIER

- Signet Mastery: Signet cooldowns are reduced by 25%.
- Vigorous Focus: Gain Vigor when using a Stance.
- Sharpened Axes: Critical hits with axes grant extra adrenaline.
- Mobile Strikes: Movement skills break Immobilize.

GRANDMASTER TIER

- Quick Bursts: Burst skill cooldowns are reduced by 20%.
- Adrenal Reserves: Burst skills cost less.

Warriors in PvE

Warriors have a wonderous range of weapon choices, so that's the first thing you want to get your head around. Buy as many weapon types as possible, or simply start using each weapon you find until you unlock more of your skills. Keep at least a melee weapon and a ranged weapon in your inventory at all times. It's even better if you have a defensive melee set, a ranged weapon, and something for sheer damage output. At high levels, you can even push this to have two damaging sets of equipment, so you can swap between each during battle to maximize your skill use.

Warriors have to take more risks than most professions. They get into the thick of battle very quickly, and that means your hero takes damage sooner. Choose skills to have a set of fun toys for killing and a set for lasting longer in battle. When you go through easy areas, have fun with aggressive attack skills. Buff yourself with "For Great Justice!," attack with Bull's Charge, and relax. When you're getting ready for a dungeon run or elite event, swap your abilities. Pick skills to negate conditions or keep you alive. Endure Pain is a gift from the heavens, and don't ignore choices like Balanced Stance or Dolyak Signet for staying away from crowd-control abilities.

Practice swapping weapons. It doesn't come naturally to every player, yet it's an essential skill, especially for warriors. You get even more weapon skills at your disposal by jumping back and forth, and there aren't any real downsides to doing it. If you have a good kiting weapon, like a rifle, use it to hassle targets at range, forcing them to suffer while they try to reach your warrior. When they arrive, swap to a high-damage melee weapon to obliterate wounded foes. If you enjoy melee on its own merit, use a greatsword for massive AoE damage, and switch to a hammer if you suddenly need to hit an enemy with crowd-control effects.

Your banners are fun to keep around because they let people raise their movement rate. Note that you don't have to be the one who carries the banner. All of these skills create a physical banner that allies can pick up. When you play in a group, this is a fun way to race between waypoints or events. Slot a couple of banner skills into your bar and trade off so something is up for most of the trip.

Equipment-wise, you should look for Power, Precision, and Critical Damage for a full DPS set. That's your primary focus when soloing or running basic events. Then, get a Toughness, Vitality, and Healing set of gear later on, when you start running more dungeons and elite events. These make a huge difference in your performance. A DPS warrior that switches into a full set of gear with survivability stats will have more Health and Armor than someone with defensive traits wearing Power, Precision, and Critical Damage equipment.

You don't always have to switch your traits around to survive! Just make sure you have the gear for it.

Warriors in PvP

In PvP, many of your neglected skills come to the forefront. Anything that applies or breaks crowd control is suddenly quite useful. "Shake It Off!" is just amazing because it helps your team avoid a number of negative effects. If you're supporting a group that doesn't have much anti-crowd-control power, you can have a bar with that and additional skills to break Stun.

On the offensive, as a warrior, you want to be the one messing with the enemies. Throw Bolas is a sweet kiting skill. Use this to Immobilize foes out in the open, when they can't do much but soak up damage from everyone who sees them. Stomp gives you AoE crowd control, and you shouldn't ignore that, either. You can throw around groups that stack up near doors and chokepoints without much preamble. However, give yourself time to escape, or push into the group with high damage and your allies' support.

Battle Standard is a glorious elite skill for PvP. In a full group, this ability lets everyone avoid crowd control while upping damage and helping bring back downed buddies. You can turn around an entire battle by timing this properly. "I Will Avenge You!" is similarly wonderful as a last-ditch way to get your team back on its feet.

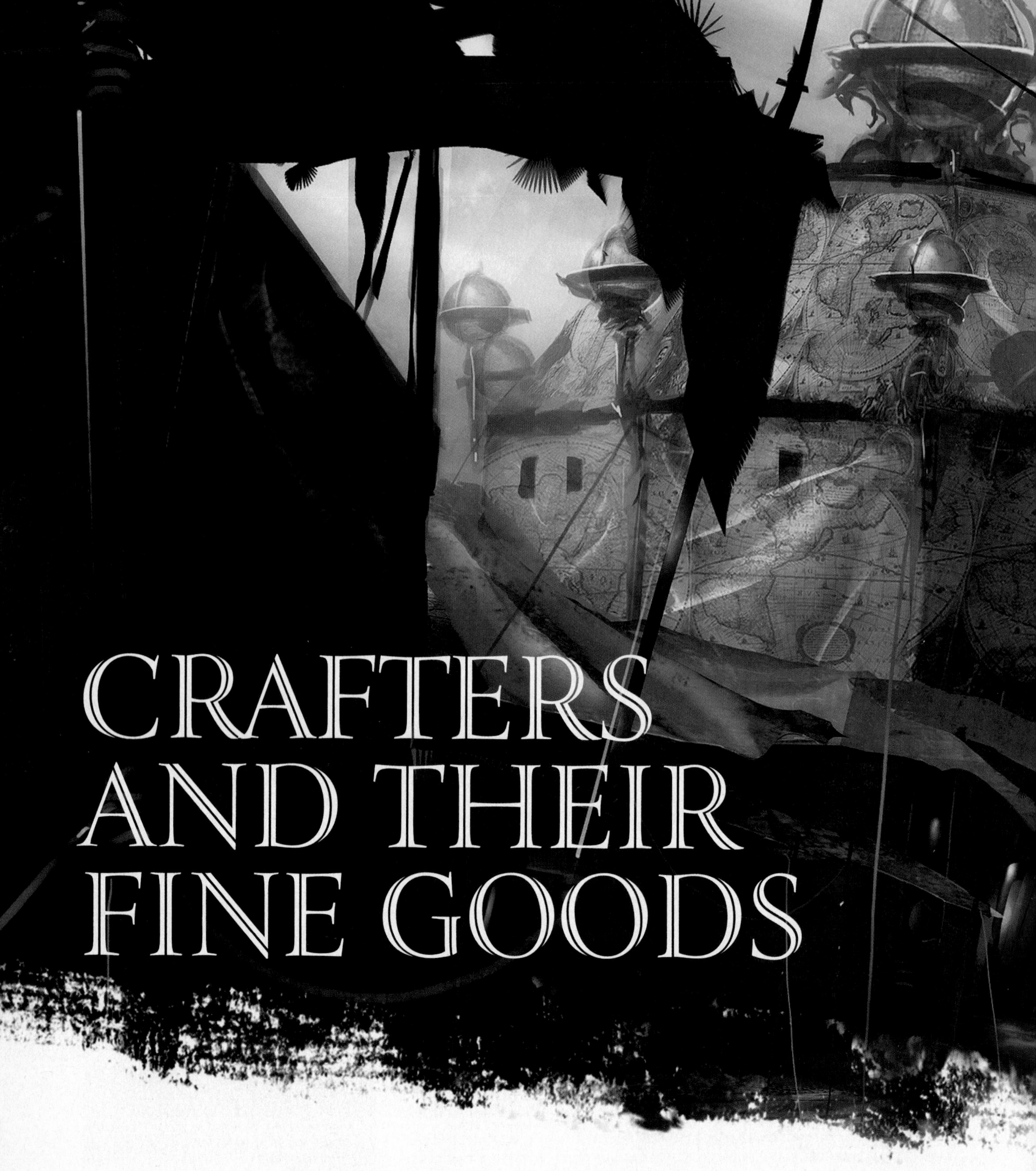

CRAFTERS AND THEIR FINE GOODS

Crafting is a good way to expand the independence of your character or your guild. The skills you learn make it easier to transform "worthless" items into usable equipment. Even if you aren't turned on by the idea of making goods for yourself, you might be interested in what others do. Read through this chapter to learn about the eight crafting disciplines and to find out whether you'd like to become a crafter.

If not, you can still learn what items are needed by crafters. This helps when selling things on the Trading Post or if you're supporting guild crafters by mailing them items or leaving items in the guild bank. You'll also get an idea of what each craft can do, making it easier to approach other people when you want something made.

TRAINERS

You can't teach yourself everything in this life or in *Guild Wars 2*. To take up a crafting trade, you need to visit a major city and look for the district that has all of the crafting trainers. These NPCs are always grouped together in a place that has forges, looms, and various other implements of trade.

Talk to the trainers to see what they teach, and pick up two crafts that fit your character well. If you have friends or a guild with specific needs, you might choose your crafts based on those people as well.

It doesn't cost anything to take up a trade. You just get the early recipes from your trainer and start making things whenever you want. In the future, you can come back to your trainer to procure goods that assist in your crafting. There are also rare recipes in cities that can be purchased with karma. Those are nice to have!

CRAFTING RECIPES

Please visit **www.bradygames.com/GW2updates** for a downloadable list of crafting recipes and other updates as they become available.

WHERE TO CRAFT

The crafting stations near your trainer are ideal for building anything from that given craft. You cannot make items out in the field, even if you have the proper ingredients. So, it's good to stash spare crafting items in your bank so you have relatively clean bags to adventure with.

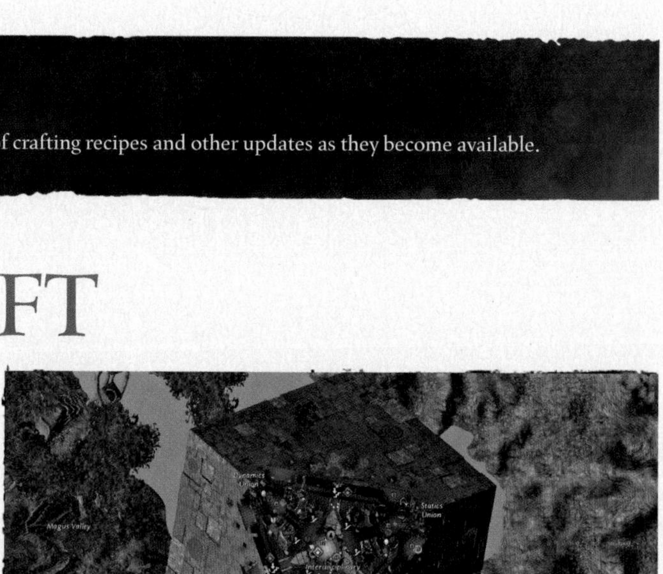

When it comes time to make something, get everything you need from the bank and then go to your crafting station. Every major city has what you need, but it's better to go to the same city every time (this cuts down on confusion as you travel back and forth, since you'll learn the best routes rather quickly).

Take the items to your crafting station and interact with the object to open the crafting window. You're ready to go!

RAW MATERIALS

It's nice to know what raw materials to gather. You can purchase things from the Trading Post or look out in the world to find everything you need. While deciding where to shop and hunt, open your Hero window ("H") and then click on the hammer on the left side of the screen. This opens the crafting tab. Look at all of the recipes you know and see what items are required for them. Click on each item in turn, and start to memorize the ingredients that are most common.

Food ingredients, cloth, leather, wood, and metal are the most common base items in crafting. There are many specific items within each of these categories, but they'll all be used in similar ways to create items of varying levels and quality.

Read through the description of your specific crafts to see which raw materials are important to you. It's fine to gather everything you come across, but some ingredients aren't necessarily worth saving. For example, if your character doesn't use wood, it might be better to sell the wood you collect (through the Trading Post). The money you make from auctioning off unneeded crafting items helps to fund your progress.

CRAFTING YOUR OWN INGREDIENTS

Raw materials aren't usually the only thing you need. These often are refined into more advanced items before being made into an actual piece of equipment. Thus, you might take Copper Ore, make it into a Bronze Ingot by adding some Lumps of Tin to it. Then, your Bronze Ingot might go on to make even more advanced ingredients, such as a Bronze Pauldron Casing.

This is where some people start to find the process complex. Don't worry! It's not that bad and you just need to play around with the system for a while until things become more intuitive.

To start learning, make one of EVERYTHING your character knows how to craft. Trainers teach you the base components for all of your normal items. As long as you keep a little bit of everything around, you'll have the ability to discover more advanced recipes.

MAKING INSIGNIAS & INSCRIPTIONS

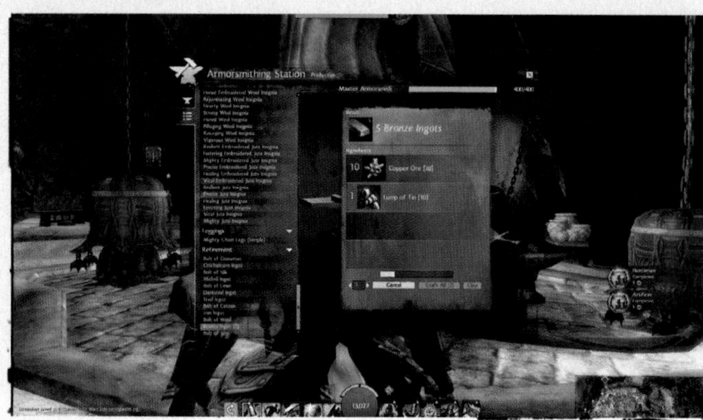

Once you're comfortable making components for your equipment, it's time to start creating insignias/inscriptions (the first affect armor, the latter affect weapons). These are the final ingredients for a piece of equipment. They determine the attributes of your final piece. They can raise power, precision, toughness, and vitality (or mixtures of these attributes). They also affect condition damage, healing, and other specific functions of a character. Crafters use these to help their clients build up specific attributes to make themselves deadlier or tougher.

Insignias are made by taking pieces you harvest from monsters and combining them with basic items (pieces of cloth or spools that you can purchase from trainers).

Here are the major types of items you harvest for making insignias: Venom Sacs, Claws, Bones, Vials of Blood, Fangs, Totems. There are tiers for each of these items, so you have to hunt tougher monsters if you need items for more powerful insignias.

For example, Vials of Blood might be listed as "Vial of Weak Blood," "Vial of Thin Blood," or "Vial of Potent Blood." There are six tiers for each category. Highlight these items when you find them. Each one lists the level of crafting they're associated with. If it says "Armorsmithing (100)," then you know your armorsmith can't start working with that item before passing 100 in that crafting skill.

DISCOVERY

You're almost good to go. Now that you can make basic ingredients, advanced items, and insignias, you can craft equipment for your characters. There's only one rub. You don't have any recipes for actual equipment. What gives? Let's explain the final step.

When you're at a crafting station, look for the Discovery tab and click on it. You'll be taken to a screen that shows all of the ingredients you're carrying. Double click to add these, in turn, to your work bench. The interface tells you if there aren't any viable combinations with the items you've selected. If the combination turns red, double click on something you've already added to pull it out of the recipe you're creating.

Mix and match until you start finding new recipes that work. If you need to craft more components, you can do it from inside the Discovery screen by clicking on the advanced ingredient in question and using the "+" icon to craft more instantly.

When trying to discover new recipes, keep one of every advanced ingredient around so you can try each possible combination.

Most equipment recipes come in intuitive groups. For instance, some Chain Shoes are made by adding Bronze Chain Boot Panel + Jute Boot Lining + any level-appropriate insignia.

So look for descriptions that seem to go together. Boot + Boot, Chest + Chest, etc. Toss in the insignia last and see what happens.

You get a minor amount of bonus experience (toward your craft and for general leveling) when you find a new recipe. Use a combination of insignias to uncover different recipes with the same ingredients. Iron Scale Chest Panel + Wool Chest Padding + a second tier insignia gets you a Scale Coat. However, there are a number of insignias that complete this recipe. Each one is unique, ensuring you can get tons of bonus experience even if you don't have many different ingredients.

After you've discovered a recipe, that combination of ingredients is saved for your character. You can now make those items at any time, assuming you have the base components in your inventory. You won't get bonus experience, but that's not a huge problem.

LEVELING YOUR CRAFT

Though each craft differs to a small extent, there are general tactics that help your characters go through the system as painlessly as possible. Here are a few ideas to get you started.

WORK TOGETHER

Talk to people you know: friends, guildies, or other crafters. Figure out who needs which items and go out harvesting together. Not only is this more fun, but everyone comes back with a considerable number of items because the group kills faster and can survive in a wider range of locations.

This is compounded if you then trade items you don't need to your harvesting buddies and get their unneeded items in return. A fair distribution of metal, leather, cloth, wood, food, and insignia ingredients can make for a lucrative session.

Because this game allows everyone in a group to harvest from nodes and loot monsters, you benefit more from a larger party than you do from just having a single ally. The more, the merrier. Convince friends that don't carry harvesting tools to start buying them, or offer to buy the items for your friends as long as they pass a decent portion of the harvested items to you. They get free experience for the harvesting, and you get your materials without having to spend even more time looking for items.

FIND GOOD HARVESTING SPOTS

If you know what you need, look for spots that have a lot of that item specifically. Learn the best locations for metal, wood, or whatever you seek. If there are specific insignias you like making, figure out the best creatures to kill for dropping your ingredients. Write down when you find an area with a large number of those monsters, and come back to that spot periodically. A fast run in a high density area is often better than spending an hour generally hunting around the wilderness and grabbing what you need whenever it drops.

In addition, there are special areas in each region that have a higher density of items. Tough monsters often guard passages filled with crafting materials. Assemble crafting groups to take down these areas.

MAKE ADVANCED PIECES EARLY

Experience for crafted items diminishes as your character gets better and better at the craft. Items you can barely make show up in orange, and eventually the colors fade to yellow, blue, toward white, and into grey. Eventually, you won't get any real points for making something.

Therefore, you want to carefully stockpile ingredients early in a crafting tier. Roughly for every 25 points in a craft, you unlock more recipes. When a new metal becomes available, the first thing you can do is transform the ore into ingots. Do that exclusively and stash the ingots away while you raise crafting points quickly. Then, you'll unlock a tier with advanced items that require those ingots. Make a ton of those advanced pieces. You still won't be making useful equipment in that tier, but you're grabbing points and saving everything.

When you finally get to the stage where equipment can be created in a given tier, you'll have everything you need (ingots and advanced ingredients). Make insignias and start throwing everything together. That's how you normally get the points that get you all the way into your next type of metal/wood/etc.

LOVE YOUR SALVAGE KITS

Salvage kits break down common metal, leather, and cloth items. This is a great way to get more material to work with. Always salvage these simple items in your inventory, and consider salvaging cheaper pieces of equipment as well. If you're crafting equipment that doesn't have an intended user, you can even break your own gear down to recover some of the component pieces that went into making it.

ADVERTISE

Agree to make equipment for others without charge as long as they bring you the ingredients. This is especially helpful early in your career, when money is so tight and getting free experience and crafting skill points is a major timesaver. Do work like this for your friends and guild mates. Let others know in cities that you're available for work and see if you get any takers.

Try not to bug people. If no one seems to want your services in a given day, so be it. They'll come around eventually, and it's really not that big of a deal.

BIG BAGS FOR EVERYONE!

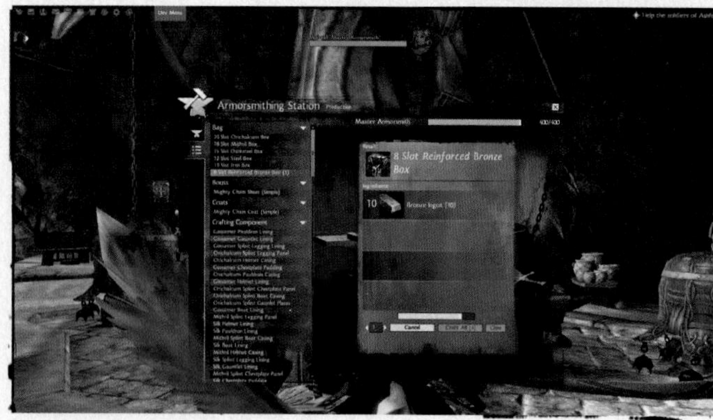

If you don't know what to take as a secondary craft, strongly consider one of the armor trades (Armorsmithing, Leatherworking, Tailoring). These are useful for making a huge number of equipment items, but they're also capable of making storage gear: boxes, bags, and packs. Everybody needs better bags than the little ones you buy early in your career. Making these for yourself and your friends is a great way to save money on the Trading Post.

Once you're finished making these for buddies, start selling excess bags for profit!

WHAT IS THE HARDEST CRAFT?

That's a matter of opinion. But in our opinion, it's Cooking. The recipes are a little more complex, there isn't as much you can figure out through pure intuition, and the benefits are both minor and temporary early on.

HOW DO I GET RICH CRAFTING?

Honestly, you don't. Some people will do a great job cashing in on their work, but most players end up spending money on ingredients and losing cash to items that are salvaged instead of sold. You also lose time while crafting when you could be adventuring and looting more monsters.

Don't think of crafting as a way to make money. Usually, it's just another way of helping yourself and others to find new items.

CAN I KEEP UP WITH MY CHARACTER'S LEVELING?

It's extremely hard to level your crafting enough to stay current with your character's equipment. Making your own gear is awesome, but this should only be a goal if you're a glutton for punishment. It's far easier to make equipment for your second character while leveling; you'll have a stronger character for gathering materials, and he or she will have more money to spend.

SWITCHING CRAFTS

Though characters can only learn two crafts and use them at the same time, you can switch to other crafts in the future; you just have to drop one of the skills you've already been using. You never lose the points that you gained in your earlier crafts, but it costs money to reactivate them.

CRAFTING DISCIPLINES

ARMORSMITHS

Raw Materials needed	Cloth, Metal
Primary Goods	Heavy Armor
Secondary Goods	Boxes

ARTIFICERS

Raw Materials needed	Wood, Metal
Primary Goods	Focuses, Scepters, Staves, and Tridents
Secondary Goods	None

COOKS

Raw Materials needed	Food Ingredients
Primary Goods	Food (Temporary Boon Items)
Secondary Goods	None

HUNTSMEN

Raw Materials needed	Wood, Metal, Leather
Primary Goods	Guns, Bows, Warhorns, Torches
Secondary Goods	None

JEWELCRAFTERS

Raw Materials needed	Metal, Stones
Primary Goods	Rings, Amulets, Trinkets
Secondary Goods	Item Upgrades

LEATHERWORKERS

Raw Materials needed	Cloth, Leather
Primary Goods	Leather Armor
Secondary Goods	Packs

TAILORS

Raw Materials needed	Cloth, Leather
Primary Goods	Cloth Armor
Secondary Goods	Bags

WEAPONSMITHS

Raw Materials needed	Wood, Metal
Primary Goods	Melee Weapons
Secondary Goods	None

THE MONSTERS OF TYRIA

It always helps to know what you're getting into, especially in battle. This chapter is all about the monsters of *Guild Wars 2*. Individual creatures vary in terms of their level, skill, and sometimes profession. However, there are similarities within most groups of monsters that let you anticipate their locations, methods of attack, and possible treasures. Read this chapter to learn how and where to hunt!

ABOMINATION

Where Found:	Orr and the Lower Steamspur Mountains
Useful Items:	N/A
Common Attacks:	Melee, Frenzy, Ground Slam
Locations:	Sparkfly Fen, Straits of Devastation, Cursed Shore, Bloodtide Coast, Timberline Falls, Gendarran Fields

These massive undead are found in large concentrations of Orrian military troops. Lesser undead are used like fodder during Orrian battles, while abominations are sent to take out the tougher enemies. Expect these monsters to hit hard and make themselves felt. Use ranged attacks against them, or dodge carefully when in melee to make sure you don't take as many hits.

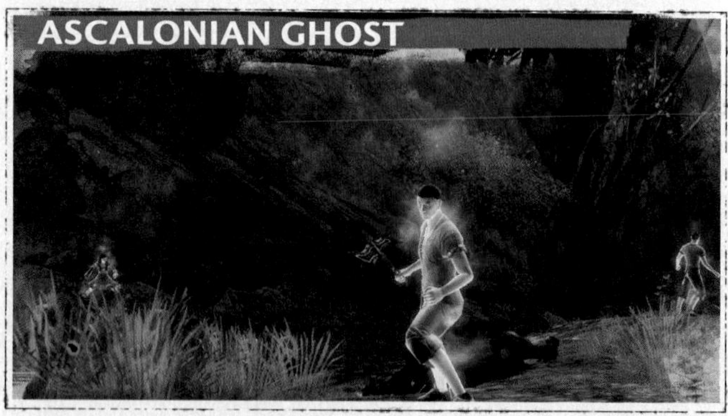

ASCALONIAN GHOST

Where Found:	Ruins Around Ascalon
Useful Items:	N/A
Common Attacks:	Profession Based
Locations:	Black Citadel, Blazeridge Steppes, Diessa Plateau, Eternal Battleground (WvW), Gendarran Fields, Harathi Hinterlands, Iron Marches, Kessex Hills, Plains of Ashford

Ascalonians died by the thousands during their war with the charr. Because of the violence and magic involved in their destruction, many of the Ascalonians are not resting peacefully. Their blue apparitions are a common sight throughout Ascalon. Often they're found in groups but can still be fought in isolation if you attack carefully.

TYPE	ATTACKS
Ascalonian Archer	Range, Ignite Arrows, Cripple
Ascalonian Captain	Melee, Weakness, Knockdown
Ascalonian Cultist	Range, Poison, Steals Health, Summons Minions
Ascalonian Enchanter	Range, Consumes Boons, Reflects Projectiles
Ascalonian Fighter	Melee, Fiery Block, Bleeds
Ascalonian Healer	Range, Heals Allies, Weakness
Ascalonian Mage	Range, Firestorm
Ascalonian Peasant	Melee

BANDIT

Where Found:	Throughout Kryta
Useful Items:	Cloth, Leather Scrap, Totems
Common Attacks:	Profession Based
Locations:	Brisban Wildlands, Cursed Shore, Harathi Hinterlands, Kessex Hills, Queensdale

Bandits are a major problem in the human lands. These criminal elements are usually located in small bases near the roadways, allowing them to plunder and steal to their hearts' content. Expect fairly large groups of targets, and bring a friend or two if you really want to hunt bandits and rake in the coin and cloth items they frequently drop.

TYPE	ATTACKS
Bandit Bruiser	Melee, Champion
Bandit Cutpurse	Melee, Steals
Bandit Highwayman	Melee, Flurry, Immobilize
Bandit Poisoner	Melee, Veteran, Poison, Blind
Bandit Rifleman	Range, Champion, Knockback, Immobilize
Bandit Saboteur	Melee, Drops Bomb
Bandit Scout	Range, Starts Fires
Bandit Thug	Melee, Stun, Vulnerability

BARRACUDA

Where Found:	Underwater
Useful Items:	Scales
Common Attacks:	Melee, Bleed, Frenzy, Summon Other Barracudas
Locations:	Gendarran Fields, Harathi Hinterlands, Kessex Hills, Queensdale, Caledon Forest, Metrica Province

Barracuda are a little tougher than the mainstream fish; they'll summon additional enemies and attack with reckless abandon. They're still low on health, so they're the best target for learning underwater weapon skills. Fast kills and large groups get you in and out of the water quickly!

BASILISK

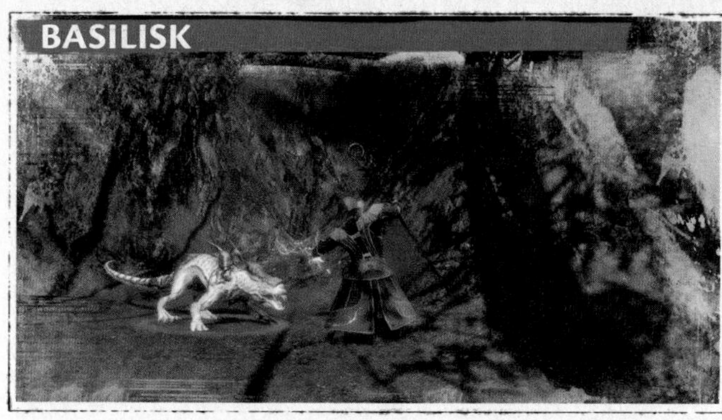

Where Found:	Craggy Areas, Mountains
Useful Items:	Scales
Common Attacks:	Melee, Immobilizing Breath
Locations:	Bloodtide Coast, Eternal Battleground (WvW), Fields of Ruin, Harathi Hinterlands, Kessex Hills, Lornar's Pass

Basilisks are a major nuisance to fight in melee combat. Their gaze Stuns targets for several seconds, and it doesn't take long for the basilisks to recharge their ability. Dodge to the sides to evade the attack; stay mobile if you're at range.

BAT

Where Found:	Primarily Caves
Useful Items:	Vials of Blood, Leather Salvage
Common Attacks:	Melee, Evasion, May Have Health Steal
Locations:	Bloodtide Coast, Brisban Wildlands, Caledon Forest, Dredgehaunt Cliffs, Eternal Battleground (WvW), Gendarran Fields, Harathi Hinterlands, Kessex Hills, Lornar's Pass, Metrica Province, Queensdale, Snowden Drifts, Sparkfly Fen, Timberline Falls, Wayfarer Foothills

Bats are frustrating to fight because they almost immediately try to evade once they're attacked. This provides a brief period of immunity to damage, so don't use your best attacks until the bats have wasted their evasion. AoE weapons are useful because you can thin a flock of bats without worrying about the ones that are immune to damage.

BEAR

(ARCTODUS, BLACK BEAR, MURELLOW, PLATED BEHEMOTH, POLAR BEAR)

Where Found:	Forests, Hills
Useful Items:	Leather Salvage
Common Attacks:	Melee, Maul, Damage Over Time
Locations:	Wayfarer Foothills, Queensdale, Kessex Hills, Timberline Falls, Gendarran Fields, Eternal Battlegrounds (WvW), Frostgorge Sound, Snowden Drifts, Dredgehaunt Cliffs, Lornar's Pass, Fields of Ruin, Diessa Plateau, Iron Marches, Plains of Ashford, Sparkfly Fen, Hoelbrak

Bears wander around the wilderness, usually by themselves (though they're found in similar areas and can be hunted specifically if you know where to look). Bears have high health, so it takes a moment to kill them. Use healing skills between fights, because bears do a fair amount of damage. You might also want to slot a damage mitigation skill or something to remove conditions.

BOAR

(FOREST BOAR, JUNGLE BOAR, WARTHOG, DIRE BOAR)

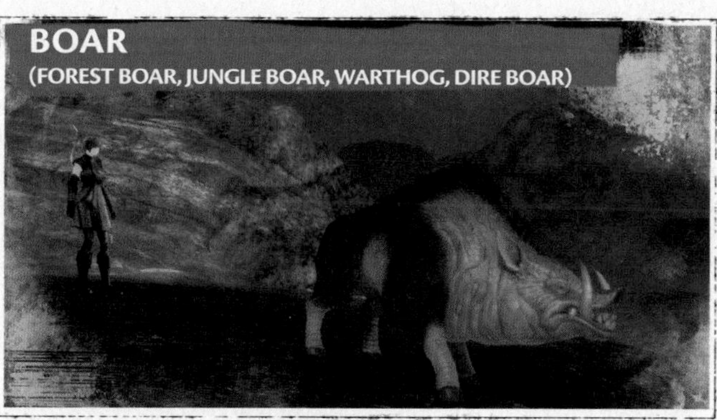

Where Found:	Grazing Land
Useful Items:	Fangs, Leather Salvage
Common Attacks:	Melee, Charge, Knockback
Locations:	Blazeridge Steppes, Brisban Wildlands, Caledon Forest, Diessa Plateau, Eternal Battlegrounds (WvW), Fields of Ruin, Fireheart Rise, Gendarran Fields, Harathi Hinterlands, Iron Marches, Lornar's Pass, Metrica Province, Mount Maelstrom, Plains of Ashford, Queensdale, Sparkfly Fen, Straits of Devastation

Boars rush to attack anyone who starts a fight with them, making a fast charge toward their victim. They knock targets around, making them a somewhat frustrating enemy to fight. Evade their charge and stick to ranged attacks if you want to kill the boars safely.

Where Found:	Branded Lands
Useful Items:	N/A
Common Attacks:	Depends on the Species
Locations:	Blazeridge Steppes, Brisban Wildlands, Fields of Ruin, Iron Marches

Branded is a title bestowed on any living creature that has been corrupted by the influence of a dragon. Even sentient beings, such as humans and charr, can be changed into twisted beasts. The branded have abilities according to the creature or racial type they were before the change. Many of the world's' best minds are working to understand and undo the influence the branded have on the land.

TYPE	ATTACKS
Branded Charr	Champion, Melee, Launch
Branded Devourer	Range, Bleed
Branded Devourer Hatchling	Range, Bleeds on Critical Hit
Branded Earth Elemental	Melee
Branded Fish	Melee
Branded Griffon	Melee, Flight (Evasion)
Branded Lieutenant	Veteran, Melee
Branded Minotaur	Melee, Throw
Branded Ogre	Melee, Powerful Punch
Branded Rock Dog	Melee, Leap
Branded Siege Devourer	Range
Branded Spark	Range

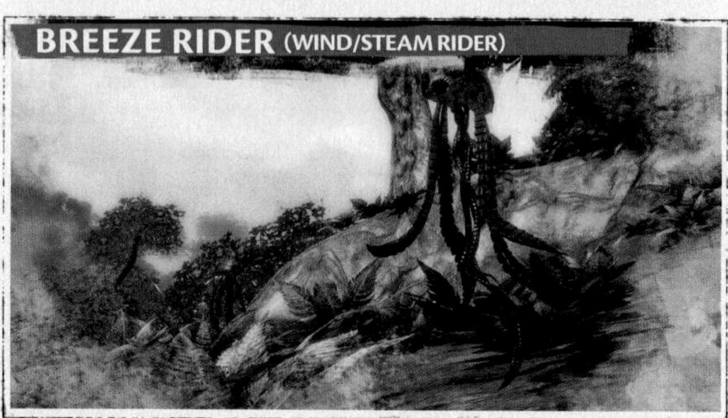

Where Found:	Plains, Caves
Useful Items:	Venom Sac
Common Attacks:	Melee, Often Have Immobilize
Locations:	Blazeridge Steppes, Brisban Wildlands, Caledon Forest, Fields of Ruin, Fireheart Rise, Lornar's Pass, Mount Maelstrom

Breeze riders are bizarre creatures. They float silently in the air and attack their prey with long tentacles, like a nightmarish squid. Breeze riders also use an Immobilizing poison to prevent their victims from escaping. Thankfully they are not very tough, and are at a big disadvantage if they don't get the drop on you. Keep your eyes open and fight smart, and breeze riders are easily defeated.

Veterans from this family are tougher and have an eye beam attack that should be dodged whenever possible. Be careful of these guys, as they're a great deal meaner than their cousins.

Where Found:	Queensdale, Kessex Hills, Diessa Plateau, and Snowden Drifts
Useful Items:	Leather
Common Attacks:	Varies by Profession
Locations:	Gendarran Fields, Harathi Hinterlands, Kessex Hills, Queensdale, Snowden Drifts

Centaurs are most often seen in human lands, though they're a threat in Snowden Drifts as well, where a clan of them is causing trouble. Centaurs are hard to fight because they work as a team, move quickly, and often have ranged attacks, Immobilize, or Knockdowns. Use cover and ranged attacks to pull centaurs back to a safe location and then kill them there. Because centaurs are seen in large groups, they're great for harvesting leather. You can kill quite a few enemies without having to hunt for more than a minute or two. Bring allies to make your work even faster!

When you're close to centaur siege weapons, make these devices your first priority. Rush into close range to stay under their line of fire, and break the weapons so your group can fight safely for a little while.

TYPE	ATTACKS
Harathi Commander	Melee, Champion, Bleed, Immobilize, Daze, Trample, Buffs Allies
Harathi Lancer	Melee, Blocks, Launches
Harathi Trampler	Melee, Trample
Modniir Beastmaster	Range, Summon War Beasts
Modniir Berserker	Melee, Champion, Frenzy, Bleed, Vulnerability
Modniir High Sage	Range, Champion, Bleed, Immobilize
Modniir Hunter	Range, Champion, AoE, Cripple
Modniir Sage	Range, Bleed, Immobilize
Tamini Archer	Range, Bleed
Tamini Chieftain	Melee, Stun, Buffs Allies
Tamini Warrior	Melee, Cripple, Power Attack

Where Found:	Beaches, Rocky Areas
Useful Items:	Meat
Common Attacks:	Melee, Block Attacks
Locations:	Bloodtide Coast, Caledon Forest, Fields of Ruin, Fireheart Rise, Frostgorge Sound, Gendarran Fields, Harathi Hinterlands, Kessex Hills, Lion's Arch, Lornar's Pass, Metrica Province, Mount Maelstrom, Snowden Drifts, Sparkfly Fen, Timberline Falls

Crabs are frequently found along coastlines. They're neutral until you attack them. They're easy to hunt, and cooks can get meat from them to use for inexpensive recipes. Thundershrimp, though aquatic, are quite similar to hunt. Both types of monsters are fairly passive until you engage them. They use evasive tactics to draw out the fight, so they're slow to kill. Use weapons with the highest possible burst damage to try and kill the enemies before they get a chance to evade, or switch targets and fight a couple at a time so you have something to hit while you wait for a target to stop its immune phase.

DESTROYER

Where Found:	Breaches In the Ground
Useful Items:	N/A
Common Attacks:	Melee, May Have Fire Attacks
Locations:	Brisban Wildlands, Eternal Battleground (WvW), Kessex Hills, Lornar's Pass, Mount Maelstrom, Timberline Falls

Destroyers are creatures of mindless terror that boil up from the ground to attack whatever gets in their way. You often know destroyers are in the area because there are broken sections of ground with fire and magma surrounding them. All destroyers attack at close range, and the big threat is often their numbers. Pull these enemies away from their buddies so you aren't overwhelmed by them.

DEVOURER

Where Found:	Ascalon, Plains, Rocky Areas
Useful Items:	Claw
Common Attacks:	Usually Melee, May Have Poison, Burrowing, or Ranged Attacks
Locations:	Black Citadel, Blazeridge Steppes, Bloodtide Coast, Citadel of Flame, Diessa Plateau, Eternal Battleground (WvW), Fields of Ruin, Fireheart Rise, Gendarran Fields, Iron Marches, Plains of Ashford

Devourers look like scorpions, but they're larger and meaner. In addition to being armored and wielding sharp mandibles and claws, devourers often Poison their prey to weaken and hurt it throughout the fight. The charr consider these to be redeeming qualities and tame devourers as war beasts. Trained or wild, these oversized insects are vicious and should be approached with caution.

Be even more careful than usual if you bump into giant devourers. These veteran beasts have long-range attacks that can put a hurt on the group if you aren't careful. Spread out and attack them from multiple points to avoid this threat.

DOLPHIN

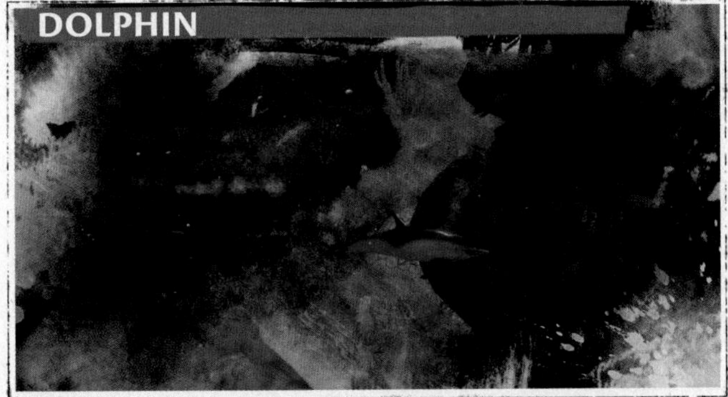

Where Found:	Underwater	Common Attacks:	Melee, Bite
Useful Items:	N/A	Location:	Bloodtide Coast

These uncommon creatures are specific to the Bloodtide Coast. They fight in a standard underwater manner; they try to close the distance quickly and bite your character. Back away to buy yourself time with ranged weapons.

DOLYAK

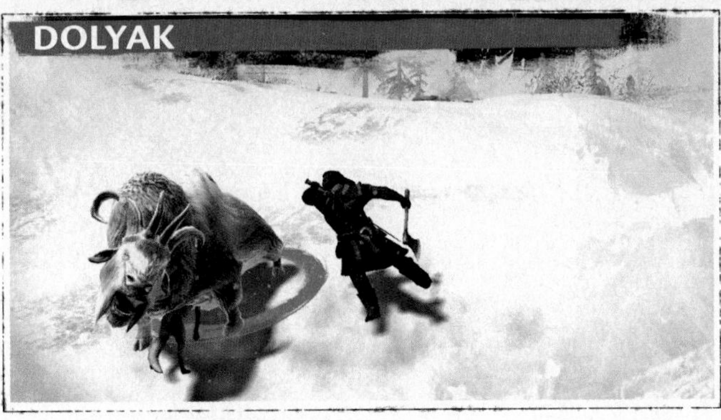

Where Found:	Cold Outdoor Areas
Useful Items:	Meat, Leather Salvage
Common Attacks:	Melee, Initial Charge
Locations:	Wayfarer Foothills, Snowden Drifts, Dredgehaunt Cliffs, Frostgorge Sound, Lornar's Pass, Timberline Falls

Dolyaks are heavy beasts of burden. Norn tame them for a variety of tasks, but you're allowed to attack any that are seen out in the wild. These creatures won't come after you unless you strike first, but they drop enough goodies that they're good targets for crafters.

Try not to tick off too many dolyaks at the same time. They frontload their damage, so it's easy to get smashed down if you aren't careful. This is doubly true if the dolyaks are higher level than your hero.

DRAKE

Where Found:	Waterways
Useful Items:	Scales, Claws, Meat
Common Attacks:	Melee, May Have Knockdowns or Breath Weapons
Locations:	Blazeridge Steppes, Bloodtide Coast, Brisban Wildlands, Caledon Forest, Diessa Plateau, Dredgehaunt Cliffs, Eternal Battleground (WvW), Fields of Ruin, Fireheart Rise, Frostgorge Sound, Gendarran Fields, Harathi Hinterlands, Hoelbrak, Iron Marches, Kessex Hills, Lornar's Pass, Metrica Province, Mount Maelstrom, Plains of Ashford, Queensdale, Snowden Drifts, Sparkfly Fen, Timberline Falls, Wayfarer Foothills

Drakes wander in wetland areas and look for trouble. Smaller members of the species usually travel with their broodmothers, making for large and enjoyable battles. Adult males stick to themselves and can be killed more safely. Not all drakes have breath weapons, so you might think of them as somewhat easier targets. Don't be complacent! Attack each new variety of drake cautiously so you can find out what they're capable of before you let your guard down.

Larger drakes may be veterans or champions, so check your target before engaging them by yourself. For drakes that have breath weapons, be sure to strafe around them while fighting. Like moas, it's possible to avoid these attacks even without dodging as long as you're fast and stay mobile.

DREDGE

Where Found:	In and Around Caves
Useful Items:	Metal Salvage, Cloth Salvage
Common Attacks:	Varies by Profession
Locations:	Diessa Plateau, Dredgehaunt Cliffs, Frostgorge Sound, Lornar's Pass, Snowden Drifts, Sorrow's Embrace, Timberline Falls, Wayfarer Foothills

The dredge are major enemies of the norn. They used to be enslaved by the dwarves, but now there aren't any dwarves hanging around the surface of Tyria. This has freed the dredge and given them time to build their forces. You almost never see individual dredge just hanging around. They're usually seen in large groups, mining or attacking an area. Their use of ranged attacks makes it hard to fight just a single dredge, as you often end up moving into range of additional enemies. Pull the dredge back to your location or kill them at range to avoid long chains of encounters.

While fighting dredge, watch out for their siege weapons. Dredge turrets hit hard and should be destroyed as soon as possible. The only thing more dangerous in a dredge cave is a dredge warrior in a mining suit. Those suits have an incredible amount of health, and they cut through things pretty quickly. Kite dredge when they're wearing the suits and drag them away from areas with reinforcements and turrets.

TYPE	ATTACKS
Dredge Disaggregator	Melee, Immune to Blind, Daze, Play Gong
Dredge Diving Suit	Melee, Immune to Blind
Dredge Excavator	Melee, Immune to Blind, Tunnel, Bleed
Dredge Mining Suit	Melee, Immune to Blind, Stun, Bleed, Summon Dredge
Dredge Oscillator	Melee, Veteran, Immune to Blind, Knockback
Dredge Ratnik	Range, Immune to Blind, Bleed, Vulnerability
Dredge Resonator	Range, Immune to Blind, Knockdown
Dredge Reverberant	Range, Immune to Blind, Bleed, Vulnerability
Dredge Strazar	Range, Knockdown

EAGLE AND HAWK

Where Found:	Mountainous or Hilly Terrain
Useful Items:	N/A
Common Attacks:	Ranged Attacks
Locations:	Queensdale, Fields of Ruin, Timberline Falls, Queensdale

These birds of prey have low health but are pesky adversaries. They often live in clusters, and you should pull them carefully to avoid fighting a few at once. Because they're not especially large, it can be hard to spot them if you're busy looking at other monsters (or exploring casually). If you aggro one, kill it where you stand and then proceed. Don't try to kite them or take up too much space, as you might get into more trouble.

ELEMENTAL

Where Found:	Anywhere They're Summoned
Useful Items:	Gems, Glittering Dust
Common Attacks:	Changes by Type
Locations:	Brisban Wildlands, Citadel of Flame, Cursed Shore, Diessa Plateau, Dredgehaunt Cliffs, Fireheart Rise, Frostgorge Sound, Gendarran Fields, Harathi Hinterlands, Iron Marches, Kessex Hills, Lornar's Pass, Malchor's Leap, Metrica Province, Mount Maelstrom, Plains of Ashford, Snowden Drifts, Timberline Falls

Elementals are animated beings with the force of some aspect of nature. Be prepared to fight enemies that are tough and deadly. The properties of various elements can be infused into the summoned creature, so expect different battles depending on which type of elemental you encounter.

TYPE	ATTACKS
Air Elemental	Range
Earth Elemental	Melee, Heavily Armored
Ember	Ranged, Immune to Burning
Ice Elemental	Melee, Ice Explosions
Lava Elemental	Melee
Lightning Elemental	Range, Champion
Pyrite Elemental	Melee, Heavily Armored
Spark	Range
Tar Elemental	Melee

Because elementals are somewhat challenging and don't offer much reward for your time in battle, they're not a good target for crafters hunting for drops. Unless you're doing an event or task, give elementals a wide berth and stick to easier prey if you want ingredients, easy money, or fast kills.

ETTIN

Where Found:	Caves and Forests
Useful Items:	Bones
Common Attacks:	Melee, Knockback
Locations:	Gendarran Fields, Kessex Hills, Lornar's Pass, Mount Maelstrom, Queensdale, Timberline Falls

Ettins aren't found in too many areas, so they're an unusual sight. Eccentric looking and quite aggressive, they're not monsters to be trifled with. Expect heavy attacks that knock your characters around. Melee fighters have to practice their dodging to ensure they don't get splattered and left on the ground for a few seconds. Roll away from the ettins so the attack misses harmlessly, and then resume your assault.

FISH

Where Found:	Tend to be Aquatic
Useful Items:	Scales
Common Attacks:	Nothing Scary
Locations:	Most of the World

Fish aren't very hard to kill. They're basic attackers that have to close the distance and bite you to death. Kite them or simply out-damage them to get your victory. Unless you're hunting for scales, it's not worth attacking most fish.

FLAME LEGION (CHARR)

Where Found:	Ascalon
Useful Items:	Claws, Garments
Common Attacks:	Profession Based
Locations:	Citadel of Flame, Diessa Plateau, Fireheart Rise, Iron Marches, Plains of Ashford

Charr from the Flame Legion have been cast out of the Black Citadel. They're a defunct legion as far as other charr are concerned, but that doesn't stop them from being a threat. Flame Legion soldiers use magic and melee fighting to kill anyone who gets in their way. They're always found in groups, and they sometimes have siege weaponry to back up their attacks. If you have any healing abilities that remove conditions, ready those before you fight the Flame Legion. Their abilities and turrets have a tendency to set people on fire. Remove this Burning condition whenever possible.

TYPE	ATTACKS
Flame Legion Axe Fiend	Melee, Rapid Attacks
Flame Legion Blademaster	Melee, Stun, Bleed
Flame Legion Bladestorm	Melee, Whirl, AoE Attacks
Flame Legion Effigy	Melee, Veteran, Burn, Buffs Allies
Flame Legion Fire Shaman	Range, Launch
Flame Legion Igniter	Melee, Burn
Flame Legion Lava Shaman	Range, Launch
Flame Legion Shadowblade	Melee, Bleed
Flame Legion Smoke Shaman	Range, Blind, Stealths Allies
Flame Legion Stalker	Range, Ignites Arrows

FLY (WASP, MOSQUITO, FIREFLY)

Where Found:	Open or Wet Areas
Useful Items:	Venom Sacs
Common Attacks:	Melee, May Have Charge or Rapid Attacks
Locations:	Bloodtide Coast, Brisban Wildlands, Caledon Forest, Divinity's Reach, Fields of Ruin, Gendarran Fields, Harathi Hinterlands, Lornar's Pass, Metrica Province, Mount Maelstrom, Queensdale, Snowden Drifts, Sparkfly Fen, Straits of Devastation, Timberline Falls, Wayfarer Foothills

These oversized insects are found in open plains, marshes, or caves. They are usually non-aggressive unless provoked and are not too difficult to swat down. Crafters hunt them as a resource for ingredients for inscriptions. Gathering a large group and blasting them with a burst of AoE damage is low risk and fun.

Though fast to kill, some creatures from this family are high on damage output. Ranged attacks soften the nastier targets, and you can switch to melee for the kill when they get close. That's a good way to keep the risk low while fighting and still get fast kills.

GIANT

Where Found:	Wandering through Kessex
Useful Items:	N/A
Common Attacks:	Melee, Stomp, Shout
Locations:	Kessex Hills

There aren't many living giants in this section of the world. Orr used to have problems with giants, and the good news is that all of those monsters died when Orr was destroyed. The downside is those giants came back and are now undead. Yeesh, that's rough.

Living giants are only seen in Kessex Hills. They're tall, tough, and can fight groups rather effectively. Ranged attacks and kiting tactics make fights much easier against these formidable opponents.

GOLEM

Where Found:	Asura Lands
Useful Items:	Glittering Dust, Metal Salvage
Common Attacks:	Melee or Range, Whirlwind Attack, Shoot Fists

Golems are part magical and part mechanical creations. Golems are often created by the asura for what they consider menial tasks, such as housework and combat. The most common types are MK I and MK II. MK I golems are large and thickly built. They perform a wide range of tasks and attack by swinging their arms around in combat. MK II golems are more specialized for fighting, and they look the part. They perform ranged attacks by shooting out their fists.

Kiting works extremely well against golems; they're not very fast, and you can avoid some of their more troublesome attacks by staying at range.

GRAWL

Where Found:	Hilly or Cavernous Areas
Useful Items:	Bones, Leather Salvage
Common Attacks:	Profession Based
Locations:	Blazeridge Steppes, Diessa Plateau, Dredgehaunt Cliffs, Fireheart Rise, Frostgorge Sound, Lion's Arch, Lornar's Pass, Plains of Ashford, Snowden Drifts, Timberline Falls, Wayfarer Foothills

The grawl are a race of hairy humanoids who live in loose tribes. They are uncivilized, but don't make the mistake of underestimating them. Since they can't fight smarter, they just fight harder. They tend to travel in small packs that make the most of their special attacks. Grawl berserkers take turns knocking a hero down. Grawl shamans practice magic that can be very powerful. Hit grawl from range, retreat around corners to force them forward and into a small cluster, and then switch to AoE attacks to kill the groups quickly.

TYPE	ATTACKS
Grawl Berserker	Melee, Frenzy, Massive Attack
Grawl Hunter	Range, Cripple, Bleed, Summon Birds
Grawl Priest	Range, Summon Totem, Heal
Grawl Raider	Range, AoE, Immobilize
Grawl Shaman	Range, Summon Totem, Knockdown
Grawl Trapper	Range, Frost Trap, Baits Wurms

GRIFFON

Where Found:	Hill Country
Useful Items:	Claws
Common Attacks:	Melee, Evade, Knockdown
Locations:	Blazeridge Steppes, Bloodtide Coast, Dredgehaunt Cliffs, Fields of Ruin, Fireheart Rise, Frostgorge Sound, Gendarran Fields, Harathi Hinterlands, Iron Marches, Lornar's Pass, Snowden Drifts, Timberline Falls, Wayfarer Foothills

These majestic beasts jealously guard their roosts. Since they are territorial, it's easy to fight griffons one at a time. Griffons like to knock their targets down to make them vulnerable to attack from beaks and claws. Griffons also have the ability to evade your attacks, causing your hero to swing at nothing but air. Wait them out and resume your attacks when the griffons descend. If there are multiple targets in the battle, switch to something vulnerable while your original enemy evades. This prevents your hero from wasting his time while there are enemies still attacking.

GRUB

Where Found:	Caves, Swampy Areas
Useful Items:	Venom Sacs, Fangs
Common Attacks:	Range, Poison
Locations:	Bloodtide Coast, Brisban Wildlands, Caledon Forest, Diessa Plateau, Eternal Battleground (WvW), Fields of Ruin, Fireheart Rise, Gendarran Fields, Harathi Hinterlands, Iron Marches, Kessex Hills, Metrica Province, Mount Maelstrom, Plains of Ashford, Queensdale, Straits of Devastation, The Grove

These giant bugs hide in dark areas and prefer to be left alone. They don't attack unless threatened, but they have a ranged spit attack that carries poison. Be ready to remove that condition from your characters if you're hunting grubs, as crafters sometimes do. Any skills that automatically clear conditions every few seconds make grubs easy prey.

HARPY

Where Found:	Hilly and Elevated Rocky Areas (Common in Charr Lands)
Useful Items:	Claw
Common Attacks:	Usually Melee, Evade, May Summon Allies
Locations:	Blazeridge Steppes, Diessa Plateau, Eternal Battleground (WvW), Fields of Ruin, Fireheart Rise, Harathi Hinterlands, Plains of Ashford, Queensdale, Timberline Falls

These filthy creatures make their roosts on high and rocky areas. Harpies are pests because they attack aggressively and use flight to evade enemies' responses. There are many tasks that involve killing harpies or retrieving goods they've stolen. That's the great thing about harpies; you can do horrible things to them and not feel bad. A fun strategy is to attack a harpy nest and slaughter the harpies that come to its defense. Unleash your most powerful AoEs and rake in experience and loot.

HUNTING CAT
(JAGUAR, SNOW LEOPARD, STALKER)

Where Found:	Open Outdoor Areas
Useful Items:	Hides
Common Attacks:	Melee, Pounce
Locations:	Brisban Wildlands, Caledon Forest, Dredgehaunt Cliffs, Eternal Battlegrounds (WvW), Fields of Ruin, Frostgorge Sound, Hoelbrak, Lornar's Pass, Snowden Drifts, Sparkfly Fen, Timberline Falls, Wayfarer Foothills

A variety of large cats live throughout the world. All are solitary hunters that will attack if you get close. Watch when they prepare to pounce. It's a devastating hit that should be evaded whenever possible. Many types of crafters value the hides gathered from hunting cats.

HYLEK

Where Found:	Forests and Marshes
Useful Items:	N/A
Common Attacks:	Vary by Profession
Locations:	Bloodtide Coast, Brisban Wildlands, Caledon Forest, Kessex Hills, Metrica Province, Mount Maelstrom, Sparkfly Fen, Straits of Devastation

The hyleks are large humanoid frogs. They are not a playable race but can be found in many of the capital cities as travelers or envoys. Hyleks live in tribal villages, often near water, and they can be quite civilized. However, there are some tribes that are aggressive to you. Make sure to kill hyleks armed with blowguns first. They fire a series of poison darts that make fights much more difficult.

TYPE	ATTACKS
Hylek Amini	Melee, Immune to Poison
Hylek Caster	Range, Burn, Poison
Hylek Cuicani	Range, Burn, Poison
Hylek Nahualli	Range, Chill, Shoots Darts
Hylek Tlamatini	Melee, Immune to Poison

ICEBROOD

Where Found:	Shiverpeak and Steamspur Mountains
Useful Items:	N/A
Common Attacks:	Vary by Profession
Locations:	Brisban Wildlands, Dredgehaunt Cliffs, Fireheart Rise, Frostgorge Sound, Honor of the Waves, Mount Maelstrom, Snowden Drifts, Wayfarer Foothills

The icebrood are a group of creatures twisted and bound to Jormag, or have willingly sworn themselves to serve the dragon. These are your enemies! Destroy them wherever you find them, for they stand to do a great amount of harm to the world.

TYPE	ATTACKS
Corrupted Fish	Melee, Cripple
Corrupted Quaggan	Melee
Icebrood Colossus	Melee
Icebrood Elemental	Melee, Summons Minions, Chill, Bleed
Icebrood Goliath	Melee
Icebrood Kodan	Melee, Champion
Icebrood Norn	Melee, Frozen Ground
Icebrood Wolf	Melee, Lunge, Bite

IMP

Where Found:	Usually in Caves
Useful Items:	Glittering Dust, Gems
Common Attacks:	Range
Locations:	Brisban Wildlands, Caledon Forest, Citadel of Flame, Dredgehaunt Cliffs, Fireheart Rise, Frostgorge Sound, Iron Marches, Lornar's Pass, Metrica Province, Mount Maelstrom, Timberline Falls, Wayfarer Foothills

Imps are flying elemental creatures. They attack from range using whatever element they're affiliated with. Often imps are summoned by magic users to perform guard duty or to power a magical artifact. While individual imps aren't very tough, others may join the fight and ramp up the damage. If this happens, retreat around an obstacle. When the imps follow, they'll naturally group up around the corner and will be vulnerable to AoE attacks.

INQUEST

Where Found:	Asura Lands, Laboratories, Underground Volcano Bases
Useful Items:	Glittering Dust, Metal Salvage, Totems
Common Attacks:	Profession Based
Locations:	Blazeridge Steppes, Bloodtide Coast, Brisban Wildlands, Divinity's Reach, Malchor's Leap, Metrica Province, Mount Maelstrom, Rata Sum, Sorrow's Embrace, Sparkfly Fen, Timberline Falls

The Inquest is a faction of asura that tries to harness magic and technology in dangerous ways. While all asura value the pursuit of knowledge, the Inquest wants it only to acquire power. The result is mad science run amok. Take care when getting too close to an area where the Inquest is performing experiments. They will attack with technologic weaponry and their golems.

When in doubt, kill Inquest agents before dealing with the golems they have in the area. The asurans aren't that hard to take down directly, and many of them have ways to make the golems stronger. Once they're dead, it will be a little easier to strip down the golems for parts.

TYPE	ATTACKS
Head Analyst	Range, Veteran
Inquest Assassin	Melee, Stealth
Inquest Assistant	Range, Champion, Bleed, Shields
Inquest Engineer	Melee, Drops Turrets
Inquest Extinguisher	Range, Champion, Chill, Pull, Removes Conditions
Inquest Golemancer	Range, Stun, Buffs Golems
Inquest Golemcaster	Range, Applies Conditions
Inquest Grenadier	Range, Champion
Inquest Powersuit	Melee, Whirlwind, Pilot Ejects
Inquest Technician	Range, Heals Allies
Mark I Golem	Melee, AoE, Self Repair
Mark I Golemite	Melee
Mark II Golem	Range, Stun
Mark II Golemite	Range, Shoots Fists
Prototype Incinerator Golem	Melee, Fiery Attacks

JOTUN

Where Found:	Tundra
Useful Items:	Bones, Cloth Salvage
Common Attacks:	Melee, Knockback
Location:	Dredgehaunt Cliffs

The jotun are easy to recognize. They look like giant humans with bluish skin and tattoos. The jotun live on the frozen tundra in simple huts. If you get too close, jotun become very aggressive and will fight you with whatever they have at hand, even if that means going hand-to-hand with their victims. What they lack in technique they make up for in strength and ferocity. Jotun are highly vulnerable to kiting attacks if you have a clear area behind your character.

KRAIT

Where Found:	Humid and Watery Areas
Useful Items:	Bones, Scales, Cloth Salvage
Common Attacks:	Profession Based
Locations:	Eternal Battleground (WvW), Kessex Hills, Malchor's Leap, Metrica Province, Mount Maelstrom, Timberline Falls

Of all the creatures and races that live in or near the water, few are as dangerous as the krait. With the upper torso of a humanoid and a powerful tail, the krait are ungainly on land but lethal underwater. Depending on their profession, individual krait have vicious attacks including magic, summoning allies, pulling targets in with their tridents, and inflicting all kinds of conditions. If your normal gear is better than your aquatic weaponry, pull these enemies up to the shore and fight them there. It's often easier than killing them in their preferred environment.

TYPE	ATTACKS
Krait Damoss	Melee, Bleed, Poison
Krait Hypnoss	Range, Champion, Poison, Summons Minions
Krait Nimross	Range, Pull, Bleed, Immobilize, Knockback
Krait Slaver	Melee, Immobilize

MANTA RAY

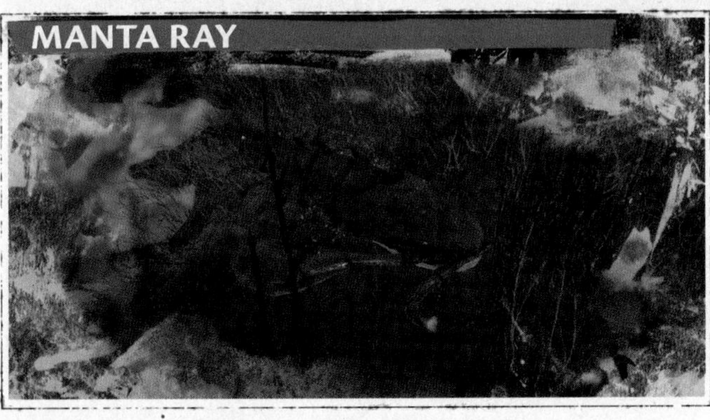

Where Found:	Underwater
Useful Items:	N/A
Common Attacks:	Melee
Location:	Sparkfly Fen

These rare creatures should be kited to avoid their fairly damaging melee attacks.

MASTIFF (ROCK DOG, WARG)

Where Found:	Forests and Rocky Land
Useful Items:	Meat, Bones
Common Attacks:	Melee, Lunge, Bite, Bleed
Locations:	Blazeridge Steppes, Brisban Wildlands, Diessa Plateau, Fields of Ruin, Gendarran Fields, Harathi Hinterlands, Iron Marches, Kessex Hills, Plains of Ashford, Queensdale

Mastiffs are canines that are larger than wolves and have a thick mane of fur along their shoulders. The sylvari, Nightmare Court, and Sons of Svanir train their own breeds as combat animals. Use AoE attacks to kill these hounds while attacking their masters.

In other areas, you find rock dogs and wargs that are more independent but just as dangerous and feral. All of these monsters are lethal if you let them get too close to your character. Either exploit their lack of range or keep them disrupted in melee combat.

MINOTAUR (BULL, IRATE BULL, BROWN COW)

Where Found:	Hilly Terrain
Useful Items:	Vials of Blood, Meat
Common Attacks:	Melee, Charge, Frenzy, Enrage
Locations:	Diessa Plateau, Fields of Ruin, Lornar's Pass, Plains of Ashford, Queensdale, Brisban Wildlands

Minotaurs are found in the open hilly areas of the world. They fight aggressively, rushing foes and breaking them with powerful melee attacks. These beasts also have the ability to give themselves Frenzy and Enrage boons. This allows them to increase their already substantial damage. When facing minotaurs, keep moving and try to stay out of reach. Immobilize, Stun, or knock them around to make it easier to do this. Ranged characters have an edge in this, but melee characters with damage mitigation also do well.

MOA (FLAMINGO, ETC.)

Where Found:	Open Terrain
Useful Items:	Meat, Eggs
Common Attacks:	Short Range, May Have Breath Attacks, Daze, Frenzy
Locations:	Sparkfly Fen, Snowden Drifts, Divinity's Reach, Bloodtide Coast, Lion's Arch, Caledon Forest, Queensdale, Gendarran Fields, Kessex Hills, Metrica Province, Mount Maelstrom, Straits of Devastation, Wayfarer Foothills, Dredgehaunt Cliffs, Frostgorge Sound, Lornar's Pass, Timberline Falls, Harathi Hinterlands, Fields of Ruin, Brisban Wildlands, Blazeridge Steppes, Diessa Plateau, Fireheart Rise, Plains of Ashford

Moa are flightless birds that are stunningly tough for their size. Many have breath weapons they use to Stun their foes and deal damage at the same time. You can easily be killed if you attack several moa at once. Fight them on their own and evade to the side the moment they set up their breath attack.

There are many different colors of moa, and you end up finding different varieties of these birds in almost every part of the world.

MOOSE

Where Found:	Open Areas
Useful Items:	Meat
Common Attacks:	Melee, Kick, Calls Allies if Nearby
Locations:	Snowden Drifts, Wayfarer Foothills, Frostgorge Sound, Timberline Falls, Lornar's Pass, Dredgehaunt Cliffs

Though neutral until attacked, moose are a brave species. They'll come to the aid of nearby moose. Be wary of this before you end up fighting an entire herd!

Use ranged attacks to get a major edge on the beasts, because they are entirely dependent on melee attacks to defeat their enemies.

NIGHTMARE COURT

Where Found:	The Tarnished Coast and Steamspur Mountains
Useful Items:	Bones, Cloth Salvage
Common Attacks:	Profession Based
Locations:	Brisban Wildlands, Caledon Forest, Mount Maelstrom, Sparkfly Fen, The Grove

The sylvari believe that during the time before they are born they are part of the Dream of the Pale Tree. Most describe it as a time of light, growth, and hope. But others seem to have experienced something darker. These sylvari leave the presence of the Pale Tree and the Grove and have created the Nightmare Court. Members of the Nightmare Court have been attacking villages and taking captives in order to "turn" them. Through torture, they work to corrupt their victims to their own twisted image.

Put a condition-clearing skill on your bar before going into Nightmare Court areas. Many of these sylvari have abilities that do damage over time or otherwise mess with your hero. Clear these conditions quickly and fight back with raw damage output!

TYPE	ATTACKS
Nightmare Court Executioner	Melee, Bleed, Poison, Cripple
Nightmare Court Bowman	Range, Bleed, Knockback
Nightmare Court Page	Range, Evade, Poison
Nightmare Court Ebon Knight	Melee, Weakness, Vulnerability, Launch
Nightmare Court Kennelmaster	Melee, Buffs Allies, Frenzies Pets
Nightmare Apprentice	Range, Poison, Steals Health
Nightmare Court Squire	Melee, Counters Attacks
Dark Count	Range, Inflicts Random Conditions, Turns Boons to Conditions
Nightmare Court Marquis	Melee, Confuse, Cripple, Teleport, Buffs Self
Nightmare Court Knight	Melee, Bleed, Block
Nightmare Court Tormentor	Range, Burn, Steals Health
Nightmare Court Torch	Range, Burn, Steals Health
Nightmare Hound	Melee

OGRE

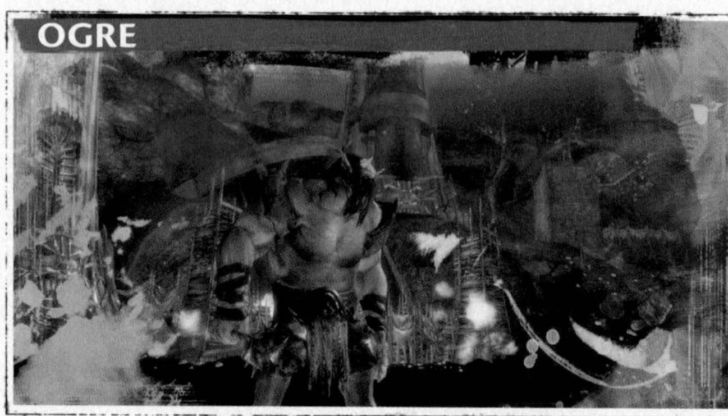

Where Found:	In Small Communities (Commonly in Ascalon)
Useful Items:	Bones
Common Attacks:	Melee, Ground Slam, Throw Boulder
Locations:	Blazeridge Steppes, Eternal Battleground (WvW), Fields of Ruin, Plains of Ashford

Ogres don't look very bright, but they're smart enough to know they accomplish more as a group than as individuals. Ogres often have animal companions that fight alongside them (ogres try to buff these pets to make them more powerful, so take out the pets quickly to make the battles safer).

Ogres build crude yet effective settlements along mountainsides. Expect heavy resistance if you invade their homes; this is a very lucrative activity because ogres drop bones quite often. These are prized by crafters and can be sold at the Trading Post for a tidy sum. Because there are usually tasks and events surrounding these communities, you can get paid as you hunt to make even more money.

OOZE

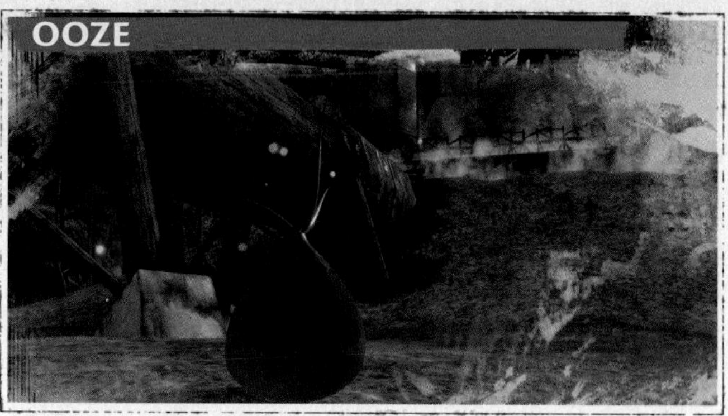

Where Found:	Varies
Useful Items:	Metal Salvage
Common Attacks:	Melee, Immobilize
Locations:	Bloodtide Coast, Brisban Wildlands, Citadel of Flame, Cursed Shore, Diessa Plateau, Fireheart Rise, Frostgorge Sound, Harathi Hinterlands, Kessex Hills, Lornar's Pass, Metrica Province, Mount Maelstrom, Plains of Ashford, Queensdale, Sorrow's Embrace, Straits of Devastation, Timberline Falls

Oozes are a pain in the rump. They often have the ability to stop you dead in your tracks, and this gets more daunting if you fight too many of them in a tight space. You won't get a moment to yourself, and their damage adds up quickly. Ranged attacks help to pull oozes safely. Melee AoEs are better for the fast kills. Combine the two for an easier time with these monsters.

Beware of champion oozes. These larger versions have so much health that it takes a small army to bring them down. Running away from them is difficult, so if things go poorly you aren't likely to survive the experience. Bring your friends. Heck, bring your guild!

ORRIAN (RISEN)

Where Found:	All Over Orr and The Steamspur Mountains
Useful Items:	Metal Salvage, Cloth Salvage, Bones
Common Attacks:	Profession Based
Locations:	Bloodtide Coast, Brisban Wildlands, Caledon Forest, Cursed Shore, Gendarran Fields, Kessex Hills, Malchor's Leap, Mount Maelstrom, Sparkfly Fen, Straits of Devastation, Timberline Falls

Orr was an ancient civilization that was destroyed and sank to the bottom of the sea. Foul magic corrupted the dead entombed within and they have risen to conquer the living. Orrians are undead from all the races of the world. Do not mistake them for mindless zombies; they work in groups, call for help, and members fight with the skills they still knew while alive. Orrian brutes, for example, are tough melee warriors that knock their victims down with hammer strikes. Heroes looking to add to their prestige should fight these menaces wherever they're found. Orrians are a threat to every living being in the world.

TYPE	ATTACKS
Orrian Spectral Guard	Melee
Orrian Spectral Juggernaut	Ranged
Risen Abomination	Melee, Unstoppable, Frenzy
Risen Acolyte	Range, Frenzy
Risen Archmage	Range, Champion, Frenzy
Risen Baron	Melee, Champion, Frenzy
Risen Baroness	Melee, Champion, Frenzy
Risen Brute	Melee, Knockdown
Risen Bull	Melee
Risen Bull Shark	Melee, Toxic Bite
Risen Captain	Melee, Champion, Frenzy
Risen Chicken	Melee, Explodes

TYPE	ATTACKS
Risen Corrupter	Melee, Champion, Chill, Self Boons
Risen Despoiler	Melee, Champion, Teleport, Blind, Daze, Stun
Risen Drake	Melee, Knockback, Bleed, Summon Flies
Risen Drake Broodmother	Melee, Breathes Fire
Risen Drake Hatchling	Melee, Launched When Hit
Risen Eagle	Melee, Drops Bombs
Risen Executioner	Melee, Champion, Frenzy
Risen Farmer	Melee, Frenzy
Risen Giant	Melee, Veteran, Knockdown, Vulnerability, Poison, Throw Grubs
Risen Gorilla	Melee, Throw, Weakness, Cripple
Risen Grub	Range, Spit Draws Undead
Risen Hylek	Range, Poisons, Immune to Poison
Risen Jester	Range, Frenzy
Risen Knight	Melee
Risen Megalodon	Melee, Champion, Toxic Bite, Steals Health, Eats Foes
Risen Noble	Melee, Frenzy
Risen Pirate	Melee, Frenzy
Risen Plague Carrier	Melee, Explodes
Risen Plaguebearer	Range, Champion, Steals Life, Transfers Conditions
Risen Preserver	Range, Champion, AoE Heals, Removes Conditions, Mist Form
Risen Priest of Balthazar	Melee, Champion
Risen Priestess of Dwayna	Range, Champion
Risen Priestess of Lyssa	Range, Champion
Risen Putrifier	Melee, Champion, Pull, Steal Life, Reflect
Risen Quaggan	Melee
Risen Raptor	Melee, Dazes Wounded Enemies
Risen Sea Scorpion	Melee, Bite, Poison Sting
Risen Sea Turtle	Melee
Risen Servant	Melee, Frenzy
Risen Shark	Melee, Toxic Bite
Risen Spider Hatchling	Melee
Risen Spider Queen	Melee, Lays Eggs, Pull
Risen Squire	Melee, Frenzy
Risen Statue of Dwayna	Range, Champion
Risen Subjugator	Range, Champion, Fear, Steals Life
Risen Thrall	Melee, Frenzy
Risen Villager	Melee, Frenzy
Risen Wizard	Range, Frenzy
Risen Wraith	Range, Teleport, Steals Health

PINESOUL
(MOSSHEART, OAKHEART, WILLOWHEART)

Where Found:	Forested Regions
Useful Items:	Food
Common Attacks:	Melee, Knockdowns, Immobilize
Locations:	Brisban Wildlands, Caledon Forest, Dredgehaunt Cliffs, Eternal Battleground (WvW), Frostgorge Sound, Gendarran Fields, Harathi Hinterlands, Lornar's Pass, Metrica Province, Mount Maelstrom, Queensdale, Snowden Drifts, Timberline Falls, Wayfarer Foothills

Pinesouls and their cousins are usually found in forested areas. They're safe to walk around but deadly if angered. These enemies have high health and are great at knocking people around. Even while dying they're able to toss everyone away from their bodies. Evade backwards anytime a pinesoul charges for a stronger attack. If you have skills that make your hero immune to positional attacks, use them early in a pinesoul fight and lay on the direct damage.

Even in death these forces of nature have plenty of power. They often throw melee characters back in a final death frenzy as they go down. Back off to avoid this if it bothers you.

Watch out for a champion in Queensdale that is even more powerful than most creatures of this variety. None of the pinesoul variants are low on health, but that one has healing pods and won't quit without a serious fight.

PIRATE

Where Found:	Coastal and Riverside Areas
Useful Items:	Cloth (Excellent Source)
Common Attacks:	Profession Based
Locations:	Bloodtide Coast, Cursed Shore, Gendarran Fields, Lion's Arch, Lornar's Pass, Snowden Drifts

Pirates inhabit the rivers and coastline around the Steamspur Mountains. You might expect them to be poorly equipped, but that's not the case. Many pirates have turrets, military training, and even siege weaponry (such as cannons). They fight in groups and may have veterans to lead their forces. Expect them to use Stun attacks and a mix of melee and ranged weaponry. Because pirates build small settlements, you can usually find places to hide inside their towns. Use these buildings to break line of sight and force all of your attackers to come forward as a group. This is ideal for AoE attacks and for resting afterward.

Pirates may be the best source of cloth in the entire game. They drop it like nobody's business, so tailors love to kill them for fun and profit.

TYPE	ATTACKS
Buccaneer Captain	Range, Champion, Shoots Lightning
Buccaneer First Mate	Range, Veteran, Throws Foes
Buccaneer Pirate	Range, Throws Daggers
Buccaneer Sapper	Melee, Frenzy
Buccaneer Sniper	Range, Immobilize
Covington Pirate	Range, Throws Daggers
Covington Pirate Thug	Melee
Cutthroat Captain	Range, Champion, Throws Bombs
Cutthroat First Mate	Range, Veteran, Launch
Cutthroat Pirate	Range, Throws Daggers
Cutthroat Sapper	Melee, Frenzy
Cutthroat Sniper	Range, Immobilize
Jackdaw Captain	Range, Champion, Rapid Attacks, Buffs Allies
Jackdaw First Mate	Range, Veteran, Burning
Jackdaw Pirate	Range, Throws Daggers
Jackdaw Sapper	Melee, Frenzy
Jackdaw Sniper	Range, Immobilize

RAPTOR

Where Found:	Jungles, Grasslands
Useful Items:	Claws, Meat
Common Attacks:	Melee, May Have Daze or Chill
Locations:	Blazeridge Steppes, Bloodtide Coast, Brisban Wildlands, Caledon Forest, Diessa Plateau, Dredgehaunt Cliffs, Fields of Ruin, Fireheart Rise, Frostgorge Sound, Gendarran Fields, Harathi Hinterlands, Iron Marches, Kessex Hills, Lornar's Pass, Metrica Province, Mount Maelstrom, Queensdale, Snowden Drifts, Sparkfly Fen, Straits of Devastation, Timberline Falls

Raptors are a mix between a flightless bird and a lizard. They have few feathers on their forearms, which are better for clawing than flapping. Raptors are found in a wide range of areas, and many of them share the same characteristics. They're usually going to close with your hero, attack in melee, and Daze people they hit. Some raptors have Chill instead, but both major archetypes are best killed with either very long range weapons, or high-damage melee skills. Characters that let raptors get too close are going to lose their kiting potential and get gobbled up. Switch to melee to burn down these targets if you get caught out in the open.

SEA SCORPION

Where Found:	Underwater
Useful Items:	N/A
Common Attacks:	Melee, Poison, Temporary Immunity to Damage
Locations:	Bloodtide Coast, Frostgorge Sound, Mount Maelstrom, Lion's Arch, Caledon Forest

These heavily armored creatures are tough to take down. Thankfully they keep to themselves and will only fight when provoked. It's better to focus on burst damage when fighting a sea scorpion. Try to kill them before they go immune to damage and then deal with your conditions once the fight is over.

SEPARATIST

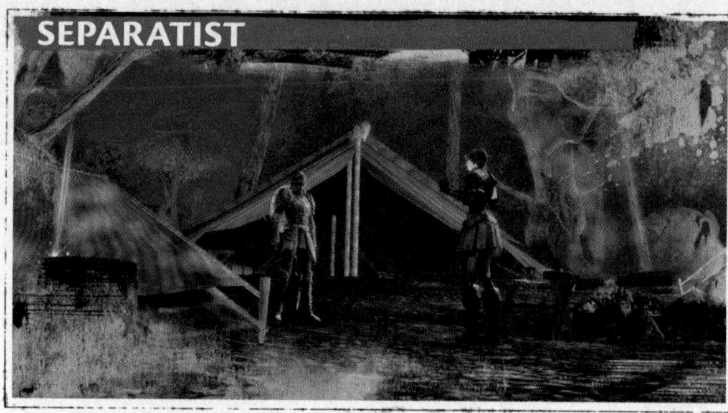

Where Found:	Ascalon
Useful Items:	Cloth
Common Attacks:	Profession based
Locations:	Blazeridge Steppes, Diessa Plateau, Fields of Ruin, Harathi Hinterlands, Iron Marches, Plains of Ashford

The peace treaty between the charr and the humans of Ebonhawke is a good thing for both peoples, but not everyone is ready to put down their weapons. Human separatists are trying to erode support for the treaty and the government that signed it. Don't expect these humans to give you any chances; they'll murder charr and human alike if it furthers their cause.

TYPE	ATTACKS
Separatist Basher	Melee, Knockdown, Reflect Projectiles
Separatist Engineer	Range, Chill, Launch
Separatist Marksman	Range, Knockback
Separatist Stormcaller	Melee, Champion, Teleport, Cripple, Bleed
Separatist Thaumaturge	Range, Champion, AoE Lightning, Knockback, Tornado

SHADE

Where Found:	Swamps
Useful Items:	N/A
Common Attacks:	Melee, Charge Attack
Locations:	Iron Marches, Kessex Hills, Lornar's Pass, Queensdale

Shades are large ape-like creatures made of dark energy. They're often found prowling around swamps, fens, and bogs. Watch out when these creatures charge, because they can toss adventurers quite far. You won't usually see large groups of these enemies, so they're difficult to kill en masse. Their attacks can sometimes apply Weakness, making the rest of the fight more difficult because your character does less damage for a short time. Hold off on your strongest attacks during this period, and then unload on the Shades as soon as the Weakness wears off.

SHARK

Where Found:	Deep Water
Useful Items:	N/A
Common Attacks:	Melee, High Damage, Bleed
Locations:	Plains of Ashford, Gendarran Fields, Iron Marches, Timberline Falls, Kessex Hills, Frostgorge Sound, Fireheart Rise, Lornar's Pass

Sharks are often quite large. They're easy to spot, even at long range. Inflict early damage from range, as sharks can't hit back until they get close. Once they do, it's a race to deal damage. Heal to stay ahead, and resume kiting if you can quickly vacate its melee range.

Champion sharks can be found in Harathi Hinterlands and the Bloodtide Coast. They're brutally tough and should only be engaged with a fairly large group. Soloers and duos just end up being lunch, even if they do have good kiting skills.

SHEEP (AND OTHER LIGHT COMBATANTS)

Where Found:	Open Areas
Useful Items:	N/A
Common Attacks:	Melee Attacks
Location:	Everywhere

Many animals of this type, including deer and does, exist in Tyria. They're hardly worth fighting because they're so easy to kill and have precious little treasure to dispense. Though they are worth a small amount of experience, you'd be better off fighting something more valuable as part of an event.

SIAMOTH

Where Found:	Open Areas
Useful Items:	Meat
Common Attacks:	Melee, Charge
Locations:	Mount Maelstrom, Sparkfly Fen, Caledon Forest, Brisban Wildlands, Metrica Province, Bloodtide Coast, Lornar's Pass, Gendarran Fields, Timberline Falls

Siamoths are large, armored rodents. They're fairly hardy for glorified rats, but you won't have too much to fear from them. They're rarely found in large numbers, and individuals don't pose a huge risk to seasoned heroes.

SKALE

Where Found:	Bogs, Rivers, Coastlines
Useful Items:	Scales, Vials of Blood, Leather Salvage
Common Attacks:	Melee, Health Regeneration, May Have Knockdown
Locations:	Blazeridge Steppes, Bloodtide Coast, Brisban Wildlands, Divinity's Reach, Eternal Battleground (WvW), Fireheart Rise, Gendarran Fields, Harathi Hinterlands, Iron Marches, Kessex Hills, Metrica Province, Plains of Ashford, Queensdale

Skales are amphibious creatures found in wetlands of the world. Like salamanders, they have the ability to heal wounds and regenerate health at an accelerated rate. They are lucrative targets for hunting because of all the resources that can be gathered from them. Though very aggressive, you're unlikely to end up fighting very many skales simultaneously. This makes them relatively safe so long as you don't kite them far and wide, accidentally drawing more enemies into the conflict.

SKELK

Where Found:	Often Near Water
Useful Items:	Fangs, Venom Sacs, Leather Salvage
Common Attacks:	Melee, Often Have Teleport or Shadow Step
Locations:	Bloodtide Coast, Brisban Wildlands, Caledon Forest, Diessa Plateau, Eternal Battleground (WvW), Fireheart Rise, Frostgorge Sound, Gendarran Fields, Harathi Hinterlands, Iron Marches, Lornar's Pass, Metrica Province, Mount Maelstrom, Plains of Ashford, Queensdale, Snowden Drifts, Sparkfly Fen, Straits of Devastation, Timberline Falls, Wayfarer Foothills

Skelks are small sneaky lizards that stand on their hind legs. In combat they have abilities that let them appear behind you and rake you with their claws. When they start this disappearing act, dodge out of the way so the cowards can't slash into your back. Lay into them when the skelks reappear and ensure you keep the upper hand in the battle. These monsters don't have particularly high health, so they die quickly as long as you stay on your toes.

SKRITT

Where Found:	Caves and Mountainous Areas
Useful Items:	Scales, Totems, Leather Salvage, Metal Salvage
Common Attacks:	Profession Based
Locations:	Blazeridge Steppes, Brisban Wildlands, Caledon Forest, Dredgehaunt Cliffs, Fields of Ruin, Lornar's Pass, Metrica Province, Queensdale, Timberline Falls

These rat-like humanoids are as much pests as the four-legged creature they look like. Skritt make homes in areas that are either dark or hard to get into. They prefer homes close to living spaces of other humanoids. This helps them hide with the things they steal, which tend to be anything not nailed down. Skritt may appear silly and cute, but they can do real damage with their makeshift weapons. In addition, they fight in groups whenever they can. You might have trouble getting just one or two skritt at a time if you don't pull carefully when entering their areas.

For a laugh, engage a group of skritt and then run away from them. See what they yell as you get away.

TYPE	ATTACKS
Skritt Bottle Lobber	Range, Throws Junk, Buffs Allies
Skritt Forager	Melee, Big Damage
Skritt Gear Lobber	Range, Sets Bombs, Deploys Turrets
Skritt Pistolier	Range
Skritt Sentry	Melee

SONS OF SVANIR

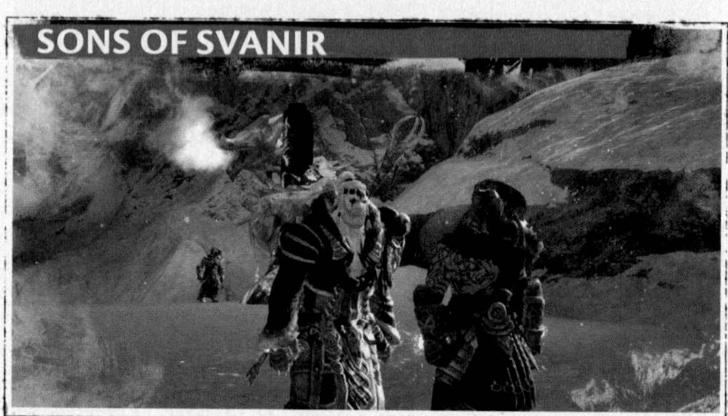

Where Found:	Norn Lands
Useful Items:	Totems, Metal Salvage
Common Attacks:	Often Warriors or Rangers
Locations:	Dredgehaunt Cliffs, Frostgorge Sound, Hoelbrak, Honor of the Waves, Snowden Drifts, Wayfarer Foothills

These norn have chosen to follow the teachings of their dead leader Svanir who was corrupted by the Elder Dragon Jormag. This faction is tolerated, minimally, in norn society. However, outside of the norn capital city, the Sons of Svanir will attack anyone on sight.

Almost all Sons of Svanir are brutal damage dealers. Whether up close or at range, expect these guys to pack a mighty punch. Fight them conservatively, heal often, and break line of sight to ensure the ranged members of their groups have to come to you. Kiting is hard against Sons of Svanir teams, as many of them have Cripple or Chill to make your escape more difficult. Melee AoE attacks are often more successful against these jerks.

TYPE	ATTACKS
Son of Svanir	Range, Cripple, Chill
Icebrood Berserker	Range, Champion, Cripple, Chill, Reflect Projectiles
Icebrood Hunter	Range, Chill, Summon Wolf
Icebrood Claymore	Melee, AoE, Bleed
Icebrood Mauler	Melee, Knockdown, Freeze
Icebrood Seer	Range, Champion, Chill, Summon Minions

SPIDER

Where Found:	Caves, Forests
Useful Items:	Venom Sacs
Common Attacks:	Melee, Poison, Pull
Locations:	Blazeridge Steppes, Bloodtide Coast, Dredgehaunt Cliffs, Fields of Ruin, Fireheart Rise, Frostgorge Sound, Gendarran Fields, Harathi Hinterlands, Iron Marches, Lornar's Pass, Snowden Drifts, Timberline Falls, Wayfarer Foothills

Spiders are foul pests that use damage over time and sometimes positional attacks to disrupt heroes. Healing abilities that remove conditions are extremely useful when fighting spiders; their poison isn't enough to kill with a single application, but it drags you down eventually, unless you stop to rest between every battle. High-damage melee weapons are the best for killing spiders because many of them can pull you into melee, limiting the value of ranged weapons and kiting techniques.

TROLL

Where Found:	Frozen Tundra, Forests, Caves
Useful Items:	Vials of Blood, Bones, Venom Sacs, Cloth Salvage
Common Attacks:	Melee, Knockdown, Self Healing
Locations:	Bloodtide Coast, Brisban Wildlands, Caledon Forest, Dredgehaunt Cliffs, Fireheart Rise, Frostgorge Sound, Gendarran Fields, Kessex Hills, Lornar's Pass, Metrica Province, Mount Maelstrom, Plains of Ashford, Snowden Drifts, Sparkfly Fen, Timberline Falls, Wayfarer Foothills

Trolls are hunchbacked and brutish-looking humanoids. They have bad posture and are large and thickly built. They don't wear much more than rags and don't carry any weapons. Trolls can speak, but don't expect any meaningful conversations; they will attack you on sight. They're renowned for their fortitude. Expect them to regenerate and heal their wounds.

Conditions that cause damage over time are very effective against trolls because these skills keep the troll's healing in check. Instead of spreading your damage around, focus on a single target and bring it down as fast as possible.

Though trolls aren't usually found in high numbers, they're still a great target for crafters hunting through the wilderness. Use them as targets of opportunity because they drop such a large number of useful ingredients.

WAVE RIDER

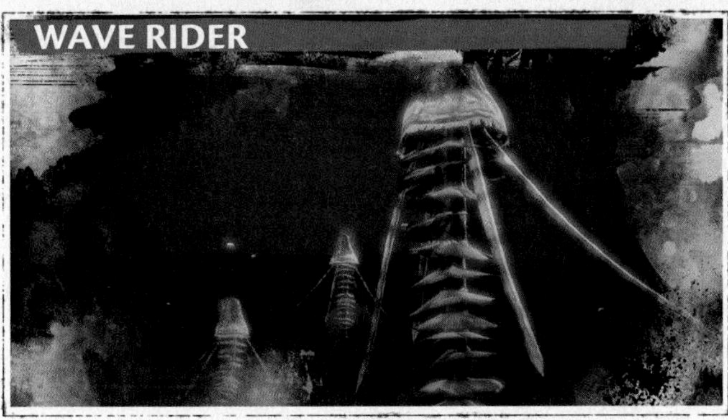

Where Found:	Deep Water
Useful Items:	Scales
Common Attacks:	Melee, Poison AoE
Locations:	Bloodtide Coast, Snowden Drifts, Kessex Hills, Lion's Arch, Frostgorge Sound, Lornar's Pass

Wave riders are large jellyfish that trail a long line of poisonous tentacles behind them. These are not passive creatures that wait for prey. Wave riders swim up to their victims to whip them with their tentacles and let their poison do its work.

Unless your hero is able to remove conditions painlessly, and frequently, it's smart to switch to ranged weapons for these fights.

WOLF (COYOTE)

Where Found:	Forests and Open Land
Useful Items:	Fangs, Leather Salvage, Meat
Common Attacks:	Melee, Summon Allies
Locations:	Brisban Wildlands, Caledon Forest, Cursed Shore, Eternal Battleground (WvW), Fields of Ruin, Frostgorge Sound, Gendarran Fields, Harathi Hinterlands, Hoelbrak, Iron Marches, Lornar's Pass, Mount Maelstrom, Queensdale, Snowden Drifts, Sparkfly Fen, The Grove, Timberline Falls, Wayfarer Foothills

Wolves live in packs and can be killed in high numbers when you find their dens. They're hunted for fangs and pelts so crafters can make insignias. Because they rely on melee damage, it's easy to group wolves together for AoE attacks. Another technique is to allow wolves to use their howl ability to summon more wolves. That way, you get to kill more enemies without having to hunt them down. If you do this, be very careful of getting into fights that are too big or too long for your character to handle. This is a better technique when you have a group, so there are characters to back each other up if/when things go wrong.

WURM

Where Found:	Colder Climates
Useful Items:	Fangs, Venom Sacs
Common Attacks:	Ranged, Tunnels, Bites, Back Away, May Have Knockdowns
Locations:	Brisban Wildlands, Caledon Forest, Diessa Plateau, Dredgehaunt Cliffs, Fireheart Rise, Frostgorge Sound, Gendarran Fields, Kessex Hills, Lornar's Pass, Metrica Province, Queensdale, Snowden Drifts, Sparkfly Fen, Straits of Devastation, Timberline Falls, Wayfarer Foothills

Wurms are a massive threat to melee troops. They hide in the ground and then burst up to deal damage to everyone nearby. Stay away from wurms when they submerge and wait to reengage them until they've come back to the surface! Even after that, they knock people around and automatically back away from your characters when struck. That frustrates any melee attacks that are channeled. It's quite a hassle.

Switch to ranged weapons and kill the wurms from medium range. That keeps them from backing up out of your attack range during the early hits of the fight. Ranged characters with mobility also benefit from this because some wurms have slow ranged attacks that miss strafing characters. Use this to great advantage by circling around the wurms and shooting them from a safe distance.

PLAYER VS. PLAYER WARFARE

Guild Wars 2 provides challenges to a variety of players. Dungeon delvers, PvE guilds, and soloists are happy to wander around the world, fighting monsters and saving the day. But what about the players who want to test each other and find out who is the best? That's what PvP is for, and there are several ways to go about it.

This chapter takes you through the major battles found in WvW (when servers compete against each other) and then it covers the smaller and more controlled matches for more organized PvP.

GETTING READY TO FIGHT

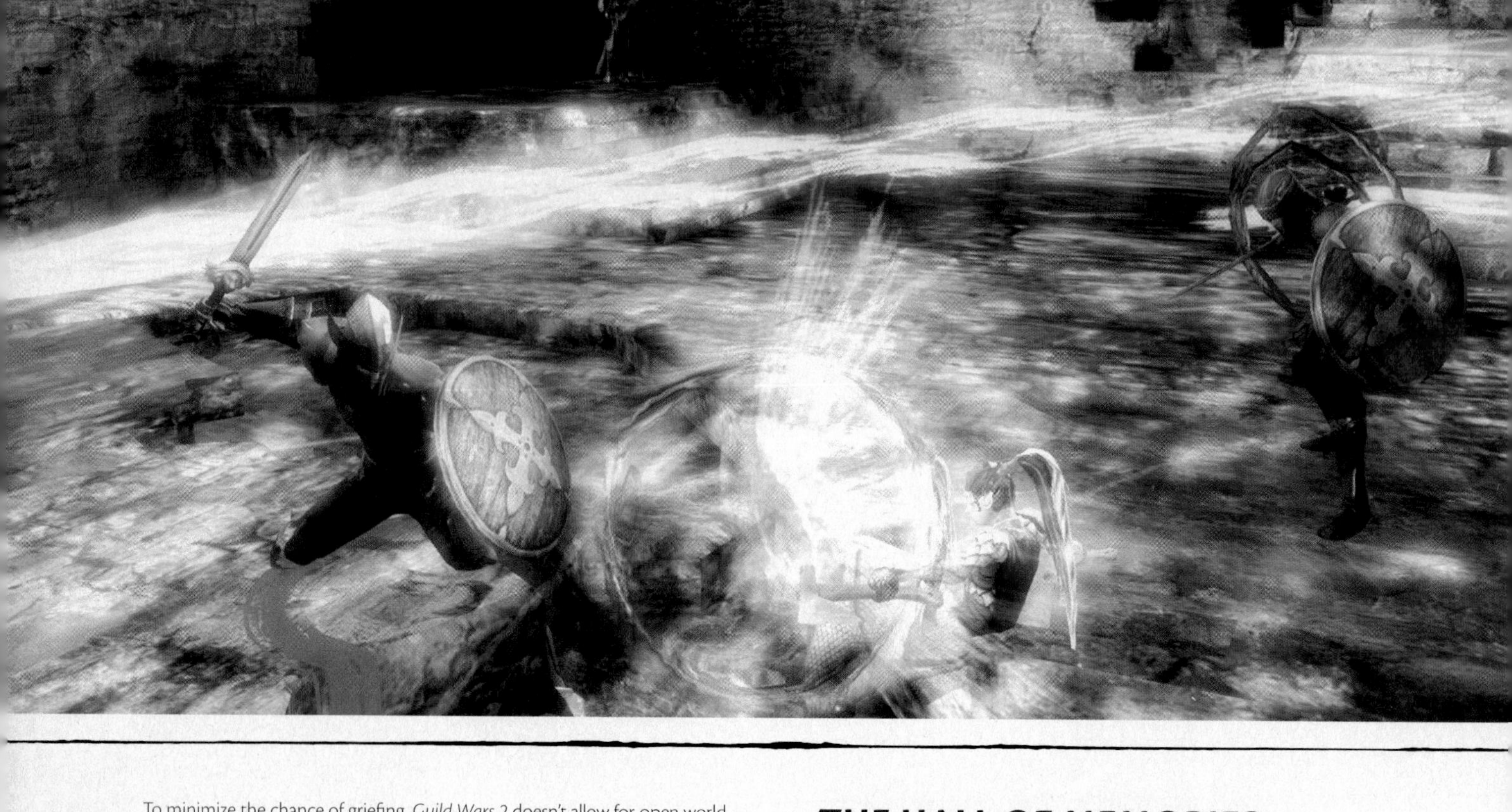

To minimize the chance of griefing, *Guild Wars 2* doesn't allow for open world fighting in its PvE zones. Characters in Tyria are fully cooperative, cannot hurt each other, and that's it. You never have to worry about friendly fire, being ganked (attacked and murdered by higher-level characters), or any other negative character interactions.

To access PvP, use the PvP tab in your Hero screen. Pressing "H" brings up the Hero window; click on the PvP tab on the left, and then select "Go to the Mists." From there you can find smaller battles, or just mess around with your character at level 80 with all of their skills unlocked. The PvP screen is also where you can see your stats for this part of the game. Glory, in case you're wondering, is like a currency. You accrue it while fighting enemies in PvP matches, and it's used to upgrade your equipment.

If you want to enter WvW and fight in the Eternal Battlegrounds, open the WvW tab in the upper left portion of the screen, and use the interface there to teleport into these contested maps.

During your first trip into the Mists, the game puts you through a minor tutorial in PvP combat. Your character gets simple weaponry that suits your profession, and a number of quick events pop up as you move through the outer section of the Mists. Follow the directions onscreen to learn about this style of gameplay, or walk to the far side of the map to enter a gate and leave the tutorial. You're now in the normal lobby that the other PvPers access.

THE HALL OF MEMORIES (THE PVP LOBBY)

Going straight into matches is fine, but you can get your feet wet first if you'd like to have a more controlled entry into this style of play. The first area of the Mists is essentially a PvP lobby. That's where you should start unless you really know what you're doing. The lobby has testing dummies to try out various weapon skills. You can trade for different weapons and armor, and then switch around traits and skills to your heart's content.

Everyone is set to level 80 in the lobby, so you can compare damage and general fighting capabilities between your various characters without it being an apples and oranges type of issue.

Another aspect of the lobby is that it's a hub for all PvP services. There are Asura Gates to take your character back to Tyria (specifically, to Lion's Arch). Use NPCs in the area to start special matches, join others in PvP, buy PvP weapons and armor, or wander around the island and improve your skills.

An instructor, near the entrance, shows you the locations of all pertinent training groups and vendors in the lobby. You can train for ground combat, underwater fighting, use of siege equipment, practice on simple dummies, change gear at the vendors, spend Glory, or talk to other players and trade stories and tactics.

Talk to the vendors in the area to outfit your character for any style of fighting. Make sure you have the weapon types you prefer, and don't be afraid to try out new combinations over time. The things you fall in love with in PvE may not be the ones you enjoy for PvP.

The base tier of PvP items is free, so you're never going to be stuck without appropriate gear. You can stock up on weapons of various types, and try out each to see how well they work for you against other people.

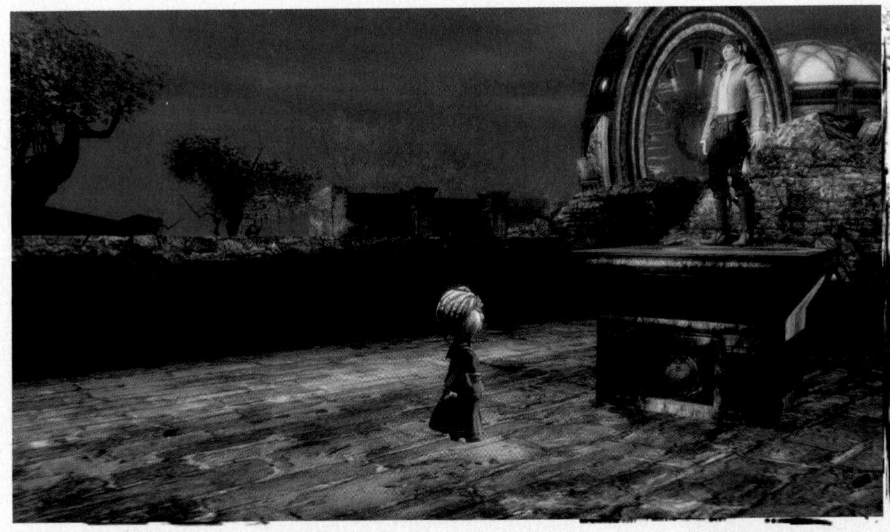

High mobility is incredibly useful and important when fighting other players, so strongly consider one or more ranged weapons that look like they'd be good for kiting or anti-kiting work. Your enemies are quite likely to be doing the same thing!

Make sure to set up your skills. You have access to everything that your profession has to offer, including elite skills. Set up a strong default bar that has at least some healing, condition removal, and damage immunity/mitigation. That's your default for PvP. While you might find something preferable over time, it's good to start out with these types of abilities until you know exactly what you're doing.

When you want to leave the PvP side of the game, go back to your Hero screen and exit from there. Or, take the Asura Gate back to Lion's Arch.

COMMON TIPS

Before talking about specific types of PvP, we'll go over some of the general rules and tactics you'll need for your early engagements.

KEEP MOVING!

Mobile targets are harder to hit with AoEs and a number of short-range attacks. If you plant your feet for a channeling skill, realize that your opponents are quite likely to move and cause most of the effect to miss.

Counter speed with speed. Make sure you move fast, use obstacles to break line of sight at critical moments, and try to get behind enemies whenever possible. The more attacks your opponent wastes, the more likely your hero will win the fight.

> "If you are about to go down, try to do so near an ally so they can revive you!"
>
> —*Peter Larkin*

SLOW OR IMMOBILIZE ENEMIES

When you do need to attack with short-range skills or channeled abilities, consider leading with attacks that Daze, Chill, Immobilize, or Cripple your target. If they can't run away, they'll have to eat the damage from your heaviest attacks. Melee characters have to fight like this all the time in PvP. Jump/shadowstep over to opponents, keep them from getting away, and lay into the fools. That's how it's done.

Also remember that a slow/disabled enemy looks vulnerable to more than your hero. Other players are more likely to jump in and trash your enemy when they look weak. This is a good way to have your team focus fire on individual targets.

DON'T LET THEM DO IT TO YOU

Evade early and often if you think someone is setting up a heavy attack run. As soon as he starts closing aggressively, dodge behind something, roll through the person, or otherwise get out of the way. Skills that Stun give you a golden opportunity to escape as well. Even a second or two can be enough to disrupt someone's best attack routine.

KILL THE OWNER, NOT THE PET

Various monsters can be summoned during battle. They'll hassle your character, and it seems tempting to go after them. If you're behind cover, that's fine. Kill the offending creature when you aren't taking fire from anything else. However, don't waste attacks on these lesser enemies when there are bigger fish to fry. When you're out in the open, direct your damage toward the hero who summoned those pets. That's who you need to kill to stop the creatures for more than a few moments. Don't get distracted!

KEEP YOUR MIND ON THE PRIZE

Whether you're sieging a keep, going after a supply caravan, or capturing a location in PvP, you have to think about your objective. Don't let stray enemies draw you away from your group or your goal. Out in the open you're just fighting meat. You aren't getting substantial points for your team, and you're left vulnerable while your allies stay on task and do the real work.

Stay with your group, fight near the objectives, and don't give in to the temptation to fight for sheer combat's sake. Odds are, your enemy is just manipulating you into doing something silly. That lone mesmer could have two buddies waiting around the corner to rip you in half.

THIS ISN'T A DPS RACE

"Glass cannons may do a lot of damage, but they're not so good at holding objectives. Consider adding some survivability to your build!"

—Peter Larkin

Sheer damage output is NOT the way to survive PvP engagements. It's nice to kick people around and look like the bad guy on campus, but you won't live for long. Abilities that provide Protection, Invulnerability, Stuns, and good healing are much more important. Many foes can start a war of attrition with you, and that's when survival and mitigation are of the utmost importance.

CONDITIONS ARE NOT YOUR FRIEND

Make sure at least one of your skills can clear conditions from your character. You can't afford to meet enemies that rely on conditions for damage without such a skill on your bar. They'll eat you alive!

AND SPEAKING OF CONDITIONS...

Poison, Burning, and Bleeding go right through armor. When you're hunting heavy metal (i.e., warriors and guardians), it's great to use these damage over time abilities. That extra armor won't mean nearly as much.

DON'T BE PREDICTABLE

Use multiple routes to get through each map. Mix up the attack routines you use, especially later in each fight. Don't give enemies time to adapt to your style; otherwise they'll start figuring out the best counters to your tactics.

SWITCH SKILLS WHEN NECESSARY

You can't alter your traits during a PvP engagement, but skills are another story. If your current configuration doesn't meet your team's needs, change your bar. This is also a good way to surprise enemies who think they know what you're capable of.

BE POLITE (OR EVEN FRIENDLY)

Teams that work well together can take out opponents who are distracted with whining and in-fighting. Avoid language that is going to disrupt your allies. "You need to do X" may not sound that rude, but is it likely to work? People don't listen when you bark commands. Not many players are going to be real-life military commanders, right? The way to get people listening is to use cooperative language that doesn't trigger defensive thinking.

"We could use more healing and condition clearing. I've slotted another skill for that. Could you put X on your bar for the next fight?"

GETTING GLORY

Unlike most online games with a PvP element, the reward currency in *Guild Wars 2* is NOT given for completing matches. Most games give you a greater amount for winning, a lesser amount for losing, and a very modest amount during a match for completing various objectives.

This has led to a major and consistent problem in online PvP: some people join matches and don't bother participating. They'll get various rewards just for standing on the spawn point and taking up space. It's very unpleasant to watch, especially if you're losing because your team doesn't have enough real players.

That's not a big problem in *Guild Wars 2*. Glory is only awarded for actions the player actually takes. You are rewarded for killing enemies, taking territory, and defending your areas against other attackers. You won't have to wait for the end of matches—you can leave any time—and everything you've done still counts. Players who don't work with the team get very little Glory (if any).

Stay with allies, take and defend areas together, and watch the rewards come in.

WORLD VS. WORLD

ETERNAL BATTLEGROUND

Red Hill
Mendon's Gap
Veloka Slopes
Speldan Clearcut
Pangloss Rise
Zraith's Beacon
Red Overlook
Red Home
Ogrewatch Cut
Anzalias Pass
Orgoth Uplands
Molevek Work
Umberglade Woods
Rogue's Quarry
Stonemist Castle
Wildcreek Run
Durios Gulch
Aldon's Ledge
Bravost Escarpment
Green Lowlands
Klovan Gully
Quentin Lake
Blue Lowlands
Green Hill
Jerrifer's Slough
Golanta Clearing
Darkrait Inlet
Danelon Passage
Blue Hill
Langor Gulch

BORDERLAND

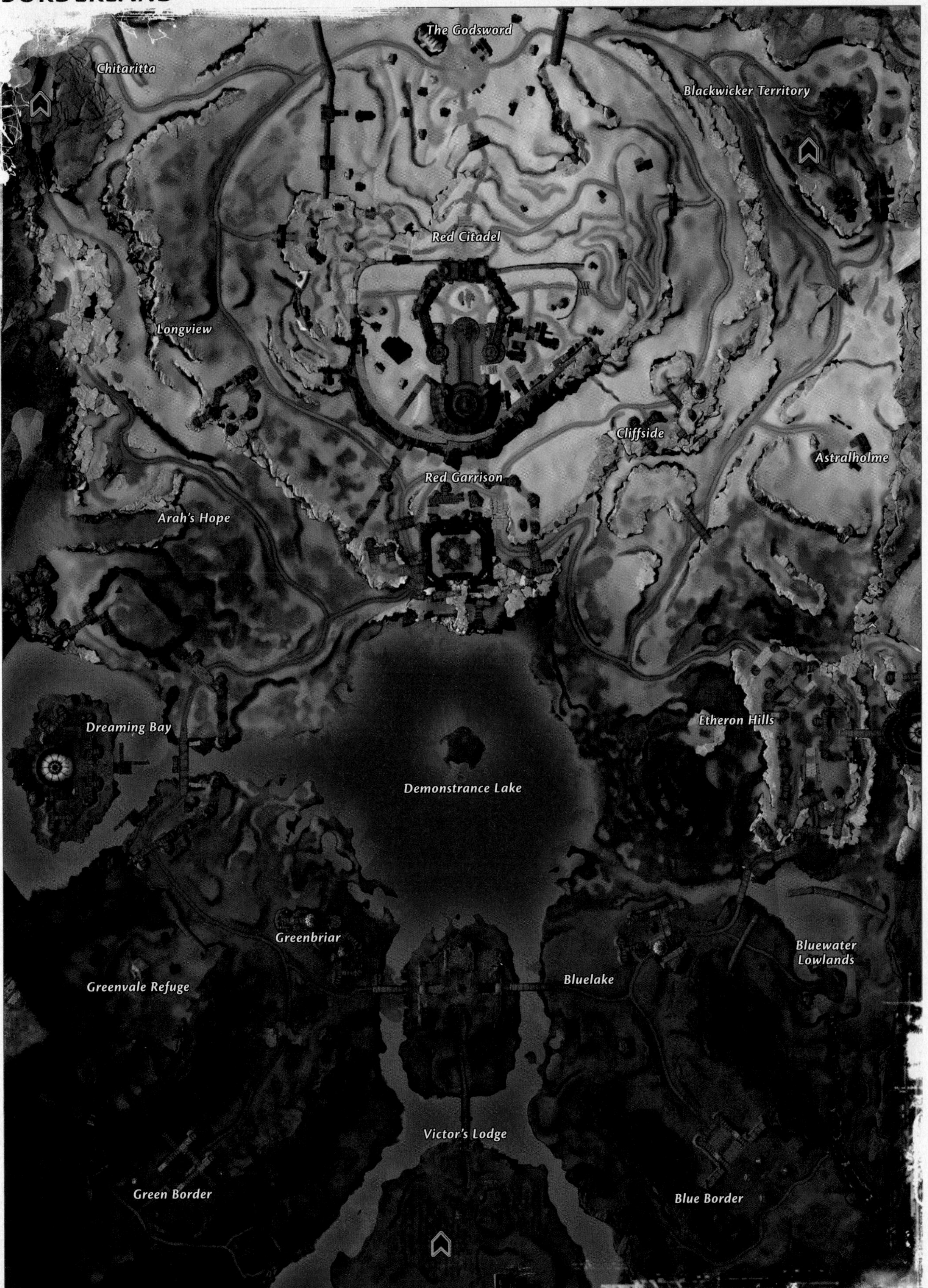
The Godsword
Chitaritta
Blackwicker Territory
Red Citadel
Longview
Cliffside
Astralholme
Red Garrison
Arah's Hope
Etheron Hills
Dreaming Bay
Demonstrance Lake
Greenbriar
Bluewater Lowlands
Greenvale Refuge
Bluelake
Victor's Lodge
Green Border
Blue Border

The Eternal Battlegrounds pits three servers against each other for a two-week period. In-game, each server is called a world, so three worlds will be competing against each other for dominance of the Eternal Battlegrounds.

In this form of PvP, your character won't have new equipment, traits, and skills. You have to outfit yourself properly for your engagements (though everyone is still fixed at level 80 to provide a somewhat even playing field).

DYNAMIC LEVEL ADJUSTMENT IN WvW

True level-80 characters have better gear, full access to their traits, and are ready for anything the other worlds have to throw at them. Lower-level heroes are raised to 80, but they don't have high-end equipment, the best traits, and so forth. They can still contribute, but it's rewarding to level up and see your character get better and better over time.

If you find that you're losing more fights than you win, take heart and don't get upset with yourself. You're leveling up, learning how to play, and may be facing people with multiple advantages. Keep trying and you'll soon find that your hero is on par (or superior) to the enemies you face.

To see how your team is doing or to enter WvW (whether in the Mists or not), press "B," though your personal keyboard settings may differ. All three servers and their points are shown there. At the top, there are tallies for the cumulative points the teams have earned during the battle. Below is a breakdown of the assets each team has conquered.

WvW has tangible benefits for everyone on the server (not just for participants). Taking and holding territory gets your server bonuses for crafting, fighting, and survival. These affect players in PvP, PvE, and for item creation. Because of this, you have every reason to want your side to do well.

These bonuses are not set up in a way that steals from other servers when you take the lead. No one's values go down because the other side is doing well. Your numbers just won't go up as quickly. This is also nice for teams that do well for a few days and then lose the lead; all of the bonuses you gain will stay for the entire duration of the battle. This encourages even a losing server to rally for a day or two. The more people they bring into the fight, the easier it is to get some of their perks before the more dangerous server reasserts itself.

THE LAYOUT

WvW is set up as a series of four connected regions. The Eternal Battlegrounds' primary combative area is a central region with a massive keep and a number of lesser fortresses throughout the zone. Towers and resource points are available as well. Each side region has resources, though to a lesser degree than the central area.

Each server that is participating in the WvW action takes one of the side areas (Red, Blue, or Green). You'll be assigned to the same one as your server mates. Though your enemies may change every two weeks, your allies will be the same. This makes it easier to form lasting alliances and learn how to best cooperate with your team.

THE BASIC GOAL

Put simply, you want to take over more territory than your enemies. Under ideal circumstances, you want to hold everything in your color's starting region, everything in the center, and as much as possible in the other two sides' territory.

Doing that every time, at all hours, isn't going to be easy. But that's still your basic goal. Your team could lose fights constantly, have four deaths to every kill, and still be winning the WvW fight. This isn't about kills. Everything rests on land control.

GETTING POINTS

Points are given out every five minutes based on the number of areas your team controls at that time. The more structures you control, the better. More powerful and important areas are worth even more points.

Supply Camps are worth five points per cycle. Defensive areas are worth 10, 25, or 50, depending on the size of the fortress. The Castle is the only building worth a full 50 points, so it's contested at all times.

POINT VALUES FOR STRUCTURES

Area	Point Value
Supply Camp	5
Tower	10
Keep	25
Castle	50

If your team looks like the strongest or second-strongest one in the match, go ahead and battle it out for the biggest and most valuable locations. The weakest team may want to set its goals lower. Why fight and continually lose against a superior force? Instead, make sure to attack supply areas and less-defended keeps. Grab locations and hold them long enough to score some points. Have your main force stay mobile and take whatever is weak. You might not get to usurp the number one spot, but this ensures that even a side with lower numbers or weaker gear can compete, have fun, and get bonuses for its server.

Another way to earn points is to kill sentries at key points through the map, escort Dolyaks, or kill Dolyaks that are being escorted by other teams. Sentries and enemy Dolyaks are worth 1 point each. Successful Dolyak escorts are worth 3 points!

HOW TO PROCEED

Organize into groups with other members of your server. It's very important to work together; individual characters can be picked off easily by enemy groups, and it's impossible to take most areas without the help of other people. An individual can, at best, harass supply routes, scout, and report information back to other people so they can better organize their assaults or counter the other team's attacks.

Voice communication is essential. Getting it for your group is a must, and it's even better if you can field a server for even more of your team. Having 30-40 people work together is a major boon; you can have strike teams at multiple points in the map that turn on a dime when they need to switch targets or unite for a larger strike against a heavy target.

The most mobile characters should slot skills for swiftness, bonuses to base movement speed, and stability. Have them race across the map, reporting targets and enemy movement.

Larger groups should grab defensive bonuses, AoE attacks, healing, and group boons. These are the teams that stick together and siege neutral or enemy-controlled fortresses. Be prepared to fight against extremely high-level enemies—even the guards are high level and deal serious damage. The lords that protect the larger structures pack a huge punch.

SUPPLIES

Protect caravans that travel between supply points and the structures your team controls. These supplies are then collected at depots within the buildings; they're used to repair and improve structures and weapons at that location. All of this is controlled by individual players, so it won't happen without your help.

For example, walls can be repaired after taking damage. Have someone withdraw supplies from the depot and walk over to the wall. Interact with the wall to use the supplies and fix the damage that's been done. You can only carry 10 supplies at a time, so larger projects require multiple trips to the depot.

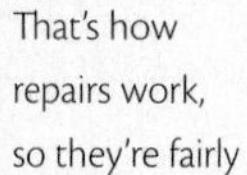

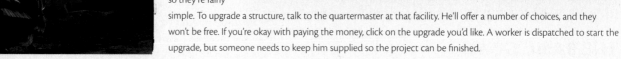

That's how repairs work, so they're fairly simple. To upgrade a structure, talk to the quartermaster at that facility. He'll offer a number of choices, and they won't be free. If you're okay with paying the money, click on the upgrade you'd like. A worker is dispatched to start the upgrade, but someone needs to keep him supplied so the project can be finished.

QUARTERMASTER UPGRADES

- **Hire Outfitter:** Sells supplies (Costs 5 Silver, 100 Supplies).
- **Hire Siegemaster:** Sells siege weapon blueprints (Costs 10 Silver, 200 Supplies).
- **Hire Patrol:** Guards wander around the keep, protecting it from attack (Costs 20 Silver, 300 Supplies).
- **Hire a Second Worker:** Structural upgrades are completed faster (Costs 10 Silver, 100 Supplies).
- **More Guards:** Adds more guards to the keep (Costs 25 Silver, 250 Supplies).
- **Raise Guard Level:** Increases the level of keep guards (Costs 50 Silver, 500 Supplies).
- **Build Waypoint:** Adds a waypoint for your team (Costs 20 Silver, 500 Karma, and 100 Supplies).
- **Build Cannons:** Adds new cannons to defend the area.
- **Build Mortars:** Adds new mortars to defend the area.
- **Reinforce Keep:** Upgrades the walls and doors of the fortress (Costs 10 Silver, 50 Supplies).
- **Reinforce Doors:** Strengthens the doors of the keep (Costs 20 Silver, 100 Supplies).
- **Fortify Keep:** Makes the walls harder to destroy.

All of these help to ensure your structure can defend against larger and larger attacking forces without falling. The teams that are already winning have the most reason to invest in this way. Their soldiers are already stretching themselves thin by having to defend more structures over a wider area. That means they'll have to hold against more people with fewer and fewer troops.

ALWAYS LOOK FOR A NEW PLACE TO STRIKE

Teams that aren't doing as well should instead group together into massive strike forces, break through poorly defended fortresses (even when they're well upgraded), and then move on to repeat the assault somewhere else. Force the other team to waste time and resources on their upgrades. That can be demoralizing, and it's a decent way to rally your people. Even if you can't win the war, make sure your team can focus fire and win individual battles.

You might be wondering why a losing team wouldn't want to upgrade the few structures they still control. They still can, certainly, and that's fine. It's just that holing up in one keep doesn't guarantee you'll be able to hold that point. It's a dangerous type of thinking. If a losing force goes on the defensive, they're more likely to stay on the bottom. They're already either outnumbered or outskilled (that's why they're having trouble in the first place). If another team sees that they're all in one place, they might just decide to break the group's morale even further.

By spreading out, you make it harder to tell where your team will strike next. And then, if you come together quickly, the other sides won't have as long to react before you've grabbed something. Also, the other teams have to keep fighting each other. If your side picks off little keeps while the number one and two teams batter each other, it's all to your benefit.

SIEGE MASTERS

SIEGE MASTER BLUEPRINTS

Item	Cost
Flame Ram	4 Silver
Arrow Cart Blueprints	4 Silver
Ballista Blueprints	6 Silver
Catapult Blueprints	8 Silver
Siege Golem Blueprints	100 Silver
Trebuchet Blueprints	16 Silver

Siege Masters are an upgrade you grab from the Quartermaster. Once completed, these new NPCs sell blueprints for new weapon emplacements. Buying one puts it in your inventory; using it allows you to place the structure. Then you must use supplies to build the item. This often requires several trips back to the supply depot, so don't deploy something too far from there and end up being unable to finish it while it's still needed.

SIEGING A FORTRESS

Siege assault and defense is a major aspect of WvW. The attackers can break through doors or walls to gain entry to the fortress, and the defenders work to repair these structures while killing members of the attacking force.

There are multiple ways to get into an enemy fortress, so make sure to scout the building and look for weak points. You can focus on a single entry point and try to overwhelm the defenders, or attack one point as a feint and have another team break in from a hidden direction. Doors and walls can be damaged with your weapons and spells, but siege weapons are much more powerful. The blueprints for siege weapons don't cost much money, but they require more effort in bringing supplies to build them and defend them.

Watch out for enemy players and guards. Make sure patrols are killed off as quickly as possible, especially if there is a lull in the fighting. If your opponents ever back off, use the time to restore fallen teammates, kill guards, and assess how the battle is going.

Defending a keep can be hard work. Several players will have to be on repair duty to keep the walls and doors from falling down. Other players have to man the walls to fire down on enemies attacking the door. Defensive siege weapons can be built or upgraded as well. Just keep in mind that your amount of supplies will be limited. Using siege weapons on the walls will greatly increase your range and damage. If you need to get out of the keep, use the teleportation points that only work for defenders to pop in and out of the area. A well-timed charge can roll through an attacking force and destroy its siege weapons.

You can use AoEs through doors, so be careful if you're close to a door and start taking sudden damage. Break off to the side to heal and avoid future damage if things start getting too intense.

Attackers shouldn't let supplies reach an area they're trying to siege. Kill any bulls that approach to ensure the defenders cannot upgrade their building while you're trying to fight them. This also castrates their ability to repair damages.

Defenders should use any deployed mortars, cannons, and such to deal more distant AoE damage while fighting against superior numbers.

SQUAD COMMANDERS

Groups in WvW are led by a squad commander. This person is able to designate areas for attack and defense. This helps organize the squad so it can come together for important tasks. Choose structures to attack or defend, protect or ambush supply caravans, and help the general war effort.

This is not a duty to be taken lightly. You need considerable experience in WvW to lead squads properly. In addition, it costs 100 gold pieces to purchase the tome that lets you become a squad commander. That's a great deal of cash, so think long and hard before you make the big leap.

SMALL-SCALE PvP

Organized PvP is an entirely different animal. These matches have set levels, team sizes, and are generally more controlled. You'll never have to deal with radically unfair set-ups, so personal skill plays a huge part in whether your side wins or loses.

Unlike WvW, your team isn't decided by server. It might be different each time you play, so look at your armor to quickly tell which side you've joined. Everyone looks red or blue, making it easy to tell who's fighting whom.

If your character goes down, enemies are likely to try and finish you off. They'll get a "Finish Them!" interaction any time they get close to your fallen character. Allies should attack the enemies that approach so they are driven off or downed before they can do this.

"If you can, save any skills that grant stability for finishing enemy players. Doing so ensures others cannot interrupt your *coup de grâce* with crowd control."

—Peter Larkin

Slain characters are out of the fight for a few moments. They get the option to respawn in their team's fortress after a short delay.

THE BATTLE OF KYHLO

This match pits two teams against each other for small-scale territory control. Both sides are racing to get 500 points before the other, and there are several ways to go about this.

Time Limit	15 minutes
How to Get Points	Hold control points (each area grants 1 point/2 seconds)

"In structured PvP, you get 10 points for finishing an enemy player, but you get more points for capturing and holding objectives. Fight on the objectives to maximize point gain!"

—Peter Larkin

There are three control points on the map. The Windmill (WM) is on the northern side of the map. The Clocktower (CT) is in the center, dominating the area. Over by the southern end of the map is a Mansion (MN). The red team starts in the northwest, and the blue team starts in the southeast.

It's quite possible to win by grabbing two control points and defending them for the remainder of the match. This is a conservative plan, but it's very effective if you have a patient team.

More aggressive players try to shut out the other force entirely by going after every point. This is very challenging unless you're facing an extremely unskilled enemy force. If you think your people have a huge edge, go ahead and try it. Just remember that it's easy to lose multiple battles if you spread your team across the entire map.

ARTILLERY DUELS

Each team has a trebuchet to assist in their efforts. The red team has theirs just south of the red base. The blue team's is north from their home. These weapons are amazingly powerful, especially if your opponents bunch together to try and seize a capture point. The downside is that these weapons can be destroyed.

Make sure that your enemies don't have free rein to fire on your buddies. Send people over to kill siege gunners and trash the trebuchet. If it's undefended, that's even better. Once destroyed, these weapons must be repaired by a kit that spawns. These repair kits have to be brought out to the trebuchet, and the person carrying the kit can't fight. They're easy prey unless another character tries to escort them, and that leaves at least two opponents out of the fight for a little while.

"Learning how long to charge trebuchet shots is key. For example, launching a half-power shot into the clock tower will land directly on the center control point."

—Andrew Freeman

Communication, as always, is an essential part of victory. Have your team members divide up. One person grabs the trebuchet, another three scout the capture points (and take them if possible), and a fifth goes after the enemy trebuchet. If the enemies bunch up, avoid the area where they're at their strongest. If they spread out too, figure out which of your buddies can win on their own and have the other players retreat and wait for help. Don't stay in any one place for long, or you'll end up being trebuchet food.

In the same mindset, call out large clusters of enemies so that your team's treb gunner can target them. Let your friend know if they're on-target, and help them make their fire as accurate as possible.

The trebuchets do enough damage to break through water pipes and buildings, so experiment with firing these weapons all over the map.

CONTROL POINTS

Capture territory by entering the designated circle and staying there until the area converts to your team's control. Try to fight within the circle whenever possible, so your team doesn't lose control while the skirmish rages. This gives reinforcements more time to hurry to your aid, whether you're on attack or defense.

It's not a huge run between the control points, so you should focus your troops on areas that are highly contested. If the enemies run around and get the area behind your force, retreat, smash them, and return to the center afterward. Swapping control points often risks losing the match, but it's extremely good for Glory (since each capture gives a bonus to your Glory).

The Mansion is surrounded by stairs, columns, and walkways that players with ranged weapons and spells can use to gain an elevation advantage. Use this to support allies attacking the center against a superior force. Hit the enemies with ranged AoEs to hurt the group quickly.

Scouts on top of the Clocktower roof can quickly look over the entire map. This is an excellent point for someone on voice chat. Call out enemy movements to your allies and prevent friends from walking into ambushes.

RAID OF THE CAPRICORN

Raid of the Capricorn is an interesting battleground because it features terrestrial and aquatic environments. You have to master the art of fighting other players with a wider range of weaponry, so practice your underwater fighting heavily to improve your performance here.

Time Limit	15 minutes
How to Get Points	Holding control points (each area grants 1 point/2 seconds) Killing enemy players (5 points)

There are three points of control in this raid. The Dock is near the red team's starting point. The Ruins (R) are in the center, submerged. And blue's starting point is closer to the Beach . There are cannons spread throughout the map; use these to launch AoE attacks against clusters of enemies. Even if you have decent skills of your own for this purpose, make sure enemies don't get to the cannons unimpeded.

Watch the Ruins carefully. They're easy to take with even a single character if people are getting bogged down in the overland section of the map. Don't cede this point to your enemies.

> "If the enemy is overwhelming one capture point, don't be afraid to avoid them and capture one of the points they're neglecting."
>
> —*Karl McLain*

In addition, you can save time moving from the Beach to the Dock by swimming under the boat in the center. Going around takes longer and leaves you exposed to ranged attacks. You're also easier to spot, so enemies have more time to prepare themselves for your arrival.

FOREST OF NIFLHEL

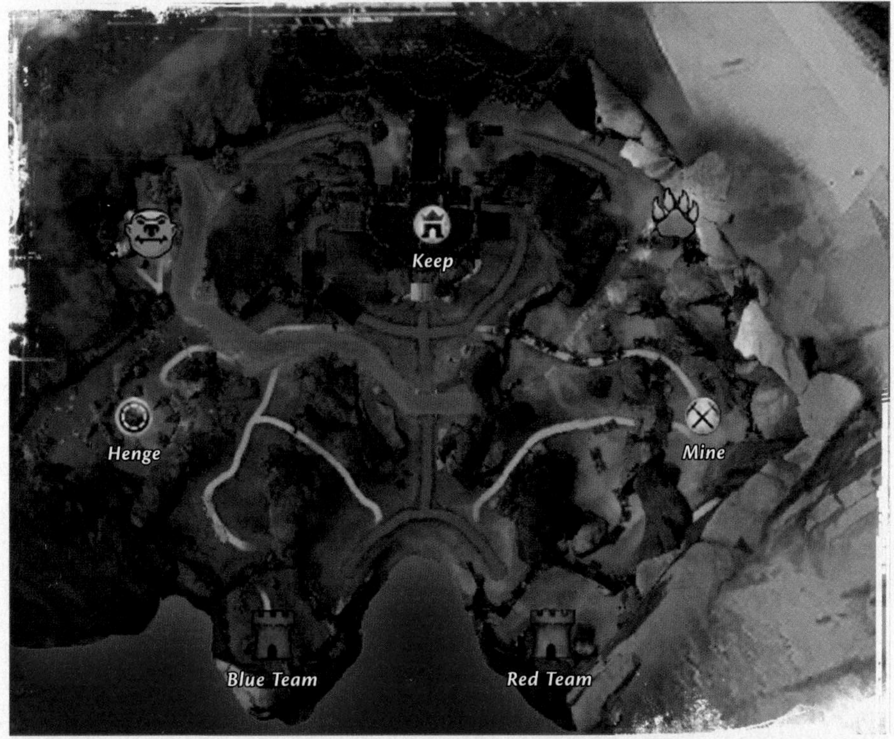

This conquest map features area control, standard combat rules, and special NPCs that spawn and can be killed for additional points, and boons, throughout the fight. The winner is declared when one team reaches 500 points or the time limit ends (at which point the leading team is declared the winner).

Time Limit	15 minutes
How to Get Points	Hold capture points(each area awards 1 point/2 seconds) Kill NPCs (25 points) Kill enemy players (5 points)

The Henge (H) is near the blue base. The Keep (K) is near the middle of the map, and Mine (M) is by the red base. Try to get the control points in two locations and hold them while killing players who come to attack.

If you're barely holding on to two control points, do not break off to kill the NPCs. Make sure your areas are locked down before dedicating forces to do this; otherwise you end up losing players at the control points and then the areas fall to your enemies. This ends up getting the other team even more points than you get from attacking and killing the NPC.

By the same token, watch your enemies' positions and exploit their mistakes. If they are dedicated to attacking an NPC, hit their control points *or* attack them while they're engaging the enemy. Distracted opponents make the most enjoyable targets.

It's easiest to win when your enemies focus on sheer combat. This map is large enough that troops can end up in long-term battles for territory between the capture points. Don't let your team fall for that. If multiple enemies are ambushing people in those spots, have one of your allies attack them there while the rest of you grab capture points and win the game. Periodically switch off which person is being sacrificed to the losing team so no one has to lose out on Glory.

Even if the enemies wise up to what you're doing, that's fine. You've gotten to score easy points for a while. If they charge your points in earnest, then fight them there. You get more Glory for that anyway!

LEGACY OF THE FOEFIRE

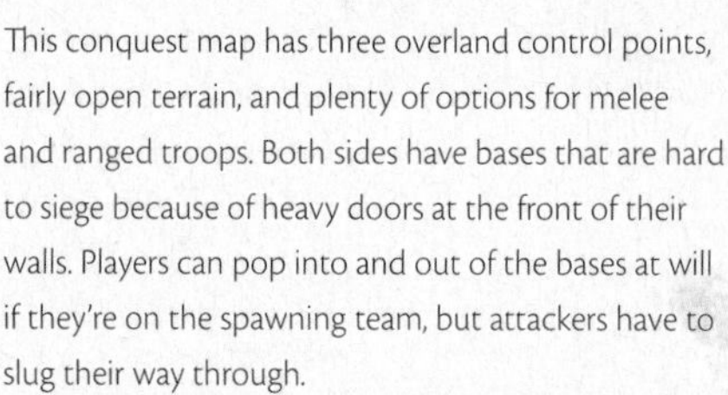

This conquest map has three overland control points, fairly open terrain, and plenty of options for melee and ranged troops. Both sides have bases that are hard to siege because of heavy doors at the front of their walls. Players can pop into and out of the bases at will if they're on the spawning team, but attackers have to slug their way through.

Control territory, kill the lord of the enemy's base, and defeat other players to earn points. The winner is declared when one team reaches 500 points or the time limit ends (at which point the leading team is declared the winner).

Time Limit	15 minutes
How to Get Points	Hold capture points (each area awards 1 point/2 seconds) Kill enemy players (5 points) Kill the enemy Lord (100 points)

All three control points are lined up between the two sides' bases. The central point is the best to have because it can reinforce either the northern or southern point without much delay. It's also a good area to start an attack on your enemy's base. Therefore, you can expect that this area will be contested throughout the engagement.

The enemy Lord is there to distract you. He is a tempting target (worth a huge sum of points), and it's possible to pull off an amazing turnaround if you get him. But, going after the Lord can also be a losing strategy. It normally takes two players to kill the Lord and his guards (two soldiers and two casters). If you take too long to succeed, you'll lose territory and points during the attempt, *and* the enemies might reinforce just in time to save their leader.

If you're going to hit the Lord, do it quickly and aggressively. The four guards tend to splatter if you go after them with everything you have. Even a single player can carefully pull them (one or two at a time), and kill them out in the courtyard. Everyone else that shows up can attack the Lord directly. Though high on health, he won't last for long against three players. Even two can dispatch him with considerable speed.

Though a small map, scouting is still immensely important here. Have people call out enemy attacks so you know if your Lord is in danger. Hit enemy groups from the rear after they've engaged the Lord. This is a great way to ruin their fun and pick up some free points.

Grab the middle and control the map for as long as possible. If you hold two control points the entire time while your opponent goes after one point and the Lord, your team is still going to win (unless deaths are extremely lopsided). Use the Lord as a distraction or as a target of opportunity. Don't make him your death ground.

TOURNAMENTS

There is a Tournament NPC on the eastern side of the entry area. Talk to him if you want to set up a specific PvP engagement between individuals wanting to see who can end up on top of the pile. This is particularly exciting for guilds or hotshot duelists who are trying to prove that they've got what it takes.

Expect this to be an area that develops heavily in the months after launch.

This chapter contains information about the many regions available for exploration and adventure within Tyria. The earlier zones, with content for levels 1-25, are covered in great depth. This is done to help new players learn the ropes by leading them through the first section of the game.

Later areas are described in far less detail because there isn't room to have an entire walkthrough for the entire game of *Guild Wars 2*! That would take up more space than the entire book, and there are plenty of other subjects we want to cover.

This chapter is organized by major regions. We talk about all of the regions within Ascalon (charr lands), Kryta (human), The Shiverpeaks (norn), the Tarnished Coast (sylvari and asura), Steamspur Mountains, and Orr.

THE WORLD OF GUILD WARS 2

SUBJECT TO CHANGE

Part of a multiplayer online game's appeal is that it can evolve. Content can be added or changed over time; indeed, players expect this to happen. This presents a unique set of challenges to a strategy guide. How can a guide provide adequate coverage when some of its information may become outdated due to game updates—sometimes as early as its initial release? We created this guide with these challenges in mind.

Our goal is to cover enough areas and events to help you become very comfortable with the game and level your character from 1-25 (and a little beyond). Providing 100% completion is not our intent, nor is this possible with an ever-evolving game environment. You can expect some locations, such as waypoints, renown hearts, skill challenges, and others to shift, thus contradicting some of the map markings on these pages. Nevertheless, this guide's event and map coverage will take you well past the point of establishing confidence in your gameplay and being ready to continue your adventures at will.

JUMPING PUZZLES

For the explorer in each of us, jumping puzzles are located throughout the world. You don't often find them on the beaten paths. Instead, they're hidden here and there, behind tiny nooks and on top of hills and cliffs that are easily missed. It takes patience and skill to navigate these tricky areas, but inquisitive adventurers will love the challenge!

To search as thoroughly as possible, don't simply aim for points of interest, renown tasks, and waypoints. Walk along the edges of maps, explore caves, and especially poke your head into any breaks in tree lines and mountains. Also, see if you can bounce your way up into areas that otherwise seem inaccessible. Not all of these are off limits, after all!

You can find some nifty events and places to wander if you put in the effort—have fun!

ASCALON

Ascalon was once a place of tremendous power for the Humans who lived there. They fought to hold off the warlike Charr who came to conquer and burn, but the Humans were not strong enough. Many died, and their spirits stir in the shadows. Old hatreds die hard, and the Charr may have hurt themselves more in victory than they would have suffered in defeat. A curse rests upon this land, calling the dead to forever rise in vengeance.

BLACK CITADEL

LEVEL RANGE:	Charr Capital City
WAYPOINTS:	11

The Black Citadel is a wonder of engineering. Built upon the ruins of the human city of Rin, the charr capital is almost a living machine, dominated by a black sphere, called the Imperator's Core, that can be seen from a great distance. The city was forged by the Iron Legion, and the charr believe that even gods cannot stand against the power of their armies and technology. In the past, that's proven true.

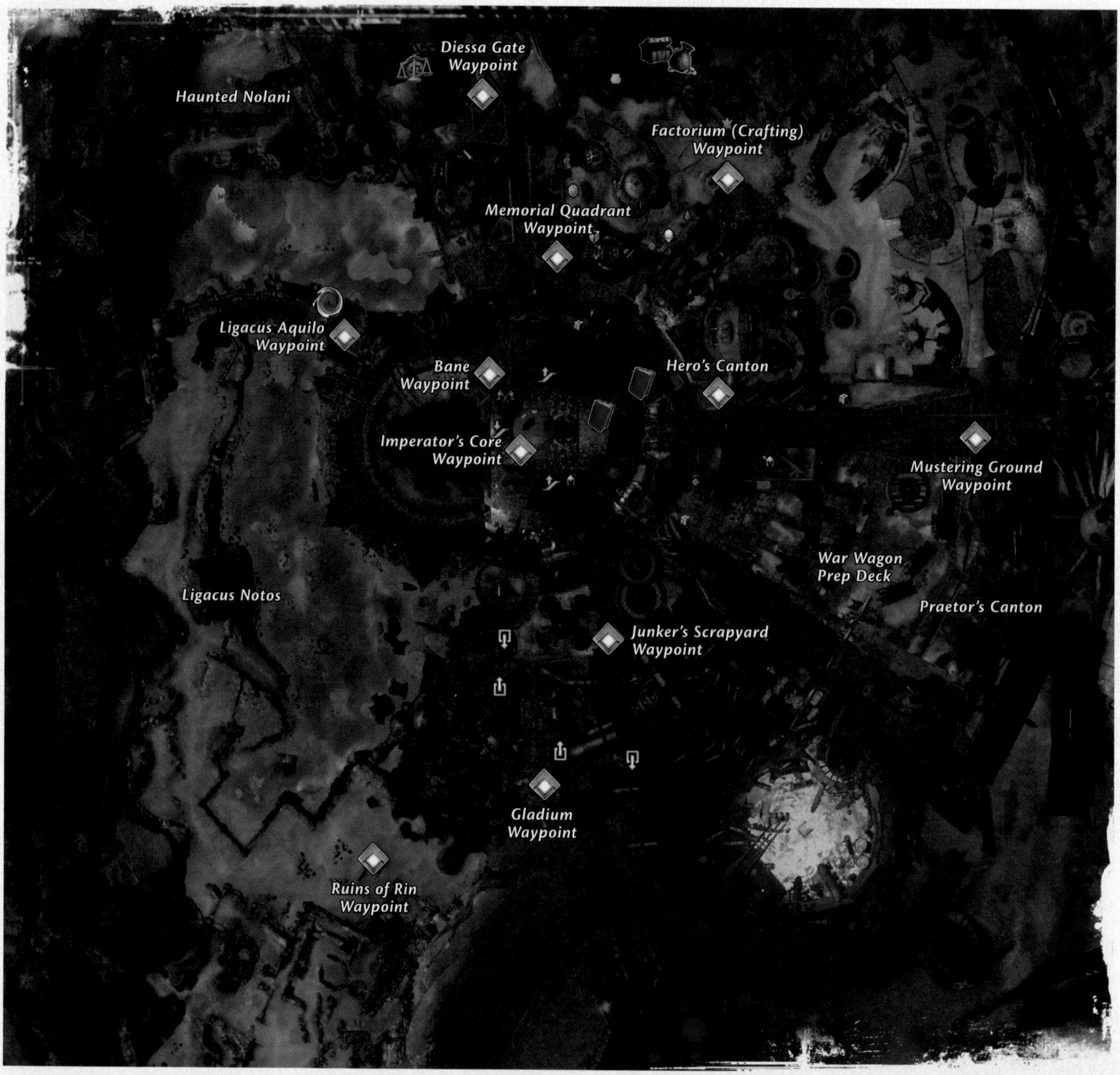

Diessa Gate Waypoint
Haunted Nolani
Factorium (Crafting) Waypoint
Memorial Quadrant Waypoint
Ligacus Aquilo Waypoint
Bane Waypoint
Hero's Canton
Imperator's Core Waypoint
Mustering Ground Waypoint
War Wagon Prep Deck
Praetor's Canton
Ligacus Notos
Junker's Scrapyard Waypoint
Gladium Waypoint
Ruins of Rin Waypoint

MUSTERING GROUND WAYPOINT (EAST SIDE)

SERVICES	Weaponsmith, Armorsmith, Equipment Repair, Assorted Merchants
TRAVEL	Path to Village of Smokestead (E)

The Mustering Ground is a parade area near the eastern exit of the city. Warbands gather at this point between Hero's Canton and the exit to the Village of Smokestead. To the south is a parking area for charr vehicles. It's a fun place to look around, but try not to touch anything!

HERO'S WAYPOINT (CENTER AREA)

SERVICES:	Weaponsmith, Armorsmith, Merchant, Profession Trainers
TRAVEL:	Path to Village of Smokestead

This is the crossroads of the city. From here you can go pretty much anywhere, so it's a good waypoint to get as soon as you reach the Black Citadel. Charr characters have houses here that are a focal point for their personal stories, dye merchants, and so forth.

MEMORIAL WAYPOINT (NORTH OF CENTER)

SERVICES:	Weaponsmith
TRAVEL:	Gate to Diessa Plateau (N), Elevator to The Bane (S)

Memorial Waypoint stands near the center of the citadel. Along this raised avenue, charr gaze at statues of heroes past. Speak to Salinus Warbreaker to learn recent charr history. Nearby, to the south, are stairs to the Bane. Profession trainers stand by the entrance to the sphere. You can also read inscriptions on the statues to learn more about the charr culture.

DIESSA GATE WAYPOINT (NORTH SIDE)

SERVICES:	Armorsmith, Weaponsmith
TRAVEL:	Path to Village of Smokestead

As the name says, this waypoint stands next to the gate to Diessa Plateau, a zone that is perfect for players of levels 15 through 25. To the west is the city's Trading Post, if you're looking to sell something valuable. Further west is a ramp to a platform that overlooks the old city ruins, but you can't go down into them.

FACTORIUM WAYPOINT (CRAFTING FLOOR, NORTHEAST SIDE)

SERVICES:	Salvage Merchant, Equipment Repair, Crafting Trainers
TRAVEL:	Gate to Diessa (NW), Bank (N)

This is the city's production area. Craftsmen of all trades come here to produce new items and to learn recipes. You can talk to trainers from every craft, and there are stations to ply your trade as well. This is also a place where you can repair your armor.

To learn about the Durmand Priory, go north and a little east into the Durmand Scriptorium. Also along the west side is an entrance to the Hero's Canton. Along the northern wall is a Bank.

LIGACUS AQUILO WAYPOINT (NORTHWEST SIDE)

SERVICES:	Salvage Merchant
TRAVEL:	Asura Gate to Lion's Arch (W)

West of the sphere is the Ligacus Aquilo Waypoint. The Asura Gate to Lion's Arch is here along with a salvage merchant. Going to Lion's Arch is valuable for players because it acts as a crossroads to other lands and the capital cities of other races.

IMPERATOR'S WAYPOINT (CENTER OF TOWN)

SERVICES:	Armorsmith, Weaponsmith, Equipment Repairs, Salvage Merchant, Guild Weaponsmith, Guild Armorsmith, Guild Registrar, Guild Promoter, Profession Trainers, Food Ingredient Merchant
TRAVEL:	N/A

The charr leadership resides at the top of the great sphere. Follow the spiral staircase up to find the waypoint. At the bottom is everything a group needs to set up a guild, and there are vendors as well. Just outside the sphere are profession trainers.

JUNKER'S WAYPOINT (SOUTH OF CENTER)

SERVICES:	Food Merchants
TRAVEL:	Elevator Down to Gladium Canton (S)

A group of merchants sell their wares along the Perimeter Loop, on the southern side of town. Many of these foodstuffs grant different boons for a short time. They offer a small advantage in a tough fight. To the west is an ancient artifact known as the Stormcaller. Speak with nearby charr to learn its history and to gain a speed boon.

BANE WAYPOINT (BELOW THE IMPERATOR'S CORE)

SERVICES:	Food Ingredient Merchant
TRAVEL:	Elevator Up to Memorial Waypoint

This fighting pit is a place where the charr stage gladiatorial combat for both entertainment and to settle disputes. There are several charr in the stands who are very interesting to talk to. What they say helps explain how much combat means to the charr.

GLADIUM WAYPOINT (SOUTH SIDE)

SERVICES:	Salvage Merchants, Cooking Ingredient Karma Merchant, Food Merchant
TRAVEL:	Elevator Down to Ruins of Rin (SW), Elevator Up to Perimeter Loop (N), Elevator Up to Scrapyard (NE)

The Gladium Canton is a place where many disgraced charr and refugees make their home. The mixture of races and cultures has made a mark on this place, adding greenery and magical technology to the black metal of the citadel. Sadly, poverty has turned the Gladium into a dark and desperate place.

RUINS OF RIN WAYPOINT (SOUTHWEST SIDE)

SERVICES:	N/A
TRAVEL:	Elevator Up to Gladium Canton (N)

Located at the southwestern point of the Black Citadel, this area contains the ruins of the old city of Rin. It's a dead area with little of interest to anyone but the scholars of the Durmand Priory.

PLAINS OF ASHFORD

LEVEL RANGE:	1-15
TASKS:	16
WAYPOINTS:	18
SKILL CHALLENGES:	6
HARVESTING INFO:	Copper Ore, Aspen Saplings, Early Cooking Ingredients

SKILL CHALLENGES

- Centurion Titus Gearclaw (Northwest of Greysteel Armory) (NW)
- Barradin's Statue (Inside Vault Waypoint, Underground) (W)
- Centurion Micka Thickblood (Northwest of Ashford Waypoint, Inside the Camp) (S)
- Ethereal Vanguard Monument (Northeast of Ashford Waypoint, Along the Hills) (S)
- Ruins of Ascalon City (Southeast of Ascalon City Waypoint, In the Water) (NE)
- Effigy Core (South of Adorea Waypoint, Inside a Cave) (S)

WEST SIDE

In olden days, charr once held the lands of Ascalon until being pushed out by the human civilization. Now they've returned, and their legions have successfully combated the human populace. However, Ascalon didn't fall easily; King Adelbern's last attack unleashed a horrific spell that blackened and burned the land. Worse still, the spirits of the Ascalon refuse to rest quietly, and they'll attack anything or anyone.

Charr heroes are now needed to defend their people and help solidify the hold of the legion. They also face the remnants of a now-outcast part of their military: the Flame Legion. More than a few dangers prowl in the fields, canyons, and historic ruins of this open land.

EAST SIDE

SMOKESTEAD WAYPOINT (WEST SIDE)

SERVICES:	Waypoint, Profession Trainers, Weaponsmith, Armorsmith, Equipment Repair, Salvage Merchant
TRAVEL:	Entrance to the Black Citadel (Charr Capital City) (W)
HARVESTING INFO:	N/A

Smokestead is more of a gathering place for warbands before they move to the front lines. It is just a short walk away to the entrance to the Black Citadel, the capital city of the charr. The waypoint is a mere stroll along a ramp. To the southwest is a tavern that houses several merchants; you can find weapons, armor, and equipment repair services there.

HERD CATTLE (Repeatable)

GOAL:	Herd cattle back into their pen
LEVEL:	2

Description: This event is north of the waypoint. A small enclosure holds a number of cows as well as some wurms, and cattle are scattered outside—exactly where they aren't supposed to be. Inside the pen are several cattle prods. Pick one of these up and use its abilities to get the cattle back inside their pen. Try to use the first ability around groups of cattle; you can't scare them away from the pen, so even hitting them at weird angles helps. If anything attacks you during this time (such as a wurm), use the second ability to fight back. It's not long before the cows get a moooove on.

GREYSTEEL ARMORY WAYPOINT (NORTHWEST SIDE)

SERVICES:	Waypoint, Karma Weapon Merchant, Karma Armor Merchant, Food Merchant
TRAVEL:	Smokestead Waypoint (S), Feritas Waypoint (E)
HARVESTING INFO:	Copper Ore (N) (Common), Onions, Herb Patches, Blueberries, Aspen Saplings (NE)

Greysteel Armory Waypoint is but a jump from the armory, where the charr smiths work to outfit the military. As such, it's a perfect place for the Flame Legion to make trouble. They want that equipment for themselves! Because of that, the armory sometimes meets with Flame Legion resistance, which has to be overcome, hopefully by helpful adventurers.

In addition, Greysteel Armory Waypoint is nicely situated for a bit of weapons testing. It's close enough to the armory to get munitions and far enough away that it won't bother the harvesters in the region. Besides, the cubs seem to find it exciting, and anything that gets them excited about the life of a soldier...well, that's second nature for a charr. Maybe even first.

North of the waypoint you can fight Centurion Titus Gearclaw in a Skill Challenge. Strafe around him to avoid the mines he throws at you.

HELPING THE ARMORY (Renown Task)

GOAL:	Help Crucibis Forgeweld run the armory.
LEVEL:	2

Description: This task requires you to pick up tools and unexploded mortar shells, return metal bars, deposit scrap metal in the forge, and guard against the Flame Legion. While this task may seem like busywork, every scrap of metal is crucial to the charr war effort. Simply picking up the junk around the armory may complete this task. However, the armory might not be available to you; you may have to recapture it before you are able to turn everything in. Tools go in the tool rack, bars go in the metal bar barrel or forge, and scrap metal goes into the huge forge. If you want a bit of fun, try manning one of the two cannons or throwing around the unexploded mortar shells. You can also try the experimental mortar.

PROTECT THE ARMORY (Repeatable)

GOAL:	Prevent the Flame Legion from capturing the armory.
LEVEL:	2

Description: The Flame Legion is making an assault on the Greysteel Armory. You have to stop them from gathering on the armory proper and killing all of the guards. One strategy is to use CC abilities to stop them at the ramp. Assist any allies in the area; you are going to need their help in dealing with the multiple Flame Legion warriors. You can also use the armory's cannons in their defense.

RECLAIM THE ARMORY (Repeatable)

GOAL: Reclaim the armory from the Flame Legion.

LEVEL: 2

Description: Flame Legion warriors have taken the armory! That can't be allowed to continue. On its face, this one isn't too tough; kill as many of the Flame Legion as you can. However, you can be overwhelmed pretty easily (just like the armory guards). It might be nice to have a friend or two, just to watch your back. Keep the Flame Legion out long enough and the armory will be reclaimed.

COLLECTING DEVOURER EGGS (Repeatable)

GOAL: Lure devourers out to get to their eggs (and snatch them).

LEVEL: 3

Description: North of the armory is a canyon called Devourer's Mouth. Drottot Lashtail is teaching the proper way to gather eggs to some young cubs. Use the nearby devourer lures to distract the lashtail females. When they come out, destroy the nests and steal their eggs. You may uncover a hatchling when you destroy a nest but feel free to ignore them; they won't hurt you too much. Once you've collected several eggs, turn them in to Drottot!

KILL THE ENRAGED SKALE (Group)

GOAL: Slay the giant skale.

LEVEL: 4

Description: In a tunnel next to the devourer pen is Kalare the Intrepid. She asks for your aid in killing a giant skale. It's a nasty creature. Go through the tunnel and into a cave to the northeast, which is hidden behind a waterfall. The area is filled with skale, but only the enraged veteran skale (your target) is aggressive. Still, you don't want interference in this fight, especially if you have area-of-effect attacks. Get the enraged skale's attention and draw it out so you can fight it alone. This fight isn't too bad, and with the big guy down, Kalare will retrieve the treasure.

RECOVER CANNONBALLS (Repeatable)

GOAL: Recover cannonballs from the skritt.

LEVEL: 3

Description: To the northwest of the Greysteel Armory Waypoint is Tela Range, where the charr Iron Legion practices with their artillery. Pick up cannonballs from the ground in Mock's Niche to the north, and run them back to Seph Blackblood. If you can't find any, just take a look around. Some of the skritt are carrying them! These enemies have the ability to knock you down; practice dodging so they don't get the drop on you. You get an exploding cannonball as a reward.

ORGANIZE THE WRECKING YARD (Renown Task)

GOAL: Help Scar Stripeclaw organize the wrecking yard.

LEVEL: 3

Description: Go southeast from the Greysteel Armory Waypoint and walk around the horseshoe-shaped wall. This is a scrapyard for the Iron Legion. Your job here is to help Scar Stripeclaw. To do this, clear out rats (by killing them or setting rat traps), clean up gears and junk, and help workers in the yard. You can also help by keeping any pesky Flame Legion away from the wrecking yard. This task can be completed in no time and without any fighting.

CLEAR THE FLAME LEGION CAVE (Repeatable)

GOAL: Kill 5 Flame Legion inside the cave.

LEVEL: 4

Description: A Flame Legion squad that raided the scrapyard is holed up in a cave to the east. Keep an eye out for a veteran igniter that patrols the area. The Flame Legion are spread out far enough apart that it's possible to take each one at a time. Once they have all been slain grab a package of weapon parts and return to the scrapyard. Place the parts into the appropriate barrel to earn some reputation.

PROTECT THE WEAPON PARTS FROM THE FLAME LEGION (Repeatable)

GOAL:	Prevent the Flame Legion from stealing all six weapon parts.
LEVEL:	3

Description: The scrapyard contains more than just junk; it's also a dumping ground for broken weaponry. Stop the Flame Legion from taking valuable parts that may be used against your people later. Flame Legion attackers come in pairs from either entrance until the time limit expires. Take them out before they can run off with six weapon parts. During the attack, don't forget to revive any fallen scrapyard workers so they can help in the fight.

FERITAS WAYPOINT (NORTHWEST SIDE)

SERVICES:	Waypoint, Karma Armor Merchant
TRAVEL:	Greysteel Armory Waypoint (W)
HARVESTING INFO:	Onions, Blueberries, Aspen Saplings

Lake Feritas lies to the east of Greysteel Armory Waypoint. Several fisherfolk make their living by fishing here, and there are more than a few drakes as well. However, it is a fragile environment, and one that can be easily polluted. To make matters worse, the Flame Legion has set up a base on the shoreline. There's no shortage of allies needing your assistance.

SECURE LAKE FERITAS (Renown Task)

GOAL:	Help Strum Bassclash secure Lake Feritas.
LEVEL:	4

Description: The fisherfolk around Lake Feritas could certainly use a hand. The drakes in the area aren't usually aggressive, but they do enjoy breaking equipment, and every so often, they just get ornery. Circle around the lake fixing traps, cleaning up tar, and protecting the fishers from drakes. Cleaning up the tar is a good way to raise your reputation, which has definite benefits. If you are looking for a fight, stick around the fisherfolk. Attack any drakes that turn aggressive and revive the fisherfolk if they fall. Once the job is done, Bassclash becomes a reputation vendor.

DESTROY FLAME LEGION BRAZIERS (Repeatable)

GOAL:	Destroy 5 Flame Legion braziers.
LEVEL:	5

Description: The shoreline above Lake Feritas is now home to a Flame Legion base. The base has its own artillery, using (you guessed it) flame attacks. The flame braziers require a beating to be brought down, and the Flame Legion force in the area isn't about to make it easy. Entering the cave to the northeast is dangerous; the Flame Legion is there in numbers and their turrets are damaging. If you have trouble finding the braziers look on your minimap.

CLEAR THE LAKE OF TAR ELEMENTALS (Repeatable)

GOAL:	Destroy tar elementals until Lake Feritas is clean.
LEVEL:	4

Description: A Flame Legion shaman has fouled the lake with corrupted tar. Help Legionnaire Sparclash kill tar elementals to clean the lake. This is pretty straightforward; the elementals aren't too difficult by themselves, and if you get overwhelmed, you can always pull back. Once this is done, a team of legionnaires will set out to attack the Flame Legion shaman directly.

DEFEAT THE FLAME LEGION SHAMAN (Group)

GOAL:	Defeat the Flame Legion shaman.
LEVEL:	5

Description: After fouling Lake Feritas, the shaman has the audacity to taunt you from his hideout on the other side of the lake. Try to take out as many Flame Legion warriors and turrets as you can before engaging him directly. You need to have room to maneuver. The shaman can throw multiple fireballs and has a melee attack that can send you tumbling. His deadliest trick is his Fire Shield; it reflects damage back to the attacker. When he does this, stop your attack; it's not hard to kill yourself with your own damage. Use your free time while his fire shield is up to revive any fallen allies. With this shaman dead, the Flame Legion has surely suffered a definite blow.

FIGHT THE FLAME LEGION (Renown Task)

GOAL:	Help Latera Painstorm fight the Flame Legion.
LEVEL:	5

Description: With all the fighting in this area, you might find yourself completing this task before you even know it. All you have to do is kill Flame Legion and destroy their equipment. This includes turrets and any of their magical devices, such as those near the cave mouths on the other side of Lake Feritas. It's better to kill Flame Legion patrolling the shore. While you can destroy the turrets, they are tough and can kill you if you aren't careful. Latera Painstorm becomes a karma merchant selling useful armor when you are done.

VIR'S GATE WAYPOINT (WEST SIDE)

SERVICES:	Waypoint, Skill Challenge (Skill Book), Karma Armor Merchant
TRAVEL:	Smokestead Village (NW), Guardpoint Decimus Waypoint (S)
HARVESTING INFO:	Copper Ore, Aspen Saplings, Blueberries, Root Vegetables

Travel southeast from the village of Smokestead through Vir's Gate to reach this waypoint. This area is not a flat plain but a land spotted with rocks, woods, and ruins. The charr would have fully claimed this region long ago if it weren't for the vengeful ghosts. These hostile spirits attack anything they encounter, and while they can be dispersed, they are doomed to return and haunt the area again.

HELP BRYLLANA DEEPMIND (Renown Task)

GOAL:	Assist the Iron Legion with their mission of taming the wilds outside Smokestead Village.
LEVEL:	6

Description: Bryllana Deepmind is working on reclaiming the old Ascalonian vineyard. Unfortunately, Ascalonian ghosts keep attacking her troops. But Bryllana has a theory: if all the remnants of the past are gone, maybe the ghosts will leave too. Head into the ruins and start wrecking things. Torches and casks get you the most appreciation for your work, but hammers and bottles can also be destroyed. Whether this marks the end of the spirits in the area is debatable, but Bryllana is certainly appreciative.

PROTECT THE CRUSH CUBS (Repeatable)

GOAL:	Stay near the cubs and keep ghosts away.
LEVEL:	6

Description: Near Bryllana Deepmind you may see some charr cubs daring each other to explore the Old Duke's Estate. The cubs will head out and take a path that circles the estate. Stay near the cubs to reduce their fear level and kill any ghosts that get close. Stay with them until time expires and maybe you will learn something about life, courage, and growing up.

LODESTONES FOR TATSU FARKILL (Repeatable)

GOAL:	Kill earth elementals and gather lodestones for Tatsu Farkill.
LEVEL:	6

Description: A few steps north of Vir's Gate Waypoint, Gaerra Farshot needs ammunition for her mortars. Earth elementals, whose lodestones would be perfect ammunition, are just to the east, south of Old Duke's Estate.

Destroy the elementals for their lodestones and turn them in to Tatsu who is to the west of the elementals across an old road (on your minimap). The elementals themselves are powerful with a damage reflect shield, an AOE attack, and a ground pound attack. If you see a bubble of energy surround the elemental, stop your attack. The damage will be reflected and you don't want to learn how much damage you do the hard way. Their area-of-effect attack is a line of churning earth that harms anyone standing on it. When you see them start to raise their arms, dodge aside to avoid the pound. More elementals can be summoned by interacting with the mounds of earth.

BREAK THE MORALE OF THE ATTACKING HARPIES (Repeatable)

GOAL:	Break the morale of the attacking harpies and defend the mortars.
LEVEL:	6

Description: Gaerra Farshot hates harpies and is itching for the chance to use her mortars on their nests. Once Tatsu Farkill returns with the lodestones, she begins the bombardment. Gaerra is a little too good at her job and riles the entire nest. The harpies come in waves from either side in increasing numbers and toughness. They will go straight for the mortars, and you have to hit them pretty hard to get their attention. The attacks continue until the harpies lose heart or all four mortars are destroyed. Afterward, head south to Victor's Presidium.

VAULT WAYPOINT (WEST OF CENTER)

SERVICES:	Skill Challenge (W)
TRAVEL:	Vir's Gate Waypoint (W), Temperus Waypoint (E)
HARVESTING INFO:	Copper Ore (W)

This waypoint is underground in Barradin's Vaults. Travel deeper into the vaults to find an old soldier who will sell you a creature codex.

BATTLE IN THE VAULT (World Event)

GOAL:	Capture the vaults from Barradin's Army.
LEVEL:	10

Description: Follow the road out of Vir's Gate to find the stairs down to the vault.

DEFEAT THE ASCALONION SOLDIER, IVOR TRUSHOT (Part of World Event)

GOAL:	Beat boss.
LEVEL:	10

Description: Kill this patrolling enemy near the waypoint. He'll have multiple guards with him, so area-of-effect attacks are useful to quickly thin their ranks.

GUARDPOINT DECIMUS WAYPOINT (SOUTHWEST SIDE)

SERVICES:	Karma Masterwork Armor Merchant, Salvage Merchant
TRAVEL:	Vir's Gate Waypoint (N), Temperus Waypoint (E)
HARVESTING INFO:	Blueberries, Aspen Saplings, Copper Ore

South of Vir's Gate is Guardpoint Decimus Waypoint. Along the way you will pass through a charr camp named Victor's Presidium. It overlooks the rocky and wooded area around the waypoint. Further south of the waypoint are the Decimus Stones, a group of ruins that holds strange power.

HELP KYRA SHARPTRACKER (Renown Task)

GOAL:	Fight with the Ash Legion as they attempt to reclaim Victor's Presidium from ghosts.
LEVEL:	6

Description: Between Vir's and Guardpoint Decimus Waypoint is Victor's Presidium. Here, patrolling spirits and living predators attempt to overwhelm Ash Legion agents. Travel east to get started. Revive any fallen scouts you find and stick by them. They will help you fight, and if they fall again you can revive them for further gratitude.

FIND THE MISSING SCOUT (Repeatable)

GOAL:	Find the missing scout and escort her back to Sharptail.
LEVEL:	7

Description: When you arrive at Victor's Presidium you may hear that a scout has not returned from her mission. Her objective was to scout an old mining cave to the east. Her warband is worried because the cave has been known to contain ghosts and trolls. Follow the road out of Victor's Presidium south, then east. The road will lead directly to the mine entrance and you will find the scout unconscious inside. Kill any enemies nearby and revive her. Protect her as she heads north from the cave. She's going to need your help because groups of ghosts will ambush her at several points along the way.

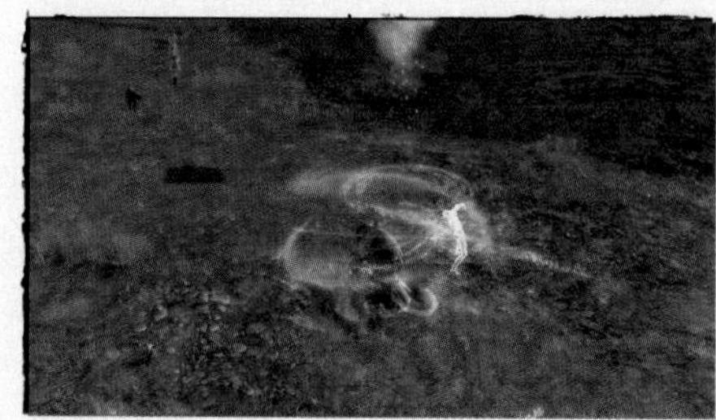

ESCORT VHES AND HER WARBAND (Repeatable)

GOAL:	Protect the warband as it travels to Guardpoint Decimus Waypoint.
LEVEL:	6

Description: Talk to Vhes Hauntslayer in Victor's Presidium. She is very vocal regarding her concerns about ghosts and their interactions with the Decimus Stones. Agree to join her warband as they investigate this possible threat. The group will be attacked multiple times by Ascalonian ghosts along the way. Once Guardpoint Decimus Waypoint has been reached, she will set up camp.

PROTECT HAUNTSMASH AS HE PLANTS CHARGES (Repeatable)

GOAL:	Keep Hauntsmash alive long enough for him to plant four explosive charges.
LEVEL:	6

Description: After Vhes sets up camp, talk to Furore Hauntsmash. He's going to fix the Decimus Stone problem, and he's going to do it with a bang. Follow him as he plants explosive charges on each of the Decimus Stones. Walk ahead of him to encounter any ghosts first so Hauntsmash gets in fewer fights. Watch his health, because if he dies, the mission is a failure. When all the charges are planted, follow Hauntsmash back to the camp to see the fireworks.

DEFEND THE ASH LEGION CAMP (Repeatable)

GOAL:	Protect the tents in the forward camp near Guardpoint Decimus Waypoint.
LEVEL:	8

Description: After the Decimus Stones have been destroyed and Hauntsmash has returned to the camp, the spirits in the area mount a counterattack. To succeed, you must prevent them from destroying all of the camp structures. Grab the attention of the Ascalonian peasants and fighters and pull them toward the archers and mages. Once you have them in a group, use any area-of-effect attacks you have. There are a number of enemies and they are truly intent on destroying those tents, but once they're gone, the area will be a lot safer.

TEMPERUS WAYPOINT (WEST OF CENTER)

SERVICES:	Waypoint, Karma Boon Merchant, Merchant, Weaponsmith
TRAVEL:	Guardpoint Decimus Waypoint (SW), Vir's Gate Waypoint (W), Adorea Waypoint (SE), Martyr's Waypoint (NE)
HARVESTING INFO:	Copper Ore (N), Aspen Saplings (NE)

Follow the road east out of Vir's Gate; Tempurus Waypoint is along the ramp by a charr outpost. There are two charr war camps nearby, and plenty of work is needed to tame this region. Ghosts haunt the north and the Flame Legion patrols the south.

HELP THE BLOOD LEGION (Renown Task)

GOAL:	Prove yourself to the Blood Legion by culling hostile creatures and ghosts by Temperus Point.
LEVEL:	7

Description: Talk to the legionnaires standing around before you leave Temperus Point. You can gain their respect by sparring with Blood Legion braggarts and pointing Blood Legion loafers in the right direction. Talk to Tesserarius Drivenhail to learn about a grawl problem to the northeast; Jenk Cutspecter may also have a task for you. And if you haven't had your fill of fighting ghosts yet, they can be found to the north. Spiders and their eggs need to be destroyed in that direction as well.

DISPATCH CAPTAIN CALHAAN'S GHOST (Repeatable)

GOAL:	Disperse the ghost of Captain Calhaan and those of his squad.
LEVEL:	7

Description: Head north from Temperus Waypoint and into some ruins. There you will find Calhaan's Haunt. Stick around and you may run into the spirit this place is named after. Like so many other ghosts of Ascalon, he is cursed to relive battles of the past, with you taking the place of his enemy. Several of his spirit allies follow him. To keep from being overwhelmed, clear the area before you take on this group. Send Captain Calhaan's shade to a temporary rest to finish this repeatable.

KILL THE GRAWL MARAUDING THROUGH MARTYR'S WOODS (Group)

GOAL: Kill the elite grawl that is attacking supply caravans.

LEVEL: 7

Description: Tesserarius Drivenhail needs someone to take out the grawl leader (Badazar's Champion). This nasty guy has been attacking supply caravans traveling Martyr's Woods in the north. Follow the road northeast to the Toppled Wall and you may find this tough grawl and his two henchmen. Concentrate on the boss; once their leader is slain, the others turn tail and flee. The leader is a powerful magic user that casts spells at a distance and can use a splash attack to launch heroes that get too close.

KILL THE GRAWL SHAMANS (Repeatable)

GOAL: Kill the grawl shamans before they complete their ritual.

LEVEL: 7

Description: Southeast of Martyr's Waypoint there is a group of grawl shamans performing a ritual around a statue of Balthazar. You can't be sure what the result will be, but you know it won't be good. The shamans are at points around the statue. Try to kill the packs of grawl berserkers before you take on the shamans.

DRIVE THE GRAWL FROM BALTHAZAR'S STATUE (Repeatable)

GOAL: Kill the grawl until they leave the area.

LEVEL: 8

Description: A nearby tribe of grawl has come to revere a statue of Balthazar as their new deity, "Badazar." Circle the statue and kill Grawl until their morale breaks. Be wary of fighting too many at once; their Knockdown and CC abilities can kill you if you're not careful.

CAPTURE THE GHOSTS FOR JENK CUTSPECTER (Repeatable)

GOAL: Capture ghosts for Jenk Cutspecter using the ghost collector.

LEVEL: 6

Description: Jenk has an idea that may lock away the ghosts for good. Talk to Jenk and he will give you a ghost collector. Use its abilities, like proton bolts, to bring any ghost nearby to less than half health. Once they are weakened, the Capture ability stores them away. If you lose your ghost collector, pick up any of the spares lying around. Once you have a full load, return to Jenk and follow him to Exterminatus HQ.

PROTECT THE CONTAINMENT UNIT (Repeatable)

GOAL: Defend the containment unit from multiple waves of Flame Legion attacks.

LEVEL: 6

Description: To the south of Temperus Waypoint is Exterminatus HQ, which houses Jenk Cutspecter's Ghost Containment Unit. After he has filled it with the ghosts you have collected, Flame Legion invaders attempt to break the base's defenses. They must be stopped before they break the containment unit and free the ghosts! The large doors are a good place to make a stand; there are several guards there, and it lets you keep a good eye on the containment unit. Withstand all of the Flame Legion attack waves and the containment unit will be safe.

DESTROY THE GHOSTS IN THE CONTAINMENT UNIT HANGAR (Repeatable)

GOAL: Clear the containment unit hangar of ghosts.

LEVEL: 7

Description: If the Flame Legion was successful in destroying the containment unit, the freed ghosts must be cleared out of the Exterminatus HQ hangar. The spirits are spread about the room, and taking them out one by one is time consuming. All of the ghosts must be dispersed; otherwise, they re-materialize. The fast way is to try to grab the attention of multiple ghosts and get them to chase you back to the guards near the hangar doors. When the hangar is completely empty of ghosts, your job is done.

HELP THE IRON LEGION (Renown Task)

GOAL:	Join with the Iron Legion to protect the area from the Flame Legion.
LEVEL:	8

Description:

Head south from Temperus Waypoint to Exterminatus HQ. Killing Flame Legion and disabling their power sources in the area will earn you the Iron Legion's respect. You can also talk with nearby legionnaires to find other ways to help. There's plenty to do!

KILL THE LAVA SHAMAN (Repeatable)

GOAL:	Follow the Iron Legionnaire to Igni Castrum and kill the lava shaman.
LEVEL:	8

Description: In Exterminatus HQ, there is an Iron Legionnaire looking to take the fight to the Flame Legion. Talk with him and agree to join his assault. His path goes through Flame Legion-patrolled lands to the southwest. You will end up in a cave (Igni Castrum), which is protected by turrets and Flame Legion warriors. Get the defenders and turrets out of the way before you fight the lava shaman inside the cave. His ranged magma attack does damage to you over time, and you don't want to be dodging into other enemies while trying to avoid the shaman. Keep moving and fighting until the shaman is dead. You're done teaching the Flame Legion a lesson (for now, at least), so go back to Terminus Waypoint.

DESTROY THE EFFIGY (Group)

GOAL:	Destroy the effigy before it reaches the Victory Cenotaph.
LEVEL:	8

Description: Aurelia Stonegazer needs volunteers to defend the charr Victory Cenotaph from a giant walking effigy created by the Flame Legion. Someone killed the Flame Legion shaman in Igni Castrum, and now they're ticked off. This burning creation is slowly making its way along the road from Igni Castrum to the Victory Cenotaph. With it is a small escort of Flame Legionnaires. Take the escort out first or the combined damage will be overwhelming. While fighting the effigy, you have to keep moving and be ready to evade. It throws fireballs and can rain fire over a wide area. Try to distract the effigy and bring it in range of the cannons at Exterminatus HQ. If the effigy is not stopped before it reaches the Cenotaph, it will destroy the statue. Bring down this monstrosity and show the might of the charr!

PROTECT THE ENGINEERS (Repeatable)

GOAL:	Protect the engineers repairing the Victory Cenotaph.
LEVEL:	8

Description: If the effigy succeeds in destroying the Victory Cenotaph, this mission becomes available. The Iron Legion aren't the type of charr to mope around after such a loss! Three engineers concentrate on repairs while a few guards protect them. The Flame Legion is trying to take advantage of this vulnerable position and will attack in mixed groups of up to five. Try to keep at least one of the engineers revived and working along with two guards. The time available to complete the repairs is limited, and the Flame Legion keeps coming. However, as long as you have at least one engineer working and the help of a couple guard defenders, you can get the job done.

ADOREA WAYPOINT (SOUTH SIDE)

SERVICES:	Waypoint
TRAVEL:	Temperus Waypoint (NW), Ashford Waypoint (E)
HARVESTING INFO:	Aspen Saplings (limited), Copper Ore (limited)

Head south of Tempurus Waypoint to the shores of Lake Adorea. Adorea Waypoint overlooks the small body of water. While the drakes that live in and around the lake are the main threat, there is also the mystery of the ruins on the small island. This is a good place to practice amphibious combat if you have not done so already.

HELP PAENULA (Renown Task)

GOAL:	Help Paenula train the troops by fighting in the pit and capturing creatures.
LEVEL:	9

Description: You can find Paenula north of Adorea Lake at the bottom of a ramp. She runs the battle simulation pit at the top of the hill. It's a great way to train soldiers against real enemies in controlled situations. You can help her by training with the soldiers in the pit or capturing creatures for it. To help train the soldiers, head up the ramp and select your challenge. You can make a lot of progress on this task in a single fight. Or you can go out and catch creatures with a modified rifle that Paenula gives you. Head south and use the Bleeding Shot and Blunderbuss abilities to reduce the health of drakes and minotaurs. Once they are below half health, use Net Shot ability to send them to the pit.

ASHFORD WAYPOINT (SOUTH SIDE)

SERVICES:	Waypoint, Weaponsmith, Armorsmith, Merchant, Karma Tool Merchant, Skill Challenge
TRAVEL:	Adorea Waypoint (W), Spirit Hunter Camp Waypoint (N)
HARVESTING INFO:	Copper Ore (Abundant) (E)

This waypoint is inside Ashford Forum, north of Lake Adorea. Here you can test your skills and upgrade your equipment. You can also buy tools that increase your chance to get higher-quality materials. If you follow the road northeast, you can have your first contact with separatist forces. Follow the road further north to encounter the ghosts that fill the Devast District and Abbey Ruins.

DESTROY THE SEPARATIST CATAPULTS AND ROADBLOCK (Repeatable)

GOAL:	Smash the separatists and the barriers they have placed on the road.
LEVEL:	10

Description: Follow the road east of Ashford Forum and you may come upon the injured engineer Lynnka Steelbender. Help her and she will tell you that separatists are blocking the road. They have a catapult on either side, so don't stand still for too long. A circle on the ground around you is your cue to move your feet! Start with one of the catapults. If you are feeling lucky, you can use area-of-effect attacks to take out the catapult and the separatists guarding it at the same time. The safer way to do it is to pull away the separatists so you can dodge the catapult shot and the separatist basher hammer swings. Once you clear both sides, take out the roadblock.

SPIRIT HUNTER CAMP WAYPOINT (CENTER)

SERVICES:	Waypoint
TRAVEL:	Ashford Waypoint (S)
HARVESTING INFO:	Copper Ore, Root Vegetables

North of Ashford Forum and at the center of the region is the lonely Spirit Hunter Camp Waypoint. South of here, charr legionnaires patrol the rocky plains and ruins, trying to control the ghost population. This is dangerous duty; Ascalonian spirits glide silently through the perpetual fog that covers much of the area. North of the waypoint is given over to wilderness and the mortal threats of the grawl, wurms, and devourers.

HELP GAVROS SPIRITFOE AND THE CHARR PATROLS

(Renown Task)

GOAL:	Support charr patrols by fighting ghosts, searching for Ascalonian hammers, and lighting torches.
LEVEL:	10

Description: This task covers a large area, but the best way to help the legionnaires is to head south, to Abbey Ruins. It's easy to find patrolmen to help and torches to light there. Using the dropped hammers can be fun, but they aren't your main focus. Instead, hunt around the ruins and make a beeline for the torches. Of course, the ghosts are thick in the region, and they'll try to stop you, but they were targets anyway.

MARTYR'S WAYPOINT (NORTH SIDE)

SERVICES:	Waypoint
TRAVEL:	Temperus Waypoint (S), Entrance to Diessa Plateau (Level 15-25 Charr Region) (N), Spirit Hunter Camp Waypoint (SE), Ascalonian Catacombs Waypoint (E)
HARVESTING INFO:	Copper Ore (W), Aspen Saplings (S)

This waypoint stands at the northern end of the map, guarding the path through the Toppled Wall to Diessa Plateau (a likely place for you to explore when you're ready to leave the Plains of Ashford). But you probably aren't quite ready for that! Enemies are nearby, and you can still make a difference here. Cursed spirits guard Calhaan's Haunt, spiders skitter in Martyr's Woods, and the grawl make a nuisance of themselves everywhere else.

ASCALONIAN CATACOMBS WAYPOINT (NORTH SIDE)

SERVICES:	Waypoint, Armorsmith, Weaponsmith, Skill Challenge
TRAVEL:	Ascalonian Catacombs (Dungeon: Level 30 for Story Mode and Level 35 for Exploration Mode), Spirit Hunter Camp Waypoint (W), Phasmatis Waypoint (E), Ascalon City Waypoint (NE)
HARVESTING INFO:	Copper Ore, Aspen Saplings, Root Vegetables

Travel northeast of Spirit Hunter Camp Waypoint to find the entrance to Ascalonian Catacombs. The Durmand Priory has set up camp here to study the catacombs and the wall, and their representatives, an armorsmith and a weaponsmith, can be found outside. Once you've gotten more experienced, think about gathering a few friends and venturing inside the catacombs. It's a place of danger and a definite chance at adventure and treasure.

That's getting a bit ahead of things, though. Outside the catacombs, charr patrols are attempting to set up a forward camp to the south. Ghosts and harpies are this area's principle dangers, and you can stand with the legionnaires against their foes.

ASCALONIAN CATACOMBS

Groups of players with five members that are around level 30 (or above) can come to this area to seek greater adventures. The Ascalonian Catacombs are north of the waypoint, and you can't miss them!

HELP SAGUM RELICSEEKER OF THE DURMAND PRIORY

(Renown Task)

GOAL:	Fight back the harpies along the wall and help the Durmand Priory recover artifacts.
LEVEL:	10

Description: North of the waypoint, harpies have built roosts along the toppled wall. The Durmand Priory cannot continue their excavation and research while these pests attack their agents and steal artifacts. Climb the stairs to the higher sections of wall and attack harpy nests. The waves of angered harpies this brings makes completing the task more difficult, but it's a fast and fun way to complete it quickly.

RECOVER STOLEN SUPPLY CONTAINERS (Repeatable)

GOAL:	Recover stolen supply containers from harpies for Explorer Erin.
LEVEL:	10

Description: Erin is standing by the Toppled Wall; she's trying to recover artifacts stolen by the harpies. While you are helping Sagum Relicseeker kill the pests, you can turn over any artifacts you have collected to Erin. Artifacts can be gathered in three ways. The most common way is to loot them from harpy corpses. The second easiest is to pick them up along the upper parts of the walls. The final way is to grab any of the shovels lying around and use them to dig up rubble.

DEFEND SWORDCROSS COMMAND POST FROM GHOSTS (Repeatable)

GOAL:	Stop Ascalonian ghosts from destroying all four command post buildings.
LEVEL:	11

Description: The charr have built a forward command post to the south of Ascalonian Catacombs Waypoint. Spirits in the area have sensed the disturbance and have come to tear it down. Ghosts in groups of three from the surrounding area come in through the north and south entrances. You will have to run between the two openings, killing ghosts and reviving fallen allies. When Ascalonian peasants take too much damage, they will run away for a bit. Switch to a more aggressive target and kill the peasants only when they come back. When all of the spirits in the area have been dispersed, you will be victorious.

PROTECT THE SIEGE TEAM (Repeatable)

GOAL:	Protect the four members of the siege team as they approach the wall.
LEVEL:	11

Description: After the command post at Swordcross has been defended, members of a siege team decide to take the fight to the Ascalonian ghosts. Once you agree to join them, the team will head north, to the wall. This is a difficult task because ghosts will attack multiple times along the way. When team members fall, they cannot be revived. Bring all your damage or healing abilities! If the last team member falls, the mission has failed.

IRONDOCK SHIPYARD WAYPOINT (SOUTHEAST OF CENTER)

SERVICES:	Waypoint, Skill Challenge
TRAVEL:	Spirithunter Waypoint (N), Loreclaw Waypoint (S)
HARVESTING INFO:	Copper Ore (SW), Aspen Saplings (S)

South of Spirithunter Waypoint, past Lamia Mire, is Irondock. Various weapon experiments are happening at this beautiful body of water, including the testing of a prototype vehicle. There are multiple ways to help in the experiments. Speak to Sesto Headsplitter to help directly, or talk to Mei or Burnwhite to handle the separatist nuisance.

ASSIST SESTO HEADSPLITTER WITH HIS WORK (Renown Task)

GOAL:	Test out Sesto Headsplitter's experimental weapons and help keep the experiments at Irondock functional.
LEVEL:	11

Description: Talk to Sesto Headsplitter to find out how you can help. If you ask, he will equip you with his experimental grenades. You can practice on any of the practice dummies in the area or get real-world data by using them on aggressive creatures. Another way to help is to repair malfunctioning equipment and to destroy tar elementals (sometimes these appear when you interact with the equipment). You can also take a dip in the basin and pick up submarine parts. Return the parts to Sesto.

KILL THE SEPARATISTS BEFORE THEY DESTROY THE IRON BARRACUDA (Repeatable)

GOAL:	Kill all of the attacking separatist saboteurs before they critically damage the Iron Barracuda.
LEVEL:	12

Description: On the south end of the island is the docking point for the submersible prototype, the Iron Barracuda. Jump in the water; separatist saboteurs are trying to destroy the Iron Barracuda from underneath! Protect the submarine by distracting the saboteurs and killing the entire attacking force. Win and get the thanks of the Iron Barracuda's crew...but if you fail, all is not lost.

ASSIST LEGIONNAIRE BURNWHITE IN REPAIRING THE IRON BARRACUDA (Repeatable)

GOAL:	Gather submarine parts and return them to Legionnaire Burnwhite.
LEVEL:	12

Description: If the separatists succeed in damaging the Iron Barracuda, Legionnaire Burnwhite will ask for your help to repair it. Search at the bottom of the basin for the scattered submarine parts around the dock. While you can loot parts from drakes, it's much easier to swim along the bottom and pick up parts as you pass over them. Climb back on the dock and hand them off to Burnwhite. Once she has enough parts, head back into the water to protect her from separatist attacks while she makes the repairs.

HELP MEI HAWKSLAYER DISRUPT SEPARATIST ACTIVITY (Renown Task)

GOAL:	Disrupt separatist activities at the nearby camp.
LEVEL:	12

Description: South of the Irondock Shipyard Waypoint, Mei Hawkslayer stands at the Loreclaw Expanse, observing the separatist camp. Head south up the path but watch your step: separatists have laid mines. Destroy the catapult at a nearby overlook or it will continually harass you. Then, make your way into the camp proper. At the center of the camp are two tents that contain separatist battle plans. Mei would like these destroyed. Head east and you will find a small stockade. Kill the guards, break down the door, and release the prisoners inside. If you still haven't fully disrupted the camp, rustle the separatists out of nearby bushes. When you're done with the task, head east to grab Loreclaw Waypoint. You'll need it later.

DESTROY THE SEPARATIST CAMP (Repeatable)

GOAL:	Destroy the two tents at the center of the camp.
LEVEL:	12

Description: Talk to Legionnaire Burnwhite. Her request is very simple: smash the two tents at the center of the separatist camp. The difficulty is that the structures are built pretty tough, and the separatist archers, bashers, and catapult attacks continually distract you. Get inside the tents to use them as cover while you destroy them from within. If the separatists are still a problem, try to pull them in with you and use area-of-effect attacks to save time.

PHASMATIS WAYPOINT (EAST OF CENTER)

SERVICES:	Waypoint
TRAVEL:	Irondock Shipyard Waypoint (S), Ascalonian Catacombs Waypoint (NW), Watchcrag Tower Waypoint (E), Ascalon City Waypoint (N)
HARVESTING INFO:	Copper Ore (Common), Aspen Saplings (Common), Root Vegetables (Common)

North of Irondock and east of Spirithunter Waypoint, Phasmatis Waypoint is on the edge of a heavily Ascalonian-controlled area. Ghosts abound here, and they aren't happy with being disturbed.

But, there are some rewards to be had for all the danger. Harvesting gets better from here. While previous areas have been sparse, harvesting sources become more plentiful to the north and east.

ASCALON CITY WAYPOINT (NORTHEAST OF CENTER)

SERVICES:	Waypoint, Skill Challenge (E)
TRAVEL:	Iron Marches (N)(Level 50-60 Region), Ascalonian Catacombs Waypoint (W), Phasmatis Waypoint (S)
HARVESTING INFO:	Copper Ore (E), Aspen Saplings (Common), Root Vegetables (Common)

This waypoint stands at the entrance to the Ascalon City Ruins on the northeast end of the map. To the north lies a path to the Iron Marches region, but that's probably a bit too dangerous for now. Closer to your position, along the ancient walls, the area swarms with Ascalonian spirits. They have even materialized ghostly trebuchets!

HELP GHYRTRATUS FIENDMAULER (Renown Task)

GOAL: Wipe out the ghosts haunting Ascalon City and help the Blood Legion retake the city for the charr.

LEVEL: 12

Description: The Blood Legion needs assistance retaking these old ruins; they are covered in Ascalonian ghosts. The easy way to help is by repairing flags and reviving injured soldiers along the roadways. For a Skill Challenge, head east into the Ascalon City Ruins and fight the packs of ghosts within the walls. To really impress the Blood Legion, pick up the battle plans you find in the ruins and hand them over to Ghyrtratus. When you are done helping the legion in this area, teleport to Loreclaw Waypoint.

DEFEAT THE FORCES DEFENDING ASCALON CITY (World Event)

GOAL: Destroy Ascalonian structures.

LEVEL: 12

Description: World events, if you have not encountered them before, are made up of many smaller events that revolve around a pivotal story within a region. Everyone in a large area can be involved and complete a component of the event while working toward the greater goal. With teamwork, a group can split up and complete parts faster. There are several obstacles in the way of the charr conquest of the ruins. Ghosts are rallying around ancient statues. Ghostly trebuchets are pounding on legionnaire forces. By destroying two Ascalonian statues and trebuchets, the spirit of Siegemaster Lormar will be made to appear. Kill him and bring the charr closer to complete domination of the region.

DESTROY THE GHOSTLY ASCALONIAN TREBUCHET (Part of the World Event)

GOAL: Destroy the first trebuchet.

LEVEL: 11

Description: This is part of the region's world event. It seems that the Ascalonian curse is powerful enough to bring back ethereal siege weaponry. You can see the trebuchet from Phasmatis Waypoint. Fight the ghosts guarding it at a distance so you have time to dodge the trebuchet shots. Then, close the distance and smash it as fast as you can. With the trebuchet down, the ghosts can't depend on their heavy artillery anymore.

DESTROY THE GHOSTLY ASCALONIAN TREBUCHET ON THE HILL (Part of the World Event)

GOAL: Destroy the second trebuchet.

LEVEL: 12

Description: This trebuchet stands at a break between the walls of the Ascalonian City Ruins. The slow way of doing this is to fight the ghosts guarding it at a distance so you have time to dodge the trebuchet shots. Then, close the distance and destroy it. The faster, but more dangerous, way is to run in and hit the guards and trebuchet simultaneously with area-of-effect attacks.

DESTROY THE FIRST STATUE (Part of the World Event)

GOAL: Destroy the statue of the Ascalonian soldier.

LEVEL: 12

Description: Ascalonian spirits are rallying around statues dedicated to their past. This particular statue stands on a rise to the southwest of the Ascalon City Waypoint. Clearing the ruins requires the removal of these ghostly attractors. Try to fight only a few ghosts at a time. When the area is clear, smash the statue.

DESTROY THE SECOND STATUE (Part of the World Event)

GOAL: Destroy the statue of the Ascalonian scholar.

LEVEL: 12

Description: Ascalonian spirits are gathering around a statue in honor of an Ascalonian scholar. This statue stands on the eastern side of the lake, south of the Ascalon City Ruins. Kill the surrounding ghosts to give yourself room, and then smash the statue.

KILL SIEGEMASTER LORMAR (Part of the World Event)

GOAL: Kill Siegemaster Lormar.

LEVEL: 12

Description: This is the last part of the region's world event. When all four structures (two trebuchets and two statues) have been destroyed, the ghost of Siegemaster Lormar makes his appearance in the Ascalonian City Ruins. Lormar himself isn't very tough, but he has his own personal guards and a horde of regular ghosts surrounding him. Clear an area of the normal wandering ghosts before taking on his group, or you risk being overwhelmed. When the spirit of Siegemaster Lormar has been dispersed, the charr have secured their victory in this region.

LORECLAW WAYPOINT (SOUTHEAST SIDE)

SERVICES:	Waypoint
TRAVEL:	Irondock Shipyard Waypoint (NW), Duskrend Overlook Waypoint (E)
HARVESTING INFO:	Aspen Saplings (Abundant)

Loreclaw Waypoint is in a quiet spot at the southern shore of Ascalon Basin. Head west to encounter a separatist camp or east to help Researcher Irkz.

HELP WITH RESEARCH ON THE SKALE (Renown Task)

GOAL: Assist Researcher Irkz in his study of the skale.

LEVEL: 13

Description:
Researcher Irkz is at the southeasternmost spot of Ascalon Basin. The fastest way to complete the research is to kill skale and pick up their oil sacs while resetting traps and reviving allies. If you travel in a full circuit, by the time you return to Irkz and hand over the skale oil sacs, you'll be done. In addition, you can help the charr nearby by giving them pep talks. Food samples can be found in skale nests. They can also be turned over to Irkz, but it's much more fun to use them as improvised weapons. When you're finished, travel north to Duskrend Overlook Waypoint.

DUSKREND OVERLOOK WAYPOINT (EAST SIDE)

SERVICES:	Waypoint, Merchant (Salvage), Armorsmith, Weaponsmith, Karma Supply Merchant
TRAVEL:	Blazeridge Steppes (E), Loreclaw Waypoint (SW), Watchcrag Tower Waypoint (N)
HARVESTING INFO:	Copper Ore (Common), Aspen Saplings (Common), Root Vegetables (Common)

Head east from Loreclaw Waypoint to an area of stone hills. Overlooking Ascalon Basin, protected by these outcroppings, is Duskrend Overlook. This is a perfect place to upgrade your equipment. Take the time to go over what the merchants have to offer, and grab any salvage kits you need before you head out. Activity at the northern ogre kraal is what everyone is talking about here. Speak to Ahneta Duskclaw; she tells you about some legionnaires on a dangerous mission.

HELP ANDROCHUS THE HIDDEN (Renown Task)

GOAL: Help lessen the ogre control of Cadem Forest.

LEVEL: 14

Description: The ogres of Watchcrag Kraal are fortifying their control of Cadem Forest. Androchus the Hidden is spying on their activities north of Duskrend Overlook. If you kill enough ogres and smash enough of their structures, he'll have far better news to report. The best way to finish this task is to talk to Dyrala Ogrestalker and assist in her mission. Along the way, you can defeat enough ogres and break plenty of stuff so you can finish this task in no time.

DRIVE THE OGRES FROM THEIR WATCHTOWER (Repeatable)

GOAL:	Drive the ogres from their watchtower by killing their scouts.
LEVEL:	13

Description: Dyrala Ogrestalker has a plan to herd the ogres back into their kraal. Talk to her and agree to join her team. Her plan, in good legion fashion, is to rampage through the ogre camp, killing ogre scouts. Make sure to keep up, because these charr are not stopping until they are done. When all the ogre scouts are slain, the group stops at Watchcrag Tower for the next phase in their endeavor.

WATCHCRAG TOWER WAYPOINT (EAST SIDE)

SERVICES:	Waypoint
TRAVEL:	Duskrend Overlook Waypoint (S), Phasmatis Waypoint (W), Ascalon City Ruins (NW)
HARVESTING INFO:	Copper Ore (Abundant), Aspen Saplings (Abundant), Root Vegetables (Abundant)

North of Duskrend Overlook is this often-contested waypoint. It's on a rise next to Watchcrag Tower, which is just inside ogre territory. The scenery is beautiful and verdant. Unfortunately, the ogres and their animal companions aggressively guard their new home.

DRIVE OFF THE OGRES ATTACKING WATCHCRAG TOWER (Repeatable)

GOAL:	Keep the charr guards alive until ogre morale breaks.
LEVEL:	14

Description: After completing the mission to take Watchcrag Tower with Dyrala Ogrestalker, you can help defend it. Ogres will come up the hill from alternating directions. Don't let any of the guards get isolated; they can't be revived, and if they all die, the tower is lost. The trick is to concentrate your fire on the ogres, because once they die, so does their pet. Slay enough ogres and their spirit will break, leading to a full-on rout.

CAPTURE STONECRAG KRAAL (Repeatable)

GOAL:	Capture the kraal and defeat the ogre chieftain.
LEVEL:	15

Description: After driving the ogres from Watchcrag Tower, you now have the ability to directly attack their kraal. Travel northeast from Watchcrag Tower Waypoint and break down the kraal door. You have to kill ogres in this area as fast as possible; otherwise, reinforcements will arrive and you'll make no progress in capturing it. Adding to the challenge are the multiple veteran ogre hunters that appear here. They have much more health and do more damage than the normal ogre hunters and ogre bruisers.

A useful strategy is to focus your damage on only the ogres. When they die, their pet does as well. Stay light on your feet as you attack the ogres, and evade away from their jumping ground smashes. Also, consider keeping one target at a sliver of health to help you Rally if you fall.

Once the area is captured, the Stonecrag Chieftain arrives with two hunters to kick you out of the kraal. He's more dangerous than the veterans you fought earlier. Get ready to evade! He doesn't fight fair, and neither should you. If you have attacks that knock down, Stun, or apply conditions, this is the time to use them. Defeat the Chieftain and the kraal is yours.

DEFEND STONECRAG KRAAL (Repeatable)

GOAL:	Prevent ogres from recapturing the kraal until the time limit expires.
LEVEL:	15

Description: After you succeed in capturing Stonecrag Kraal, charr reinforcements arrive. You will need them—those ogres want their kraal back! Ogres will be coming in the two entrances, trying to recapture their former home. Most of the attacks come from the eastern gate, but every so often there's an engagement to the west. Keep the guards on their feet and active, or you might find yourself overwhelmed. When you succeed, Maren Silentstrike arrives and sells celebratory fireworks. Congratulations! Thanks to you, the charr have Ashford Plains well in hand.

DIESSA PLATEAU

LEVEL RANGE:	15-25
TASKS:	15
WAYPOINTS:	19
SKILL CHALLENGES:	8
HARVESTING INFO:	Copper Ore, Iron Ore, Silver Ore, Gummo Saplings, Vine Vegetables, Herb Patches, Blueberries

Diessa Plateau is north of the Black Citadel. The ranches and mills of this area supply the charr legions with the food and materials they need. This land is under constant threat of attacks from separatists, the Flame Legion, and Ascalonian ghosts.

SKILL CHALLENGES

- Shaman Purda (West of Charrgate Haven Waypoint, Inside the Keep) (NW)
- Sharptail's Nest (Northwest of Bloodcliff Waypoint, Out in the Open) (NW)
- Ascalonian Aqueduct (North of Blasted Moors Waypoint, Reached Via the Tunnels Underneath That Area) (Center)
- Roj the Rowdy Butcher (South of the Blasted Moors Waypoint, On a Hill Near a Tower) (Center)
- Place of Power (East of Breached Wall Waypoint, Atop the Ruins) (S)
- Rancher in Training Poisonwill (Southwest of Dawnright Estate Waypoint, Out in the Open) (Center)
- Veruta Beefhawker (North of Manbane's Waypoint, Deep Inside the Cave) (N)
- Bogfang the Skale (Southeast of Font of Rhand Waypoint) (NE)

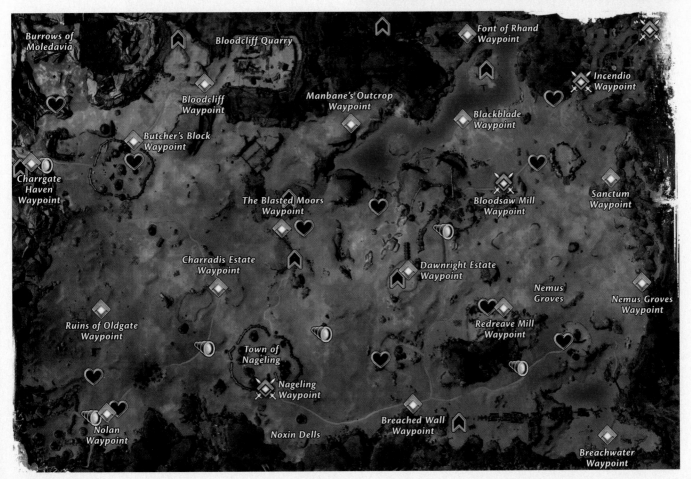

NOLAN WAYPOINT (SOUTHWEST SIDE)

SERVICES:	Weaponsmith, Merchant, Equipment Repair
TRAVEL:	Gate to Black Citadel (Charr Capital City) (S), Oldgate Waypoint (N), Nageling Waypoint (E)
HARVESTING INFO:	Copper Ore (N), Aspen Saplings (N), Gummo Sapling, Vine Vegetables, Blueberries

The town of Nolan is the last truly safe point in Diessa Plateau. Check your equipment and speak to Padar Grindaxe before you head out.

ASSIST THE BLOOD LEGION (Renown Task)

GOAL:	Keep the road free of separatist threats.
LEVEL:	15

Description: Separatists are harassing travelers along the road east out of Nolan. They are putting mines and wreckage along the roadway and attacking caravans. A fun way to fight the separatists is to turn their mines against them. Pick up the mines and place them at their feet. For less violent assistance, salvage scrap from the wreckage on the roadside and take it to Tiga Fierceblade.

The most efficient way of completing this task for the Blood Legion is to follow a patrolling legionnaire, help him fight the separatists, and revive him if he falls.

ATTACK THE FLAME LEGION HIDEOUT (Repeatable)

GOAL:	While disguised as a separatist, destroy supplies and plant evidence of a separatist attack.
LEVEL:	15

Description: Speak with Sonja Redclaw to hear her plan to get the Flame Legion and separatists at each other's throats. When you are ready to go undercover, tell her to put you in a separatist disguise. The Flame Legion hideout is in a small cave to the southwest. Be ready to fight; there are many Flame Legionnaires packed in a small area. This can be put to your advantage. Lead your enemies to the cave walls near the supplies and let loose with your area-of-effect attacks. You will have killed most of your witnesses while destroying the supplies. You need to destroy eight supplies in total. Once you're done, to ensure the separatists are blamed, plant evidence at the markers indicated on your minimap. Return to Sonja for more cloak-and-dagger fun.

ATTACK THE SEPARATIST CAMP (Repeatable)

GOAL:	While disguised as a Flame Legionnaire, kill 10 separatists and place Flame Legion emblems in the camp.
LEVEL:	16

Description: Speak with Sonja Redclaw to start part two of the plan. Let her put you in a Flame Legion disguise and break down the southeastern gate to the separatist camp. Start this part of the deception by slaying some separatists. Once the camp is emptied, place some Flame Legion emblems at the spots marked on your minimap. Once all the emblems are planted, the separatists will attack the Flame Legion and both threats will be neutralized.

ASSIST THE ASH LEGION (Renown Task)

GOAL:	Take out separatists at Dunrock Gulch.
LEVEL:	17

Description: Vasher Shadowsinner has been ordered to observe the nearby separatist camp. But why observe separatists when you can eliminate them? Break down the gate and cause chaos by killing the separatists and destroying their structures and supplies. Deep inside is a small prison. Get inside and free the prisoners so they can start fighting too. Under a tent is a barrel of explosives. Use the bombs in the barrel to quickly destroy supplies, wagons, and tents, and to kill separatists.

OLDGATE WAYPOINT (WEST SIDE)

SERVICES:	Waypoint
TRAVEL:	Nolan Waypoint (S), Charradis Waypoint (E), Butcher's Block Waypoint (N), Charrgate Waypoint (N)
HARVESTING INFO:	Copper Ore (W), Aspen Saplings (Common), Gummo Saplings, Mushrooms (W)

The Ruins of Oldgate sulk beneath the trees. Its location north of the town of Nolan makes it a threat to civilians and ranchers. The dead are restless in Oldgate, and a detachment of the Iron Legion is working to control the ghosts. The normal way of attacking the spirits to dispel them works, but you can talk to Rhell Crankmane for a more high-tech option.

ASSIST THE IRON LEGION (Renown Task)

GOAL:	Minimize the ghostly forces in the Ruins of Oldgate.
LEVEL:	16

Description: The Iron Legion here is following the basic method for controlling a ghost population. They are lighting torches and killing the ghosts that are attracted to them. You can impress the legion by running along the line of torches and lighting them quickly (by pressing the Interact key). Kill any ghosts you encounter or find by clearing rubble. Clearing rubble may cause more ghosts to appear. Rhell Crankmane is nearby, and he has his own ideas for controlling the ghosts.

DEFEND RHELL CRANKMANE (Repeatable)

GOAL:	Defend Rhell Crankmane while he sets up his ghost control machines.
LEVEL:	16

Description: Speak with Rhell Crankmane about getting started. Rhell says he has created a "Ghost Control Machine," which creates a sound that ghosts can't resist. It neutralizes the ghosts for a short period of time. The problem is he needs someone to fight off the ghosts while he works. Follow him into the woods and protect him while he sets up two machines. Mixed groups of ghosts will attack; take out the archers and mages first because of their area-of-effect attacks. Once he is done, all of the ghosts in the ruins are Stunned, letting you pass safely through for a short period.

HELP KARRIS QUICKCALM (Repeatable)

GOAL:	Help Karris Quickcalm hunt for wurm eggs inside Wurm's Gullet.
LEVEL:	16

Description: Karris has to collect wurm eggs for Meatoberfest. Agree to help her and head into the cave first. Collect wurm eggs from the cave floor and wurm corpses, and hand them over to Karris. Going in front is much faster than following her because she walks so slowly. Once she has enough, Karris turns around and goes to Butcher's Block.

BUTCHER'S BLOCK WAYPOINT (NORTHWEST SIDE)

SERVICES:	Waypoint, Merchant
TRAVEL:	Oldgate Waypoint (S), Charrgate Haven Waypoint (W), Bloodcliff Waypoint (NE)
HARVESTING INFO:	Aspen Saplings (W), Vine Vegetables

The village of Butcher's Block is filled with celebrants. Hooray for Meatoberfest! There is a great deal to see and do here. Helping out is a good way to make a name for yourself. Once you are done partying, you can fight the separatists hiding in the woods.

ASSIST LAKOR GRIZZLEMOUTH (Renown Task)

GOAL:	Help Butcher's Block celebrate Meatoberfest.
LEVEL:	16

Description: Be the life of the party at the happiest time of the year, Meatoberfest! An easy way to do this is to make sure no one's hungry or thirsty. Grab meat from the meat racks to give to hungry soldiers. Grab a drink from the ale cart and hand it to a thirsty soldier. There are some inebriated soldiers who are getting too rowdy. Start a fight with a few to get out their aggression.

THE CELEBRATION OF MEAT (World Event)

GOAL:	Give a helping hand during the celebration.
LEVEL:	N/A

Description: There is so much to do during Meatoberfest that it's tough keeping track of it all. Never fear: the world event list can help you know what's going on in the area.

HELP KIBOZ RAPIDEATER (Part of the World Event)

GOAL:	Help Kiboz Rapideater herd cattle to Butcher's Block.
LEVEL:	16

Description: Kiboz needs to get his cattle to Meatoberfest. You can find him on the road north to Butcher's Block. Protect him and his cattle from wolves and separatist attacks. Take out wolves quickly because their howls bring more wolves. Revive Kiboz if he gets injured; otherwise, his caravan won't move forward.

PROTECT RADARR BOOMMAKER'S FIREWORK LAUNCHERS (Part of the World Event)

GOAL:	Defend five firework launchers from separatist attacks.
LEVEL:	16

Description: Radarr Boommaker has set up his firework launchers to the east, outside of the walls of Butcher's Block. While this is safe for the celebrants of Meatoberfest, the separatists lurking in the woods threaten Boommaker's launchers. Slay the entire attacking separatist force before they destroy all five launchers. Luckily the launchers are pretty sturdy. Boommaker fights alongside you, and the separatists only attack in small groups. Once they are all dead, hang around a minute to watch the fireworks show.

DEFEAT AZALUS POISONTONGUE (Part of the World Event)

GOAL:	Teach this guy a lesson in manners.
LEVEL:	16

Description: This veteran is ruining Meatoberfest by hurling insults at anyone in range. Pick a fight with him to knock him down a peg. He may be drunk, but he's no pushover; just when you think you have him down, he gets a second wind and restores his health. You can grab meat from the nearby meat racks to restore your health if you get in trouble. Defeat Azalus and save Meatoberfest!

DEFEAT THE PLAINS WURM (Group)

GOAL:	Defeat the plains wurm before Karris Quickcalm must return to Butcher's Block.
LEVEL:	16

Description: While in Butcher's Block, talk to Aynna Quicksight. She sent Karris Quickcalm to gather wurm eggs near Wurm's Cleft, and Karris is late getting back. Travel southwest out of Butcher's Block. A champion plains wurm is blocking the entrance to the cave! This huge beast tosses boulders at you, so stay on your toes. Once it's defeated, Karris can bring its eggs to Meatoberfest.

CHARRGATE HAVEN WAYPOINT (NORTHWEST SIDE)

SERVICES:	Waypoint, Equipment Repair, Merchant, Weaponsmith
TRAVEL:	Wayfarer Foothills (Level 1-15 Region) (W), Butcher's Block Waypoint (E)
HARVESTING INFO:	Copper Ore (S), Iron Ore (N), Silver Ore (Rich) (N), Mushrooms (N)

West of Butcher's Block is a guardpost called Charrgate Haven. It guards the pass to Wayfarer Foothills. The land turns from plains and forests to rocky hills and mountains. The charr are trying to mine for ore to the north, but the subterranean threat of the dredge keeps them from holding to the area.

DEFEND RIMTOOTH (Repeatable)

GOAL:	Defend Rimtooth from dredge.
LEVEL:	15

Description: Terje Strongarm and Oxnard Bonestrap are trying to get a shipment of ale from Charrgate Haven to Butcher's Block in time for Meatoberfest. It's not far, but the dredge are attacking anything that travels on the road. Halfway to Butcher's Block, a dredge APC will surface and attack Rimtooth, the group's pack marmoth. If Rimtooth takes too much damage, the ale shipment is destroyed and Terje and Oxnard will have to return to Charrgate Haven. Strike at the dredge to draw their attention away and slay the entire dredge force.

ASSIST THE IRON LEGION (Renown Task)

GOAL:	Deal with the dredge nuisance.
LEVEL:	16

Description: The charr are fighting to run the dredge out of the mines to the north. Slay any dredge you see and destroy their structures to drive them away. The dredge turrets should be taken out first. These machines have high range and hit hard! The guard towers are tough, but they don't hit back and it's satisfying when they fall.

DESTROY THE DREDGE BARRICADE (Repeatable)

GOAL:	Destroy 10 dredge wall segments.
LEVEL:	17

Description: Arcaris Clashcaller is looking for volunteers to fight the dredge. The dredge have overrun a mine and have put up a wall separating the charr from their equipment. Deal with the pulse cannons first and then kill nearby dredge. Revive fallen allies to help you knock down the wall sections. Area-of-effect attacks are helpful here; you can hit wall segments and dredge attackers in one nice blast.

RETRIEVE THE STOLEN MINING EQUIPMENT (Repeatable)

GOAL:	Collect hammers in the mine.
LEVEL:	17

Description: Once the dredge wall has been broken down, legionnaires move into the mines to retrieve the mining equipment. Follow them in and bring them any sledgehammers you find. A great deal of footwork is needed because you can only carry one hammer at a time. To make things more fun, use the sledgehammers as weapons on the dredge. If you can't find any on the ground, sometimes the dredge drop sledgehammers when they die.

BLOODCLIFF WAYPOINT (NORTHWEST SIDE)

SERVICES:	Waypoint, Skill Point, Tool Merchant
TRAVEL:	Butcher's Block Waypoint (SW), Blasted Moors Waypoint (SE)
HARVESTING INFO:	Iron Ore (Abundant)

Bloodcliff Quarry is a strip mine that feeds the hefty iron needs of the charr legions. This place needs to be running at full productivity, but the dredge have been staging raids. Fight off the dredge, and then head north of the waypoint. There's a Durmand Priory scribe nearby who's willing to share some lore (and give you a Skill Point).

ASSIST THE QUARRY WORKERS (Renown Task)

GOAL:	Increase worker productivity in the quarry.
LEVEL:	17

Description: Worker productivity needs to be improved at the quarry. Talk to lazy miners and convince them to get back to work. To aid in the quarrying operation, fix the drilling machines. This makes them produce boulders, which you can then use to fill dredge tunnels. Once things are running smoothly, talk to Wagh Nearshot to buy useful items.

THE DREDGE ASSAULT (WORLD EVENT)

GOAL:	Protect Bloodcliff Quarry and keep it operational.
LEVEL:	17

Description: When you get close enough to the Bloodcliff Quarry, this world event appears. The dredge are making an assault on the quarry, and it's up to you to stop them!

STOP THE DREDGE (REPEATABLE)

GOAL:	Stop the dredge from stealing equipment.
LEVEL:	17

Description: The dredge are raiding Bloodcliff Quarry and stealing equipment. You must prevent the dredge from getting 12 pieces of equipment back to their personnel transports within the time limit. Don't try to take out the transports; there are too many, and the thief will just go to the next-nearest one. Watch the minimap to find where the thieves are and cripple them to slow them down.

DRIVE THE DREDGE FROM BLOODCLIFF QUARRY (Repeatable)

GOAL:	Block dredge tunnels and slay the dredge.
LEVEL:	17

Description: The dredge have dug tunnels into Bloodcliff Quarry. The legion force defending the quarry is almost overwhelmed by the attackers coming from these tunnels. Like many other assaults, you have to break the attackers' morale to drive them off. However, the fighting spirit of the dredge cannot be dampened while they have access to reinforcements. The first thing you have to do is take out those tunnels! Revive any downed allies you come across to help. Once the tunnels are gone, the remaining dredge must be slain. Fight next to Wagh Nearshot at the center of the quarry to finish up quickly.

CHARRADIS ESTATE WAYPOINT (WEST OF CENTER)

SERVICES:	Waypoint
TRAVEL:	Butcher's Block Waypoint (NW), Blasted Moors Waypoint (NE), Nageling Waypoint (SE)
HARVESTING INFO:	Vine Vegetables

When you're done with Bloodcliff Quarry, travel southeast to this waypoint. Some of Ascalon's finest cattle come from the Charradis Estate. It's surrounded by good grazing land on the rolling hills of Diessa Plateau. With the legions occupied by the ghosts, separatists, and flame legion, the ranchers must defend the estate themselves. Some very interesting tasks can be found here.

HELP THE RANCHERS (Renown Task)

GOAL:	Help Charradis Estate ranchers attend to the cattle.
LEVEL:	17

Description: With so much aggressive wildlife in the area, the ranchers are having a tough time getting all the chores done. If you don't feel like fighting, grab hay from nearby hay bales and use ranch hand Spring to bring it to the cows. Otherwise, go outside of the ranch fence and help the ranchers with the wolves and wurms. Stomp on any wurm mounds you see to bring them to the surface.

CLEAR THE FIELD OF WURMS (Repeatable)

GOAL:	Clear the field of wurms and wurm mounds for the cow race.
LEVEL:	17

Description: The ranch hands are trying to hold a cow race, but the field is infested with wurms and their mounds. To make matters worse, there is a huge veteran wurm creating hatchlings. Revive any fallen ranchers you find to help you with the clean up. Kill the veteran wurm first to stop it from throwing rocks at people and from spawning more wurms. Then, stomp on any wurm mounds to bring them up and squish them. Once all the wurms are dead, the race can begin.

NAGELING WAYPOINT (SOUTH SIDE)

SERVICES:	Waypoint, Equipment Repair
TRAVEL:	Charradis Estate Waypoint (NW), Blasted Moors Waypoint (N), Breached Wall Waypoint (E), Dawnright Waypoint (NE)
HARVESTING INFO:	Iron Ore (W)

Nageling is more of a small fortress than a town. Legion patrols, turret cannons, high walls, and thick doors make it an imposing place. Nageling needs these defenses because it is constantly harassed by separatist attacks.

HELP NAGELING'S RESIDENTS (Renown Task)

GOAL:	Help the residents of Nageling.
LEVEL:	18

Description: Separatists are skulking outside of the town walls, probing for weaknesses. The town guards are doing their best, but they are getting caught in separatist ambushes. An effective way to protect the town is to revive guards and stay with them to help them fight the separatists. You may even be able to use the town's defensive turrets.

DEFEAT THE SEPARATIST BRIGADE (Group)

GOAL:	Defeat the separatist brigade assaulting the town of Nageling.
LEVEL:	18

Description: A brigade of 10 veteran separatists is trying to break into and rampage through the town. They travel in a pack, and their combined damage can be overwhelming. Grab their attention and retreat a bit to separate the melee fighters from the ranged attackers. Kill the melee group first. With the brigade whittled down, the rest should be less of a problem.

DEFEND MAD MARDINE'S COWS (Repeatable)

GOAL:	Keep enough cows alive to complete five tests.
LEVEL:	20

Description: Mad Mardine has created a cattlepult that has interesting applications. It's a weapon, food transport, and entertainment all in one. One of his ballistic bovines has struck a harpy nest, and its occupants are coming for vengeance. The harpies aren't too bright, but they keep attacking the cows. Help by defending the cows and keeping at least five of them alive. You can't protect them all, so choose a set of cows you want to defend. If you succeed, the harpies get spooked and Mad Mardine sends for more "ammunition." If any cows are left you can wager with Mardine on how far a launched cow will go.

BLASTED MOORS WAYPOINT (WEST OF CENTER)

SERVICES:	Waypoint, Skill Challenge (S), Skill Point
TRAVEL:	Charradis Waypoint (SW), Nageling Waypoint (S), Manbane's Waypoint (NE)
HARVESTING INFO:	Iron Ore, Silver Ore, Gummo Saplings, Herb Patches, Mushrooms

This waypoint is on the outskirts of Ascalon ruins. There is more about this place than meets the eye. If you jump down the well, you can find some ancient aqueduct tunnels. Within the tunnels are Mushrooms, metal ore veins, interesting enemies, and a place of power to commune with and gain a Skill Point. South of the waypoint is a lookout tower. Defeat Roj the Rowdy Butcher to win a Skill Challenge.

FONT OF RHAND WAYPOINT (NORTH SIDE)

SERVICES:	Waypoint, Skill Challenge (Skill Book)
TRAVEL:	Blackblade Waypoint (S), Incendio Waypoint (E)
HARVESTING INFO:	Blueberries (Abundant)

Not far from this waypoint is a strange sunken structure called the Font of Rhand. Animals avoid the area, leaving only the rumbling sound of rushing water. The Flame Legion has taken over this old Ascalonian tomb and sealed the entrance with magic. The source of the magic is coming from Incendio Templum.

MANBANE WAYPOINT (NORTH SIDE)

SERVICES:	Waypoint, Karma Vendor, Karma Weaponsmith, Skill Point
TRAVEL:	Blackblade Waypoint (E), Blasted Moors Waypoint (S), Butcher's Block Waypoint (W)
HARVESTING INFO:	Gummo Saplings (Common), Vegetables (Common), Rich Iron Vein (N)

Manbane Waypoint is north of Blackblade Lake, at the top of the Diessa Plateau. The northern shore is quiet and verdant, with bears being the most dangerous creature you find. North of the waypoint is Spider Nest Cavern, where Mushrooms and rich Iron veins can be found. The southern shore is a dangerous area, filled with earth elementals, more bears, and Flame Legion forces.

ASSIST STOUT DARKMIND (Renown Task)

GOAL:	Keep Ebonshore Plant operational and Blackblade Lake free of contaminants.
LEVEL:	20

Description: Before meeting up with Darkmind, follow the shore and collect water-testing kits. Swim to the bottom of the lake to fix chemical dispensers. Clear the Ebonshore Plant of Flame Legion and tar elementals so you can turn in the water-testing kits to Darkmind. Kyron Darkshield may also need help. Once Stout Darkmind is satisfied, she becomes a karma vendor.

PREVENT THE FLAME LEGION RITUAL (Repeatable)

GOAL:	Prevent the Flame Legion from completing a ritual to pollute Blackblade Lake.
LEVEL:	20

Description: Smogan Darkhorn has spotted a group of Flame Legion gathering at the island north of the water processor. Veteran Flame Legion ritualists are summoning darkness and corruption from the depths. The only way to stop the ritual is to slay them. Sap their determination by killing all the ritualists. Once they've lost heart, they retreat, and you have saved the lake from an icky fate. If the Flame Legion completes their ritual, the lake will swarm with tar elementals.

DEFEND THE WATER-PROCESSING MACHINES (Repeatable)

GOAL:	Prevent tar elementals from destroying the water-processing machines.
LEVEL:	20

Description: Kyron believes the water processors can clean out the contaminants produced by the Flame Legion ritual. While the machines do their work, you must protect them from the tar elementals that ooze from the lake. Both processors will be attacked with waves of two elementals each. Unless you have a good ranged weapon that lets you stand on the ramp between the two, this means there will be a lot of running around trying to kill the tar elementals as fast as you can. While you are fighting, the processors are cleaning the water. If you lose a processor, the fight will be longer but easier since you only have one point to guard. When the water is purified, the lake will be returned to its pristine beauty, although the Flame Legion might try their ritual again. If both processors are destroyed, Kyron moves to fix them.

DEFEND KYRON DARKSHIELD (Repeatable)

GOAL:	Protect Kyron Darkshield as she fixes the east and west water processors.
LEVEL:	20

Description: If the Flame Legion succeeds in damaging the water processors, Kyron needs someone to guard her back while she repairs them. The Flame Legion attacks her in mixed groups of three. There are two strategies to handle them. The first is to let them cluster around Kyron and cut them down with area-of-effect damage. The other way is to kill or cripple them before they reach Kyron. Once one water processor is finished, Kyron moves on to the second. Stay with Kyron; the Flame Legion will focus on her instead of attacking the processors. Once Kyron's work is complete, the lake will be cleaned and the Flame Legion will leave, promising vengeance.

BLACKBLADE WAYPOINT (NORTHEAST SIDE)

SERVICES:	Waypoint
TRAVEL:	Font of Rhand Waypoint (N), Manbane Waypoint (W), Bloodsaw Mill Waypoint (SE), Dawnright Waypoint (SW)
HARVESTING INFO:	N/A

To reach this waypoint, travel south of the Font of Rhand or west of Manbane's Outcrop. A Skill Point can be found at Skerry Isle to the north. Travel south to Dawnright Waypoint while avoiding the skelks in the water and Flame Legion in the forest.

DAWNRIGHT WAYPOINT (EAST OF CENTER)

SERVICES:	Waypoint, Skill Challenge, Salvage Merchant
TRAVEL:	Blasted Moors (W), Blackblade Waypoint (N), Redreave Mill Waypoint (W), Breached Wall Waypoint (S)
HARVESTING INFO:	Vine Vegetables, Herb Patches

At the Dawnright Estate, rancher-in-training Posionswill has a Skill Challenge for you: defeat his prized bull. Show that bovine who's boss, and then move along to Stonefall Estate. You can pass the time by picking some herbs and vegetables along the way. Enjoy the brief respite while you can; you are heading into territory that is threatened by separatists and spirits of Ascalon.

HELP RAK DEATHMANE (Renown Task)

GOAL:	Protect Stonefall Estate's livestock from separatists.
LEVEL:	21

Description: Stonefall Estate is south of the Dawnright Estate. You can help the ranchers in the area by preventing separatists from driving off livestock and stealing chickens. One way to take care of the livestock is by carrying chickens back inside the fence. The fastest method is to get hay from Dahala Lasherpaw and give it to nearby cows or add it to bedding in the barn. Outside the fence, you can help by killing separatists and protecting the ranchers.

DRIVE OFF THE SEPARATIST CATTLE RUSTLERS (Repeatable)

GOAL:	Kill all the separatists trying to steal the cattle.
LEVEL:	21

Description: A force of separatists is attempting to make off with the entire herd! Slay them so the ranchers of the Stonefall Estate can recover their cows.

BREACHED WALL WAYPOINT (SOUTH SIDE)

SERVICES:	Waypoint
TRAVEL:	Dawnright Waypoint (N), Redreave Mill Waypoint (NE), Breachwater Waypoint (E)
HARVESTING INFO:	Iron Ore (E), Blueberries

A long wall of Ascalon ruins follows the southeastern edge of Diessa Plateau. Separatists have set up in Camp Althea, and the Ash Legion and ghosts fight for control of the ruins to the east.

ASSASSINATE THE SEPARATIST INSTIGATOR (Group)

GOAL:	Kill the separatist instigator before he can escape.
LEVEL:	21

Description: An important separatist leader is moving near Camp Althea. There is only a limited amount of time before he travels out of reach, but make your approach carefully. The separatist instigator is surrounded by a mass of guards. Kill them first and then take on the leader. He can strengthen himself, which makes this a tough fight.

BREACHWATER WAYPOINT (SOUTHEAST SIDE)

SERVICES:	Waypoint
TRAVEL:	Breached Wall Waypoint (W), Nemus Grove Waypoint (N)
HARVESTING INFO:	Iron Ore (Common), Silver Ore (Common), Vine Vegetables, Herb Patches

Aid the Ash Legion as they fight the Ascalon ghosts in the area. The harvesting is pretty good here.

REDREAVE MILL WAYPOINT (SOUTHEAST OF CENTER)

SERVICES:	Waypoint
TRAVEL:	N/A
HARVESTING INFO:	Iron Ore (limited), Silver Ore (limited)

Travel northeast of Breached Wall Waypoint to reach this mill. Redreave Mill is in a bad position; it's backed against a cliff wall and under siege from separatists.

ASSIST REDREAVE MILL (Renown Task)

GOAL:	Protect workers and the machinery from separatists.
LEVEL:	22

Description: Redreave Mill is in competition with the other mills in the area. Speak to Attis Ricsaw to find out how to help. Before you head out of the mill, convince apathetic workers to get back to their tasks. Once you're outside, kill any separatists in the area and revive any injured workers.

DESTROY SEPARATIST TREBUCHETS OUTSIDE THE MILL (Repeatable)

GOAL:	Destroy the three trebuchets bombarding the mill.
LEVEL:	22

Description: Separatist trebuchets are firing into Redreave Mill. They never actively target you, so run out of the mill and circle around to attack the trebuchets from behind. You avoid most of the separatist guards this way.

NEMUS GROVE WAYPOINT (SOUTHEAST SIDE)

SERVICES:	Waypoint, Tool Merchant, Pendant Merchant, Salvage Merchant
TRAVEL:	Breachwater Waypoint (S), Sanctum Waypoint (N), Redreave Mill Waypoint (W)
HARVESTING INFO:	Iron Ore (N), Silver Ore (N), Gummo Saplings (NW), Vine Vegetables (Abundant), Herb Patches

This is the farthest southeastern point of the region. The forests to the west supply the lumber mills in the area. The nearby cliffs are rich in ore resources.

HELP RAINTIMBER MILL (Renown Task)

GOAL:	Keep the skelk problem under control.
LEVEL:	23

Description: Ever since the mill workers began clearing trees north of the mill, the skelk in the forest have become more aggressive. Give Raintimber Mill a hand by culling their numbers. Go into the woods north of the mill and reset skelk traps. Kill any skelk you see and protect the workers.

KILL THE SKELK ASSAULTING RAINTIMBER MILL (Group)

GOAL:	Kill the champion putrescent skelk before it destroys the saw conveyor and other equipment.
LEVEL:	23

Description: If you are south of Raintimber Mill, you may find Tharus Fiendstalker muttering about hunting a dangerous beast. It isn't long before a huge putrescent skelk rises up out of Breachwater Lake and starts rampaging through the mill, followed by a mass of regular skelk. Focus your damage on the champion and make sure you evade its leap attack. You can sometimes get the beast caught on the mill structures, allowing you to attack it safely from range. Once the monster goes down, the rest of the skelk do not pose a problem.

PROTECT THE TRAINED SKELK (Repeatable)

GOAL:	Protect the trained skelk gathering kindling for Raintimber Mill.
LEVEL:	24

Description: One of the workers at the mill has turned the presence of skelk to an advantage. A number of skelk have been tamed and trained to gather kindling and return it to the mill. Unfortunately, they get attacked by the wild skelk in the forest. Your job is to stand guard and protect the trained skelk while they work. They spread out, so it's easier to guard only a small group of them. Just remember that the fewer you have, the slower the job gets done. Take out the wild skelk lurking in the trees and nests to make your job easier.

DEFEND THE ENGINEERS (Repeatable)

GOAL:	Defend the engineers repairing Raintimber Bridge.
LEVEL:	24

Description: Charr engineers are working to repair Raintimber Bridge. You have to stand guard on either side of the broken bridge and stop the separatists from reaching them. Revive any allies if they go down, and use crowd control abilities to slow down the separatists. Keep the engineers alive until they complete their work.

WARD OFF SEPARATISTS ATTACKING RAINTIMBER BRIDGE (Repeatable)

GOAL:	Prevent the separatists from destroying the bridge with their catapult or explosive charges.
LEVEL:	24

Description: Separatists are trying to destroy Raintimber Bridge. You have to protect the bridge and slay enough separatists to drive them away. They have a catapult on the ridge north of the bridge. You can remove the threat by taking it out; just make sure to keep moving to avoid its fire. Or, you can ignore the catapult and fight the separatists trying to place bombs on the bridge. It's a faster way to break their morale, but it's riskier.

SANCTUM WAYPOINT (EAST SIDE)

SERVICES:	Waypoint
TRAVEL:	Nemus Grove Waypoint (S), Bloodsaw Mill Waypoint (W), Incendio Waypoint (NW)
HARVESTING INFO:	Iron Ore (Abundant), Silver Ore (Abundant), Gummo Saplings (NW), Vine Vegetables, Mushrooms

This out-of-the-way area is great for harvesting. Travel east to enter Holystone Caves. This network of tunnels contains a large amount of both ore veins and grawl. Adventure waits to the west at Bloodsaw Mill Waypoint.

BLOODSAW MILL WAYPOINT (EAST OF CENTER)

SERVICES:	Waypoint, Karma Vendor, Merchant, Equipment Repair, Weaponsmith
TRAVEL:	Blackblade Waypoint (NW), Incendio Waypoint (NE), Sanctum Waypoint (E)
HARVESTING INFO:	Gummo Saplings, Vine Vegetables

This lumber mill has been turned into a fortress, as a solid response to the Flame Legion coming from Incendio Templum. If it's not under assault when you arrive, it will be soon. That means this waypoint will often be contested. Make sure to grab Blackblade Waypoint to the northwest so you have another one close by in case things go wrong.

ASSIST BLOODSAW MILL (Renown Task)

GOAL:	Assist the workers and protect them from enemies.
LEVEL:	23

Description: Regardless of the danger of Flame Legion attacks and mauling by bears, work still has to get done around here. Create a safer environment by slaying either of these threats. Reviving downed workers is greatly appreciated. Help out around the mill by disposing of wood in the fire pits in the area. Wood can be gathered from the Bloodsaw saplings or picked up off the ground. Often some pieces are next to the fire pits to save you a little running. If you see any workers lazing around, get them back to work before they set a bad example. Pick up an explosives pack and use the Plant Bomb ability to destroy tree stumps. Use Throw Grenade to blast the wasp nests in the trees. Remember that it's not overkill, it's fun!

FLAME LEGION BATTLES (World Event)

GOAL:	Help the charr fight against the Flame Legion.
LEVEL:	N/A

Description: There is a series of tasks in this area to strengthen the charr position at Bloodsaw Mill and support an assault on the Blood Legion HQ. Incendio Templum must be conquered in order to open up the portal to the Font of Rhand.

DEFEND BLOODSAW MILL FROM THE FLAME LEGION (Part of the World Event)

GOAL:	Prevent the Flame Legion from capturing Bloodsaw Mill.
LEVEL:	23

Description: A Flame Legion invasion force is attempting to take over and wreck Bloodsaw Mill! Revive as many downed allies as possible to get the balance of force in your favor. Keep slaying Flame Legion forces until the time expires.

RECAPTURE BLOODSAW MILL FROM THE FLAME LEGION (Part of the World Event)

GOAL:	Capture Bloodsaw Mill.
LEVEL:	23

Description: Force the Flame Legion from Bloodsaw Mill. Revive as many allies as you can to help you fight. When you have more allies than enemies in the capture zone, you make progress toward taking the mill back. Once the mill is free, more tasks become available to you.

RECOVER SCRAP METAL (Part of the World Event)

GOAL:	Recover the scattered pieces of scrap metal for Savor Foulnight.
LEVEL:	23

Description: Talk to Joda Barbsaw. She will tell you she is getting impatient awaiting the return of the mill's engineer, Savor Foulnight. Hurry him up by gathering scraps of metal so he can fix the mill. You can find scraps in the forest north of the mill. The easy way to do it is to run through the woods and pick up the scrap (with your Interact key) without stopping. This will keep you one step ahead of the Flame Legion and bears in the forest. Bring what you've gathered to Savor, who is standing on a ridge south of the forest. Once he has enough, he sets out to fix the mill. When he's done, Savor joins Rankar Harrownight at the front of the mill.

DEFEAT HAZARAR RAZENIGHT (Part of the World Event)

GOAL:	Defeat Hazarar Razenight in combat.
LEVEL:	24

Description: Hazarar thinks he's too tough to join the fight against the Flame Legion. Burst this guy's bloated ego by challenging him to a fight. He's not just boasting. He hits hard, can knock you down, and can heal himself multiple times during the fight. Before you take him on, decide on your strategy, either offense or defense. Set yourself up with equipment or talents accordingly, and take him down. Win, and he'll join Rankar Harrownight.

DEFEND FAINT GHOSTNIGHT (Part of the World Event)

GOAL:	Defend Faint Ghostnight as he searches for devourer eggs.
LEVEL:	23

Description: Faint Ghostnight's last devourer pet, "Grr," has died. Faint has decided to raise a new one, but he needs to find the right egg. Watch his back while he searches five devourer nests. The devourers are protective of their territory, so try to attack them first before they get to Ghostnight. Once he has the perfect egg, he will join Rankar Harrownight.

HELP THE NIGHT WARBAND (Part of the World Event)

GOAL:	Help the Night Warband reach Incendio Templum.
LEVEL:	24

Description: Once you have completed the tasks for Savor Foulnight, Faint Ghostnight, and Hazarar Razenight, they will gather with Rankar Harrownight at the flagpole at Bloodsaw Mill. Together, they will form the Night Warband and set out to conquer the Flame Legion headquarters. Follow them as they head north and join in the fighting. Revive any of them if they go down, and proceed to Incendio Templum.

INCENDIO WAYPOINT (NORTHEAST SIDE)

SERVICES:	Waypoint
TRAVEL:	Sanctum Waypoint (SE), Bloodsaw Mill Waypoint (SW), Blackblade Waypoint (W), Portal to Font of Rhand (NE)
HARVESTING INFO:	Iron Ore (Abundant), Silver Ore (Rich) (NE)

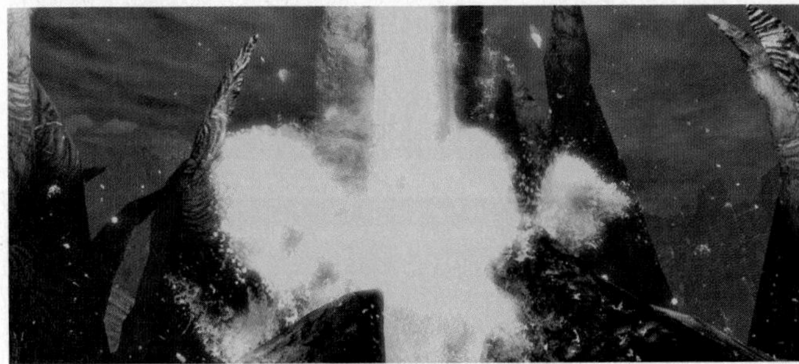

This is the headquarters of the Flame Legion in the region. Flame Legion guard the waypoint, and your foes get tougher the further you go in. If you have captured Incendio Templum with the Night Warband, a portal to the Font of Rhand will open up. The plentiful Silver and Iron veins are rewards for those who dare venture inside.

ASSIST THE ASH LEGION (Renown Task)

GOAL:	Infiltrate, sabotage, and destroy Incendio Templum.
LEVEL:	25

Description: Remaris Earshot is on reconnaissance duty at the entrance to Incendio Templum. She can't leave her post, so she asks for your help in weakening the Flame Legion. If you're not with the Night Warband, it's best to head down to Bloodsaw Mill and start that chain of tasks, which brings you back here (but not alone). If you want to go it alone, move inside, slay the Flame Legion, and destroy any braziers and supply carts. You can find battle plans in Flame Legion fonts, which you can bring back to Remaris. Stay on your guard; the further you go into Incendio Templum, the tougher the enemies become.

CAPTURE INCENDIO TEMPLUM (Repeatable)

GOAL:	Capture Incendio Templum from the Flame Legion before reinforcements arrive.
LEVEL:	25

Description: The Night Warband is going to capture Incendio Templum. Climb up to the upper level with the Fountain of Flame and capture that area first. It only has a few points of entry, and with your two allies it's easier to maintain control. Once the upper level is yours, jump down to the lower level. This area is tougher because it's a ring around the upper area. You can't see allies or enemies on the other side, and it takes time to run around. Focus on keeping downed allies revived and you can win.

DEFEND INCENDIO TEMPLUM (Repeatable)

GOAL:	Prevent the Flame Legion from retaking Incendio Templum.
LEVEL:	25

Description: The Flame Legion isn't going to take the loss of their headquarters lying down. You have to prevent the Flame Legion from taking both the upper and lower areas until the time limit expires. Unless you are extremely fast, holding the lower area is hard because of its ring shape. It's tough keeping the Flame Legion out of the area. Focus on holding the upper templum and keeping your allies alive. Use crowd control abilities to keep the enemies out of the capture zone, and you should succeed.

DESTROY THE EFFIGIES (Repeatable)

GOAL:	Take down the effigies before the Flame Legion recaptures Incendio Templum.
LEVEL:	25

Description: The Flame Legion is making a second try at recapturing Incendio Templum, and this time they've brought some effigies. The bad news is pretty bad, but the good news is that as soon as you defeat the two effigies, you win! Attack the effigy at the lower ring first and try to fight and defeat it before it can get into the capture zone. Take on the effigy at the upper templum next. Revive your allies if they go down, and keep moving. Once both effigies are destroyed, victory is yours. Congratulations! You've bested the Flame Legion twice!

FIELDS OF RUIN

LEVEL RANGE: 30-40

This region is along the eastern wall of Tyria. It's a large plain dominated by Ebonhawke, a free human city at the southern end of the map. Ogres are a major threat here, as are human separatists and charr renegades (who ironically agree that their governments are both wrong about peace and that they should keep killing each other). You can reach the Fields of Ruin by porting through an Asura Gate in Divinity's Reach or by walking south through the higher-level Blazeridge Steppes.

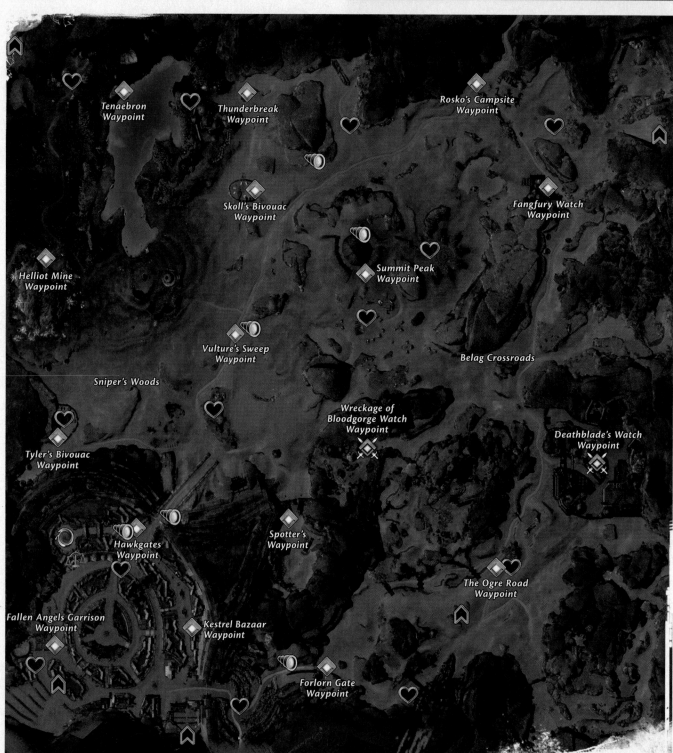

Tenaebron Waypoint
Thunderbreak Waypoint
Rosko's Campsite Waypoint
Skoll's Bivouac Waypoint
Fangfury Watch Waypoint
Helliot Mine Waypoint
Summit Peak Waypoint
Vulture's Sweep Waypoint
Belag Crossroads
Sniper's Woods
Wreckage of Bloodgorge Watch Waypoint
Deathblade's Watch Waypoint
Tyler's Bivouac Waypoint
Hawkgates Waypoint
Spotter's Waypoint
The Ogre Road Waypoint
Fallen Angels Garrison Waypoint
Kestrel Bazaar Waypoint
Forlorn Gate Waypoint

BLAZERIDGE STEPPES

LEVEL RANGE: 40-50

Travel north from the Fields of Ruin to continue adventuring in charr lands. Or, walk east through the Plains of Ashford to get to Blazeridge Steppes. Blazeridge Steppes has suffered from years of magical warfare and influence from the Elder Dragons. The conflict between the charr and humans did substantial damage to the area, and the taint from the dragons has created creatures here that are Branded. Be careful of them; the Branded are the enemies of all free people.

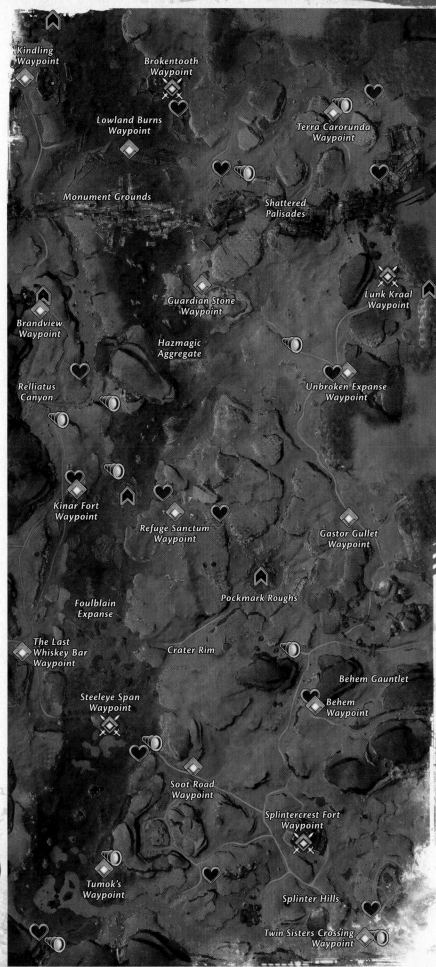

Kindling Waypoint
Brokentooth Waypoint
Lowland Burns Waypoint
Terra Carorunda Waypoint
Monument Grounds
Shattered Palisades
Guardian Stone Waypoint
Lunk Kraal Waypoint
Brandview Waypoint
Hazmagic Aggregate
Relliatus Canyon
Unbroken Expanse Waypoint
Kinar Fort Waypoint
Refuge Sanctum Waypoint
Gastor Gullet Waypoint
Foulblain Expanse
Pockmark Roughs
The Last Whiskey Bar Waypoint
Crater Rim
Behem Gauntlet
Steeleye Span Waypoint
Behem Waypoint
Soot Road Waypoint
Splintercrest Fort Waypoint
Tumok's Waypoint
Splinter Hills
Twin Sisters Crossing Waypoint

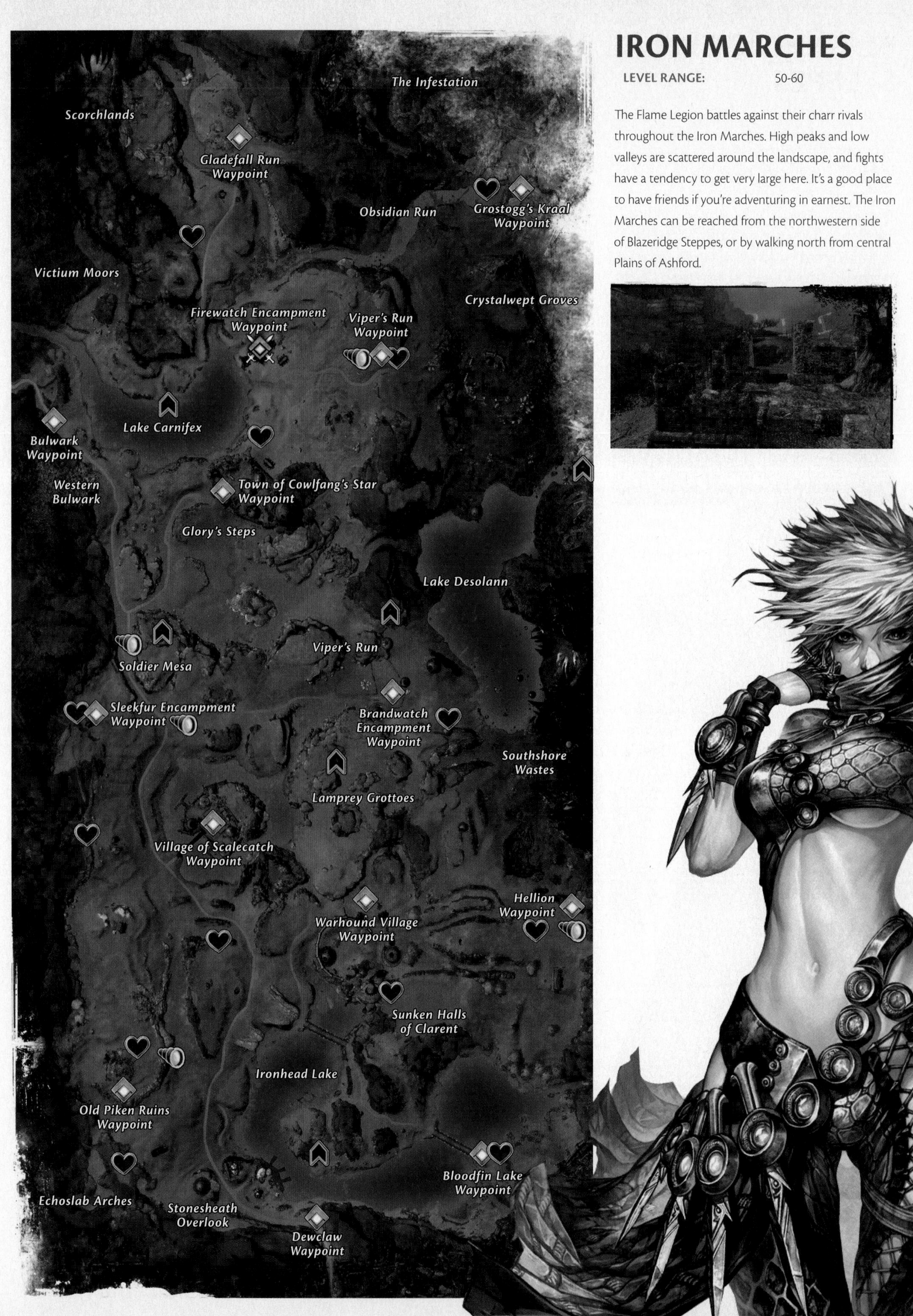

IRON MARCHES

LEVEL RANGE: 50-60

The Flame Legion battles against their charr rivals throughout the Iron Marches. High peaks and low valleys are scattered around the landscape, and fights have a tendency to get very large here. It's a good place to have friends if you're adventuring in earnest. The Iron Marches can be reached from the northwestern side of Blazeridge Steppes, or by walking north from central Plains of Ashford.

FIREHEART RISE

LEVEL RANGE: 60-70

The last stretch of charr territory is northwest from the Iron Marches. Enemies get extremely powerful that far north, so don't try to explore there until you're good and ready. The Flame Legion is still a horrible threat to anyone who dares enter their territory. It will take great tenacity to drive them away once and for all.

Kryta is a section of green hills and arable land that supports the last great bastion of human civilization here in Tyria. Though the centaurs push to wipe the humans off the map, the people of Divinity's Reach won't go without a fight. The humans of Kryta have kept their faith in the gods, and even in these times of crisis they may yet flourish.

DIVINITY'S REACH

LEVEL RANGE:	Human Capital City
WAYPOINTS:	13
POINTS OF INTEREST:	20

UPPER FLOOR

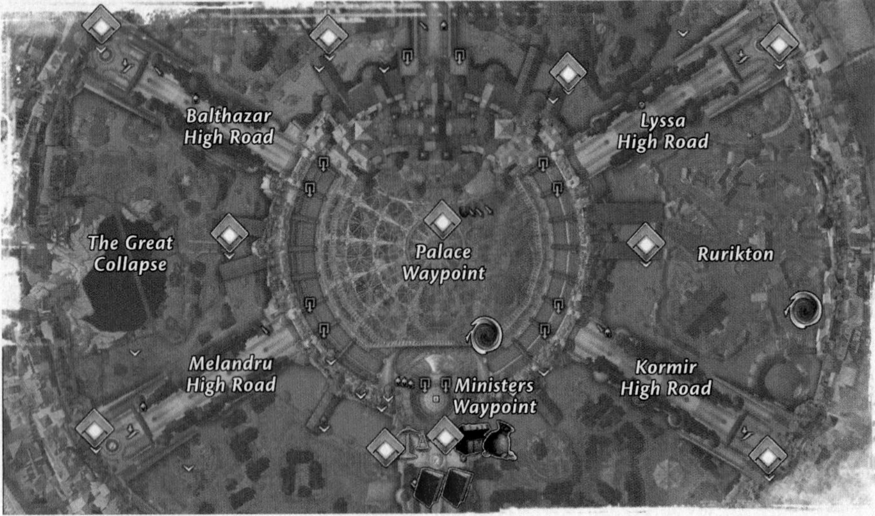

LOWER FLOOR

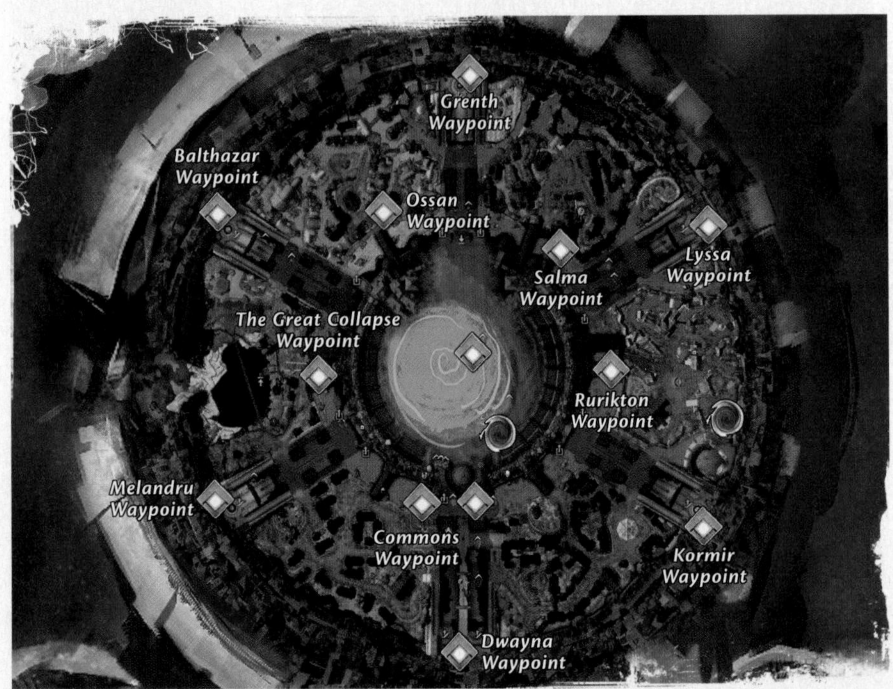

There are few symbols that demonstrate the diversity and unity within humanity better than the capital of Divinity's Reach. Six high roads, each dedicated to one of the True Gods, divide the lower city into districts. Each of the districts has its own atmosphere and ambience, reflecting the various refugees who have settled there. And yet, despite their different cultures, philosophies, and spiritual leanings, the people of Divinity's Reach are all part of the same whole—just like the wheel of the city.

DWAYNA WAYPOINT (SOUTHSIDE)

SERVICES:
Waypoint, Guild Services, Bank, Trading Post, Armorsmith, Weaponsmith, Trainers for All Professions, Karma Merchant, Divinity Guide, Carnival Worker, Equipment Repair, Food Merchant, Cooking Merchant

TRAVEL:
Entrance to Queensdale (Level 1-15 Region), Path to the Upper City, Path to Commons Waypoint

Dedicated to the Goddess of air and life, Dwayna, this major high road leads into the city (toward the Central Plaza) from the region of Queensdale. At the midpoint, opposite the city, stands a Divinity Guide eager to give directions and a Karma Merchant willing to speed you on your way.

LIFE IS TOO SHORT

Divinity's Reach is an enormous city, and there's a lot to see and do. To help you reach your destination faster, the Karma Merchants at the midsections of each of the high roads can grant you a speed boost for a short while. All you have to do is talk to them.

On the ascending path, armorsmiths, weaponsmiths, and trainers for all professions can be found. Not all the profession trainers are in the same place, but take a moment and you'll find each and every one of them on this set of ramps. At the top, near the Statue of Dwayna, are the Guild Registrar and Promoter, Bank, and Trading Post.

On the lower path, carnival workers can mark points of interest on your map, as long as you're looking for the carnival. Farther down, shopkeepers sell everything from salvage kits and leather bags to sticks of butter and vegetables.

COMMONS WAYPOINT (SOUTH CENTRAL)

SERVICES:	Waypoint, Crafting Trainers and Services, Armorsmith, Salvage Merchant, Food Merchant, Divinity Guide
TRAVEL:	Elevators to the Upper City, Path to Melandru Waypoint, Path to Dwayna Waypoint, Path to Collapse Waypoint, Path to Rurikton Waypoint

The Commons Waypoint services two districts of Divinity's Reach: the Western and Eastern Commons. These districts are where the real work is done to keep a city this size running. Crafters of every discipline can be found here along with shops lined against the inner circle. It's little surprise that the carnival is located throughout these two districts; it's an obvious place to entertain people. Stop by and check out each of the four attractions. If you have trouble finding any of them, carnival workers are positioned strategically throughout the districts and will happily put you on the right path.

MELANDRU WAYPOINT (SOUTHWEST SIDE)

SERVICES:	Waypoint, Karma Merchant, Armorsmith, Weaponsmith
TRAVEL:	Path to the Upper City, Path to Commons Waypoint, Path to Collapse Waypoint

Melandru, the Goddess of Nature and Growth, looks after the gardens and terraces of the city. The Plaza of Melandru, at the end of the road, lies between the Western Commons and the Great Collapse. There, a statue dedicated to the deity keeps watch near the outer wall of the city.

COLLAPSE WAYPOINT (WEST SIDE)

SERVICES:	Waypoint, Karma Merchant
TRAVEL:	Elevators to the Upper City, Path to Balthazar Waypoint, Path to Melandru Waypoint, Path to Ossan Waypoint, Path to Commons Waypoint

This entire district was ravaged by a massive sinkhole caved all the way through into the crypts beneath the city. Workers and architects are striving to fix the damage. Queen Jennah was able to warn the guard and have the district evacuated before the collapse. Talk to the people around the area. Some of them have heard odd things.

A statue of Balthazar stands along the intact northern edge of the district. If you talk to his priestess, she'll grant you a speed buff.

BALTHAZAR WAYPOINT (NORTHWEST SIDE)

SERVICES:	Waypoint, Karma Merchant, Divinity Guide, Weaponsmith, Armorsmith, Food Merchant
TRAVEL:	Path to Collapse Waypoint, Path to Central Plaza, Path to Ossan Waypoint

Another statue of Balthazar dominates the bottom of this high road. The God of War and Battle is an extremely popular deity with champions of all types, and many visit His monument here to pray for His guidance and assistance. Perhaps as a sign of His power, the road up to the Central Plaza is straight and relatively free of obstacles. On the north side of the road, you can find a shopkeeper, weaponsmith, and armorsmith selling their wares.

OSSAN WAYPOINT (NORTH CENTRAL)

SERVICES:	Waypoint, Food Merchant, Salvage Merchant, Armorsmith
TRAVEL:	Elevators to the Upper City, Path to Grenth Waypoint, Path to Balthazar Waypoint, Path to Salma Waypoint, Path to Collapse Waypoint

The Ossan Quarter was named for the Ossa family, and many of the residents are former Elonian refugees. This is reflected in the architecture of the district; it's substantially different than in other parts of Divinity's Reach. Here, the buildings have more rounded roofs with higher peaks and doors and windows of odd shapes. The streets are also a little cleaner, and there's a well-kept market in the center of the quarter.

GRENTH WAYPOINT (NORTH SIDE)

SERVICES:	Waypoint, Karma Merchant, Divinity Guide, Weaponsmith, Armorsmith
TRAVEL:	Path to the Upper City, Path to Salma Waypoint, Path to Ossan Waypoint

Grenth, the God of Death and Ice, holds dominion over the most northern plaza; as testament, the cemetery and entrance to the crypts are not far away. Within the city, His territory marks the separation between the Ossan and Salma districts. The Salma district is where many of the noble families reside, and the Grenth High Road is populated mostly by aristocrats in fine suits and gowns.

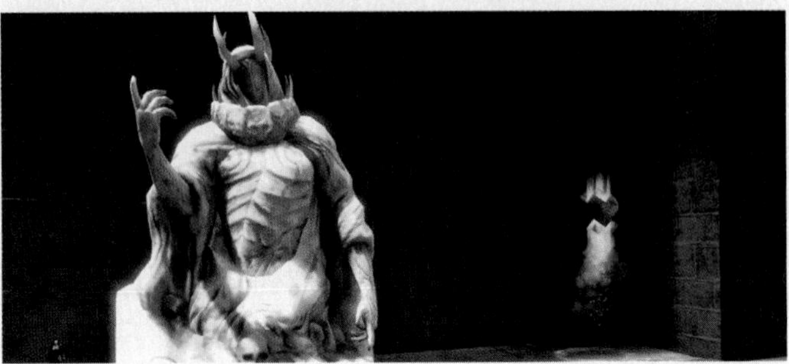

SALMA WAYPOINT (NORTHEAST CENTRAL)

SERVICES:	Waypoint, Equipment Repairs, Food Merchant, Salvage Merchant, Armorsmith, Weaponsmith, Homes (for Human Characters)
TRAVEL:	Elevators to the Upper City, Path to Lyssa Waypoint, Path to Grenth Waypoint, Path to Rurikton Waypoint, Path to Ossan Waypoint

Named for the famous Queen Salma, the Salma district is where most of the aristocracy make their homes. Not surprisingly, you can also find locations run by people who cater to them...as well as those who prey on them. Whether you were born a noble, commoner, or street urchin, there is a place for you in the Salma district. All human characters have their residences here.

The Salma Waypoint also has access to one of the most convenient Equipment Repair services in Divinity's Reach.

Be sure to stop at the market in the center of the district for some of the local food and drink. To get there, take the door facing the inner circle of the city. The architecture of the buildings on the edges of the district is not to be missed.

LYSSA WAYPOINT (NORTHEAST SIDE)

SERVICES:	Waypoint, Divinity Guide, Salvage Merchant, Weaponsmith, Armorsmith
TRAVEL:	Path to the Upper City, Path to Rurikton Waypoint, Path to Salma Waypoint

Lyssa is the twin Goddess of beauty and illusion, and her statue is a common place for lovers to meet or the lovesick to hope. She is also seen as a personification of luck, with one twin representing good fortune and the other bad. Although somewhat chaotic, Lyssa is one of the most popular of the Six Gods, and, historically, her followers have guided some of the most important events in the world. Families and groups of children are common sights along this high road.

RURIKTON WAYPOINT (EAST SIDE)

SERVICES:	Waypoint, Salvage Merchant, Cooking Merchant
TRAVEL:	Asura Gate to Ebonhawke, Elevators to the Upper City, Path to Kormir Waypoint, Path to Lyssa Waypoint, Path to Commons Waypoint, Path to Salma Waypoint

Named in honor of the brave Prince Rurik, Rurikton is the most elegant of the districts by far. Plazas with amazing statues are flanked with beautiful buildings. Many of these buildings have higher floors with balconies, giving panoramic views of the city. As if that weren't enough, wander down to the amphitheater in the southeast corner. It is impressive!

Rurikton also holds the Asura Gate to Ebonhawke, a human city to the far east (in the Fields of Ruin, level 30-40 zone). This represents a significant diplomatic tie for Divinity's Reach; Ebonhawke is the only remaining human city in Ascalon, and it's a dangerous place.

KORMIR WAYPOINT (SOUTHEAST SIDE)

SERVICES:	Waypoint, Karma Merchant, Divinity Guide, Weaponsmith, Armorsmith
TRAVEL:	Path to the Upper City, Path to Commons Waypoint, Path to Rurikton Waypoint

The statue of Kormir stands with open arms, welcoming the residents of Divinity's Reach and visitors. Once a mortal woman, a Spearmarshal with the Order of the Sunspears, Kormir is now the Goddess of Truth and Knowledge. As such, Her plaza is a place for scholars, debaters, and wisdom seekers of all types. In keeping with the Goddess' martial background, an armorsmith and a weaponsmith can be found at the top of the road, just outside the Central Plaza.

PALACE WAYPOINT (CENTRAL)

SERVICES:	Waypoint, Equipment Repairs, Cultural Armorsmith (Tiers 1-3)
TRAVEL:	Asura Gate to Lion's Arch, Elevators to the Lower City, Paths to All High Roads

It is here that visitors from other nations arrive, through the Asura Gate to Lion's Arch. Their first sight is one of splendor and natural beauty. The Palace Gardens make for a peaceful and beautiful backdrop to the Shrine of the Six.

The Seraph Headquarters nearby is the base of the largest military organization of Kryta, captained by Logan Thackeray. Not far away is the Royal Palace, from where Queen Jennah guides her people. This is the seat of the human race in all its glory.

MINISTER'S WAYPOINT

SERVICES:	Waypoint, Banker, Trading Post, Guild Registrar
TRAVEL:	Road North toward the Palace, South Route toward the Edge of Town

For people who are using the Trading Post and Bank, this is the perfect spot. Come here for the waypoint and stay for the convenience. You can shop till you drop and finish off a great day of touring Divinity's Reach.

QUEENSDALE

LEVEL RANGE:	1-15
RENOWN TASKS:	17
WAYPOINTS:	16
SKILL CHALLENGES:	7
HARVESTING INFO:	Copper Ore, Aspen Saplings, Carrots, Button Mushrooms, Beetletun Lettuce, Blueberry Bush, Herb Seedlings, Onion

SKILL CHALLENGES

> Defeat Franklin Quickblade and His Band (West of Center, Below Bandit Caves).
> Erts Jug of Power Unguent (West Side, Near Vale Waypoint).
> Commune with Earthen Magic (Center, Near Scaver Waypoint).
> Defeat the Windmill King (Center, also Near Scaver Waypoint).
> Fight Carnie Jeb, the Strong-Man (Northeast Side, Near Caudecus's Manor).
> Commune with the Temple of Ages (South Side, Near Godslost Waypoint).
> Commune with Tamini Place of Power (Southeast Side, in Taminn Foothills).

The rich and fertile plains of Queensdale offer humanity a chance to recover from the many battles against the charr. However, even with Divinity's Reach to the north and the Seraph guards protecting Queensdale, the people are not safe.

Bandits patrol the roads as often as the Seraph do, and centaurs attack and burn anything they can. The Seraph are pushed to their limit combating these evils. They need help.

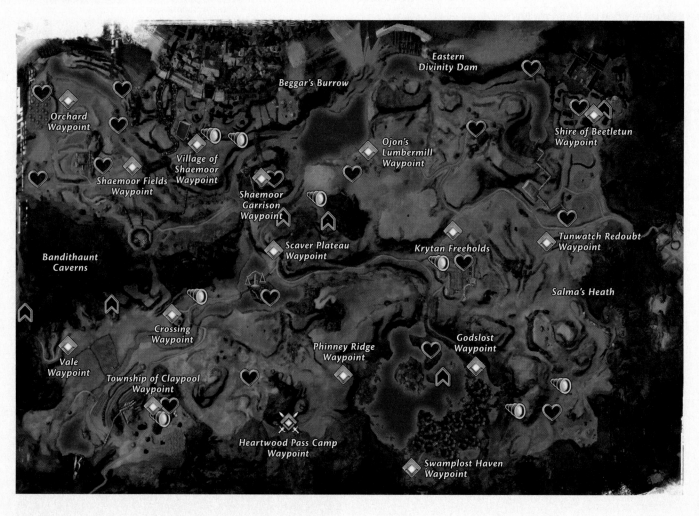

Eastern Divinity Dam
Beggar's Burrow
Orchard Waypoint
Ojon's Lumbermill Waypoint
Shire of Beetletun Waypoint
Village of Shaemoor Waypoint
Shaemoor Fields Waypoint
Shaemoor Garrison Waypoint
Scaver Plateau Waypoint
Krytan Freeholds
Tunwatch Redoubt Waypoint
Bandithaunt Caverns
Salma's Heath
Crossing Waypoint
Godslost Waypoint
Phinney Ridge Waypoint
Vale Waypoint
Township of Claypool Waypoint
Heartwood Pass Camp Waypoint
Swamplost Haven Waypoint

SHAEMOOR WAYPOINT (NORTH)

SERVICES:	Waypoint, Trainer, Cooking Merchant, Salvage Merchant, Weaponsmith, Armorsmith, Equipment Repair, Scout
TRAVEL:	Divinity's Reach (Human Capital) (N), Fields Waypoint (W), Garrison Waypoint (SE)
HARVESTING INFO:	Copper Ore, Aspen Saplings, Herb Seedlings, Onion

The village of Shaemoor has grown around the gates to Divinity's Reach. With the capital this close, bandits avoid the village and centaur incursions are dealt with quickly. Some of the largest problems here are with crops.

FIELDS WAYPOINT (NORTHWEST OF CENTER)

SERVICES:	Waypoint
TRAVEL:	Shaemoor Waypoint (E), Orchard Waypoint (NW), Crossing Waypoint (S)
HARVESTING INFO:	Copper Ore, Aspen Saplings, Carrots, Herb Seedlings, Onion

Fields Waypoint is surrounded by a number of farms and has quick access to the river and dam. Everyone in the area could use some help, so head west to Jeb's Wheatfield to aid the farmers before turning north to help at the dam. Once these are all squared away, Orchard Waypoint is to your west, with more work for you.

HELP FARMER DIAH (Renown Task)

GOAL:	Help Diah by watering corn, stomping wurm mounds, feeding cattle, and defending the fields.
LEVEL:	2

Description: Farming is a lot of work. Farmer Diah will take any and all help you're willing to give. Kicking over wurm mounds, defeating the wurms, giving bags of feed to the cattle, and using a water bucket to water the withered-looking plants all count toward completion. The fastest by far is to find a brown cow near several feed bags and keep feeding it. The cows never say no to food, and Diah doesn't mind them having their fill. (Plus, the little hearts around the cows are so cute!)

CROP BURNERS! (Repeatable)

GOAL:	Protect the hay bales from bandits.
LEVEL:	2

Description: If things weren't bad enough, bandits are destroying Diah's crops. The bandit crop burners attack in pairs for 10 waves. They split their attacks between the upper and lower fields. If you are alone, stick with the upper field and sacrifice the lower field. The bandits have to burn all 10 bales for you to fail. Catch the bandits before they light the bales when you can, but they can attack at range. Don't panic if they light a bale or two. Kill the bandits and then run for a water bucket. Use the water to douse the fire. When more bandits come, drop the bucket, deal with them, and pick up the bucket again. Even if no bales are currently on fire, the water bucket will vanish if you leave it on the ground too long. Why run back to get another one if you don't have to? The good news about all this is that defeating the bandits counts toward finishing your renown task.

KILL THE GIANT WURM (Repeatable)

GOAL:	Kill the plains wurm queen.
LEVEL:	2

Description: A giant wurm is tearing up Jeb's field. This is a job for a hero! (If you don't have a hero around, an adventurer will do.) This wurm does incredible damage and takes a good bit, as well. Both of her attacks are telegraphed by the wurm rearing back. She spits poison at ranged characters and slams melee characters by knocking them down and away (and then spitting poison again). Evading the queen wurm's attacks is the key to winning the fight. When the wurm rears back, dodge to the side.

THE FISHERMEN (Renown Task)

GOAL:	Help Fisherman Travis and Fisherman Justin.
LEVEL:	3

Description: Fishing has been more difficult with the rapid increase of drakes and skales in the river. The fishermen need you to cut back their numbers while checking traps for hostile creatures. If the broodmother is around, this renown task is very fast because you get so much credit for killing her and her little buddies. If she isn't, head east across the river to the drake nests. Several drakes and many drake eggs are here. Kill the drakes and break the eggs. Head north to the dam when you're finished.

THE BROODMOTHER (Repeatable)

GOAL: Kill the drake broodmother.

LEVEL: 3

Description: A drake broodmother is moving along the river with her young. This can be a very tough fight; the broodmother has high health and high damage, and her young attack with her. The crucial part of this fight is to deal with the broodmother on her own. Kill the little drakes at range before engaging the broodmother, or use area-of-effect attacks to kill the little drakes quickly. They will overwhelm you if you leave them alive.

Once the smaller drakes have been dealt with, concentrate on the Broodmother herself. When she breathes in and puffs up, she's about to breathe fire. Avoid her flame breath by dodging and keep hitting her until she's defeated. With her down, the area becomes a lot safer.

THE DAM (Renown Task)

GOAL: Help Foreman Flannum.

LEVEL: 3

Description: Western Divinity Dam isn't new, and it needs quite a bit of maintenance—leaks need to be plugged, rockslides need to be cleared. Earth elementals make this work difficult. Head north along a ledge of the dam, killing hostile creatures and fixing the dam. Awakening earth elementals are great targets, as you get credit for waking them and again for killing them. From the northern edge of the dam, cut south across the river toward Orchard Waypoint and see what you can do to help Eda.

UNWELCOME GUESTS (Repeatable)

GOAL: Drive the harpy flock from the dam.

LEVEL: 3

Description: Young harpies have infested the dam and are making work impossible. Killing some will show the others that the dam isn't worth it. Each kill reduces the overall morale by 10%, so 10 kills will get your point across.

ORCHARD WAYPOINT (NORTHWEST SIDE)

SERVICES:	Waypoint
TRAVEL:	Fields Waypoint (SE)
HARVESTING INFO:	Copper Ore (Abundant) Carrots, Mushrooms, Herb Seedlings, Onion

Orchard Waypoint offers a shortcut to the more distant farms of Queensdale. As these farms are farther from Divinity's Reach, they are also farther from what little protection the Seraph can manage. While Eda needs the more mundane help of harvesting apples and killing pests, Mepi is dealing with constant bandit raids. Head west to help Eda and then south to help Mepi with Bandithaunt Caverns.

THE APPLE ORCHARD (Renown Task)

GOAL: Assist Farmer Eda.

LEVEL: 4

Description: Drive bats and spiders from the orchard and squish spider egg sacs. While the harvesting is time consuming, Eda knows the business of running an orchard. Killing pests, however, is a bit out of her league, especially when spiders are as big as she is! March into the orchard and start slaying spiders. If you run out of targets, hit the eggs around the trees on the southern edge. Watch for trees that start to shake, as these produce spiders or bats. Once the orchard is in shape, head south to help Mepi.

EIGHT-LEGGED FREAKS (Repeatable)

GOAL: Clear the orchard of spiders for Farmer Eda.

LEVEL: 4

Description: The spiders are absolutely out of control and Eda won't enter the orchard until they are dealt with. It's a good thing you were already going to kill them anyway.

YOU MADE SOMETHING MAD (Repeatable)

GOAL: Kill the huge spider in Eda's orchard.

LEVEL: 4

Description: This orchard has real spider problems, culminating in one big creepy-crawly. The huge orchard spider can pull you toward it, so kiting is much more difficult. If you need to kite the spider, be ready to evade when its mandibles start glowing to avoid getting pulled back to it. Instead, the best course of action is to run in with your highest-damage abilities blazing! This fight can't last long, as the spider summons pairs of hatchlings periodically. Hit the spider hard and fast, and bring it down as soon as possible.

ASSIST RANCHER MEPI (Renown Task)

GOAL: Kill bandits and destroy their supplies in Bandithaunt Caverns.

LEVEL: 5

Description: Mepi has had quite enough of the constant raids by bandits. He's found their hideout, Bandithaunt Caverns, just south of his ranch. Now he needs help ending the raids for good. Head south and enter Bandithaunt carefully. The initial tunnels are pretty narrow, but they open up into a cave system packed with enemies. Kiting in the caverns will get you far more trouble than you can handle. If you need to kite, kite back the way you came. More than anything else, choose your targets carefully and try to pick bandits by themselves or in pairs. It's easy to get overwhelmed, so advance through the cavern slowly and methodically. Once inside, look for the supplies and destroy them as they become available.

MEPI'S MOAS (Repeatable)

GOAL: Rescue Mepi's moa herd from the bandit caves.

LEVEL: 4

Description: The bandits have really outdone themselves now. They've stolen Mepi's entire herd of moas. Moas are powerful creatures when they feel safe, but the constant poking of the bandits keeps them cowed. You need to make them feel safe before they'll bolt for the exit. You need to defeat all the bandits within the area and then hold the region until the completion bar fills.

THE BAR ISN'T MOVING

When holding an area, the completion bar will only move if there are no enemies and at least one ally in the circled area. The color of the border is red if one of these conditions is not met, but it turns blue as soon as both are filled. The completion bar then begins moving.

The moas become invincible once you've fully claimed the area, and they'll leave and knock down any enemies that get close. With the moas heading out to safety, head south further into the caverns. There's another way out and perhaps some revenge to get on the way.

THE BOSS (Group Event)

GOAL: Eliminate the bandit lieutenant.

LEVEL: 5

Description: This event is extremely difficult to do alone, but it's possible if you are fast on your feet. First, pull the bandits across the bridge toward you to clear the bridge. A bandit turret will attack if you try to cross the bridge, and you don't want any distractions while you destroy this siege engine.

Once the bridge is clear of bandits, run up to the turret and blast away. Don't fight the turret from range; it can knock you down, deal a lot of damage, and light you on fire. Be ready to use defensive skills or healing skills when the turret goes down.

Bodyguards all along the wooden walkway like to light things on fire from range. The bandit lieutenant is a champion, and he can root you in place and shoot you from range. Use any abilities you haven't used already and kill him. Abilities that knock the lieutenant down or otherwise hold him in place are wonderful.

There are two skill challenges on the southern side of the caverns, but they're in dangerous territory. It's better to get them when you come around from the other side of the map.

REPAIR THE PUMPING STATION (Repeatable)

GOAL:	Defend workers repairing the Pumping Station.
LEVEL:	3

Description: Bandits have blown the three pipes at the Pumping Station and are keeping workers from repairing them. Head up the path to the south and revive any downed workers. Defending all three pipes alone isn't possible. Defend one pipe at a time and wait until the worker is finished before heading to the next pipe.

A TOXIC PROBLEM (Repeatable)

GOAL:	Bring blobs of toxin to Apprentice Jameson.
LEVEL:	3

Description: Toxic oozes have infested the Pumping Station. Slay the oozes and collect blobs of toxin for Jameson. There are oozes everywhere, and Jameson only needs 10 toxin blobs to clear the Pumping Station and cleanse the water. Finish helping at the Pumping Station before jumping back to Shaemoor Waypoint and traveling east to Shaemoor Garrison.

GARRISON WAYPOINT (NORTH OF CENTER)

SERVICES:	Waypoint, Scout
TRAVEL:	Shaemoor Waypoint (NW), Scaver Waypoint (S), Ojon's Lumbermill Waypoint (E)
HARVESTING INFO:	Copper Ore, Herb Seedlings, Onion

Shaemoor Garrison is all that stands between the Tamini centaurs and the verdant fields of Queensdale you've been helping. The garrison is under constant siege and needs help. After you've seen the garrison, walk south to push the centaurs back.

ASSIST THE SERAPH AT SHAEMOOR GARRISON (Renown Task)

GOAL:	Drive back centaur forces and secure the farmlands.
LEVEL:	6

Description: The Tamini have pushed far into Queensdale and the Seraph have been too undermanned to resist them effectively. They need some big guns. They need you. Head south and start killing centaurs indiscriminately if none of the repeatable events are available. Fight your way south to Scaver Waypoint.

WHOSE GARRISON IS THIS? (Repeatable)

GOAL:	Liberate Shaemoor Garrison.
LEVEL:	6

Description: Sometimes the centaurs take hold of Shaemoor. Fight your way into Shaemoor Garrison and hold it until the Seraph can reinforce the fort. Once you break down the door, destroy the prison door to the east. This releases Seraph guards to help you. Your primary targets should be the Tamini shaman and archers, as these do the most damage to the Seraph that followed you in. Once the keep has been restored, revive any downed allies and head south to finish your renown task.

GUARD BARTHOL (Repeatable)

GOAL:	Defend Barthol on his way to the Old Armory.
LEVEL:	6

Description: Speak with Guard Barthol (near the garrison's southern exit) to begin this event. Guard Barthol knows of weapons in a burned-out building that the Seraph could really use right now. He's very headstrong, so keeping him alive might be a bit difficult. He cannot be revived. If he goes down, you fail the event. It's imperative that you keep him from taking damage, as he only heals between fights and he'll pick fights with a few veteran Tamini chieftains on the way. Use ranged attacks to get enemy attention, use snares and roots to keep archers from getting more enemies, and follow Barthol until he gets to the armory.

SCAVER WAYPOINT (CENTER)

SERVICES:	Waypoint, Salvage Merchant, Armorsmith, Weaponsmith, Equipment Repair
TRAVEL:	Garrison Waypoint (N), Crossing Waypoint (W), Phinney Waypoint (SE), Krytan Waypoint (E)
HARVESTING INFO:	Aspen Saplings, Herb Patches, Blueberry Bush, Herb Seedlings, Onion

Scaver Waypoint is south from the garrison. Get down there to secure the spot. It's useful because the road heads out in multiple directions from there, so it's a nice hub for the future.

Protected by water, bridges, walls, and a rocky shore, Altar Brook Trading Post is a safe resting point for any caravans moving from Divinity's Reach to southern Queensdale. There are several merchants buying and selling to travelers and adventurers passing through. Empty your bags while you're here and continue west. That is, unless the darn centaurs have taken it over!

PROTECT THE TRADE ROUTE (Renown Task)

GOAL: Help Lexi Price protect the trade route.

LEVEL: 7

Description: Kill vermin, clean up the Trading Post, eliminate threats along the trade route, and destroy Tamini stakes and death markers. There are a couple groundspawns, including Rat Traps and Document Bins, that can be set/cleaned up before you leave the Trading Post. Speak with Mona to start the caravan event. Escorting the caravan will finish the renown task. If Mona is not available, follow the river west. Clear Tamini stakes and death markers along the road while killing skales and drakes in the river.

ESCORT MONA'S CARAVAN (Repeatable)

GOAL: Escort the Trading Post caravan to Claypool.

LEVEL: 7

Description: Mona has supplies that need to get to Claypool. She's gotten them as far as the Trading Post, but the road ahead is too dangerous for her and the single guard. Packs of wolves cross the road ahead and will attack your small band. As the wolves summon allies when low on health, the packs are always larger than they first appear.

However, the real danger is the centaur. Two waves of centaurs (with two Tamini warriors) attack on your way to the bridge. A third group of attackers is just across the bridge, and three more groups attack before you finally reach Claypool. The final two waves also have a Tamini archer in them. You fail when the pack bull dies, but it heals between fights so it can take a little bit of damage without your needing to panic. Kill the centaurs as fast as you can. Let the pack bull take a few hits, but don't let it get below half health before you pull all remaining enemies off of it. Revive the caravan guard if he goes down, as he's very good at keeping attackers away from the bull.

> **WALK-BY WAYPOINT**
>
> Protecting the caravan takes you past Crossing Waypoint but not close enough to activate it. If the Seraph are in control of the tower, take a moment to run over and activate the waypoint when the caravan turns toward the bridge.

REBUILDING ALTAR BROOK (Repeatable)

GOAL: Escort and defend workers sent to rebuild the guard tower.

LEVEL: 8

Description: Altar Brook Crossing has fallen and the Seraph are sending workers to rebuild it. Escort them through multiple waves of centaur attacks to Crossing Waypoint. There are three repair workers and they can be revived if they fall, but you fail if all of them are killed. Once the workers get to the remains of the tower, defend them until they rebuild the Altar Brook Guard Post.

CROSSING WAYPOINT (WEST OF CENTER)

SERVICES:	Waypoint
TRAVEL:	Scaver Waypoint (E), Fields Waypoint (N), Vale Waypoint (W), Claypool Waypoint (S)
HARVESTING INFO:	Copper (Abundant, in a Cave to the North), Blueberry Bush, Herb Seedlings, Onion

Crossing Waypoint sits at the bottom of a small watchtower. This rickety tower is all that defends the bridge from Tamini control. This waypoint is often contested.

CLAYPOOL WAYPOINT (SOUTHWEST)

SERVICES:	Waypoint, Equipment Repair, Scout, Salvage Merchant, Cooking Merchant, Armorsmith, Weaponsmith
TRAVEL:	Kessex Hills (Level 15-25 Region) (S), Crossing Waypoint (N), Vale Waypoint (NW), Heartwood Pass Waypoint (E)
HARVESTING INFO:	Carrots, Blueberry Bush, Herb Seedlings, Onion

The walled and fortified town of Claypool marks the southern end of Queensdale and the entrance to Kessex Hills. Here, Seraph train the militia and guard the pass. With so many guards and volunteers, merchants are safe to hawk their wares and adventurers can put their feet up for a moment…but not too long. No place is truly safe in these times. Get the militia in better shape before heading east to deal with the centaurs. Once the centaurs have been beaten to a manageable level, travel north to help at Curtis's Ranch on your way to Vale Waypoint.

TRAIN WITH THE MILITIA (Renown Task)

GOAL: Train with the militia.

LEVEL: 8

Description: The Seraph have their work cut out for them. The militia is composed of a bunch of farmers with little knowledge of combat. While the Seraph are good teachers, they need a student to teach by example. There are three Seraph representatives drilling the recruits.

Sergeant Liddy is teaching the use of shields and blocking. Grab a Seraph Training Shield and step close to the Shield Drill Sergeant. When the Sergeant telegraphs his attack, block with the shield. The Sergeant hits so hard that your shield is destroyed and you need to get another one, but the workers have seen what the Seraph want.

Sergeant Soto is training with rifles. More specifically, he's teaching how to charge up attacks. Grab a rifle and target a Training Target. Watch and listen for the commands given by the Rifle Drill Sergeant. Press and hold the attack button until he shouts, "Fire!" Let up on the button and grab another rifle.

Sergeant Neal is teaching swordwork on the far north side, but it's more about attacking when the time is right. Grab a sword and face the Sword Drill Sergeant. Wait for her to drop her guard, then attack! Move between the three training sessions or stick to your favorite until the renown task is done.

PROTECTING CLAYPOOL (Renown Task)

GOAL: Help the Seraph protect Claypool from centaurs.

LEVEL: 9

Description: Defeat centaurs, destroy their holdings, and find ways to weaken their presence in the area. A great many centaurs are to the east of Claypool, and the Seraph need help dealing with them. Kill centaurs and break their equipment in the area before you jump back to Claypool Waypoint and travel north.

CURTIS'S RANCH (Repeatable)

GOAL: Drive the bandits from Curtis's Ranch.

LEVEL: 8

Description: Bandits have taken Curtis's Ranch. As an important source of livestock for Claypool, this cannot be allowed. The bandits will only stay as long as it is profitable, so you won't need to kill every single one. The biggest challenge is getting them away from each other. They've heard about you and are unwilling to travel alone. They use ranged weapons and work in groups of two or three. Be ready for tough fights and pull the smaller groups around the edges first. Each kill reduces morale by around 8%. This means that 13 deaths should show them that the ranch isn't worth it for them.

EVENT SCALING

If there are more heroes in the area, you'll notice that it might take more kills to complete the event. That's because events increase in scope and difficulty when more people are present. Our guide tries to give you an idea of what things are like when you're out on your own, but having a group around will slightly change the situations you encounter.

VALE WAYPOINT (SOUTHWEST)

SERVICES:	Waypoint
TRAVEL:	Crossing Waypoint (E), Claypool Waypoint (SE)
HARVESTING INFO:	Copper Ore, Aspen Saplings, Carrots, Mushrooms, Blueberry Bush, Herb Seedlings, Onion

Vale Waypoint sits at the bottom of a harpy-infested ridge. Adventurers looking for Copper veins and Mushrooms are in luck: check the caves to the north. Those looking to expand their knowledge should head into the highest of the harpy caves and defeat veteran Ert (and Burt) to gain access to the Jug of Power. Once you're stronger and more refreshed, jump back to Claypool Waypoint and head east to reinforce Heartwood Pass.

OL' SAWTOOTH (Repeatable)

GOAL:	Slay a powerful giant fish.
LEVEL:	10

Description: In the lake formed at the bottom of Clayent Falls, Ol' Sawtooth is making life difficult for the fishers. Sawtooth is a veteran and summons barracuda to his aid. Bring a friend or be ready to immediately unload with your most damaging abilities.

RUNESTONES (Repeatable)

GOAL:	Slay the enraged cave troll.
LEVEL:	10

Description: Be careful picking up Embedded Troll Runestones in the caves. A champion cave troll attacks if you take his things! Throwing a runestone at him will knock him down and start the fight in your favor. If you are alone, this is your chance to run away. If you are with friends, let him have it! He telegraphs his knockdown attack and, aside from his high health and immense damage, that's all you have to worry about. When you're ready, jump back to Claypool Waypoint and head east toward Heartwood Pass Waypoint.

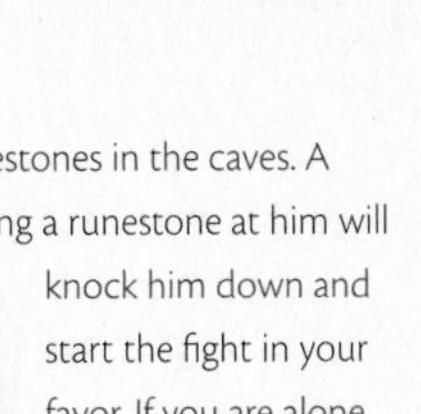

HEARTWOOD PASS WAYPOINT (SOUTH)

SERVICES:	Waypoint, Weaponsmith
TRAVEL:	Claypool Waypoint (W), Phinney Waypoint (NE)
HARVESTING INFO:	Aspen Saplings, Carrots, Herb Patches, Blueberry Bush, Herb Seedlings, Onion

Heartwood Pass has been a contested stronghold for as long as anyone can remember. The Seraph constantly drive the Tamini centaurs from it, but they can't hold it for long. Take the camp and defend it as long as you can before continuing northeast to Phinney Waypoint.

CAPTURE HEARTWOOD PASS (Repeatable)

GOAL:	Capture Heartwood Pass Camp from the Tamini.
LEVEL:	9

Description: The Tamini centaurs have made camp in Heartwood Pass. Fight your way in and assault the leader's tent. The Tamini chieftain summons and buffs allies. Hit him with your fastest high-damage abilities and Stun him if possible. The longer this centaur lives, the lower your chances of success.

HOLD HEARTWOOD PASS CAMP (Repeatable)

GOAL:	Hold Heartwood Pass Camp.
LEVEL:	10

Description: The Seraph have come to hold Heartwood Pass Camp as long as they can. Seven waves of centaurs attack. The waves can approach from either the east or west. Engage the centaurs outside the blue border with the help of the Seraph when you can and revive any nearby Seraph guards between waves. Strike out northeast once the camp is yours. Activate Phinney Waypoint before jumping back to Garrison Waypoint (or Scaver Waypoint if the garrison is contested) and head east to Ojon's Lumbermill Waypoint.

PHINNEY WAYPOINT (SOUTH)

SERVICES:	Waypoint
TRAVEL:	Heartwood Pass Waypoint (SW), Scaver Waypoint (NW), Godslost Waypoint (E), Swamplost Waypoint (SE)
HARVESTING INFO:	Carrots, Herb Patches, Blueberry Bush, Herb Seedlings, Onion

Phinney Waypoint overlooks the eastern edge of Godslost Swamp. It's a good place to jump to if things go wrong at either Heartwood Pass or Godslost Swamp.

OJON'S LUMBERMILL WAYPOINT

SERVICES:	Waypoint, Salvage Merchant (Hunting Lodge), Food Merchant (Hunting Lodge)
TRAVEL:	Garrison Waypoint (W), Krytan Waypoint (SE), Beetletun Waypoint (E)
HARVESTING INFO:	Copper Ore, Aspen Saplings, Carrots, Redcap Mushrooms, Blueberry Bush, Herb Seedlings, Onion

Ojon's Lumbermill supplies most of the wood used in Divinity's Reach. With the Queen's Forest so close, there is an abundance of available wood. As luck would have it, the Tamini don't give the workers any problems. Instead it's the skritt and common wilderness insects. Get the lumberjacks back on schedule before heading east, past the Hunting Lodge, to Beetletun Waypoint.

OJON'S LUMBERMILL (Renown Task)

GOAL:	Assist Laborer Cardy and Ojon's Lumbermill.
LEVEL:	8

Description: The skritt live in the caves just south of the lumbermill and have become quite a nuisance. They're constantly stealing tools and pestering the workers. The wasps are no better; they're huge, and they attack anything that gets close. Kill any skritt and wasps near the camp. Heading into the caves is really only necessary if you're doing the repeatable event.

STOLEN TOOLS (Repeatable)

GOAL:	Retrieve stolen logging tools from the skritt hideout.
LEVEL:	7

Description: The lumberjacks can't work without their tools. Head into the caves and get them back. Valerius stands just east of the caves, waiting for the tools. Nearly every skritt has at least one tool, and some are left on the floor of the caves. Valerius only needs 10 tools, so this is very quick. Make your way to the lumbermill and head northeast to the Hunting Lodge.

THE HUNTING LODGE (Renown Task)

GOAL:	Assist Hunter Block and the Hunting Lodge.
LEVEL:	9

Description: Divinity's Reach is constantly in need of meat and furs. Hunter Block and his associates are generally able to fill this need, but some of the boars have gotten rather large and aggressive of late.

Hunt boars, help hunters, fix traps, and watch out for the veteran dire boars. Once the hunters are back on schedule, continue your journey east along the river toward Beetletun.

THE GIANT BOAR (Group)

GOAL:	Hunt and slay the giant boar.
LEVEL:	10

Description: One of the boars has gotten much larger and even more aggressive than the others. If you have a friend or two, take on the champion giant boar. Don't try to do it alone; this giant boar has high health and deals quite a lot of damage.

THE FISHERMEN OF BEETLETUN (Renown Task)

GOAL:	Assist Fisherman Will and the Fishermen of Beetletun.
LEVEL:	10

Description: It takes quite a lot of work to keep Divinity's Reach fed. The fishermen of Beetletun work hard to feed themselves and send food to the capital. Recently, the crabs have been getting aggressive and the skales are encroaching into the fishing area. Protect the fishermen by eliminating the more dangerous animals there. You can also help by harvesting crabs. To do this, get their attention and pull them close to a trap; activate it to capture the shellfish. When you're done here, finish your journey to Beetletun Waypoint.

AN OOZING PROPOSITION

The pipe leading up from the river is filled with toxic oozes. It is also an excellent place for Copper Ore and Rich Copper Ore if you can kill the oozes (levels 12-14) fast enough. If you have a partner, take a quick detour through the pipe!

BEETLETUN WAYPOINT (NORTHEAST)

SERVICES:	Waypoint, Cooking Merchant, Armorsmith, Weaponsmith, Equipment Repairs, Salvage Merchant
TRAVEL:	Ojon's Lumbermill Waypoint (W), Tunwatch Redoubt Waypoint (S)
HARVESTING INFO:	Aspenwood Saplings, Carrots, Blueberry Bush, Herb Seedlings, Onion

The Shire of Beetletun is the largest city in Queensdale next to Divinity's Reach, and they won't let you forget it. The troubles of the centaurs and bandits are kept far enough away that Beetletun can maintain two social classes. The Lords and Ladies of Beetletun maintain the prosperity of the town, while the workers and villagers keep it running on a day-to-day level. Help out in town before heading south toward Tunwatch Redoubt Waypoint, where your help is needed more.

CAUDECUS'S MANOR

Groups of five adventurers (levels 40 and higher) can make a call on Caudecus. His manor is immediately northeast of the waypoint and takes up the entire northern part of town. Caudecus is one of the most powerful ministers of Kryta, and his influence rivals that of Queen Jennah herself. In fact, there are even some rumors that he fancies himself royalty in the making, which may lead to some interesting political developments.

BEETLETUN AT LAST (Renown Task)

GOAL:	Help Beetletun maintain its prosperous reputation.
LEVEL:	13

Description: Beetletun is one of the most beautiful cities in Kryta, but it doesn't stay that way on its own. The workers slave away day and night to keep the streets clear, and the children do chores so the parents can keep their minds on larger matters. Help out by crushing wasp nests, erasing graffiti, and sending hiding children back to their chores.

AID THE BEETLETUN FARMERS (Renown Task)

GOAL:	Assist the Beetletun Farmers in their resistance against the centaurs.
LEVEL:	12

Description: The Tamini centaurs are constantly attacking the Beetletun Farmers and the Seraph are not anywhere close. Kill any centaurs you see.

RETAKE BEETLETUN FARMS (Part of the World Event)

GOAL:	Retake Beetletun Farms and bring Sprinkler Pieces to Clarence.
LEVEL:	12

Description: This event is more complicated as it has two goals that need to be completed. You need to clear out 12 centaurs from the field and collect and return five Sprinkler Pieces. Work on the Sprinkler Pieces first and only kill the centaurs as you need to. More Tamini centaurs are slowly adding to the area, and if you kill them all without turning in the Sprinkler Pieces the event won't end and more Tamini will appear.

Once Clarence has enough parts, kill the Tamini as quickly as you can without getting overwhelmed. Be wary of the Tamini archers. There are quite a few of them, and they run around a lot. This tends to make any fight with one centaur become a fight with the four others he bumped into while you were killing him. With the Tamini dispersed and Clarence repairing the sprinkler, things resume a sense of normalcy for the farmers.

TUNWATCH REDOUBT WAYPOINT (EAST)

SERVICES:	Waypoint
TRAVEL:	Gendarran Fields (Level 25-35 Region) (E), Krytan Waypoint (W), Godslost Waypoint (SW)
HARVESTING INFO:	Copper Ore, Blueberry Bush, Herb Seedlings, Onion

Tunwatch Redoubt is on the frontlines of the war with the Tamini. This fort is responsible for keeping the centaurs from getting any substantial force into the Beetletun area. It's a heavy responsibility, and help from adventurers is more than welcome. Touch base here before heading west toward Krytan Waypoint.

RETAKE TUNWATCH REDOUBT (Part of the World Event)

GOAL:	Retake Tunwatch Redoubt.
LEVEL:	12

Description: The Tamini have taken the fort and need to be removed. Attack tentatively to reduce their numbers without getting into a fight with the whole fort. Slowly kill your way in and revive the fallen defenders. If too many Tamini archers are attacking you, consider pulling back around the wall and forcing them to come to you (or at least minimizing their damage until a healing skill recharges). Once you stand in the center of the fort, this becomes a defensive event until reinforcements arrive.

RESCUE THE CAPTIVES (Part of the World Event)

GOAL:	Rescue the captive farmers.
LEVEL:	13

Description: The Tamini centaurs have taken some of the Beetletun farmers south past Salma's Heath. Follow the mountains south and start killing the Tamini. Ten farmers were captured and all must be released. The farmers are behind prison gates deep in Hidden Cliff Camp. Break the gates to free the farmers. Once all are free, jump back to Tunwatch Redoubt Waypoint.

KRYTAN WAYPOINT (EAST OF CENTER)

SERVICES:	Waypoint, Salvage Merchant
TRAVEL:	Ojon's Lumbermill Waypoint (NW), Tunwatch Redoubt Waypoint (E), Godslost Waypoint (S), Scaver Waypoint (W)
HARVESTING INFO:	Copper Ore, Aspen Saplings (Abundant), Carrots, Blueberry Bush, Herb Seedlings, Onion

Eldvin Monastery is known worldwide for its fabulous alcoholic beverages. Though centaur camps are very close, this walled monastery remains safe and productive thanks to passing adventurers willing to help. There are also several caravans transporting barrels and kegs to other parts of Queensdale, and they need guards. Help the monastery brewers and then do northern escort before jumping back to do the southern escort. If the escorts are unavailable, follow the road south past Godslost Waypoint to Swamplost Waypoint.

HELP THE MONASTERY BREWERS (Renown Task)

GOAL:	Fight centaurs, recover stolen ale, protect the monastery, clear grubs from the fields, and taste test new ale.
LEVEL:	11

Description: There's a lot of work to be done at the monastery. Whether you're more interested in killing things or breaking your back, the Brothers and Sisters of the monastery appreciate your assistance. Wander through the fields and vineyards in the courtyard, looking for Grubs. Both pulling them out and killing them give credit. As you are moving through the courtyard, keep your eye open for shady people. They're looking to steal ale kegs! Run down the thief and bring the Abbey Ale back to Sister Liz, in the small room near the front of the monastery. You can also get a taste test of a new drink from Sister Liz while you're there. For those of the killing persuasion, the cave to the southeast has a number of Tamini that need to die. In addition, there are sometimes attacks by Tamini looking to grab kegs. Defend the monastery from them for more credit toward the renown task.

CARAVAN TO BEETLETUN (Repeatable)

GOAL:	Escort the caravan to Beetletun.
LEVEL:	10

Description: Charice is part of the troupe performing in Beetletun and she has supplies that need to get to the city. Give her and the single Seraph guard a hand. The Seraph guard can be revived, so don't worry too much about him. Instead, make sure the Tamini don't get free hits on Charice or her ox, Shau. The Tamini attack in five groups of two to five centaurs with a mix of warriors and archers. Your first target should be a centaur that isn't being attacked by the Seraph guard. The escort ends just north of Beetletun Farms.

CARAVAN TO SWAMPLOST HAVEN (Repeatable)

GOAL:	Protect the brew shipment.
LEVEL:	14

Description: Sister Brenda is supervising a shipment of brew to Swamplost Haven and needs a bodyguard. This escort takes you by two waypoints and across Godslost Swamp. The Tamini send three waves of enemies (between two and three centaurs per wave) to capture the brew before it is out of their hands. Once you're in the swamp, the denizens attack at several intervals. Skelk lurkers and scaled drakes jump onto the wooden walkway. Don't worry if Sister Brenda's health goes down; she can be revived once the fight is over. Even she tells you that the beer is what needs to be kept safe. With Brenda ensconced at Swamplost Haven, jump to Godslost Waypoint and head east.

SWAMPLOST WAYPOINT (SOUTHEAST OF CENTER)

SERVICES:	Waypoint, Armorsmith, Weaponsmith, Salvage Merchant
TRAVEL:	Kessex Hills (Level 15-25 Region) (S), Godslost Waypoint (N), Phinney Waypoint (NW)
HARVESTING INFO:	Copper Ore, Aspen Saplings, Carrots, Bluebery Bush, Herb Seedlings, Onion

Swamplost Haven is one of the final strongholds before Kessex Hills. The Seraph here are charged with holding the centaurs to the east at bay. Head east and climb the hills to discover unlikely allies and something very dangerous. Jump to Godslost Waypoint once the centaur plans of conquest have been set back a bit.

UNITE THE ETTINS AND BATTLE CENTAURS (Renown Task)

GOAL: Help Krug by uniting the ettins and battling centaurs.

LEVEL: 14

Description: The centaurs are casting something, and chances are it won't be good for the populace of Kryta. Head up the hills past the aggressive ettins and speak with the nonaggressive ones. Convince them to attack the centaurs as you continue east to the ritual itself. Follow the ettins in and let them go first. Groups of Tamini run around the ritual site in constant patrols. These fights are very difficult alone. Pull some centaurs away from the path of the others and kill the archers first. You don't need to get to the center of the ritual to complete the renown task, but there is a Skill Challenge there! If you are alone, kill Tamini on the outskirts to complete the quest. Then run to the Tamini Place of Power between the patrols to get the Skill Challenge. Once you're finished there, jump to Godslost Waypoint.

GODSLOST WAYPOINT (SOUTH)

SERVICES:	Waypoint
TRAVEL:	Krytan Waypoint (N), Phinney Waypoint (W), Swamplost Waypoint (S)
HARVESTING INFO:	Aspen Sapling (Abundant), Copper Ore, Carrots, Blueberry Bush, Herb Seedlings, Onion

Godslost Waypoint stands on the northern edge of Godslost Swamp. Tortured spirits, fireflies, and aggressive monsters make this swamp a place to be avoided at the best of times, but now rifts to the Underworld have released additional horrors. Someone has to keep what is happening here from spilling any further into the area.

GODSLOST SWAMP (Renown Task)

GOAL: Help Historian Garrod investigate Godslost Swamp.

LEVEL: 15

Description: You can help the investigation of the area by closing portals to the Underworld, vanquishing portal minions, and putting tortured spirits to rest. Speak with the tortured spirits to find out why they cannot pass on. Kill the shade and help the spirit rest. As you move around through the deeper portion of the swamp, watch for green portals to the Underworld. Defeat the shades nearby and destroy the rifts.

UNDERWORLD CREATURES (Group)

GOAL: Stop Underworld creatures by destroying portals in the swamp.

LEVEL: 15

Description: Things are going very wrong in Godslost Swamp. There are far more portals and aggressive creatures than normal. Start killing anything in the area, but watch out for any veterans. They can add to a fight easily, and they can quickly change a battle from easy to exhausting.

THE SHADOW BEHEMOTH (Part of the World Event)

GOAL: Defeat the Shadow Behemoth.

LEVEL: 15

Description: Something is stirring in the swamp, and now it's awakened. That's why you're here—and why you've brought friends. This creature is mean, nasty, and powerful, and you shouldn't fight it alone.

The Shadow Behemoth cannot be damaged while the portals remain open. However, aatxes and shades, creatures of the Underworld, guard the portals. Use ranged attacks to pull the Underworld minions to you and kill them. Then, use ranged attacks to destroy the portals. You can also use ranged area-of-effect abilities to hit the portals at the same time as the minions.

If you see a red circle around you, dodge! The Shadow Behemoth doesn't like your messing about with its portals, and it uses ranged attacks that can knock you down and inflict a lot of damage.

Avoid engaging the portals in melee. This forces the Shadow Behemoth to use its claws, and if it hits you, it will almost certainly kill you. A purple swirling vortex appears where the Behemoth's claws are about to be. You need to evade as soon as you see it.

Once all three portals are down, the Behemoth becomes targetable for a short period. Use your high-damage abilities and any skills that boost damage as your window is short. After a few moments, the Shadow Behemoth breathes poison gas and summons three new portals to restart the cycle. Keep at it until the monster falls.

KESSEX HILLS

LEVEL RANGE: 15-25

TASKS: 14

WAYPOINTS: 18

SKILL CHALLENGES: 5

HARVESTING INFO:
Aspen Sapling (Greenwood Log, Cinnamon Sticks), Gummo Sapling (Soft Wood Log, Amber Nugget, Chanterelle Mushroom), Root Vegetables (Head of Garlic, Turnip, Beet), Vine Vegetables (Cucumber), Mushrooms (Mushroom, Chanterelle Mushroom), Herb Patch (Oregano Leaf), Onion, Strawberries, Clam, Copper Ore (Copper Ore, Gems), Iron Ore (Iron Ore, Gems), Silver Ore (Silver Ore, Gems)

Kessex Hills is a land under siege. The centaurs are taking territory at every opportunity. Ruins of human towns are scattered across the landscape and the overworked Seraph can barely protect them. The Lionguard, who have a treaty with the centaurs, maintain the road connecting Divinity's Reach and Lion's Arch. It's a mess out there, but you're here to help.

HOW DID I GET HERE?

Kessex Hills is in the middle of a war between the Seraph and both the Tamini and Harathi centaurs. This area borders other maps. To the north is Queensdale, the lowest-level human territory (1-15). There are exits to Queensdale in the northwest and northeast (near Fort Salma and Sojourner's Way). To seek other challenges, leave Kessex by taking the northwestern road into Brisban Wildslands (15-25). In the south, the road near Ireko Tradecamp leads into Caledon Forest (1-15). For tougher fighting, the eastern side of the map has a road into Gendarran Fields (25-35). That's where you can get into some real trouble!

WEST SIDE

EAST SIDE

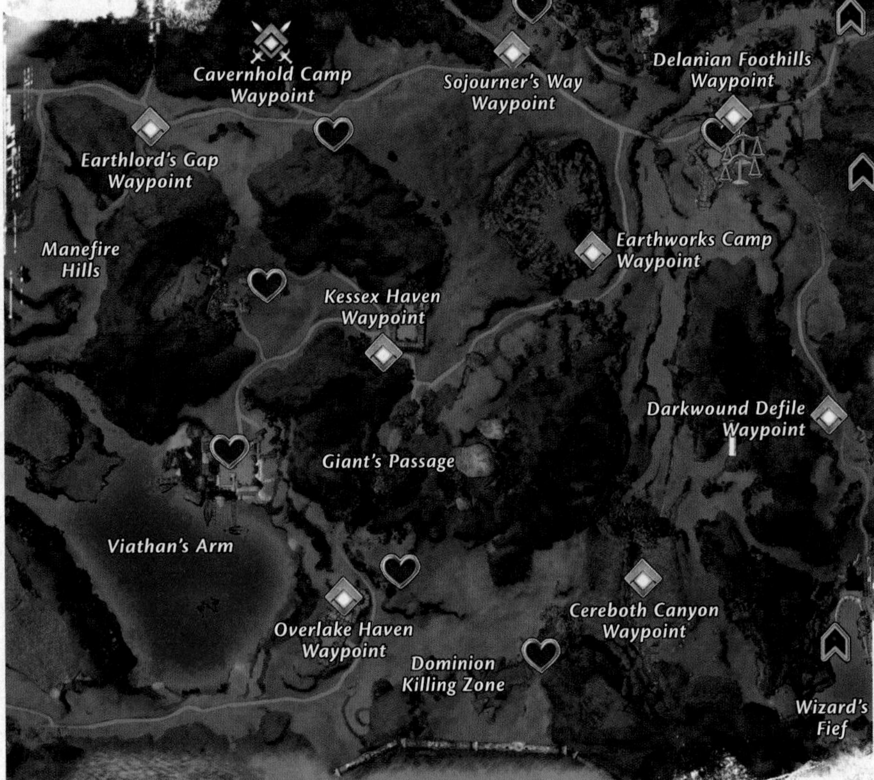

SKILL CHALLENGES

- Eternal Portal (Northeast of Delanian Waypoint) (NE)
- Draithor's Lab Meat (Southeast of Delanian Waypoint) (NE)
- Master Elementalist Dylane (South of Darkwound Waypoint) (SE)
- Tocatl's Challenge (Northeast of Ireko Tradecamp Waypoint) (S)
- Gathering Site (Southwest of Overlord's Waypoint) (SW)

SOJOURNER'S WAYPOINT (NORTHEAST SIDE)

SERVICES:	Waypoint, Scout, Jewelry Merchant (Traveling Noble)
TRAVEL:	Entrance to Queensdale (Levels 1-15) (NW), Delanian Waypoint (E), Earthworks Waypoint (SE), Cavernhold Camp Waypoint (W)
HARVEST INFO:	Silver Ore, Copper Ore, Iron Ore, Aspen Sapling, Vine Vegetables, Herb Patch

Sojourner's Waypoint stands just inside Kessex Hills. Expect to find some bandits watching for undefended travelers. The bandits have set up camp just north of the road. Fight them to keep the road safe before you head on to Delanian Waypoint.

REVENGE! (Renown Task)

GOAL:	Help Waldo Flood take revenge on local bandits.
LEVEL:	15

Description: Kill bandits, steal bandit supplies, destroy bandit cannons, and check bushes for hiding bandits. It sounds like a lot of fun. Head north from the waypoint and start killing everything that moves. There are bandits everywhere, so take it slow and be cautious. While the waypoint is close by, there's no use getting killed for nothing. Pull bandits away from the cannons until the cannons are isolated. Run around to the back and kill the bandit gunner to silence these dragons of iron.

RANSOM (Repeatable)

GOAL:	Rescue the traveling child's mother.
LEVEL:	15

Description: Not everyone gets the message when the Seraph say, "The roads aren't safe to travel." A noble and her son are traveling along the road, and there's a chance the mother will be captured by bandits. If you see this happening, kill the veteran bandit lieutenant and all three bandit kidnappers to reunite mother and son. Look at the map carefully to find your targets. The lieutenant hides around the trees to the side of the road.

DELANIAN WAYPOINT (NORTHEAST SIDE)

SERVICES:	Waypoint, Armorsmith, Weaponsmith, Salvage Merchant, Equipment Repair, Scout
TRAVEL:	Gendarran Fields (Levels 25-35) (E), Sojourner's Waypoint (W), Earthworks Waypoint (SW), Darkwound Waypoint (S)
HARVEST INFO:	Aspen Sapling, Gummo Sapling, Copper Ore, Silver Ore, Iron Ore, Herb Patch

Black Haven is a place of safety for travelers. The massive stone walls and gates are nigh impregnable by the likes of centaurs and bandits. This protection only reaches so far. The roads and hills outside the walls are rife with bandits, basilisks, bats, and other unpleasantness. Help clean the area up and grab the two nearby Skill Challenges before heading to Earthworks Waypoint.

BLACK HAVEN (Renown Task)

GOAL:	Help Lionguard Micah keep the Black Haven area safe for travelers.
LEVEL:	16

Description: The roads have been getting progressively more dangerous around Black Haven. Kill aggressive enemies around the haven and let everyone breathe a sigh of relief. This task is very fast when other events are available. The south side of the castle holds a great many dangers (of the two- and four-legged variety) for the times when the caravan is unavailable.

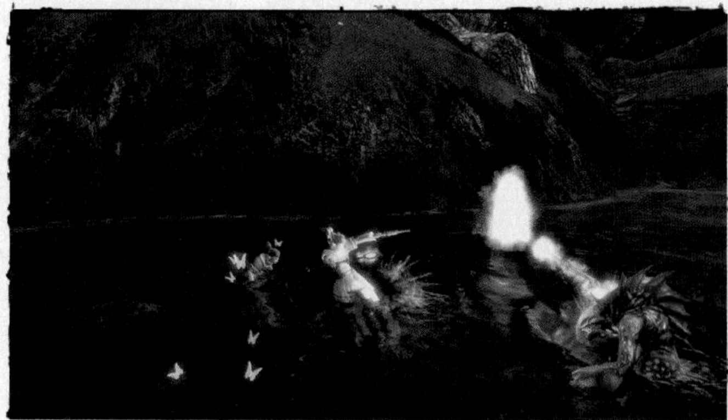

CARAVAN (Repeatable)

GOAL: Escort the caravan to Kessex Haven.

LEVEL: 16

Description: Anytime there is money to be made, there are merchants paying for escorts. Irvine is no different. He has a single guard and would like another (or more if he could get them). Grab the Delanian Waypoint before you start this event.

Once you've talked to Irvine and initiated the event, follow the pack bull. Irvine, the merchant, and even the guard don't matter. You will succeed or fail based on the pack bull's survival. The bull regenerates health between fights so it can take a bit of damage, but don't let it drop below half or you might be too late to save it. If you're alone, let the guard and bull hold aggro for a moment while you start killing enemies. Use your most damaging attacks, as there is plenty of time for them to recharge between fights. As soon as the third wave is killed, run up the hill and activate the Earthworks Waypoint and then return to the caravan. The fourth and final attack comes as a pack of four Tamini. Once the escort completes, run just a little further to activate the Kessex Haven Waypoint and then jump back to Delanian Waypoint to finish the task.

ROADBLOCK (Repeatable)

GOAL: Clear the bandit roadblock from the road to Lion's Arch.

LEVEL: 16

Description: Nearly a dozen bandits guard a roadblock near the Earthworks and are prepared to prey on any unfortunate travelers. Pull the first several away from the roadblock and dispatch them before attacking the roadblock itself. The bandits do not flee when the roadblock is destroyed. They will continue to fight even after their plans have been smashed. Do not charge in and get overwhelmed unless you have friends to help. Because the caravan (mentioned earlier) comes down the road, it's possible to finish both events at the same time. Though dangerous, it's incredibly fun and can get you a fair amount of money and experience.

THE LIONGUARD (Repeatable)

GOAL: Accompany the Lionguard patrol.

LEVEL: 16

Description: Two visiting Lionguard are patrolling outside the keep. They're brave men, but their route is a dangerous one. Talk to the Lionguard to initiate this patrol, and follow them closely. You only fail the event if both soldiers fall. They heal between fights, so that helps considerably. Follow them around the keep and help vanquish pretty much everything around the area. When you're done, grab the two Skill Challenges in the northeast and head to Earthworks Waypoint.

THE DRILL (Group)

GOAL: Slay Draithor before he experiments on captives.

LEVEL: 16

Description: A centaur madman is killing captives in a gruesome way. There are only five captives and you need to save them. Champion Draithor the Drill deals immense damage, steals life to heal himself, and has an amazing amount of health. Be ready to revive allies as they fall, and do not attempt this alone. Use any skills available to keep him Stunned or knocked down when he starts stealing life, and then unload with every damaging attack you have.

THE REMAINS (Repeatable)

GOAL: Take remains from Draithor's Demesnes to Aria Venom.

LEVEL: 16

Description: Should Draithor the Drill kill his captives, Aria shows up at the entrance hoping to put the spirits to rest. The Merchant's Remains can be found on the ground or on the corpses of Draithor's minions. Get 10 sets of remains and Aria will be happy. The people don't come back in a pretty way, but at least you get another shot at Draithor!

THE DRILL: TAKE TWO (Group)

GOAL: Help Aria Venom slay Draithor the Drill.

LEVEL: 16

Description: Aria is a little twisted, but she has a mission. She's used the remains you collected to fashion three flesh golems and is going to attack Draithor. Help her kill him! With the flesh golems absorbing the life-stealing, he's a much easier opponent. Keep from being in front of him and avoid his helpers. Just kill the fiend and run out of the area to collect your reward.

EARTHWORKS WAYPOINT (EAST SIDE)

SERVICES:	Waypoint
TRAVEL:	Sojourner's Waypoint (N), Delanian Waypoint (NE), Kessex Haven Waypoint (W)
HARVEST INFO:	Iron Ore, Gummo Sapling, Onion

A crude wooden palisade juts from the ground around the Earthworks. The Tamini aren't very good at building their own cities or towns, but they're great at taking land. Keeping the centaurs out of the Earthworks on a long-term basis is almost impossible, but it's worth a try. Do what you can before heading northwest toward Cavernhold Camp Waypoint and another Tamini stronghold.

CAPTURE HARATHI EARTHWORKS (Part of World Event)

GOAL: Capture all three sections of the Harathi Earthworks.

LEVEL: 16

Description: The Earthworks are so big that you have to capture all three major entrances before the Tamini will retreat to regroup. Pick an entrance and run in. Trebuchets bombard any non-centaurs who stay outside and they do very high damage. Do not attempt to kite centaurs while dodging the siege engines. One failure spells doom. Clear the centaurs from a capture point and keep it until the area converts. When you're done, move to the next and repeat the process. Be careful of the centaurs' ranged troops; they have deadly attacks, and they just keep coming. Duck out of the contested areas to heal if you think your hero isn't going to survive the encounter. When all three points are yours, take a moment to loot corpses. Don't take long, as the Tamini haven't left permanently.

HOLD THE EARTHWORKS (Part of World Event)

GOAL: Repel the centaur attack and hold the Earthworks.

LEVEL: 16

Description: Twelve waves of Tamini try to retake the Earthworks. If you are alone, be ready to move around. The enemy uses all three entrances and there are very few Seraph to help. Worse yet, you cannot revive the Seraph once they fall. Each wave has three or four centaurs. Keep an eye on the health of any Seraph helping you. Make sure the centaurs die before the Seraph do. Once a wave is down, immediately check the other entrances. If things are getting out of hand, grab the enemies and kite the Tamini while the guards kill them. You have a healing skill, but the guards don't. It's "safer" for your hero to take the hits. Once the Tamini fail to recapture the Earthworks, the Seraph loot the place and throw it all on a cart that needs to be escorted to friendlier territory.

THE SUPPLY BULL (Part of World Event)

GOAL: Escort the supply bull to Quarryside.

LEVEL: 17

Description: The two Seraph guarding this caravan know how dangerous the mission is and keep the bull moving at speed. The guards can be revived and the bull heals between fights. Keep the Tamini off the bull whenever possible. Sacrifice the guards if you need to, but the bull falling means failure. While the guards are good at keeping melee centaurs off the bull, ranged centaurs are another matter. These should be your first target. Escort the group all the way to Quarryside before heading north to Cavernhold Camp Waypoint to help Guard Barnaby.

CAVERNHOLD CAMP WAYPOINT (NORTH SIDE)

SERVICES:	Waypoint, Armorsmith (with Barnaby), Weaponsmith
TRAVEL:	Sojourner's Waypoint (E), Gap Waypoint (W), Kessex Haven Waypoint (S)
HARVEST INFO:	Silver Ore

The Tamini have set up residence in a large cave and can retreat back to it whenever they start suffering losses. Pry them out of this spot and destroy any other camps in the area on your way west to Gap Waypoint.

BARNABY (Renown Task)

GOAL:	Help Guard Barnaby.
LEVEL:	17

Description: Pushing the Tamini out of the Earthworks is not enough. You need to hunt them wherever they run. Help the Seraph assault centaur camps, destroy centaur weapons and supplies, ensure the safe delivery of supplies to the mine, and defeat centaurs wherever you find them.

DEFEND CAVERNHOLD (Part of World Event)

GOAL:	Maintain control of Cavernhold Camp.
LEVEL:	17

Description: Stand against seven waves of centaurs as they try to siege the cave. There is only one entrance into the area, which makes it easier to see the enemies approaching. Don't let them get past you and into the open; they'll be more of a pain to weed out if that happens.

GAP WAYPOINT (NORTH SIDE)

SERVICES:	Waypoint, Rock Merchant (Quarryside), Weaponsmith (Quarryside)
TRAVEL:	Cavernhold Camp Waypoint (E), Kessex Haven Waypoint (SE), Viathan Waypoint (SW), Greyhoof Camp Waypoint (W)
HARVEST INFO:	Silver Ore (Abundant in Quarryside), Gummo Sapling, Root Vegetables, Mushrooms

Gap Waypoint stands at a crossroads. North is the cave of Goff's Bandits. Southeast is the town and mine of Quarryside. West is Greyhoof Camp. Teaching the bandits a lesson sounds like a good idea, but Quarryside could use your help a lot more. Head southeast to keep this valuable resource in the right hands before turning fully east toward Kessex Haven Waypoint.

ENGINEER GILLI (Renown Task)

GOAL:	Help Engineer Gilli.
LEVEL:	18

Description: Quarryside exists to maintain the mine and the workers within. Help Engineer Gilli by protecting the perimeter from centaurs, clearing vermin from the mine and fields, and motivating the workers. The cave bats at the bottom of the mine make excellent targets. Watch for rock piles. These innocent looking ground spawns are elementals in hiding and give you credit toward the task both when you wake them and again when you defeat them.

DEFEND QUARRYSIDE (Part of World Event)

GOAL:	Defend Quarryside from the centaur invaders.
LEVEL:	18

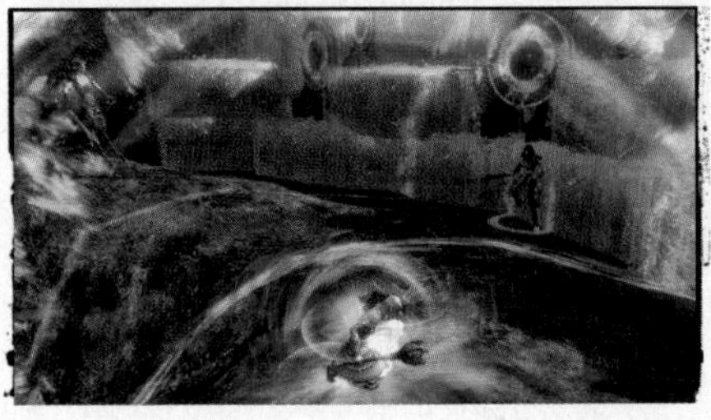

Description: Centaurs sometimes gather to attack the mine. They attack in eight waves. The enemies run into the town primarily from the north and east but take up a position at the mine entrance. Intercept them there, and keep the centaurs from sneaking past you to take the mine. If the mine is being taken, head inside to stop the enemies before it's turned.

RETAKE THE QUARRY (Part of World Event)

GOAL:	Defend Quarryside from the centaur invaders.
LEVEL:	18

Description: Not all is lost even if the Tamini take the quarry. Fight your way down the ramps and start killing centaurs. The fighting gets much easier once the first enemies are dead and you only have to deal with the single enemies coming from deeper in the mine or down the ramps. Push the invaders out of Quarryside, and then head east to Kessex Haven Waypoint.

KESSEX HAVEN WAYPOINT (EAST OF CENTER)

SERVICES:	Waypoint, Equipment Repair, Armorsmith, Salvage Merchant, Food Merchant
TRAVEL:	Gap Waypoint (NW), Earthworks Waypoint (E), Overlake Haven Waypoint (S)
HARVEST INFO:	Onion, Iron Ore

Kessex Haven stands as a bastion in a troubled area. Triskell Quay is to the southwest, where there are some new enemies to deal with. When you're finished with the krait, head east to Overlake Haven Waypoint and take on bigger game.

TRISKELL QUAY (Renown Task)

GOAL:	Help the fishers of Triskell Quay.
LEVEL:	19

Description: Head to the water to fight krait, destroy their nets, and check the fishermen's shrimp traps. Very little of this task can be done above water; only reviving fishermen gets you credit. It's faster to dive into the water and take a look around. There are krait nets and shrimp traps near the docks. Checking the traps might start a fight, so be careful. Grab any groundspawns you see and swim out to Krait's Larder.

HORRIBLE NEIGHBORS (Repeatable)

GOAL:	Free villagers from Krait's Larder.
LEVEL:	19

Description: The krait have kidnapped a number of villagers and taken them to Krait's Larder. Kill the krait slavers to release the citizens. Release all 10 to complete the event. Not all the citizens are underwater. A few are in cages above. Killing the slavers doesn't get the job done. Instead, grab a metal bar from the platforms and pry the cage doors open. With the villagers free and the town in better shape, turn east and head up the cliffs to Overlake.

OVERLAKE HAVEN WAYPOINT (SOUTHEAST OF CENTER)

SERVICES:	Waypoint, Equipment Repair, Explosive Merchant, Salvage Merchant, Armorsmith, Scout
TRAVEL:	Entrance to Caledon Forest (Levels 1-15) (SW), Kessex Haven Waypoint (N), Cereboth Waypoint (E), Ireko Tradecamp Waypoint (W)
HARVEST INFO:	Iron Ore, Silver Ore, Mushrooms

Overlake Haven stands atop the cliffs watching over Viathan's Arm and the road to Caledon Forest. The walls of the keep are built high and thick as a tribe of ettins live nearby and are not the best of neighbors. The ettins have been especially aggressive recently. Is something driving them toward the settlement? Smoke billows from the ground to the east. Travel that way and see what you can find out before continuing east to Cereboth.

GOT ETTIN? (Renown Task)

GOAL:	Assist Overlake Haven with the ettin nuisance.
LEVEL:	20

Description: Help recover supplies, eliminate ettins, and attract rabbits to make the ettins less aggressive. Head northeast from Overlake and up the hill. Kill the ettins and watch for Rabbit Bait Points along the ground. Use the points as you pass them. If there are no targets, grab the Lion's Arch Supply Boxes on the ground and run them back to Overlake. There are also ettins and Rabbit Bait Points through the tunnel farther northeast.

ROADBLOCK (Repeatable)

GOAL: Clear the ettin roadblock.

LEVEL: 20

Description: Ettins have blocked Giant's Passage to the north of Overlake. Four ettins caused a rockslide to cut off trade. Kill the ettins and destroy the rockslide to complete this quick event. Remember to dodge backward whenever ettins charge for a heavy blow; heroes don't like taking hits on the chin, especially from these giant monsters.

THAT'S A LOT OF ETTIN! (Group)

GOAL: Defeat the brutish ettin chieftain.

LEVEL: 20

Description: Use explosives to damage the thick-skinned ettin. In the cave northeast of the keep, the brute has made his home. This event is monumentally easier if you have a second person or a pet. Pull and kill the normal ettins when the veteran brutish ettin chieftain is on the other side of the cave until he only has his bodyguard with him. Have your friend (or pet) attack the chieftain while you grab the nearest Stolen Explosives and put them at his feet. These deal immense damage! If you are alone, kite the two ettins until only the chieftain stands. Use slowing abilities to give yourself time to pick up the explosives, and then kite him onto the barrels. Loot the corpses when you're done.

DESTROYERS (Renown Task)

GOAL: Assist Sangdo Swiftwing.

LEVEL: 21

Description: Collect volcanic rocks, investigate suspicious mounds, and destroy fissures. Head farther east from Overlake and into the giant fissure in the ground. Destroyers roam freely and are spawning from small fissures. It's your job to put a stop to it. Head inside and start killing destroyers. Investigate any suspicious mounds, as you get credit for the investigation and for killing the destroyer that often spawns.

COLLAPSE THE FISSURE (Repeatable)

GOAL: Collapse the destroyer fissure.

LEVEL: 20

Description: A giant destroyer fissure is spawning an army of destroyers. Attacking the fissure summons all nearby enemies. Clear the area a bit before you deal any damage to the fissure directly or a rather large fight ensues. As you're already down there killing destroyers, this is mostly just a free event to do while you're having fun.

IREKO, HO! (Repeatable)

GOAL: Escort the merchant pack bull to Ireko Tradecamp.

LEVEL: 21

Description: A merchant needs to get to Ireko Tradecamp, but most of the Lionguard are busy with the ettins. One Lionguard is already helping, and two more join the group. There are four waves of enemies as you travel, but only two are difficult. If you have a skill that clears conditions, prepare it now by slotting it before your fights. Some of the enemies rely on Poison! The guard dies instantly when wave two happens and six krait attack. Let the bull take a few hits, as taking on six enemies at once is very difficult. Pull everything off the bull if it starts getting near half health. Wave four only has one enemy, but it's a veteran krait. Fight at range when he drops the Poison cloud on himself and kill him like any other tough enemy. High damage attacks and skills that Knockdown, Daze, Stun, or Cripple are very useful.

LOST AND ALONE (Repeatable)

GOAL: Help Kari back to Overlake Haven.

LEVEL: 20

Description: Kari is lost in the tunnels beneath Cereboth and needs help getting home. Kari is only brave enough to move if you're nearby. If you get too far away, she will run back to where you first found her. She'll also cower in fear if any destroyers are nearby. Kill the destroyers and keep her moving all the way back to Overlake Haven, then jump back to Cereboth Waypoint and continue northeast.

DESTROY THE DESTROYER (Group)

GOAL:	Kill the Champion Harpy Destroyer.
LEVEL:	21

Description: Fight down through the craggy depths until you reach the Mafic Core. Within, there is sometimes a champion harpy. It's ready to attack you and any other heroes nearby. This enemy is a tough one, being able to summon lava fonts that damage groups and heal the creature as it passes over them. Bring a team of adventurers and spread out to ensure that the harpy can't hit all of you at once. To keep your character safe and healthy, stay on your feet and make sure not to stand in the lava. Use ranged weapons when you aren't close to the beast, as it frequently flies through the cavern and can be hard to hit in melee.

CEREBOTH WAYPOINT (SOUTHEAST SIDE)

SERVICES:	Waypoint
TRAVEL:	Overlake Haven Waypoint (W), Earthworks Waypoint (N), Darkwound Waypoint (NE)
HARVEST INFO:	Strawberries, Silver Ore, Iron Ore, Gummo Sapling, Mushrooms

Cereboth Waypoint stands in a very scenic part of Kessex Hills. You can barely tell there's a war on. Take a moment to enjoy the region before turning northeast toward Darkwound Waypoint.

STRAWBERRIES AHOY!

If you're looking for strawberries, head southeast through the ettin area and on toward the Floating Castle. The cliffs along Isgarren's View are covered in these tasty treats!

DARKWOUND WAYPOINT (EAST SIDE)

SERVICES:	Waypoint, Salvage Merchant, Armorsmith, Weaponsmith
TRAVEL:	Cereboth Waypoint (SW), Delanian Waypoint (N)
HARVEST INFO:	Root Vegetables, Mushrooms, Silver Ore, Copper Ore, Iron Ore

Darkwound Waypoint appears at first to be in the middle of nowhere. Only one merchant and some farm animals stand near the waypoint. The other merchants and a Skill Challenge, however, are south along the road in Garenhoff. This is a moderate-sized scholarly town, but they do not have their own waypoint. Once your selling is complete, jump back to Gap and travel south to Viathan Waypoint.

GORT'S REQUEST (Repeatable)

GOAL:	Clear ettins from Gort's Pit.
LEVEL:	17

Description: Ettins have infested Gort's Pit (just north of the waypoint) and he wants them gone! There are six ettins that need to be defeated and occasionally a veteran appears. Ettins are tough enough without being veterans, so clear the bats in the area to give yourself kiting room. Take the ettins one at a time and this event becomes very simple. Wait in the pit for a few moments after the final ettin is dead. Gort makes his way back and uncovers his treasure as your reward.

VIATHAN WAYPOINT (CENTER)

SERVICES:	Waypoint
TRAVEL:	Gap Waypoint (NE), Greyhoof Camp Waypoint (N), Moogooloo Waypoint (W), Ireko Tradecamp Waypoint (S)
HARVEST INFO:	Silver Ore, Iron Ore, Onion, Gummo Sapling, Clam

Viathan Waypoint stands on the northeast shore of Viathan Lake. Charred rubble to the west mars this otherwise picturesque view. Head northeast through Auld Red Wharf toward Greyhoof Camp Waypoint. This isn't friendly territory, so don't let your guard down.

GREYHOOF CAMP WAYPOINT (NORTH SIDE)

SERVICES:	Waypoint, Weaponsmith
TRAVEL:	Gap Waypoint (E), Viathan Waypoint (SE), Moogooloo Waypoint (SW), Meadows Waypoint (W)
HARVEST INFO:	Silver Ore, Iron Ore

Greyhoof is the Seraph's nightmare made real. Bandits have teamed up with centaurs. Working together, they have become a force the Seraph can't deal with. Help Sergeant Rane wage war against Greyhoof and clear a path to the waypoint. Once Greyhoof is taken care of, head west to Meadows Waypoint.

LOOKING FOR A CHALLENGE?

A champion bandit bruiser lives in a cave between Greyhoof Camp Waypoint and Gap Waypoint along the northern mountains. This bandit has exceptionally high health and deals tremendous damage, but has rewards for those able to best him. Call some friends if you want to start trouble here!

DEALING WITH GREYHOOF (Renown Task)

GOAL:	Help Sergeant Rane.
LEVEL:	22

Description: Clear out unexploded shot, recover the badges of fallen Seraph, and defeat as many centaurs and bandits as possible. If the centaurs control Greyhoof, take it back to make substantial progress on this event. If the Seraph control the camp, stay outside the walls, picking off enemies and recovering Seraph badges.

CAPTURE GREYHOOF (Part of World Event)

GOAL:	Capture Greyhoof Camp.
LEVEL:	21

Description: To break the siege on Fort Salma, Greyhoof Camp must be taken. The Seraph will help as they can, but you have to lead the charge. Fight your way into Greyhoof Camp and team up with any Seraph. These allies cannot be revived if they go down, but their damage is very welcome in this fight. Keep them alive as long as you can without jeopardizing the larger objective. Once the camp is taken, a weaponsmith appears to sell centaur weapons to you.

MEADOWS WAYPOINT (NORTHWEST SIDE)

SERVICES:	Waypoint
TRAVEL:	Entrance to Queensdale (Levels 1-15) (N), Greyhoof Camp Waypoint (E), Moogooloo Waypoint (S), Overlord's Waypoint (SW), Fort Salma Waypoint (W)
HARVEST INFO:	Gummo Sapling, Herb Patch

If it weren't for the bridge to the south, Fort Salma to the west, or Greyhoof Camp to the east, Meadows Waypoint wouldn't even be a footnote. As it is, this waypoint is surrounded by events that are crucial to the Battle of Fort Salma (World Event). While there is little to do here directly, it makes for a very convenient staging area when centaurs are on the move. Continue moving west to Fort Salma after you unlock the point.

TAKE THE BRIDGE (Part of World Event)

GOAL:	Take the bridge before Greyhoof Camp is attacked.
LEVEL:	22

Description: Time limit (5 minutes). The centaurs control the bridge that gives them easy access to retake Greyhoof Camp. The good news is you only have to chase them off (by killing defenders and any reinforcements that approach). The bad news is they have siege engines. Keep moving and consider killing the engineers first so the siege weapons fall silent.

LOST HEIRLOOMS (Repeatable)

GOAL:	Protect Webb as he recovers his heirlooms.
LEVEL:	22

Description: Mr. Daukins comes from an old family that used to live in Auld Red Wharf and he wants a couple of his heirlooms back. Keep him in view; he moves pretty quickly until he gets to Auld Red Wharf. The man only helps with fights that he starts, so let him begin the encounters. He heals between engagements and can be revived if he falls, so there isn't any worry about keeping him alive. Once he reaches the wharf he slows down to search buildings for his two heirlooms. You get full credit after he's found them both.

FORT SALMA WAYPOINT (NORTHWEST SIDE)

SERVICES:	Waypoint, Armorsmith, Equipment Repair, Scout
TRAVEL:	Meadows Waypoint (E), Overlord's Waypoint (S), Halacon Waypoint (SW)
HARVEST INFO:	Silver Ore, Iron Ore, Herb Patch, Gummo Sapling

Fort Salma is in trouble. The centaurs are constantly sieging the compound. They work diligently to cut off any supplies or reinforcements from arriving. Fort Salma is also the last holdout between this tribe of centaurs and Queensdale. Push the enemies away from Fort Salma and out of Wallwatcher Camp before grabbing Halacon Waypoint to the west.

FORT SALMA (Renown Task)

GOAL:	Aid Fort Salma.
LEVEL:	23

Description: Help battle centaurs, disarm their traps, and repair the damage from their assaults. First deal with any centaur attacks. If the enemies aren't nearby, grab a bucket from the well to put out fires or repair damaged houses.

BREAK THE SIEGE (Part of World Event)

GOAL:	Break the siege on Fort Salma.
LEVEL:	23

Description: Three trebuchets are bombarding Fort Salma. All three need to be destroyed to break the siege. Be ready for a good bit of running as Harathi siege masters arrive to repair any destroyed siege weapons. You have to obliterate all three weapons as fast as you can. Alternatively, you can destroy two of them, go back and kill the siege masters at the first, and then proceed to the third for the victory.

WALLWATCHER CAMP (Part of World Event)

GOAL:	Drive the centaurs from Wallwatcher Camp before reinforcements arrive.
LEVEL:	24

Description: The siege is broken and now is the time to strike back. Reinforcements arrive in 10 minutes. You have that long to drive the centaurs from Wallwatcher Camp.

HOLD THE CAMP (Part of World Event)

GOAL:	Prevent the centaurs from recapturing Wallwatcher Camp.
LEVEL:	24

Description: This event starts with six Seraph soldiers alive. They're led by Lieutenant Gregoire. To win, at least one of these allies needs to survive eight waves of centaur attacks. Keep an eye on Lieutenant Gregoire and stay mobile. Centaurs attack in pairs from three entrances. If the Lieutenant starts taking damage, immediately break off from your skirmishes and go to assist him. These Seraph cannot be revived once they fall, so do your best to use AoE healing and boons to assist them. Or, keep the centaurs' attention so your hero takes the brunt of the damage. Once you hold the camp, a merchant selling centaur weapons arrives.

HALACON WAYPOINT (NORTHWEST SIDE)

SERVICES:	Waypoint
TRAVEL:	Entrance to Brisban Wildlands (Levels 15-25) (W), Fort Salma Waypoint (NE), Overlord's Waypoint (SE)
HARVEST INFO:	Iron Ore, Herb Patch

Halacon Waypoint is the last waypoint before entering sylvari/asuran lands. If you want to see how the other half lives, take a peek in there. The level range is similar to Kessex, so it's a fun way to break up your events and face some new enemies.

After you unlock Halacon, backtrack and look at your map. Your next goal is Ireko Tradecamp Waypoint.

IREKO TRADECAMP WAYPOINT (SOUTH SIDE)

SERVICES:	Waypoint, Food Merchant, Salvage Merchant, Weaponsmith, Armorsmith, Scout
TRAVEL:	Caledon Forest (Levels 1-15) (SE), Overlake Haven Waypoint (E), Shadowheart Site Waypoint (W), Viathan Waypoint (NE), Moogooloo Waypoint (N)
HARVEST INFO:	Iron Ore, Gummo Sapling, Mushrooms, Onion

Ireko Tradecamp is one of the more important trade areas in Kessex Hills. Both asura and tengu join humans here. There's plenty of work for adventurers in this area. Head east into some caves to help Matlal before you jump back to Ireko and head west to Shadowheart Site Waypoint.

COLLECTING TRUFFLES (Renown Task)

GOAL:	Help Matlal collect truffles for her starving tribe.
LEVEL:	22

Description: Matlal needs food to feed her tribe, but there are veteran ettins wandering the cave. She has a plan and needs someone to carry it out. Speak with Matlal and have her use her "Pig Magic." Take a moment to acquaint yourself with your new abilities before looking for truffles. Use Smell to get an idea where nearby truffles are located. This shows a plume of smoke where you need to use Forage to get the truffle. Once you have it in your mouth, return to Matlal and speak with her to give her the truffle. Do this several times to supply the starving tribe.

To speed this up substantially, look for burrows along the walls. Enter the burrows to scare out aggressive grubs and find a couple truffles. Bite is your primary attack in this form and it deals a good bit of damage. This gives you credit for entering the burrow, killing the grub, and each truffle you return! With the tribe in better shape, swim out and climb atop the cave to speak with Tocatl before jumping back to Ireko and running east to Shadowheart Site Waypoint.

SHADOWHEART SITE WAYPOINT (SOUTHWEST SIDE)

SERVICES:	Waypoint, Salvage Merchant, Weaponsmith, Armorsmith
TRAVEL:	Ireko Tradecamp Waypoint (E), Overlord's Waypoint (N)
HARVEST INFO:	Gummo Sapling

Shadowheart Site is a village under attack. The risen boil up from the swamp and infect everything they touch. The sylvari work hard to keep them in check and will never turn down a helping hand. Help where you can before heading northwest toward the Skill Challenge. Afterward, jump to Meadows Waypoint and travel south to Moogooloo.

SHADOWHEART (Renown Task)

GOAL:	Aid the warden of Shadowheart.
LEVEL:	22

Description: Fill gourds at the fountain to cure sick sylvari, stop the spread of corrupted fungus, and defeat the undead plaguing the swamp. The gourds are around the fountain and can be filled under the falling water. Splash the healing waters on corrupted sylvari to cleanse them. A faster way to complete this task is to look for Pus Shrooms just outside the village. Squash these and kill any grubs that appear!

RETAKE SHADOWHEART SITE (Repeatable)

GOAL:	Liberate Shadowheart Site from the risen.
LEVEL:	22

Description: The sylvari can't keep the risen at bay without help. Sometimes help gets there too late, leaving a lot of downed sylvari that need to be revived. Carefully kill your way into the village, as there are risen brutes mixed in with the thralls (brutes are much stronger enemies). Killing a dozen or so undead will convince them to regroup and come back another time.

STOPPING AN ARMY (Group)

GOAL:	Stop the risen krait from building their army.
LEVEL:	22

Description: Four veteran risen krait hypnosses are raising an army in the swamp to the west of Shadowheart. These foes summon allies, and they're even pretty tough by themselves. Come here with friends if you want a better chance at victory. Clear an area initially and have one group member hold the hypnosses in place while the rest of the group unloads on them. Rinse and repeat to complete the event.

MOOGOOLOO WAYPOINT (WEST OF CENTER)

SERVICES:	Waypoint, Salvage Merchant
TRAVEL:	Viathan Waypoint (E), Ireko Tradecamp Waypoint (S), Overlord's Waypoint (SW), Meadows Waypoint (N)
HARVEST INFO:	Clams, Silver Ore

Moogooloo is your last stop before taking the fight to the centaurs, but the quaggan need your help. As a peaceful people, the quaggan are being murdered and enslaved by the nearby krait. Help by inflicting horrible casualties on the krait; this encourages them to leave the quaggan alone. Afterward, make your way southwest to Overlord's Waypoint.

HELP THE QUAGGAN (Renown Task)

GOAL:	Help Doolsileep protect the quaggan of Moogooloo Village.
LEVEL:	23

Description: Free slaves from the krait, kill the quaggans' predators, clear krait nets, and collect tasty crab meat for Doolsileep. Head south from Moogooloo toward the krait cave. Kill hermit crabs near Doolsileep, as you need to talk with him to get credit for the meat. Then head into the krait area for even more killing. Watch for nets to clear and other predators to attack, but the krait are your primary target.

RETAKE MOOGOOLOO (Repeatable)

GOAL:	Clear the krait from Moogooloo to rescue the quaggan slaves.
LEVEL:	23

Description: The krait have tired of raiding for slaves and have decided to take up residence in Moogooloo. Kill any krait you see to teach them the error of their ways. All krait must be dead at the same time to fully free Moogooloo Village. Because krait reinforcements trickle in over time, you have to work quickly to defeat all of the enemies. Once Moogooloo is freed, travel southwest to Overlord's Waypoint.

STOP THE KRAIT BLOOD WITCH (Group)

GOAL:	Kill the blood witch.
LEVEL:	23

Description: This uncommon event is a challenge. Make sure you have a solid group before attempting it. One of the hardest steps is simply getting into the blood witch's lair. Barracuda and krait pour out of the lair in a constant stream. They summon additional barracuda when engaged, so a direct attack is hard to pull off. Stay low on the lake floor and fight your way in as best you can. Rest once you're there and have one person start pulling the remaining krait away from the champion blood witch to give yourselves some room. This will be a hard fight as the already tough blood witch summons friends and allies that call even more enemies. Healing is essential, because the blood witch likes to Bleed her victims. Kiting is nearly impossible because of her Immobilizing attacks, so make sure someone in your group is tough enough to handle her blows for as long as possible.

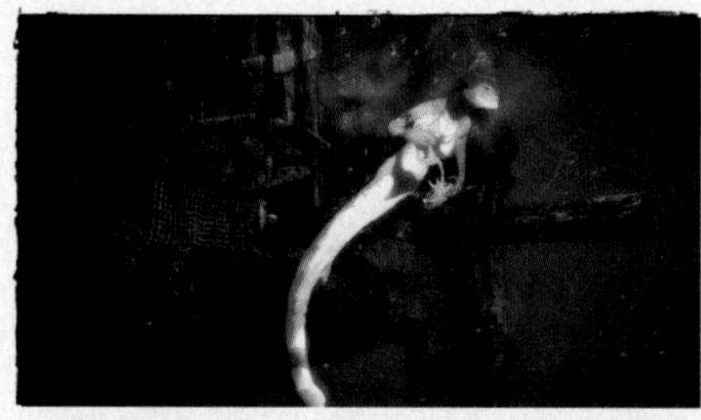

OVERLORD'S WAYPOINT (SOUTHWEST SIDE)

SERVICES:	Waypoint, Scout
TRAVEL:	Moogooloo Waypoint (NE), Shadowheart Site Waypoint (S), Halacon Waypoint (NE), Fort Salma Waypoint (N)
HARVEST INFO:	Iron Ore, Rich Iron Ore, Silver Ore, Rich Silver Ore, Onion, Root Vegetables, Gummo Sapling

All your hard work has come down to this. The Harathi foothold in Kessex can be seen from Overlord's Waypoint. After pushing them out of Greyhoof, away from Salma, and out of Wallwatch, it's time to take the fight to them. Kill the horsemen and free Kessex!

OPERATION OVERLORD (Renown Task)

GOAL:	Help Seraph Tripp.
LEVEL:	25

Description: Destroy the siege engines, defeat centaur guards, and then assault the camp. This is pretty straightforward. Get inside and start breaking things! Your biggest concern is the siege engines. The Harathi trebuchets have long range and a large blast radius, and they deal tremendous damage. However, they have a tough time targeting things close to the weapons themselves and have a long reload time. Exploit these minor weaknesses by fighting near the weapons and then destroying them whenever you get a chance. Watch out for bandit cannons as well. The cannons fire in all directions and have a faster reload time. Enter the camp from the north gate; the southern gate leads to a gauntlet of siege weapons and patrols. Once inside, throw your most damaging abilities at the siege engines. Start killing centaurs and don't stop until the Seraph mail you a reward.

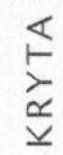

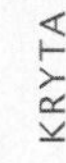

JUST REWARDS

Rich ore veins await those who brave the deepest parts of Overlord's Greatcamp.

GENDARRAN FIELDS

LEVEL RANGE: 26-32

Gendarran Fields is where the centaurs start to have even more sway. Their battles aren't just local concerns for the militia. Centaurs have taken territory, constructed more fortifications, and made travel quite precarious. Watch yourself on the road, and don't assume that each camp is a safe haven for your people. You can reach Gendarran Fields by walking east from Queensdale, north out of Lion's Arch, or coming west out of Snowden Drifts. It's a very accessible and central location in Tyria.

WEST SIDE

EAST SIDE

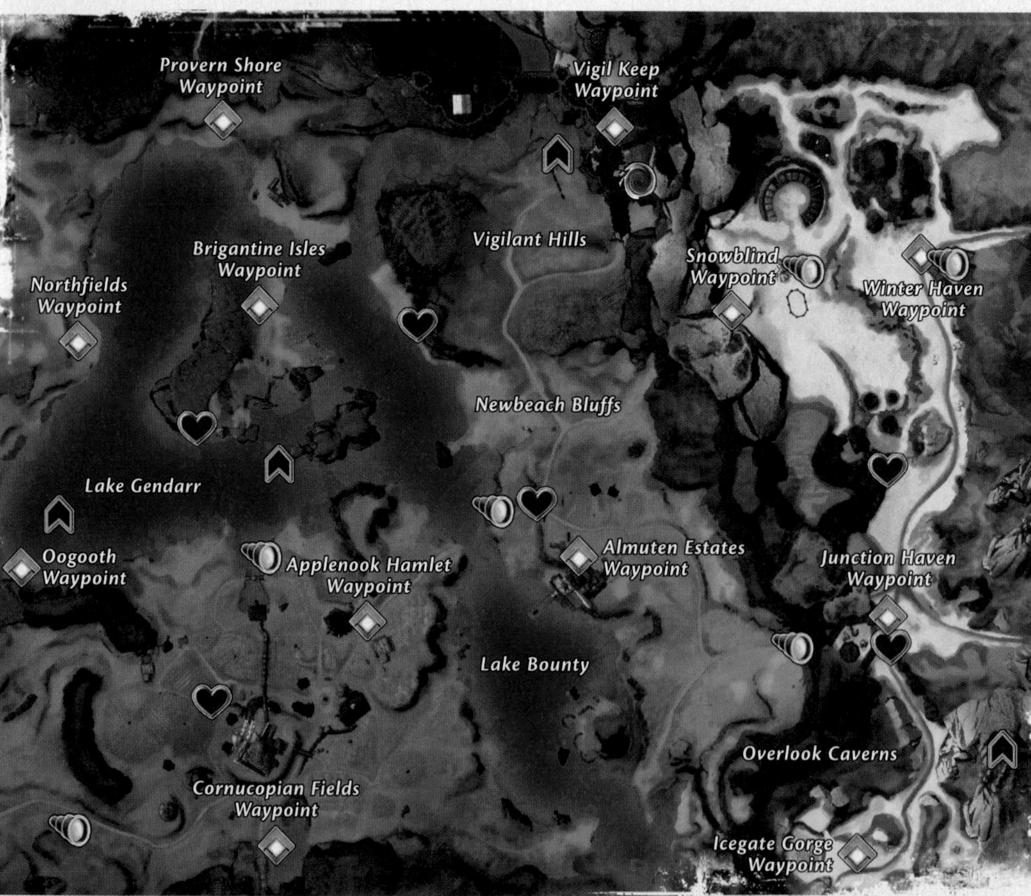

HARATHI HINTERLANDS

LEVEL RANGE: 35-45

Scoured to the dirt by war, siege weaponry, and trampling hooves, Harathi isn't a beautiful sight. It's a sad reminder that the land suffers in times of war almost as much as the people who have to fight. Harathi Hinterlands is quite challenging for single adventurers. Many of the events involve nasty attacks against (or from) groups of centaurs. This is a great place to take guild members for exciting PvE challenges. Harathi Hinterlands is on the northern end of Kryta, above Gendarran Fields.

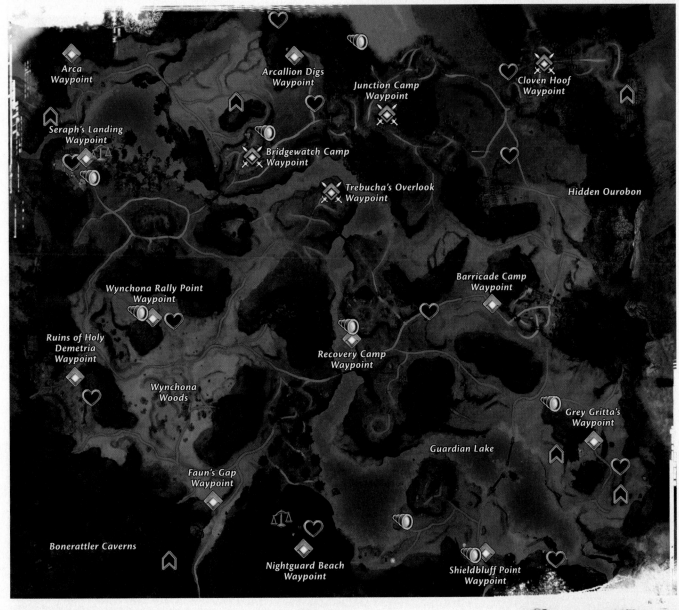

Arca Waypoint
Arcallion Digs Waypoint
Junction Camp Waypoint
Cloven Hoof Waypoint
Seraph's Landing Waypoint
Bridgewatch Camp Waypoint
Trebucha's Overlook Waypoint
Hidden Ourobon
Barricade Camp Waypoint
Wynchona Rally Point Waypoint
Ruins of Holy Demetria Waypoint
Recovery Camp Waypoint
Wynchona Woods
Grey Gritta's Waypoint
Guardian Lake
Faun's Gap Waypoint
Bonerattler Caverns
Nightguard Beach Waypoint
Shieldbluff Point Waypoint

THE CITY OF LION'S ARCH

WAYPOINTS: 13

Lion's Arch has become a crossroads for the intelligent races of the world. The city was built on ruins and founded by pirates and tradesmen. If something can be bought, it can be found in Lion's Arch…if you have enough coin!

With Asura Gates to the capital cities of all major races, Lion's Arch has become both a highway for travelers and a haven for those who don't quite fit in. Even cities and people who want little to nothing to do with each other are connected to Lion's Arch because the trade is just too good to pass up.

Lion's Arch is also home to many brave heroes who are trying to stem the tide of undead from the south. The Lionguard are constantly vigilant in their watch. For over one hundred years these soldiers have held a difficult line, but never once have they faltered.

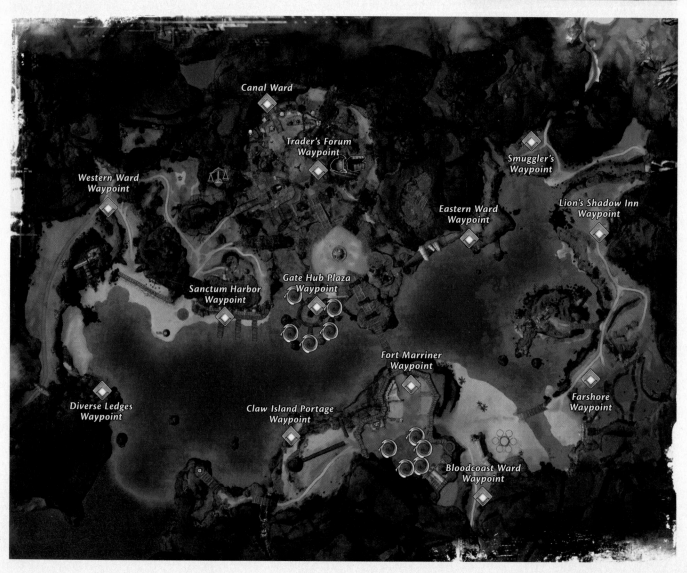

GATE HUB PLAZA WAYPOINT (CENTER OF TOWN)

SERVICES:	N/A
TRAVEL:	Asura Gates to Black Citadel, The Grove, Rata Sum, Divinity's Reach, and Hoelbrak; Path to Trader's Forum Waypoint, Path to Eastern Ward Waypoint

Most travelers enter Lion's Arch by an Asura Gate. With so many gates packed close together, the Grand Piazza is where adventurers cross paths on their way to other regions. The gates of the Grand Piazza can take you to nearly any major city in Tyria. Ebonhawke is the exception (to get there, take the gate to Divinity's Reach and walk east to another Asura Gate).

Coriolis Plaza is east of Gate Hub Plaza. While none of the Asura Gates here are functioning, Coriolis Plaza is the next major expansion for Lion's Arch. Captain's Council is northeast of Gate Hub Plaza; just run up some scaffolding. The Crow's Nest Tavern there is the cleanest of all the bars in the city.

Be sure to stop at Lion's Court and speak with the Vigil Crusader to learn more about the city before you inevitably head to the market.

TRADER'S FORUM WAYPOINT (NORTH OF CENTER)

SERVICES:	Salvage Merchant, Bank, Trading Post, Profession Trainers (All), Weaponsmith, Armorsmith, Equipment Repair, Craft Masters and Stations (All)
TRAVEL:	Path to Gate Hub Plaza Waypoint, Path to Canal Ward Waypoint

The northern side of town is the heart of Lion's Arch. Revered masters of every profession and craft are willing to take on students with potential. You can also find merchants and smiths of every calling, a Bank, and a Trading Post.

The Bank of Lion's Arch sits up a ramp just beside the waypoint. Here you can deposit your most valued possessions without worry. The Trading Post is to the west.

For the explorer in you, take a look in the sewers beneath the Bank. Sadly, this isn't a back way into the vault. There certainly are a lot of Order of Whispers personnel in the Lost Grotto, though. What are they up to?

CANAL WARD WAYPOINT (NORTH SIDE)

SERVICES:	N/A
TRAVEL:	Path to Trader's Forum Waypoint, Portal to Gendarran Fields (Level 15-25 Region)

This is the last stop before entering Gendarran Fields. Inexperienced adventurers and civilians are better off using a gate to leave Lion's Arch than trying to cross the fields on foot. There are centaur raiders out there!

SANCTUM HARBOR WAYPOINT (WEST OF CENTER)

SERVICES:	Equipment Repair
TRAVEL:	Path to Trader's Forum Waypoint, Path to Western Ward Waypoint

Sanctum Harbor Waypoint looks over the northern beach of Sanctum Harbor. It's an area of remembrance. There are memorials to the north, and those willing to swim can see what the city must have been before it was destroyed. Sanctum Harbor is littered with ruins. Anyone who played through the events from the original *Guild Wars* should really take a swim down there.

There's a quaggan on the western docks who can repair equipment.

WESTERN WARD WAYPOINT (NORTHWEST SIDE)

SERVICES:	Salvage Merchant, Armorsmith, Weaponsmith
TRAVEL:	Path to Sanctum Harbor Waypoint, Path to Hooligan's Route

There is little of note at Western Ward Waypoint. Life slows down a bit, and this area is away from the hustle and bustle of central Lion's Arch. Here, there are more animals than people and there's nothing in the way of merchants.

For a bit more adventure, look in the caves to the north. Pirates don't like selling their ill-gotten goods in daylight or where there are too many guards. The Undermarket is perfect for them. Keep an eye on your purse and a hand on your weapon.

White Crane Terrace is quite isolated. The tengu have closed the Shuttered Gate to outsiders.

DIVERSE LEDGES WAYPOINT (WEST SIDE)

SERVICES:	Diving Goggles
TRAVEL:	Path to Sanctum Harbor Waypoint

The long walk and climb to Diverse Ledges Waypoint is well worth your time. The view of Lion's Arch is unparalleled. At the very top of the scaffolding are Diving Goggles and a diving board. This is one of Lion's Arch's "must-dos" for every traveler. Grab the goggles and dive into Sanctum Harbor. While you're down there, take a look at Old Lion's Arch beneath the waves.

EASTERN WARD WAYPOINT (EAST OF CENTER)

SERVICES:	N/A
TRAVEL:	Path to Smuggler's Waypoint, Path to Gate Hub Plaza Waypoint

Eastern Ward Waypoint is a quick stop between the Grand Piazza and Smuggler's Waypoint.

SMUGGLER'S WAYPOINT (NORTHEAST SIDE)

SERVICES:	N/A
TRAVEL:	Path to Eastern Ward Waypoint, Portal to Gendarran Fields (Level 15-25 Region), Path to Lion's Shadow Inn Waypoint

Smuggler's Waypoint sits right by the Portal to Gendarran Fields. Be careful if you're heading out there. If you're a young hero, there's plenty of danger to be found there.

Some of the less common denizens of Lion's Arch make a home behind the waterfall to the east of Smuggler's Waypoint. Don't stare at them. They don't like it.

LION'S SHADOW INN WAYPOINT

SERVICES: N/A

TRAVEL: Path to Smuggler's Waypoint, Path to Farshore Waypoint

Farmer Hogg has given up his former profession; there wasn't enough money in it. His house has been converted from a farmhouse to an inn.

Deverol's Island is across a bridge just south of Lion's Shadow Inn Waypoint. The island stands on stony legs a dozen feet above the sandy beach.

FARSHORE WAYPOINT (SOUTHEAST SIDE)

SERVICES: N/A

TRAVEL: Path to Lion's Shadow Inn Waypoint, Path to Bloodcoast Ward Waypoint

Tokk's Mill is an agricultural and technological wonder. Wind-driven sprinklers irrigate its terraced fields. Tokk's Mill produces enough food to keep all of Lion's Arch fed.

BLOODCOAST WARD WAYPOINT (SOUTH SIDE)

SERVICES: N/A

TRAVEL: Path to Lion's Shadow Inn Waypoint, Path to Fort Marriner Waypoint, Portal to Bloodtide Coast (Level 45-55 Region)

Bloodcoast Ward is home to some of the less socially conscious entertainment of Lion's Arch. Tenanera's Pit is used for creature fighting of all kinds. There are ledges for many people to have a good look at the action, and drink to be had for a few copper.

South of the Waypoint is the portal to Bloodtide Coast. This should only be taken by the stoutest of adventurers, as the enemies beyond are quite powerful.

FORT MARRINER WAYPOINT (SOUTH OF CENTER)

SERVICES: Salvage Merchant, Equipment Repair, Practice Dummy

TRAVEL: Asura Gate to the Mists, Path to Bloodcoast Ward Waypoint, Path to Claw Island Portage Waypoint

The smell of blood and sweat permeate Fort Marriner. Adventurers from all lands and professions come here to practice their fighting abilities.

CLAW ISLAND PORTAGE WAYPOINT (SOUTH SIDE)

SERVICES: N/A

TRAVEL: Path to Fort Marriner Waypoint

Claw Island Portage sits just inside Lion's Gate harbor. These are the closest docks to Fort Marriner and are often used for military ships.

SHIVERPEAK MOUNTAINS

The Shiverpeak Mountains are home to the norn, a race of giant humanoids whose strength and determination are known throughout Tyria. The norn were driven from their previous homes by Jormag, the Elder Dragon. Undaunted, the norn have rebuilt, making Hoelbrak a new capital for their people.

But there is trouble in the mountains. The Sons of Svanir foment rebellion. These norn worship Jormag and his corrupting power. Deep in the mountains, the jotun are also being swayed by the dragon's taint. As if these threats weren't enough, the dredge burrow beneath the soil and stone, waiting to strike wherever they sense vulnerability.

The norn have their work cut out for them if they wish to bring peace to the Shiverpeak Mountains.

HOELBRAK

LEVEL RANGE:	Norn Capital City (All Levels)
WAYPOINTS:	14

UPPER FLOOR

LOWER FLOOR

Hoelbrak is built high in the mountains, making it almost impossible to siege. The only way into the city by land is from the southeast (leading into the Wayfarer Foothills or the Dredgehaunt Cliffs). Otherwise, visitors have to use the Asura Gates to jump here from Lion's Arch.

This city is known for its longhouses, brutal weather, and hard drinking. Those with a more philosophic leaning might also come here to learn about the norn's animal totems. During the harsh times when the norn were driven out of the mountains, they found solace and guidance in the spirits of the animals. They now revere these creatures and have built great lodges in their honor. The bear, wolf, raven, and snow leopard are held in the highest regard.

To stop at a norn's personal residence, go to the Great Lodge in the southern part of town. Crafters reside in the Trade Commons, on the middle level and toward the center of Hoelbrak. The Asura Gate to Lion's Arch is to the west; go there to reach other capital cities throughout the land.

EASTERN WATCHPOST WAYPOINT (SOUTHEAST SIDE)

SERVICES:	Waypoint, Merchant (Salvage), Armorsmith, Weaponsmith
TRAVEL:	Passage to the Wayfarer Foothills (Level 1-15 norn region) (E)

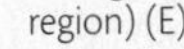

The Eastern Watchpost is at the edge of Hoelbrak. A path leads residents out of town and into the wilderness. The main road west goes into the city and passes by a number of important merchants, including those who sell weapons and armor. You can also purchase salvage kits here!

The northern road leads toward the Hall of Legends, and the southern path takes one closer to the bank.

HALL OF LEGENDS WAYPOINT (EAST SIDE)

SERVICES:	Waypoint, Equipment Repairs, Profession Trainers, Merchant (Booze)
TRAVEL:	City Exit (S), Shelter Rock (N)

The Hall of Legends is a small area with a tavern and a number of trainers. Heroes who want to reset their traits or purchase trait guides should come here to meet their trainers and learn from them. This doesn't come without cost; you need to spend some coin to get the job done, so think carefully before you dedicate to your traits.

The tavern sells booze for anyone who enjoys short-term buffs. The drinks are quite cheap, so you won't break the bank to get a few of these.

This area doesn't connect well to the rest of the city unless you're willing to walk all the way through the northern caverns. That's a long trek unless you want to see Skarti along the way. After visiting the Hall of Legends, return to the Eastern Watchpost and explore elsewhere.

SOUTHERN WATCHPOST WAYPOINT (SOUTH SIDE)

SERVICES:	Waypoint, Bank
TRAVEL:	Entrance to the Dredgehaunt Cliffs (Level 40-50 norn region) (S), Eastern Watchpost (NE), Trade Commons (N)

The Southern Watchpost guards the more dangerous exit from the city. The Dredgehaunt Cliffs have deadlier enemies compared with the Wayfarer Foothills. Novice adventurers should only go this way if they have no love for life itself!

To the west is the Vigil Armory, where people can store their items for future use. The Southern Watchpost Waypoint is the closest one to this bank, so it gets a lot of traffic. Note that all of your heroes share a single bank account, so it's possible to trade items between your characters without mailing all of the equipment back and forth.

TRADE COMMONS WAYPOINT (SOUTH OF CENTER)

SERVICES:	Waypoint, Equipment Repairs, Merchants (Food), Stations and Trainers for Every Craft
TRAVEL:	City Exit (Down the Ramp and Then East), The Great Lodge (S), Peeta's Gate (W)

The Trade Commons is one of the most important sections of Hoelbrak. Here, trainers are constantly teaching their crafts to new apprentices. You can pick up the methods for making weapons, armor, accessories, and just about anything else you can imagine. There are stations for each craft, so you don't need to wander back and forth trying to make various items. The only hassle is that the bank isn't right there in the middle of the commons. You should get the Southern Watchpost Waypoint so you can pop back and forth between this area and the bank without any delay.

To get into the main portion of the city, use the ramp here in the commons. It leads down to the main floor of Hoelbrak. From there, you can leave town by walking east or continue north to Might and Main, where there are even more merchants.

The western path from the Trade Commons Waypoint leads toward the Asura Gate to Lion's Arch.

GREAT LODGE WAYPOINT (SOUTH SIDE)

SERVICES:	Waypoint, Merchants (Food, Salvage, Booze)
TRAVEL:	Trade Commons (N)

The Great Lodge is a massive building at the southern end of town. Slip through the main doors; they're never open wide because of the cold and foul weather. Once you're in, it's a constant party. Merchants sell food and drink, and everyone is gathered around to talk, joke, and feast.

Norn characters can enter their private homes from this building. Look on the eastern side of the room where you first enter. That's the entrance.

UPPER BALCONY WAYPOINT (SOUTH SIDE)

SERVICES:	Waypoint
TRAVEL:	Great Lodge (Down)

The Upper Balcony is above the Great Lodge entrance. It presents an ideal view over Hoelbrak, so it's perfect for tourists. Climb up there and look around for a few minutes before returning to the middle tier of the city.

PEETA'S GATE WAYPOINT (WEST OF CENTER)

SERVICES:	Waypoint, Asura Gate to Lion's Arch, Trading Post
TRAVEL:	Trade Commons (E), Hero's Compass (NW)

Peeta's Gate lets tourists leave Hoelbrak and visit other cities. It's also where foreigners

first arrive in town. There isn't much to do here besides pass through. There's a Trading Post to the south, and most of the people you see coming by Peeta's Gate are going down there. Check out the variety of goods for sale, or post a few auctions of your own.

The road northwest continues on toward Hero's Compass.

HERO'S COMPASS WAYPOINT (WEST SIDE)

SERVICES:	Waypoint, Merchant (Booze)
TRAVEL:	Peeta's Gate (SE), Veins of the Dragon (NE)

The norn hold some of their grand events out here. Personal fortunes rise and fall with the gladiatorial events that are held each year. This location doesn't get many visitors except during those special times, during players' stories. There isn't much to do normally.

A frozen river leads into a cave to the northeast. Be sure to check out that route if you're looking for special areas. A brave Son of Svanir hides in that cave, but he's more interested in talking than fighting.

MIGHT AND MAIN WAYPOINT (CENTER OF TOWN)

SERVICES:	Waypoint, Weaponsmith, Armorsmith, Merchants (Salvage and Food), Equipment Repair, Guild Services
TRAVEL:	Trade Commons (S), The Animal Lodges (W/N/E/SE)

The great fire and avenue through the center of Hoelbrak is called the Might and Main. You can buy weapons and armor there or sell anything you no longer want. There are merchants for salvage kits, and a few snacks are available too. You can get almost anywhere quickly once you have this waypoint, as it connects with everything in the northern section of town.

SNOW LEOPARD RISE WAYPOINT (NORTHWEST OF CENTER)

SERVICES:	Waypoint
TRAVEL:	Might and Main (E)

Stealth, prowess, and subtlety are the ways of the snow leopard. Visit the ledge on the western side of Might and Main to find out more about this totem animal.

RAVEN RISE WAYPOINT (NORTH OF CENTER)

SERVICES:	Waypoint
TRAVEL:	Might and Main (S), Bear Lodge (E), Snow Leopard Lodge (W)

Those who favor cunning and wisdom will be more at home in the lodge of the ravens. Age, experience, and a clever mind are all lauded here. You can find the lodge by walking north from Might and Main, the central square of Hoelbrak.

BEAR RISE WAYPOINT (NORTHEAST OF CENTER)

SERVICES:	Waypoint, Merchants (Food)
TRAVEL:	Might and Main (SW), Shelter Rock (N)

The bear is a creature of strength, both in mind and body. It has ferocity and the confidence that comes from these mighty traits. There aren't many good merchants here, but it's still a fun place to visit. Everybody likes the bears (as long as they're on your side, right?).

WOLF RISE WAYPOINT (SOUTHEAST OF CENTER)

SERVICES:	Waypoint, Merchants (Food and Salvage), Karma Merchant (Booze)
TRAVEL:	Might and Main (NW)

Courage and loyalty are the way of the wolf. It is only through cooperation that true strength is found. Learn this from the wolves and their worshippers.

SHELTER ROCK WAYPOINT (NORTHEAST SIDE)

SERVICES:	Waypoint
TRAVEL:	Bear Lodge (S)

The northeastern section of Hoelbrak is hidden from view. A large cave network is up there, and you can reach it by walking into the tunnel north of Bear Rise or by the entrance north of the Hall of Legends. There aren't many people to talk to inside the caves, but there is a waypoint. South from Shelter Rock is a small building where Skarti lives. Talk to Skarti and Ingrid to find out more about the political situation in Hoelbrak. They'll also talk to you about the Wolfborn and the history of the city. It's neat stuff.

WAYFARER FOOTHILLS

LEVEL RANGE:	1-15
TASKS:	16
WAYPOINTS:	17
SKILL CHALLENGES:	8
HARVESTING INFO:	Copper Ore, Aspen Saplings (Green Wood Logs), Early Cooking Ingredients

SKILL CHALLENGES

- Bear Shaman Marga (East of Grawlenfjord Waypoint, Underwater) (SE)
- Issormir's Body (Northeast of Horncall Waypoint, At the Top of the Stairs) (SW)
- Veteran Blane the Insane (Northeast of Darkriven Waypoint) (SE)
- Burrisson the Blue (West of Zelechor Hot Springs Waypoint) (W)
- Corrupted Spike (East of Krennak's Homestead Waypoint) (E)
- Barrels of Ale (Southeast of Lostvyrm Cave Waypoint, Inside the Cave) (N)
- Ancient Cave Spring (East of Solitude Waypoint, At the Back of the Cave) (NE)
- Bjord's Banner (Northeast of Dawnrise Waypoint) (N)

The Wayfarer Foothills are east of the norn capital city of Hoelbrak. Norn adventurers who desire honor and glory come to this place to hunt and battle. The southern section of this territory is green and fruitful, though the upper reaches of it are cold and merciless. Expect to meet the mighty jotun, the dragon-worshipping Sons of Svanir, and many fierce beasts.

Solitude Waypoint
Dolyak Pass Waypoint
Dawnrise Pass Waypoint
Crossroads Haven Waypoint
Lostvyrm Cave Waypoint
Halvaunt Snowfield
Halvaunt Waypoint
Krennak's Homestead Waypoint
Moleberia
The Icesteppes
Vendrake's Homestead Waypoint
Zelechor Hot Springs Waypoint
Twinspur Haven Waypoint
Taigan Groves Waypoint
Osenfold Waypoint
Darkriven Waypoint
Doldenvan Passage
Horncall Waypoint
Kresdor Kenning
Hero's Moot Waypoint
Grawlenfjord Waypoint
The Grekvelnn Burrows
Outcast's Cleft Waypoint
Molensk

HORNCALL WAYPOINT (SOUTHWEST SIDE)

SERVICES:	Waypoint, Merchant (Salvage), Armorsmith, Karma Merchant, Scout, Skill Challenge (NE)
TRAVEL:	Entrance to Hoelbrak (Norn Capital City)(W)
HARVESTING INFO:	N/A

Horncall Village is a small settlement on the western edge of the foothills. It's a base of operations for people who are just starting their adventure in the Wayfarer Foothills. The road out of Hoelbrak leads southeast through Snowlord's Gate. Talk to the scout in town before leaving; he'll show you where some of the tasks are located in the surrounding territory.

A small set of stairs is built into the mountain, northeast of the waypoint. Climb these switchbacks until you reach the top, and search for the body of Issormir. Commune with the body for a free skill point.

The easiest task is to your east, up in the hills. After completing that task, use the road to travel southeast. Look for the village of Hero's Moot.

HELP SHAMAN FREYGIRR (Renown Task)

GOAL:	Honor Raven by helping his flock, hunting skelk, retrieving eggs, and repairing broken roosts.
LEVEL:	2

Description: Travel east from Horncall and climb the hill along the mountainside. Raven's statues are up there. Fulfill this event by delivering eggs to Freygirr (they are found on the ground along the hill). Fight skelks in the area if you prefer combat, or answer riddles from Raven's statues for even more experience. If you have extra karma, you can buy a Precision buff from Freygirr.

ANSWER RIDDLES (Repeatable)

GOAL:	Answer Raven's riddles.
LEVEL:	2

Description: The hills east of Horncall Waypoint are home to a number of statues. Approach these and interact with them. You are given a number of riddles. Read each one carefully because a wrong answer disables the statues for a short period. Answer several of the riddles correctly to complete this event. Doing so also helps to complete the "Help Shaman Freygirr" task.

BOREALIS WAYPOINT (SOUTH SIDE)

SERVICES:	Waypoint, Merchant, Karma Merchant, Equipment Repair
TRAVEL:	Horncall (W), Outcast's Waypoint (S), Grawlenfjord Waypoint (E)
HARVESTING INFO:	N/A

The road from Horncall leads down into the Borealis Waypoint, by the town of Hero's Moot. After getting the waypoint, search through the forest in several directions. There are important tasks all over the place. For the easiest progression, travel southwest and help the snow leopard shaman, and then hit the bear shaman to the northeast to gain even more favor.

When you're done with all of their tasks and events, travel east. There is a waypoint across a small river, and that's your next target.

HELP SHAMAN SIGARR (Renown Task)

GOAL:	Honor Snow Leopard.
LEVEL:	2

Description: Walk southwest from Hero's Moot and look for Shaman Sigarr. Talk to the shaman and be transformed into a snow leopard. In this state, you can hunt dredge and moas all around the area. Killing the dredge gets you credit for the task and for the repeatable event in the area. Moas are only good for the task itself, but there are plenty of them and they're fast to kill. Get out of leopard form as soon as you're done with both events.

HUNT DREDGE AS A SNOW LEOPARD (Repeatable)

GOAL:	Become a snow leopard and kill dredge.
LEVEL:	2

Description: After talking with Sigarr, on the southwestern hill, you become a snow leopard. In this form, search the area and use Snarl (your fourth weapon attack) to scare dredge out of their hiding places, usually holes in the ground. Kill several dredge like this to complete the event. Your first and second attacks are more than enough to cut these weak mole people to shreds.

HELP SHAMAN FREYGUNN (Renown Task)

GOAL:	Honor Bear by protecting her children and proving your strength to her acolytes.
LEVEL:	3

Description: Bear's shrine is northeast of Hero's Moot. It's a quick journey through the woods, and you'll soon find plenty to do. Talk to acolytes to challenge and then impress them. Or, fight the Sons of Svanir nearby and kill them for points. If the Sons of Svanir launch a serious assault, you can finish this task by completing the repeatable event.

THE HIDDEN PATH

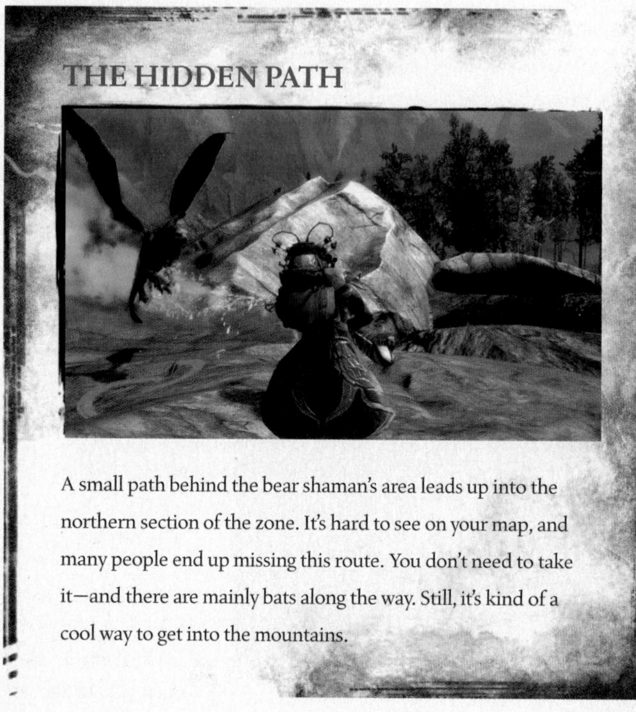

A small path behind the bear shaman's area leads up into the northern section of the zone. It's hard to see on your map, and many people end up missing this route. You don't need to take it—and there are mainly bats along the way. Still, it's kind of a cool way to get into the mountains.

DEFEND THE SHRINE FROM THE SONS OF SVANIR (Repeatable)

GOAL:	Kill the Sons of Svanir to prevent them from taking Bear's shrine.
LEVEL:	3

Description: Every few minutes, the Sons of Svanir mount an assault on Bear's site. This launches a repeatable event that you win by killing the Sons of Svanir as they arrive. Stay near the acolytes for help with the fighting, and watch the progress on both your event and the main task in the area. This completes them both rather quickly.

GRAWLENFJORD WAYPOINT (SOUTHEAST SIDE)

SERVICES:	Waypoint
TRAVEL:	Borealis Waypoint (W)
HARVESTING INFO:	N/A

Grawlenfjord is east of Hero's Moot. It doesn't look like there is much to do there until you arrive. Search along the eastern cliffs to find more to do, including another task. There are grawl to slay and jotun to play with even farther north.

After exploring this area thoroughly, seek the Outcast's Waypoint south of Hero's Moot.

ASSIST KANI (Renown Task)

GOAL:	Fight the grawl that have chosen to worship a demon and destroy all signs of their new god.
LEVEL:	3

Description: Kill grawl in their cave. It's northeast from the Grawlenfjord Waypoint. You get points for each death, and there are bonus points if you destroy the offerings and totems that litter their den.

KILL THE WINGED HORROR (Repeatable)

GOAL:	Defeat the winged horror north of the waypoint.
LEVEL:	3

Description: The winged horror flies outside of the northern cave. It takes a while to respawn if killed, so you won't always see it there. Once you find the winged horror, use ranged attacks to stay outside of its aura and destroy it. You can also rush in and cut the demon to pieces.

STEAL FOOD FROM THE GRAWL (Repeatable)

GOAL:	Steal food sacks from the grawl.
LEVEL:	3

Description: Kani sometimes wants to push things further in her aggression against the grawl. She'll ask that adventurers gather grawl food sacks from inside the cave to the east. Go in there and get sacks, one at a time. Use the second ability that pops up on your weapon bar to get a speed boost while ferrying the sacks back to Keni. After she gets about four sacks from each person working on the event, she'll start a countdown! This triggers a new event.

DEFEND KANI'S STOLEN FOOD (Repeatable)

GOAL:	Protect Kani and her food from the grawl.
LEVEL:	3

Description: After gathering grawl food sacks for Kani, you should stay and defend your ill-gotten gains. Grawl raiders attack from the cave and come in waves (with a few members in each strike force). Stay and hold the area throughout these waves and enjoy the fighting. Once the grawl numbers have dwindled, you get credit for the event.

KILL THE ICE DRAKE BROODMOTHER (Repeatable)

GOAL:	Defeat the broodmother.
LEVEL:	3

Description: Every few minutes, the ice drake broodmother spawns on the southern end of the river. She'll have four hatchlings with her, and all of them patrol together along the waterway. Ambush them for a fast event and some fun fighting. If you have trouble with this group, take one run to pick off the hatchlings. Run away when they're dead and come back to kill the broodmother while she's still by herself.

OUTCAST'S WAYPOINT (SOUTH SIDE)

SERVICES:	Waypoint, Karma Merchant, Scout
TRAVEL:	Borealis Waypoint (N)
HARVESTING INFO:	N/A

Outcast's Waypoint is at the end of the southern road, leading down from Hero's Moot. This is a good staging area for assaults on Molensk, the large dredge mine. Come here when you're close to level 5. Take care of business and then consider going back to a capital city.

To move on, return to Horncall Waypoint and use the northern road to leave. That's how you reach the more difficult parts of the Wayfarer Foothills.

BUY SOMETHING MEAN!

Level 5 is a good time for this because you can purchase a better weapon from a weaponsmith. Unless you have something better, a vendored weapon every five levels will keep you adequately up to date.

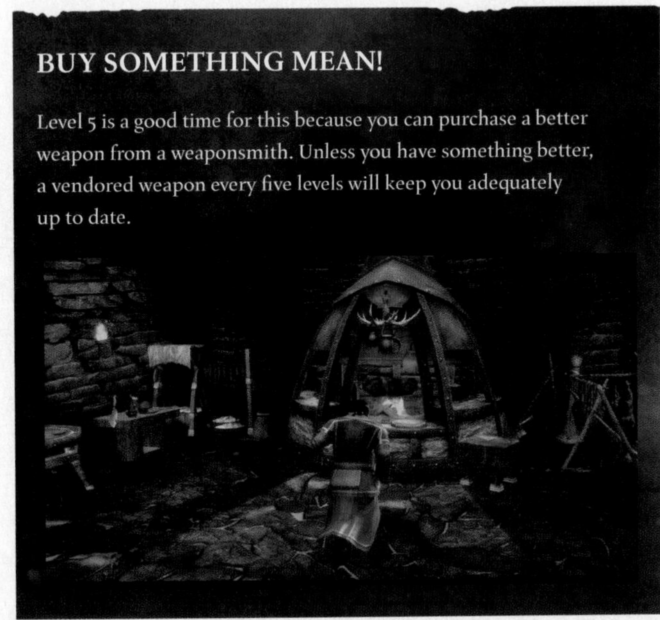

HELP SHAMAN VIGMARR (Renown Task)

GOAL:	Honor Wolf by fighting the Sons of Svanir.
LEVEL:	4

Description: There's a task east of Outcast's Waypoint. Go around the hill and meet the Wolf's shamans. Talk to Vigli at the back of the small camp. He'll summon a few wolves and get them to attack the Sons of Svanir. Follow them so you can get this task done while completing a repeatable event. You get credit for killing Sons of Svanir, destroying their tents and banners, and by releasing wolves from the cages in the area.

DESTROY THE SONS OF SVANIR TENTS (Repeatable)

GOAL:	Break down three tents in the Sons of Svanir encampment.
LEVEL:	4

Description: Follow the wolves after they're spawned by the shaman and attack the encampment. You only need to break the three tents to get credit for this event. Everything else is just for fun or to complete the main task in the area. Target the buildings after you've killed the Sons of Svanir; that way you won't lose any wolves or get yourself hurt.

ASSIST GRIMARR MOLESMASHER (Renown Task)

GOAL:	Push back the dredge who are invading norn lands and destroy their vile machines.
LEVEL:	5

Description: There is a small cave to the west of the snow leopard area. You can enter this place (called Molensk) from up there or from an entrance beside Outcast's Waypoint. Dredge have taken over the mine. You need to kill a pile of these mole people to complete your task. This is a higher-level event compared with some of the other ones in the area. If you find this too difficult, back off and return later. While fighting in the mines, use ranged attacks to lure dredge back to your character. This averts the situation where you attack one dredge and end up fighting nearby enemies, as well. Destroy any mining machines you come across to complete the task even sooner.

DESTROY THE DREDGE TOWER (Repeatable)

GOAL:	Obliterate the dredge tower outside of the mine.
LEVEL:	4

Description: The dredge sometimes erect a siege tower to the west of Outcast's Waypoint. Jump down the hills, kill the gunners who defend it, and then work on the two turrets that flank the tower. Once those are down, you're free to destroy the emplacement at will. As soon as it falls, you get a new event to stop the dredge from repairing the tower.

STOP THE DREDGE FROM REPAIRING THE TOWER (Repeatable)

GOAL:	Kill dredge until they stop trying to work on the tower.
LEVEL:	4

Description: Dredge come out in packs to replace their precious tower. Thwart them in this by killing the repair crews. Area-of-effect attacks are very useful because the crew members build up quickly. If the repairs are going too well, be sure to attack all the enemies as soon as possible to pull them onto your character. This is risky, but it might be the only way to win if you're not killing them fast enough!

GATHER DREDGE ORE (Repeatable)

GOAL:	Pick up dredge ore inside the mine and take it to Sven.
LEVEL:	5

Description: Sven is waiting outside of the mine, on a hill southeast from the snow leopards. He wants you to harvest ore from inside the nearby mine. Kill the dredge while you're searching through the area, and look for chunks of ore on the ground. You won't get credit until you actually take the ore to Sven. You need about 17 pieces of ore to complete the event.

KILL THE DREDGE COMMISSAR (Group)

GOAL: Kill the commissar who is overseeing the mine.

LEVEL: 5

Description: A powerful dredge leader is in the southwestern part of the mine. He has a couple of buddies back there, and you should kill them as soon as possible. The commissar takes a long time to bring down, and having additional targets is only a good thing if you want to rally by killing them later (when you go down). It's easier to just bring a friend or two and hack through the commissar. Failing that, use ranged attacks and kite the big guy back through the part of the mine you just cleared.

HEADING NORTH FROM HORNCALL

SERVICES:	N/A
TRAVEL:	Horncall (S), Taigan Groves (NE)
HARVESTING INFO:	Copper Ore, Aspen Saplings, Hoarfrost Thistle

Take the northern road out of town and talk to fellow travelers along the way. You'll soon find that the way ahead is blocked by the rebellious Sons of Svanir. Someone is going to have to deal with those creeps.

CLEAR THE ROADBLOCK (Repeatable)

GOAL: Destroy the roadblock on the northern path.

LEVEL: 6

Description: Sons of Svanir rebels have taken the road and constructed a barricade. They're manning it well and have a number of troops in the pass. Kill these creeps and then work on the barricade. Attack that until more enemies spawn, and then switch to the living targets. Burn through them and finish off the roadblock at your convenience. The event finishes as soon as the barricade is destroyed.

TAIGAN WAYPOINT (SOUTH OF CENTER)

SERVICES:	Waypoint, Merchant, Karma Merchant, Armorsmith
TRAVEL:	Horncall (SW), Darkriven Waypoint (SE), Twinspur Haven (N)
HARVESTING INFO:	Root Vegetables, Aspen Saplings

The Taigan Waypoint is your first foothold into the northern part of the zone. The waypoint is just off of the road, so you can't miss it while coming north. There are Sons of Svanir and some wild beasts in the area, but nothing is terribly dangerous unless you attack the peaceful pinesouls that tromp through the forest.

There are many root vegetable harvesting areas to the east of the waypoint. If you prefer wood, look to the northwest. There are many trees to fell near the creek.

PROTECT GARETH'S FAMILY (Renown Task)

GOAL: Entertain Gareth's children and hunt down wild beasts nearby.

LEVEL: 7

Description: Gareth's wife has gone out for the day, and that's left the hunter in a bit of a quandary; he's not very good at watching his kids, and they need to be entertained. Complete this task by killing aggressive animals in the nearby wilderness, by playing with the kids, or by bringing dolyak meat to Gareth. You can also take honey from the hives around the stead and give it to Sigmy, the little girl.

COLLECT DOLYAK MEAT (Repeatable)

GOAL: Hunt dolyak and bring their meat back to Gareth.

LEVEL: 7

Description: Dolyak are a common sight in the woods near Gareth's stead. While hunting aggressive creatures to fulfill the task in the area, you should also kill dolyak. This gets you meat to turn in to Gareth. Seven pieces should be more than enough for his family.

KILL LONGSHANKS FOR JAFRI (Repeatable)

GOAL:	Escort Jafri into the woods and kill longshanks for him.
LEVEL:	7

Description: Jafri is one of Gareth's children. He is sometimes found outside of the family home. Talk to him and agree to escort the boy. He'll take you into the forest and point out longshanks, a veteran beast. Kill one and let Jafri bring the head back to his father.

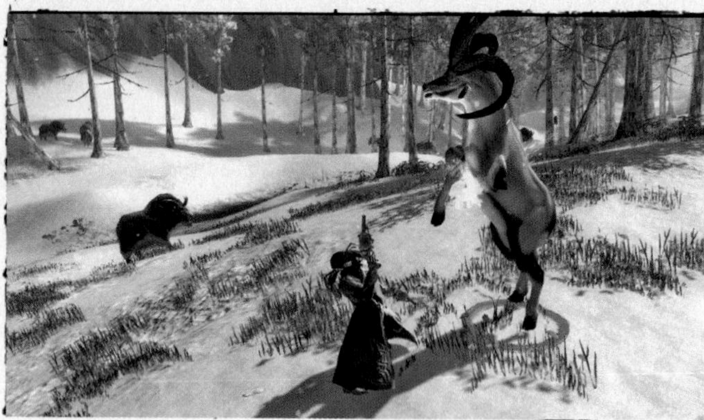

DEFEND THE LODGE FROM BEARS (Repeatable)

GOAL:	Fight off a few waves of bear attacks.
LEVEL:	7

Description: Give honey to the children and complete other tasks in the area while you wait (e.g., collect dolyak meat and hunt aggressive monsters nearby). Eventually, the kids' actions (Sigmy, in particular) trigger a bear assault. Several waves of the creatures attack the family home. Keep the bears off of the house doors and use area-of-effect attacks to thin their numbers quickly. This finishes off the main task of the area better than anything else; there are so many targets that you get pretty much full credit just for fighting the waves. Once it's done, you can leave the farmstead without issue.

HELP LINNEA AND BJARNI (Renown Task)

GOAL:	Honor Hare by protecting rabbits, killing minotaur, and helping with the yeti hunt.
LEVEL:	6

Description: Linnea and Bjarni are on top of the mountain that's south from Taigan Waypoint. Climb up the path that leads there and kill minotaur as you go. This helps to complete the primary task for these two norn. You can protect rabbits from the minotaur for even more credit, but there are so many targets that you won't need much help. Minotaur are everywhere in these mountains. Also, if you find any injured rabbits, you can carry them back to the norn, who are pleased with your assistance.

COLLECT FUR SAMPLES FOR LINNEA (Repeatable)

GOAL:	Bring piles of strange fur back to Linnea.
LEVEL:	6

Description: Talk to Linnea near the top of the path. She'll ask you to look for fur nearby. Piles of fur are on the ground here and there; many are on the plateau south of Linnea. You won't see many of them on the trail, but you only need several to complete Linnea's event. Bring the fur to her and turn in the items. When she's done examining it, talk to her again. This begins another event. Linnea leads your hero south, down the mountain.

DARKRIVEN WAYPOINT (SOUTHEAST OF CENTER)

SERVICES:	Waypoint
TRAVEL:	Taigan Waypoint (NW)
HARVESTING INFO:	Aspen Saplings, Copper Ore

Anyone looking for wood to harvest has come to the right spot. Darkriven is located down a road to the southeast from Taigan Waypoint. Aspen saplings cover the area, and there aren't many monsters to slow your harvesting run.

A cave to the south houses quite a few dredge. Look in there for a bit of action. You can also start mining Copper Ore from that cave.

BRING PLANTS TO LUNT (Repeatable)

GOAL:	Gather pungent flowers and bring them to Lunt, inside the cave.
LEVEL:	6

Description: There is a cave south of Darkriven Waypoint. Go inside and start looking for flowers to pick. The flowers you need are on the western side of the cave, with a bunch of dredge. Kill the dredge that get in your way, but focus on the green plants. They spawn on the ground all over that side of the cave. Get eight plants and bring them to Lunt, by the bridge. This starts a new event after a short time.

PROTECT LUNT'S FIRE (Repeatable)

GOAL:	Keep the fire lit while holding off waves of dredge.
LEVEL:	6

Description: After getting flowers for Lunt, wait around for a minute. He'll light the flowers on fire and lure the dredge over to his side of the bridge. Your job is to keep the fire lit by killing the dredge that come over. Don't worry about keeping Lunt alive; that isn't part of the event, and it's something you can do or not do without any consequences. Kill about a dozen attackers to complete the event. You can stand on the bridge and just wait for them to come to you. It's much safer than following Lunt into the enemy camp.

STENCH BOMBS

If you complete the events for Lunt, he'll give you bombs to play with. These create a cloud of smoke, and they're fun toys. You only get one throw per bomb, so play around and then move out.

OSENFOLD WAYPOINT (SOUTHWEST OF CENTER)

SERVICES:	Waypoint
TRAVEL:	Take the Bridge East to Get onto the Mountains or Walk North to Find Haivoissen Kenning
HARVESTING INFO:	Copper Ore, Hoarfrost Thistle

This waypoint is tucked out of the way and can easily be missed. You reach it by crossing the bridge near Linnea if you're already up in the mountains. Or, come south from the jotun if you're exploring the western edge of the map.

Cooks must absolutely explore Haivoissen Kenning; there are many ingredients to harvest from the jotuns' small encampment and down the minotaurs' hill to the east. It's well worth your time to loot the place. Even if you aren't a cook, go in there and harvest for your friends. They'll appreciate the help if they're just starting to learn the culinary arts.

ZELECHOR HOT SPRINGS WAYPOINT (SOUTHWEST OF CENTER)

SERVICES:	Waypoint, Merchant, Skill Challenge (W)
TRAVEL:	Osenfold Waypoint (S), Twinspur Haven (E)
HARVESTING INFO:	Hoarfrost Thistle (E), Aspen Saplings (E), Copper Ore (Near the Waypoint)

The Zelechor Hotsprings are tucked away in a small part of the western zone. It's a pretty spot, but there isn't a task nearby. People end up missing the area sometimes because of that. Make sure that you don't, because there is a Skill Point to be gained here. Talk to Burrisson the Blue to face your challenge. He's bathing on the western side of the springs.

TWINSPUR HAVEN WAYPOINT (SOUTH OF CENTER)

SERVICES:	Waypoint, Scout, Equipment Repair, Merchant, Karma Merchant
TRAVEL:	Taigan Waypoint (S), Crossroads Haven (N), Vendrake's Waypoint (E)
HARVESTING INFO:	Copper Ore, Hoarfrost Thistle

Twinspur Haven is a fortified town along the northern road. It's a rare place of safety in the cold steppes of the north. Sell excess loot and repair while you're here, and talk to the scout to learn more about the tasks nearby. There are interesting events to the east and west. Explore both sides thoroughly so you don't miss any of the fun.

ASSIST THE LIONGUARD (Renown Task)

GOAL: Patrol the road and eliminate enemies of the Lionguard.

LEVEL: 8

Description: The road north connects Twinspur Haven and the Crossroads. Every hostile along that route counts as a target for this task. Aggressive monsters that wander too close to the road are fair game, but there isn't much of a perimeter on the task; you can't leave the road and hunt in the fields. You have to kill your targets within close sight of the path. Walk up to any trees along the route; Sons of Svanir hide in the trees, and they're worth quite a bit to the Lionguard. Don't worry if it takes a couple of passes to get all of your points; your character passes through this area a few times while doing local events.

ESCORT ALFRAD BREWERSON (Repeatable)

GOAL: Help Alfrad get his mead to the Crossroads.

LEVEL: 9

Description: Alfrad Brewerson is waiting in the center of Twinspur Haven. He's the guy with an event icon over his head. Talk to him and agree to escort his mead along the northern road. This is great to do while you're working on the task for this area (to keep the roads clear for the Lionguard). You can kill two birds with one stone.

KILL THE SON OF SVANIR (Group)

GOAL: Kill the corrupted wolfmaster and his wolf pack.

LEVEL: 8

Description: It isn't often that you see this task, but there is a Son of Svanir champion that spawns near Twinspur Haven. He'll wander around the area outside the town, bringing with him a few wolves. Use area-of-effect attacks to kill the pack quickly, and then kite their master around the open fields to get an edge on him. For a champion, he isn't too hard to kill, and the wolves are extremely low on health. You can keep them up for rally fodder if you think the fight is going to be a close one.

VENDRAKE'S WAYPOINT (SOUTHEAST OF CENTER)

SERVICES:	Waypoint
TRAVEL:	Twinspur Haven (W), Krennak's Homestead Waypoint (N)
HARVESTING INFO:	Aspen Saplings, Hoarfrost Thistle, Copper Ore (not much)

Leave Twinspur Haven via its northern gate and walk east through the wilderness. Vendrake's Homestead is out there, though you won't usually spot it until you're almost on top of it. There are a few tasks along the river nearby, so this is a good rallying point.

FIGHT THE GRAWL TRIBES (Renown Task)

GOAL: Kill grawl and elementals near the eastern river.

LEVEL: 9

Description: Grawl and their elemental summonings are all over the river and the eastern cliffs near Vendrake's Waypoint. Go over there and fight these enemies while looking for repeatable events. The event to kill shamans is often up, and that's something to do while finishing the primary task. It helps to have a ranged weapon ready in this area because there are groups of enemies and wurms as well. Wurms are a pain to fight in melee, so spells and ranged attacks make your life easier.

KILL GRAWL SHAMANS (Repeatable)

GOAL: Look by the cliffs to the east and hunt grawl shamans.

LEVEL: 9

Description: This repeatable pops up frequently. You just need to tackle grawl shamans and kill them. About half of the grawl are shamans, so finding the targets isn't too bad. The camp tucked into the eastern mountains is ideal for finishing the event quickly. The fighting is tough and the monsters respawn quickly there, but it's fun stuff. If you get stuck in the grawl's magical prison, wait for a few seconds and then attack the crystal to break free. Remember to look behind your character often: you need to keep an escape path clear so your character doesn't get overwhelmed from behind!

KILL STIGAND THE DRAGONTOUCHED (Group)

GOAL:	Fight champion Stigand near the river.
LEVEL:	10

Description: Stigand the Dragontouched is a vicious caster who leads the Sons of Svanir in this area. Look on the eastern bank of the frozen river to find this vile opponent. If there are downed norn in the area, check to see if they're green when you highlight their bodies. If so, revive them before starting the fight. Any help is a good thing!

Also, bring friends for this encounter. Some group events aren't that hard to solo if you're tough. That's not the case with Stigand. This fight is mean, and you're going to take a ton of damage if you're alone. Get a couple more people and focus fire on Stigand the entire fight. Let the elementals in the area take some damage so they're quick kills for anyone who needs to rally. Their damage output is pitiful compared with Stigand, so it's good to keep them around in this way.

KRENNAK'S HOMESTEAD WAYPOINT (EAST OF CENTER)

SERVICES:	Waypoint, Merchant (NW)
TRAVEL:	Vendrake's Waypoint (SW), Lostvyrm Cave Waypoint (NW)
HARVESTING INFO:	Aspen Saplings, Copper (N)

Krennak's Homestead Waypoint is along the eastern wall of the map, near the grawl areas. Get this waypoint before fighting the enemies in Hunter's Lake. This isn't a great spot for gathering materials or doing long-term activities. It's more of a location to find and finish the task nearby, and then leave.

If you want to sell anything, go toward the task icon northwest of the waypoint. Tor the Tall is there, and he sells basic goods and lets you sell anything you want to get rid of.

FIGHT THE ICE DRAGON'S CORRUPTION (Renown Task)

GOAL:	Kill worshippers of the Ice Dragon and destroy signs of corruption.
LEVEL:	10

Description: Walk around the frozen lake and kill icebrood wolves while trashing any corrupted ice you see. The eastern side of the lake is the easiest for this task because there are plenty of icebrood wolves, but they're spread out and make for soft targets. For more fun, look along the eastern cliffs and enter the Frozen Maw. That cave has additional targets and is ideal if you want to hunt more Sons of Svanir.

HALVAUNT WAYPOINT (WEST OF CENTER)

SERVICES:	Waypoint, Scout
TRAVEL:	Crossroads (N), Twinspur Haven (S)
HARVESTING INFO:	Aspen Saplings (All Over), Copper Ore

Halvaunt Waypoint is west of the road as you head farther north. It's close to the Crossroads, but you still want to get this waypoint as soon as possible. The Crossroads are contested on an almost constant basis, so you can't jump up there a fair amount of the time. Having this waypoint lets you get close enough.

AID THE MINERS (Renown Task)

GOAL:	Kill dredge, destroy their machines, and free prisoners.
LEVEL:	11

Description: The mines southwest of Halvaunt Waypoint are infested with dredge. That happens a lot in this part of the world. You have to go in there and kill as many dredge as possible while destroying their equipment. Talk to Agivor outside and go into the mines with him; this triggers a repeatable event that nets you more experience for your time spent inside. It's also a tiny bit safer because Agivor gets some of the dredges' attention. Attack the gun turrets as soon as you see them. They're the nastiest thing in the mine. With them down, the enemies won't be able to hit you and your buddies with area-of-effect attacks. In addition, the turrets are worth points toward your task. Look for small rooms locked behind gates. Destroy these gates to release prisoners and gain additional points.

HELP AGIVOR REWIRE THE DRILLING MACHINE (Repeatable)

GOAL: Escort Agivor so he can repair the drill.

LEVEL: 11

Description: Agivor is with the miners outside of this area. He'll have a quest marker over his head, so you know he's important. Talk to him and start the event when you're ready to go into the mines. Agivor rushes forward without much regard for his safety, so stay close to him and kill off anything that gets on his back. Don't pick any extra targets of your own (lest the two of you be overwhelmed). If Agivor falls, that's okay. It gives you time to rest after a big fight. Revive him when you're back at full health.

Take the big guy down into the depths of the mine and then around to the back. That's where he finds the drilling machine he's looking for. Guard him while he repairs it; this triggers a few waves of dredge to attack, so be on your guard even if you cleared the area. Use the machine to break line of sight if you want to pull the dredge toward your character; this helps for hitting them with area-of-effect attacks.

Once the machine has been repaired, Agivor activates it and frees a whole slew of miners. This ends the event and triggers the next stage of it.

DEFEND MINERS AND GRAB ORE (Repeatable)

GOAL: Collect ore and bring it to Agivor.

LEVEL: 11

Description: Chunks of ore are hidden in the back room, where the miners were held. Get a few pieces of ore from there, and then escort the newly freed miners. They'll knock additional pieces of ore from the walls (as long as you keep at least one of them alive). They are revivable, so that makes things a little easier. Get roughly 10 pieces of ore for Agivor and then turn them in. Agivor gives you your reward and heads out of the mine.

CROSSROADS HAVEN WAYPOINT (NORTHWEST OF CENTER)

SERVICES:	Waypoint, Equipment Repair
TRAVEL:	Endenvar (S), Twinspur Haven (S), Lostvyrm Cave Waypoint (E), Dawnrise Waypoint (NW)
HARVESTING INFO:	Aspen Saplings

Crossroads Haven is a fortress along the northern road of the zone. It's where the north-south and east-west roads meet, thus giving the location its name. Sadly, the fortress is attacked on almost a constant basis. Unless players are actively holding the area, the waypoint is likely to be contested when you want to get there. Use Halvaunt Waypoint instead, if that happens.

HELP THE LIONGUARD AT CROSSROADS HAVEN (Renown Task)

GOAL: Kill Sons of Svanir and revive fallen defenders.

LEVEL: 13

Description: Whether the fortress is under attack or being held, you get credit for slicing apart the Sons of Svanir. They're a common sight around (and sometimes inside) the city. When you see defenders fall, revive them for extra credit.

DEFEAT TAF THE TERRIBLE AND RECAPTURE THE CROSSROADS (Repeatable)

GOAL: Kill Taf and hold the castle until it returns to norn control.

LEVEL: 13

Description: Taf is the leader of the enemy assault force. You can find him on the upper walkways inside Crossroads Haven (after the fortress has fallen). Kill him before trying to seize the lower ground. Once Taf is slain, come into Crossroads Haven from the southern side and push slowly through the courtyard; don't come down Taf's stairs and tick off all of the enemies at once. It's better to be slow and methodical (otherwise you're likely to get killed). Slay all of the enemies and wait for the fortress to convert back to norn control.

PROTECT GINNA STONESKAALD (Repeatable)

GOAL: Help Ginna restore the shrine near Crossroads Haven.

LEVEL: 12

Description: The shrine referenced here is southeast of Crossroads Haven. It's on a hill that can be seen from the southern gates of the town. Go out there and revive Ginna if she has fallen to the Sons of Svanir. Afterward, stay and protect her from assaults while she repairs the shrine. It takes only a couple of minutes. The enemies come in small groups, so they aren't a huge threat. If Ginna falls, she can be revived to continue her work.

LOSTVYRM CAVE WAYPOINT (NORTH OF CENTER)

SERVICES:	Waypoint, Skill Challenge (SE)
TRAVEL:	Crossroads Haven (W), Krennak's Homestead Waypoint (SE), Dolyak Pass Waypoint (NE)
HARVESTING INFO:	Minimal

Lostvyrm Cave Waypoint is at the top of the frozen lake, on the eastern end of the map. A nearby cave has a Skill Point challenge and a task, so this place is a must-see location even though it's in the middle of nowhere and doesn't have a road of its own.

HELP LODGE KEEPER KEVACH (Renown Task)

GOAL: Kill wurms, wake up norn, and outdrink any of the norn that are left standing.

LEVEL: 12

Description: Before going too far into this task, look for the cave southeast of the waypoint. Go inside and walk slowly as you descend. There are wurms in there, and they don't always pop up until they've noticed you. It's easy to collect several of them without knowing it until they all jump you. Fight them as they come to avoid being mobbed, and then go to the bottom of the cave. That's where you find a brewer who gives you a Skill Challenge. Drink up to learn more about yourself.

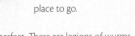

Kevach's Homestead is to the east. You don't need to go there, but the people inside have a number of stories to share. If you'd like to learn more about the area and its people, that's a good place to go.

For finishing the task, the upper part of the lake is perfect. There are legions of wurms to fight. You'll be done in moments.

HELP OSBORN FIGHT A GIANT WURM (Repeatable)

GOAL: Kill a veteran wurm with Osborn.

LEVEL: 12

Description: Osborn gets up some serious courage and goes out on the ice to fight a large wurm. You'll find him west of Kevach's Homestead. Join in to help defeat the mighty beast. Ranged weapons are superior due to the Knockback that wurms use as a protective measure. If you only have melee attacks, don't try prolonged weapon skills. Hit the wurms with short, simple strikes. Winning this fight triggers another event, to gather wurm eggs.

GATHER WURM EGGS FOR CHEF ALDIS (Repeatable)

GOAL: Go into Lostvyrm Cave and gather wurm eggs.

LEVEL: 12

Description: Chef Aldis approaches Lostvyrm Cave and asks adventurers to go inside. There are ice wurm eggs that spawn on the ground, and they're quick to steal. You don't even need to fight the wurms that spawn. Run through while picking up the eggs, or sick a pet on the wurms to distract them. Either way, you can finish the event without a single fight.

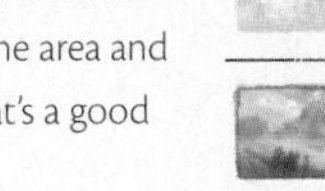

DEFEND THE LODGE FROM ICE WURMS (Repeatable)

GOAL:	Protect the doors from an ice wurm assault.
LEVEL:	12

Description: If you bring the ice wurm eggs back to Chef Aldis, she'll take them up to the lodge. Follow her and wait for ice wurms to follow. Make sure you're outside before the fighting starts; otherwise, you can't participate in the event—you get locked in! Keep the wurms off of the doors and use area-of-effect attacks to bring them down quickly.

DOLYAK PASS WAYPOINT (NORTHEAST SIDE)

SERVICES:	Waypoint
TRAVEL:	Entrance to Diessa Plateau (Level 15-25 Charr Region)(E), Crossroads Haven (W), Lostvyrm Cave Waypoint (SW), Solitude Waypoint (N)
HARVESTING INFO:	Copper Ore (Nearby)

Dolyak Pass is near the northeastern corner of the Wayfarer Foothills. It's by the junction between this region and Diessa Plateau, where the charr hold more sway. If you'd like a major change of scenery for your next adventuring region, that's a good place to go. The climate is warmer, and both the land and enemies are quite different.

ESCORT TALON KILLPEACE TO CROSSROADS HAVEN (Repeatable)

GOAL:	Help Talon get his caravan down the western road.
LEVEL:	13

Description: Talon Killpeace runs a caravan between Diessa Plateau and Crossroads Haven. If you escort him along the western road, you'll get a moderate amount of experience for your efforts. This isn't an especially fast event, so impatient adventurers may want to skip it.

SOLITUDE WAYPOINT (NORTHEAST SIDE)

SERVICES:	Waypoint, Skill Challenge (E)
TRAVEL:	Entrance to Frostgorge Sound (Level 70-80 Norn Region) (N), Dolyak Pass Waypoint (S)
HARVESTING INFO:	Copper (Along the Edge of the Mountains)

Solitude Waypoint is even farther north than Dolyak Pass. There isn't much up there except for Copper, wild beasts, and a transition to Frostgorge Sound. If you've been leveling here in the Wayfarer Foothills, don't go through that entrance. Frostgorge is way over your level, and there isn't anything to do there until your hero has become much more powerful. It's better to get this waypoint and then leave it alone for quite some time.

If you'd like another Skill Point, look along the eastern mountain wall. A small valley leads into Warmspring Grotto. Cave spiders are all over that place, but they don't attack in large groups (especially if you use spells or ranged attacks to get their attention). Switch to healing abilities that cleanse status effects, if possible. Spiders love their Poison.

There are veteran cave spiders on the upper tiers of the cave. Avoid them by jumping up the right side of the cave. Hop all the way to the top and then commune with the spring there to earn your Skill Point.

DAWNRISE WAYPOINT (NORTHWEST SIDE)

SERVICES:	N/A
TRAVEL:	Entrance to Snowden Drifts (Level 15-25 Norn Region) (W), Crossroads Haven (SE)
HARVESTING INFO:	Copper Ore (Best Location in the Zone) (S)

Dawnrise Waypoint is at the end of the road in the northwestern corner of the map. This is where you go to continue adventuring in the norn lands past level 15 or so. This is also a great waypoint for metal harvesters. The Copper Ore is better than anywhere else in the zone. There are veins of it bursting out of the ground in all directions.

ASSAULT ON SVANIR'S DOME (WORLD EVENT)

SERVICES:	N/A
TRAVEL:	Crossroads Haven (S), Dolyak Pass (E), Lostvyrm Cave (SE)
HARVESTING INFO:	Copper Ore

There isn't a particularly good waypoint for the events at Svanir's Dome, so you have to leg it there from one of the northern waypoints. This place is tough because there are cold winds, few allies, and a horde of Sons of Svanir. Expect fierce resistance if you try to quell their rebellion.

CHALLENGE THE MINIONS OF JORMAG (Renown Task)

GOAL:	Destroy the Sons of Svanir and any signs of corruption in their area.
LEVEL:	15

Description: Kill icebrood elementals, icebrood wolves, and Sons of Svanir along the southern edge of the dome. That's the easiest way to complete the task. Take out dragon banners whenever you see them; they give you a huge boost.

TAKE OUT THE TOWERS (Part of World Event)

GOAL:	Destroy the east and west towers.
LEVEL:	15

Description: Norn attack the Sons of Svanir towers periodically. Help them take down these towers by killing enemies and destroying banners in the area. You have help from NPCs, though your enemies come in considerable numbers, so don't let your guard down.

A veteran appears at the western tower. He can be soloed by a skilled hero, but having buddies around to help isn't a bad thing. Some of the events that follow are extremely challenging, so you might as well call in friends for the whole run!

CAPTURE THE DOME (Part of World Event)

GOAL:	Capture the center of the encampment.
LEVEL:	15

Description: After the towers are down, make your way to the center of the Sons of Svanir camp. Large groups of Sons of Svanir guard the camp, and they get multiple waves of reinforcements. Fight with area-of-effect weapons and skills to make your life easier, and flee if the battle gets too intense. This is a wonderful place to rack up high kill counts, if you're working on various achievements.

KILL THE MARAUDER (Part of World Event)

GOAL:	Slaughter the champion marauder.
LEVEL:	15

Description: Almost immediately after you seize the center of the camp, a massive marauder bursts from the ice and attacks your party. Fight back to continue the assault! Use your best skills for burst damage, healing, and single-target attacks.

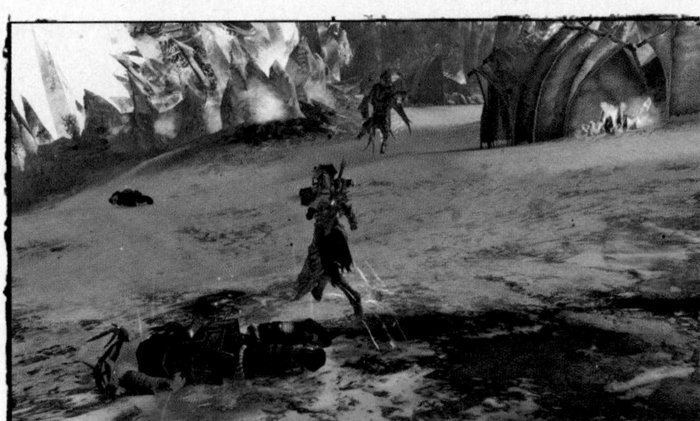

SNOWDEN DRIFTS

LEVEL RANGE:	15-25
TASKS:	13
WAYPOINTS:	18
SKILL CHALLENGES:	6
HARVESTING INFO:	Copper Ore, Iron Ore, Silver Ore, Gummo Saplings (Soft Wood Logs), Aspen Saplings (Green Wood Logs), Strawberries, Early Cooking Ingredients

SKILL CHALLENGES

- Devotee of Owl (Southeast of Owl Waypoint) (SE)
- Stinging Wind (North of Lost Child's Sorrow Waypoint) (NE)
- Rum from Corvin the Skaald (North of Isenfall Waypoint) (N)
- Grawl Totem (South of Skradden Waypoint) (SW)
- Razorwing's Nest (North of Seraph Outriders' Waypoint) (W)
- Raven Shaman's Power Source (Northeast of Scholar's Cleft Waypoint, Inside an Imp Cave) (NW) (Bring Some Friends)

Snowden Drifts is the zone that's west from the Wayfarer Foothills. The path is located in the northwestern part of Wayfarer Foothills, and you arrive on the new zone's northeastern edge.

Snowden Drifts is cold, snowy, and mountainous. It's a good zone for miners, as you can find veins of ore throughout the area. The Sons of Svanir are still a big problem, as are dredge, minotaur, and quite a few wild beasts.

The zone's northern side has easier targets and lower-level events. We suggest doing these before you venture south to take on the more serious attractions. Still, if you're a bit over-leveled, are well equipped, or have a group, you can begin almost anywhere you like. Let's get hunting!

HIGHPASS HAVEN WAYPOINT (NORTHEAST SIDE)

SERVICES:	Waypoint, Equipment Repair, Karma Merchant, Food Merchant, Weaponsmith, Armorsmith, Scout
TRAVEL:	Snowhawk (SW)
HARVESTING INFO:	Aspen Saplings (abundant), Root Vegetables

Highpass is the first place you stop while coming into Snowden Drifts. It's a good town, and you'll probably come back here often. Sell goods, repair your equipment, and talk to the scout in town to find out more about the region. She directs you southwest.

If you haven't purchased a new weapon in quite some time, buy one at the local weaponsmith. The level-15 gear is good enough to keep you up to date if you haven't gotten anything awesome from the Trading Post or during your adventures.

Before you go too far from Highpass, walk north and look for a kodan warrior named Horn. The kodan are bear-men on the Shiverpeak Mountains; they're an impressive race, and you'll do well to court their favor.

ASSIST LIONGUARD HARAL (Renown Task)

GOAL: Remove dangers around the roads.

LEVEL: 15

Description: Kill enemies close to the roads and assist Lionguard forces in the area.

The road out of Highpass splits before too long. Take the southern route to meet Haral, a Lionguard who wants help. You get credit for his task by killing Sons of Svanir to the west or south. Look for hunter's traps on the ground, because you get credit for opening those, as well. If an icebrood wolf pops out of the trap, kill it for extra credit.

PUSH BACK THE CORRUPTION (Renown Task)

GOAL: Destroy sources of corruption around Blasted Haven.

LEVEL: 17

Description: Walk west along the upper road in Snowden Drifts to find this task. When you reach the proper area, start to kill icebrood elementals, icebrood wolves, and Sons of Svanir around Blasted Haven. You should also destroy formations of ice while you're exploring. This task is dangerous if you're alone and push too far, too fast. The mix of wandering enemies and ice formations with their own defenses makes this a little tricky. If you have trouble, stay on the hillside and avoid the main road—it's well defended. Pick off stragglers to get credit without as much risk.

HELP AN EBON VANGUARD CONVOY (Repeatable)

GOAL: Protect a convoy against the Sons of Svanir.

LEVEL: 15

Description: A convoy appears on the road out of Highpass from time to time. The guards who travel in this group aren't prepared to face the Sons of Svanir. They end up being overwhelmed by five waves of attackers. If you rush to defend the group, you can get credit for this event and score a huge number of points toward Lionguard Haral's task.

TRAPPER'S LABYRINTH (NORTHEAST SIDE)

SERVICES:	N/A
TRAVEL:	Entrance to Frostgorge Sound (Level 70-80 norn region)
HARVESTING INFO:	Copper Ore, Iron Ore

Trapper's Labyrinth is a massive cave complex that dominates the northern wall of Snowden Drifts. The entrance is west from Highpass. You fight wild beasts initially, but dozens of dredge lurk deeper in the tunnels. Be wary of going through a transition to a new zone; the gateway at the back of the labyrinth takes you to a place with very powerful enemies (Frostgorge Sound). You don't want to go there just yet.

This is a very good place to grab metal. Iron ore veins, including one that's usually a rich vein, are common sites in the caverns. For more efficient mining, enter the labyrinth via its western entrance, near the Lost Child's Sorrow Waypoint. This gets you into iron territory much faster.

LOST CHILD'S SORROW WAYPOINT (NORTHEAST SIDE)

SERVICES:	Waypoint, Salvage Merchant
TRAVEL:	Highpass Haven Waypoint (E), Njordstead (W)
HARVESTING INFO:	Gummo Saplings, Copper Ore, Iron Ore

Continuing west along the northern stretch, you find a waypoint with a few kodan. This is called Lost Child's Sorrow Waypoint. You can pop in to get metal from the caverns to the east. Alternatively, you can walk to the west and deal with the contested areas and their plethora of repeatable events.

NJORDSTEAD WAYPOINT (NORTH SIDE)

SERVICES:	Waypoint
TRAVEL:	Lost Child's Sorrow Waypoint (E)
HARVESTING INFO:	Gummo Saplings, Iron Ore, Silver Ore

If you stay on its northern side, the western road continues from Lost Child's Sorrow Waypoint and eventually leads you into Njordstead. Icebrood enemies frequently take over this area. You sometimes have to fight through them to retake the settlement.

HELP MALIK NJORDSON (Renown Task)

GOAL:	Kill the full range of icebrood enemies that litter this area.
LEVEL:	17

Description: Malik has more than enough problems. Icebrood elementals are around his stead, and the icebrood wolves up there aren't friendly, either. Kill these targets on sight to help Malik. While you do this this, see if Njordstead needs clearing. If it doesn't, look to the west, where you can find normal wolves. Those count for Malik, as well. They're ideal if none of the repeatable tasks is running. The corrupted area southwest of town is also a good place to rack up points for the task.

DEFEND THE VILLAGERS OF NJORDSTEAD (Repeatable)

GOAL:	Fight off eight waves of attackers before the villagers are killed.
LEVEL:	17

Description: If you're around when Njordstead is attacked, rally to its defense. Eight waves of icebrood elementals and icebrood wolves are on the way. Keep the villagers at the center of town safe.

Don't worry too much about the ones on the periphery. They're likely to die, but you'd lose more by protecting them. It's safer to stay in the center and let the waves of enemies come to you. You get credit for the event as soon as the last wave falls. Hold your area-of-effect attacks until the enemies bunch up around the villagers; you can clear entire waves in mere seconds by doing this.

CLEAR THE ICEBROOD FROM NJORDSTEAD (Repeatable)

GOAL:	Kill 10 enemies in Njordstead and then eliminate the veteran leading them.
LEVEL:	17

Description: You can score fast experience every time this town is captured. To clear it out, you only have to kill 11 enemies: the 10 normal targets and the veteran with them. It's an incredibly fast event, especially if other people are around to help with the veteran. If not, kill targets around the edge of Njordstead until you have an open space for the veteran fight. Pull the veteran over, preferably to the southern side of town, where you can run if things get ugly.

DESTROY THE ICE CORES (Repeatable)

GOAL:	Blast all four of the corrupted ice cores.
LEVEL:	17

Description: The corrupted area we mentioned earlier is southwest of Njordstead. Occasionally, an event starts that tells you to destroy the large cores of ice down there. It doesn't take long to find them, and all of the shards are marked on your minimap. Go after the four corrupted ice cores and kill elementals while you're there. The ice cores don't have any of their own defenses, so kill any active enemies before you bother with them. If you want to be even more efficient, use area-of-effect attacks while you fight the elementals near the ice cores. You can damage the cores while you're killing things that would attack you anyway.

SODERHEM STEADING WAYPOINT (NORTH OF CENTER)

SERVICES:	Waypoint, Weaponsmith, Armorsmith, Karma Merchant
TRAVEL:	Lost Child's Sorrow Waypoint (NE), Njordstead (N), Torstvedt (S)
HARVESTING INFO:	Minimal

Soderhem is a small town on the region's northern side. This area doesn't have many merchants otherwise, and that gives Soderhem some utility. You can jump to the area, sell, and get back out in a flash. That is, unless enemies take over the town. That happens from time to time, and cleaning it out is a good way to accrue extra experience.

HELP AUDA (Renown Task)

GOAL:	Keep the roads clear.
LEVEL:	17

Description: While you're on the roads east of Soderhem, kill snow leopards, wolves, and any Sons of Svanir you see. All of them are targets of opportunity that Auda wants to eliminate. Talk to Auda—the person marked with this task—to start a secondary event that helps you find the target. Doing so initiates "Escort Wise Keeper."

ESCORT THE WISE KEEPER TO BLASTED HAVEN (Repeatable)

GOAL:	Take the Wise Keeper from Njordstead to Blasted Haven.
LEVEL:	17

Description: Talk to Auda to start this escort. Then hurry to Njordstead to meet the Wise Keeper and his small group of followers. This party walks east toward Blasted Haven and must endure attacks by wolves and Sons of Svanir. Each enemy wave has several members, so area-of-effect attacks are essential for clearing their ranks quickly. Try to defend the bodyguards as much as you defend the Wise Keeper. Though you don't fail the event if they fall, the extra firepower is useful against nastier attacks later.

CLEAR THE SOUTH

If you continue west after you complete the events around here, the enemies start to get tougher. You're better off turning south and completing the lower areas before you progress to the western side of Snowden Drifts.

SNOWHAWK LANDING WAYPOINT (EAST OF CENTER)

SERVICES:	Waypoint, Equipment Repairs, Armorsmith, Weaponsmith, Scout
TRAVEL:	Highpass (NE), Owl Lodge (SE), Jotun's Vista (SW)
HARVESTING INFO:	Iron Ore, Silver Ore

Snowhawk Landing is a town in the middle of the map. You bump into this trading center while you patrol the roads southwest from Highpass. Take care of any chores and then move on. There isn't much to do here. If you're looking for work, continue southwest along the roads.

ASSIST LIONGUARD NADEL (Renown Task)

GOAL:	Make Jotun's Vista safer for travelers.
LEVEL:	18

Description: Nadel is a Lionguard on the road west from Snowhawk Landing. She needs help clearing the roads. To do this for her, light detour markers along the road's southern branch. The markers are just beside the road, and they can be hard to see if you aren't looking for them. Nearby, you find both wolves and jotun. Kill them to make Nadel even happier. Stay on the roads; you can't get credit for kills you make out in the northern hills.

TORSTVEDT HOMESTEAD WAYPOINT (EAST OF CENTER)

SERVICES:	Waypoint
TRAVEL:	Valslake Waypoint (SW), Snowhawk Waypoint (E)
HARVESTING INFO:	Gummo Saplings, Herb Patches

Torstvedt Homestead Waypoint is west of Snowhawk Landing. Look for it after you clear Nadel's task and kill plenty of jotun in the area. The waypoint is up in the hills to the north of the main road. This isn't a major resting point because there aren't services up here. You can continue west or turn north to find several more events.

REAVER'S WAYPOINT (SOUTHEAST SIDE)

SERVICES:	Waypoint, Scout, Karma Merchant
TRAVEL:	Owl Lodge (SE), Snowhawk (N), Griffonfall (SW)
HARVESTING INFO:	Gummo Saplings, Root Vegetables

Reaver's Waypoint is in the middle of nowhere, but it's a useful jumping point between areas. Look for it while you travel south from the Villmark Foothills. There isn't a road, so you have to go overland, unless you're coming from the west instead.

Continue toward Owl Lodge in the south if you're looking for events.

OWL WAYPOINT (SOUTHEAST SIDE)

SERVICES:	Waypoint, Skill Challenge (S)
TRAVEL:	Highpass (N), Reaver's Waypoint (NW)
HARVESTING INFO:	Gummo Saplings (abundant), Root Vegetables

Owl Lodge is in the southeastern part of the zone. Go there for a fun race of repeatable events and fighting with the Sons of Svanir. Don't even worry about the task in the area; there are so many events that the task pretty much completes itself while you do the events.

Fox Shaman Reva is outside Owl Lodge, on the western slope of a hill. Talk to him and complete a quick Skill Challenge to earn a Skill Point!

HELP OWL'S FOLLOWERS (Renown Task)

GOAL:	Help Lahri by killing Sons of Svanir and protecting the followers of Owl.
LEVEL:	17

Description: Sons of Svanir are all over the zone's southeastern side. They've taken over Owl Lodge, and you can help your people by killing these creeps. The repeatable events in the area are worth a huge bonus toward your task. Even random Sons of Svanir are worth enough to help you finish the task without any trouble.

PROTECT THE OWL SHAMAN (Repeatable)

GOAL:	Defend Shaman Ulgadis while she purifies the sacred owls of the area.
LEVEL:	17

Description: Shaman Ulgadis occasionally appears and tries to help the area's owls. You can see Ulgadis on your map because she has a shield icon over her head. Go to her and agree to escort the shaman while she runs around the area and purifies the owls. Kill any Sons of Svanir who get too close, and you'll be in good shape. The event takes a few minutes to finish, but it leads to additional events, so that's nifty!

HELP THE SHAMAN BANISH THE DRAGON TOTEM (Repeatable)

GOAL:	Escort Shaman Ulgadis to the Dragon Totem.
LEVEL:	18

Description: After purifying the sacred owls, Ulgadis wants to rid the area of corruption on a long-term basis. Escort her to the totem in front of Owl Lodge. Help her kill a veteran there, fight off a few more Sons of Svanir, and then destroy the Dragon Totem itself. You get credit immediately upon the shrine's destruction, but escort Ulgadis back to her camp if you'd like a free blessing from her!

KILL THE HUNTERS (Elite)

GOAL:	Kill the Sons of Svanir hunters before they kill the sacred owls in the area.
LEVEL:	17

Description: When this event is triggered, a veteran Son of Svanir starts hunting owls in the area around Owl Lodge. Look for your target on the map, go to him, and kill the creep. He often has allies nearby, so clear space for the fight ahead of time. Take out targets behind the veteran and then pull him back to your safe spot. Once he's gone, you get credit for the event.

GRIFFONFALL (SOUTHEAST SIDE)

SERVICES:	N/A
TRAVEL:	Owl Lodge (E)
HARVESTING INFO:	Strawberries (everywhere!), Gummo Saplings

Griffonfall is a wonderful place to hunt griffons or harvest strawberries for cooking. There isn't much else to do there, so it's quite skippable if you don't care about either of these attractions.

EXILE WAYPOINT (SOUTH SIDE)

SERVICES:	Waypoint, Salvage Merchant, Equipment Repairs, Class Trainers
TRAVEL:	Valslake Waypoint (N), Reaver's Waypoint (E)
HARVESTING INFO:	Minimal

Enthusiasts of kodan history and lore will be overjoyed with the events near Exile Waypoint. This is where the kodan have set up a small city for their people. They came down from the north to gain allies against the tyranny of Jormag! That makes them friends in pretty much every way.

HELP DECIDE THE FATE OF THE KODAN (Meta)

GOAL:	Assist the kodan in choosing a new leader.
LEVEL:	19

Description: A mysterious creature appeared out of thin air and assassinated the previous leader of these kodan. They're now in the process of choosing the next Claw.

DEFEND SILENT SNOWFALL (Part of the Meta Event)

GOAL:	Defend Silent Snowfall before the tournament.
LEVEL:	19

Description: Silent Snowfall will be attacked before the tournament begins. As soon as this event starts, hurry to her position. She's northeast of the main town, and it isn't long before she's overcome.

DEFEAT ICE RAKING (Part of the Meta Event)

GOAL:	Teach Ice Raking a lesson about failure.
LEVEL:	19

Description: Ice Raking is a powerful kodan warrior. He's never known defeat, and that is what worries him. He knows that a good leader must understand consequences. Battle Ice Raking so he can learn about failure and defeat. Afterward, escort him to the arena north of town and start the next part of the meta event.

WITNESS THE CEREMONY AND DEFEAT AN ASSASSIN (Part of the Meta Event)

GOAL:	Watch the Claw's battles and then defeat the new Claw.
LEVEL:	19

Description: A trial by combat determines the next Claw. Watch as this event proceeds, and then stick around afterward. The new leader will have some serious trouble. A largos assassin attacks, and you have to kill him before the Claw falls. Having a few friends (or even just one) makes a huge difference, because the fight is over so quickly. You have to deliver major damage to kill the assassin in time.

VALSLAKE WAYPOINT (SOUTH SIDE)

SERVICES:	Waypoint
TRAVEL:	Exile Waypoint (E)
HARVESTING INFO:	Iron and Silver Ore (abundant), Herb Patches

The Waypoint for Valslake is on the lake's western side. This is a major location for anyone interested in mining. A nearby dredge cave has a rich source of iron, and the hills around the lake are similarly wonderful. Be careful of the veteran at the back of the dredge cave. He's beatable, but take him seriously.

MOVING WEST

Now that you've hit the southern side of Snowden Drifts, turn your attention to the western side of the map. The hardest events are over there.

ISENFALL WAYPOINT (NORTH SIDE)

SERVICES:	Waypoint, Salvage Merchant, Skill Challenge, Scout
TRAVEL:	Njordstead (E)
HARVESTING INFO:	Iron Ore (W), Gummo Saplings, Root Vegetables

Isenfall Waypoint is up on the northern side of Snowden Drifts. It's above Isenfall Lake, and you should seek out this place as soon as you come west from Njordstead or up from Snowdrift. The walk takes a couple minutes, so you'll be happy to have a Waypoint in this part of the map.

Talk to a shaman inside the small settlement and answer his riddle to get through a Skill Challenge. We won't spoil the riddle for you, and don't worry—it's not hard if you keep your wits about you.

Before you head out, talk to a scout in the southeast. He'll show you more of the area.

CLEAR THE URCHINS (Repeatable)

GOAL:	Destroy nine poisonous urchins.
LEVEL:	21

Description: Swim down into Isenfall Lake and look for the urchins. They belch poison if you get too close, so it isn't hard to find them. Destroy these from maximum range and keep moving as you hit them. Their poison is vicious. If you're taken down, swim to the top of the lake as quickly as possible. You can escape their range and recover without dying. Destroy nine of the urchins to get credit and finish the event.

AID THE DURMAND PRIORY AGAINST THE CENTAURS (Renown Task)

GOAL:	Kill centaurs and recover priory items.
LEVEL:	23

Description: The centaurs have taken over an area of gullies west of Durgar. Every target is worth points toward your task. You can also destroy supplies and pick up artifacts while you move through the camp. Be careful! Centaurs are a massive pain to fight. Their mobility, high damage, and potential for large encounters pose a threat to solo adventurers. Avoid areas where a fight may draw four or more enemies, because even victory might not be enough as patrolling centaurs have a chance to hit you from behind.

FROZEN SWEEPS WAYPOINT (WEST SIDE)

SERVICES:	Waypoint, Scout
TRAVEL:	Isenfall Waypoint (NE), Snowdrift Waypoint (E)
HARVESTING INFO:	Iron Ore

The southern road eventually gets you to this waypoint. It's near a few important tasks (to your north), so make Frozen Sweeps a staging ground. Talk to the scout beside the waypoint to learn more about the zone's southwestern portion.

FIGHT THE DENIZENS OF JORMABAKKE STEAD (Renown Task)

GOAL:	Kill the corrupted enemies near the stead.
LEVEL:	24

Description: Icebrood elementals and wolves litter the area south from the gullies. Infiltrate that area, kill any enemies you find, and destroy dragon banners. Then continue up toward the main part of Jormabakke Stead (farther south). Kill the Sons of Svanir at their base and show the traitors how weak they really are.

SERAPH OUTRIDERS' WAYPOINT (WEST SIDE)

SERVICES:	Waypoint
TRAVEL:	Frozen Sweeps Waypoint (E), Skradden Waypoint (S), Scholar's Cleft Waypoint (N)
HARVESTING INFO:	Iron Ore, Silver Ore

This area is on the western side of the map. It's a hilly area known for its fierce enemies. The centaurs and Sons of Svanir are quite close to the waypoint, and they're targets for your task in this area. As far as friendly faces go, ranchers eke out a living to the northwest of the waypoint, and seraph guards hold the waypoint itself.

HELP THE SERAPH OUTRIDERS (Renown Task)

GOAL:	Fight back the Sons of Svanir and the centaurs.
LEVEL:	24

Description: The seraph camp here has seen better times. They're under constant assault by the centaurs. They can't pursue their attacks on the Sons of Svanir with half their people lying on the field. Revive fallen soldiers while you kill their attackers. The small road north sees constant action, but you can kill Sons of Svanir to the south while you break their dragon banners. Either route gets the job done.

SCHOLAR'S CLEFT WAYPOINT (NORTHWEST SIDE)

SERVICES:	Waypoint, Salvage Merchant, Skill Challenge (NE)
TRAVEL:	Seraph Outriders' Waypoint (S), Isenfall Waypoint (E)
HARVESTING INFO:	Minimal

Scholar's Cleft Waypoint is tucked into the region's northwestern corner. It's a place where Durmand Priory scholars come to study and contemplate the world. There are centaur problems in the area, but attacks up there are usually light.

For a skill point, search along the eastern line of hills and look for a cave that's filled with imps. Kill the ones inside and jump up the pillars of stone on the cave's left wall. A ledge above takes you deeper into the area. A place of power is back there, but a powerful villain guards it. You have to face two tough norn and a flock of summoned birds. Area-of-effect attacks and damage mitigation are essential. A group to help you is also a worthy consideration.

SNOWDRIFT WAYPOINT (WEST OF CENTER)

SERVICES:	Waypoint, Equipment Repairs, Armorsmith, Weaponsmith, Salvage Merchant
TRAVEL:	Valslake Waypoint (SE), Frozen Sweeps Waypoint (W)
HARVESTING INFO:	Iron Ore, Silver Ore, Gummo Saplings, Root Vegetables

Snowdrift Waypoint is in almost the dead middle of the map. It's a fortified location with all of the amenities. Take the southern road west to get there. You can branch off afterward to explore the zone's northern or southern sides.

LORNAR'S WAYPOINT (SOUTH SIDE)

SERVICES:	Waypoint
TRAVEL:	Route to Lornar's Pass (Level 30-40 norn region) (S), Snowdrift Waypoint (N)
HARVESTING INFO:	Iron Ore, Silver Ore, Gummo Saplings

The road south from Snowdrift Waypoint gets you down to this area. It's near the transition to Lornar's Pass, a slightly higher-level area that's worth seeking when you get close to level 30. Two tasks are directly west from this waypoint, so you have plenty to do down there even if you're staying in Snowden Drifts.

PROVE YOUR MIGHT (Renown Task)

GOAL:	Kill aggressive enemies and help hunters to impress the norn of Mennerheim.
LEVEL:	24

Description: Look for animals while you walk west from Lornar's Waypoint. Revive any fallen hunters while you do this. Arctodus are your best prey, but even moose count toward the task. Try to finish the entire event before you go all the way west to the next town. You can't find any targets either north or west of Mennerheim, so it's better to finish by the time you arrive.

DONATE SOME MEAT

If you're almost finished but are tired of hunting, donate any meat you found recently to the chef in Mennerheim. He appreciates your help, and that might finish the task without having to turn around and wait for new targets.

DISRUPT THE DREDGE IN MOLENGRAD (Renown Task)

GOAL:	Fight dredge and destroy their machines in and around Molengrad.
LEVEL:	23

Description: Molengrad is west of Mennerheim. You can walk over there and kill dredge to complete the task immediately, but there's a better way. If you're patient, you can kill two birds with one stone. Go northwest to Podaga Steading Waypoint. Doing the repeatable events there lets you siege Molengrad as well, and then you can get even more experience.

PODAGA STEADING WAYPOINT (SOUTHWEST SIDE)

SERVICES:	Waypoint, Merchant, Weaponsmith, Armorsmith, Skill Challenge (SW)
TRAVEL:	Lornar's Waypoint (E), Skradden Waypoint (W)
HARVESTING INFO:	Iron Ore, Silver Ore

Dredge attack the town of Podaga Steading quite often. Having Molengrad on your border doesn't facilitate a peaceful life! When the dredge invade, an event to retake the town commences. Afterward, the events chain so that you push into Molengrad to destroy the tunnels. Use Podaga to race through these events as you go through the region.

To get the Skill Challenge in this area, walk west out of town and hug the southern mountains. Find a cave of grawl out there that isn't easy to see until you're on top of it. This is called Glisterice Caves. Kill the grawl inside while you look for a wooden walkway that leads upward. The Skill Challenge is above the small camp.

DESTROY THE DREDGE TUNNELER (Repeatable)

GOAL:	Take out the dredge tunneler before it breaks through into the area near Podaga Steading.
LEVEL:	24

Description: The dredge don't always have a northern tunnel that leads into Podaga Steading. They have to break through the rock to get there, and they use a mighty tunneler to achieve this end. Go into Molengrad through the mines' eastern entrance.

DRIVE THE DREDGE FROM PODAGA STEADING (Repeatable)

GOAL:	Kill dredge in this area.
LEVEL:	24

Description: Dredge morale plummets once you walk west and start attacking their people at Podaga Steading. Though it's risky, a mobile offense is much faster. Avoid the turrets and kill only the dredge to finish the event sooner. The town's northern side is a little easier because it has more dredge and fewer turrets. Be extra careful if you see ant foes in mining suits; they have considerable health and take quite a while to kill. Once you reduce the dredge's morale to 0%, the event ends and the next one starts.

DESTROY MOLENGRAD'S CEILING SUPPORTS (Repeatable)

GOAL:	Bring down four ceiling supports.
LEVEL:	24

Description: The tunnel into Molengrad isn't far from Podaga Steading. Walk down there while the dredge flee from their recent defeat. Follow the northern tunnel and kill the dredge guarding it. Area-of-effect attacks are extremely useful because the dredge are numerous there. Try to hide along the cavern walls to avoid turret fire that originates further down. When you're clear, take out all four of the marked supports and watch the tunnel collapse.

PROTECT THE PEOPLE OF PODAGA STEADING (Repeatable)

GOAL:	Drive off the dredge attackers.
LEVEL:	24

Description: Minutes after a victory in the dredge tunnels, the molemen mount an assault on Podaga. They'll win if you don't intervene. Watch out for rising turrets and a veteran in a mining suit. These are the big targets, and you must take them down. The only problem is that it's easy to get overwhelmed if you stand in the center of the street and face everything at once. Groups can handle that, but solo characters should take to the town's higher sides and pull targets up to their positions. Help any villagers being overrun, and do your best. Failure starts the event chain over from the beginning. Success staves off the dredge for several more minutes—and then they attack the town once more.

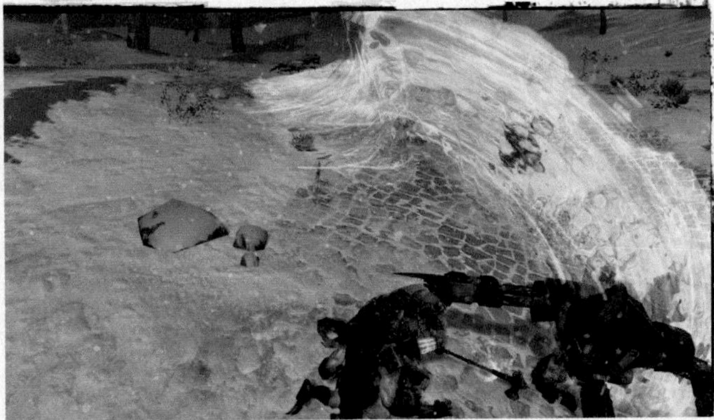

SKRADDEN WAYPOINT (SOUTHWEST SIDE)

SERVICES:	Waypoint
TRAVEL:	Exit to Gendarran Fields (Level 25-35 human region) (W)
HARVESTING INFO:	Gummo Saplings (N), Herb Patches (N)

Skradden Waypoint is on the map's southwestern side. It's near the exit to a new zone. Travel here if you're reaching the end of your time in Snowden and don't have your next destination planned in advance.

LORNAR'S PASS

LEVEL RANGE:	25-40
TASKS:	15
WAYPOINTS:	16
SKILL CHALLENGES:	9
HARVESTING INFO:	Iron Ore, Silver Ore, Gold Ore

SKILL CHALLENGES

- Dwarven Relic (East of Thunderhorns Waypoint, Inside the Dredge Cave) (NE)
- Heart of the Priory (North of Durmand Priory Waypoint, Inside the Priory) (W)
- Steam Portal (Southwest of Lamentation Waypoint, In a Narrow Pass) (E)
- Grenth's Door (South of Lamentation Waypoint, In Reaper's Gate) (E)
- Peg Leg (East of False Lake Waypoint, Underwater) (W)
- Frozen Portal (Southeast of Thunderhorn's Waypoint)
- Mysterious Meat (North of Durmand Priory, inside the grawl/fleshreaver cave system)
- Lionguard Mette (South of Stonescatter Waypoint, north of False Lake Waypoint)
- Skillet (East of Nentor Waypoint, inside the skritt cave)

Lornar's Pass is to the west of Hoelbrak. You reach it by walking through Snowden Drifts and then down past Lornar's Waypoint. Come here in your late 20s or early 30s and look for more fun fighting the dredge. They're a major threat in this area.

MAYBE JUST ONE MORE!

Lornar's Pass is a region with higher levels than the rest of the ones we've written up for this guide. For people who still want a bit of guidance before they get to their elite skills, this is a final place you can go and get some experience while we show you the ropes.

NORTH SIDE

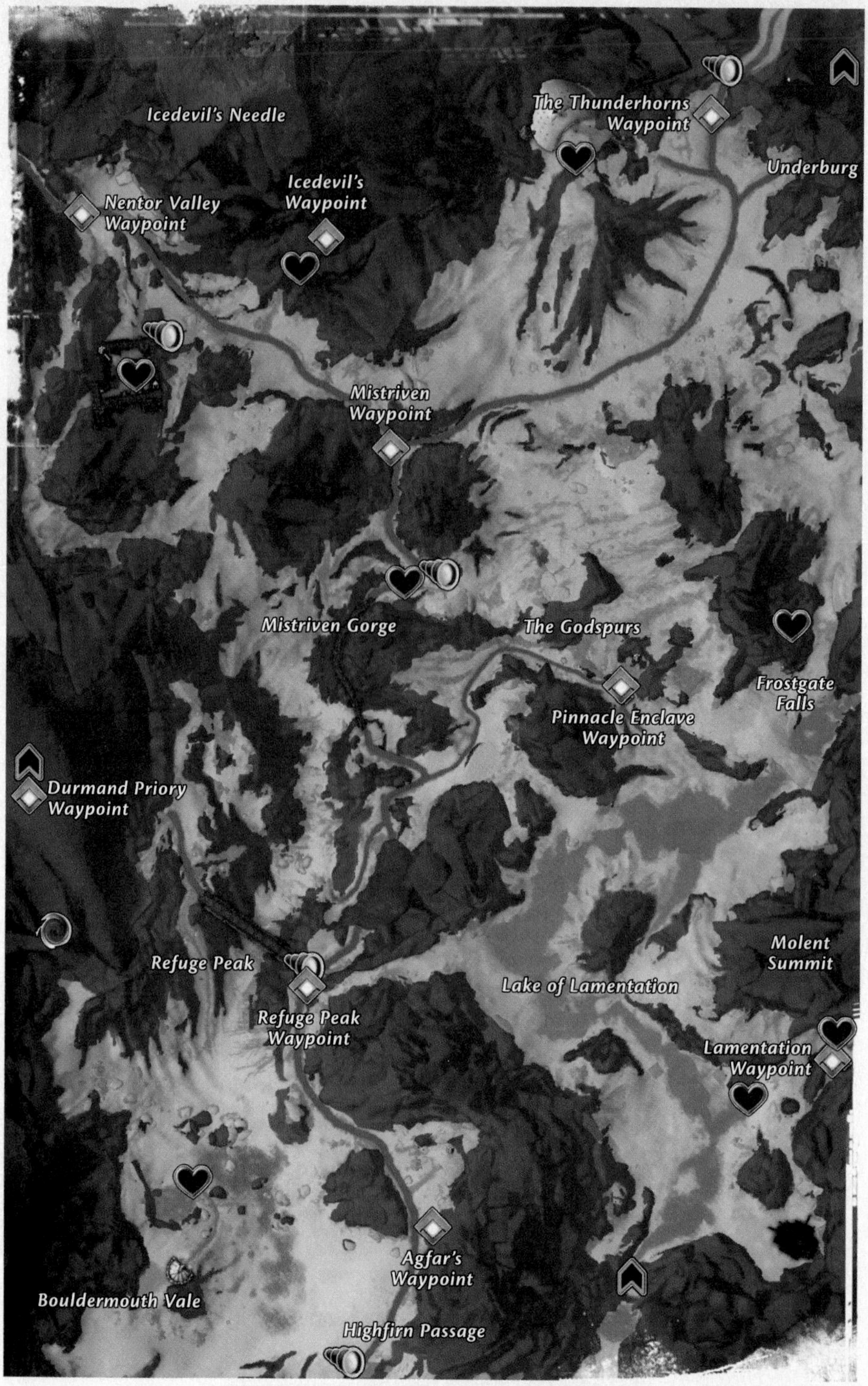

THUNDERHORNS WAYPOINT (NORTHEAST SIDE)

SERVICES:	Waypoint, Food Merchant (W), Skill Challenge (W)
TRAVEL:	Entrance to Snowden Drifts (Level 15-25 Norn Region) (N)
HARVESTING INFO:	Minimal

Thunderhorns Waypoint is where most norn start their work in this region. It's a quiet waypoint near the Snowden Drifts entrance. There are dredge to the east and a friendly hall to the west. Get your bearings before picking a direction, and then set off when you're ready.

When you visit Korakatt's Hall (to the west), make sure to stop and talk to one of the residents. They'll tell you about dwarven history, and your character gains a Skill Point!

SOUTH SIDE

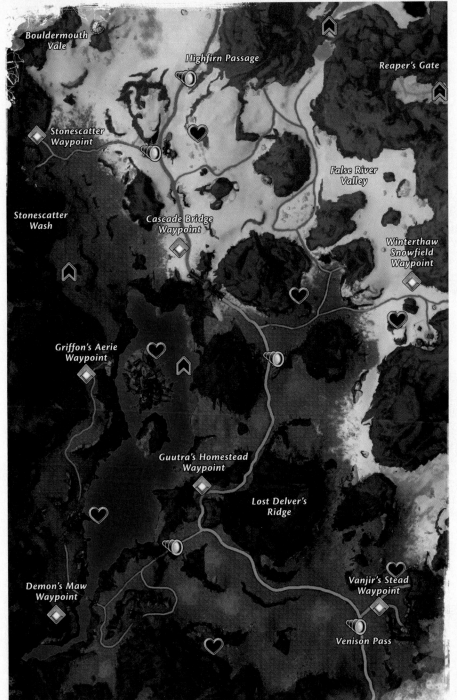

Bouldermouth Vale
Highfirn Passage
Reaper's Gate
Stonescatter Waypoint
False River Valley
Stonescatter Wash
Cascade Bridge Waypoint
Winterthaw Snowfield Waypoint
Griffon's Aerie Waypoint
Guutra's Homestead Waypoint
Lost Delver's Ridge
Vanjir's Stead Waypoint
Demon's Maw Waypoint
Venison Pass

HELP HUNE MANAGE THE LODGE

(Renown Task)

GOAL:	Help with Korakatt Hall activities.
LEVEL:	26

Description: Feed dolyaks, stomp dredge mounds, and calm rowdy patrons inside the hall. All of these help you complete this task. If you can't find enough things to do, kill any dredge that are close to the hall. Any time you're back at the main building, look for feed bags and give those to the dolyaks. It's fast and gets you quite a few points, and it makes the dolyaks happy!

DEFEND LORELA FROM THE DREDGE

(Repeatable)

GOAL:	Protect Lorela while she gathers 12 griffon eggs.
LEVEL:	26

Description: Lorela is a sous chef with a rough boss. She's been sent out to gather griffon eggs, regardless of the danger she faces. If you see her out by the Thunderhorns Waypoint, meet with her and escort the girl on her quest for proper ingredients. She'll go around to a dozen griffon nests, steal their eggs, and keep going until she can bring everything back to Korakatt Hall. Keep her protected and alive so you have assistance in all of the fights along the way: dredge pop out of the ground quite often, and griffons are par for the course. This is a slow event, but the fighting keeps it from lagging.

DRIVE OFF THE DREDGE AT KORAKATT HALL (Repeatable)

GOAL:	Reduce dredge morale and prevent them from doing any damage to Korakatt Hall.
LEVEL:	26

Description: A couple minutes after you return to the hall with Lorela, the dredge mount an assault on the place. They'll deploy a roadblock across the eastern bridge, and that's where the dredge start to appear. Attack them with the residents of the hall at your side. Destroy the roadblock as soon as possible to help curtail dredge morale, and then work on their stragglers until the event is done. This event helps with the local task, so it's quite useful. Beating this starts Lorela's event chain back at the beginning (after a few minutes).

UNDERBURG (NORTHEAST SIDE)

SERVICES:	N/A
TRAVEL:	N/A
HARVESTING INFO:	Minimal

If you're in the mood to hunt dredge, lay siege to Underburg and go to town. There are dozens of them there, and they'll die in droves if you're tough enough to take them on. Although there isn't as much metal to mine as you might like, the dredge here drop Iron Ore and metal scraps. If you can't mine it, kill for it!

MISTRIVEN WAYPOINT (NORTH OF CENTER)

SERVICES:	Waypoint
TRAVEL:	Thunderhorns Waypoint (NE), Pinnacle Enclave Waypoint (SE)
HARVESTING INFO:	Minimal

Take the road south from Thunderhorns Waypoint to reach this area. The way is reasonably safe, though there are some griffons and grawl close enough to hassle you if you're concerned about that type of thing. Once you unlock this waypoint, look north for a fast task before continuing along the road.

If you started Lornar's Pass from Nentor Waypoint, the road also brings you here (just from a different angle). Both paths converge and go into the southern section of the map.

NENTOR WAYPOINT (NORTHWEST SIDE)

SERVICES:	Waypoint
TRAVEL:	Exit to Gendarran Fields (Level 25-35 Human Region)
HARVESTING INFO:	Minimal

If you're coming in from human territory, Nentor Waypoint is where you'll begin. The waypoint is feet away from the transition between the two regions. A mining camp is to the south. You can climb the hillside or use the road to get there. Both have enemies, and they all count toward the local task.

HELP THE MINERS (Renown Task)

GOAL:	Assist the mining camp by organizing tools and killing local threats.
LEVEL:	27

Description: The mining camp is in the northwestern part of this map. There are bandits, raptors, trolls, and grawl all over the area (even on the road itself). Kill these enemies, destroy their roadblocks, and finish the event whenever you like. If you'd prefer a peaceful method to earn credit, go up to the mining camp and look for scrap and tools. Collect these and bring them to the top of the camp. Put the tools on a rack and leave the metal right next to that. Both give you fair credit, and there are a number of places to pick up these items within the camp. You won't have to do any fighting.

HELP KELGG (Renown Task)

GOAL:	Go into the infested mine and aid miners, kill bats and skritt, and close sink holes.
LEVEL:	28

Description: There's a small mine to the northeast of Nentor Waypoint. It's hard to see, so walk up to the cliffs and follow the sounds of bats. They infest the narrow passage that leads into the cave. Once you're inside, kill the bats and skritt while looking for miners to save.

PINNACLE ENCLAVE WAYPOINT (NORTHEAST OF CENTER)

SERVICES:	Waypoint
TRAVEL:	Thunderhorns Waypoint (N), Lamentation Waypoint (SE)
HARVESTING INFO:	Minimal

Pinnacle Enclave Waypoint is far to the south of Thunderhorns Waypoint. The road gets you there eventually if you take it all the way around (to the west and then south). If you're impatient, walk overland for a faster and somewhat more exciting trip!

Once there, look east for a fun task and some exploration.

HELP THE PRIORY FIGHT THE DREDGE (Renown Task)

GOAL:	Clear out the ruins and stop dredge encroachment.
LEVEL:	30

Description: The area between the Godspurs and Frostgate Falls is filled with dredge and wolves. Both need to be killed in droves to complete this task. If you see dredge equipment on the eastern side of the area, trash it for bonus points. A small cave to the west of the falls is home to many additional wolves. If you're hunting them for crafting materials, that's a great place to stop.

DURMAND PRIORY WAYPOINT (WEST SIDE)

SERVICES:	Waypoint, Equipment Repair, Skill Challenge
TRAVEL:	Pinnacle Enclave Waypoint (E), Rocklair Waypoint (S)
HARVESTING INFO:	Minimal

Durmand Priory is a massive landmark, and you should go there even if you don't need another Skill Point or a new waypoint. It's a beautiful building, high on the side of a mountain. If you're coming from Pinnacle Enclave Waypoint, stay on the road and take the bridge across the large chasm. This is a time saver. Otherwise, people on the floor of the valley have to go south of the priory and take the snowy road that leads up Refuge Peak.

The waypoint is inside the building, at the back of the temple. A Skill Challenge is nearby, so get that done before you leave the area.

Look south for a fast task with Herder Lyot, and then backtrack to Pinnacle Enclave Waypoint so you can clear the eastern side of the region.

HELP HERDER LYOT (Renown Task)

GOAL:	Maintain the dolyak ranch, feed dolyaks, and fight wurms nearby.
LEVEL:	33

Description: A dolyak ranch is down the mountain, south of Durmand Priory. Carefully descend the mountain and look for wurms to kill while you approach the ranch. Not only are there wurms above the ground, but there are also mounds to kick. Look for these, because they get you more credit than a normal wurm kill. Then, go to the ranch itself (near the task icon). Kill wurms inside the pen, revive any dead dolyaks, and then bring feed to the creatures. The feed is right outside of their pen, so it only takes a moment. That should finish the task for you! Keep going south afterward until you get to Rocklair Waypoint. That'll be much more convenient. Then come back to the priory later on.

LAMENTATION WAYPOINT (EAST SIDE)

SERVICES:	Waypoint, Skill Challenge (x2) (S)
TRAVEL:	Pinnacle Enclave Waypoint (NE)
HARVESTING INFO:	Minimal

Lamentation Waypoint is on the eastern side of the map. It's tucked into an area of crags and monsters. Griffons fly over the hills, and the lowlands are held by dredge and ice elementals. You don't have a road for safe passage to this new area, but at least it's revealed on your map from quite a distance away (so you know where you're going).

For a Skill Point, search the southern hills. Reaper's Gate is down there, with a villager who can help you learn new knowledge. For a second Skill Point, use the tunnel south to reach Grenth's Door. Kill the aatxes and shades to the east and commune by the statue of Grenth.

SLOW THE STEAM INVADERS (Renown Task)

GOAL:	Kill steam creatures, close portals, and gather specimen parts.
LEVEL:	32

Description: After getting Lamentation Waypoint, move west onto the lake that gives the area its name. There are important things to do on the Lake of Lamentation. Ice elementals, steam-driven monsters, and other various foes are all over the frozen lake. Kill them for points while looking for portals to close or specimens to pick up. The steam parts that spawn on the ground are dark; it's easy to see them against the light background of the snow and ice. You get points for picking up the parts, and then even more if you put them in the collection barrel next to Scholar Darkpaw (the task giver).

DESTROY THE STEAM CREATURES' PORTALS (Repeatable)

GOAL:	Destroy three steam portals.
LEVEL:	32

Description: Steam portals are summoned on the Lake of Lamentation. They won't always be up, but their appearance is fairly common. If you see them, go after the portals on the central part of the lake. They're maintained by large structures that are easy to see (and they're marked on your minimap). Watch carefully while attacking; enemies spawn inside the portals and immediately attack your hero. Switch fire to them so you don't get killed, and then finish off the portals after the battle. Once you take out all three portals, the area will be cleared for a little while.

PREVENT A BUILDING FROM BEING CONSTRUCTED (Repeatable)

GOAL:	Kill all of the steam fabricators before the building is completed.
LEVEL:	32

Description: Steam fabricators attempt to construct a base if there aren't major portals in the area. A team appears on the western end of the lake and starts work on a large building. You can trash the building easily enough, but you have to kill the fabricators to complete the event. A veteran also appears with the fabricators. Leave the veteran for last (because the creep respawns rather quickly). It's better to take out the regular fabricators. As soon as you kill the last living fabricator, you win the day! Fight near the building so any area-of-effect attacks damage the structure; this sets the enemies back, ensuring you have more time if there are any problems.

AGFAR'S WAYPOINT (WEST OF CENTER)

SERVICES:	Waypoint, Scout
TRAVEL:	Entrance to Bloodtide Coast (Level 45-55 Region) (W), Winterthaw Waypoint (SE)
HARVESTING INFO:	Minimal

This could hardly be called a town. It's more of a glorified camp for people who are traveling to or from the Durmand Priory. The most important thing about it is its waypoint. There aren't many similar travel points anywhere nearby, so getting this waypoint saves you a huge amount of time.

ESCORT PRIORY EXPLORER GILLARD (Repeatable)

GOAL: Talk to Gillard and complete the escort event to the south.

LEVEL: 35

Description: Priory Explorer Gillard is inside the Rocklair encampment. Look for an event icon to find Gillard. If you're under level 33 or so, it's better to handle events on the eastern side of the zone or to work on repeatable events elsewhere before doing this. Gillard wants an escort all the way south, into territory with level 35+ enemies. As long as you're appropriately leveled, it's a decent way to get karma, money, and experience while exploring new terrain. There are imps, jotun, and other groups of monsters to fight. Once you cross Cascade Bridge, wurms, dredge, and wolves come after you as well. You can revive the dolyaks and the guards if they fall, so it's more important to protect your hero than to save the NPCs.

PROTECT THE WORKERS (Repeatable)

GOAL: Approach Cascade Bridge and make sure the workers finish their repairs.

LEVEL: 35

Description: If Cascade Bridge has been destroyed by monsters, a number of workers will come to rebuild it. These workers are attacked frequently by Covington pirates, and anyone in the area should help to keep them safe. Those doing the escort mission for Explorer Gillard have to get the bridge back up before they can finish their original event, so they don't have much of a choice in the matter. Note that you have to be careful; the pirates' attacks are heavy enough that a single hero might be overwhelmed. Try to get at least some of the workers revived if they fall; that way, progress continues on the bridge at all times. The pirates have unlimited numbers, so workers take precedence over fallen defenders.

WINTERTHAW WAYPOINT (EAST SIDE)

SERVICES:	Waypoint
TRAVEL:	Rocklair Waypoint (NW), Entrance to Dredgehaunt Cliffs (Level 40-50 Region) (E), Guutra's Homestead Waypoint (SW)
HARVESTING INFO:	Minimal

The road down from Rocklair Waypoint eventually turns east or bends south. The eastern route ends at Winterthaw Waypoint, an out-of-the-way area with multiple events nearby. It's a great place for fast leveling, if you're up to the task.

If you're looking for somewhere to adventure after completing Lornar's Pass, there is an entrance to Dredgehaunt Cliffs near this waypoint. Walk east and start your exploits there some time around level 40.

HELP ARCANIST KRUPPA WITH DESTROYERS (Renown Task)

GOAL: Battle destroyers and collapse their burrows.

LEVEL: 36

Description: Arcanists are fighting a variety of destroyers to the south of Winterthaw Waypoint. Walk down to the scene of the conflict and kill destroyers (they come in several varieties, but none of them has special powers that make them more dangerous than the others). To get additional credit for the task, knock over their piles of rocks, destroy their burrows, and revive any arcanists that have fallen in the area. Watch out for large groups; if you kick over a mound of rocks while standing near a burrow, you can end up with many enemies at once.

HELP PRIORY EXPLORER LEANDRA (Renown Task)

GOAL: Weaken dredge and recover relics in the area.

LEVEL: 35

Description: Leandra is near the road, west from Winterthaw Waypoint. Her area is covered in dredge troops. Damage their air vents on the ground to summon additional dredge and get bonus credit. While doing that, kill dredge that are already topside. Many targets are north from the task icon, so hunt up there if you're trying to finish the event quickly.

GUUTRA'S HOMESTEAD WAYPOINT (SOUTH OF CENTER)

SERVICES:	Waypoint, Skill Challenge (NW)
TRAVEL:	False Lake Waypoint (W), Winterthaw Waypoint (NE), Vanjir's Stead Waypoint (SE)
HARVESTING INFO:	Gold Ore (N)

Guutra's Homestead Waypoint is on the southern branch of the road. Leave Winterthaw and take the road as it turns in that direction; you can't miss it. There aren't any good services there, but you're darn close to the pirates on False Lake. That's a good thing because they're great targets. They drop raw coin, wool scraps, and goodie bags, so they're wonderful sources for crafting items. As long as you're tough enough to endure their turrets and patrollers, it's a great place to farm for loot!

For another Skill Point, swim down to the bottom of False Lake and meet Peg Leg. Complete his Skill Challenge before you head off to explore the island at the center of the lake.

HELP QUELDIP (Renown Task)

GOAL:	Defeat pirates, steal treasure, and destroy turrets on the island.
LEVEL:	36

Description: The Covington pirates control the entire area due to their fortified island. Queldip wants you to shake up the pirates, but it's going to take some careful work. Pirate turrets have considerable range, and anyone going across the island's bridges will be subject to attack. It's sometimes easier to attack from the east, by swimming across the lake and onto the lower portion of Jetsam Island.

To kill the turrets safely, rush past the pirates and fight next to the turrets. They can't fire at someone standing that close, so you only have to kill the pirates who follow you back. Kill them, destroy the turret next, and then look for bags of goods on the ground. Stay in the lower part of the island or use the buildings above for cover. More pirates and turrets attack if you're out in the open. Keep killing until you've finished the task.

COLLECT DWARVEN ARTIFACTS (Repeatable)

GOAL:	Search False Lake for dwarven artifacts and bring them to Innkeeper Klement.
LEVEL:	37

Description: Sometimes Innkeeper Klement leaves Guutra's Homestead and rushes to the bank of the lake (on the southeastern side of it). Swim down into the water and look for piles of sand or actual dwarven artifacts along the bottom. If you swim quickly, you won't even have to fight any drakes that attack your character along the way. You only need to get about 10 of the items if you're by yourself. Bring these back to the innkeeper and hand them over. Follow Klement back to the stead and hang around for a minute; he might need some help!

DEFEND KLEMENT AND FABRI (Repeatable)

GOAL:	Protect the stead from pirate attackers.
LEVEL:	37

Description: A couple minutes after you finish collecting the artifacts, a pirate captain comes up to Guutra's Stead and tries to extort some tribute from Klement and Fabri. This can't be a coincidence! Stand with the people of the stead and repel a series of attackers. They'll trickle in if you kill them one at a time, so it's better to kill them en masse (if you can). Don't waste time attacking the pirate captain; he's not really taking part in the skirmish. As soon as enough pirates are killed, he'll head off on his own.

ESCORT THE ARTIFACT TO VANJIR'S STEAD (Repeatable)

GOAL:	Take the artifact down to Vanjir's Stead, in the southeast.
LEVEL:	38

Description: Researchers arrive to take the artifact away. If you hang around after the pirate captain leaves, this event begins within a minute or so. Pirates, earth elementals, and raptors attack while your convoy makes its way along the roads to the southeast. The fights often have four enemies, so you need to be very careful if you're alone.

Fight for maximum survivability. Only protect the dolyaks if things get especially heated. The trip ends when you get down to the stead, near Vanjir's Stead Waypoint.

DEFEAT LORD IGNIUS (Group)

GOAL:	Slay champion Lord Ignius.
LEVEL:	38

Description: The job isn't done even after the package is delivered down at Vanjir's Stead. Follow Jodd and the others to see what this artifact is all about. Before too long, the group stops in the wilderness and summons the creature bound inside the stones. You have to fight this powerful beast, a champion named Lord Ignius. The fight is soloable, so you won't need a group unless things go all pear-shaped. The asura from your escort as well as a norn from the stead all jump in to help out. When Lord Ignius is slain, the event chain ends.

FALSE LAKE WAYPOINT (SOUTHWEST OF CENTER)

SERVICES:	Waypoint
TRAVEL:	Guutra's Homestead Waypoint (E), Rocklair Waypoint (N)
HARVESTING INFO:	Minimal

False Lake Waypoint isn't far from Guutra's Homestead Waypoint, but it's still quite valuable. This area is on the western side of the river, making it possible to reach the high ground quickly. Get this by running south from Rocklair or by swimming across the river from Guutra's and climbing up the northern bank. Walk south from False Lake Waypoint to find your next task.

HELP DUIDDA (Renown Task)

GOAL:	Hassle pirates, destroy more turrets, shred pirate flags, and steal rum.
LEVEL:	37

Description: Another band of Covington pirates is south of False Lake Waypoint. They're up on the western side of the water. These pirates are slightly higher level, so watch yourself if you haven't gained any levels while fighting the others. To keep the task safe, fight the single pirates higher on the shore. If you're tough, gutsy, or have a group, rush into the main compound. There are more enemies, and the mix of flags and rums let you complete the event in under half the time.

DEMON'S MAW WAYPOINT (SOUTHWEST SIDE)

SERVICES:	Waypoint
TRAVEL:	False Lake Waypoint (N), Vanjir's Stead Waypoint (E), Entrance to Bloodtide Coast (Level 45-55 Region) (SW)
HARVESTING INFO:	Minimal

Monk's Leap is at the southern end of False Lake. It's near a huge collection of earth elementals, on the western side of the map. It's an unremarkable location until you find the passage out to Bloodtide Coast, a narrow waterway southwest of the waypoint.

To continue working with events in Lornar's Pass, take the bridge east after killing its guards. That puts you back on the road.

VANJIR'S STEAD WAYPOINT (SOUTHEAST SIDE)

SERVICES:	Waypoint, Merchant (Salvage), Armorsmith, Weaponsmith, Equipment Repair
TRAVEL:	Demon's Maw Waypoint (W), Guutra's Homestead Waypoint (NW), Entrance to Timberline Falls (Level 50-60 Region) (S)
HARVESTING INFO:	Minimal

Vanjir's Stead is on the southeastern end of Lornar's Pass. This place is incredibly important because it's near the passage to Timberline Falls. It has a merchant, you can repair there, and it's relatively safe at all times. You couldn't ask for much more.

HELP HUNTER NEIDA (Renown Task)

GOAL: Battle jotun and ice wurms.

LEVEL: 38

Description: Walk northeast from Venison Pass to kill the wurms and jotun up there. If possible, start Armas' event (described next). You can often get full credit for this task just by completing that event. Otherwise, stay in the snowfields and hunt targets for a few minutes.

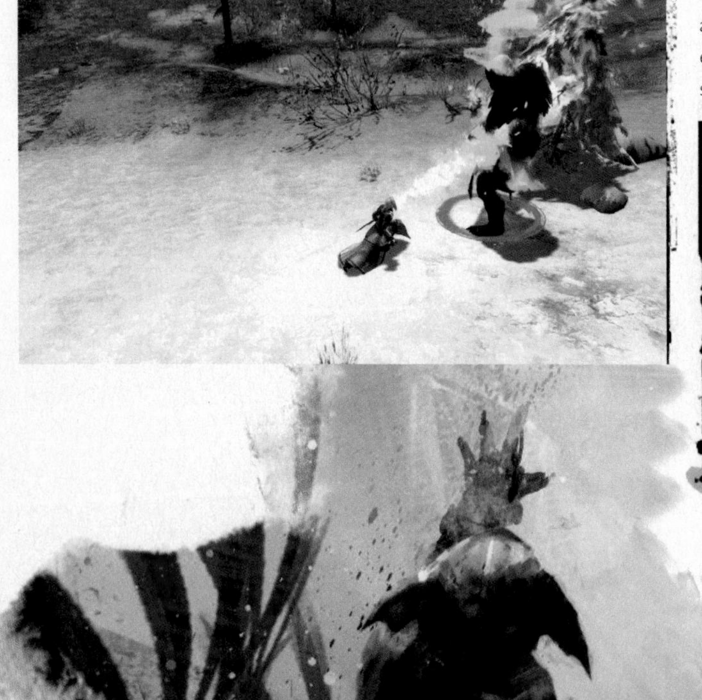

JOIN ARMAS AGAINST THE JOTUN CHIEFTAIN (Repeatable)

GOAL: Kill the jotun chieftain.

LEVEL: 38

Description: Armas is a norn hunter on the northern end of town, in the stead. Talk to him before you work on Neida's task so you can get credit for both events simultaneously. As soon as you begin to help him, the lunatic charges north into jotun territory. Follow the hunter and defend him from jotun attackers. He'll drive into the heart of their territory and kill the chieftain (so long as you can survive the push). If things are getting tense, let Armas fall so you have time to rest. Revive him afterward to continue the event. The chieftain is in a cave along the eastern edge of the map. He's a veteran, but with Armas' help it's a manageable fight. Getting there is harder than killing him!

HELP RESEARCHER BRAMM (Renown Task)

GOAL: Activate surveillance equipment, revive fallen researchers, and kill ettins.

LEVEL: 39

Description: Follow the southern line of mountains while moving west from Venison Pass. Halfway along the southern side of the map there are ettins with a bunch of research equipment nearby. Use the equipment while fighting the ettins to complete this task. Although the ettins are spread out, they're high level and have knockdown attacks that cover a huge area of effect. Use ranged attacks whenever you can, and draw them out toward your position. This lowers the chance of having to fight more than one of them at a time. The fallen researchers aren't near the front of the ettins' pass; they're deep in the crags. Push far into the ettins' area to finish the task quickly, but jump to a waypoint as soon as you finish so you don't have to fight your way back out.

DREDGEHAUNT CLIFFS

LEVEL RANGE: 40-50

The Dredgehaunt Cliffs divide the Shiverpeak Mountains from the Steamspur Mountains. They're reachable from the southern exit of Hoelbrak or by leaving the eastern end of Lornar's Pass. As you'd expect, the norn continue to have dredge problems throughout these mountains. The Moletariat is a serious threat to travelers and adventurers alike.

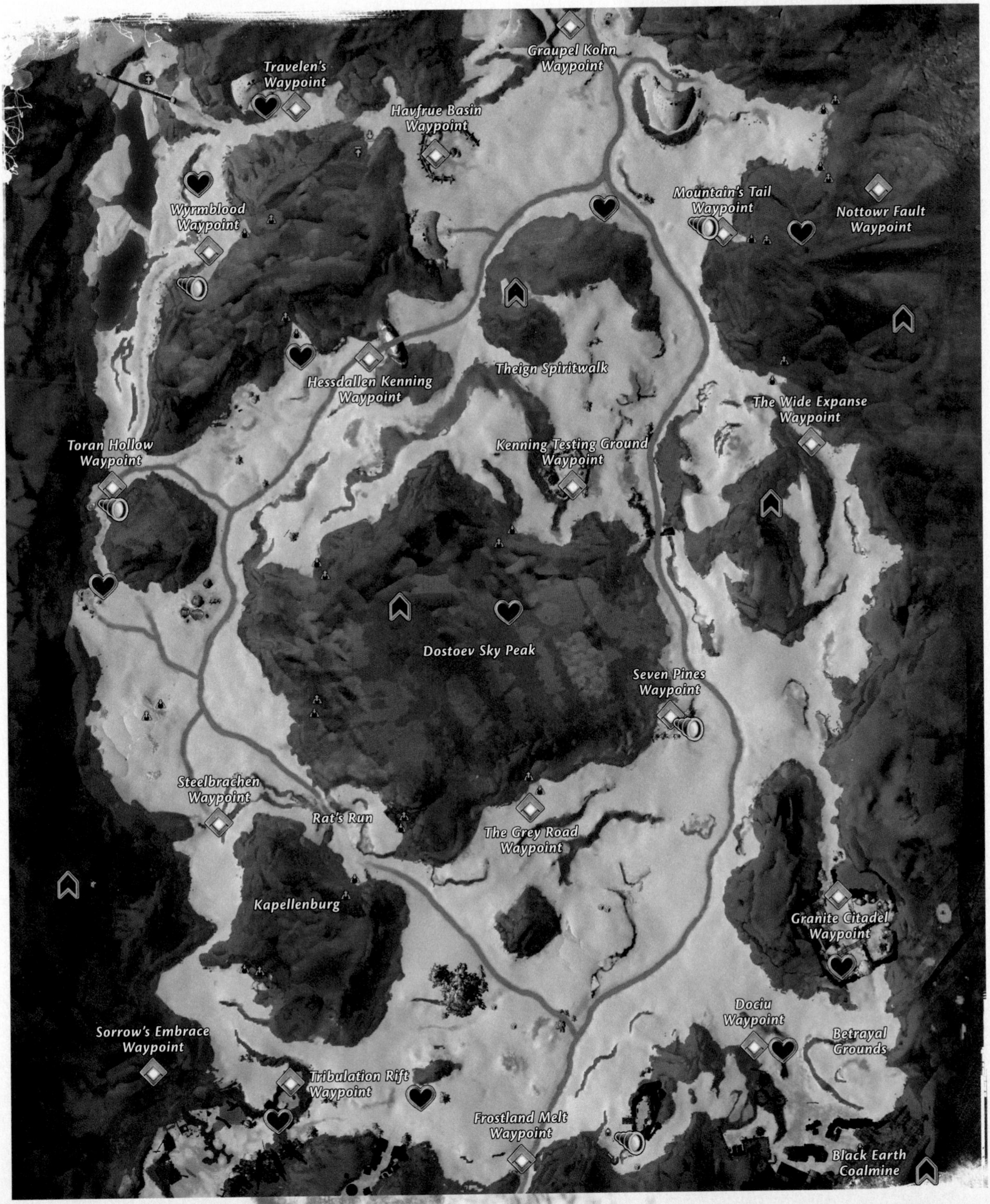

Graupel Kohn Waypoint
Travelen's Waypoint
Havfrue Basin Waypoint
Wyrmblood Waypoint
Mountain's Tail Waypoint
Nottowr Fault Waypoint
Theign Spiritwalk
Hessdallen Kenning Waypoint
The Wide Expanse Waypoint
Toran Hollow Waypoint
Kenning Testing Ground Waypoint
Dostoev Sky Peak
Seven Pines Waypoint
Steelbrachen Waypoint
Rat's Run
The Grey Road Waypoint
Kapellenburg
Granite Citadel Waypoint
Sorrow's Embrace Waypoint
Dociu Waypoint
Betrayal Grounds
Tribulation Rift Waypoint
Frostland Melt Waypoint
Black Earth Coalmine

FROSTGORGE SOUND

LEVEL RANGE: 70-80

The toughest area in the Shiverpeak Mountains is all the way up top, at the northern end of the chain. Travel north from the Wayfarer Foothills or west from Fireheart Rise to get there. Swim through the chilly waters to find some impressive enemies and face rare challenges. Or, face off against the best that the Sons of Svanir have to offer. Just be careful of the dragons' influence there in the north. It's a palpable threat at every turn.

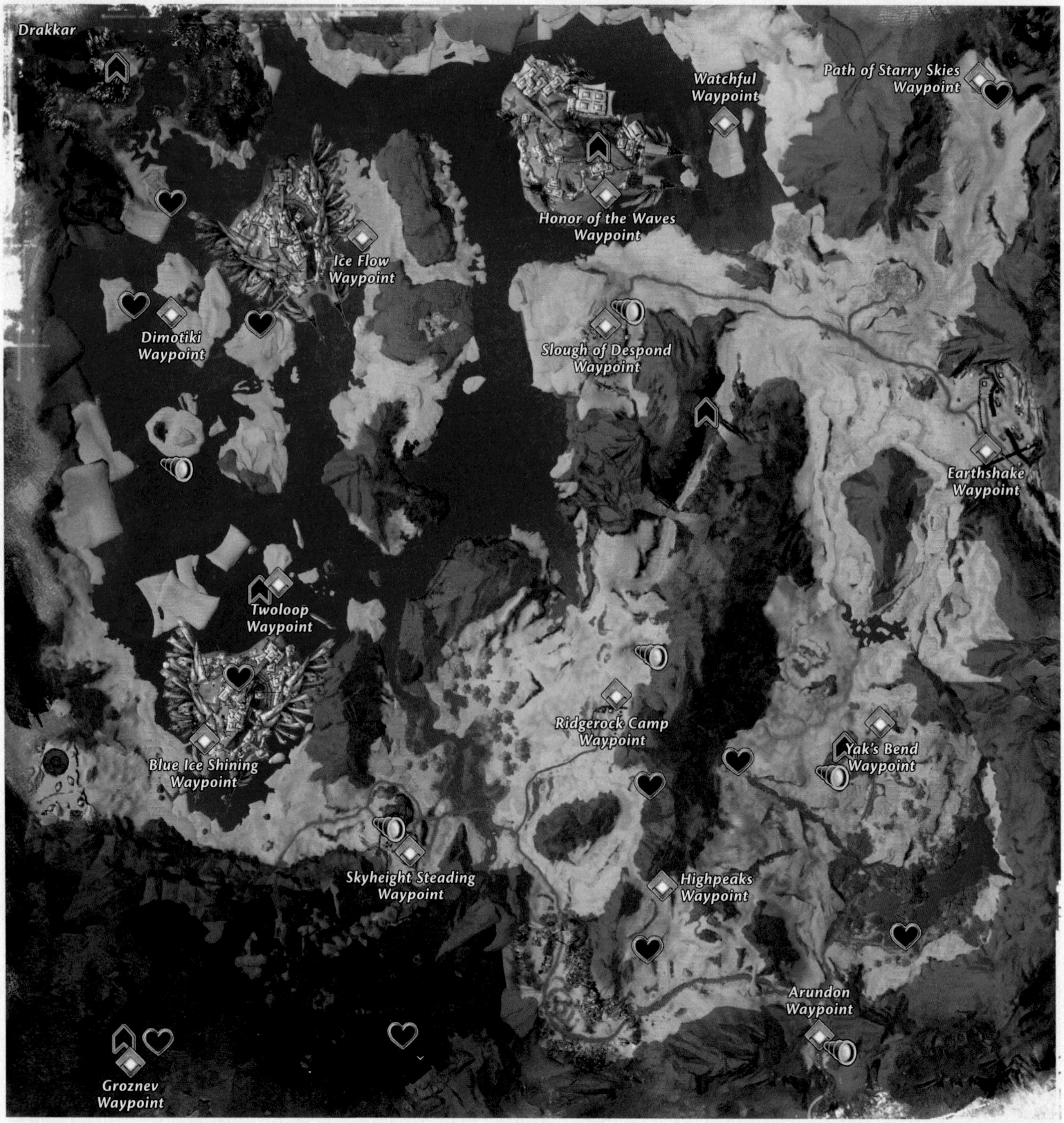

Drakkar
Watchful Waypoint
Path of Starry Skies Waypoint
Honor of the Waves Waypoint
Ice Flow Waypoint
Dimotiki Waypoint
Slough of Despond Waypoint
Earthshake Waypoint
Twoloop Waypoint
Ridgerock Camp Waypoint
Yak's Bend Waypoint
Blue Ice Shining Waypoint
Skyheight Steading Waypoint
Highpeaks Waypoint
Arundon Waypoint
Groznev Waypoint

TARNISHED COAST

RATA SUM

LEVEL RANGE:	Asuran Capital City (All Levels)
WAYPOINTS:	11
SKILL CHALLENGES:	3

The Tarnished Coast of Tyria has a warm climate, verdant growth, and abundant natural resources. Not surprisingly, it is also home to many intelligent races. Both the asura and sylvari live here, and many smaller groups, such as the krait, skritt, and hylek, have found refuge within the wilderness.

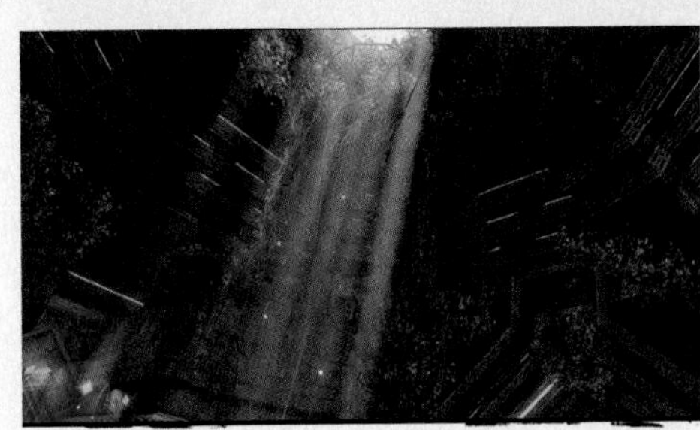

TOP FLOOR

The most dangerous threats to travelers, apart from the aggressive wildlife, are Inquest loyalists, members of the Nightmare Court, and the legions of Orrian undead. There are several small towns to take refuge in for an evening, but none compare with the cities of Rata Sum and The Grove. These are the home cities of the asura and sylvari and are marvels of technology and nature, respectively.

Rata Sum is both the capital of the asuran race and one of their greatest achievements. Built as a floating cube suspended over an asuran-made mountain, which itself was created over an inland river, the city stands as a marvel of arcane construction and power.

Rata Sum is divided into five primary floors, which are separated by order of importance to the city. The top two floors are dedicated to the ideals of the asura; the highest pinnacle holds the Council chambers of asuran government, while the public top floor has passages to great laboratories and through the Asura Gates to the world beyond.

The middle level holds crafting and manufacturing stations. It is here that asuran masterworkers go to learn and perfect new techniques.

SECOND FLOOR

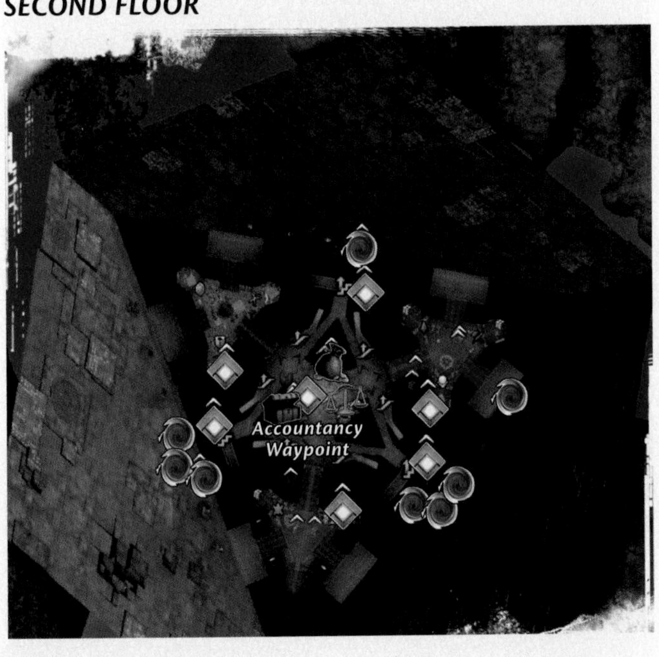

BOTTOM FLOOR

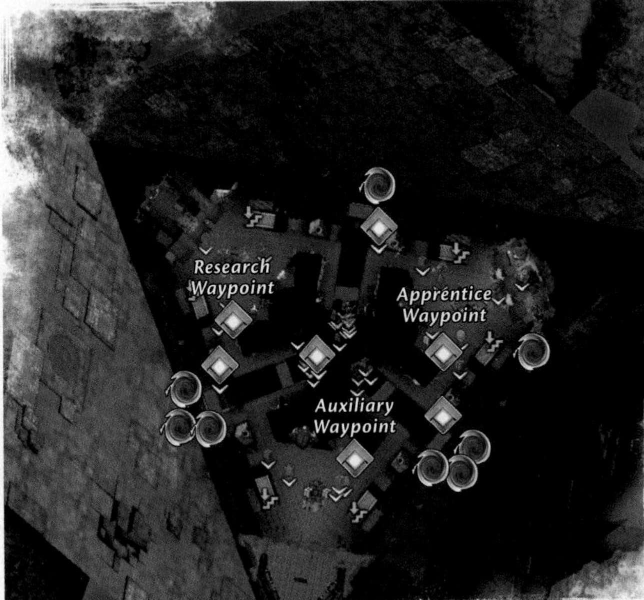

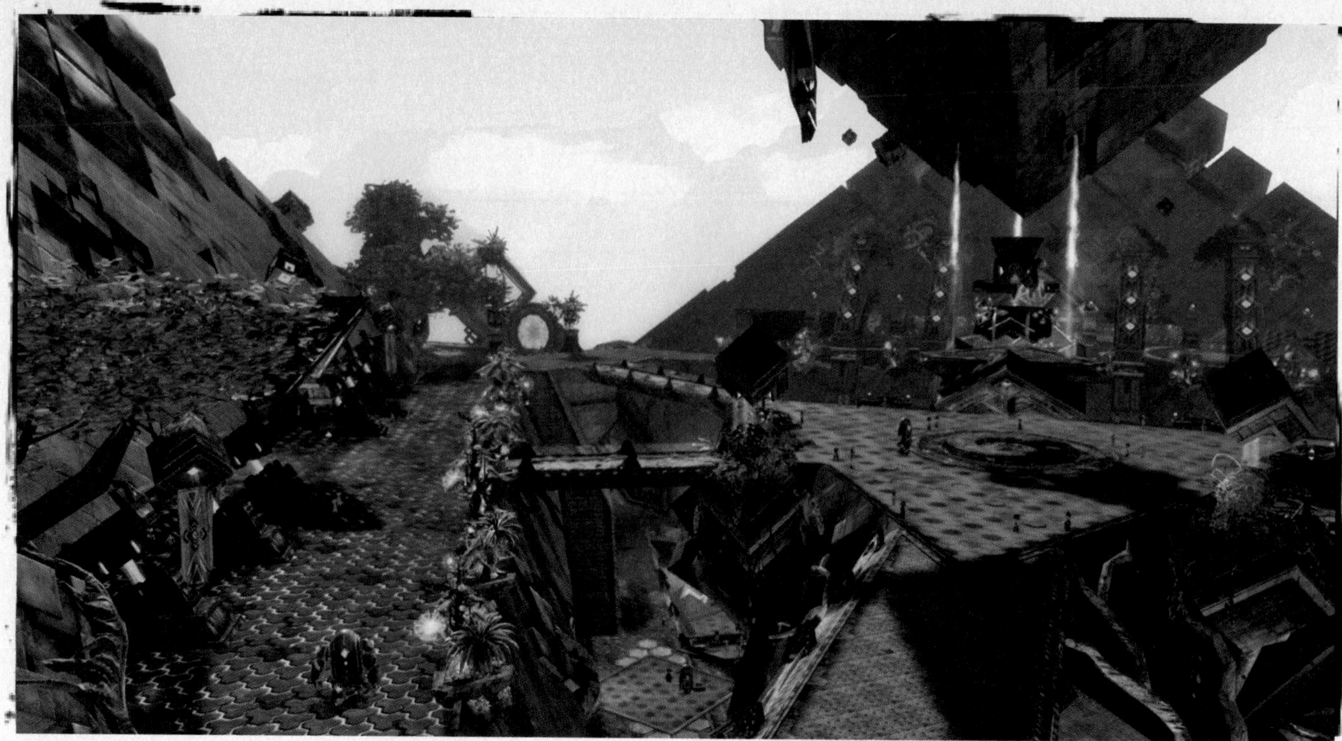

The bottom two levels are centered more on the daily life of the city. The bottom level is home to novice apprentices, researchers, and other auxiliary staff that don't belong to a lab yet. It is also a recruiting place for the Peacemakers (and others). The lowest floor, the Substrata, is the foundation of the city. It holds individual laboratories and residences for the populace, but it is not considered a prestigious location by most.

ARCANE COUNCIL CHAMBERS (COUNCIL LEVEL)

SERVICES:	N/A
TRAVEL:	Asura Gate to Beol Fountain

The general affairs of Rata Sum are governed by the Arcane Council. From the very top of the city, the members of the Council can look out over their capital and the surrounding land. Most asura attempt to avoid membership in the Council, as it takes them away from their own individual experiments or those of their laboratory krewes.

CREATOR'S COMMONS (TOP FLOOR)

SERVICES:	Weaponsmith, Armorsmith, Merchant (Salvage), Equipment Repairs
TRAVEL:	Asura Gate to the Council Level (in the Center of the Fountain), Metrica Square (SE), Magustan Court (N), Magicat Court (SW), Ramps to Crafting Floor

Beol Fountain decorates the center of Creator's Commons, at the middle of the top floor. The bottom of the fountain is an Asura Gate to the Council Level, from where the leaders of the city govern.

At the fountain itself, a knowledgeable villager is attempting to sell a Skill Book. The merchant nearby sells salvage kits, and there is even a place to repair equipment.

Arrayed around the fountain are armorsmiths and weaponsmiths, who sell a variety of goods.

Walkways connect Creator's Commons to the three waypoints on this floor: Magustan Court, Metrica Square, and Magicat Court. Ramps leading down to the crafting floor aren't far, either.

METRICAL WAYPOINT (TOP FLOOR)

SERVICES:	Waypoint, Profession Trainers (Necromancer, Elementalist, and Mesmer)
TRAVEL:	Asura Gate to Idea Incubation Lab, Asura Gate to Metrica Province (City Exit), Ramps to Crafting Floor

Metrical Court, on the southeast corner of the top floor, holds Metrical Waypoint. The Asura Gates to the Idea Incubation Lab and Metrica Province immediately flank the waypoint. Travelers making their way into the city from Metrica Province can ask a nearby tour guide for directions.

To the west is the College of Synergetics. Within this building are three villagers willing to sell information and an alcove for mystic profession trainers. Necromancers, elementalists, and mesmers can speak with their mentors here.

To depart the top floor to the crafting floor, simply follow the ramps leading down from the waypoint.

MAGICAT WAYPOINT (TOP FLOOR)

SERVICES:	Waypoint, Profession Trainers (Ranger, Engineer, Thief)
TRAVEL:	Asura Gate to Applied Development (Homes), Asura Gate to Snaff Memorial Lab, Ramps to Crafting Floor

Magicat Court is on the western edge of the top floor of Rata Sum. The waypoint stands across from the Asura Gates to Snaff Memorial Lab and the Applied Development Lab.

Asuran characters never feel more at home than when they are in the Applied Development Lab. It is here that they took their first steps in experimentation, and got their first taste of well-deserved recognition.

The ramps to the crafting floor are just past the stairs from Magicat Court. The College of Dynamics is immediately north. Here, some of the more subtle professions can find mentors. The trainers for rangers, engineers, and thieves are ready and willing to impart their knowledge.

MAGUSTAN WAYPOINT (TOP FLOOR)

SERVICES:	Waypoint, Profession Trainers (Warrior, Guardian)
TRAVEL:	Asura Gate to the Advanced Metamystics Lab, Asura Gate to Lion's Arch (City Exit), Ramps to Crafting Floor

Magustan Court has Asura Gates to the Advanced Metamystics Lab and Lion's Arch. As this is the first place where most visitors from other areas set foot, a Tour Guide is ready to answer questions or give directions. Nearby ramps lead down to the crafting floor.

East of the court stands the College of Statics, home of the Magihedron. This place is dedicated to the martial professions. A warrior trainer and a guardian trainer stand in an alcove, ready to impart their wisdom.

ACCOUNTANCY WAYPOINT (CRAFTING FLOOR)

SERVICES:	Waypoint, Trading Post, Bank, Guild Services, Equipment Repairs
TRAVEL:	Statics Union (NE), Dynamics Union (NW), Synergetics Union (S), Ramps to Top Floor, Stairs to Bottom Floor

The Interdisciplinary Accessium is the financial heart of Rata Sum. The Accountancy Waypoint at its center provides ease of travel for buyers and sellers alike. It is where the Bank and Trading Post stand, and there is a place for travelers to repair their equipment.

For those wishing to create their own guilds, the Guild Registrar and Promoter are both here and ready to help.

The ramps from here lead up to the top floor, along the sides of Creator's Commons. The paths lead to the unions and the three other waypoints on this floor. Just beside the ramps are paths to the north, southeast, and southwest. These lead to stairs to the bottom floor.

STATICS WAYPOINT (CRAFTING FLOOR)

SERVICES:	Waypoint, Stations and Trainers (Artificer, Huntsman, Weaponsmith)
TRAVEL:	Path to Accountancy Waypoint

Statics Waypoint sits on a ledge outside Forge Hall. Take a moment to admire the view before heading inside the hall and starting your business. The Statics Union plays host to a number of craftmasters that aid the college above. Huntsmen, artificers, and weaponsmiths all find both Masters to teach them and stations to practice their craft here. With the Accountancy Waypoint, Bank, and Trading Post a short run away, crafters spend a great deal of time here.

DYNAMICS WAYPOINT (CRAFTING FLOOR)

SERVICES:	Waypoint, Stations and Trainers (Jeweler, Tailor, Armorsmith)
TRAVEL:	Path to Accountancy Waypoint

The Dynamics Waypoint is just outside Artisan Hall. Be mindful of the railings, as they are only high enough to trip you and not high enough to keep you from taking the fast route to the bottom of Rata Sum. Inside Artisan Hall are Masters of crafts supported by the College of Dynamics. A Master Jeweler, Master Tailor, and Master Armorsmith occupy the three corners of the hall. The Tailoring Station, Armorsmithing Station, and Jeweler's Station dominate the floor. The path to the Accountancy Waypoint (and its various services) completes the dream of these crafters.

SYNERGETICS WAYPOINT (CRAFTING FLOOR)

SERVICES:	Waypoint, Stations and Trainers (Leatherworker, Cooking)
TRAVEL:	Path to Accountancy Waypoint

Overlooking Skinner's Hall is Synergetics Waypoint, named for the college this hall supports. The Master Leatherworker and Master Chef are happy to share their Leatherworker's Station and Cooking Fire with those who are willing to listen and work. The Synergetics Union doesn't turn anyone away. Only a hop, skip, and jump separate Skinner's Hall from the Accountancy Waypoint. If the hall doesn't have what you need, the Bank and Trading Post almost certainly will.

RESEARCH WAYPOINT (BOTTOM FLOOR)

SERVICES:	Waypoint
TRAVEL:	Path to Apprentice Waypoint, Path to Auxiliary Waypoint, Stairs to Crafting Floor, Ramp to Lower Research Stacks

The Research Waypoint doesn't hold much for anyone not part of a krewe. The merchants are so pushy that it's impossible to buy anything. The wavering wall to the north holds the ramp to the Lower Research Stacks where a warden keeps test subjects locked in cages.

AUXILIARY WAYPOINT (BOTTOM FLOOR)

SERVICES:	Waypoint
TRAVEL:	Path to Apprentice Waypoint, Path to Research Waypoint, Stairs to Crafting Floor

There are recruiters and other krewe-related people in this area. It's not a stop for the average traveler unless you have specific business to attend to.

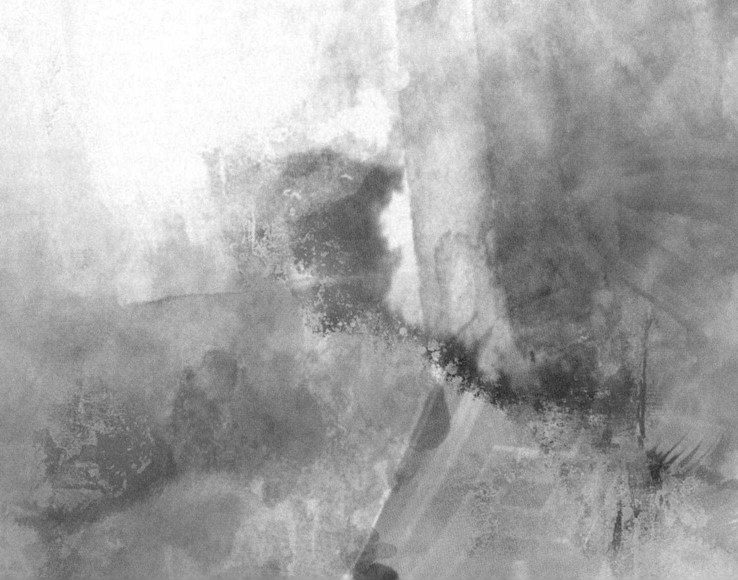

APPRENTICE WAYPOINT (BOTTOM FLOOR)

SERVICES:	Waypoint
TRAVEL:	Path to Research Waypoint, Path to Auxiliary Waypoint, Stairs to Crafting Floor

At the Apprentice Waypoint travelers can learn more about the major schools of thought for krewe apprentices. Krewe apprentices Gorqi and Lunq are eager to explain in depth the differences between the two schools. Take a moment to listen to each if you're interested. This is also where most apprentices come to relax. There is a waitress serving apprentices (she won't serve travelers), and the Aquatarium is a good place to keep thoughts calm and off research for a few moments.

METAMYSTICS WAYPOINT (SUBSTRATA)

SERVICES:	Waypoint
TRAVEL:	Asura Gate to Magustan Waypoint

The Advanced Metamystics Lab works tirelessly to better the lives of asura everywhere. (Actually, they just research and experiment for the sake of advancing science.)

INCUBATION WAYPOINT (SUBSTRATA)

SERVICES:	Waypoint
TRAVEL:	Asura Gate to Metrical Waypoint

The Flaxx Compound stands a short walk from the Incubation Waypoint. Don't bother trying to get in without an appointment, as there is a guard with golems that can't be cajoled into letting anyone in.

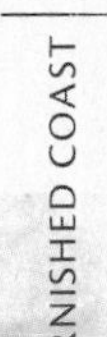

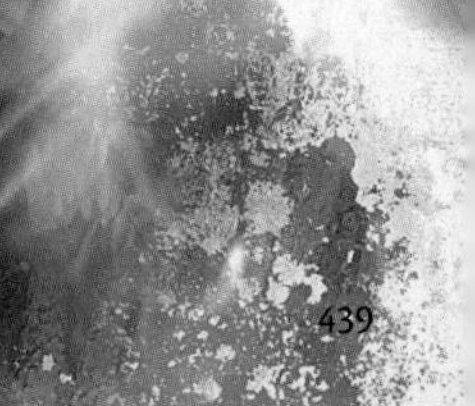

THE GROVE

LEVEL RANGE:	Sylvari Capital City (All Levels)
WAYPOINTS:	4
SKILL CHALLENGES:	1

The Grove has grown and developed around the roots and under the branches of the Pale Tree. Rather than staircases, sweeping ramps connect the three primary floors of the city. It can be difficult for newcomers to the Grove to navigate. We suggest taking the time to get one waypoint on each of the three floors first, and then using these to explore one floor at a time.

As new sylvari awaken from their shared dream, they are brought to the Grove to be educated before making their way into the world. While physically fully grown, there is a great deal these saplings don't know about the world. Teachers of all types and styles bestow their wisdom to these new additions to the sylvari populace.

CALEDON WAYPOINT (TOP FLOOR)

SERVICES:	Merchant (Salvage)
TRAVEL:	City Exit to Caledon Forest (Level 1-15 Sylvari Region), Path to Watchgate Waypoint

Caledon Waypoint sits just at the exit to Caledon Forest. It's both the first stop for adventurers entering the Grove and the last stop for adventurers leaving. At first look, there doesn't seem to be much here, but Dreas (the merchant) sells leather bags and all levels of salvage kits. He's also willing to buy pretty much anything and everything a traveler might find along the road or in an enemy's pockets. To the south is the bulk of the Grove.

TOP FLOOR

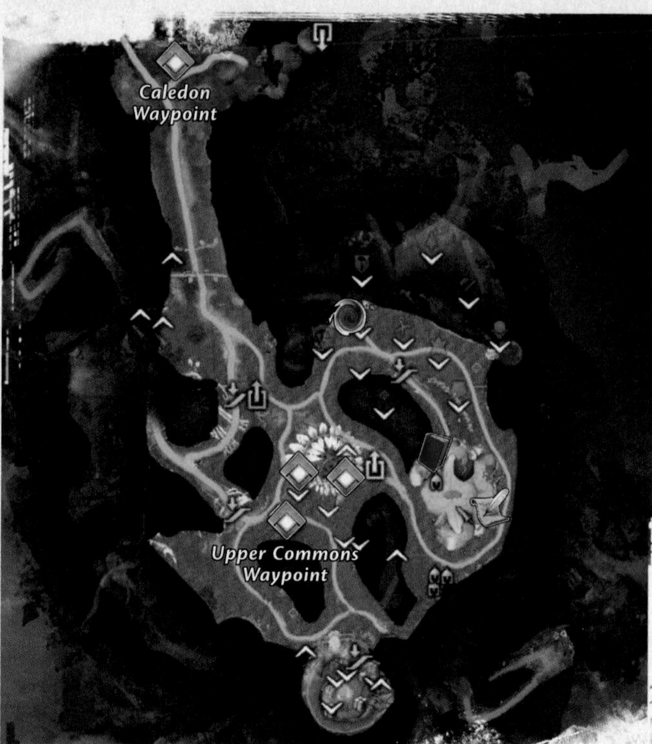

SECOND FLOOR

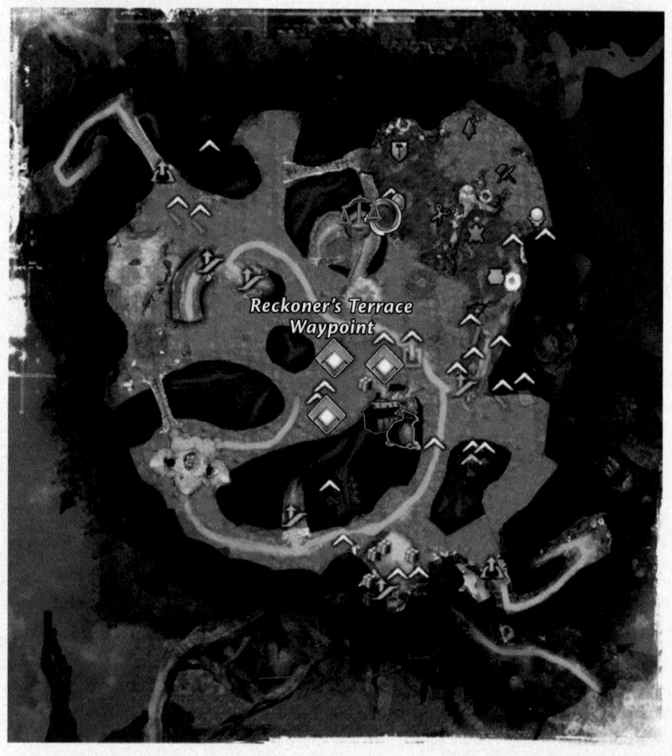

BOTTOM FLOOR

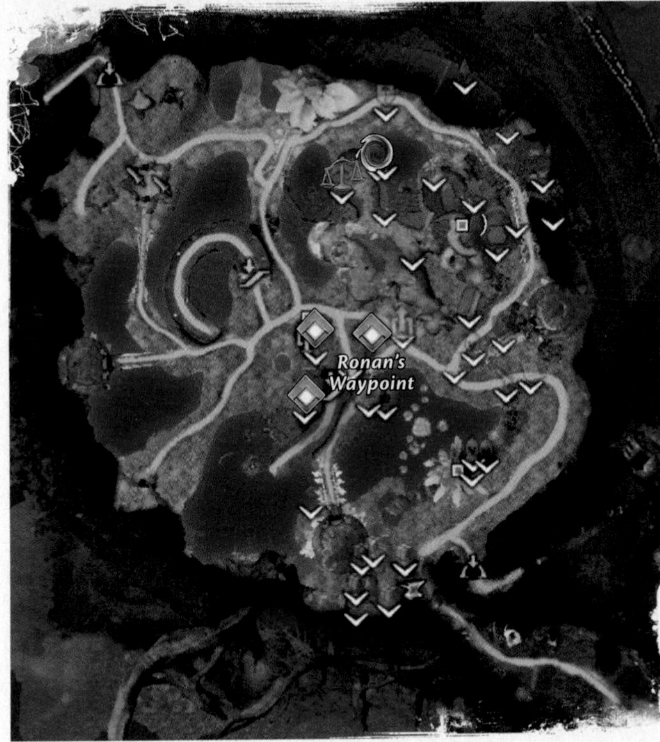

UPPER COMMONS WAYPOINT (TOP FLOOR)

SERVICES:	N/A
TRAVEL:	Path to Entry Gate Waypoint, Path to Watchgate Waypoint

The Pale Tree Circle sits to the northeast of Upper Commons Waypoint. This is the center of sylvari life in the Grove; it holds two lifts that take sylvari to the Soul of the Pale Tree, where they commune with their progenitor.

Use these lifts to ascend and look in the circle above for Ventari's Tablet. Be sure to visit this special place. To the north of the waypoint is a gentle ramp down to the lower floors, while to the south is Silliari's Tavern. This place of relaxation connects the top and middle floors of the Grove, so no matter where you are, relaxation is close by.

ENTRY GATE WAYPOINT (TOP FLOOR)

SERVICES:	Weaponsmith, Armorsmith, Equipment Repair, Profession Trainers for All Professions, Guild Services
TRAVEL:	Asura Gate to Lion's Arch (City Exit), Path to Watchgate Waypoint, Path to Upper Commons Waypoint, Ramp to Middle Floor

Purple energy swirls inside the Asura Gate to Lion's Arch. The Entry Gate Waypoint stands beside it. For new visitors to the city, this marks their first contact with the sylvari and their tree home.

At first look, there aren't very many services, but a little bit of walking to the southeast brings you to the Envoy's Shelter. Only nature can pack so much into such a small place. The Envoy's Shelter houses a weaponsmith, an armorsmith, equipment repairs, guild functions, and trainers for all eight professions! If you can't find the trainer you're looking for inside the shelter, check just outside, as many of them stand by the entrances. For those looking for a wonderful view, visit Mentor Arduine to the east of Entry Gate Waypoint.

WATCHGATE WAYPOINT (TOP FLOOR)

SERVICES:	N/A
TRAVEL:	Path to Upper Commons Waypoint, Path to Entry Gate Waypoint, Ramp to Middle Floor

Entering from Caledon Forest, one must pass under Warden's Watchgate. This is the last line of defense before reaching the Pale Tree itself. Just inside the passageway is Watchgate Waypoint. As the first stop in the Grove proper, there are several paths available from here. To the immediate south is a ramp to the middle floor. To the east is Entry Gate Waypoint. On the other side of the Pale Tree Circle, to the south, is the Upper Commons Waypoint.

TENDER'S WAYPOINT (MIDDLE FLOOR)

SERVICES:	Trading Post
TRAVEL:	Path to Maker's Waypoint, Ramps to Top and Bottom Floors

There are several places connected to this waypoint. To the southeast is the Trading Post, while across a bridge to the north is the back door to the crafting area, and south leads to Maker's Commons. For those on missions, the east holds the Durmand Posting as well as members of the Order of Whispers. Take the bridge to the northwest to enter the Gardenroot Tunnel. Here the sylvari tend the grubs that live within the Pale Tree between the middle and bottom floors.

MAKER'S WAYPOINT (MIDDLE FLOOR)

SERVICES:	Bank, Equipment Repair, Crafting Trainers and Services
TRAVEL:	Path to Scholar's Waypoint, Path to Tender's Waypoint

There are few places in the Grove busier than Maker's Waypoint. Here, once again, The Pale Tree boggles the mind by putting so much in one location. Directly north of Maker's Waypoint is Maker's Terrace, complete with a Trainer and Station for every crafting profession. To the south is the Bank, and to the southeast is a path leading to Scholar's Waypoint and Blackroot Tunnel (which leads to the bottom floor).

SCHOLAR'S WAYPOINT (MIDDLE FLOOR)

SERVICES:	N/A
TRAVEL:	Path to Maker's Waypoint, Ramp to Bottom Floor

Scholar's Waypoint sits between the ramps between the middle and bottom floors, near a few important areas. A Vigil Warpost is up the ramp to the west, while Silliari's Tavern and the entrance to Blackroot Tunnel are up to the east. Be sure to visit Silliari, as he's a good conversationalist; he also gives you a Skill Challenge.

NOON WAYPOINT (BOTTOM FLOOR)

SERVICES:	N/A
TRAVEL:	Path to Dawn Waypoint, Path to Ronan's Waypoint, Ramp to Middle Floor

The Noon Waypoint sits on the bottom floor of the Grove. This is primarily a residential area for the populace, and there are few services for travelers this deep. The entrances to Blackroot Tunnel and the ramp to the middle floor are immediately south. Just past the entrance to the tunnel is the entrance to Nightshade Garden, where the wardens imprison the enemies of the Pale Tree. The House of Niamh is to the north of the waypoint. Here you can learn more about the Cycle of Noon from Gardener Laidir.

DAWN WAYPOINT (BOTTOM FLOOR)

SERVICES:	Weaponsmith, Armorsmith
TRAVEL:	Path to Noon Waypoint, Path to Ronan's Waypoint

The entrance to the House of Aife is immediately to the south. This is one of the many houses dedicated to educating the saplings. Further south is the Great Helix, which connects all three floors of the Grove. To the west are armorsmiths and weaponsmiths who help the citizens of the Grove arm themselves. Further west are the entrances to the Gardenroot Tunnel (which connects to the middle floor) and the Yew Circle.

RONAN'S WAYPOINT (BOTTOM FLOOR)

SERVICES:	Equipment Repairs
TRAVEL:	Path to Dawn Waypoint, Path to Noon Waypoint, Ramp to Middle Floor, Entrance to the House of Riannoc (Homes)

Ronan's Waypoint is the closest waypoint to the center of the bottom floor and, as such, gets the most use. Ronan's Bower and the entrance to the House of Riannoc, where many sylvari live, are to the northeast. South leads to the House of Caithe. (Caithe was one of the Firstborn.) The Garden of Night is to the west. Immediately north is the Great Helix, which connects all three floors of the Grove.

METRICA PROVINCE

LEVEL RANGE:	1-15
TASKS:	14
WAYPOINTS:	16
SKILL CHALLENGES:	8
HARVESTING INFO:	Copper Ore, Aspen Saplings, Early Cooking Ingredients

SKILL CHALLENGES

- Control Node (North of Soren Draa Waypoint, Inside Inquest Base) (SW)
- Utcua (East of Jeztar Falls Waypoint, Swim to a Cave Underneath the Lake) (S)
- Oola (Southeast of Cuatl Waypoint, In a Secret Lab: Talk to a Researcher to Open the Door) (E)
- Cuatl Health Goo (Northwest of Cuatl Waypoint, In the Open) (E)
- Suspicious Control Panel (Northeast of Rana Landing Complex Waypoint, Inside Biocauldron Alchemics) (Center)
- Black Ice 4444 (North of Hexane Regrade Waypoint, Inside the Large Complex) (NE)
- Ancient Elemental Fire Energy (West of Muridian Waypoint, In the Wetlands Beneath the Base) (NW)

Metrica Province is a land at war; conflict is constant in this grassland wilderness. While once fully subterranean, the asura have now expanded above ground, and their laboratories are sprouting up in every nook and cranny. This has pushed the local wildlife as well as the hylek and skritt natives into smaller and smaller territories throughout the province.

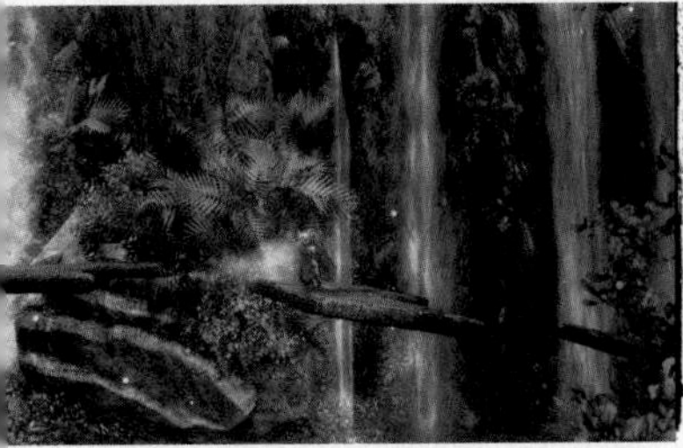

These other races raid the asuran labs, and that isn't the only problem for the asura. Internal strife is growing. The Inquest have gained a huge number of followers, and their policies are not friendly, even to others of their own kind. They believe research should be protected by any means possible. If this includes killing fellow asura, or anything else that gets in their way, well, that's a small price to pay for progress.

Inquest Outer Complex
Muridian Uplands Waypoint
Thaumanova Reactor
Hexand Regrade Waypoint
Artergon Waypoint
The Anthill Waypoint
Survivor's Encampment Waypoint
Luminates Plant
Arterium Haven Waypoint
Michotl Grounds Waypoint
Cuatl Morass Waypoint
Fisher's Beach Bend
Rana Landing Complex Waypoint
Desider Atum Waypoint
Old Golem Factory Waypoint
The Funhouse
Akk Wilds Waypoint
Loch Jezt Waypoint
Hydrone Unit Waypoint
Sunshade Caves
Soren Draa Waypoint
Calx's Hideout
Jeztar Falls Waypoint
Wildflame Caverns

SOREN DRAA WAYPOINT (SOUTHWEST SIDE)

SERVICES:	Weaponsmith, Armorsmith, Equipment Repair
TRAVEL:	Entrance to Rata Sum (Asura Capital City) (W), Wildflame Caverns (S), Jeztar Falls Waypoint (E), Old Golem Factory Waypoint (N)
HARVESTING INFO:	N/A

Soren Draa sits at the bottom of Rata Sum. Recruiters from the city and its various labs try to get travelers' attention. Though this is a small town compared with the city above, you can get a good look at the glory and dangers of technology. Nearby, golems malfunction and labs wage constant war with each other in the race for the next discovery.

Take care of the malfunctioning golems before progressing any further. Go farther west to start "Experimenting on Golems" and "Defending Etheropods."

When you're finished here, check the Wildflame Caverns to the south. It's easy to miss if you aren't looking for it, and it's got a fun repeatable event that pops up fairly often.

EXPERIMENTING ON GOLEMS (Renown Task)

GOAL:	Perform golem experiments and hinder the Inquest.
LEVEL:	2

Description: Golems are here to experiment on! They're everywhere in this area. Weaken the PM-900a and experiment on the SRV 3296 as you go. Watch for the broken golems; there are often Inquest saboteurs responsible. Revive the golems and kill the saboteurs that become visible to get double credit toward this task.

MALFUNCTIONING GOLEMS (Repeatable)

GOAL:	Help peacemakers weaken malfunctioning PM-900a golems.
LEVEL:	2

Description: PM-900a golems are attacking the guards here. This is horrible! Without functioning guards, anyone could slip into Rata Sum. There are two primary ways to deal with the golems: beat them down with your character's abilities, or get a neuromitigator from the ground by Peacemaker Chief Grumm. If you're working alone, eight golems need to be weakened to get full credit for the event.

WHY USE A SMALL STICK?

The neuromitigator does more damage than your starting weapon skills, and it hits with a cone effect. As such, you can disable multiple golems at once.

The event demands that you disable the golems instead of killing them, so you don't get credit for killing blows either way. There's no reason NOT to use the neuromitigator.

DEFEND THE ETHEROPODS (Repeatable)

GOAL:	Defend the etheropods while Bluz harvests breeze rider eyes.
LEVEL:	3

Description: Bluz is using etheropods to attract breeze riders so he can harvest their eyes. He needs you to kill waves of enemies for him. As long as one etheropod is still standing when he collects the last eye, you win. Fight aggressively to ensure this happens!

WILDFLAME CAVERNS (SOUTHWEST SIDE)

SERVICES:	N/A
TRAVEL:	North to Soren Draa Waypoint, West to Jeztar Falls Waypoint
HARVESTING INFO:	N/A

The Wildflame Caverns are nestled between Soren Draa and a nearby lab. Embers live inside the cave. They're a minor hassle and don't drop much loot, but each target is fast to kill, so you can wade through them.

The caves produce fire opals, which are used to power a number of mechanical constructions in the region. If it's available, the "Fire Opals" event is a quick repeatable that should be done before traveling further west to the Opticalium.

FIRE OPALS (Repeatable)

GOAL:	Help Chott collect fire opals for a prototype golem weapon.
LEVEL:	3

Description: Chott and the Incinergen Lab krewe are working on a new weapon; they need fire opals to get it to work. Kill the embers in the cave for their opals.

There are also fire opals on the ground. Pass them to Chott, who wanders throughout the area, to increase your contribution.

HYDRONE UNIT WAYPOINT (SOUTH SIDE)

SERVICES:	Waypoint
TRAVEL:	West to Soren Draa Waypoint, Northeast to Loch Waypoint
HARVESTING INFO:	N/A

This waypoint is a middle spot between many of Metrica's southern points. Grab it while you're moving toward Jeztar Falls to cut down on travel times through here in the future.

JEZTAR FALLS WAYPOINT (SOUTH SIDE)

SERVICES:	Waypoint, Karma Vendor
TRAVEL:	East to Soren Draa Waypoint, North to Loch Waypoint
HARVESTING INFO:	N/A

There is a great deal to do around the Jeztar Falls Waypoint. Start at Opticalium Labs on the way from Soren Draa (to the west of Jeztar Falls); there's always something going on at the Opticalium. If you wait for a minute, you'll often find a new event to work on.

Once the Opticalium is safe, travel southwest to Incomp Labs and make sure everything is quiet over there. If the golem generators are under Inquest attack, help defend the laboratory before moving down to the beach near the waypoint.

There's a hylek village to the north, along the beach. These hylek have had their territory encroached upon by the Inquest, and they're rather displeased. Deal with the hylek chief and the Inquest in the water before moving to the northern edge of the lake (directly northeast of the waypoint).

PR&T Labs could use some assistance before you leave the area. Give them a hand before jumping back to the Soren Draa Waypoint; then your work here is done.

ASSIST THE OPTICALIUM (Renown Task)

GOAL:	Help maintain Opticalium Lab's field equipment and prevent Inquest interference.
LEVEL:	3

Description: The Inquest doesn't like competition, and they're here to cause trouble. Kill Inquest operatives while you revive fallen researchers and repair lab equipment. Depending on when you get here, the lab may have already fallen and you get to complete two events at once! Retake the lab while fighting and repairing equipment to get even more money and experience.

RETAKE THE OPTICALIUM (Repeatable)

GOAL:	Retake the Opticalium Lab from the Inquest.
LEVEL:	3

Description: Inquest agents have taken the Opticalium and it's up to you to see that their stay is short. Pay special attention to the Inquest turrets; they're incredibly mean. If you have powerful ranged attacks, take out the turrets first. If you're a close-range combatant, pull the Inquest attackers away from the turrets and kill them away from the artillery; you can then go in, destroy the turret itself, and attempt to hold the area. Note that the turrets are not considered part of the Inquest forces; they can appear at your back to fire on you even if you control the area, but they can't hold the territory without support from Inquest personnel.

Keep new enemies outside the circle to retake the lab. When there are other players holding the area, you can afford to stay outside the highlighted zone; this way you can attack Inquest agents before they enter the circle.

DEFEND THE OPTICALIUM (Repeatable)

GOAL:	Drive off the Inquest when they invade the Opticalium.
LEVEL:	4

Description: The Inquest is tired of waiting for subtle attacks to take care of the Opticalium. They sometimes make a direct assault on the building. Kill the attackers to score credit for this defensive operation. The Inquest invade from literally all directions, but the agents from the south won't count toward the main offense. Don't worry about them unless there are a lot of defenders. Target the golems that come in from the east. They have whirlwind attacks and bring down defenders quickly. If there are multiple characters defending, take the time to revive the fallen researchers around the compound. Each slain Inquest agent reduces its comrades' morale by 4%. Kill 25 of them and the Inquest will realize this prize isn't worth the cost.

GOLEM GENERATORS (Repeatable)

GOAL:	Defend the golem generators.
LEVEL:	4

Description: The Inquest is making a run against Incomp Optic's golem generators. Defend these from eight waves of Inquest attackers. The generators are spread out in several buildings, so don't try to defend all four generators; pick one and hold your ground. As long as the last generator doesn't fall, you can still complete the event without any lost experience or money.

HYLEK POISON (Renown Task)

GOAL:	Stop the Inquest from using hylek poison.
LEVEL:	4

Description: Grab hylek poison from the ground or from the hylek themselves. Give the poison to Blopp, the task giver (he's marked on your map). There are two good places to get this event done. If the Incomp Optics Lab is under attack, kill Inquest there to get credit for this task. Or, pick up underwater filters near the Inquest aqua lab; the Inquest you kill there also count.

CHIEF CIPACTLI (Repeatable)

GOAL:	Defeat Chief Cipactli.
LEVEL:	4

Description: Watch out for Chief Cipactli while heading into the hylek camp. He isn't any tougher than the other hyleks; he's just bigger, and you get bonus experience for taking the sucker down. Cut him down to size for an instant reward.

INQUEST BEACONS (Repeatable)

GOAL:	Destroy the beacons powering the Inquest aqua lab.
LEVEL:	5

Description: The lake by the hylek village is being used by the Inquest. There are three beacons underwater that need to be destroyed. Approach each one slowly to give yourself a chance to get used to underwater movement. Be similarly careful when using your weapon (this is likely your first chance to use your aquatic weapon). Watch for Inquest attackers and practice underwater fighting to unlock extra weapon skills. The more kills you get, the sooner you'll be able to use better underwater attacks.

ASSIST PR&T ESOTERICS (Renown Task)

GOAL:	Help the PR&T krewe collect sludge samples and create ooze from engineered plants.
LEVEL:	5

Description: The PR&T krewe have a lab across the river and up the hill. Go over there and grab an Oozone Alternator (there are many lying around). Start shooting the plants all along the hill. This turns them into oozes, which you can also shoot. It's pretty simple to get credit for this task. If "Put Them Back" is available at the same time, do that simultaneously, because it also counts toward this event.

PUT THEM BACK! (Repeatable)

GOAL:	Return toxic oozes to the storage tanks inside PR&T Esoterics.
LEVEL:	5

Description: When this event is available, grab the oozes near the compound whenever you see them. Run them to the storage tanks inside the lab. The oozes jump out of your hands and attack if you take too long, so take the most efficient path you can find. When you have to fight, beat the oozes quickly and hurry up the path before they make more trouble. While carrying these things, you get access to a run speed increase. Each ooze goes in a different tank, so watch what you're doing to avoid any frustrations or complications.

OLD GOLEM FACTORY WAYPOINT (SOUTHWEST OF CENTER)

SERVICES:	Waypoint
TRAVEL:	Soren Draa Waypoint (S), Rana Landing Complex Waypoint (NE)
HARVESTING INFO:	Copper Ore (Abundant), Aspen Saplings (Abundant)

Obscura Incline and the Old Golem Foundry are north from Soren Draa. Few people know that there are actually two groups working at the Obscura Incline. The Old Golem Foundry is being combed by salvage experts from Shoon's krewe, but some of the workers aren't what they seem. More Inquest problems?

To the west is a large door that leads to an Inquest base. Assault the base and finish the events inside after you help the workers at Obscura Incline. There's a lot to do here, so be patient and wait for those repeatable events. You miss out on serious experience by racing through the area.

SHOON'S SALVAGE (Renown Task)

GOAL:	Help Shoon's salvage krewe deal with Inquest interference.
LEVEL:	6

Description: There is a closed gate on the west side of Obscura Incline. Behind it is a hidden Inquest lab. Break through the gate with normal weapon attacks. Once

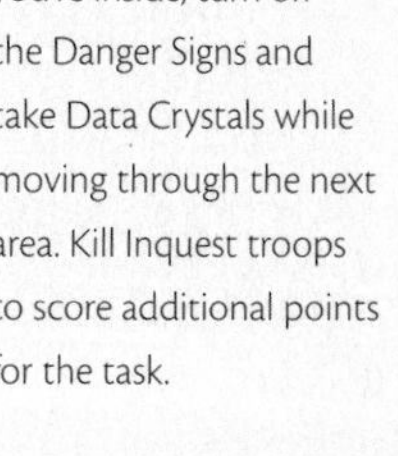

you're inside, turn off the Danger Signs and take Data Crystals while moving through the next area. Kill Inquest troops to score additional points for the task.

An alternative to sieging the base is to look for spies within Shoon's salvage krewe. Look for suspicious salvage specialists and reveal them as Inquest spies. Be ready to fight them, as they'll get violent when their cover is blown.

FREE THE SPECIALISTS (Repeatable)

GOAL:	Destroy cage control nodes to free the salvage specialists.
LEVEL:	6

Description: While you're inside the Inquest lab, destroy the three control nodes to free Shoon's specialists. The nodes are shown on your minimap, so it doesn't take long to find them.

HARVESTING

Now that you're out of the starting section, there are harvesting locations throughout the world. Watch your minimap for trees to cut down, ore to mine, and herbs to pick. Don't pass these up unless you are in an extreme hurry, as even non-crafters benefit by selling the materials or using the upgrades on equipment.

Everyone can harvest these materials. In addition, the harvesting points are not going to disappear for other people when you access them. Each member of a group can (and should) use each mine, tree, or plant they come across. This grants a small experience bonus, so you're even being rewarded for the brief time expended.

ROJ'S REVENGE (Repeatable)

GOAL:	Destroy the Inquest research pods.
LEVEL:	6

Description: Shortly after Roj and the specialists are freed, a new event begins. Roj intends to do more damage to the Inquest's research. Help him destroy six research pods. The specialists make good distractions if you're having any issues killing the enemies. Keep reviving the asura if they go down. They'll contribute a little damage to your battles and prevent all of the enemies from attacking your character.

THE ESCAPE (Repeatable)

GOAL:	Destroy Inquest golems.
LEVEL:	6

Description: This event begins after "Roj's Revenge." As you and the specialists try to escape, Inquest agents catch you in a trap. They have several new golems ready to make your life difficult. This is a tougher fight if you go after the MK II golem immediately. It has the most health of all the enemies. Luckily, that golem isn't especially deadly; let it wait until the other targets are destroyed. The MK I golems have a whirlwind Knockback attack. Kill them first and then target the Inquest extinguisher. That foe slows your characters and hassles people from range. Once the fight is under control, deal with the MK II. Be ready to evade its rapid-fire punches.

COPPER ORE AND ASPEN SAPLINGS IN ABUNDANCE

Once you pass through the Inquest lab, take a look around the exit passage. There is often a rich Copper vein there. Even when there isn't, you can find a great deal of Copper Ore and trees by following the west side of the lake (going north into Fisher's Beach Bend). The enemies are level 8, so be ready for some tough fights.

RANA LANDING COMPLEX WAYPOINT (SOUTHWEST OF CENTER)

SERVICES:	Waypoint, Armorsmith, Weaponsmith, Salvage Merchant
TRAVEL:	Old Golem Factory Waypoint (SW), Mochotal Waypoint (N), Akk Wilds (SE), Loch Waypoint (S)
HARVESTING INFO:	Copper Ore, Aspen Saplings, Mushrooms

Brill Alliance Labs and the Rana Landing Complex sit along the Voloxian Passage between Soren Draa and Desider Atum. Both of these buildings are very secure and offer travelers a place to rest. You can also find merchants here! Rana Landing is a good place to sell excess goods before heading back out into the wild.

With empty bags and full health, head south to the Serpentwind; it's full of skritt and allows you to complete a task while traveling to Dr. Bleent's Encampment. After setting things right with Dr. Bleent, travel southeast to the Akk Wilds Waypoint.

SKRITT STUDIES 101 (Renown Task)

GOAL:	Help the Brill Alliance study the skritt.
LEVEL:	7

Description: Look for lone skritt standing by mysterious devices up a nearby hill. Talk to the captivated skritt to make them mad. Once they're enraged, bash them until they become docile again. Though this can be done in the immediate area, the tunnel nearby is much more fun. Head southeast to the tunnel and activate monitors as you go; they're small machines pushed into the ground and appear fairly often. This lets you complete the task much sooner.

YERKK'S RESEARCH (Repeatable)

GOAL:	Defend Yerkk while he isolates skritt for his IQ experiment.
LEVEL:	7

Description: Yerkk and his assistant Lemm need skritt subjects; Yerkk walks through the Serpentwind getting them. Protect him from attackers, because he's very weak and goes down easily if attacked for long. The good news is you can revive him when he's knocked out. Follow Yerkk and help him subdue 10 skritt test subjects.

SKRITT LOVE FUNGUS

Skritt tunnels are good places to look for harvestable fungus. The ones here provide Mushrooms for any cooks you know!

ECOSYSTEM HELP (Renown Task)

GOAL:	Help Hrouda maintain the ecosystem in spite of Dr. Bleent's research.
LEVEL:	8

Description: To the southeast of Rana Landing is an area with many oozes and eggs. To complete the task in that area, eliminate rogue oozes, return evidential wurm eggs, and clean up ooze remnants. Dr. Bleent's camp also has puddles that can be cleaned up. Wurm eggs are found all over the ground and often reveal an ooze when you pick them up. Use these to finish the task as quickly as possible.

AN OOZING PROPOSITION (Group)

GOAL:	Defeat the giant ooze at Doctor Bleent's camp.
LEVEL:	8

Description: On occasion, a champion giant ooze appears in Dr. Bleent's camp, on the far side of the skritt tunnel (or around the hills). Do not take this target lightly! Dodge its attacks while you clear the smaller oozes from the area, and then engage the big one last. You probably can't tackle this nasty fellow by yourself. Ask for help from other players in the area, form a group, or get some guild buddies to come out and squish the giant ooze with you. Characters with healing abilities or damage mitigation are useful, because the giant ooze hits quite hard for such a low-level monster.

To make the fight more interesting, the giant ooze can summon two regular oozes at regular intervals. The only good news is that these extra oozes die when the giant one does. If you're almost done with the fight, let the little guys take their attacks while you focus on the boss. Or, let area-of-effect attacks from your group kill the lesser oozes throughout the fight so no one has to switch targets and thin his ranks.

AKK WILDS WAYPOINT (SOUTHEAST SIDE)

SERVICES:	Waypoint
TRAVEL:	Rana Landing Complex Waypoint (NW), Desider Atum (NNW), Cuatl Waypoint (N)
HARVESTING INFO:	Copper Ore, Aspen Saplings, Mushrooms, Root Vegetables

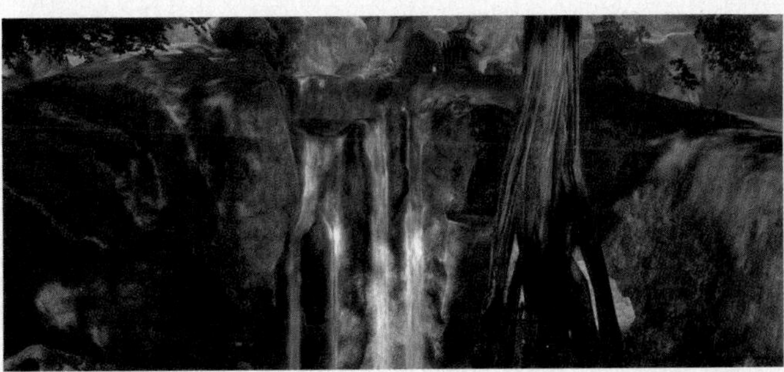

There's a bit of history in the southern Akk Wilds. Legends say there is a secret lab in the Sunshade Caves. A girl named Parnna is looking into it. She's on the right track, but someone has to help her deal with the skritt first. Head southeast to Parnna's Gate and give her a hand. If the gate is damaged, you'll have to head into the skritt tunnel farther southeast to get the pieces back.

When you're finished there, it's time to jump back to Rana Landing, empty your bags, and follow the road east. Alternatively, you can take an overland route north.

THE TRANSFER CHAMBER (Renown Task)

GOAL:	Aid Parnna's research into the ancient transfer chamber.
LEVEL:	9

Description: Look for this task southeast from the Akk Wilds Waypoint. When you get into the area, recover gate pieces and defeat the skritt who try to stop Parnna from collecting data inside the chamber. Fight your way into the room while killing all of the skritt nearby. Look for gate pieces on the ground and pick them up between fights.

STOP THE FORAGERS (Repeatable)

GOAL:	Stop skritt foragers from destroying the Asura Gate.
LEVEL:	9

Description: This event is sometimes triggered while you're in Parnna's area. The event is on a 5-minute timer. Skritt foragers and bottle lobbers come into the area in a steady stream. They're trying to take out the Asura Gate. Foragers are the ones that damage the gate, but they aren't your primary concern. The bottle lobbers stay at the back and can knock you down. Use your best burst-damage attacks on the bottle lobbers to kill them quickly and then use normal attacks on the foragers between waves of bottle lobbers. That's the safe way to win.

PARNNA'S ROOTS (Repeatable)

GOAL:	Escort Parnna into Calx's ancient lab.
LEVEL:	10

Description: After successfully completing "Stop the Foragers," you get a chance to continue the event chain. Move through the gate into a new area. Collect Data Crystals from the ground and give them to Parnna. Oozes boil out of the floor at regular intervals and Parnna can't be revived if she falls, so watch her back while you're gathering materials. Stay near her and only go off to grab Data Crystals when they are close by or just after a wave of oozes has been killed.

SAVE PARNNA (Repeatable)

GOAL:	Kill enough destroyers that the golems release Parnna.
LEVEL:	10

Description: Things aren't finished with this event chain yet! Parnna has triggered a security program and is trapped until the golems are sure the area is cleansed. To stop the alert, kill destroyers throughout the area. They're sometimes found in clumps. Use ranged attacks to pull the destroyers toward you. This averts larger fights if you're worried about being overwhelmed. The event is completed as soon as enough of the destroyers are slain.

DESIDER ATUM WAYPOINT (SOUTHEAST OF CENTER)

SERVICES:	Waypoint, Equipment Repair, Merchant (Salvage), Crafting Trainers (Huntsman, Weaponsmith, Armorsmith, Jeweler, Artificer, Tailor, Leatherworker, Chef), Armorsmith, Weaponsmith, Scout
TRAVEL:	Rana Landing Complex Waypoint (W), Akk Wilds Waypoint (S/SE), Cuatl Waypoint (E), Michotl Waypoint (NE)
HARVESTING INFO:	Copper Ore, Aspen Saplings, Root Vegetables

Desider Atum is a home away from home for many Rata Sum scholars. Craftmasters from every school have workshops here, along with merchants from many trades. If you can't find something in Desider Atum, you'll have to head to the capital.

To the east is Cuatl Morass. This area is slightly lower level, and it's a good place to start. When you return from clearing that region, speak with Caracotl outside the town. Escort him toward the Michotl Grounds Waypoint. Help the hylek and then return to Desider Atum. Only then should you set your sights farther north, toward Arterium Haven Waypoint.

ESCORT CARACOTL (Repeatable)

GOAL:	Escort Caracotl to Michotl Grounds.
LEVEL:	10

Description: Follow Caracotl as he makes his way to the Michotl Grounds. Fight off anything that gets too close, and wait for the event to finish. Make sure you're patient during the trip.

CUATL WAYPOINT (EAST SIDE)

SERVICES:	Waypoint
TRAVEL:	Desider Atum Waypoint (W)
HARVESTING INFO:	Copper Ore

The Lionguard have bottled up the Cuatl Tribe in this area, but they haven't been able to eliminate the Cuatl hylek completely. The further the Lionguard pushes, the more intense their opposition. As if the hylek weren't enough of a problem, Inquest agents are doing something with a cannon close by. Help the Lionguard deal with the hylek before jumping back to Desider Atum.

THE CUATL HYLEK (Renown Task)

GOAL:	Help the Lionguard keep the Cuatl hylek in check.
LEVEL:	10

Description: Eliminate the Cuatl hylek, smash their eggs and turrets, and protect the haven from raids. Watch out for flame spitters; these turrets deal damage over a wide area and hit targets with an effect that damages over time. Kill your way to the bottom of the area and start smashing eggs. Kill the flame spitters first in any engagement. If the area is cleared out already, climb the hill on the northeast side of the area. There are additional targets there. Go into the tunnel and follow that to reach the area between Artergon Woods and the Luminates Plant.

THE HYLEK CHIEF (Repeatable)

GOAL:	Defeat the hylek chief.
LEVEL:	11

Description: Friendly attackers occasionally start an attack on the hylek camp. If you're bold, follow them in and help the group kill the chief. Once the area is clear, look for some Michotl Brew to complete a Skill Challenge.

MICHOTL GROUNDS WAYPOINT (WEST OF CENTER)

SERVICES:	Waypoint, Armorsmith, Weaponsmith, Karma Merchant
TRAVEL:	Rana Landing Complex Waypoint (S), Desider Atum Waypoint (SE)
HARVESTING INFO:	Minimal

Michotl Grounds Waypoint is a desolate section of Metrica. The marsh is untamed, mostly because it's an unsuitable area for construction. As the asura don't have much interest in the wetlands, other creatures have moved in. There is a hylek village in the marsh and a krait settlement in the lake to the west. Help the peaceful Michotl tribe before jumping back to Desider Atum for the trip north.

AID THE MICHOTL TRIBE (Renown Task)

GOAL:	Assist in dragonfly hunts and protect the Michotl tribe from hylek and krait invaders.
LEVEL:	11

Description: Kill monsters on your way across the swamp. The repeatable events in the area help you finish this task, so it's a good opportunity to get a few things done at the same time.

KILL THE CUATL THIEVES (Repeatable)

GOAL:	Kill Cuatl thieves.
LEVEL:	10

Description: Attack the rampaging thieves before the Michotl supplies are depleted. If the enemies get all of the supplies, the event fails and you only get a portion of the money, karma, and experience for your work. To win, kill roughly 16 of the thieves. Abilities that slow or Stun targets are useful because they give you more time to attack the enemies before they make their escape.

SAVE THE EGGS (Repeatable)

GOAL:	Stop the krait from destroying hylek eggs.
LEVEL:	10

Description: Several waves of krait attempt to swarm a group of 11 hylek eggs. The eggs are all in one place, so you can plant your feet, deploy any banners, and go to town on the enemies that approach.

ARTERIUM HAVEN WAYPOINT (CENTER)

SERVICES:	Waypoint, Karma Merchant
TRAVEL:	Desider Atum (S), Artergon Waypoint (N)
HARVESTING INFO:	Copper Ore, Aspen Saplings, Leafy Vegetables (Abundant)

At first glance, the Arterium doesn't look like much; the action is to the east of this waypoint. That's where you find the Luminates Plant. Be sure to take a circuit of the plant if you're interested in seeing a beautiful waterfall or harvesting crafting materials. Once the Inquest have been dealt with, return to Arterium Haven Waypoint and head north to Artergon Waypoint.

REQUISITION GONE WRONG (Repeatable)

GOAL:	Drive off the Inquest before they steal all of the LUM0009 golems.
LEVEL:	12

Description: The Inquest have come to the Luminates Plant with an offer the technicians can't accept. Inquest agents are trying to take this lab's golems without paying! Drive off the Inquest to finish the event. You need to kill roughly 15 of the enemies before they steal the golems.

ARTERGON WAYPOINT (NORTH OF CENTER)

SERVICES:	Waypoint
TRAVEL:	Arterium Haven Waypoint (S), Hexane Regrade (E), Muridian Waypoint (N/NW), Survivor's Encampment Waypoint (W)
HARVESTING INFO:	Copper Ore, Aspen Saplings, Herb Patches, Root Vegetables, Leather (from Panthers in the Northern Cave)

The power grid for the Luminates Plant dominates this area. The woods give way to rolling plains, which are only noteworthy for their power conduits and mosquitoes. This waypoint is a hub, so it's useful for finishing nearby tasks. Return here before setting off again. This cuts down on travel time. After finishing the local events, travel east to reach Hexane Regrade Waypoint.

THE POWER GRID (Renown Task)

GOAL:	Help the Luminates Plant krewe maintain the power grid.
LEVEL:	12

Description: Activate mini-conduits, stop Inquest interference, and destroy the energy distortions and mosquitoes that are drawn to the grid. There are so many groundspawns and enemies that you won't have any trouble finishing this task. Watch your back, as the mosquitoes roam in groups of three. Characters with area-of-effect attacks can wipe them out in a flash.

THEY CUT THE POWER (Repeatable)

GOAL:	Protect Zoydd's efforts to restart the power grid.
LEVEL:	12

Description: The baseline event in this area starts with Zoydd trying to get the grid working. Each tower nearby has a Repairatron that starts working to fix it. Defend these golems while the towers are fixed. The golems will not help you fight. Start your patrol in the northwest and finish in the southeast. This puts you in a good position for the second part of the event. Zoydd runs from the Luminates Plant to Transformer Hub Kachong and begins repairs. Waves of Inquest attack him. Fight them off!

KILL THE AIR ELEMENTAL (Repeatable)

GOAL:	Kill the air elemental.
LEVEL:	13

Description: This event begins after the grid powers back up. An air elemental spawns during this power surge, and two sparks accompany it. Ranged characters should kill the sparks first, as they coat the area in an electrical field that inflicts damage over time. The sparks don't deploy the electric field against melee enemies, so close-range attackers can afford to rush the air elemental immediately. Kill this group of enemies to finish the event.

HEXANE REGRADE WAYPOINT (NORTHEAST SIDE)

SERVICES:	Waypoint
TRAVEL:	Exit to Caledon Forest (Level 1-15 Sylvari Region) (E), Artergon Waypoint (W)
HARVESTING INFO:	Copper Ore, Aspen Saplings

Hexane Regrade lies in the shadow of an immense Inquest base. Be careful in these hills, because Inquest agents are out there.

Of course, if you want a change of pace, you can take the nearby exit to Caledon Forest. This wilderness is home to the sylvari, but they could always use help in safeguarding their area.

DISRUPT THE INQUEST (Renown Task)

GOAL:	Help Researcher Owta disrupt the Inquest.
LEVEL:	13

Description: Take out Inquest operatives, destroy lab equipment, and rescue prisoners. Make your way into the Inquest lab. Watch for grenadiers, as they can sit at range and blast your party with area-of-effect damage. Spread out if you have any allies; this makes it easier to kill the grenadiers quickly.

RECOVERY OF STOLEN GOODS (Repeatable)

GOAL:	Recover stolen LUM0009 golems from the Inquest.
LEVEL:	13

Description: The Inquest have managed to get ahold of several of the LUM0009 golems from the Luminates Plant and returned to their headquarters with them. The golems have already been reprogrammed, so you need to bring them to low health to restart their ordinary orders. Find and recover all three golems to complete this event.

THE BOMB (Repeatable)

GOAL:	Intercept Inquest saboteurs before they reach the power station.
LEVEL:	13

Description: Occasionally, Inquest engineers craft a mobile bomb that starts heading toward the power station. The Mark IV Mobile Bomb then appears on your map, and you need to stop it as soon as possible. Inquest troops defend this special golem. Take out these guards first, and then trash the golem as soon as they're dead.

MURIDIAN WAYPOINT (NORTH SIDE)

SERVICES:	Waypoint
TRAVEL:	Brisban Wildlands (Level 15-25 Asura/Sylvari Region) (N), Arterium Haven Waypoint (SE), Survivor's Encampment Waypoint (S)
HARVESTING INFO:	Copper Ore, Aspen Saplings

This waypoint is in a section of plains between the Thaumanova Reactor and a small Inquest lab. Recently, the reactor has started spewing poisonous gases—and that can't be allowed to continue. Finish the events at the reactor and then travel south to Survivor's Encampment Waypoint.

GATHER PARTS (Repeatable)

GOAL: Collect golem parts for Walla's H.A.Z.M.A.T. suits.

LEVEL: 13

Description: Golem parts are scattered on the ground throughout the area. They can also be torn from enemy golems. Both methods give you credit. It takes about 12 parts to finish the event. Turn these in to Walla (on the minimap).

HELP THE C.L.E.A.N. KREWE (Renown Task)

GOAL: Kill Inquest agents, destroy chaos rifts, kill the beasts that emerge from the rifts, and detoxify researchers.

LEVEL: 14

Description: The lab is hosed. Rifts are randomly opening and spitting out creatures from who knows where. Kill these enemies as you go. All the mobs are neutral until you attack, so there's no chance of getting swarmed here. Look for researchers while clearing the area; helping them gives you a quick boost toward the task's completion. You can also stick around and look at the different creatures that come out of the rifts. It's a fun place to rack up kill variety while you're hunting.

DESTROY THE CHAOS (Repeatable)

GOAL: Destroy the chaotic materials created by the reactor meltdown.

LEVEL: 14

Description: The chaotic materials are found on the ground, often surrounded by chaos beasts. These beasts die when the chaotic material is destroyed, so a fast rush against the material is fairly effective. Area-of-effect attacks are good, too. The material deals damage every few seconds to everything close by; the damage isn't high, but it's worth noting. Don't start these fights unless you have all of your health. There are six sets of chaotic materials that need to be destroyed.

ESCORT THE C.L.E.A.N. GOLEM (Repeatable)

GOAL: Escort the C.L.E.A.N. 5000 golem while it absorbs clouds of chaos magic.

LEVEL: 14

Description: The next event in the lab area is to escort a golem while it soaks up chaos magic. Locate the golem on your minimap, go to it, and then protect the machine. Inquest operatives come after the golem repeatedly. All you have to do is fight them off until the event completes.

DEFEND THE C.L.E.A.N. GOLEM (Repeatable)

GOAL: Defend the golem as it cleans the core.

LEVEL: 15

Description: Victory in the previous event starts a timed section. For 5 minutes, you have to protect the golem from a major Inquest assault. Operatives port in all over the room, but they won't come at you in large groups. The fire in the room doesn't hurt you, so don't worry about bumping into it.

KILL THE FIRE ELEMENTAL (Group)

GOAL:	Destroy the fire elemental.
LEVEL:	15

Description: Beating the previous events turns you into the victim of your own success. The final stage of this chain is tricky and dangerous. A fire elemental appears, and it summons embers all over the room. The elemental blasts different sections of the chamber with fire, dealing damage to anyone standing inside the area of effect. It also tosses waves of fire. Dodge to avoid the attacks, because they deal a huge amount of damage.

Clear an area of embers so there is more room to maneuver. Watch the ground for red circles (these are the warning signs that a flame burst is about to land). Ranged characters are more effective against the elemental because they have more time to react before being hit by the fire attacks. Even melee characters should consider switching to ranged weapons. Work in conjunction with any other players in the area to defeat the fire elemental and complete the chain.

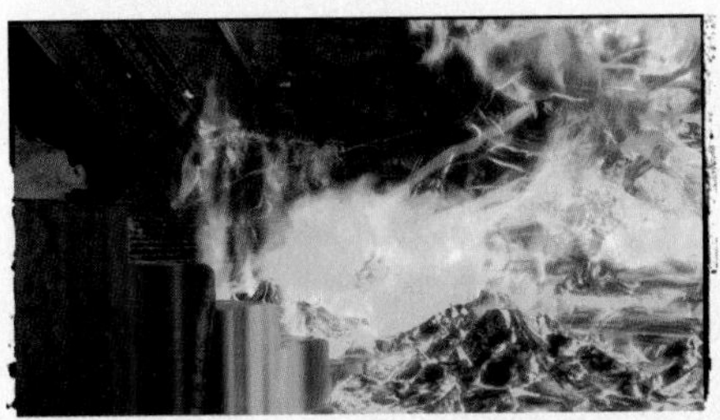

SURVIVOR'S ENCAMPMENT WAYPOINT (NORTHWEST OF CENTER)

SERVICES:	Waypoint, Salvage Merchant, Karma Merchant
TRAVEL:	Muridian Waypoint (N), Arterium Haven Waypoint (E), Anthill Waypoint (S)
HARVESTING INFO:	Copper Ore (Abundant), Aspen Saplings (Abundant), Root Vegetables, Herb Patches

This area lies between the reactor, the anthill, and an Inquest lab. The Greyfern Expanse isn't a safe place! Inquest agents raid the area for prisoners, and jungle wurms are everywhere. Once you've handled the events here, head south to the anthill and continue cleaning up the fallout of the reactor.

DRAIN THE MARK II (Renown Task)

GOAL:	Drain the Mark II golem's power before it reaches the Inquest gate.
LEVEL:	14

Description: The Inquest has imbued a golem with great power. Now they're trying to get it home, along with a group of test subjects. Damage the golem to force it to repair itself (which takes away some of its power). Each time you defeat the golem, reinforcements arrive. Be ready for a hard fight, as the golem doesn't have far to go and you need to defeat it again and again. Anyone using attacks that push enemies around should keep the golem from making progress. Knockdowns are also quite useful.

DESTROY ALL INTRAFLUXION NODES (Repeatable)

GOAL:	Destroy all intrafluxion nodes before the golem's energy core is fully charged.
LEVEL:	14

Description: You have to enter a small instanced area to continue this line of events. A timer begins, and you have 7 minutes to destroy eight power nodes. Kill the enemies that guard each area before attacking the nodes directly. Your foes are able to sense when the nodes take damage, and they'll come to investigate (you end up with larger fights because of this). Clearing the guards ahead of time ensures you don't have to fight everyone at once. Leave the instanced area after the event completes.

LEAD THE IMBUED GOLEM (Repeatable)

GOAL:	Lead the imbued golem's energy core to the Survivor's Encampment.
LEVEL:	14

Description: The event chain continues. You now have to escort the energy core out of the area. Its goal is to reach the Survivor's Encampment, but teams of Inquest agents attack. Each group has three or four members, and they sometimes have golems with them. Target MK I golems as soon as possible because of their pesky knockdowns. If your golem takes too much damage, back off. The construct shuts down for a time and then wakes back up with an electrical burst. Avoid the damage from this and then continue your escort.

ANTHILL WAYPOINT (WEST SIDE)

SERVICES:	Waypoint, Weaponsmith, Armorsmith, Salvage Merchant
TRAVEL:	Survivor's Encampment Waypoint (N)
HARVESTING INFO:	Copper Ore, Mushrooms (Abundant)

The Anthill is the largest skritt settlement in Metrica Province. The local skritt are busy collecting interesting rocks; they're a friendly bunch, so you're free to talk to them.

This is the last place that truly needs an adventurer's help in Metrica. You're almost ready to move on to bigger problems!

AID THE CHOAS KREWE (Renown Task)

GOAL:	Clean up chaotic material, kill chaos beasts, and try to convince the skritt to stop collecting these materials.
LEVEL:	13

Description: Destroying chaos material creates chaos beasts (levels 13-14), but they're very weak. Kill these creatures and look for skritt foragers to talk to. The foragers won't always give up their rocks, so it's kind of a random event. When the skritt are convinced to stop what they're doing, you get credit toward this task.

KILL CHAOS (Group)

GOAL:	Kill the chaos creature.
LEVEL:	13

Description: A chaotic monster appears here from time to time. The beast has a good amount of health, but it's still squishy if you kill its summoned allies quickly and keep pressure on it. As with many group events, you may need to grab buddies from the area or ask a guild member to come by and help during the fight. Putting one person on dedicated add duty (to kill summoned creatures) makes it much easier to finish the event.

CALEDON FOREST

LEVEL RANGE:	1-15
TASKS:	18
WAYPOINTS:	18
SKILL CHALLENGES:	7
HARVESTING INFO:	Copper Ore, Aspen Saplings, Early Cooking Ingredients

SKILL CHALLENGES

- Morgan's Orchid (North of Spiral Waypoint, In the Open) (SE)
- Dark Thorn (Far North from Spiral Waypoint, Inside the Briarthorn Den) (E)
- Waterfall (West of Caer Astorea Waypoint, On a Small Hill) (SW)
- Mysterious Patch of Ground (East of Brigid's Overlook Waypoint, Near the Cliffs) (Center)
- Swift Arrow (East of Titan's Staircase Waypoint, At the End of the Bridge) (E)
- Krait Altar (East of Kraitbane Haven Waypoint, At the Bottom of the Lake) (NE)
- Powerful Darkness (North of Twilight Arbor Waypoint, Out in the Open) (NW)

Caledon Forest is a wilderness under siege. While the sylvari and the Nightmare Court battle for supremacy, the skritt continue to be a nuisance and the Orrian undead boil up from the ground itself. Copses of trees and marsh give way suddenly to rotten soil.

These are not the only major players in the region, however. Hylek, soundless, and tengu all try to eke out a living within and along the edges of this verdant area. Their goal: to settle far enough away from the fighting that they can expand and be themselves but remain close enough to ask for help when things go wrong.

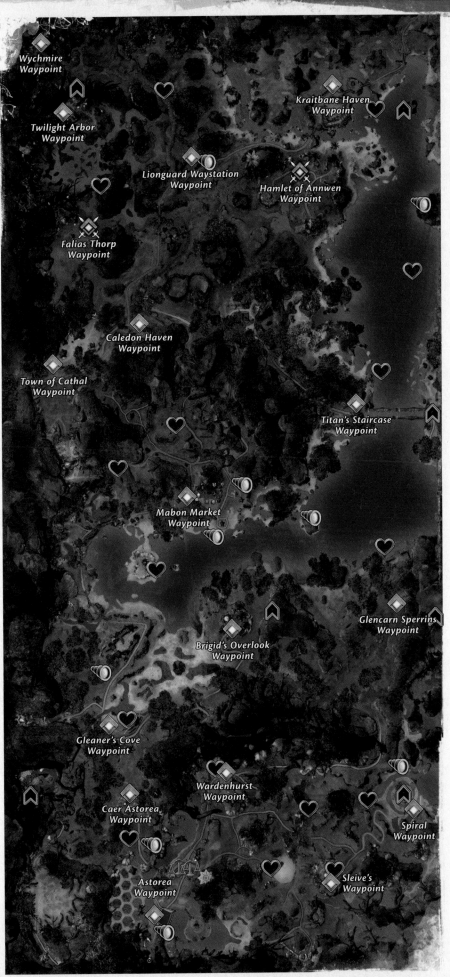

Wychmire Waypoint
Kraitbane Haven Waypoint
Twilight Arbor Waypoint
Lionguard Waystation Waypoint
Hamlet of Annwen Waypoint
Falias Thorp Waypoint
Caledon Haven Waypoint
Town of Cathal Waypoint
Titan's Staircase Waypoint
Mabon Market Waypoint
Glencarn Sperrins Waypoint
Brigid's Overlook Waypoint
Gleaner's Cove Waypoint
Wardenhurst Waypoint
Caer Astorea Waypoint
Spiral Waypoint
Astorea Waypoint
Sleive's Waypoint

TARNISHED COAST

ASTOREA WAYPOINT (SOUTH SIDE)

SERVICES:	Waypoint, Black Lion Trading Company, Equipment Repair
TRAVEL:	The Grove (S), Wardenhurst Waypoint (N)
HARVESTING INFO:	N/A

Astorea is a small village dominated by Rime's Garden on one side and Solitaire Island on the other. The primary purpose of Astorea is simply growing produce and supplying the populace of the Grove with food and materials.

In such a peaceful area, there is little to do in Astorea that isn't directly related to supplying the Grove. Help the workers in Astorea before heading north along the road to Wardenhurst.

Here you get the combat you've been craving, as Orrian undead work hard to take the small outpost.

NOT THE TREE! (Repeatable)

GOAL: Stop termites from consuming the Wardenlight Tree.

LEVEL: 2

Description: Termites and termite larvae come from three sides to attack the tree. Kill the larvae before they get a chance to burrow. If they burrow, grab a shovel (which are found all around the area) and dig them out.

LIGHTING THE WAY (Repeatable)

GOAL: Give firefly luminescence to Warden Annwyn.

LEVEL: 2

Description: Kill fireflies for their essence and submit it to Warden Annwyn. If there are no fireflies alive, search for firefly nests; you can get at least one firefly luminescence and often a firefly with another. If a lot of people are doing this event, be sure to turn it in often so the event doesn't end before you get credit.

WARDENHURST WAYPOINT (SOUTH OF CENTER)

SERVICES:	Waypoint, Salvage Merchant, Karma Merchant
TRAVEL:	Astorea Waypoint (SW), Spiral Waypoint (E)
HARVESTING INFO:	N/A

Wardenhurst is one of the more dangerous towns near the Grove. The Orrian undead have pushed pretty far into Caledon Forest, and Wardenhurst is under constant harassment. It even occasionally falls before reinforcements can get there. For this reason, Wardenhurst is populated almost entirely by guards. Have your weapons ready when you approach this town.

Once you've secured the area a bit better, head southeast along the roads to the Verdence. The Verdence is a lush area of growth, one the most pleasant places in Caledon Forest. It's easy to see what the forest was before the undead threat arose here. Valiant Estiene is looking for hardy adventurers here; give him a hand before heading to Grenbrack Delves.

SUPPORTING THE WARDENS (Renown Task)

GOAL: Help Gemai support the wardens of Wardenhurst.

LEVEL: 2

Description: Wardenhurst is under constant attack by undead. Dig up Grasping Hands to expose the undead (and kill them), replenish withered territory markers, and spar with local wardens. There are plenty of Orrian undead and Grasping Hands, so you won't need to look for territory markers or spar with the locals often.

LIBERATE WARDENHURST (Repeatable)

GOAL:	Liberate Wardenhurst from the undead.
LEVEL:	2

Description: Wardenhurst has fallen and you need to get it back. Start at the edge of town and kill your way toward the center, reviving fallen sylvari as you go. These revived guards will aid in the retaking.

DEFEND WARDENHURST (Repeatable)

GOAL:	Defend Wardenhurst from the undead.
LEVEL:	2

Description: There is little rest in Wardenhurst. By the time you have retaken the guardpost, more waves of Orrian undead have assembled and thrown themselves at the defenders. You have to defeat eight waves of attackers. Stick near the guards, as they can hold an enemy until you can get around to killing it.

MASTIFFS (Renown Task)

GOAL:	Help Danador tend the Sylvan Mastiffs.
LEVEL:	3

Description: Danador is raising the sylvan mastiffs that help guard the borders of sylvari lands. Help raise and protect the sylvan mastiffs by removing local pests, tending to the pack, and finding lost dogs. The bags of feed and pest repellant are along the fence. Grab the feed and take it to the nearest mastiff. You can feed the same mastiff multiple times, so don't run farther than you have to. Do this task before the following repeatable, as the escort takes you well away from here and you'll have to backtrack. The only entrance in the fence is near the task (on the map).

TAKE THE FIGHT TO THEM (Repeatable)

GOAL:	Defend Valiant Estiene as he attacks the undead.
LEVEL:	3

Description: It's time to get a bit of your own back from the undead. Valiant Estiene knows where some of the undead are coming from and wants to try and weed them out in a more permanent fashion, but he needs help: he needs you.

This is a long trek north to an undead stronghold with small waves of Orrian undead along the way. If you need to rest, let Estiene take some hits while you heal; he'll start moving again as soon as the enemy is dead. You are also assisted by the Valiant's pet broodmother. She's able to attack the undead with cone-ranged fire breath, so try to keep the enemies in front of her.

NOT THE DRAKE! (Repeatable)

GOAL:	Slay the undead drake broodmother.
LEVEL:	4

Description: After you fight your way to the back of the cave, something really unfortunate happens. A corpse caller runs up and infects the pet broodmother, turning it into an undead drake broodmother. She then turns on you to attack and immediately starts spawning smaller undead drakes. Use all your burst attack abilities to bring the broodmother down. Poor thing! Head out of the cave and southwest to Grenbrack to continue.

GRENBRACK DELVES (SOUTH OF CENTER)

SERVICES:	N/A
TRAVEL:	Wardenhurst Waypoint (W), Spiral Waypoint (E), Sleive's Inlet (S/SE)
HARVESTING INFO:	N/A

Enormous flowers bloom over still water and keep Grenbrack Delves in a state of constant shadow. This habitat is wonderful for both the scaled drakes who make their home under the petals and the spiders that live in the cave to the north. The spiders are getting awfully big, though.

OF COURSE THERE ARE SPIDERS (Renown Task)

GOAL: Help Elain clear the spider cave.

LEVEL: 4

Description: Gather mushrooms as you delve into the cave. Kill spiders, tear down their webs, destroy any toxic mushrooms, and look for people trapped (freeing the trapped people also contributes to the next event). This is pretty straightforward.

Head to the cave in the north. Aim for the trapped people first as you have to fight your way to them, and freeing them spawns spiders. Don't worry about squishing spider egg sacs or toxic mushrooms, or picking edible mushrooms, unless there are no spiders. It's just faster to kill things.

AND PEOPLE TRAPPED (Repeatable)

GOAL: Rescue sylvari trapped in webs.

LEVEL: 4

Description: Look for sylvari webbed against the walls; there are eight of them in total. Don't attack the webs if you are low on health, as up to four spiders can spawn from each web.

AND A QUEEN (Repeatable)

GOAL: Kill the enraged spider queen.

LEVEL: 4

Description: The spider queen comes to attack you with four hatchlings in tow once you've rescued the last sylvari. The spiderlings drop pretty quickly and the queen doesn't do huge damage, but she has quite a bit of health and can poison you. She can also summon more spiderlings if the fight lasts too long.

SLEIVE'S INLET (SOUTHEAST SIDE)

SERVICES:	Salvage Merchant
TRAVEL:	Spiral Waypoint (NE), The Verdence (E), Grenbrack Delves (N/NW), Sleive's Waypoint (SE)
HARVESTING INFO:	N/A

Follow the road from Grenbrack Delves east and then turn southwest. This isn't the quickest route, but there is only one way to the top of the bluff overlooking Sleive's Inlet. From here the wardens watch the undead menaces teem out of the swamp, but they are too few in numbers to actually stop the incursion.

Deal with the undead threat before talking to Brugh, as he is heading north and there are people who need help here.

CLEANING HOUSE (Renown Task)

GOAL: Assist Wyld Hunt Valiant Caillech with the undead.

LEVEL: 4

Description: To the southeast is a bog with many Orrian undead and noxious plants. You can kick the plants apart as you encounter them, but the fastest way to complete this task is to kill the undead.

UNFRIENDLY NEIGHBOR (Repeatable)

GOAL: Defeat the undead abomination.

LEVEL: 4

Description: Along with the smaller undead, an abomination has decided to move in. As you're killing the undead horde, watch for the abomination. It doesn't move (so it won't sneak up on you), but you don't want to stumble onto it by accident when there are a couple fast patrols of thralls nearby. Even an adventurer would have trouble with so many foes simultaneously. Pick off the outer enemies as you are able to until you can fight the abomination alone. Unless you choose to kite the abomination, start the fight by closing with the abomination and pushing it against the nearby tree. This will keep you out of range of the patrols. With the abomination dead, you can now push the undead out of the swamp entirely.

GET OUT! (Repeatable)

GOAL: Drive off the remaining undead horde.

LEVEL: 4

Description: There's no subtlety to this. Pick off the Orrian undead along the fringe if you want to be safe, or dive in and murder them as a group if you feel powerful. Watch out for the brutes, though. They move slower, but they are extremely durable and deal more damage. With the undead threat at a level that the wardens can handle alone, speak with Brugh and head north.

BRUGH (Repeatable)

GOAL: Escort Brugh to Morgan's Spiral.

LEVEL: 4

Description: Brugh is on his way to build/grow a tower in Morgan's Spiral. The undead, however, are trying to stop him, and they attack him several times along the way. Brugh is kinda squishy, but he can be revived. The undead attack in groups with three types of enemies: thralls, plague carriers, and brutes. The plague carriers need to be killed first, as they will run up to either Brugh or you and explode! The thralls are pretty straightforward, but they can distract you from a brute that is lumbering in. Once the thralls are down (or sooner if the thralls live very long), look around and locate the brute. This enemy can knock you down; it is disastrous to get caught off guard by one.

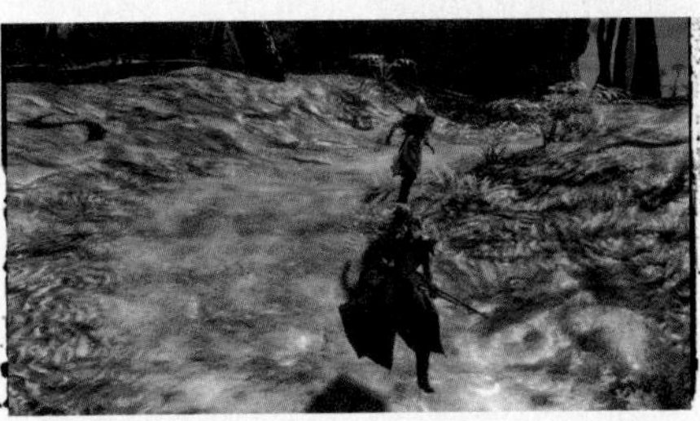

SPIRAL WAYPOINT (SOUTHEAST SIDE)

SERVICES:	Waypoint
TRAVEL:	Grenbrack Delves (W)
HARVESTING INFO:	N/A

Why is it that the most beautiful of places are always targets for undead incursions? Morgan's Spiral is a picturesque area with the Morgan's Orchid at its center. With so much beauty and so many undead, a battle is bound to begin. As soon as Brugh gets here and starts growing his tower, things begin to heat up. Help contain the undead threat before heading on.

While there are no merchants to be seen near the tower, rest assured that they're only in hiding. Head north into the canyon infested with undead. At the north side of the canyon is a group of wardens and merchants. When you are fully finished, jump to Astorea Waypoint, cross the bridge to the northwest, and follow the road north.

HELP WARDEN BRULIANS (Renown Task)

GOAL: Help Warden Brulians.

LEVEL: 5

Description: Kill Orrian undead, clear corrupted grub holes (which reveal hostile undead grubs), and destroy Orrian artifacts. If you help Brugh, this event is very easy.

DEFEND THE TOWER (Renown Task)

GOAL: Defend the sylvari tower from the undead.

LEVEL: 5

Description: Once Brugh arrives at the center of Morgan's Spiral, he raises a tower. The undead don't like this at all. Take a moment to run around and activate the mortar pods nearby; they'll make your life much less stressful by lobbing area-of-effect attacks at incoming enemies. While the faster undead don't get hit, the brutes take a good bit of damage. Keep the undead off the tower for six waves. The seventh wave is a single abomination. Don't let him close with you if you can avoid it, as his damage is pretty high.

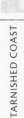

CAER ASTOREA WAYPOINT (SOUTHWEST OF CENTER)

SERVICES:	Waypoint, Armorsmith, Karma Weaponsmith
TRAVEL:	Astorea Waypoint (S), Gleaner's Cove Waypoint (N), The Grove (through Ogham Wilds) (S)
HARVESTING INFO:	Copper Ore, Aspen Saplings, Root Vegetables

Caer Astorea is the last bulwark against the Nightmare Court, keeping them from marching over Astorea and into the Grove. As such, the outpost of Caer Astorea has most of its forces out in the field; only a few guards remain to hold the constant vigil at the keep. Attacks come often, and any help retaking or defending Caer Astorea is greatly appreciated.

Once Caer Astorea is secure, head west down into the Ogham Wilds. There are two Skill Points to be found there. Commune with a waterfall on the northern edge, and then travel south. Kahedins stands in the open, selling a creature book. With your work here done, it's time to head further north and get your hands dirty.

VARIETY IS THE SPICE OF LIFE

The Ogham Wilds holds a great many types of enemies—everything from breezeriders, spiders, and grubs to fireflies and mosshearts. With such a cornucopia of monsters, this area is very good for crafting: you can acquire trophies from the monsters you defeat while harvesting the primary materials of the region.

RETAKE CAER ASTOREA (Repeatable)

GOAL:	Retake Caer Astorea from the Nightmare Court.
LEVEL:	6

Description: The Nightmare Court have taken Caer Astorea, and the corpses of the defenders are scattered on the ground. Just south of town, Captain Uathach stands near the road looking to add her strength to the retaking effort. Get her assistance and head into the town.

As the road bisects the town, it makes sense to retake one side of the village at a time. Follow Captain Uathach up the mushroom steps on the west side of the road directly to the Caer Astorea Watchtower. Move slowly and revive fallen defenders as you go. Charging in will likely get you far too many ranged opponents to handle. Once the enemies are cleaned out of the Watchtower, you need to hold it before moving across the bridge to Caer Astorea Armory and eliminating the rest of the undead.

DEFEND CAER ASTOREA (Repeatable)

GOAL:	Defend Caer Astorea from the Nightmare Court.
LEVEL:	6

Description: With so much strategic value placed on Caer Astorea, the Nightmare Court is not about to let it go. They will continue the siege until they prevail. It's your job to ensure they don't.

The enemy comes at the north side of town in eight waves. The enemies come in pairs, but two groups attack at once (four enemies total). The first group consists of two Nightmare Court kennelmasters and two Nightmare Court pages. The kennelmasters are casters, while the pages are archers. Kill the kennelmasters quickly or they will buff the archers; things get very dangerous after that.

The next set has a Nightmare Court page leading three Nightmare Court squires. Wait for the squires to engage the wardens guarding Caer Astorea; rush past them and kill the lone archer before he deals too much damage. The third and fourth groups have an even balance of squires and pages. Continue allowing the wardens to occupy the melee troops while you kill the archers. You can then help the defenders finish their fight.

A group will not spawn until the current group is dead. If you are low on health and need a break, let the wardens handle things themselves. You can restore yourself while letting the wardens take a beating from the final enemy in a group.

GLEANER'S COVE WAYPOINT (SOUTHWEST SIDE)

SERVICES:	Waypoint, Salvage Merchant, Scout
TRAVEL:	Caer Astorea Waypoint (S), Brigid's Waypoint (E), Mabon Waypoint (N)
HARVESTING INFO:	Copper Ore, Aspen Saplings, Root Vegetables

Only harvesters and other people willing to put in a hard day's work come to Gleaner's Cove. Much of the food for the Grove is harvested here, and there is only a small fort on the nearby hill to defend the region. Natural predators are a threat, but the greater danger comes from invading Orrian undead.

Adventurers are welcome to help the workers gather natural resources or safeguard the territory. When you visit Bay Haven, there is a soundless villager looking for help on the north side; don't agree to help just yet, as this escort takes you away from the region. Instead, head east to Brigid's Overlook first.

HELP HARVESTER MAVAD (Renown Task)

GOAL:	Help Harvester Mavad.
LEVEL:	7

Description: The harvesters can always use a hand gathering lavender, searching sand piles, and dealing with the wildlife. A shovel (they lie scattered on the ground) is required to search the sand piles, so don't worry about them unless you are finding it difficult to accomplish the other parts of the task. Fortunately, you can work on this task at the same time as the following repeatable.

SPIKEROOT FRUIT (Repeatable)

GOAL:	Protect the harvesters as they collect spikeroot fruit.
LEVEL:	7

Description: Keep Harvester Calla and Harvester Eyal safe while they gather spikeroot fruit. The two set a pace that is easy to keep up with, until they walk right into aggressive enemies. Like most harvesters, they tend to focus on what they're looking for and not the dangers nearby. In addition to the wildlife that the harvesters directly upset, there are several waves of scaled drakes that take a direct interest. These kills count toward the area task, so you get a double bonus.

Keep the harvesters in sight; they take sharp turns and can duck out of sight very quickly if you're not careful. You only have to protect them until they harvest the 10 fruits of the current crop.

BRIGID'S OVERLOOK WAYPOINT (SOUTH OF CENTER)

SERVICES:	Waypoint, Salvage Merchant
TRAVEL:	Gleaner's Cove Waypoint (SW), Sperrins Waypoint (E)
HARVESTING INFO:	Copper Ore, Aspen Saplings

As one of the sylvari's newer settlements, Brigid's Overlook has more problems than people to deal with them. The beautiful view of Ventry Bay and Sandycove Beach is marred by the presence of Orrian undead. While this might have been a scenic place to build the settlement, it's too far from Bay Haven for the wardens to guard effectively.

THE SIEGE (Repeatable)

GOAL:	Stop the undead attackers.
LEVEL:	8

Description: Nine waves of Orrian undead are heading to Brigid's Overlook. Activate the mortar pods placed around the settlement as soon as possible and then join Saraid on the south side of town or on the beach (she shows up on your minimap).

Saraid plants mortar turrets and can also supply you with the seeds needed to grow them. There is a maximum number of turrets you can have down at once; make sure there are at least three turrets up at all times.

The turrets will deal significant damage to the brutes as they advance, but the thralls move too quickly. Make the thralls your primary targets. Use ranged attacks and Knockback (if you can) to keep the thralls from destroying the turrets. You need those turrets to keep the brutes back; they have high hit points and deal high damage, so they are a real threat.

THE ATTACK (Repeatable)

GOAL:	Defend the settlers from the undead horde.
LEVEL:	8

Description: If Saraid cannot defeat the undead outside of Brigid's Overlook, you'll have to fight them inside the settlement. Eight waves of undead need to be defeated, while six settlers need to be defended. Take a moment to activate the mortar pods surrounding the settlement (they become turrets once activated). Holding the undead at the entrance to town and letting the mortars pound them is your best bet. Hold the line!

Once the Overlook is safe, move west and help the soundless villager on the north side of Bay Haven.

SOUNDLESS AND ALONE (Repeatable)

GOAL:	Help the soundless villager return home.
LEVEL:	8

Description: A soundless villager stands on the north side of Bay Haven, looking longingly at her home to the north. Escort her along the road toward Mabon Waypoint. Three waves of enemies greet you along the way. All three waves can be seen and engaged before the soundless villager actually gets to them.

The first wave is composed of three skales, while the second and third waves are from the Nightmare Court. Use your most damaging attacks to end the enemies quickly, as you'll have time for them to recharge between the fights. After the three waves have been defeated, the soundless villager runs on ahead, and your task is done. Follow the road to Mabon Waypoint; this will be your hub for a bit.

MABON WAYPOINT (CENTER)

SERVICES:	Waypoint, Armorsmith, Weaponsmith, Salvage Merchant, Scout (x2), Karma Weaponsmith (Weeping Isle)
TRAVEL:	Brigid's Waypoint (S), Town of Cathal Waypoint (NW), Titan's Staircase Waypoint (E/NE)
HARVESTING INFO:	Copper Ore, Aspen Saplings

Mabon Market is a crossroad for several merchants and an asuran researcher. The merchants' guards make this small point of civilization fairly safe, and the merchants do good business with travelers and adventurers alike. This is one of the last safe havens between the Grove and Kraitbane...and that's because of adventurers like you.

Start by backtracking a little and heading southwest to Weeping Isle, where you can help the soundless. Helping them leads you north from the Weeping Isle to attack the Nightmare Court. Once the soundless are in a better position to defend themselves, swing back by Mabon Market to sell.

You can then decide whether you are interested in helping the hylek at Sperrins Waypoint. It's a bit out of the way, but if the fights have been difficult, you might want the extra experience. To help the hylek, jump to Brigid's Waypoint and travel east to Sperrins Waypoint; you can return to Mabon Market after you are finished.

HELP THE SOUNDLESS (Renown Task)

GOAL: Help the soundless.

LEVEL: 8

Description: The soundless have been ousted from their lands by the Nightmare Court, and there is a lot needed to be done to help them get back on their feet. You can repair fishing nets and traps (which reveal enemies), cull the wave rider population (underwater combat), help divers (by reviving them underwater), and fend off Nightmare Court raids (on land).

As long as you are comfortable underwater, that's the best way to go here. There are nets and traps to fix, enemies to kill, and allies to revive. If you aren't used to underwater combat, or want to learn more of your abilities, this is a good time to practice. Despite appearances, the water isn't that dangerous; land is close by, and the water isn't very deep. Spend your time circling around Weeping Isle, repairing nets and traps while killing wave riders and saving divers.

GET THEM BACK (Repeatable)

GOAL: Help Talaith liberate soundless prisoners.

LEVEL: 9

Description: The Nightmare Court isn't willing to let the soundless go. They've captured some of the unfortunate citizens. Follow Talaith to the north into the Nightmare Court's base and keep her alive long enough to free the prisoners. There are turrets all over this place, and Talaith is more concerned with her liberation mission. The turrets do incredible damage. It's up to you to destroy the turrets before they kill you. The good news is that you can revive Talaith when she drops.

Follow Talaith as she fights her way northwest into the camp. At the top of the camp are three prisons with soundless in them. Destroy the doors to set them free and start the final stage of the event. With the prisoners free, it's time to get Talaith back home. Escort her back toward the Weeping Isle and then jump back to Mabon Waypoint. If you're heading to Sperrins Waypoint to help the hylek, you can save a little copper by jumping straight to Brigid's Waypoint and traveling east.

HARASS THE NIGHTMARE COURT (Renown Task)

GOAL: Help Tovar harass the Nightmare Court.

LEVEL: 9

Description: The Nightmare Court will never let the soundless be without the proper encouragement. It's a lucky thing you're good at this kind of diplomacy. Kill anything that looks nasty, free prisoners, and destroy turrets. Basically, it's the same stuff you're already doing to help Talaith. Nice!

SPERRINS WAYPOINT (EAST SIDE)

SERVICES:	Waypoint
TRAVEL:	Brigid's Waypoint (W)
HARVESTING INFO:	Copper Ore, Aspen Saplings, Root Vegetables

North of Sperrins Waypoint is the home of the Zopatl Tribe. As one of the few friendly hylek villages, it's a shame they have to compete with the krait for room to live.

THE ZOPATL TRIBE (Renown Task)

GOAL:	Help Atzintli and the Zopatl Tribe battle the krait.
LEVEL:	10

Description: This hylek village is under attack by the hostile krait. Your job is to fight the krait, rescue captive hylek, and repair territory markers. If krait are close to the village entrance, use the hylek poison turrets for some safe fun. Your best bets are to grab territory markers, revive fallen hylek, and fight the few krait that are on the surface. If you're having difficulty finding targets, venture into the water for the captives. Be careful, though: the krait are dangerous foes, and the water is very deep. You might not want to go it alone. When you are finished here, jump back to Mabon Waypoint.

DEEP WATER

Your character cannot drown, but deep water can still be very dangerous. If you are not careful, you can find yourself under attack from several directions, including above and below. Travel carefully whenever you enter deep water and clear everything around you to avoid unpleasant ambushes.

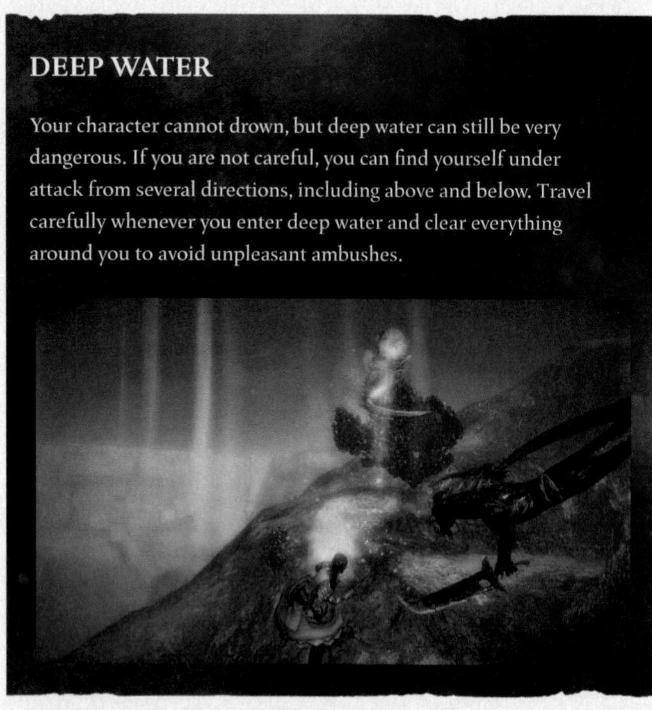

HANTO TRADING POST (CENTER)

SERVICES:	Armorsmith
TRAVEL:	Mabon Waypoint (S), Titan's Staircase Waypoint (SE), Caledon Haven Waypoint (W)
HARVESTING INFO:	Copper Ore, Aspen Saplings, Mushrooms, Herb Patches

Jump back to Mabon Waypoint to begin your journey to Hanto Trading Post. Researcher Widd has some research he needs to get to Hanto. Speak with him to begin the escort. Keep pace with the mosshearts and make your way to Hanto Trading Post.

Though Hanto is in the middle of Caledon Forest, there is a remarkable lack of sylvari here. That's because Hanto exists through a trade agreement between the tengu and the asura. The asura have agreed to construct a gate that the tengu can use to trade. This is a huge deal, as the tengu don't generally leave their city, and they have closed the doors to all outsiders.

This would be a wonderful arrangement if the asura were actually building a gate. They're not. Their research is along an entirely different arc and the constant skritt attacks aren't helping. See what you can do about lightening the burden of defense before continuing on. Before heading east to Titan's Staircase, run west and grab the Caledon Haven Waypoint. This will come in handy in the future.

CARAVAN WORK (Repeatable)

GOAL:	Guard the mosshearts carrying Widd's research.
LEVEL:	11

Description: Just east of the waypoint, Researcher Widd has work for you. Guard his caravan as it travels north. Several waves of skritt attack throughout the journey. The normal skritt are not the problem. The skritt saboteurs, however, are a real concern. They run at the caravan with lit bombs. The bombs inflict a lot of damage if they hit the caravan. Fortunately, the skritt saboteurs show up on your minimap, and you can take the damage if you kill them before they reach the mosshearts. The wonderful news about this event is the skritt you fight here also count toward the task below.

HYPER-AGGRESSIVE SKRITT (Renown Task)

GOAL:	Help Zippti study the hyper-aggressive skritt.
LEVEL:	11

Description: The skritt have infested the Ruins of the Unseen and are far more aggressive than normal. If caravan work is available, this task almost completes itself. If it is not, head north up the road from Mabon Waypoint and watch for the break in the ruins to the west. Move into the ruins and start fighting the skritt. Watch for shiny tracking devices and piles of gears on the ground. Activate the tracking devices and knock over the piles of gears for added completion while you battle the skritt.

TRACKING DEVICES (Repeatable)

GOAL:	Collect data cores from tracking devices for Apprentice Vee.
LEVEL:	12

Description: Apprentice Vee has work while you're in the Ruins of the Unseen fighting skritt. Grab the data cores from the corpses and turn them in to Vee whenever he passes by. You can also collect them from shiny tracking devices (on the ground). As this is a contribution event, keep track of Vee and turn in if the event is near finishing. Once you get to Hanto Trading Post, things can go a bit wrong, as the skritt don't appreciate how the asura do research.

M.A.D. WORK (Repeatable)

GOAL:	Protect the M.A.D. from skritt while Dekkti works.
LEVEL:	11

Description: The asura have set up a machine called the M.A.D., which affects the skritt. What could possibly go wrong? Waves of skritt teem from the ruins and attack the outpost. Much like the caravan escort, the skritt saboteurs are the real problem. The other skritt engage the defenders and swing at the M.A.D., but the saboteurs head straight for the machine and explode for considerable damage. Luckily, the saboteurs show up on the minimap, allowing you to intercept them. Keep the saboteurs away and fight off the other skritt as you have time. When all your work here is done, follow the road southeast to Titan's Staircase Waypoint.

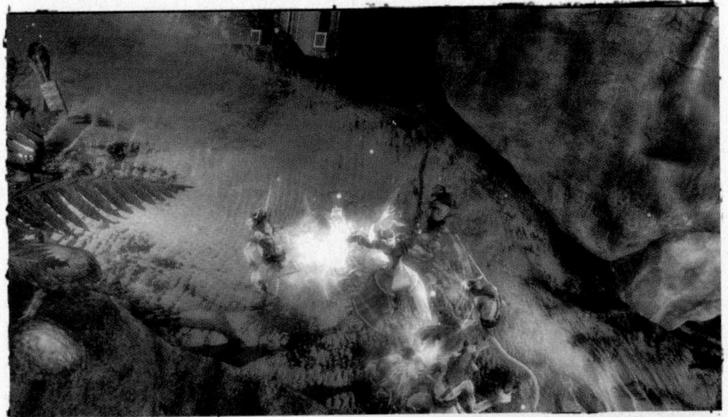

BUILDING A BETTER PATH

Though you aren't ready for the fights in the northwest just yet, follow the road west and activate the Caledon Haven Waypoint before you head southeast to Titan's Staircase. This will save you a lot of travel time later.

TITAN'S STAIRCASE WAYPOINT (EAST SIDE)

SERVICES:	Waypoint, Weaponsmith, Salvage Merchant
TRAVEL:	Hanto Trading Post (W)
HARVESTING INFO:	Copper Ore, Root Vegetables

The tengu don't trust the sylvari (or the rest of the world). A huge wall protects them from the ravages of the other races. Although they won't let you in, you can cross the bridge and speak with Swift Arrow for a Skill Challenge.

Swift Arrow challenges you to a duel to teach you how to evade. Many of his attacks knock you down, so be ready. Don't use attacks that take time to charge up; he won't give you the opportunity. Once you put Swift Arrow in his place, head north and help the hylek deal with the krait. There will be a good bit of underwater combat in the next few tasks.

SAVE THE HYLEK (Renown Task)

GOAL:	Help Yoal weaken the krait and recover kidnapped hylek.
LEVEL:	11

Description: The krait have taken the water territory along the Dominion of Winds. Killing krait and freeing hylek within this stretch of water will work toward completing the task. To free the hylek, simply destroy the cages holding them. Attacking a cell alerts nearby krait to your presence. As you save prisoners, keep your eyes open for hylek chests. These have items stolen by the krait, which you can return to Yoal. As you're dealing with the krait, move northeast to rescue Cueyatl.

CUEYATL'S ESCAPE (Repeatable)

GOAL: Help Cueyatl escape the krait.

LEVEL: 11

Description: Cueyatl has been captured and is being held in one of the deeper sections of the krait area. Break her cage and escort her back to the surface. She's very vulnerable and can go down quickly. Be ready to revive her. Once she's on land, witness how distrustful her camp is. Follow Cueyatl back to the edge of the water and help her prove a point.

CUEYATL'S PLAN (Repeatable)

GOAL: Bring krait skins to Cueyatl.

LEVEL: 11

Description: Cueyatl wants to prove to her camp that not all outsiders are evil. Help her show the others that your people and hers can band together against a common enemy: the krait. Head into the water and start killing krait for their skin. This is a contribution-based event, so be ready to run back if someone else finishes it. If you're having trouble finding targets, remember that hitting a cell calls nearby krait. For a single player, getting 11 skins completes the event.

Follow Cueyatl back to the camp and watch what happens when she presents the evidence to the others. You're let into the camp! A weaponsmith and a merchant are up the ramp. Time to enjoy the fruits of your labors!

HELP THE QUAGGANS (Renown Task)

GOAL: Help Fisher Leudap support the fishers of Soggorsort.

LEVEL: 12

Description: You need to light fishing lanterns, check quaggan traps, and kill krait. Killing poisonous urchins also counts. The urchins and lanterns can be on several ledges along the walls. Find a ledge or the floor and follow it for a bit. This gives you the opportunity to find poisonous urchins and traps while letting you see any lanterns near the floor. Kill krait as you see them and revive any dead fishers.

DEFEND THE QUAGGANS (Repeatable)

GOAL: Defend the Soggorsort quaggans from krait slavers.

LEVEL: 12

Description: Eight waves of krait slavers attack Soggorsort. These come from several directions and attack the villagers. The villagers who need to be defended have shields over their heads. You fail if 10 villagers are captured at any one time. The good news is that captured villagers show up on your minimap (as a pair of tied hands). Defeating the slaver that grabbed them and cutting the captive free counts as a full rescue.

Find an area where several villagers can be easily seen, and set up a defense. The more mobile and comfortable you are underwater, the larger this area can be. Kill the slavers quickly and keep villagers from being taken to succeed. If you fail, the event below becomes available. If you succeed, swim north to Kraitbane Haven Waypoint.

FREE THE QUAGGAN (Repeatable)

GOAL: Free quaggan slaves from Slaver's Deep.

LEVEL: 13

Description: Watch for Jubjup. She can be found swimming around and asking for help. She'll point you north, in the direction of Slaver's Deep. You need to destroy 10 cells for victory. Hitting the cages upsets nearby krait, and they'll attack you (this is almost identical to freeing the hylek in other tasks). Swim north to Slaver's Deep and free the quaggan. When you've finished, continue north to Kraitbane Haven Waypoint.

KRAITBANE HAVEN WAYPOINT (NORTHEAST SIDE)

SERVICES:	Waypoint, Armorsmith, Weaponsmith, Equipment Repair, Salvage Merchant
TRAVEL:	Kessex Hills (NE), Hamlet of Annwen Waypoint (S)
HARVESTING INFO:	Copper Ore (Abundant Underwater), Root Vegetables, Berry Patches, Lettuce (Abundant to the North)

This fortified keep stands at the edge of Treemarch Estuary and near Slaver's Deep. The guards work day and night to keep the krait from encroaching any further into the estuary.

Clear the krait and then speak with Lionguard Kady, who patrols around the outside of Kraitbane Keep. Something is wrong in the Hamlet of Annwen. Head south to check it out.

SLAVER'S DEEP (Renown Task)

GOAL:	Assist Lionguard Hester in weakening the krait of Slaver's Deep.
LEVEL:	13

Description: This job requires you to defeat krait, rescue slaves, and put slave remains to rest. This occurs mostly underwater. If you aren't comfortable underwater, head east. There is a construct rising out of the water with krait and slaves on it. There isn't enough to finish the event, but it gets you very close and thus minimizes how much time you spend underwater. Those at home underwater can just dive down and start clearing the area.

HAMLET OF ANNWEN WAYPOINT (NORTHEAST SIDE)

SERVICES:	Waypoint
TRAVEL:	Kraitbane Haven Waypoint (N), Lionguard Waystation Waypoint (W)
HARVESTING INFO:	Copper Ore, Aspen Saplings, Mushrooms

Building outside fortified walls is seldom advisable, but someone always does it. The people of this small village sit within sight of Kraitbane Haven, but they are too far away for help to arrive in a timely fashion. Give Annwen a hand before heading northwest into the estuary. There are a number of Orrian undead waiting to ambush anyone who happens to get too close. See what you can do to limit their ability to do so before following the road west to Lionguard Waystation Waypoint.

LIBERATION! (Repeatable)

GOAL:	Liberate the Hamlet of Annwen from hylek invaders.
LEVEL:	13

Description: While the Hamlet of Annwen is very large and there are an incredible number of hylek attackers involved, you do not need to kill all of them. Each hylek killed reduces the overall morale by 10%; thus, you only need to kill 10 attackers. Avoid rushing in and trying to kill them in large groups, as several of the hylek can Stun you for several seconds. If you have any utility or healing traits that remove conditions, this can do a great deal to mitigate this. If you do not, you'll have to soak the damage until you can act again. With Annwen liberated, move northwest toward the Treemarch Estuary.

TOUGH FIGHTS?

The Treemarch Estuary is some of the higher-level content in Caledon Forest. If you have any difficulty with it, skip the following repeatable and task ("Undead in Treemarch Estuary" and "Wyld Hunt"). Instead, head to Lionguard Waystation Waypoint; complete the repeatables there before coming back.

UNDEAD IN TREEMARCH ESTUARY (Renown Task)

GOAL:	Help Lionguard Messina cull the undead of Treemarch Estuary.
LEVEL:	14

Description: This is very straightforward and can be completed while assisting the Wyld Hunt. If the following repeatable is not available, move north into the estuary and watch for any of the Orrian undead. The waterways are the best place to find targets. There are noxious mushrooms to be destroyed and undead in abundance. Watch for any downed Lionguard, but be wary, as some of the bodies are undead lying in wait for a kind heart.

WYLD HUNT (Repeatable)

GOAL:	Help the Wyld Hunt Valiants clear undead from Treemarch Estuary.
LEVEL:	14

Description: Clear three locations and revive the fallen valiants. Once you revive the valiants, follow them from one Orrian spider den to the next. The last location has a veteran abomination, several thralls and brutes, and three undead grubs—lots of poison! Be sure to have an ability to clear poison conditions or let the valiants take the brunt of the attacks. When this is done, flee south back to the road or jump to the Kraitbane or Hamlet of Annwen Waypoint and continue your journey into Lionguard Waystation Waypoint.

LIONGUARD WAYSTATION WAYPOINT (NORTH OF CENTER)

SERVICES:	Waypoint
TRAVEL:	Kraitbane Haven Waypoint (E), Hamlet of Annwen Waypoint (E), Caledon Haven Waypoint (S), Wychmire Waypoint (NW)
HARVESTING INFO:	Copper Ore, Aspen Saplings, Mushrooms

At a crossroad near the Wychmire Swamp, there is little excess at Lionguard Waystation. The guards keep watch over the wooden palisade and do their best to make a safe place for travelers to stop. To the south, fire and forest are mixing in an unhealthy way. Deal with the fires before jumping to Caledon Haven Waypoint: you'll be back.

SAVE THE TREES (Repeatable)

GOAL:	Protect local mosshearts from fire imps.
LEVEL:	12

Description: South of the waypoint, fire imps are attacking the mosshearts in the area. There are four mosshearts total, and you need to keep at least one of them alive for 6 minutes. The mosshearts can mostly fight the imps off, but the imps light the mosshearts on fire. Keep an eye out for gourds around the area to put out the flaming mosshearts. The damage over time by the fire will eventually kill these gentle tree creatures.

STOP THE FIRES (Repeatable)

GOAL:	Clear the fire imp population and extinguish their fires.
LEVEL:	12

Description: Fire imps are setting the entire region ablaze. Kill 10 imps and extinguish 6 fires. This repeatable is just south of the waypoint, almost impossible to miss. Around the trees are gourds to pick up and use to douse the fires. You have to put the gourd down to fight, so keep a gourd until you're ready to engage an imp. Once the forest is safe, jump back to Caledon Haven Waypoint.

CALEDON HAVEN WAYPOINT (NORTHWEST OF CENTER)

SERVICES:	Waypoint, Salvage Merchant, Equipment Repair
TRAVEL:	Falias Thorp Waypoint (N/NW), Town of Cathal Waypoint (W), Lionguard Waystation Waypoint (N/NE)
HARVESTING INFO:	Copper Ore, Aspen Saplings, Mushrooms

There isn't much at Caledon Haven Waypoint, but it may have been a while since you last visited a merchant or repaired your equipment. Do so before heading on. To the west is Town of Cathal Waypoint, an armorsmith, and the pass to Metrica Province.

To the northwest is Falias Thorp. This bastion of defense is often under attack, and the Falias Thorp Waypoint is rarely functional. When you're ready to move on, make your way north to Falias Thorp and the Wychmire Swamp.

TOWN OF CATHAL WAYPOINT (WEST SIDE)

SERVICES:	Waypoint, Armorsmith
TRAVEL:	Falias Thorp Waypoint (N), Metrica Province (Level 1-15 Asura Region) (W), Caledon Haven Waypoint (E)
HARVESTING INFO:	Negligible

Town of Cathal Waypoint stands at the pass between Caledon Forest and Metrica Province. If you're interested in moving to another zone, now is a good time to do so. Metrica Province is home to the asura, and they have their own problems, but it does make for a change of scenery (especially because the content is of similar level). If you're not done in Caledon Forest, though, it's time to head north to Falias Thorp. Either way, visit the villager for a creature book before moving on.

FALIAS THORP WAYPOINT (WEST SIDE)

SERVICES:	Waypoint
TRAVEL:	Town of Cathal Waypoint (S), Lionguard Waystation Waypoint (E)
HARVESTING INFO:	Negligible

This outpost guards the area against the Nightmare Court lurking in the Wychmire Swamp. As the primary defense of the area, Falias Thorp is often under attack or occupied by hostile forces. If the waypoint is contested, use Town of Cathal Waypoint as a springboard to retake the area and push into Wychmire Swamp.

RECAPTURE FALIAS THORP (Repeatable)

GOAL:	Drive the Nightmare Court from Falias Thorp.
LEVEL:	13

Description: Clearing the Nightmare Court from Falias Thorp is a difficult fight, as the enemies can enter from a few angles and your allies are mostly useless. Revive them to keep the enemies from grouping up against you, but keep an eye on the defenders, as they won't last very long against the Nightmare Court without your help.

HELP THE WARDENS (Renown Task)

GOAL:	Help the wardens in Wychmire Swamp.
LEVEL:	14

Description: Destroy summoned husks and corrupted plants, fight the Nightmare Court and their minions, and free prisoners. If Falias Thorp is captured, take it first as the kills you make there will help greatly toward completing this event. If you have Falias Thorp, head to the western part of Wychmire, where there are many summoned husks. Watch your feet, as there are corrupted plants to be destroyed as you find them. As you kill your way north into Wychmire Swamp, start swinging east as you near the completion of this task. Once you complete it, jump to Lionguard Waystation Waypoint or fight your way there. It's time to take the north road from Lionguard Waystation.

LIONGUARD WAYSTATION WAYPOINT REVISITED (NORTH OF CENTER)

SERVICES:	Waypoint
TRAVEL:	Kraitbane Haven Waypoint (E), Hamlet of Annwen Waypoint (E), Caledon Haven Waypoint (S), Wychmire Waypoint (NW)
HARVESTING INFO:	Copper Ore, Aspen Saplings, Mushrooms

This is your second time at Lionguard Waystation, and it's time for the final push against the evil in Caledon Forest. Take the road heading north. It's quite dangerous and the Lionguard need help protecting travelers. Watch for Gamarien along the road. He's trying to scout the swamp, but he's not strong enough to do it alone.

GAMARIEN (Repeatable)

GOAL:	Protect Gamarien as he scouts Wychmire Swamp.
LEVEL:	14

Description: Gamarien takes a zigzagging path through the swamp and tends to shoot at everything that moves. Get ready for quite a run as this sylvari doesn't walk like most escorts. Several skelks, a few Nightmare Court members, and some summoned husks will be dead before Gamarien finds what's causing all the problems in Wychmire. If you are alone, jump back to Lionguard Waystation Waypoint and continue north again. Do not attempt the group event solo.

GREAT JUNGLE WURM (Group)

GOAL:	Defeat the great jungle wurm.
LEVEL:	15

Description: Come with friends. This enormous wurm does massive damage, has massive health, and can fight in multiple ways. In addition to its melee attack, it also spits barbs that cause Bleeding and Poisoning and can spew area-of-effect poison clouds at range. Should you live long enough to actually hurt the thing, it will call the summoned husks to itself and consume them to heal. Bring everyone. Once the wurm has been defeated, jump back to Lionguard and continue north along the road.

SAFEGUARD THE ROAD (Renown Task)

GOAL:	Help Lionguard Cern safeguard the road.
LEVEL:	15

Description: There's a lot you can do to help here: repair warning signs, light torches, destroy skull monuments, and drive off trolls. Though the event says to safeguard the road, head off the northern side of the road as soon as possible. Warning signs and skull monuments are throughout the troll area, and you can also kill the trolls there to make this a very fast completion. With the road safer, keep following it to Wychmire Waypoint.

CHAMPION JUNGLE TROLL (Group)

GOAL:	Defeat the champion jungle troll.
LEVEL:	15

Description: Enough said, really. If you can get the jungle troll on the road, it's a much easier fight (there's more room to kite him, kill his two friends, and possibly find travelers to help with the battle). If he gets off the road, he heads back into troll territory.

The jungle troll lives pretty deep in the northern part of the swamp (far north of the zone). This guy doesn't fight fair. He can regenerate, like any other troll; he has two lesser trolls beside him (kill them first); and he's in a relatively protected location (a narrow cleft in the ground). Knock him down, snare him, and otherwise limit his actions (through crowd control abilities) as you kite him around. Evade his powerful attacks (he telegraphs quite a bit), and don't let him regenerate his health. As soon as he covers himself to heal, dive in and let loose with your high-damage abilities.

WYCHMIRE WAYPOINT (NORTHWEST SIDE)

SERVICES:	Waypoint
TRAVEL:	Lionguard Waystation Waypoint(SE), Brisban Wildlands (Level 15-25 Sylvari/Asuran Region) (W)
HARVESTING INFO:	Copper Ore, Aspen Saplings, Mushrooms, Herb Patches

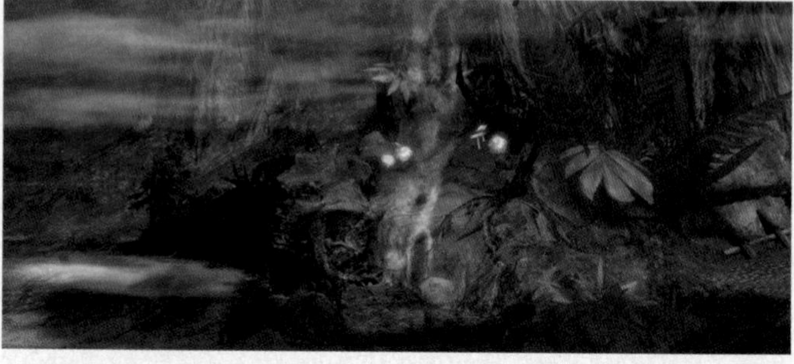

You've done it! Caledon is a safer place because of your hard work. Speak to Warden Shield just north of the waypoint for a Skill Challenge and decide where to go next. The Brisban Wildlands are just to the west; that region seems a likely proposition, and the people there are sure to need the help of adventurers.

DANGER TO THE SOUTH

The Twilight Arbor Waypoint is almost directly south from this area. It's a very dangerous spot, and heroes should only come here when they're much more seasoned. A dungeon is there, requiring a full group of adventurers.

BRISBAN WILDLANDS

LEVEL RANGE:	15-25
TASKS:	16
WAYPOINTS:	12
SKILL CHALLENGES:	6
HARVESTING INFO:	Gummo Trees (Soft Wood Logs, Soft Wood Dowels), Herb Patches (Cucumbers), Leafy Vegetables (Celery Stalks), Mushrooms (Chanterelle Mushrooms), Purple Iris Flower (Purple Iris Petals), Iron Ore (Iron Ore, Gems), Silver Ore (Silver Ore, Gems)

SKILL CHALLENGES

- Ghostly Runner Zengrade (East of Mirkrise Waypoint, Running Around the Ruins) (S)
- Henge of Denravi (Southwest of Mirkrise Waypoint, On a Hill Above the Swamp) (S)
- Place of Power (South of Triforge Point Waypoint, Inside the Thaumacore Inquiry Center) (W)
- Lady Grimassi (South of Triforge Point Waypoint, Out in the Open) (W)
- Restless Arboreal Spirit (South of Seraph Observers Waypoint, Out in the Open) (N)
- Super Shiny Thing (West of Watchful Source Waypoint, Inside Skrittsburgh) (Center)

No major nation or people lay claim to Brisban Wildlands. The reaches of both the asura and sylvari end at the borders of this vastly untamed wilderness. Without the oversight of guardians, secret laboratories and hidden villages abound between the trees and even under the mountains. Here, the skritt and hylek are among the many who have created a place to call home.

Without the law and protection of the larger nations, bandits, the Inquest, and the Nightmare Court have also made places of their own. Here, they attack unwary travelers, steal research from asuran labs, and enslave the skritt.

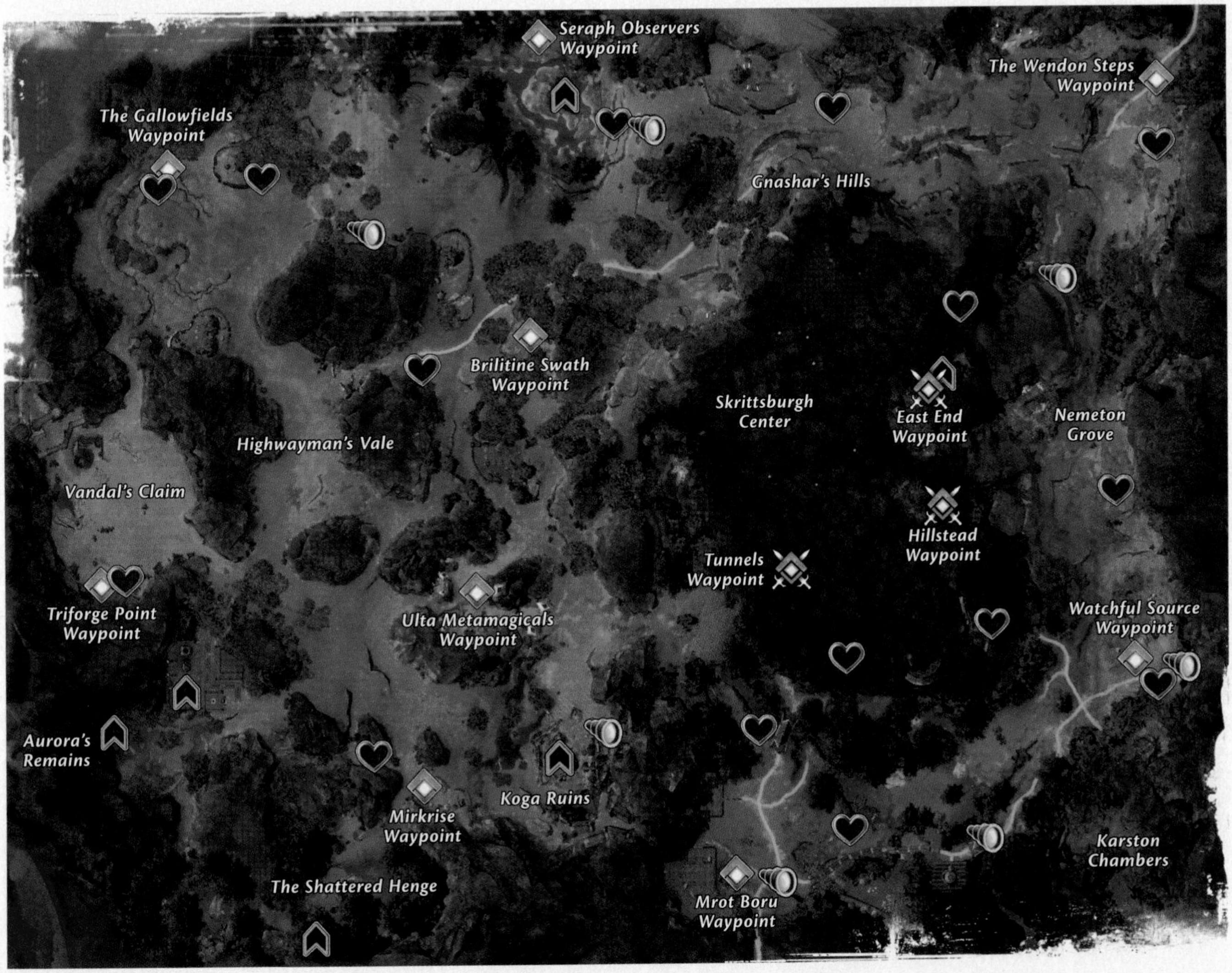

Seraph Observers Waypoint
The Wendon Steps Waypoint
The Gallowfields Waypoint
Gnashar's Hills
Brilitine Swath Waypoint
Skrittsburgh Center
East End Waypoint
Nemeton Grove
Highwayman's Vale
Vandal's Claim
Hillstead Waypoint
Tunnels Waypoint
Triforge Point Waypoint
Ulta Metamagicals Waypoint
Watchful Source Waypoint
Aurora's Remains
Koga Ruins
Mirkrise Waypoint
Karston Chambers
The Shattered Henge
Mrot Boru Waypoint

WHERE DO I START?

Brisban is the level 15-25 region for both sylvari and asuran progression; therefore, you can enter from either Caledon Forest or Metrica Province. The first several tasks are level-appropriate no matter which entrance you come in. If you are entering through Caledon Forest, skip to Watchful Source Waypoint and then come back to Mrot Boru. If you are entering from Metrica Province, just keep reading.

MROT BORU WAYPOINT (SOUTH SIDE)

SERVICES:	Waypoint, Merchant, Scout, Armorsmith, Equipment Repair, Weaponsmith (Aethervolt Lab)
TRAVEL:	Entrance to Metrica Province (Level 1-15 Asuran Region) (S), Watchful Source Waypoint (E), Mirkrise Waypoint (W)
HARVEST INFO:	Herb Patches, Gummo Trees, Silver Ore, Iron Ore

On the border of Venlin Vale, the fort of Mrot Boru is the last bastion of asuran control. The high walls and steep staircases keep most aggressors out but do nothing for the more subtle enemies—and the Inquest rarely attack head-on. Watch your pockets and your back here. Even though the citizens and their progeny run around without worry, there are daggers and spies everywhere. Help those living here and then take the road east to Watchful Source Waypoint to help the sylvari.

TEMP WORK (Renown Task)

GOAL:	Aethervolt researchers require temporary assistants.
LEVEL:	16

Description: Here you can test pigment transmogrifiers on red hylek for Aerixx, collect ooze samples for Tramma, and fight any Inquest spying in the area.

Aerixx stands in a small building at the edge of the water (he's on the road side) across the road from Aethervolt Lab. Talk to him to get a pigment transmogrifier and let the fun begin. The first ability is what changes the color of the hyleks. The second does damage with a little range. Head around the building and start spraying hylek.

There are two ways to do this, depending on your damage output. If you have high area-of-effect damage, spray several hylek while kiting them around. Once you've enraged a whole bunch, drop the transmogrifier and kill the maddened enemies. The upside to this is it's faster; the downside is that you can't pick up the transmogrifier once you've dropped it (you have to get another). However, the red hyleks will attack the blue hyleks before they attack you. (Asura note: conclusive evidence that hyleks have color vision.)

If there are no hyleks in the village or in the water, head across the river and talk to Tramma. There is an ooze cave nearby. The oozes are not naturally aggressive. Just kill them and bring them back to the ooze processors near Tramma.

While doing both of these activities, watch for Inactive aetheric observers. Activate these for more credit toward the task. If any Inquest show up to make trouble, they can be dispatched as well.

ATTACK THE INQUEST (Renown Task)

GOAL:	Keep the Inquest from endangering Mrot Boru.
LEVEL:	17

Description: Everyone has secret labs in Brisban. Even the Inquest have a lab. If the people of Mrot Boru really knew how close it was, they'd be worried. Make a left before crossing the bridge north of Mrot Boru and walk down the slope. The Inquest members are in plain view. Kill the Inquest, disable their spy transmission receivers, and destroy the Inquest power generators. This task is very quick, as there are a great many targets (mobs and two types of groundspawns). Once the Inquest are suitably set back, jump back to Mrot Boru Waypoint and head east to Aethervolt Labs. There, look for Sparkk.

GATHERING ENERGY (Repeatable)

GOAL: Gather energy for Sparkk.

LEVEL: 16

Description: Don't talk to Sparkk until you're ready to go. He won't wait for you and he quickly heads east (out of range of the other events) to the Karston Chambers. Hunt cavern scutters to collect their energy for Sparkk. The cavern scutters aren't an issue alone; they'll only attack if you hit them first or smack a friend of theirs. The real dangers in this area are the jungle wurm hatchlings. They're aggressive and can burrow under the unwary. If no scutters are around, look for larvae tails. Pull these, and one or two scutter larvae come to the surface. These have the energy also. Sparkk needs 10 energy samples before he returns to his lab.

WHERE'S SPARKK?

If someone has already started Sparkk's event, he may not be at the Aethervolt Lab. Try following the path east across the bridge and up the slope to the Karton Chambers to look for him.

WHAT WENT WRONG? (Group)

GOAL: Destroy the malfunctioning golem.

LEVEL: 16

Description: Once Sparkk gets back to his lab, he tries to repair the broken golem. He does too good a job, and it goes nuts trying to kill everything. Its attacks are pretty mean, and it has a good bit of health, but there is plenty of room to kite it. Also, if you are having trouble, position the golem so it faces one of the nearby fireflies. Once one of the golem's cone attacks hits the firefly, the insect joins the fray (and you might need all the allies you can get). With the golem now safely broken once again, you've helped Aethervolt as much as possible. Head east along the road to Watchful Source Waypoint.

WATCHFUL SOURCE WAYPOINT (SOUTHEAST SIDE)

SERVICES:	Waypoint, Merchant, Scout, Armorsmith, Weaponsmith, Equipment Repair, Karma Merchant (The Revered Terebinth)
TRAVEL:	Entrance to Caledon Forest (Level 1-15 Sylvari Region) (E), Mrot Boru Waypoint (SW), Wendon Waypoint (N)
HARVEST INFO:	Gummo Trees, Herb Patches, Iron Ore, Silver Ore

The outpost of Watchful Source stands on the top of Zinder Slope. As the last remnant of sylvari dominance in the area, there are a number of services here for the hearty adventurer. Take time to replenish your supplies and head out to face the dangers of the wilderness.

PROTECT THE WYLD HUNT (Repeatable)

GOAL: Protect the Wyld Hunt party from the unseen hunter.

LEVEL: 16

Description: The hunters are being hunted. Where the Zinder Slope meets the river (SW of Watchful Source Waypoint), four Wyld Hunt valiants are stalking an unseen hunter. The mists keep the hunter shrouded until it strikes. Follow the valiants and wait for your moment. The hunter is a veteran; it can take a lot of hits and deals heavy melee damage. Either avoid getting its attention by letting the Wyld Hunt members face it (you can let up to three of the four valiants die before the mission fails), or face it head on and kite the hunter while the valiants kill it.

KILL NIGHTMARE SPELLBINDERS (Repeatable)

GOAL: Kill nightmare spellbinders before the skritt are enslaved at Joy's End.

LEVEL: 16

Description: Kill six nightmare spellbinders as they run from Skrittsburgh to Joy's End. Failure comes if any skritt are enslaved by the time they reach Joy's End. The spellbinders come in pairs with trailing skritt slaves. If any of the spellbinders get past you, you'll need to race into Joy's End to kill them before they fully enslave any skritt.

THWARTING THE NIGHTMARE COURT (Renown Task)

GOAL:	Thwart the Nightmare Court at Joy's End.
LEVEL:	16

Description: South of Watchful Source Waypoint is a major Nightmare Court stronghold, Joy's End. Make them feel unwelcome by setting fire to the nearby brambles (and fighting the Nightmare Court executioners that come). You can also free prisoners as you advance by opening nightmare bulbs. Note that killing anything or anyone associated with the Nightmare Court counts toward this task. Mostly, you can complete this task while you do the repeatables in the area.

RESCUE THE SKRITT (Repeatable)

GOAL:	Rescue the kidnapped skritt.
LEVEL:	16

Description: Kill three jailers to access the gates and destroy all three prison gates. Fight your way to the top of Joy's End. Clear all enemies away from the jailers before engaging them, as they are all veterans of the Nightmare Court. Be very careful not to get the attention of two of them at once. Both the jailers and the prison gates count toward the "Thwarting the Nightmare Court" task. With all this done, jump back to Watchful Source Waypoint and start north.

PROTECT THE REVERED TEREBINTH (Renown Task)

GOAL:	Help Leigheara protect the Revered Terebinth.
LEVEL:	17

Description: Your task includes fighting the Nightmare Court, freeing prisoners from Beldame's Rise, and removing the pests and stranglebloom surrounding the Revered Terebinth. The Revered Terebinth is on a cliff that must be mounted from the north side. The nightmare spiders and mastiffs in the area are all targets, but your best course is to grab stranglebloom. Uprooting the stranglebloom can cause termite larvae to appear (and both count toward the completion of the task), so grab any nearby stranglebloom as you fight.

RECOVER THE REVERED TEREBINTH I (Repeatable)

GOAL:	Recover the Revered Terebinth by killing the Nightmare Court.
LEVEL:	17

Description: Kill the Nightmare Court occupiers making a home under the branches of the Revered Terebinth. Each kill counts for 10% toward the occupiers' force, so you need to kill 10 of them. While the enemies respawn fairly quickly, they do not restore the percentage of the occupiers. If you want to play it safe, pull the Nightmare Court at the edge to you and wait for respawns (they come back pretty quickly). Once the percentage is at zero, the kennelmaster and his mastiffs join the fight, but all others leave.

RECOVER THE REVERED TEREBINTH II (Repeatable)

GOAL:	Recover the Revered Terebinth by defeating the kennelmaster and his mastiffs.
LEVEL:	17

Description: To get the Revered Terebinth back, you must defeat the kennelmaster and his two mastiffs. The kennelmaster is a veteran and hits pretty hard. It's imperative to pull back and fight his mastiffs before engaging him. Defeat this last wave of enemies and the Revered Terebinth is free again (the gardeners come back and the tree becomes a karma merchant).

PROTECT THE GARDENERS (Repeatable)

GOAL:	Protect the three gardeners from the Nightmare Court.
LEVEL:	17

Description: The Nightmare Court won't let the Revered Terebinth go without a fight! You must protect the gardeners tending it. The gardeners aren't really combatants, so they need strong protection. Your best bet is to stay at the bottom of the slope and try to grab the the Nightmare Court members before they engage the gardeners. Be very aggressive; the Court has brought archers. As long as one gardener is still standing when the Nightmare Court's morale reaches zero, you win the fight. Each kill counts for about 7% of the morale, so you need to kill around 14-15 targets. Don't worry if one of the gardeners goes down. They can be revived, but bringing back a defeated ally takes a fair bit of time; only do it between waves of enemies. With the Revered Terebinth safe for the time being, travel north to Wendon Waypoint.

WENDON WAYPOINT (NORTHEAST SIDE)

SERVICES:	Waypoint, Merchant, Scout, Weaponsmith, Equipment Repair
TRAVEL:	Entrance to Kessex Hills (E) (Level 15-25 Region), Watchful Source Waypoint (S)
HARVEST INFO:	Gummo Trees, Herb Patches, Iron Ore, Silver Ore

Wendon Waypoint stands on the border of Kessex Hills and the Wendon Steps. The nearby vigil camp is working hard to battle the bandits that have settled in the area. Give them a hand defending the nearby skritt from the machinations of Willem and his band of lawbreakers before heading southwest to visit a rather large skritt city.

DRIVING OFF WILLEM'S BANDITS (Renown Task)

GOAL:	Help the Seraph fight Willem's bandits.
LEVEL:	20

Description: To aid the Seraph, check the bushes for bandit spies and ambushers, return Seraph supplies to Goran, and help the local skritt population. You can also revive downed Seraph members. Bandits don't much like to farm or harvest, so the vigil camp gets raided on a regular basis. Watch for bandit cutpurses (or the merchant assistant that hasn't been unmasked) running from the vigil with boxes of supplies. Kill them (for credit) and pick up the dropped supplies to turn in to Goran (for more credit). The other targets are the suspicious bushes. You get credit for both checking the bush and killing any bandits hiding within it. If either of the repeatable events is available, those kills count toward the completion of this task as well.

SKRITT GO BOOM! (Repeatable)

GOAL:	Prevent the bandits from poisoning the skritt foragers with traps.
LEVEL:	19

Description: The poison-based mines are truly nasty once they go off. Your best bet is to stop the bandits from putting them down at all. If you are very fast, you can kill the bandits before they drop more than four mines (they'll drop as many as eight mines if left alone). Each mine can kill at least one skritt forager, so this puts the odds much more in your favor. Have abilities ready that remove conditions, as the mines put several debuffs in addition to Poison on you. Avoid trying to disarm a mine until you've killed the nearby hidden bandit poisoner and you've returned to full health.

SKRITT NEED ANTIDOTE BADLY (Repeatable)

GOAL:	Drive out the bandits so skritt can steal antidotes to the poison.
LEVEL:	20

Description: Many of the skritt have been poisoned by the bandits, and they need the antidote. They know where it is, but the bandits must be driven out before the skritt can retrieve it. The bandit hideout is at the top of the Wendon Steps, west of the waypoint. Climb to there and start killing. Choose your targets cautiously, as the bandits are very close together and can deal moderate damage. Twelve or so kills will convince the bandits to hide until you leave and give the skritt enough time to get the antidote. Now that you're in reasonably good standing with the skritt, it's time to pay a visit to Skrittsburgh, to the southwest of Wendon Waypoint.

SKRITTSBURGH (WORLD EVENT)

SERVICES:	Waypoint (x3), Weaponsmith, Armorsmith
TRAVEL:	Wendon Waypoint (NE), Watchful Source Waypoint (SE), Mrot Boru Waypoint (SW)
HARVEST INFO:	Iron Ore, Silver Ore, Mushrooms

The skritt have closed the gates to their city to keep their enemies out. All three gates are under attack and will not open until the East End, Hillstead, and tunnels are secured. While there are three tasks in the area, it's actually the repeatable events that secure the gates. These must be done in one sitting. If you take a break in the middle, you may have to backtrack and redo an event or two. Start by helping at the East End Gate. Then go south to the Hillstead Gate, and finally west to the Tunnels Gate to demonstrate to the skritt that you can be trusted.

DEFENDING THE EAST END (Renown Task)

GOAL:	Help the skritt defend Skrittsburgh East End.
LEVEL:	20

Description: Defend East End, fight destroyers, use skritt supplies, and bring injured skritt to Bordekka's base. Make a left at the first junction in the tunnels and head south. Destroyers are digging under Skrittsburgh and need to be stopped. Watch for unconscious skritt and skritt supplies as you go. Carrying the unconscious skritt occupies enough of your attention (and your arms) that you can't do anything else while holding them. Use the run-speed boost on your ability bar and get them back to Yutatta as soon as you can. Then, return to kill the destroyers. Continue killing destroyers on your way to the Hillstead Gate.

CLEAR THE DESTROYERS (Repeatable)

GOAL:	Clear out the destroyers from the East End hub.
LEVEL:	20

Description: The fury of the destroyers must be stopped. Each kill counts for 8% of the overall fury of the destroyer invasion, so you need to kill 12 destroyers to stall the battle. Do not go further south than the destroyers until you've completed both of these events. You won't have to wait long for respawns; the destroyers appear very quickly. Don't stand right on the waypoint when you finish this event; another starts right after it, and a veteran enemy appears near the waypoint.

FINISH THE JOB (Repeatable)

GOAL:	Clear out the destroyers from the East End hub.
LEVEL:	20

Description: The destroyers make one final push and send in a veteran giant destroyer crab. This enemy has substantial health, deals moderate damage, and can evade. Clear around him and destroy the four fissures first. This will give you the space you'll need to kill him. Do not stand beside a fissure unless you have to, and watch your health if you do. The fissures shoot out gouts of flame to hurt anyone standing nearby. When the last of the destroyers are down, take the wooden bridge south.

GETTING GRUB AT THE HILLSTEAD (Renown Task)

GOAL:	Help the grub farmers in Skrittsburgh Hillstead.
LEVEL:	19

Description: This requires you to collect grub meat, light torches to draw out pests, destroy faulty turrets, and protect the skritt. Kill the Nightmare Court on your way past the waypoint and southeast to Forager Sneckit (at the center of the task). There are grubs and faulty turrets here. Destroy the turrets and harvest the grubs for their meat. Pass Sneckit the meat you have to complete the task, and then head southwest from the Hillstead Waypoint to the Tunnels Gate.

A NIGHTMARE FOR THE SKRITT (Repeatable)

GOAL:	Free Hillstead skritt from the Nightmare Court.
LEVEL:	19

Description: Nightmare Court spellbinders have enslaved the skritt. Each spellbinder has enslaved two skritt, and all three of them attack at the same time. Find the spellbinders on your minimap and hit them with your highest damage abilities at the start of the engagement. The skritt come to their senses once the spellbinder falls, so don't worry about attacking them. They've been through enough as it is.

GOING THROUGH THE TUNNELS (Renown Task)

GOAL:	Help the skritt experimenting in Skrittsburgh Tunnels.
LEVEL:	20

Description: Search through junk piles and bring undamaged baubles to Twitchok. Slay any hungry wildlife and Inquest you find. With the following repeatable having several waves of Inquest, finishing this task is pretty manageable. If the repeatable is not available, start killing everything in sight.

DRIVE OUT THE INQUEST (Repeatable)

GOAL:	Drive the Inquest from the skritt tunnels.
LEVEL:	21

Description: This event is a bit more difficult. You need to kill all the Inquest in the highlighted area and hold it until the completion bar fills. The Inquest attack from all three connecting tunnels. If you have allies, keep an eye on as many tunnels as possible. Try to keep a ranged ally within the bordered region, and have others engage the enemies outside of it. That way, there isn't any interruption in holding the area. The remaining Inquest flee when the area is obviously not worth the fight. Make your way into Skrittsburgh Center and find the awaiting merchants. Once you've finished selling your loot and buying new goodies, jump to Mrot Boru Waypoint. Head through the fort and west across the Koga Ruins, toward Mirkrise Waypoint.

THE BAR ISN'T MOVING

When holding an area, the completion bar moves only if there are absolutely no enemies and at least one ally within the bordered area. The color of the circle is red if one of these conditions is not met. It turns blue as soon as both are met, and the completion bar then begins to increase.

MIRKRISE WAYPOINT (SOUTH SIDE)

SERVICES:	Waypoint, Merchant
TRAVEL:	Mrot Boru Waypoint (E)
HARVEST INFO:	Gummo Trees (Abundant), Herb Patches, Purple Iris Flowers, Silver Ore, Iron Ore

The Durmand Priory has started a research camp deep in Brisban Wildlands. However, they haven't brought enough defenders to safeguard it, and now they're paying for it. The Inquest make constant attacks and burn down the camp whenever possible. Grab the waypoint (you may have to liberate the camp to do so) and head just northwest for the task.

HELPING THE DURMAND PRIORY (Renown Task)

GOAL:	Remove threats to Durmand Priory researchers in Toxal Bog.
LEVEL:	21

Description: Assist the priory, prevent the Inquest from draining druid husks, protect explorers in the swamp, and help them gather green stinkhorns. With so many repeatable events, this task almost completes itself. Follow the events into the swamp. As you go, grab stinkhorns and kill anything that looks like a good target.

SAVE THE CAMP (Group)

GOAL:	Save the camp from the Inquest golem.
LEVEL:	20

Description: The Inquest aren't happy, and they've shown their displeasure by sending in a veteran experimental golem to burn down the camp. For now, leave the golem and take out the Inquest first. The golem's whirlwind has a Knockback effect; it can keep you busy while the Inquest kill you. Don't play their game. Kill the softer targets first. You can let up to four tents burn before the camp fails, so you have time to take targets slowly. With the Inquest down, move to the golem. It has a great deal of health, but you have friends—members from the camp. If you are alone, consider kiting the golem around while the priory members kill it. Don't run off when it dies; it drops something very interesting.

RETURNING THE ENERGY CORE (Repeatable)

GOAL:	Help the priory return the energy core to the Henge of Denravi.
LEVEL:	21

Description: As the golem falls, an energy core comes free. A couple of the Durmand Priory researchers think they know something about this object. They ask you to follow them into the swamp to test a theory. You have three guards to help you defend the two researchers. The lifespan of the guards does not count toward the success or failure of the mission; you only need to keep the researchers alive. Keep your eyes on them at all times. Fight as close to them as you can without letting them get hit by area-of-effect attacks by the enemies. Any kills made in Toxal Bog count toward the main "Helping the Durmand Priory" task.

Once the researchers get to the middle of Toxal Bog, they kneel and pray. The Inquest uses this as a signal to make a large push. Don't follow the guards. The Inquest attackers are smart, and they try to draw the guards away from the researchers. You need to keep the Inquest off the researchers until the Denravi energy source is charged. There are several waves of Inquest, but the first is the toughest as it has a mix of golems and other troops. Once you get past the first wave, all the others contain only Inquest asura. Guard the researchers until they're done and then head west and south. You're already this far, so grab the Skill Challenge at the top of the waterfall and finish the task. When you're done, jump back and speak with the Arboreal Spirit.

DEFEND THE DURMAND PRIORY CAMP (Repeatable)

GOAL:	Defend the Durmand Priory Campsite.
LEVEL:	21

Description: If you failed to stop the Inquest golem during the "Save the Camp" mission, the Inquest has taken the priory camp and burned the tents. Fight the Inquest off, revive fallen priory personnel, and defend them while they put the site in working order. Five priory tents in total need to be set up for the researchers to secure their base.

AIDING THE ARBOREAL SPIRIT (Repeatable)

GOAL:	Help the Arboreal Spirit return to its husk and drive away the hylek.
LEVEL:	19

Description: Your goal is to escort the Arboreal Spirit to its husk and keep the hylek away until it can revive itself. Talk to the Arboreal Spirit to start the event. The spirit makes its way across the bog, angering nearly everything possible. Even fireflies and friendly hylek take a moment to attack the poor thing. Defend the spirit, but don't worry if you get a little ahead or behind. It has a good bit of health, and you monitor its condition in the event tracker. Things go a bit pear-shaped when you get to the husk. A group of hylek have made the area their home, and they are unwilling to let the spirit revive. You have to "persuade" them to leave—the rough way. Each kill is worth roughly 7%, so you need 15 kills to chase off the hylek. Melee characters should be ready for some frustration, as the spirit tends to knock enemies away. Once the hylek have left and the spirit has vanished, head northwest to Ulta Metamagicals Waypoint.

ULTA METAMAGICALS WAYPOINT (SOUTHWEST OF CENTER)

SERVICES:	Waypoint
TRAVEL:	Mirkrise Waypoint (S), Brilitine Waypoint (N)
HARVEST INFO:	Gummo Trees, Herb Patches

Asura are attempting to build gates in this rocky ravine. Give them a hand with their research as a bit of a break. Once the research is well at hand, head north to disrupt negotiations between the Inquest and the bandits of the region. While the idea of this alliance is very frightening, it's only in its first stages and can be dealt with. When you're ready to move on, head north to Brilitine Waypoint.

ASSIST ULTA METAMAGICALS (Renown Task)

GOAL:	Assist Ulta Metamagicals with their Asura Gate research.
LEVEL:	20

Description: To assist Ulta Metamagicals, use their configurators to help tune the Asura Gates. Doing so helps protect researchers from creatures and toxic material coming from the malfunctioning gates, and gathers crystals. Crystal nodes are everywhere on the ground, and they return quickly. Start by grabbing some crystals. If you enjoy math puzzles, try the lattice configurators. If math isn't your strong suit, the answers are below.

- Corrupted analysis data structure. Sequence Incomplete: 4, 8, -, 32, 64, -. Input missing data = 16, 128.
- Analyzing crystal lattice dimensions. Length: 5.8 units. Width: 3.8 units. Calculating area = 22.04 units.
- Sample 236: Crystal lattice, refractive angle 72 degrees. Crystal bisection underway = 36.
- Scaling configuration malfunctioning. Crystal lattice 14 units long, 22 units wide. Figure correct dimensions for scaling by 3 = 42 units long, 66 units wide.
- Crystal sample set inventory: 7 blue, 3 yellow. Crystals sampled 10 times. Input best prediction of selecting yellow crystals = 0.3.
- Sample 35: Crystal, 5 units long, 6 units wide, 2 units deep. Volume = 60 cubic units.
- Crystal samples observed with following number of sides: 3, 6, 8, 7, 10, 12, 4. Identify range of number of sides = 9.
- Crystal density: 2.99. Crystal density reduced by 5 percent = 2.84.

HELP TEKKI DEFEND THE ASURA GATE (Repeatable)

GOAL:	Help Tekki fight off creatures swarming through the Asura Gate.
LEVEL:	21

Description: Tekki is standing in one of the caverns. Speak with her to help test her gate. Tekki has had a bit of trouble setting the gate coordinates correctly, and she ends up opening it into unfriendly territory. Defend her while she closes it and attempts to try again. She gets it wrong three times. Each time, a different type of enemy runs through, and there's very little time to heal between waves.

The first wave is made up of griffons. Each griffon killed counts for around 12%, so you need to kill eight griffons in total to close the gate. Focus attacks on one griffon at a time, as up to two griffons can attack you at once. The second gate opening brings steam minotaurs. These hit a little harder but are very similar to the griffons. You need to kill 10 minotaurs to close the gate and start the final rush.

Tekki outdoes herself on the final set. Corrupted minions pour out of the gate. This includes icebrood wolves and norn attackers. These do more damage than the steam minotaurs, and as many as four enemies can move against you at once. If your area-of-effect attacks deal high damage, switch to them. If your single-target attacks are your damage dealers, keep focusing fire and heal yourself as fast as you can. There is almost no room to kite in here, so it's a "stand up and get knocked down" fight.

At the end of this last wave, Tekki finally manages to finish her work with the Asura Gate. Head out the north side of the area; you've now helped these asura as much as you can.

STOP THE INQUEST-BANDIT ALLIANCE (Renown Task)

GOAL:	Help Peacekeeper Klodi stop the Inquest-bandit alliance.
LEVEL:	22

Description: Peacekeeper Klodi has heard disturbing rumors of a union between the Inquest and the bandits of the region. To stop this alliance, disrupt meetings between the bandits and Inquest, destroy Inquest turrets, and steal bandit documents and deliver them to the Seraph.

The area north of Ulta Metamagicals Waypoint isn't safe. There are many turrets scattered around the area. Don't try to run through them; they don't deal high damage, but they are packed very close together. Kill them one at a time and make your way to the base.

RESCUE SKRITT FROM BANDIT KIDNAPPERS (Repeatable)

GOAL:	Rescue captive skritt from their bandit kidnappers.
LEVEL:	21

Description: This is pretty straightforward: save the captured skritt. To do so, kill the bandit kidnappers before they get to the Inquest base. There are five bandits leading a group of skritt from Skrittsburgh to the Inquest base. Start the fight by killing the ranged bandits; they deal more damage than the melee bandits, and you need to thin their numbers quickly. With the ranged bandits down, concentrate your efforts on the close-up attackers. Freedom for the skritt!

NOT THE SKRITT! (Repeatable)

GOAL:	Free captured skritt from the Inquest.
LEVEL:	21

Description: If you failed to save the skritt before the slavers got to the Inquest base, now's your chance. The Inquest has something horrible planned. In 7 minutes, the skritt will be killed. You need to destroy the containment cell power node before that time. The bad news is that the power node is at the back of the Inquest base, and it's guarded by a veteran Inquest member. The good news is that it's fragile. Fight your way to it, break it, and run! Once both the Inquest and bandits are dealt with, continue north.

BRILITINE WAYPOINT (WEST OF CENTER)

SERVICES:	Waypoint, Scout
TRAVEL:	Ulta Metamagicals Waypoint (S), Seraph Observers Waypoint (N)
HARVEST INFO:	Gummo Trees, Iron Ore, Silver Ore, Leafy Vegetables (Abundant)

There isn't much in the way of services here. Fortunately, there's a scout close at hand to tell you about nearby and faraway tasks. Speak with him for a moment and head northeast to Scotta's camp. Bandits here have been harassing the area, and it's high time someone stopped them. When the area is somewhat safer, travel east from the bandit camp to Hidden Lake and Seraph Observers Waypoint.

HINDER SCOTTA'S BANDITS (Renown Task)

GOAL:	Disrupt Scotta's bandits.
LEVEL:	21

Description: It's a simple proposition: kill bandits, destroy or confiscate bandit supplies, and smash bandit weapons and roadblocks. The most dangerous part of the camp is the static defenses. Both Inquest turrets and bandit turrets are placed strategically. Fight your way in and start breaking things. Avoid the tree in the center; there's a veteran bandit rifleman nearby waiting to make your life very difficult.

BANDITS GOTTA EAT

Bandits have built their camp where a great many leafy vegetables grow. Cooks should definitely visit this place when their bags are empty.

SERAPH OBSERVERS WAYPOINT (NORTH SIDE)

SERVICES:	Waypoint, Merchant
TRAVEL:	Brilitine Waypoint (S), Gallowfields Waypoint (W)
HARVEST INFO:	Gummo Trees, Herb Patches (Abundant)

The Seraph have set up a very small camp to keep an eye on the bandits in the area. The issue is that the bandits have a larger camp and they know where the Seraph are. Help the Seraph defend their camp.

If you have a moment's respite, fight the veteran ghostly willowheart at the center of Hidden Lake. This fight is almost identical to that of veteran Seraph Michella. Head west when this area is clear. Speak with Niamh for a creature book before you enter bandit turf (south of Niamh). Clear bandits on your way west to Gallowfields Waypoint.

HOLDING THE SERAPH OUTPOST (Renown Task)

GOAL:	Help secure and maintain the Seraph outpost.
LEVEL:	22

Description: This task consists of helping the Seraph maintain security at their outpost and attend to the ghosts in the graveyard. The Seraph outpost doesn't look like much. Immediately south of the waypoint is a small bog with aggressive enemies. Kill the aggressive enemies and revive the downed Seraph soldiers. For a noncombative means to complete the task, the northeast edge of Hidden Lake is infested with ghosts. Visit the graveyard to find how each ghost died and help them all pass on. Once the camp is in good shape, head west and take the fight to the bandits.

RETAKE THE SERAPH CAMP (Repeatable)

GOAL:	Help the Seraph retake their camp.
LEVEL:	22

Description: The bandits have taken the Seraph camp. Use your highest damage abilities to kill the occupying bandits quickly. You have to hold the position until the area returns to Seraph control. Revive the fallen Seraph as you can, but do not let enemies live inside the bordered area for long. Having multiple players on this mission makes this manageable, as a ranged character can hold the point while melee fighters keep the enemies from even entering the circle.

DEFEND THE SERAPH CAMP (Repeatable)

GOAL:	Defend the Seraph camp until reinforcements arrive.
LEVEL:	22

Description: Bandits are attacking the camp in waves! Help the Seraph hold them off for 5 minutes until reinforcements arrive. The safest way to accomplish this is to sit in the middle of the Seraph forces and let them attack the bandits first. Avoid the saboteurs (they're easy to spot as they carry kegs of explosives); they do a great amount of area-of-effect damage and can toss you around.

TAKE THE FIGHT INTO BANDIT TERRITORY (Renown Task)

GOAL:	Clear the approach to bandit territory.
LEVEL:	23

Description: You now get to take the confrontation to the bandits. Slay any hostiles, destroy bandit weapons, and capture breezeriders. This approach averts most of the bandits' static defenses, but don't let your guard down. There are bandit turrets spaced all along the other sides. If you see a circle at your feet, move! There's often a gunner in each turret as well as supplies nearby. Make the turret your first target, kill the gunner, and then destroy the supplies. Kill your way west.

GALLOWFIELDS WAYPOINT (NORTHWEST SIDE)

SERVICES:	Waypoint
TRAVEL:	Seraph Observers Waypoint (E), Triforge Point Waypoint (S)
HARVEST INFO:	Gummo Trees, Herb Patches, Iron Ore (Abundant), Silver Ore (Abundant)

A small colony of skritt lives in the caves north of the Gallowfields. They mine shinies in the canyon (as one should) but have been losing territory due to the increasing bandit presence. Help them take a stand against these aggressive interlopers. Once the skritt are in better shape, head south through the pass to the west of the bandit camp.

HELP THE SKRITT AGAINST THE BANDITS (Renown Task)

GOAL: Help the skritt challenge the bandits.

LEVEL: 24

Description: The skritt appreciate all your help. All you need to do is kill bandits, destroy their supplies and weapons, and assist the skritt in gathering shinies in the canyon. You probably already killed a few bandits on your way here, which got you started on the task. Head south from the waypoint into the canyon. Be very careful about jumping; the fall can nearly kill you. Kill the hyenas and gather relics (on the ground) while making your way south through the canyon. Get full health before grabbing relics. Removing a relic also reveals a breezerider, and they are sometimes veterans. While they sound scary, they're very squishy for veterans.

TRIFORGE POINT WAYPOINT (WEST SIDE)

SERVICES:	Waypoint, Merchant
TRAVEL:	Gallowfields Waypoint (N), Ulta Metamagicals Waypoint (E)
HARVEST INFO:	Gummo Trees (Abundant), Herb Patches, Iron Ore, Silver Ore

Do not attempt to enter Fort Vandal. This area is closed and guarded by some of the most dangerous bandits ever (level 80 champions!). Instead, go through the pass and head south to a spy base. There is a merchant there for any final supplies you need before you leave Brisban Wildlands for bigger and better things.

SECURE THE AREA AROUND THE CAMP (Renown Task)

GOAL: Help Valiant Mathair secure the area.

LEVEL: 25

Description: Valiant Mathair needs your help to revive fallen allies and escort them to the spy camp in the south. As you go, take out any hostile forces you see and destroy bandit mines. Do not attempt to disarm the mines; they must be destroyed. Revive allies as you go and get a small group going south. Your allies are much stronger as a group, and you can revive any who fall along the way. Another option is to revive them and then let them take their own chances. You only get credit toward the task for reviving them, not for the actual escort.

STEAMSPUR MOUNTAINS

The Steamspur Mountains are south from norn territory. They're warmer and more easily passable than the northern mountain range, but the monsters living there are even more dangerous. You won't find any events here for low-level adventurers. Major enemies include elementals, aggressive asura, the Nightmare Court, fierce wildlife, Orrian undead, and pirates! Many of the regions in these mountains are brightly colored and fun to look around. Enjoy some sightseeing while you take back the coastline.

BLOODTIDE COAST

LEVEL RANGE: 45-55

Momoztli Grounds
Archen Foreland Waypoint
Marshwatch Haven Waypoint
Deadend Waypoint
Sorrowful Waypoint
Moriarity's Hold
Stormbluff Waypoint
Remanda Waypoint
Merchantman's Strait
Risewild Hills
Laughing Gull Waypoint
Lostwreck Waypoint
Sanguine Bay
Firthside Vigil Waypoint
Barrier Camp Waypoint
Mentecki Pass
Mole's Head
Dredgehat Isle
Wraithwalker Woods
Bogside Camp Waypoint
Mournful Waypoint
Castavall Waypoint
Jelake Waypoint
Whisperwill Waypoint

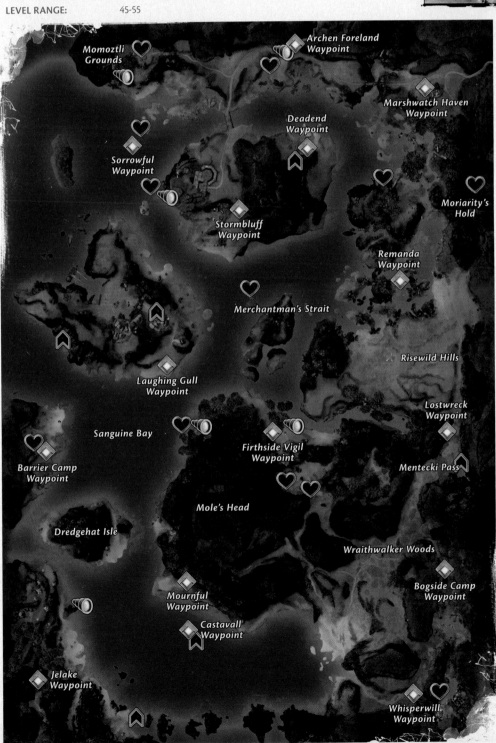

Walk south from Lion's Arch to reach the coast; this area also connects with the lower side of Lornar's Pass (in the Shiverpeak Mountains). Pirates and Orrian raiders are commonplace, so fighting on islands and rivers is almost as common as trouble on dry land. If you like fighting humanoids, you're in the right place. Make sure your aquatic weaponry is up to snuff before coming.

SPARKFLY FEN

LEVEL RANGE: 55-65

Farther south from Bloodtide Coast, this region also connects with the western side of Mount Maelstrom. Territory control is the name of the game in Sparkfly Fen. The events are very group-friendly, and it's a bit rough to solo some of them due to enemy reinforcements and the difficulty of seizing areas without getting killed in the process.

If you're trying to make your way down to Orr, go through Sparkfly Fen and look along the southern border. You can soon reach the Straits of Devastation, and that's where the battle to seize Orr begins.

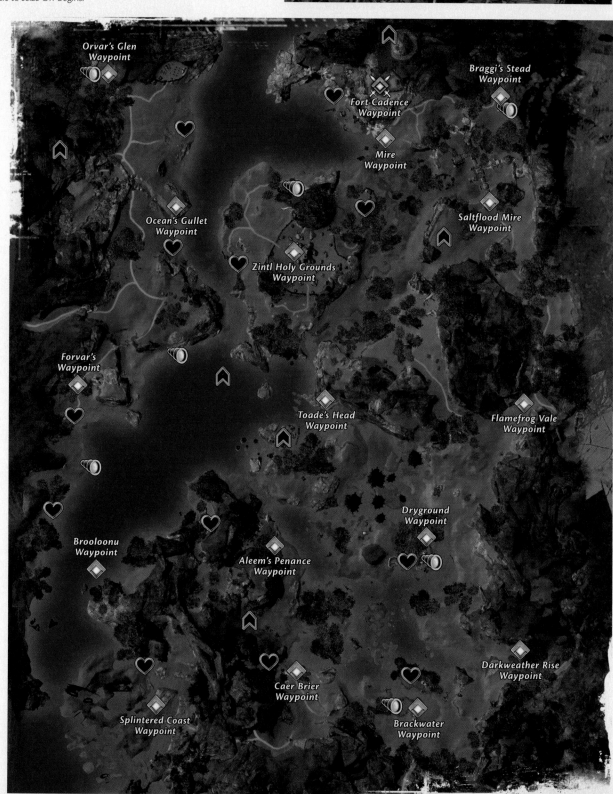

Orvar's Glen Waypoint
Braggi's Stead Waypoint
Fort Cadence Waypoint
Mire Waypoint
Ocean's Gullet Waypoint
Saltflood Mire Waypoint
Zintl Holy Grounds Waypoint
Forvar's Waypoint
Toade's Head Waypoint
Flamefrog Vale Waypoint
Dryground Waypoint
Brooloonu Waypoint
Aleem's Penance Waypoint
Darkweather Rise Waypoint
Caer Brier Waypoint
Splintered Coast Waypoint
Brackwater Waypoint

TIMBERLINE FALLS

LEVEL RANGE: 50-60

Come down from the Dredgehaunt Cliffs to explore one of the most remote areas in Tyria. Timberline Falls is a long walk from any of the civilized cities, so it's sometimes overlooked by players in its level range (they have an easier time going to the Iron Marches because it's so close to areas they're likely to have explored already). In any event, try not to miss this area. It's quite lovely, and people enjoy a good drink and a fine story of adventure down there. You meet quite a few amusing NPCs, and continuing south gets you into Mount Maelstrom, which is just an epic place to fight once you're appropriately leveled.

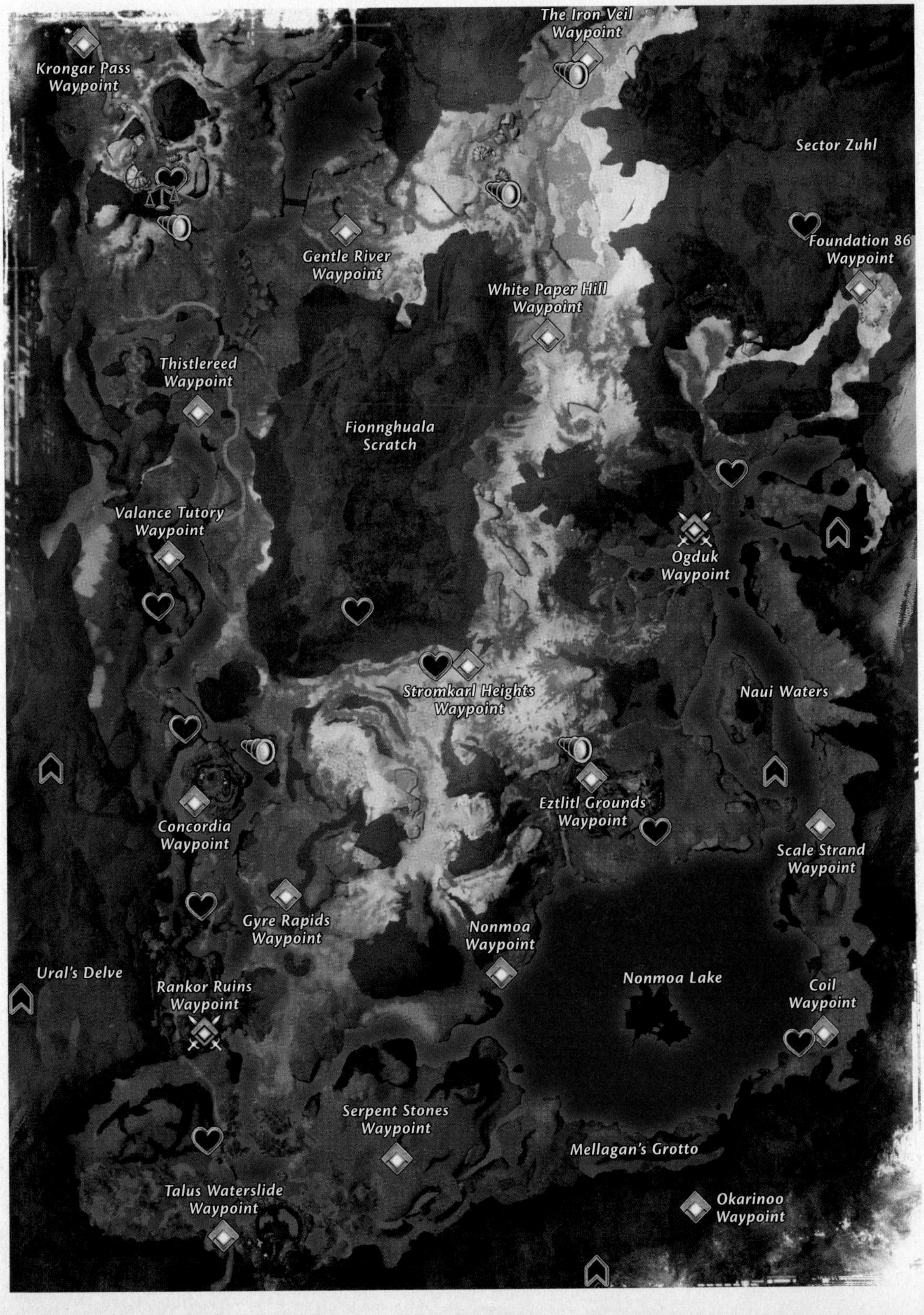

The Iron Veil Waypoint
Krongar Pass Waypoint
Sector Zuhl
Gentle River Waypoint
Foundation 86 Waypoint
White Paper Hill Waypoint
Thistlereed Waypoint
Fionnghuala Scratch
Valance Tutory Waypoint
Ogduk Waypoint
Stromkarl Heights Waypoint
Naui Waters
Eztlitl Grounds Waypoint
Concordia Waypoint
Scale Strand Waypoint
Gyre Rapids Waypoint
Nonmoa Waypoint
Ural's Delve
Rankor Ruins Waypoint
Nonmoa Lake
Coil Waypoint
Serpent Stones Waypoint
Mellagan's Grotto
Talus Waterslide Waypoint
Okarinoo Waypoint

MOUNT MAELSTROM

LEVEL RANGE: 60-70

The bottom of the Steamspur Mountains is filled with elementals, asura, and underwater adventuring. This area has more vertical content than almost any other because you can end up high above the general landscape or well beneath the waves on the eastern side of the map.

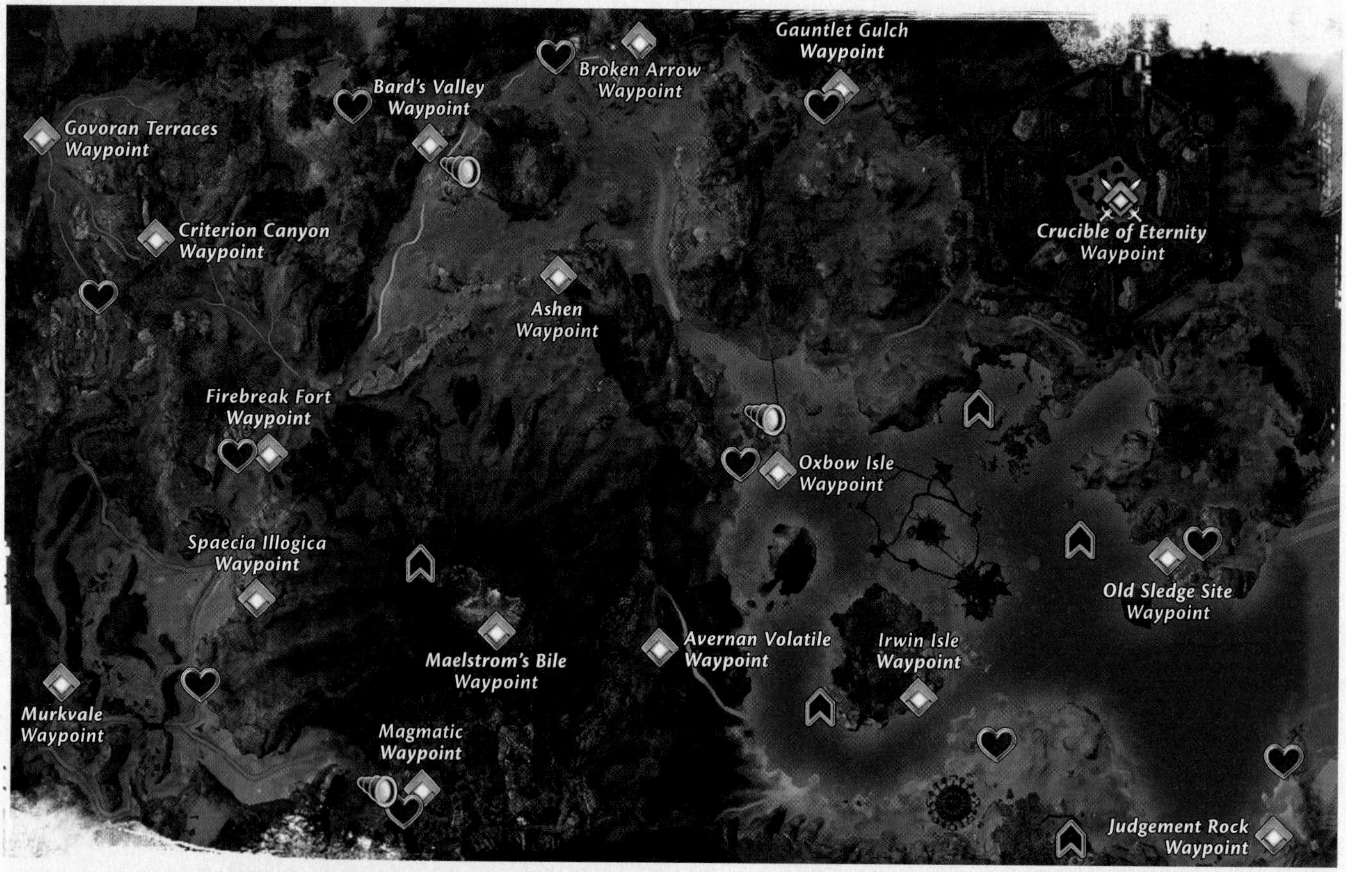

RUINS OF ORR

By level 70, you might start thinking you're kind of hardcore. You've seen much of the world and fought a legion of foes. However, the Orrians are in a league of their own. The things you'll face in their corner of the world are monstrous, brutal, and frightening. Even more than anywhere else, this is an area where you should have allies. Bring groups (preferably with a full five characters) so you can get through as many events as possible.

STRAITS OF DEVASTATION

LEVEL RANGE: 70-75

Your entrance into Orr is along the Straits of Devastation. Come south through Sparkfly Fen or west from the bottom end of Mount Maelstrom. In each case, there are major events that take your group from the coastline over to the continent of Orr. Ground and naval battles are almost constant, and these struggles push back and forth (so the lines of battle might not be the same each time you arrive).

You can earn a pile of cash by fighting hard and going through myriad events in the straits. As always, have a good set of normal and aquatic weapons; you're likely to need them all.

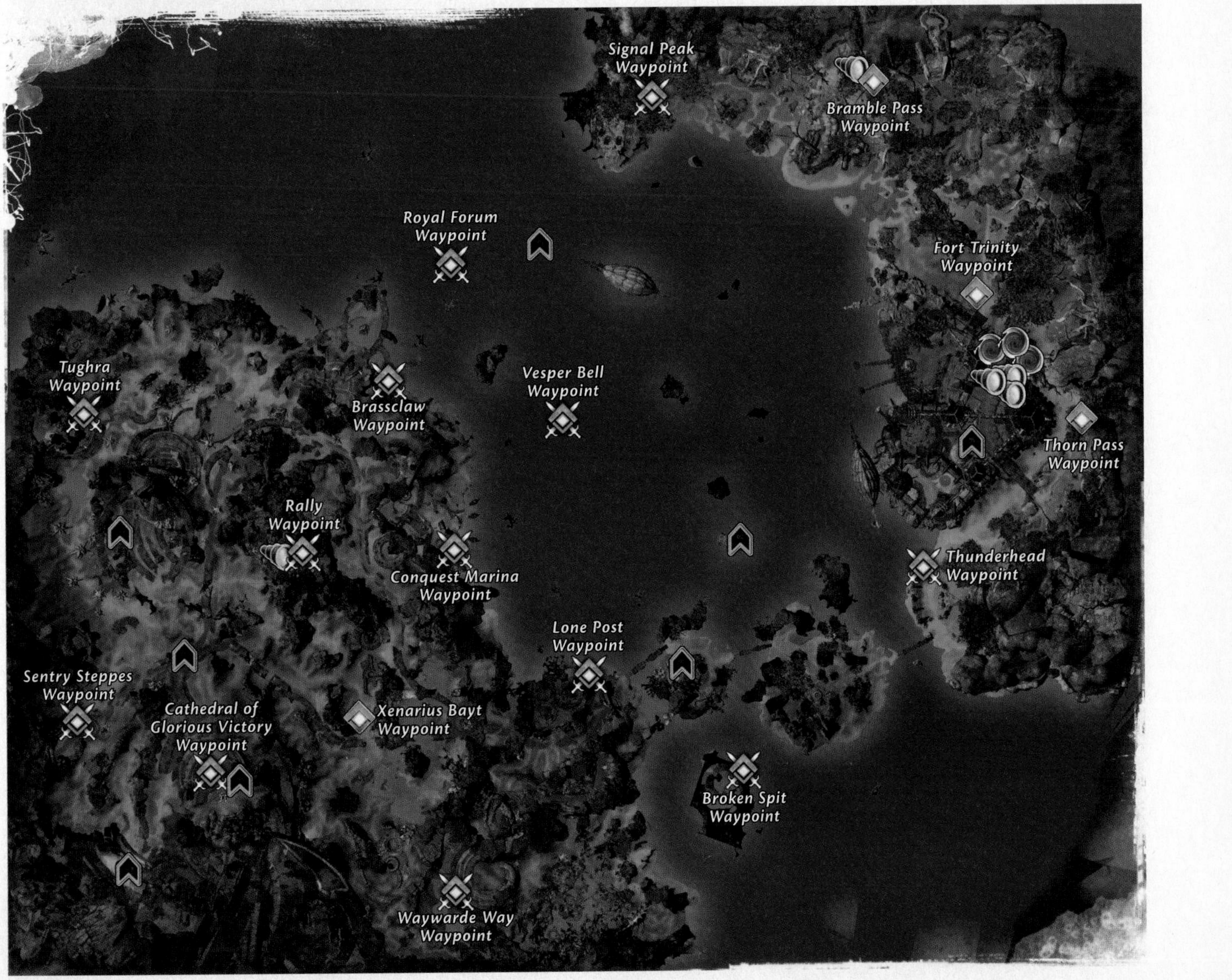

MALCHOR'S LEAP

LEVEL RANGE: 75-80

After getting to the mainland, walk west into Malchor's Leap. Escorts and both assault/defend events are commonplace, so this is also a great area to gain experience and money. Keep an AoE weapon handy; you have to fight large groups quite often, especially near the various camps being set up or sieged.

CURSED SHORE

LEVEL RANGE: 80+

Once you're near the end of leveling with a character, this is one of the best places in the world. Continue west through Malchor's Leap, and start fighting on the Cursed Shore. Treasure here is better than almost anywhere else, short of running high-level dungeons. You can get your character some powerful gear over time. Fight against giants, spiders, and undead, and see if you can help the allied forces break into the southern portion of the zone. There are good times to be had, so long as you can survive. Slot a couple extra skills for healing and survivability. All of these are useful in the Cursed Shore!

THE DUNGEONS OF GUILD WARS 2

The best test of a good PvE group is to take the players into a dungeon. *Guild Wars 2* has a solid selection of dungeons, and each one has multiple variations to keep the runs exciting and fresh. This chapter gives you a heads up for the tactics and preparation that go into a successful dungeon assault!

WHERE TO FIND DUNGEONS

Dungeons are marked on your regional maps once you've uncovered their entrances. A door icon shows up to let you know that "This is a dungeon!" Go there and look for NPCs outside the entrance. Talk to them to learn more about the dungeon and its backstory. You could meet additional players this way, as people might be hanging around to form groups.

All dungeons have their own collectible items. These let you assemble suits of special armor and a set of new weapons. These cool outfits are fun to collect even if your character has outleveled the content of the dungeon. You can always transmute the new items and combine them with higher-level gear.

Some special dungeons aren't available all the time. These mini-dungeons sometimes appear as a result of people's actions in an area. You might be working on a world event and suddenly find there is a portal to somewhere new.

DUNGEON NAME	LEVEL RANGE	LOCATION
Ascalonian Catacombs	30+	Plains of Ashford (NE Side, Ascalonian Catacombs Waypoint)
Caudecus's Manor	40+	Queensdale (NE Side, Beetletun Waypoint)
Twilight Arbor	50+	Caledon Forest (NW Side, Twilight Arbor Waypoint)
Sorrow's Embrace	60+	Dredgehaunt Cliffs (SW Side, Sorrow's Waypoint)
Citadel of Flame	70+	Fireheart Rise (NE Side, Flame Citadel Waypoint)
Honor of the Waves	76+	Frostgorge Sound (N, Honor of the Waves Waypoint)
Crucible of Eternity	78+	Mount Maelstrom (NE, Crucible of Eternity Waypoint)
Ruins of Arah	80	Cursed Shore (S Side, Arah Waypoint)

WHICH DUNGEON SHOULD WE RUN FIRST?

The first dungeon, in terms of level range, is the Ascalonian Catacombs, in the Plains of Ashford. Level 30+ characters are strong enough to complete the dungeon, and it's located on the northeastern side of the zone. Make sure everyone has at least one elite skill before going in.

STORY AND EXPLORATION MODE

When you first find a dungeon, it'll be set to story mode. Your group has to complete the area with the help of NPCs, making the experience somewhat easier. Afterward, you can return to that mode or set the dungeon to exploration mode to see higher-level enemies and new areas of the dungeon itself.

When going through each dungeon the first time, ask everyone to set their skills for a high amount of survivability and group support. With more experience, you'll learn when and where to throw in faster killing and additional damage, but simply surviving each fight is the best way to go initially. Knockdowns, Stuns, Invulnerability, healing, damage mitigation, and kiting skills are all extremely useful in dungeons.

WHO TO BRING

Don't form parties based on character professions. That's a common mistake from people who've played other online games of this type. In those games, it's sensible to say, "We need one of these, two of these, and two more of these." But that's not the way to do things in *Guild Wars 2*. Instead of bringing the right professions, bring the right people and the right tactics.

RANGED PULLERS AND KITERS

You don't need people exclusively dedicated to being pullers; pretty much anyone can pull. However, it can be helpful to have someone who is good at ranged combat. It doesn't even matter what profession that is. Almost all professions have weapons and skills that make them good at ranged combat.

They give you the option to wound enemies from distance and pull them back to a safer area. Doing this can help you avoid adds in rooms where you aren't sure where to stand in order to avoid extra foes. You don't want to fight with all sorts of enemies nearby. That leads to larger encounters, greater danger and chaos, and possible party deaths.

Attack monsters from a distance and back away to bring them out into rooms that are already cleared. Use walls and other obstacles to break line of sight so the monsters come toward you even if they have ranged attacks of their own.

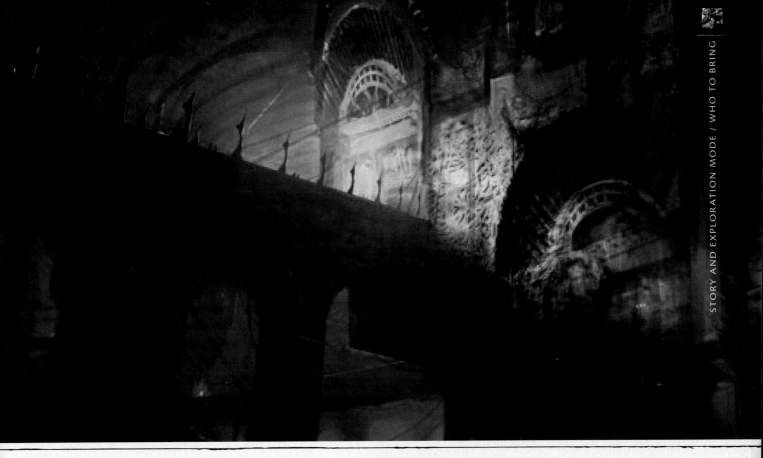

A TANK OR TWO (SOMEONE TOUGH)

The first person to engage an enemy force up close is going to get hit with conditions and direct damage out the wazoo. Don't have this be someone with pure damage skills. Even a character in heavy armor will die quickly if he or she doesn't have the right skills to mitigate damage or evade attacks during the initial few seconds of a fight. Whether by using Invulnerability, dodging, healing, or damage mitigation, you need that character to take some hits.

This process is called tanking in many games, and it's still an important concept in *Guild Wars 2*. The new spin on this is that many professions can tank. Thieves evade wonderfully, so they can kite enemies and then force them to swing at empty air if they try to stop for anything heavy. Guardians mitigate. Rangers trade damage between themselves and their pets. There are all sorts of ways to tank. Remind yourself of that often. A mesmer with pure survivability skills is going to last longer than a warrior who's slotted for raw damage output.

GROUP SUPPORT

Personal healing skills and boons are good to have in dungeons, but they're dwarfed by skills that give boons and health to your entire group. Look through your profession's listing of skills and find entries that are group friendly. Slot these to ensure you get the most bang for your cooldowns. Change to a healing skill that helps everyone. Find boons that add to the group's survival or damage output, and make those a top priority in big fights.

Most characters should have at least one or two skills dedicated to this role, but you might have a character that does nothing else.

RAW DAMAGE (DPS)

In another game, you might take three damaging characters, a tank, and a healer as a common group configuration. That's really damage-heavy for *Guild Wars 2*. Monsters die quickly if you load up on that many killers, but your people will also drop often. It's better to have one lethal character on hand; adding the other characters' moderate damage output to that usually provides a sufficient foundation for damage.

The reason for this is the flexibility of *Guild Wars 2* roles. A "Healer/Group Support" character isn't going to be sitting in the back, doing nothing except tossing health to his or her friends. It just doesn't work that way. Everyone still has damage output. As such, pure damage trades quite a bit of utility for only a moderate increase in lethality.

Be very careful about doing this with many of your characters. It's better to stop before specific fights and change your skills around to match the given needs of the battle. For example, someone lets you know that the next time is much easier if everyone frontloads their damage and burns down a certain enemy. That's when you can slot your best skills for high damage. After everything cools down, return to your normal configuration.

STAY FLEXIBLE

Groups can (and should) change their lineup to match the needs of each major encounter. If you're blowing through the dungeon without deaths or trouble, then relax and stop worrying. But when characters start dying, stop. Figure out what's going wrong and adjust your plan accordingly.

"Our tank is getting sliced in half the moment she meets the enemies." Well, try and use a fully ranged approach to see if you can kill the enemies before all of them arrive. Kiting might be preferable there.

"We're getting destroyed by these conditions." A number of professions can counter conditions for themselves and nearby allies. See if someone, like a guardian or necromancer, has a way to protect the group from whatever is crimping your style.

"This boss is killing us so fast." Talk to the group ahead of time and arrange for a number of skills with protection and healing to be used in turn. Have the other players on a voice communication program, if possible, to make it easier to trigger. "All my goodies are on cooldown. Use your group heal."

THE "HOLY TRINITY"

We've talked about the lack of hard-set roles in *Guild Wars 2*. In many games, there is a concept called the holy trinity, which is the union of healing, damage output, and damage mitigation. Or, the use of healers, DPS, and tanks to survive engagements. You need all three of these entities to be able to last long enough to overcome your enemies.

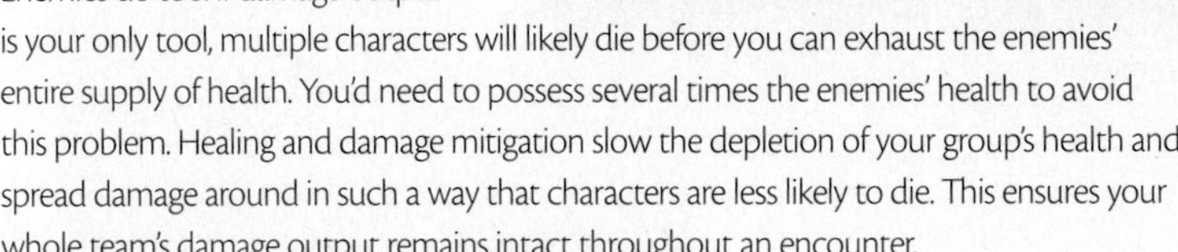

Think of this mathematically. The group has health as a resource. Enemies do too. If damage output is your only tool, multiple characters will likely die before you can exhaust the enemies' entire supply of health. You'd need to possess several times the enemies' health to avoid this problem. Healing and damage mitigation slow the depletion of your group's health and spread damage around in such a way that characters are less likely to die. This ensures your whole team's damage output remains intact throughout an encounter.

Some people assert *Guild Wars 2* does away with this model. That's only partly true, and it misses the point slightly. This game attempts to do away with absolutes. "You are the tank, you are the healer, and you guys are here just for damage." Avoiding absolutes doesn't necessarily change the nature of a fight. You still need to inflict damage and kill enemies. You still have to mitigate enemy damage as much as possible. And healing? It's never a bad thing to have! So, while you may not need to dedicate your entire character to just one of these disciplines anymore, your group must still possess and utilize them where applicable.

Now there are more ways to tip battles in your favor. Weapon swapping lets you switch duties in the blink of an eye. A guardian with a greatsword can be cutting enemies in half early in a fight, when an unseen patrol suddenly joins the encounter. Very quickly, there's too much damage for the party to withstand more than a few seconds. The guardian swaps to a scepter and a focus to help avoid damage long enough to kill off some of the newcomers.

Was that guardian there for DPS or damage mitigation? Yes, of course, the answer is that he was there for both. Almost all characters will contain elements of healing, mitigation, and DPS. Each player should shift the balance of these three elements to match the needs of the group.

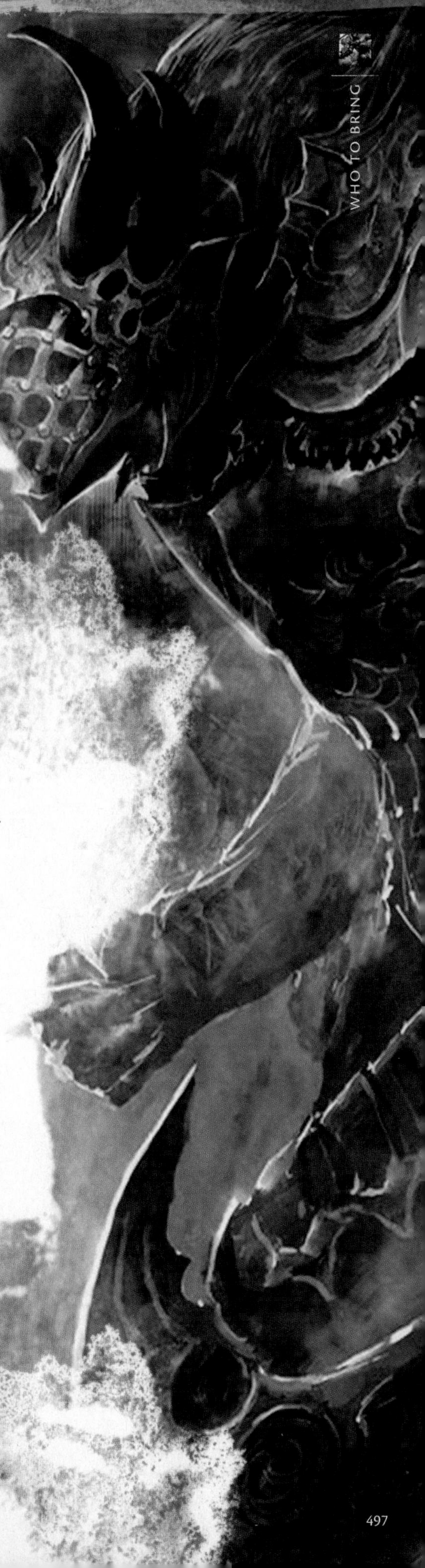

HOW TO CHANGE YOUR ROLE

METHOD	EASE OF USE	DESCRIPTION
Weapon Swapping	Instant and Easy	Use this even in the midst of combat to access a wide variety of skills.
Changing Skills	Moderate	This takes only a few seconds outside of battle, and it lets you prepare for specific encounters.
Armor Swapping	Cumbersome	Useful only outside of battle, but having an entire suit with different bonuses can make a huge difference in survivability vs. damage output.
Trait Refunds	Expensive	It's possible to visit a trainer and get a refund for your traits. Although this can be powerful in changing your character, it's not something to do lightly.

It's also possible to change the way you play to make a difference in your character's survival. Pull away from battle when you're low on health, thus avoiding AoEs and reducing the chance for enemies to attack your character. Switch to ranged combat during risky stages of an encounter.

DUNGEON SUMMARIES

If you'd like to learn about the stories for each of the dungeons, read on. There are spoilers here, so stop looking through the chapter at this point if you'd like to avoid that.

ASCALONIAN CATACOMBS

STORY MODE

Lair of the Patriarch
Graveling Tunnels
Hall of Champions
Votive Cathedral
Rockfall Chamber
Hall of Stairs
Western Chambers
Eastern Chambers
Foefire's Heart
The Lover's Crypt
Hall of Murals
Ossuary Crypts
Flooded Temple
Catacomb Entrance Waypoint
Archive of the Resting
Durmond Priory Camp

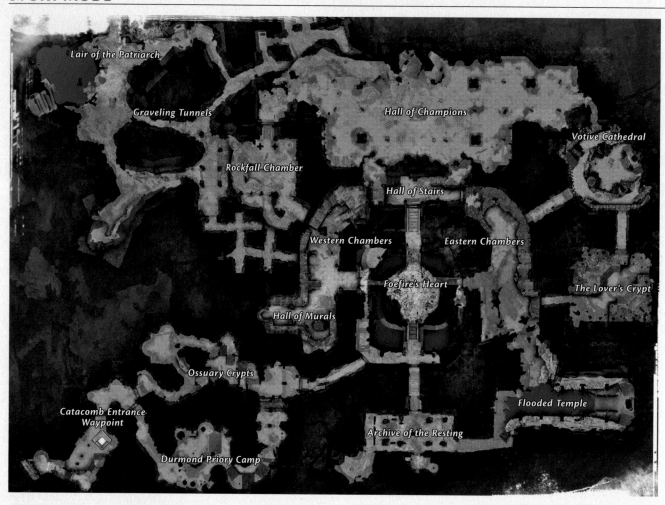

Eir Stegalkin, the norn hero, has gone into these ancient, ghost-haunted catacombs. Rytlock Brimstone wants a group of heroes to go after her, before she stirs up King Adelbern's long-dead citizens.

Rytlock meets the heroes at the entrance to the dungeon, claiming he's here to find Eir. Rytlock recounts the end of the Ascalonian war and the events of the Foefire (with a clear charr bias). As the adventurers delve deeper into the catacombs, Rytlock complains about Eir's foolishness, but on finding her, discovers she is searching for the magical sword Maegdar, which is the twin to Rytlock's own blade.

The pair are interrupted by the appearance of Adelbern's Ghost, who vows to prepare his ghostly army and eliminate the charr from Ascalon once and for all. Rytlock develops a plan to lure Adelbern out. Destroy all his lieutenants and anger him, which will draw the dead king out to fight.

EXPLORABLE MODE

King Adelbern and his ghostly citizens have been foiled, but now, even darker entities roam the Ascalonian catacombs.

After Adelbern's defeat, the ghosts have lost their driving purpose. With the decreased ghost numbers and activity, a group of unknown monsters (the "Gravelings," as they're called) have tunneled up from underneath. These creatures are thought to feed on both spirits and living beings. The Durmand Priory wants to study these dangerous creatures and, ultimately, cull their numbers. But the members of the research team have differing ideas as to how to do that. You must choose the best course of action!

CAUDECUS'S MANOR

STORY MODE

UPPER FLOOR

GROUND FLOOR

BASEMENT

Legate Minister Caudecus is hosting a party to celebrate the human-charr détente in his home, Beetlestone Manor. While a vocal opponent of Queen Jennah, Caudecus swears his loyalty to Kryta. The minister promises to unveil a new creation by his personal inventor, Uzolan.

The heroes show up for a garden party at Caudecus's Manor. The reason for the gathering is a meeting between the queen and a charr ambassador, and representatives of the other races are present, including Zojja. Logan is present as well, and suspects Caudecus of plotting something. Uzolan's invention, a golem using asuran magic, attacks the party and kidnaps the queen and several of the ambassadors.

The adventurers must ask the party guests for clues, overcome Uzolan's treachery, and rescue Queen Jenna from the human separatists who seek to destroy the human-charr efforts for peace.

EXPLORABLE MODE

Caudecus the Wise is currently accepting the hospitality of Queen Jennah while repairs are being made to his manor. Others seek to profit from the minister's absence.

Lord Caudecus is the guest of the queen, and his mansion is being watched over by the Shining Blade. However, bandits are also active in the area, seeking to pillage the unprotected mansion, capture its staff, and recover the asuran technology that Uzolan had pirated.

TWILIGHT ARBOR

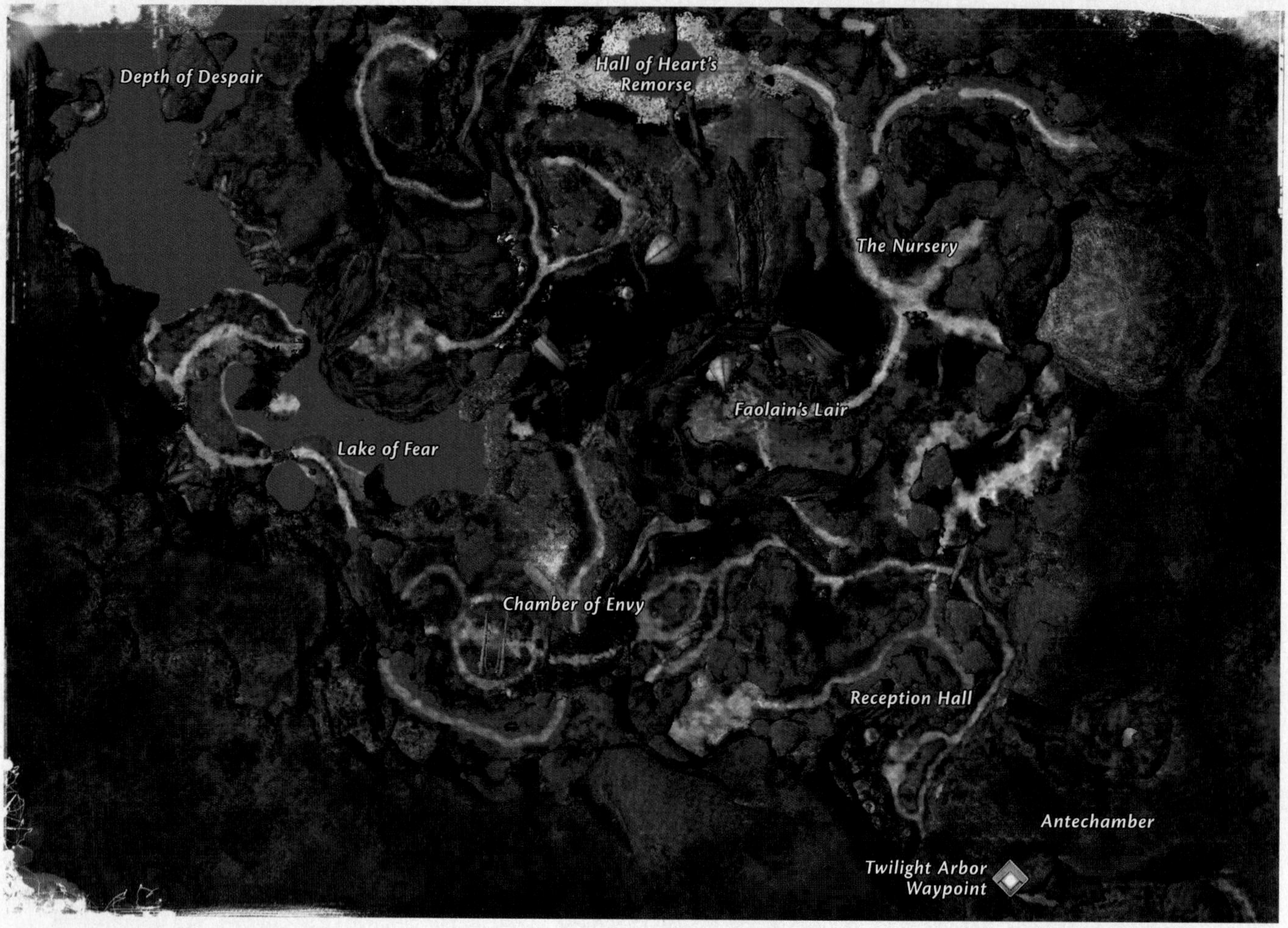

STORY MODE

The Nightmare Court consists of sylvari who turned their backs on the Pale Tree and sought their own cruel purposes in life. Their leader, Grand Duchess Faolain, makes her lair in the Twilight Arbor, surrounded by loyal minions. They have been kidnapping other sylvari for their own nefarious purposes.

The players are met at the entrance of Twilight Arbor, a twisted maze of rocks and roots in the Caledon Forest. This has become the main base for Grand Duchess Faolain, who was once close to Caithe back in the early days of the sylvari.

But Caithe has another relationship to worry about. She is attempting to mend the gap between Logan Thackeray and Rytlock Brimstone. She has invited both to help her, but told neither that the other was coming.

EXPLORABLE MODE

Faolain has fled Twilight Arbor, but the evil that infects this region remains. In her wake, other forces have now flooded in to take advantage of her foul magics to their own ends.

While Faolain has been defeated and driven out of Twilight Arbor, others of the Nightmare Court seek to move into her domain and take over. Her former allies and lieutenants conspire and compete to seize her old domain, and control the secrets she left behind.

SORROW'S EMBRACE

STORY MODE

The dredge have claimed all former lands of the dwarves. What was once Sorrow's Furnace, a place of dredge enslavement, is now known as Sorrow's Embrace. Great peril may still be found within these depths.

Zojja, pursuing clues of someone misusing her late master's research, has gone into the depths of Sorrow's Embrace, which is now a center of power for the xenophobic dredge. Caithe has convinced Eir to help rescue her, and has asked that a group of heroes come to help.

The heroes find a great dredge army massing in the depths, aided by the asuran technology of the Inquest, and further discover that the asura behind the research is one of Zojja's old rivals, Kudu. The players also discover why Logan and Rytlock are angry at each other, why Zojja is cruel to Eir, and why Destiny's Edge may never be reunited.

EXPLORABLE MODE

The Inquest have been driven out of Sorrow's Embrace, but the politics of the dredge have left the situation turbulent as various factions joust and position themselves for power. Old enmities and oppressions now come to a head, and the heroes are thrust into the middle of it.

CITADEL OF FLAME

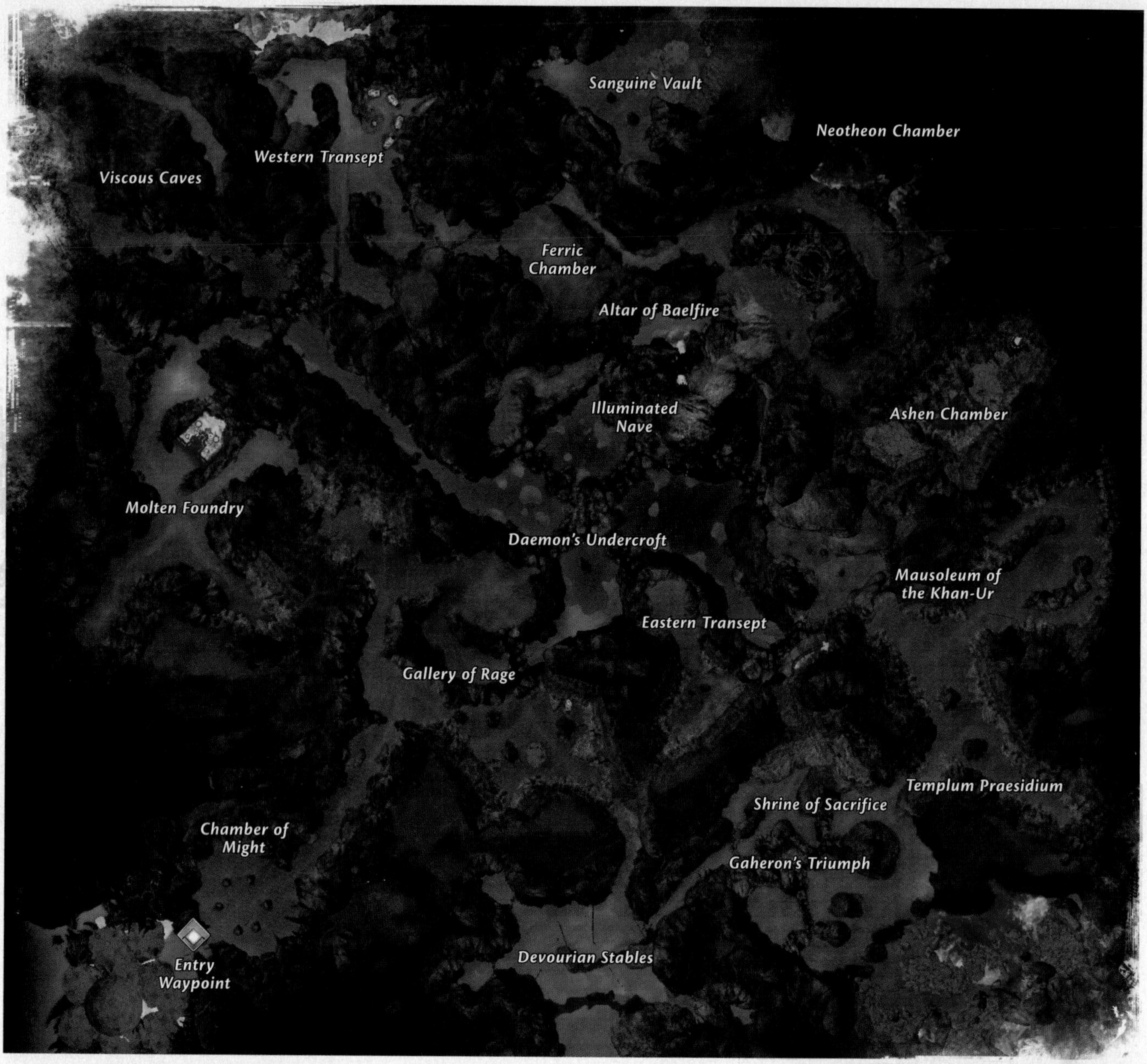

Sanguine Vault
Neotheon Chamber
Western Transept
Viscous Caves
Ferric Chamber
Altar of Baelfire
Illuminated Nave
Ashen Chamber
Molten Foundry
Daemon's Undercroft
Mausoleum of the Khan-Ur
Eastern Transept
Gallery of Rage
Templum Praesidium
Shrine of Sacrifice
Chamber of Might
Gaheron's Triumph
Entry Waypoint
Devourian Stables

STORY MODE

The Flame Citadel is the main base of the Flame Legion, the deposed former legion of the charr. It is here that Gaheron Baelfire plots to retake command of the charr and crush the humans.

The adventurers must fight alongside the united forces of the Pact to gain the gates of the Flame Citadel. There, the players must contend not only with Rytlock and Logan, who threaten to gut each other, but with the leader of the Flame Legion, Gaheron Baelfire, who aspires to ascend to godhood!

EXPLORABLE MODE

Gaheron Baelfire has been slain, but his dreams of godhood are still alive. Now the Flame Citadel is abuzz with his followers seeking to restore their lost leader.

The Flame Legion has splintered into rival factions in the wake of Gaheron's death, and each has its own plan to regain the upper hand in the battle against the other legions of the charr. Representatives of the Pact must now scramble on multiple fronts to deal with the remains of the Flame Legion.

HONOR OF THE WAVES

UPPER DECK

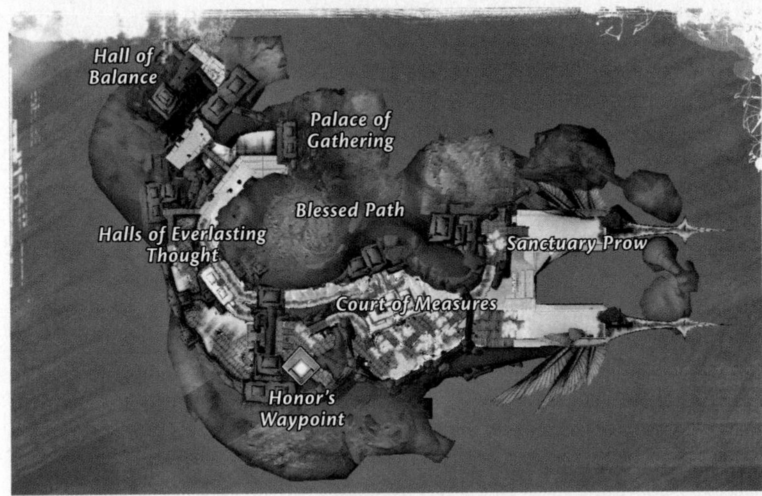

MIDSHIPS

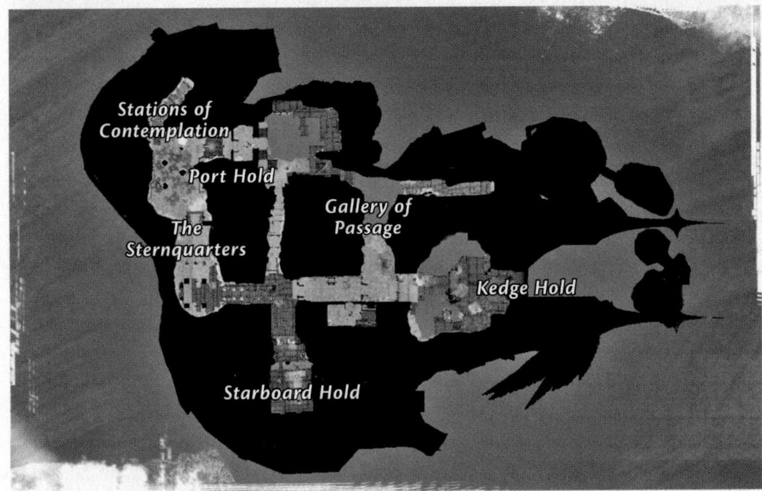

LOWER HOLD

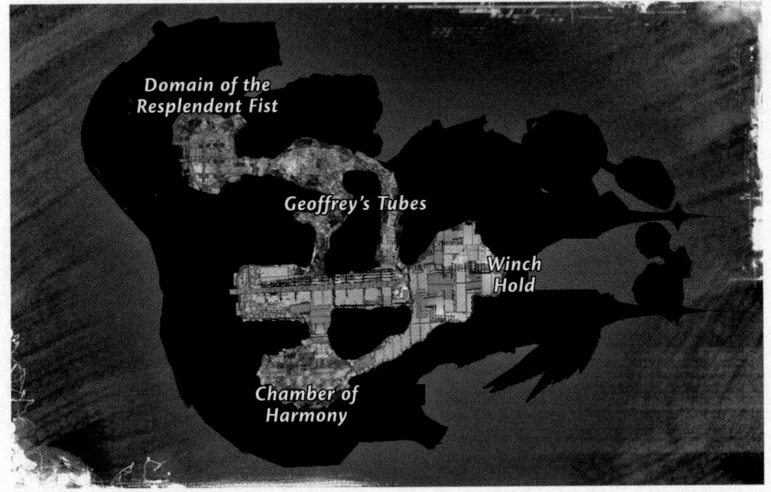

STORY MODE

The Elder Dragon Jormag has driven the kodan south in their great sanctuary ships. Now, the ship called the *Honor of the Waves* lies stricken and sinking from an assault from the dragon's minions.

The kodan are new arrivals to this part of Tyria. A dragon champion has crippled one of these ships, and ice minions have invaded its halls. One of the two leaders, the Voice, is trapped within, and her co-leader, the Claw, must rescue her before she succumbs to the power of the Jormag-worshipping Sons of Svanir.

Following her argument with Zojja in Sorrow's Embrace, Eir has fled north, and seeks to help the Claw rescue the Voice, or avenge her. Caithe is worried that the heroic norn will attempt to throw her life away.

EXPLORABLE MODE

Jormag's servants have infested the kodan sanctuary ship, *Honor of the Waves*. They must be eliminated before they corrupt all the secrets of the kodan. The Sons of Svanir are looting and pillaging the sinking ship, and the heroes must save what they can from the worshippers of Jormag.

CRUCIBLE OF ETERNITY

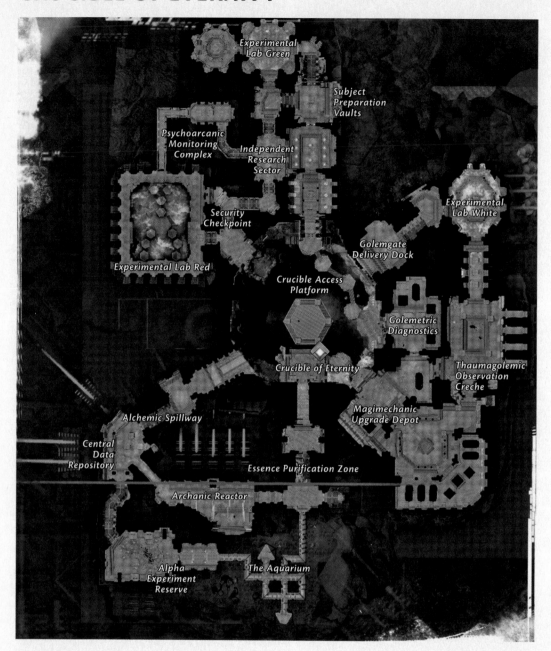

Experimental Lab Green
Subject Preparation Vaults
Psychoarcanic Monitoring Complex
Independent Research Sector
Experimental Lab White
Security Checkpoint
Golemgate Delivery Dock
Experimental Lab Red
Crucible Access Platform
Golemetric Diagnostics
Crucible of Eternity
Thaumagolemic Observation Creche
Magimechanic Upgrade Depot
Alchemic Spillway
Central Data Repository
Essence Purification Zone
Archanic Reactor
Alpha Experiment Reserve
The Aquarium

STORY MODE

The Inquest is seeking to use the power of the Elder Dragons themselves in their desire to dominate the other races. Unless they are stopped, they endanger all of Tyria with their maniacal greed.

Zojja's pursuit of Kudu and his misuse of her master's research has led her to the Steamspur Mountains, where a huge complex has been created by the Inquest. They intend to siphon the power of the dragon minions to create their own draconic servants. The heroes and Zojja are aided by the reunited Logan and Rytlock.

EXPLORABLE MODE

Even in victory there is danger inside the Crucible. The foulness at the heart of the structure is reaching critical mass, and the adventurers must go in to stop it. More importantly, they need to escape from the collapsing complex without losing their lives!

RUINS OF ARAH

STAGING AREA

POINT OF INTEREST

THE TOWER

STORY MODE

The members of Destiny's Edge have reunited. They now need to get an airship back into the fight in order to join the assault on the Elder Dragon Zhaitan. The war against the undead Elder Dragon resolves as every resource is used over the skies of the City of the Human Gods.

EXPLORABLE

There are great secrets to be had in the City of the Human Gods. The heroes must unlock these whispers of the past to find out about the races that survived before these modern times.

INTERVIEWS

LEAH RIVERA

What was the most exciting period of development for you?

The most exciting period of development for me is initial implementation of events. The problem solving required to tell the best story you can within a given space and still work within the confines of the tools is a fun challenge. The moment when you finally get it sorted out and all the characters seem alive and invested in the things around them is a great feeling!

Which areas of Tyria engage you the most, and is it their stories, monsters, or visual appeal that mean the most?

I love everything I've worked on, but if I had to pick a favorite, I'd choose Cursed Shore. It's where everything comes together from your personal story, and because Cursed Shore is an end map, I got to implement some brutal events!

Guild Wars 2 does an amazing job of redefining group roles. Someone can switch between tanking, kiting, healing, and damage during a single fight. Do you think this is where the next generation of online RPGs is heading? More player control and power, and less of "You do this, and only this."

I certainly hope so! I've never been much of an alt-aholic, but getting to play the role I feel like playing, with the character I'm most attached to, is a great step forward for me.

What is your favorite thing to do while playing the game?

I'm an explorer at heart and that manifests most prominently in gathering! I run all over the place mining, harvesting, and logging to my heart's content. The beauty of *Guild Wars 2* is that as I do that, I end up finding all the little off-the-beaten-path things like hidden events, treasure chests, veteran monsters, and other interesting things.

Early online games didn't often have deeply developed stories; they featured breadth over depth. Recent titles have been changing that and including a greater emphasis on the player's personal story. Do you think we'll see the "single-player" narrative experience and the social fun of online play continue to merge?

I love a solid narrative in my games and until we started development, I hadn't noticed how much I missed that. In other games, I end up getting so bogged down and turned around with side quests that I lose track of what the main story is supposed to be. That eventually makes me feel a lack of investment in the world and I end up getting bored. But with *Guild Wars 2*, it's very clear what your story line is from the get-go and it stays that way.

ANTHONY ORDON

What was the most exciting period of development for you?

The start of the public testing phases. It was awesome to see so many people eager to play the game that we'd been making for all these years. It was even better when they started telling us what they liked and what they didn't. Better still was when we took that feedback and improved the game.

Which areas of Tyria engage you the most, and is it their stories, monsters, or visual appeal that mean the most?

To me, the charr represent such a striking contrast to typical MMO half-man, half-beast races. When you play a charr, you're running around on four legs and roaring at your enemies. You're on the same side as the other races, but only in a self-serving sort of way. That's what the charr are all about, but instead of just talking about it they really embody it. Not just in their interactions with the player, but also with each other. The personal stories of the charr are always putting the player into a hostile, non-welcoming environment where nobody respects you until you earn it.

Guild Wars 2 does an amazing job of redefining group roles. Someone can switch between tanking, kiting, healing, and damage during a single fight. Do you think this is where the next generation of online RPGs is heading? More player control and power, and less of "You do this, and only this."

Players sometimes argue professions in *Guild Wars 2* don't have roles. This is actually true; instead of a single role, professions give you a unique set of tools that allow you to build the role you want to play. So if you like playing support classes, you actually have eight unique options in front of you instead of one or two. Some players have a hard time getting past this. They look at the thief and all they can see is a damage dealer. But if you explore the thief, you'll find a slew of abilities that do things like blind enemies and cloak nearby allies in stealth. In the past, some game would have taken this simple damage-prevention mechanic and built an entire "Blinder" class or something. But in *Guild Wars 2*, this is just one tool in a set of many. Once you get the hang of these tools, you can even start swapping between them and covering multiple roles in a single fight. Before you know it, you're mastering this and you're ready to get really crazy and do something like take a party of five thieves into a dungeon and walk away victoriously.

The distinction that *Guild Wars 2* is making is that it doesn't limit players to a single class mechanic, nor does it give them every mechanic simultaneously. You get a unique combination of mechanics and then you build combinations of combinations by grouping up together. These combinations of mechanics certainly cover the existing roles. But better yet, they allow players to creatively define new roles. It shatters the old systems that are full of single mechanic classes while simultaneously exposing a level of depth in multiplayer combat that even the developers haven't fully explored yet. You don't go backwards from this. It is the future, and it's very exciting.

Early online games didn't often have deeply developed stories; they featured breadth over depth. Recent titles have been changing that and including a greater emphasis on the player's personal story. Do you think we'll see the "single-player" narrative experience and the social fun of online play continue to merge?

I think the future holds more opportunities for interpersonal storytelling. MMOs are about virtual worlds and how you and your friends affect them. The individual player needs to be able to establish an identity, but only so they can bring that identity to the collective group that the story is about. I'm not talking about voting on conversation options. I want to see games that react to and challenge who we are as a group.

MATTHEW MEDINA

What was the most exciting period of development for you?

A game the size and scope of *Guild Wars 2* has many different cycles, and I enjoyed each of them for different reasons. But if I had to pick a favorite period, it would be the last months of development as everything begins to coalesce and the game starts to achieve the potential we've all seen it have over the last several years. When you're finally able to play a character completely through the personal story, and all the game's dynamic events are up and running, that's when you realize that this is what everyone on the team has been working towards. All the doubts and fears begin to disappear and what you're left with is simply the desire to load up the game and just play it!

Which areas of Tyria engage you the most, and is it their stories, monsters, or visual appeal that mean the most?

For *Guild Wars 2*, the areas that engage me the most are the areas that line up with the famous landmarks and ruins of *Guild Wars: Prophecies*. One of the most fun aspects for me of working on a new map was rediscovering all the areas the map artists had put in that hearkened back to the days of following Rurik as he led his people across the Shiverpeaks, or placing NPCs that tell the story of the breaking of the Henge of Denravi. The best of these areas, in my opinion, would be the sunken ruins of Lion's Arch. Long-time *Guild Wars* players will recognize all the familiar landmarks, and there's a bittersweet sense of nostalgia as you swim through areas that are now beneath the waves, where many of our players once congregated.

Guild Wars 2 does an amazing job of redefining group roles. Someone can switch between tanking, kiting, healing, and damage during a single fight. Do you think this is where the next generation of online RPGs is heading? More player control and power, and less of "You do this, and only this."

I certainly hope so! In the *Guild Wars 2* manifesto video, one of our studio founders, Mike O'Brien, talked about our desire to make a game that would appeal to players who really didn't like traditional MMO game mechanics. That's me, in a nutshell. Purely as a player, I appreciate the fact that I can be so versatile as any of the eight professions in *Guild Wars 2*, and I never feel pigeon-holed into a particular playstyle. If I'm tired of dual wielding as a warrior, I can switch to a longbow and stand back for some ranged combat, or change my utility skills and create an entirely different kind of warrior. I don't need to log out to an alt to enjoy a taste of something different. I also like not feeling as though other players will be turned off to adventuring with me if I'm not running an "optimal" build.

What is your favorite thing to do while playing the game?

Exploring. I'm that guy who will move out from the crowd and say, "Hmm, I wonder what's in that direction." I gladly put other tasks on hold so that I can run off to check out the crumbling ruins that just appeared over the horizon. I'm not averse to combat encounters, but I feel much more rewarded from finding all the nooks and crannies in each of the environments, and talking to as many NPCs as I can, just to hear what they have to say.

Early online games didn't often have deeply developed stories; they featured breadth over depth. Recent titles have been changing that and including a greater emphasis on the player's personal story. Do you think we'll see the "single-player" narrative experience and the social fun of online play continue to merge?

I do. I think that, although not every player may want a "single-player" type of experience, human beings are uniquely drawn to storytelling and playing games that allow us to take on the personality of a character we create. This is the ultimate expression of a primal need. Game developers, and games as a medium, will continue to explore ways for us to provide experiences which can meet these basic needs we all share. In effect, we humans are drawn to things like art, literature, cinema, and theatre in part because they give us a sense of meaning and purpose. Melding the social aspects of games with narrative elements provides game developers with an unprecedented opportunity to provide players with something amazing: shared meaning. I believe strongly that these are noble goals to strive for, and that this merging of narrative with social gameplay is already creating meaningful connections between individuals that transcend virtual space. How much better will that get? I'm thrilled to find out!

DEVON CARVER

What was the most exciting period of development for you?

I'd have to say the most exciting time for me was the period up to and around our first beta weekend event. We had been working our butts off to get the game ready to show to lots and lots of people and it was exciting to see everyone in the studio focusing on the same goal, polishing the heck out of those first areas we were showing off. Everyone was playing the game and providing feedback and just doing whatever they could to make sure we had the best game to show to the world. It all culminated in that insane feeling the first morning when we turned on the servers and suddenly we were playing, live, with people from all over the world. I'm not sure anything can match the feeling of playing through an area you've worked on for months with people who have never seen it and just watching them have fun. That's when you see the extra hours and all the extra work have paid off.

What is your favorite thing to do while playing the game?

It's hard to pick just one thing in a game this large and with so many fun things to do in it, but if I had to settle on just one thing, I'd say I really enjoy exploring the world that our artists have created. Every single map in the game has areas that are so incredibly beautiful and cool that I just love taking the time to explore them and see all the things our amazing art team has done. I think the first time I really noticed the scale of the central keep in one of the World vs. World maps, I honestly couldn't believe it. And to go from there to the depths of the ocean and back to the ruined city of Ascalon is just incredible. If you haven't taken the time to just soak in the things our team has put in, I'd really suggest it, because there is some jaw-dropping stuff in the game.

MATT WUERFFEL

What was the most exciting period of development for you?

The polish phase. It was a chance to revisit previous work and add all the finishing touches to take things over the top. We really got a chance to add some great stuff during polish: hidden secrets and puzzles, characters with backstories, hard to find locations, secret events, and all the little details that make the world feel handcrafted and alive.

Which areas of Tyria engage you the most, and is it their stories, monsters, or visual appeal that mean the most?

I think the most engaging aspect for me is the sense of exploration. The artists have created an absolutely stunning world that is exciting to delve into, and we've layered content over that world to create stories, context, and rewards. I always try to find the jumping puzzles in each map, because they capture that sense of exploration in a beautiful and direct way, and they're areas where we can really showcase the amazing work of the art team!

What is your favorite thing to do while playing the game?

Just finding other people and exploring together. It feels natural to group together because the incentives of the players are aligned to reward social play, and I always find myself cruising around the open world with whoever is nearby.

Early online games didn't often have deeply developed stories; they featured breadth over depth. Recent titles have been changing that and including a greater emphasis on the player's personal story. Do you think we'll see the "single-player" narrative experience and the social fun of online play continue to merge?

Combining agency, narrative, and social play in an online multiplayer game can be difficult. But playing with other people in a massive online space while retaining that sense of individual identity can really capture the imagination—the sense that there is a living-breathing world out there, where you can venture out and make your mark, is pretty powerful. I think we'll continue to see movement in that direction.

GUILDWARS 2®

OFFICIAL STRATEGY GUIDE

Written by Michael Lummis, Kathleen Pleet, Edwin Kern, and Kurt Ricketts

DK/BradyGames, a division of Penguin Group (USA) Inc.
800 East 96th Street, 3rd Floor
Indianapolis, IN 46240

ISBN: 978-0-7440-1382-5

Printing Code: The rightmost double-digit number is the year of the book's printing; the rightmost single-digit number is the number of the book's printing. For example, 12-1 shows that the first printing of the book occurred in 2012.

15 14 13 12 4 3 2 1

Printed in the USA.

Credits

Title Manager
TIM FITZPATRICK

Manuscript Editor
MATT BUCHANAN

Copy Editor
HEIDI NEWMAN

Book Designers
CAROL STAMILE
TRACY WEHMEYER

Production Designers
JEFF WEISSENBERGER
WIL CRUZ
AREVA
JULIE CLARK

BradyGAMES Staff

Global Strategy Guide Publisher
MIKE DEGLER

Editor-In-Chief
H. LEIGH DAVIS

Licensing Manager
CHRISTIAN SUMNER

Marketing Manager
KATIE HEMLOCK

Digital Publishing Manager
TIM COX

Operations Manager
STACEY BEHELER

Acknowledgments

All of us at BradyGAMES offer our sincere thanks to everyone at ArenaNet for their incredible support throughout this project. A thousand thanks to Brian Porter and Shawn Sharp—your tireless effort and dedication from start to finish made this guide possible! Very special thanks to Vicki Ebberts, Daniel Dociu, Kate Welch, David Campbell, Eric Flannum, Brian Cautrell, James Smith, Tristan Hall, Evan Teicheira, Jason King, Tim McCaughan, Cliff Spradlin, Stephen Clarke-Willson, Kevin Millard, Steve Hwang, William Fairfield, Leah Rivera, Anthony Ordon, Matthew Medina, Devon Carver, Matt Wuerffel, Aaron Sebenius, Andrew Freeman, Andrew Patrick, Bob Green, Chris Roberts, Hugh Norfolk, Peter Larkin, and Rob Thody for your help in making this guide more accurate, more thorough, easier to use, or just plain better—it has been a true pleasure working with you!

Michael Lummis: I'd like to thank my team for working above and beyond the call of duty for this entire project. Katie, Ed, and Kurt all deserve the credit for this massive, awesome guide. Black Kalagath, from the Bitplayers, was also there for us, so thanks, BK. I'm just getting started. Without Tim Fitzpatrick, Shawn Sharp, and Brian Porter, we'd still be dead in the water with only a half-awesome book to show for our time. *Guild Wars 2* has given us an amazing experience, and I hope that the fans enjoy this game as much as we have. We'll see everyone again in-game in just a few weeks. Count on it!

TM